ANNALS

OF THE

AMERICAN BAPTIST PULPIT;

OR

COMMEMORATIVE NOTICES

OF

DISTINGUISHED CLERGYMEN

OF THE

BAPTIST DENOMINATION IN THE UNITED STATES,

FROM THE EARLY SETTLEMENT OF THE COUNTRY TO THE CLOSE OF THE YEAR
EIGHTEEN HUNDRED AND FIFTY-FIVE.

WITH AN HISTORICAL INTRODUCTION.

Volume One

BY WILLIAM B. SPRAGUE, D. D.

Solid Ground Christian Books
Birmingham, Alabama USA

Solid Ground Christian Books
2090 Columbiana Rd, Suite 2000
Birmingham, AL 35216
205-443-0311
sgcb@charter.net
http://solid-ground-books.com

Annals of the American Baptist Pulpit: Volume One
Commemorative Notices of Distinguished Clergymen
of the Baptist Denomination in the United States.

William Buell Sprague (1795-1876)

From 1860 edition from Robert Carter & Brothers, New York

Solid Ground Classic Reprints

First printing of new edition June 2005

Cover work by Borgo Design, Tuscaloosa, AL
Contact them at nelbrown@comcast.net

*Special thanks to Ric Ergenbright for permission to use
the image on the cover. Visit him at ricergenbright.org*

ISBN: 1-932474-98-6

Eng.ᵈ by A.H. Ritchie.

SAMUEL STILLMAN D.D.

PREFACE.*

From the commencement of this work, I have been quite aware that nothing pertaining to it involves more delicacy than the selection of its subjects, and that no degree of care and impartiality can be a full security against mistakes. There is one reason why there seems likely to exist a greater difference of opinion in regard to the selection for this volume than any preceding one—it is that it has been necessarily determined, to a considerable extent, from mere native vigour of mind, strength of purpose, and untiring and successful devotion to the cause of Christ, without much respect to high intellectual culture. It is well known that, during a long period, comparatively few of the Baptist ministers in this country enjoyed the advantages of a collegiate education—of nearly all who *were* thus favoured I have endeavoured to form some memorial where the material could possibly be obtained—but the selection has been mainly from the ranks of those who probably never saw a College. Very few of the individuals here commemorated have been personally known to me; and though I am nominally responsible for the selection, it has really been the result of the combined judgment of distinguished living Baptist ministers in almost every part of the country. It is due to them, however, to state that they have furnished a goodly number of names as worthy, in their judgment, of

* Some things will be found in the Preface to this and some other of the volumes, which are substantially a repetition of what has already been said in the General Preface. This is rendered necessary from the fact that, as each denomination is supposed to be interested chiefly in the biographies of its own ministers, it is presumed that the General Preface will meet the eye of comparatively few except those who patronize exclusively the Congregational volumes.

being embalmed, concerning which I have been able to gather little beyond mere vague and doubtful traditions; and it has seemed more fitting to omit altogether even an honoured name, than to run the hazard of making it the subject of apocryphal statements. In regard to not a small number of deceased ministers of highly respectable standing in their day, after pursuing my inquiries to a great length, I have been forced to the conclusion that, though their record is doubtless in Heaven, they have left no record on earth out of which it is possible to frame such a memorial as they were entitled to.

The sources from which the materials for these sketches are drawn, are sufficiently indicated in the margin. It will there be seen that, in addition to the various Baptist periodicals published since the commencement of the present century, large use has been made of Backus' History of the Baptists in New England; Benedict's History of the Baptists; Morgan Edwards' Materials towards a History of the Baptists in Pennsylvania; Semple's History of the Rise and Progress of the Baptists in Virginia; Taylor's Lives of Virginia Baptist Ministers; Campbell's Georgia Baptists; Millet's History of the Baptists in Maine; Wright's History of the Shaftsbury Baptist Association; Peck and Lawton's Historical Sketch of the Baptist Missionary Convention of the State of New York; and various Biographies of greater or less extent which have appeared in almost every part of the country. It is due to candour to state, in respect to the third sketch in this volume,— that of John Clarke,—that while the statements are in accordance with the acknowledged authorities, I am assured by a distinguished Baptist clergyman, whose opinion is entitled to the highest respect, that, as the result of a somewhat extended research—not yet completed—into the life

of this veteran minister, he is likely to reach certain conclusions somewhat different from what has hitherto been
accepted as veritable history.

Somewhat less of definiteness has been reached in respect
to the period when many of the subjects of this volume
began their ministry than could be desired,—owing especially to the fact that they were often in the "exercise of
their gifts" before a regular license was conferred. The
figures on the left hand, beneath the name of each subject,
at the commencement of the sketch, always denote the
year when the individual was licensed to preach, where it
is known; in other cases, the year of his ordination; in
other cases still, the earliest ascertained date of any of his
public labours. Mistakes are more likely to have occurred
at this point than perhaps any other; though the utmost
care and effort have been used to prevent them.

It has been found necessary, in this volume, to depart
slightly, in two or three particulars, from the plan of the
work as announced in the General Preface, or as hitherto
developed. It was stated in the General Preface that the
order of the denominations would be determined by the
number of subjects which they should respectively supply.
When the Episcopal volume was published, I had no doubt
that it embraced many more names than could be legitimately gathered from among the Baptists; but the result
of a more extended examination has been to swell the list
of the Baptist ministers a little beyond that of the Episcopal; and it has seemed better to dispense with a rule that
was adopted for convenience, than to adhere to it at the
expense of omitting really deserving names. One exception also has been made from the rule that places each subject in the denomination in which he closed his career—
that exception is Roger Williams—for though his connection

with the Baptist denomination continued but a few months, yet, as he was really the father of the denomination in this country in the sense of being the founder of the first Baptist Church, and as his subsequent anomalous position would, in a strict adherence to my rule, exclude him altogether, there has seemed no alternative but that his place should be among the Baptists. The arrangement of the subjects in each denomination is designed to be strictly chronological; but from this rule also there will be found in the present volume a single exception. Owing to peculiar circumstances, no account of any of the departed Baptist worthies in Tennessee was obtained until the printing was too far advanced to allow of its finding its proper chronological place ; and rather than seem to ignore that respectable State, with whose history, from a very early period, the Baptists have been identified, a sketch of one of their venerable ministers (which, however, really includes three of them) is introduced at the close of the volume. There is little reason to apprehend that any who read the sketch will regret its insertion, even though it be a little out of place.

It will be observed that the titles *Elder* and *Reverend* are used indiscriminately, though the latter is of much more frequent occurrence. The reason is, partly that this diversity has existed among my contributors, whose taste on the subject I have felt bound to consult, and partly that it has seemed necessary, in order fairly to represent the different usages that have prevailed, and still prevail, in the denomination.

It is quite impossible for me to do justice to my sense of obligation not only for the measure of public favour—far greater than I had ventured to hope for—with which the several preceding volumes of this work have been met, but especially for the prompt and cordial aid contributed by so many worthy and honoured individuals towards the present volume. I am forbidden, as on former occasions, by the great number who have assisted me, to attempt to give a list of them; and yet I cannot forbear to mention particularly, even at the hazard of seeming invidious, the Rev. Henry Jackson, D. D., of Newport, distinguished for his successful researches into the history of the denomination in Rhode Island; the Rev. David Benedict, D. D., the well known veteran Historian, the vigour of whose faculties and the warmth of whose affections, four score years have in no degree abated; the Rev. Abial Fisher, D. D., of Massachusetts, who has not only closely observed but largely shared in all the important movements of the Baptists, especially in his own State, during an unusually protracted ministry; Horatio Gates Jones, Esq., of Philadelphia, who, amidst the pressure of professional engagements, has appropriated to me most freely and largely from the results of his indefatigable labours in this department of Biography; the Rev. Sewall S. Cutting, D. D., Professor in the University of Rochester, whose taste and studies have enabled him, as his kindly interest in my work has inclined him, to respond most satisfactorily to my numerous inquiries; the Rev. Dr. Mallary, of Georgia, who has allowed me often to put in requisition his valuable services in regard to Baptist Ministers of the South; the Rev. William Carey Crane, President of Semple Broaddus College, in Mississippi, and the Rev. S. H. Ford, of Louisville, Ky., both of whom have generously imparted to me from their ample stores of information in regard to ministers of the Southwest; the Rev. R. H. Neale, D. D., of Boston, who, in addition to other favours, has kindly furnished the original portrait from which the engraving at the commencement of this volume has been made; and the Rev. Rufus Babcock, D. D., whose excellent judgment as well as minute and extensive knowledge I have been allowed to avail myself of at pleasure. Not only for Dr. Babcock's contributions, which are so numerous as to constitute a prominent feature of this volume, but for the promptness with which he has met my almost innumerable requests, and the fraternal and genial tone by which all his communications have been marked, I beg to offer him my best thanks; at the same time assuring the public that to his untiring efforts to serve me are they indebted for no small degree of the interest that pertains to this department of the work.

In taking leave of my Baptist brethren, I cannot forbear to say that my intercourse with them in connection with the preparation of these sketches, has been a source of rich gratification to me, as I am sure it will always be a subject of grateful recollections. I heartily congratulate them that, as a denomination, they have so many bright memorials in the past, so much that is auspicious of progress and enlargement in the future. If this volume, to the production of which they have themselves been so largely auxiliary, should in any degree subserve their mission in helping forward the great cause of our common Lord and Master, my highest wish in respect to it will be answered.   W. B. S.

ALBANY, *August*, 1859.

HISTORICAL INTRODUCTION.*

The history of the Baptist denomination in the United States, like that of the other denominations, is so fully developed in the lives of its prominent ministers, that it is impossible to construct even the most general outline of the former without drawing upon material that must necessarily be embodied in the latter. The present brief sketch is framed with a view to prevent, as far as possible, repetition in the body of the work.

When the first Baptists came to this country, or who they were, it is impossible now to ascertain; though Cotton Mather says " many of the first settlers in Massachusetts were Baptists;" and he adds that "they were as holy, and watchful, and fruitful, and heavenly a people as perhaps any in the world." It may not be uninteresting to note the rise and progress of the denomination, as indicated by its introduction into the several Colonies and States, or rather by the date of the origin of the first Baptist Church in each Colony or State, in chronological order.

The first Baptist church in *Rhode Island*—which was also the first in America—was constituted by Roger Williams, at Providence, in 1636. The first in *Massachusetts* was in Swansea, and was organized in 1663, though it had been commenced by Obadiah Holmes, and others, about thirteen years before. The first in *New York*, which was the predecessor of the present Broome Street Baptist Church in the city of New York, was a General or Arminian Baptist Church, and was founded at least as early as 1669; but it seems to have existed for only a short period. About the year 1702, the Baptist interest was revived here, and in 1724 the present Broome Street Church was formed under Valentine Wightman, of Groton, and Daniel Wightman, of Newport. The first church in *Maine* was formed at Kittery in 1682, but was soon broken up and scattered, and it had no successor in the Province until 1768, when another church was constituted at Berwick, by the Rev. Hezekiah Smith, of Haverhill, Mass. The first church in *South Carolina* was the church in Charleston, founded in 1683 by the Rev. William Screven, from two separate colonies, one of which came from the West of England, the other from the District of Maine; but the early progress of the denomination in the Province was slow, as was indicated by the fact that when the Charleston Association was formed in 1751, there were only four rather small churches to compose it. The first church in *Pennsylvania* was founded at a place called Cold Spring, in Bucks County,

---

* Backus' and Benedict's Histories.—Hovey's Life and Times of Isaac Backus.—Baptist Family Magazine, 1859.—MSS. from Rev. Dr. Babcock, Professor Cutting, and H. G. Jones, Esq.

by Thomas Dungan,* who removed thither from Rhode Island in 1684. This church became extinct in 1702; but in 1688 another church—now the oldest in Pennsylvania—was formed at Pennepek or Lower Dublin, consisting chiefly of emigrants from Wales, but with a slight intermingling of English and Irish,—of which the Rev. Elias Keach † became Pastor. The first church in *New Jersey* was that at Middletown, founded in 1688, and its first settled Pastor was the Rev. John Brown ‡—the second was the Piscataway Church, organized in 1689, of which the Rev. John Drake was the first Pastor; and the third was the Cohansey Church, organized in 1690, of which the Rev. Thomas Killingsworth § was the first Pastor. The first church in *Delaware* was the Welsh Tract Church, which was formed in Wales in 1701; migrated as a colony to America, and, after lingering a while in the neighbourhood of Philadelphia, became fixed in Newcastle County, De., in 1703, being under the pastoral care of the Rev. Thomas Griffiths,‖ also an emigrant from Wales. The first church in *Connecticut* was organized at Groton in 1705, by the Rev. Valentine Wightman, who also became its Pastor—the second was gathered in New London in 1726, by the Rev. Stephen Gorton, but after a few years he disgraced himself by immoral conduct, and the church became extinct. In *Virginia*, the Baptist denomination has a triple origin. The first church was formed of emigrants from England, in 1714, at a place called Burley, in the County of the Isle of Wight, and the first Pastor was the Rev. Robert Nordin,¶ who was ordained in London with special reference to this mission. This church, and another formed shortly after in the County of Surrey, (both of

---

* Of THOMAS DUNGAN nothing more can be ascertained, except that he died at Cold Spring in 1688, was the father of nine children, and is still represented by a numerous posterity in Pennsylvania.

† ELIAS KEACH, a son of Benjamin Keach, came from London to this country, a wild and giddy youth, about the year 1686. On his arrival here, he assumed the clerical dress, with a view to pass for a minister. The project succeeded so far that large numbers were attracted to hear him. In the course of his sermon he stopped abruptly, and seemed greatly confused,—which led his audience to suppose that he had been suddenly seized by some alarming malady. Greatly to their surprise, he immediately, and with many tears, acknowledged himself an impostor; but the distress into which he was now thrown, terminated in his hopeful conversion. Having been, shortly after, baptized and ordained by Mr. Dungan, he went to Pennepek, and established the church there, and then travelled through Pennsylvania and New Jersey, preaching wherever he went with great success. In the spring of 1692, he returned to England, and afterwards became a successful minister in London.

‡ Of JOHN BROWN nothing more is known than that he was not ordained, and that he gave the lot on which the first meeting-house in the place was built.

§ THOMAS KILLINGSWORTH took the oversight of this church at its organization, and continued his connection with it till his death in 1708. He is supposed to have been a native of Norwich, in England, and to have been an ordained minister before he arrived in this country; for he was exercising his ministerial functions at Middletown as early as 1688. He was at one time a Judge of the Salem Court.

‖ THOMAS GRIFFITHS was born in Lauvernach parish, in the County of Pembroke, Wales, in 1645, came to this country with the persons who originally composed his church, and, after a faithful ministry of twenty-four years, died at Pennepek, July 25, 1725.

¶ Mr. NORDIN continued preaching at Burley and other places in Virginia until his death, which occurred in 1725.

which were of the General Baptist order,) seem not to have prospered, and most of the members subsequently removed to North Carolina. About the year 1743, a church was formed on Opeckon Creek, which was shortly after followed by two others in the same neighbourhood, consisting of emigrants from Maryland, who had been members of the General Baptist Church at Chestnut Ridge. In 1754, the Rev. Daniel Marshall and the Rev. Shubael Stearns, who had been connected with the Separates in New England, but afterwards became Baptists, went to the South, and stopped long enough in Virginia to leave a broad mark upon the character of the denomination in that State. In *North Carolina* there were a few Baptists as early as 1695; but the first church was gathered about the year 1727, by Paul Palmer,* at a place called Perquimans, towards the Northeast corner of the State, and consisted chiefly of those who had been members of the Church at Burley, Va. In *Maryland* there were a few Baptists, who had removed thither from England as early as 1709; but the first Baptist church in the Colony was founded by Henry Slator, a layman, and a General Baptist, in 1742. In *New Hampshire*, though Hansard Knollys, who was probably the first Baptist preacher who came to America, laboured there for some time, it does not appear that there was any church established until 1755, when there was one gathered at Newtown, of which the Rev. Walter Powers became Pastor. The first Baptist organization of any kind in *Georgia* was in connection with Mr. Whitefield's Orphan House, in 1757,—the leader being one Nicholas Bedgewood, who had come from England as an Agent for the Institution. Another colony began its operations higher up the country about 1771, under the Rev. Edmund Botsford, Rev. Benjamin Stirk, and others. And this ultimately coalesced with a third, consisting of Daniel Marshall and other New Lights from New England, of whom the Kiokee Church was constituted in 1772. The first Baptist church in *Vermont* was gathered at Shaftsbury in 1768; the second at Pownal in 1773; and these were the only churches in the State previous to 1780. In *Kentucky* the Rev. William Hickman, a minister from Virginia, commenced his labours as early as 1776; and a large number of Baptists removed thither from Virginia in 1780; but the first organized church—that of Gilbert's Creek—

---

* PAUL PALMER is said to have been a native of Maryland, and was baptized at Welsh Tract in Delaware, by Owen Thomas, the Pastor of the church in that place; was ordained in Connecticut; and, having exercised his ministry for some time in New Jersey, and then in Maryland, he removed to North Carolina, where he gathered the church above mentioned, and remained there, not, however, without some difficulties, till his death. His character was not entirely without spot.

OWEN THOMAS, above mentioned, was born at a place called Gwrgodilys, in the County of Pembroke, Wales. He came to America in 1707; took the pastoral care of the Welsh Tract Church, at the decease of the Rev. Abel Morgan, in which office he continued until 1748, when he resigned it to go to Yellow Springs, where he died November 12, 1760. He left behind the following singular memorandum:—"I have been called upon three times to anoint the sick with oil for recovery—the effect was surprising in every case, but in none more so than in the case of our brother, Rynallt Howel: he was so sore with the bruises he received by a cask falling on him from a wagon, that he could not bear to be turned in bed; the next day he went to meeting."

dates to 1781. In *Tennessee*, two churches are said to have been gathered some time after the year 1765, and broken up by the Indian War in 1774; but the first permanent Baptist organization here was about the year 1780, when several ministers and private members of the Church emigrated from Virginia, and were shortly after followed by an emigration from the church at Sandy Creek, in North Carolina, which, as a branch of the mother church, settled on Boone's Creek. The first church in *Ohio* was organized by the Rev. Stephen Gano, in 1790, at the mouth of the Miami River, where the town of Columbus now stands. The first church in *Illinois*—the New Design Church—was constituted in May, 1796, by the Rev. Daniel Badgley, from Virginia; and an Association called the Illinois Union was organized in 1807. The first church in the *District of Columbia* was constituted in Washington City in 1802, and the Rev. Obadiah B. Brown became its first Pastor. In the territory now included in the State of *Indiana*, several small churches were organized along the Whitewater, bordering on the State of Ohio, the first of which was in 1802. The Wabash Church, near Vincennes, was formed in 1806; and the Bethel Church, in a settlement farther down the Wabash River, was formed the same year. In *Missouri*, (then Upper Louisiana,) there were a number of Baptist families living, who had migrated thither from the Carolinas and Kentucky as early as 1796–97; and they enjoyed, during a part of the time, the labours of the Rev. John Clark; but the first Baptist, or indeed Protestant, church in the Territory was organized in 1804, under the name of Tywappity, in Cape Girardeau County. The next year, a church called Bethel was constituted near where Jackson now stands. In *Mississippi*, there were a few Baptist families in the region of Natches soon after the beginning of the present century—*when* the first church was established I cannot ascertain; but the Mississippi Association was formed in 1807. The first church in *Alabama* was organized by the Rev. J. Courtney, in Clarke County, in 1810; but there was but little increase of the denomination till 1816. In *Louisiana*, the oldest churches are those of Calvary, 1812; of Beulah, 1816; and of Aimswell, 1817. In *Michigan*, the oldest Baptist church is that of Pontiac, organized in 1822, by the Rev. Elon Galusha, who visited Michigan under the patronage of the New York Missionary Society. The first church in *Iowa* was that of Big Creek,—organized in August, 1836. The first in Wisconsin was organized in Rochester, in 1837. The first Baptist Association in *Texas* was organized in Travis, Austin County, October 8, 1840, and embraced the three churches of Travis, Independence, and Lagrange. In *Florida*, the Florida Association was formed in 1842, consisting partly of churches from the neighbouring States of Georgia and Alabama.

The "Great Awakening" which took place in connection with the labours of Whitefield, about the year 1740, gave rise to many new churches in different parts of New England, under the name of *Separate Churches*. These were formed by a secession from the regular Congregational Body, and their members claimed to hold a purer faith, as well as adopt a higher standard of Christian feeling and action, than those with whom they had previously been associated. Some of them fell into great extravagances of both doctrine and practice, but there is reason to believe that, notwithstanding the fanatical tendencies with which they may have been chargeable, they were generally sincere and devout Christians. Many of these became Baptists, among whom were Backus, of Middleborough, Hastings, of Suffield, and Marshall and Stearns, who settled in the South,—all of whom may be reckoned among the early lights of the denomination.

Several of the sketches in this volume show what has long since become matter of authentic history,—that the early Baptists in this country were emphatically a suffering people. In those Colonies or States in which Church Establishments existed, whether the form was Episcopal or Congregational, the Baptists were not only denied rights which are now universally conceded to all, but were the subjects of wrongs which none would now attempt to justify. It is not, however, to be inferred from this that either Episcopacy or Congregationalism is essentially intolerant; but only that each happened to be the medium through which the spirit of the age,—partaking, in a greater or less degree, of the darkness and severity of a yet earlier period,—acted itself out. The great doctrine of "soul freedom," of which Roger Williams was so illustrious an example and exponent, and for which the Baptists, as a denomination, have always so earnestly contended, not only frowns upon open persecution, but forbids the least violation of the rights of conscience.

It is not strange, considering the peculiar circumstances in which the Baptists were placed before and even since the Revolution, that their numerical increase should have been slow; but since the civil impediments have been removed, and the principle of universal toleration has come to be everywhere practically acknowledged, they have increased with a rapidity almost unparalleled; so that, with a single exception, they now form the largest denomination in the United States. They are spread through every State and Territory; and differ in nothing but their position in regard to Slavery. Owing to this difference, the Southern Baptists, in 1845, formed separate organizations for conducting their benevolent enterprises; and, by this means, altercations and collisions have been prevented, and thus the general efficiency of the denomination increased. In 1784, they had four hundred and seventy-one churches, four hundred and twenty-four ministers, and thirty-five thousand, one hundred and one members. In 1857, they had eleven thousand, six hundred churches, seven thousand, one hundred and forty-one ministers, and nine hundred and twenty-three thousand, one hundred and ninety-eight members.

The Baptists, as a denomination, have always attached little importance to human learning as a qualification for the ministry, in comparison with those higher, though not miraculous, spiritual gifts, which they believe it is the province of the Holy Ghost to impart; and some of them, it must be acknowledged, have gone to the extreme of looking upon high intellectual culture in a minister as rather a hindrance than a help to the success of his labours. But, if I mistake not, many of the sketches contained in this volume will show that the Baptists have had less credit as the friends and patrons of learning than they have deserved. Not a few of their preachers have been eminently accomplished as well as useful men; and some who have long since passed away, have left enduring memorials of both their scholarship and eloquence. A little after the middle of the last century, they founded Rhode Island College—this is said to have been the result of educational movements in the Philadelphia Association, continued through a number of years; and it was established in Rhode Island because that was supposed to be the only Colony in which Baptists could obtain a charter. Within a comparatively recent period, a new impulse has been given to the spirit of literary and theological improvement among them. They number at present thirty-three Colleges and Universities, more than one hundred Academies and Female Seminaries, and eleven Theological Schools. They have Publication Societies at Philadelphia, Charleston, and Nashville. They maintain forty-two periodical organs, two of which are Quarterly Reviews.

With the progress of the means of mental culture in this denomination there has been a proportional increase of the spirit of Christian and benevolent enterprise. The American Baptist Missionary Union, the American and Foreign Bible Society, the Southern Baptist Board of Foreign and Domestic Missions, the Baptist Home Mission Society, and the Bible Union, which was originated and has been chiefly sustained by Baptists, are so many several witnesses of devotion to the cause of Christ, and zeal for the diffusion of evangelical truth. Their Missions are planted in Canada, Oregon, California, New Mexico, Hayti; in France, Germany, Denmark, Sweden, Norway; in Western and Central Africa, in Southern India, Assam, Burmah, Siam, and China. The whole income of the above Societies, in 1857, was three hundred thousand dollars.

The Government of the Baptist Churches is strictly independent. Each separate church claims and exercises the right of granting license to preach the Gospel, and of ordaining Elders or Presbyters to the full work of the ministry; though this is not actually done except by the concurrence of Councils or Presbyteries. A large majority of the churches are associated in District Associations and State Conventions, which hold an annual meeting of a fraternal character for purposes of general co-operation in aid of evangelical enterprises, but have no power, legislative or judicial. In 1814, was established the Baptist General Convention, which met triennially, with exclusive reference, after the first few years, to the promotion of Foreign Missions; but that has now given place to two Conventions or Societies, one in the North, the other in the South.

The prevailing Theology of the Baptists is Calvinism—generally of the type of Andrew Fuller, but occasionally rising to that of Dr. Gill. The Philadelphia Confession,—so called from its having been adopted by the

Philadelphia Association,—the oldest Association in the country, and which agrees substantially with the Westminster, except on questions of Church constitution and Church order, has generally been regarded by the Baptists, especially in former years, as a faithful expression of their denominational belief. Somewhat more than twenty years ago, the Baptist Convention of New Hampshire adopted a Declaration of Faith, which has been extensively, though not universally, approved by the denomination. It consists of eighteen articles, all of which are in harmony with the faith of the other denominations commonly called Evangelical,* with the exception of the article on Baptism, which is as follows :—" Christian Baptism is the immersion of a believer in water in the name of the Father, the Son, and the Holy Ghost, to show forth a solemn and beautiful emblem of our faith in a crucified, buried and risen Saviour, with its purifying power," and " is a prerequisite to the privileges of a Church relation." While the Philadelphia Confession is objected to by some as too severely Calvinistic, the New Hampshire is objected to by others as at least too indefinite. Nearly all the Baptist churches in this country adopt the principle of Strict Communion, so far as regards the ordinance of the Lord's Supper ; while, in other respects, they mingle freely with their brethren of other denominations.

The Rev. Dr. Baird, in his work entitled " Religion in America,"—a work distinguished alike for the judiciousness, thoroughness, and authenticity of its details, and the high tone of candour and impartiality that pervades it,—thus concludes his account of the Baptists—"Although not a third, perhaps, of the ministers of this denomination of Christians have been educated at Colleges and Theological Seminaries, it comprehends, nevertheless, a body of men, who, in point of talent, learning, and eloquence, as well as devoted piety, have no superiors in the country. And even among those who can make no pretensions to profound learning, not a few are men of respectable general attainments, and much efficiency in their Master's work."

* Curtis, in his " Progress of Baptist Principles," presents his views of the difference between Baptists and other denominations, in four chapters: 1. " The command to baptize a command to immerse." 2. " The importance of Believer's Baptism." 3. " Infant Baptism injurious." 4. " Mixed communion unwise and injurious."

CHRONOLOGICAL INDEX.

———◆◆———

[On the left hand of the page are the names of those who form the subjects of the work—the figures immediately preceding denote the period, as nearly as can be ascer. tained, when each began his ministry. On the right hand are the names of those who have rendered their testimony or their opinions in regard to the several characters. The names in Italics denote that the statements are drawn from works already in existence— those in Roman denote communications especially designed for this work—those with a star prefixed, denote either mere *extracts* from letters or discourses not before printed, or communications not addressd to myself.]

HANSARD KNOLLYS.

1638*—1641.

FROM THE REV. J. NEWTON BROWN, D. D.

PHILADELPHIA, January 13, 1859.

Dear Sir : The sketch which I am about to furnish you of one of the arliest pioneers of Baptist principles, was originally prepared for the New Iampshire Historical Society, and in its original form appeared in one of the volumes of their Collections. I have since found new materials, of which I have availed myself, to make it more perfect, and am not aware of any remaining sources of information, which I have not explored.

The name of HANSARD KNOLLYS is eminent among the English Baptists of the seventeenth century. Of late years it has been widely spread, in connection with the issues of the Baptist "Hansard Knollys Society," a Historical Society in London, which has felt itself honoured by the selection of his name, and which, since 1845, has been nobly engaged in publishing, by subscription, accurate and annotated editions of the first Tracts on Liberty of Conscience, and other rare Baptist works of that early period,—works rarer and more precious than the purest pearls of ocean.

The life of Hansard Knollys embraced nearly a whole century,—from 1598 to 1691; and that century is the most interesting and momentous in English Annals. With most of the religious movements of that remarkable age, his biography is inwoven. His influence, like that of his great contemporary, Roger Williams, was felt both in England and America. In many points a striking resemblance might be traced, were this the place and time. One point of difference among others, is, that while the chief obscurity in the biography of Williams rests on his residence in England, the chief obscurity in that of Knollys rests on the years of his residence in America. My object, in this communication, is to throw light upon this dark period of his history.

Some preliminary statements may be necessary to do this effectually. It is important to know what he was before he came to this country; and, happily, Crosby has preserved all the facts necessary.† Mr. Knollys was born in Chalkwell, Lincolnshire, 1598. His parents were pious. They "took good care," as Crosby says, "to have him trained up in good literature, and instructed betimes in the principles of religion." While at the University of Cambridge, he was converted, and his Christian character became of the highest order. "Happy would it be for this nation," says Crosby, "if our Universities and private Academies were filled with such students." After his graduation he was chosen master of the free school at Gainsborough. In June, 1629, he was ordained as a Deacon, and then as a Presbyter, of the Church of England, and the Bishop of Lincoln gave him the living at Humberstone. His diligence was great. He preached

---

* The sketch will show that this date is assumed on *probable* grounds only.
† Crosby I. 334-344.

VOL. VI.   1

three and four times a day on the Sabbath at Humberstone and Holton, besides other seasons. as well to the poor as to the rich.   About 1632, he began to doubt the lawfulness of conformity to the Church of England, and resigned his living ; but continued to preach several years longer, with the consent, or rather connivance, of the good Bishop, though without sur- plice or prayer book.   In 1636, he was arrested at Boston, in his native county of Lincoln, by a warrant from the odious High Commission Court, and thrown into prison ; but his keeper being conscience-stricken, connived at his escape, and he went up to London to find a passage to America. There he was detained so long, with his wife and child, that, when he embarked, as he tells us himself, " he had but just six brass farthings left, and no silver or gold."   A little money of his wife paid their passage. They arrived in Boston, Massachusetts, early in 1638.   As he returned to London about Christmas, 1641, his residence in America must have been somewhat less than four years.   But he was no common man.   He was in the full vigour of life,—from the fortieth to the forty-fourth year of his age.   Where did he spend these four years, and how ?   What influence did he exert ?   What character did he sustain ?   Why did he return ? Did he leave his mark on the rising institutions of this country, and engrave his name on the foundations of American History ?   These are the questions I shall attempt briefly to answer.

All the early historians of New England mention Hansard Knollys. Winthrop, Morton, Hubbard, Hutchinson, Mather, Prince, Neal, Backus, Belknap, Eliot, Adams, Winslow, though the last four or five are comparatively modern.   Opinion is divided about him.   We must sift the facts out of them all, and make due allowance for the diversity of opinion. Some hints may be gleaned from his brief Autobiography, and some from the early New Hampshire Court Records, preserved at Exeter, in that State, to which, through the courtesy of a friend, John Kelly, Esq., I have had access.

Mr. Knollys arrived at Boston, a persecuted fugitive, in a state of utter destitution.   He had sacrificed every thing for conscience sake.   His child had died on the passage.   His wife's money was all expended.   Governor Winthrop calls him a " poor man."   Hubbard, who generally copies Winthrop, has ventured to translate this " a mean fellow."   This shows the prejudices of the time in a minister of the Pilgrims.   Knollys himself says, " Being very poor, I was necessitated to work daily with my hoe for the space of almost three weeks.   The magistrates were told by the min- isters that I was an Antinomian, and desired they would not suffer me to abide in the patent."   At that time all Boston was in a ferment on the question of Antinomianism, and hence the readiness to attach suspicion even to Cotton and Vane, much more to all new comers.   This was at the very year that Mrs. Ann Hutchinson, and her brother, the Rev. John Wheel- wright, with their friends, were banished on the same charge.   Providence interposed to save Mr. Knollys from perishing under this chilling reception from the Puritans—among whom, at the very head of the ministers indeed, was John Cotton, from that very Boston in Lincolnshire, where Knollys was first arrested for preaching the Gospel of the Son of God. God had a work for Mr. Knollys to do in America.   Two gentlemen from

Dover, N. H., (then a new settlement called *Piscataway*,* of fifteen years standing,) being at that time in Boston, invited Mr. Knollys to go with them, and preach in Dover. He, accordingly, went, but, on his arrival there, Capt. Burdet, who had usurped the government, forbid him to preach. He meekly submitted to this tyrannical interdict, and resorted to manual labour again for his subsistence. But, on Burdet's removal in September, "the people," says Winthrop, "called Mr. Knollys, and, in a short time, he gathered some of the best minded into a church body, and became their Pastor."† This was about the time that Roger Williams was baptized at Providence.

Were it certain that Hansard Knollys was a decided Baptist, when he gathered the First Church in Dover, it might be maintained with some reason that he was the first Baptist Minister in America. But there is room now to doubt. True, he is called an "Anabaptist" by Mather and Belknap, but they were not contemporary, and Winthrop, who was contemporary, neither affirms nor denies it at the time. This makes it most probable that he was not a Baptist when he arrived in Dover. Indeed we know not where, when, or by whom he was baptized. In the absence of direct testimony, it may be inferred, from various circumstances, that he became a Baptist while in Dover. It is, however, possible, that he embraced Baptist sentiments, and was baptized in London, while waiting for a passage to America.

We have seen, from Winthrop's Journal, that the Church in Dover was founded by Mr. Knollys, soon after September, 1638. This was the first Church in Dover, if not in New Hampshire. It was then a Congregational Church. The First Congregational Church in Exeter, founded by John Wheelwright, claims the priority by a few months, and is probably right in doing so.‡ This would make Knollys' Church the second in New Hampshire.

Mr. Knollys continued in the peaceful discharge of his duties as a Christian Pastor at Dover for about two years, without interruption. The settlement, during that period, in consequence of Capt. Mason's death, and the giving up of his patent by his widow, was a little independent Republic, of which Mr. Knollys was, beyond doubt, the most enlightened and accomplished citizen,—aiding, by his fine powers, in moulding its principles and institutions at the foundation. Up to this period his character appears to be established as that of a pious, learned, laborious minister of the Gospel, willingly suffering poverty, imprisonment, exile, and reproach for Christ's sake, and for conscience sake. He appears also, to be a man of peace. He did, indeed, write a letter from Boston soon after his arrival there, reflecting severely upon the manner in which things were then managed in Church and State; but, for the severity of this letter, he afterwards made an ingenuous and satisfactory confession. Few living men now would blame him for writing sharply to his friends of the oppressive system under which he suffered on his first arrival in Boston. There is yet another charge of this nature, which is not true. Both

---

* This is the original orthography. It was afterwards written *Piscataqua*, which name the river still bears.
† Winthrop, I. 326.
‡ Winthrop, I. 211.

Governor Hutchinson and Dr. Belknap have, by mistake, imputed to **Mr.**
Knollys the insolent language of Capt. Underhill, as recorded by Winthrop.* This blot does not belong to the character of Hansard Knollys,
and should be wiped away from his history.

The arrival of Mr. Thomas Larkham at Dover, in 1640, changed the
peaceful current of affairs, and put the peaceable character of Mr. Knollys
to the strongest proof. Mr. Larkham had been a minister in Northam,
England. He was a man of wealth, and popular talents. He soon formed
a party, who determined to remove Knollys. Dr. Belknap says that
" Knollys generously gave way to popular prejudice, and suffered Larkham to take his place." He further says that Larkham, when once in
power, " soon discovered his licentious principles, by receiving into the
church persons of immoral characters, and assuming, like Burdet, the
civil as well as ecclesiastical authority. The better sort of people were
displeased, and restored Knollys to his office, who excommunicated Larkham." Of course, this language of Dr. Belknap can only mean that the
church under Mr. Knollys excommunicated Mr. Larkham for his disorderly course. Upon this, Larkham and his adherents raised a riot, in
April, 1641, and, according to the reliable testimony of Winthrop, " laid
violent hands upon Mr. Knollys." This was just before the union of
New Hampshire with Massachusetts, which was already negotiating, and
was ratified in the course of the following month. The whole town was
thrown into confusion. In these exciting and critical circumstances, either
the solicitation of his fellow-citizens, or his own sense of duty, impelled
Mr. Knollys to appear in public at the head of a body of citizens, with a
flying banner, seeking to restore order. Larkham's company sent down
the river to Portsmouth for help, and a body of armed men came up, under
Williams, and, without any legal authority, assumed control, sat as a Court,
and pronounced sentence against Mr. Knollys, " fining him £100, and
ordering him to depart the plantation."†

It is worthy of consideration here, how far Mr. Knollys' sentiments as
a Baptist affected this question. That he was, at this time, (April, 1641,)
a Baptist, is quite clear, not only from the language of Cotton Mather
and Dr. Belknap, before referred to, but from the testimony of an unim-
peachable witness, who visited Dover within a year of the time,—Mr.
Thomas Lechford, an Episcopalian, who has left us some valuable information on the state of affairs throughout New England at that period.
The origin of the controversy between Larkham and Knollys is attributed
by Lechford chiefly to their different views on Baptism and Church membership. His own words are these: " They two fell out about baptizing
children, receiving of members, &c." Winthrop says, " there soon grew
sharp contention between him (Larkham) and Mr. Knollys, *to whom the*
more religious still adhered; whereupon, they were divided into two
churches."‡ This testimony is important and decisive. It proves that
Mr. Knollys had embraced Baptist views, at least so far as Infant Baptism
and the purity of church membership are concerned; that the more pious

* Vol. I. 292.
† Winthrop, II. 27.
‡ Winthrop, II. 27. Note by Judge Savage.

church members agreed with him; in short, that the First Church in Dover became a Baptist church, and that a second church was thereupon formed by the disaffected members, who, under the lead of Larkham, stirred up the prejudices of the people against Mr. Knollys, and even resorted to violent measures to put him down. And this testimony is further confirmed by the fact that, when commissioners were sent from Massachusetts, (which then claimed jurisdiction over Dover, both as included in their patent and now agreed to by the Colony,) they adjusted the difficulty by releasing Mr. Knollys from the fine and the censure of an illegal and *ex parte* Court, and requiring the church to revoke their sentence of excommunication against Larkham.*

The whole testimony, thus far, is in Mr. Knollys' favor. But at this juncture arose the cloud that, in this country, to a great extent, has overshadowed his fair fame. Both Winthrop and Belknap say that "a discovery was made of his failure in point of chastity," and that he himself confessed it before the church,—at least to the extent of some improper "dalliance" with two young women that lived in his family, and that on this account he was dismissed by the church and removed from Dover. This charge, against such a man, is a grave one. It has been reported by Hubbard in an exaggerated form; and more recently in a History of the First Church in Dover, published in 1830. I cannot, therefore, do less than examine it in this connection.

How much is meant by the term "dalliance," in the language of the Puritans of that age, we know not. But we do know that there are several circumstances which render the truth of this whole accusation very doubtful. In the first place, it rests altogether upon the testimony of prejudiced historians, who regarded him, to use the language of Dr. Belknap, as "an Anabaptist of the Antinomian cast." Even Winthrop, with all his general candour, was not free from this prejudice, and his knowledge of the case was wholly second-hand,—perhaps from the Massachusetts Commissioners, perhaps only from vague and prejudiced reports of some of his enemies, glad of an opportunity to put down the then odious and dreaded Baptists. But, in the second place, (aided by an antiquarian friend, John Kelly, Esq., of Exeter,) I have had access to the Judicial Records of New Hampshire for 1641, and there find the name of Hansard Knollys entered as *plaintiff* in an action of slander, which, though never prosecuted, in consequence of his return to England, at least implies that he regarded himself as an injured man.† Thirdly, in the "Account of his own Life," published in England, he gives this as the immediate reason of his return— "Being sent for to England, by my aged father, I returned with my wife, and one child about three years old." Fourthly, Cotton Mather, who wrote within about fifty years after the time, when the first reports had been more thoroughly sifted, and having full access to Winthrop's Journal, where the accusation in question is found, expressly excepts Hansard Knollys from the number of "scandalous" ministers, and places him in a class "whose names," he says, "deserve to live in our book for their *piety*, although their particular *opinions* were such as to be disserviceable unto the

* Winthrop, I. 27.
† Exeter News Letter, May 1, 1832.

declared and supposed *interests* of our churches. Of these," he says, "were some godly Anabaptists, as namely, Mr. Hansard Knollys, of Dover, and Mr. Miles,* of Swansea." But what seems particularly to touch the point in hand, Mather adds, "Both of these have a respectful character in the churches of this wilderness."† And to crown all, in speaking of the then recent decease of Mr. Knollys in London, Mather says he died "a good man, in a good old age." We know that there are spots on the sun, and that even great and good men have sometimes fallen in an evil hour; but I think that he who duly weighs these facts and testimonies, and compares them with all the antecedent and subsequent life of Hansard Knollys, will be slow to credit any injurious imputation on his character during the time of his residence in America.

This is not the place to follow Mr. Knollys back to England, and trace his eventful life for the next fifty years, through the most agitated period of English History. The theme is most inviting, and, at some other time, might be pursued with the greatest pleasure and profit. We should see in him one of the brightest lights of his age, one of the ablest preachers of the Gospel, one of the most accomplished teachers of youth, one of the boldest pioneers of religious liberty, one of the meekest, yet most heroic, sufferers for the truth, one of the purest and best of men. We have the testimony of Neal, in his History of New England, that "he suffered deeply in the cause of Nonconformity, being universally esteemed and beloved by all his brethren."‡ We may be permitted to cite from a sermon preached at Pinner's Hall, London, on occasion of his death, (which took place September 19, 1691,) the following testimony to the eminent purity of his character,—a character which his long and venerable life had elevated above all suspicion. "I do not say," says Mr. Harrison, "that he was wholly free from sin : sinless perfection is unattainable in a mortal state ; but yet he was one who carefully endeavoured to avoid it. He, with the Apostle Paul, did herein exercise himself to have always a conscience void of offence towards God and towards men. He walked with that caution, that his greatest *enemies* had nothing against him, save only in the matters of his God. That holy life which he lived, did command reverence even from those who were enemies to the holy doctrine which he preached. He was a preacher *out* of the pulpit as well as *in* it : not like those who press the form of godliness on a Lord's day, and as openly deny the power of it the remainder of the week ; who pluck down that in their conversations, which they build up in their pulpits. . . . . He loved the image of God wherever he saw it. He was not a man of a narrow and private, but of a large and public, spirit : the difference of his fellow Christians' opinions from his, did not alienate his affections from them. . . . He embraced *them* in the arms of his love on earth, with whom he thought he should join in singing the song of the Lamb in Heaven. It would be

---

* JOHN MILES was the founder of a Baptist church in Swansea, in Wales, 1649, and was ejected from his place, by the "Act of Uniformity," in 1662. He came to this country in 1663, accompanied by several of the members of his church, who were, immediately after, organized as the First Baptist Church in Swansea, Mass. Of this church he continued the Pastor until his death, which took place in 1683. Tradition gives him the reputation of having been an eminently useful man.

† Magnalia I. Book III. p. 221.
‡ Neal, Vol. I. p. 216.

well," continues Mr. Harrison, "if not only private Christians, but also ministers, did imitate him therein : there would not then be that sourness of spirit which is too often (with grief be it spoken) found among them. He was willing to bear with and forbear others, and to pass by those injuries which he received from them."*

Such was Hansard Knollys. Is it wonderful that God blessed him? Short as was his residence in America, the fruit of his labours remains to this day. The church which he planted in Dover, though divided on Baptism, did not perish. The Pedobaptist body now flourishes in the large Congregational church of Dover, the fruitful mother of many others, with Baptist sisters side by side. The Baptist body, composed, as Winthrop says, of "the more religious," adhered to Mr. Knollys; and, to avoid the oppressive Church and State jurisdiction of Massachusetts, under which they now came, removed to Long Island in 1641. After Long Island fell under the power of the English, in 1664, and the Episcopal Establishment succeeded that of the Dutch, under Stuyvesant, they, as soon as possible, sold out their property there, and settled on the East side of the Raritan, N. J., opposite New Brunswick, where, under Lord Carteret, they could enjoy religious liberty. To the town which they here planted, they transferred the dear old name of Dover,—*Piscataway*, (according to the original orthography,) in memory of their first home in the wilderness, where they had enjoyed, for three years and more, the ministrations of their first loved Pastor, Hansard Knollys. The church, when fully organized, and favoured again with pastoral care, under Mr. Drake,† in 1689, flourished anew, bearing much and blessed fruit. So deeply did it strike its roots into the new soil, that, to this day, no better kind of Christians grow than in Piscataway ; and not only do they fill the town, but, in the towns around it, new churches are continually springing as shoots from the parent tree, planted by Hansard Knollys, in America.‡

Affectionately yours in the Lord Jesus,

J. NEWTON BROWN.

* Crosby, I. 340.

† JOHN DRAKE laboured among this people from 1689 till his death in 1739. He sustained an excellent character. His descendants, who were numerous, claim kindred to Sir Francis Drake.

‡ Since the date of this communication, its author has found reason to modify somewhat the views here expressed, as will be seen by the following extract from a letter dated April 28, 1859, which he wrote in reply to an inquiry whether Knollys or Williams was the first Baptist minister in this country:

If the opinion of the Rev. Dr. Belcher, (to which I now incline,) could be proved, that Knollys was actually baptized in London, while awaiting his passage to America, it would settle the question of priority by some months in his favour. The chief probabilities for this opinion are that Baptist views were rapidly gaining ground in London, at the time, among the class with which Knollys would be thrown for sympathy and safety; that Dr. Belknap calls him an Anabaptist at the time of his arrival; that he took Baptist ground in the trouble with Larkham, and ever maintained it afterwards; and that we have no account of his Baptism after his return to this country, *nor while he was here.*

I have thought, hitherto, that it was a strong negative evidence against this view,—that neither Winthrop nor he himself should mention the fact, as the ground of his rejection by the Boston ministers and magistrates. But it now seems less unaccountable than formerly,—first, because the Antinomian controversy, raised by Mrs. Hutchinson, then overruled every other consideration; and second, that the clergy of Boston, in their reply to Mr. Saltonstall's remonstrance, claim to have "tolerated peaceable Anabaptists" from the beginning, (or something to that effect). Of course, if they regarded Mr. Knollys as belonging to the "Antinomian" side in that exciting controversy, they would put their objection to him on that ground *emphatically*, if not *solely*. The laws against "Anabaptists" were not enacted until 1664, that is, six years later.

It is, then, more than *possible*,—it is rather *probable*, on the whole,—that Mr. Knollys was already a Baptist on his arrival in America, in the spring of 1638; and if so, then he was the first

ROGER WILLIAMS.*
1639—1639.

ROGER WILLIAMS, according to the traditions which have been preserved concerning him, was born in Wales, in the year 1599; but of the character or circumstances of his family, or the particular place of his birth, nothing can now be ascertained. His mind seems to have taken an early religious direction; for he says, near the close of his life,—"From my childhood, now above threescore years, the Father of lights and mercies touched my soul with a love to Himself, to his only begotten, the true Lord Jesus, and to his Holy Scriptures." He is said to have been educated at the University of Oxford, under the patronage of Sir Edward Coke; and that this was in consequence of Sir Edward's having observed his sedate appearance at church, and his taking notes of the sermon; but this is rendered somewhat improbable by the fact that Roger Williams' name does not appear on the rolls of Oxford University, and, in addition to this, Sir Edward himself received his education at Cambridge. It is, therefore, somewhat doubtful which of the two English Universities has the honour of claiming the great New England republican adventurer as an alumnus; though it is rendered certain, by some of his own writings, that he enjoyed the advantages of one or the other of these celebrated institutions.

On leaving the University, he is said to have entered on the study of the Law; but it proved incongenial with his tastes, and he soon abandoned it for the study of Theology. In due time, he was ordained as a clergyman of the Established Church, and it is said that he also took charge of a parish,—but of this no evidence is to be found in his writings. In the great contest which then convulsed the British nation, he not only identified himself fully with the interests of the Puritans, but became the staunch advocate of the largest religious liberty; and, under these circumstances and influences, he resolved to join the band of emigrants who were seeking a peaceful religious home on the shores of New England. Accordingly, he embarked at Bristol, on the 1st of December, 1630, in the ship Lion, Captain Pierce, and, after a tempestuous voyage of sixty-six days, arrived at Boston on the 5th of February, 1631. His arrival was hailed by the churches of the infant Colony of Massachusetts Bay, with great satisfaction; and Governor Winthrop, in referring to it in his journal, speaks of him as "a godly minister." He brought with him his wife, Mrs. Mary Williams, to whom he had been married a short time before, but of whose previous history nothing is now known.

Baptist minister in this country. But it is curious, if this were so, that Roger Williams did not hear of it from Clarke and others, who joined him that year from Boston. Yet, if he did know it at the time he himself was baptized by Holliman, he might not be able to reach him, or might not know where he had gone. Besides, he evidently regarded Holliman as sufficiently authorized by the vote of the Church to administer the ordinance in a case of necessity, on the same principle as Tertullian, or Thomas Aquinas and Zanchius, maintain the authority of Lay-baptism.

* Gammell's Life of Roger Williams.—Knowles' do.—Callender's Historical Discourse—Backus' History of New England, I.—Benedict's History of the Baptists, I.—American Baptist Magazine, I.—Winthrop's History of New England, I.

But Roger Williams soon discovered that his views of religious liberty were greatly in advance of those of the people among whom he came to settle. He found that they had come hither, rather to enjoy unmolested their own religious principles and modes of worship, than to practise a general toleration; while he, on the other hand, fully believed that every man has an inalienable right, in all matters pertaining to religion, to think and act for himself. His doctrine was that "the civil magistrate should restrain crime, but never control opinion; should punish guilt, but never violate the freedom of the soul." Hence, when he found that the magistrates insisted on the presence of every man at public worship, and that a decree had been passed that "no man should be admitted to the freedom of the body politic, but such as were members of some of the churches within the limits of the same,"—his judgment and heart both revolted; and he began to think that the end he had proposed to himself in coming to the new world was at best but very partially gained.

A few weeks after his arrival, Mr. Williams was invited to become Co-pastor with the Rev. Samuel Skelton of the Church in Salem; but the magistrates of the Colony, having heard of his opinions, interposed their remonstrances with the people of Salem to prevent his settlement. Their opposition, however, did not avail, and he was, accordingly, settled on the 12th of April, 1631. On the 18th of May following, he was admitted a freeman of the Colony, and took the usual oath of allegiance. Being now in the fullest sense of the word a citizen of the Colony, and a minister of its oldest church, and having secured, in an unusual degree, the confidence of the people of Salem, every thing seemed to give promise of continued and increasing usefulness.

But scarcely had his settlement here been effected, before it became manifest that causes were in operation that must soon lead to his removal. The Governor and General Court were offended that the church had disregarded their advice in calling him; and his peculiar opinions, which he did not attempt to conceal, had made him obnoxious to the elders and magistrates of the Colony; and these combined influences served to render his condition extremely uncomfortable. After the lapse of a few months, therefore,—probably in August, 1631, he removed from Salem, and sought a residence in the Colony of Plymouth, beyond the jurisdiction of the Court of Massachusetts Bay.

At Plymouth he was received with great respect and kindness, by the Governor and leading citizens, and, after being admitted to the church, was settled as Assistant to the Pastor, the Rev. Ralph Smith. Governor Bradford says,—"His teaching was well approved, for the benefit whereof," he adds, "I shall bless God, and am thankful to him even for his sharpest admonitions and reproofs, so far as they agreed with truth." But, though a more friendly disposition seemed to be manifested towards him than had been in the Colony of Massachusetts, it was not long before he discovered that he was still the object of suspicion, and that his views of religious liberty met with no response from those with whom he was now associated. His preaching, however, was so acceptable, and his life so exemplary, that he remained among them, with a good degree of comfort, for about two years. In the summer of 1633, he received an invitation from the people to whom he had previously ministered at Salem, to come and supply them,—their Pastor, Mr. Skelton, being sick. He accepted their invitation, and the more readily from the fact that his former residence among them had greatly endeared them to him, and he and they still regarded each other with undiminished attachment.

Mr. Williams resumed his labours at Salem, probably in August, and, for a year, exercised his ministry, "by way of prophecy," as it was termed, before he was settled as Pastor of the church. This event took place on the death of Mr. Skelton, in the summer of 1634.

Soon after his return to Salem, we find him joining with his colleague, Mr. Skelton, in questioning the expediency of a certain meeting of ministers, which had been established in the Colony, for discussing theological questions, and for other purposes of mutual improvement. Governor Winthrop states that the ground of their objection was a fear "that it might grow in time to a Presbytery or Superintendency, to the prejudice of the Churches' liberties." It is not strange that the magistrates, who had already shared in the suspicions of his orthodoxy which had been awakened among the clergy, should have seen in this movement a fresh cause for alarm; and no doubt it was one of the circumstances that prepared the way for his final expulsion from the Colony.

But there were other and graver matters than this to bring him into collision with the civil authorities. During his residence at Plymouth, he had written a treatise on the nature of the right claimed by the monarchs of the several nations of Christendom to dispose of the countries of barbarous tribes, by virtue of discovery; and had presented it to the Governor and Council of the Plymouth Colony. In this treatise, says Governor Winthrop, "among other things, he disputed their right to the land they possessed, and concluded that, claiming by the King's grant, they could have no title, nor otherwise, except they compounded with the natives." This manuscript, though it had never been published, and was written in another Colony, he was required to deliver to the Governor for examination; and the result of a conference with the ministers was that he was summoned to appear at the next Court to receive censure. The Governor says that the treatise contained "three passages, whereat they were much offended. First, for that he chargeth King James to have told a solemn public lie, because, in his patent, he blessed God that he was the first Christian prince that discovered this land. Secondly, for that he chargeth him and others with blasphemy, for calling Europe Christendom, or the Christian world. Thirdly, for that he did personally apply to our present King Charles, these three places in the Revelations, viz."—The passages, unfortunately, are not quoted. It is not known that the offensive treatise was ever published—certainly it has not been preserved. Mr. Williams complied with the orders of the Court, and wrote letters to the magistrates, stating that his treatise had been written "only for the private satisfaction of the Governor of Plymouth;" and, with the expression of regret, if he had committed any wrong, and of loyalty to the King,—without, however, renouncing his opinions,—he offered his manuscript to be burned. The spirit which he evinced on this occasion was highly honourable to him ; and the historian, in recording the circumstance, says,—" they found the matters not to be so evil as at first they seemed."

It has already been intimated that Mr. Williams' second settlement at Salem was strongly opposed by the magistrates of the Colony. The Court sent in a decided remonstrance, and requested the Church not to ordain him ; but the Church felt that this was an infringement of their independence, and proceeded without any regard to it. This, of course, was too palpable an act of disrespect to the civil authorities to be passed without some signal expression of displeasure. Accordingly, when the Court met at Boston, a few months after, he was arraigned on the charge of having publicly called in question the King's patent, and " for usual terming the churches of England anti-christian." Again, in April, 1635, the Governor and Assistants summoned him to appear at Boston, to answer to the charge of having " taught publicly that a magistrate ought not to tender an oath to an unregenerate man, for that we thereby have communion with a wicked man in the worship of God, and cause him to take the name of God in vain." On this occasion, Governor Winthrop states that " he was heard before all the ministers, and very clearly refuted." The magistrates enacted a law, requiring every man to attend public worship, and to contribute to its support. This law Williams denounced as utterly at war with human rights, and as tending directly to cherish a persecuting spirit—" The civil power," he said, " extends only to the bodies, and goods, and outward estates of men "—with conscience and with religious opinions " the civil magistrate may not intermeddle even to stop a church from apostacy and heresy."

At this juncture, the people of Salem preferred to the Court a claim for a tract of land lying on Marblehead Neck ; but the Court, by way of retaliation for the contempt of authority which the town had shown in settling Mr. Williams, refused the claim. Mr. W., regarding this as an act of flagrant injustice, induced the church to join with him in addressing letters to all the churches with which any of the magistrates were connected, urging them to admonish the magistrates for the wrong of which they had been guilty. This was regarded as little less than an act of open rebellion ; and, at the next meeting of the Court, the deputies from Salem were denied their seats until they had apologized for the alleged indignity. Williams now addressed a letter to his own church, urging them to renounce all communion with the other churches in the Colony ; but the power of the magistrates overawed them, and they refused any longer to second the views of their teacher.

But, notwithstanding he was left alone to maintain his views,—even his own wife, for the sake of peace, joining the multitude in protesting against his course,—yet so inwrought were these views with the very texture of his mind, that he stood forth with the most heroic firmness for their defence. The ministers, with Mr. Cotton and Mr. Hooker at their head, sent a committee to Salem to deal with him ; but he utterly denied their jurisdiction, and declared himself " ready to be bound, and banished, and even to die in New England," rather than to yield his deliberate and matured convictions. The Court now requested the ministers to assemble, and consider his case, and state their opinion as to the course proper to be pursued. They did so; and their judgment was that he deserved to be banished from the Colony, for maintaining the doctrine "that the civil magistrate might not intermeddle, even to stop a church from apostacy and heresy," and that the churches ought to request the magistrates to remove him.

In July, he was summoned to Boston, to answer to the General Court for holding the following dangerous opinions:—"First, that the magistrate ought not to punish the breach of the first table, otherwise than in such cases as did disturb the civil peace. Secondly, that he ought not to tender an oath to an unregenerate man. Thirdly, that he ought not to pray with such, though wife, child, &c. Fourthly, that a man ought not to give thanks after Sacrament, nor after meat." After a protracted and earnest debate, it was agreed to allow Mr. Williams and the Church in Salem "time to consider these things till the next General Court, and then either to give satisfaction, or to expect the sentence."

At the next General Court,—which was held in October, 1635,—Mr. Williams was present, in obedience to the summons, but his opinions remained unchanged. Though most of those who had at first made common cause with him, deserted his standard, he stood as firmly as ever,—not even seeming to falter in his adherence to the principles he had avowed. The Court accordingly decided, though not by a large majority, that he should depart out of their jurisdiction within six weeks. The sentence of banishment was passed on the 3d of November,—all the ministers but one approving of it. These proceedings awakened no little sympathy for Mr. Williams in the Colony, and especially among his old friends in Salem.

Complaints were made to the Court that he still persisted in promulgating and defending his opinions; that many people resorted to his house to listen to his teachings; and that he was preparing to withdraw with them from Massachusetts, and form a settlement upon Narragansett Bay. As they were not pleased with the prospect of having a new Colony in their neighbourhood, established upon such principles as he held, they determined to send him to England, by a ship then just about to sail. For this purpose, he received another summons to attend the Court at Boston. But he declined to obey it, alleging as a reason that he was suffering from ill health. The magistrates, resolved on accomplishing their object, now sent a small sloop to Boston, with a warrant to Captain Underhill to apprehend him, and carry him on board the ship, which was about to sail for England. He had, however, taken the precaution to make his escape three days before, though his wife and children were left behind. This was in the month of January, 1636.

It is difficult to conceive of a more forlorn condition, as far as external circumstances were concerned, than was that of Mr. Williams in the early part of the period of his exile. Though he has left no detailed account of his wanderings and sufferings, yet something may be inferred from occasional allusions to the subject in his writings, and especially from a letter to his friend, Major Mason, written thirty-five years afterwards, in which he speaks of still feeling the effects of what he then endured.— "I was sorely tossed," says he, "for fourteen weeks, in a bitter winter season, not knowing what bread or bed did mean."

When Mr. Williams was leaving Salem, Governor Winthrop, who, the year before, had been supplanted in the Chief Magistracy of the Colony, by Thomas Dudley, wrote to him "to steer his course to the Narragansett Bay and Indians," as a region not yet appropriated by any of the patents of the King. In accordance with this advice, he made his way through the forest to the lodges of the Pokanokets, who occupied the country North from Mount Hope, as far as Charles River. Massasoit, the famous chief of this tribe, who had known Mr. Williams, and received favours from him, during his residence at Plymouth, now welcomed him to the hospitalities of his cabin at Mount Hope, and extended to him the protection and aid which he needed. He granted him a tract of land on the Seekonk River, upon which, at the opening of spring, he commenced planting and building. A number of his friends at Salem now joined him, and he flattered himself that he should experience no further annoyance from the authorities of Massachusetts Bay.

But scarcely had he commenced his settlement here, before he received a letter from Governor Winslow of the Plymouth Colony, intimating to him that, as he was then within their bounds, and they were unwilling to incur the displeasure of their neighbours of the Bay, he had better remove to the other side of the river; and then he would be beyond the possibility of any molestation. He readily complied with this advice, and, abandoning the fields he had planted, and the dwelling he had begun to build, embarked in a canoe, upon the Seekonk River, in quest of another spot, where he might make his home, and plant a colony. He was accompanied by five others, who, having joined him at Seekonk, were more than willing still to share his fortunes. In due time, he landed at the mouth of Mooshausic River; and, upon the beautiful slope of the hill that ascends from the river, he began the settlement, which, on account of the gracious interposition of Heaven, he afterwards called *Providence*. This is supposed to have been in the latter part of June, 1636.

Mr. Williams still found that the acquaintance he had formed with the Indians, while a resident of Plymouth, was of great service to him, especially in procuring from the Sachems a grant of the land on which he settled. In all his dealings with them, he proceeded upon the principle for which he had always contended,—regarding them as the sole proprietors of the soil, and purchasing of them a clear title to the lands of which he took possession. In order to raise the funds necessary to this purpose, and for the removal of his family to their new home, he was obliged to mortgage his house and land in Salem. In the organization of the new Colony, he kept in view the great principle of religious liberty, for which he had contended in Massachusetts: he desired to offer "a shelter for persons distressed for conscience;" and all such who came to him he welcomed with open arms. Those who joined the settlement, bound themselves to conform to the principles on which it had been founded, and also to be subject to the will of the majority.

Mr. Williams was soon placed in circumstances in which he had an opportunity to render most important services to the Colony of Massachusetts, and, after the trials to which he had been subjected in that Colony, it evinced great magnanimity that he was disposed to avail himself of it.

The Pequot Indians, who had always manifested a bitter hostility to the English, had conceived the design of a universal insurrection, for the purpose of driving them from the lands they had acquired. In the summer of 1636, they attacked a party of traders in a sloop, near Block Island, and murdered John Oldham, one of the number; and, having made a treaty of peace with all the neighbouring tribes, they were endeavouring to unite them in a common effort for the extermination of the Colonies. As soon as Roger Williams became acquainted with these facts, he communicated them to the Governor of Massachusetts; and to him did the authorities of that Colony commit the work of conciliating the Indians, with a view to defeat the bloody purpose they had formed. Though the enterprise was one of extreme difficulty and peril, Mr. Williams executed it with the utmost skill, fidelity, and success. The Sachems yielded to his counsels, and he was enabled to effect a treaty of the English with the Narragansetts and Mohegans, against the Pequots. This treaty was ratified by the two contracting parties, at Boston, in October, 1636.

But Mr. Williams' service to the Massachusetts Colony did not end here. The Pequots, though foiled in their attempt to make a league with the other tribes, were still bent on executing their purposes of vengeance; and they resolved to rush at once upon their enemies, and, if possible, cut them off by one onset of savage barbarity. When this was known, the three Colonies of Plymouth, Massachusetts, and Connecticut resolved immediately to invade the territory of the Pequots, and, if possible, to effect their final extermination. The war continued nearly a year; and, during the whole period, Mr. Williams was the constant adviser of the Colonies, especially of the authorities of Massachusetts Bay, and the watchful guardian of all their interests in their relations with the friendly Indians. The war was terminated by the celebrated battle fought near the fort on Mystic River, in May, 1637; and it ended only in the complete extinction of the race. Notwithstanding the high obligations under which Mr. Williams had placed the Massachusetts Colony, by his most timely and important services, it seems strange enough that they not only never offered him the least acknowledgment, but did not even revoke their sentence of banishment.

Not long after his settlement at Providence, Mr. Williams, with several of his brethren, embraced the views of the Baptists. Wishing to be baptized by immersion, they were at first not a little embarrassed for want of a person whom they deemed qualified to administer the ordinance; and the result of considerable consultation on the subject was that, in March, 1639, they appointed Mr. Ezekiel Holliman, "a man of gifts and piety," to baptize Mr. Williams, who, in return, baptized Mr. Holliman and ten others. These were soon joined by twelve other persons, who came to the settlement for the sake of liberty of conscience. And thus commenced the first Baptist Church on this continent. With this church Mr. Williams continued to exercise his pastoral functions but about four months, when he resigned his charge on account of a change in his religious opinions. From having rejected Infant Baptism, he proceeded to discard all Baptism whatever, "because," as Governor Winthrop states, "not derived from the authority of the Apostles, otherwise than by the ministers of England, whom he judged to be ill authority." Holding these views, he left the church which he had been instrumental in forming, and became what, in the History of New England, is denominated a *Seeker*. He regarded all the churches in Christendom as, in some sense, in a state of apostacy, and all the clergy as having lost their true apostolical authority. But these strangely erratic opinions did not abate at all his interest in the general truths of the Gospel, or his zeal in the conversion of others to the Christian faith. At a later period, when he had become more deeply involved in the affairs of the State, we find him often preaching to the Indians; and he is believed to have continued this almost to the close of his life. He was succeeded in the pastoral office at Providence by Mr. Brown* and Mr. Wickendon.†

In 1643, Mr. Williams went to England to procure a charter for his Colony; but, notwithstanding his magnanimous treatment of the authorities of Massachusetts Bay, their prejudices against him did not relax even so far as to allow him to pass through their territory to take his passage; and he was consequently obliged to embark from New York. The Dutch, at this time, were engaged in a bloody conflict with different Indian tribes; and, through the mediation of Mr. Williams, whose influence with the Indians was then probably greater than that of any other man, friendly relations between the Dutch and the Indians were restored.

Mr. Williams arrived in England in the midst of the civil war which then distracted the nation, though the state of things, on the whole, proved favourable to the prosecution of his object. He obtained his charter, after a few months, and, on his return, landed at Boston in September, 1644. Though he was still under sentence of banishment, he brought with him a letter of recommendation from some of the leading members of Parliament, which secured him from any detention on his way to Providence. On his passage to England, he prepared a "Key to the Indian Languages," which was published there shortly after his arrival; and, during his sojourn in England, he published his celebrated work, entitled "The Bloody Tenet, or a Dialogue between Truth and Peace." This was subsequently answered by the Rev. John Cotton, in a work entitled "The Bloody Tenet washed in the Blood of the Lamb." Mr. Williams published a rejoinder, entitled "The Bloody Tenet yet more Bloody, by Mr. Cotton's endeavour to wash it white."

The inhabitants of the several settlements, embraced in the charter of Mr. Williams, were not prepared at once to enter on the organization of a common government; and the charter was not actually adopted by a General Assembly of the people of the Colony, until May, 1647.

Mr. Williams, now finding his pecuniary resources not a little reduced, and having a family of six young children upon his hands, erected a trading house in the Narragansett country, where he spent the greater part of his

---

* The Rev. CHAD BROWN came to Providence in the latter part of the year 1636, by reason of the persecution in Massachusetts. He was ordained in the year 1642. He was one of the town proprietors, and the fourteenth in order. He maintained a good character, and had a prosperous ministry.

† Mr. WICKENDON, who was colleague with Mr. Brown, came from Salem to Providence in 1639, and was ordained by Mr. Brown. He died on the 23d of February, 1669, after having removed to a place called Solitary Hill. He preached for some time in the city of New York, and, as a reward for his labour, was imprisoned four months.

time. Here, for several years, he carried on an honourable traffic with
the Indians, and acted as their friend in various ways, especially in communicating to them a knowledge of the truths of Christianity. But he
was still regarded as a citizen of Providence, and filled successively some
of the highest offices of the town and of the Colony.

The new charter did not meet with universal acceptance. Mr. Coddington, the leading inhabitant of the island of Rhode Island, arrayed himself
in opposition to it from the beginning. Having secured the co-operation
of certain other dissatisfied persons, he went to England, and finally
succeeded in inducing the Council of State to annul it, and, on his
return, in 1651, brought with him a commission, erecting the islands of
Rhode Island and Canonicut into a separate government, and appointing
him Governor for life of the new Colony, with a Council to be nominated
by the people and approved by himself. This proved a most unwelcome
measure; and most of the inhabitants of Newport, and a large number
of those of Portsmouth, united in appointing Mr. John Clarke to proceed
as their agent to England, to procure, if possible, a reversal of the offensive ordinance. About the same time, the two towns of Providence and
Warwick, which had still continued to maintain the government under the
original charter, earnestly requested Mr. Williams to join Mr. Clarke in
his mission; and he, finally, though not without great reluctance, consented to the proposal. It was not without much embarrassment from the
authorities of Massachusetts that he was allowed to pass through their
territory to sail for England; but he finally succeeded, and embarked with
Mr. Clarke, in November, 1651.

Soon after their arrival in England, Williams and Clarke presented a
petition to the Council of State in behalf of the Colony they had come to
represent. Though they had to encounter a strong opposition, they found
a firm friend and efficient coadjutor in Sir Henry Vane, who was, at that
time, a prominent member of the Council, and at the height of his political
prosperity. Though the main question could not be decided at once, an
order was soon passed by the Council, vacating Mr. Coddington's commission, and confirming the charter formerly granted to the Colony, until the
case could be fully and finally adjudicated. The order of the Council
reached Newport in the early part of 1653; but, though Coddington's
administration seems to have been brought to an end, yet, owing to some
jealousies which had sprung up in the mean time, the order was not at
once fully obeyed, as the settlements on the island, and those on the main
land, continued to maintain their separate governments for a year and a
half.

During his sojourn in England, at this period, Mr. Williams enjoyed
opportunities of unreserved intercourse with many of the greatest spirits
of the age; of whom it is only necessary to mention Cromwell and Milton.
It was during this period also that he found leisure to write and publish
his rejoinder to Mr. Cotton, already referred to. He published also, about
the same time, his "Hireling Ministry none of Christ's; or a Discourse
touching the Propagation of the Gospel of Jesus Christ;" and his
"Experiments of Spiritual Life and Health, and their Preservatives,"—
two controversial essays, relating to Theology and Church Government.

He returned to Providence early in the summer of 1654, leaving Mr. Clarke behind, to watch the progress of events, and use his influence to give them a right direction. Previous to his leaving England, the Lord Protector's Council gave him an order addressed to the authorities of Massachusetts, requiring them to allow him, in future, either to land or to embark, within their jurisdiction, without being molested.

The first object which engaged his attention, after his return, was the restoration of union among the several towns of the Colony, and the reorganization of the government, agreeably to the order of the Council of State, passed two years before. This was not effected without considerable opposition; but, at length, on the 31st of August, 1654, at a meeting of the Commissioners of all the towns, the articles of union were finally agreed on. At the first general election, after the Government was thus reorganized, Mr. Williams was chosen President of the Colony. Thus the division of the settlements of Rhode Island, which had been continued through several years, and had well-nigh destroyed the independent existence of the Colony, was happily terminated.

In the early part of Mr. Williams' administration, a number of persons in the Colony, by a gross perversion of the idea of religious liberty, upon which the Colony was based, maintained that it was "contrary to the rule of the Gospel to execute judgment upon transgressors against the private or public weal." The ruling spirit of this faction was William Harris, an influential inhabitant of Providence, between whom and Mr. Williams there arose a bitter and protracted controversy. Mr. W. finally entered a formal complaint against him, at the General Court of Commissioners, for high treason against the Commonwealth. The case was ultimately referred to the authorities in the mother country, but no answer was returned, and the accusation, therefore, was never prosecuted.

In July, 1656, the first Quakers arrived in Boston, and scarcely had they landed before the guardians of the Colony were on the alert for their extermination. The most cruel laws were enacted, the most rigorous measures adopted, to effect this object; and Massachusetts was heartily and vigorously joined by all the other Colonies except Rhode Island; but she, remaining true to her principles, utterly refused her co-operation. She indeed disapproved of their doctrines, and determined to require of them, as of all others who should come to her settlements, a strict performance of all civil duties; but neither the arguments nor the threats of the Commissioners of the Colonies could drive her from her cherished principles, which had been distinctly recognised in her charter, and in all her legislation. Subsequently to this,—in 1672, Mr. Williams had a public controversy with several of the leading Quakers, which was marked by great asperity, and productive of little profit. He afterwards wrote out the discussion in full, with an account of its origin, and the manner in which it was conducted. This book is entitled "George Fox digged out of his Burrowes; or an Offer of Disquisition on Fourteen Proposals, made this last Summer, 1672, (so called,) unto G. Fox, then present in Rhode Island, in New England, by R. W."

In the summer of 1675, New England became the theatre of the most furious and desolating Indian war. Philip, the powerful and aspiring chief of the Pokanokets, had undertaken to establish a league among the surrounding tribes, with a view to avenge what he conceived to be the wrongs of his race, and, if possible, to exterminate the English, or drive them from the country. Mr. Williams made a vigorous effort to avert the threatening tempest, and at first seemed likely to succeed, but the vengeful spirit could not be repressed, and four thousand warriors rushed forth, determined to spread desolation throughout New England. For a time, it seemed as if the Colonies would be absolutely annihilated. While many of the people of Providence fled, Mr. Williams remained at home, and, though upwards of seventy-six years of age, he accepted a commission as Captain in the militia of the Colony, and kept the companies in Providence in constant readiness for active service. Though the best possible preparations for defence were made, the Indians, on the 29th of March, 1676, attacked the town, and reduced twenty-nine houses to ashes. It is said that, when they appeared on the heights, North of the town, Mr. Williams went forth to meet them, thinking his influence might prevail with them as it had done in other cases; but, though some of the older chiefs seemed kindly disposed towards him, they assured him that the young men were too much exasperated for him to venture among them with safety. He returned to the garrison, and soon saw the town in flames. This terrible war, which cost the Colonies an immense amount of treasure and blood, was brought to a close by the death of King Philip, in August, 1676.

The precise time of Mr. Williams' death cannot be ascertained; but it is known to have occurred in the early part of the year 1683. He died in the eighty-fourth year of his age, but seems to have retained his intellectual faculties in their full vigour to the last. He was buried in Providence, on the spot which he had selected as the burial place of his family, with appropriate funeral honours. It is believed that his wife and all his children survived him.

There are few characters in modern times that have met with such diversified treatment at the hands of historians as Roger Williams. Besides the adverse testimonies concerning him, occasionally rendered by his contemporaries, the act of banishment by the General Court of Massachusetts was a condemnatory verdict known and read of all men. But, as the great principle, the advocacy of which chiefly signalized his life, has been brought into a brighter light,—the severe estimate of his character has not only given place to a more kindly spirit towards him, but has been changed to a tone of high, and, in many instances, unqualified, praise. Probably those who now form their judgment of his character from the most impartial view of the history of his life, will arrive at the conclusion that he was a man of extraordinary intellectual endowments; of a naturally generous and forgiving spirit; of uncompromising integrity; of courage that nothing could appal and perseverance that nothing could arrest; and above all of an intuitive discernment of the rights of the human mind, that constituted him in that respect the great light of his age. At the same time, it will be difficult to avoid the conclusion that there were acts in his life that betokened infirmity and eccentricity; particularly his leaving the Church in Providence so soon after he had founded it, and continuing, during the rest of his life, in such an anomalous ecclesiastical relation. Instead of attempting an analysis of his character, I shall content myself with quoting the opinions of a few eminent individuals, who, though they do not entirely harmonize in their estimate of him, have evidently prosecuted their inquiries with an honest desire, and the best opportunities, to reach the truth. None of them belong to the Baptist denomination.

Dr. Bentley, in his History of Salem, writes concerning Roger Williams as follows:—

" In Salem every person loved Mr. Williams. He had no personal enemies under any pretence. All valued his friendship. Kind treatment could win him, but opposition could not conquer him. He was not afraid to stand alone for truth against the world; and he had always address enough, with his firmness, never to be forsaken by the friends he had ever gained. He had always a tenderness of conscience, and feared every offence against moral truth. He breathed the purest devotion. He was ready in thoughts and words, and defied all his vaunting adversaries to public disputation. He had a familiar imagery of style, which suited his times, and he indulged, even in the titles of his controversial papers, to wit upon names, especially upon the Quakers. He knew man better than he did civil government. He was a friend of human nature, forgiving, upright, and pious. He understood the Indians better than any man of the age. He made not so many converts, but he made more sincere friends. He knew their passions and the restraints they could endure. He was betrayed into no wild or expensive projects respecting them. He studied their manners, and their customs, and passions together. His vocabulary also proves that he was familiar with the words of their language, if not with its principles. It is a happy relief, in contemplating so eccentric a character, that no sufferings induced any purposes of revenge, for which he afterwards had great opportunities; that great social virtues corrected the first errors of his opinions; and that he lived to exhibit to the natives a noble example of generous goodness, and to be the parent of the independent State of Rhode Island."

John Quincy Adams, in his "Discourse on the New England Confederacy of 1643," after eloquently vindicating the Boston magistrates and ministers, in regard to their treatment of Roger Williams, says,—

" He was an eloquent preacher; stiff and self-confident in his opinions, ingenious, powerful and commanding in impressing them upon others, inflexible in his adherence to them, and, by an inconsistency peculiar to religious enthusiasts, combining the most amiable and affectionate sympathies of the heart with the most repulsive and inexorable exclusion of conciliation, compliance, or intercourse with his adversaries in opinion."

The Hon. Daniel Appleton White, in an account of the First Church in Salem, and its ministers, appended to the Rev. J. H. Morrison's Sermon at the installation of the Rev. G. W. Briggs, after quoting the opinion of Professor Elton on the difference between Mr. Williams on the one hand, and the magistrates and clergy on the other, adds,—

" The truth appears to be that there were faults on both sides, and that they were faults of the age rather than of the heart. It is the peculiar glory of Roger Williams that, in his great doctrine that *the civil power has no jurisdiction over the conscience*, he rose above the age, and that he was stout enough to sustain himself nobly against opposition and difficulties, which would have crushed any common man."

Bancroft, in the first volume of his "History of the United States," pays the following tribute to Roger Williams:—

" Roger Williams asserted the great doctrine of intellectual liberty. It became his glory to found a state upon that principle, and to stamp himself upon its rising institutions, in characters so deep that the impress has remained to the present day, and can never be erased without the total destruction of the work. The principles which he first sustained amidst the bickerings of a colonial parish, next asserted in the General Court of Massachusetts, and then introduced into the wilds on Narragansett Bay, he soon found occasion to publish to the world, and to defend as the basis of the religious freedom of mankind; so that, borrowing the rhetoric employed by his antagonist in derision, we may compare him to the lark, the pleasant bird of the peaceful summer, that, " affecting to soar aloft, springs upward from the ground, takes his rise from pale to tree," and at last, surmounting the highest hills, utters his clear carols through the skies of morning.* He was the first person in modern Christendom to assert, in its plenitude, the doctrine of the liberty of conscience, the equality of opinions before the law; and in its defence he was the harbinger of Milton, the precursor and the superior of Jeremy Taylor. For Taylor limited his toleration to a few Christian sects; the philanthropy of Williams compassed the earth. Taylor favoured partial reform, commended lenity, argued for forbearance, and entered a special plea in behalf of each tolerable sect. Williams would permit persecution of no opinion, of no religion, leaving heresy unharmed by law, and orthodoxy unprotected by the terrors of penal statutes. Taylor still clung to the necessity of positive regulations enforcing religion and eradicating error; he resembled the poets who, in their folly, first declare their hero to be invulnerable, and then clothe him in earthly armour. Williams was willing to leave Truth alone, in her own panoply of light,† believing that if, in the ancient feud between Truth and Error, the employment of force could be entirely abrogated, Truth would have much the best of the bargain. It is the custom of mankind to award high honours to the successful inquirer into the laws of nature, to those who advance the bounds of human knowledge. We praise the man who first analyzed the air, or resolved water into its elements, or drew the lightning from the clouds; even though the discoveries may have been as much the fruits of time as of genius. A moral principle has a much wider and nearer influence on human happiness; nor can any discovery of truth be of more direct benefit to society, than that which establishes a perpetual religious peace, and spreads tranquillity through every community and every bosom. If Copernicus is held in perpetual remembrance, because, on his death bed, he published to the world that the sun is the centre of our system; if the name of Kepler is preserved in the annals of human excellence for his sagacity in detecting the laws of the planetary motion; if the genius of Newton has been almost adored for dissecting a ray of light, and weighing heavenly bodies as in a balance,—let there be for the name of Roger Williams at least some humble place among those who have advanced moral science, and made themselves the benefactors of mankind."   *   *   *   *   *   *   *   *   *   *   *   *   *

" The most touching trait in the founder of Rhode Island Colony, was his conduct towards his persecutors. Though keenly sensitive to the hardships which he had endured, he was far from harbouring feelings of revenge towards those who banished him, and only regretted their delusion. ' I did ever, from my soul, honour and love them, even when their judgment led them to afflict me.'‡ In all his writings on the subject, he attacked the spirit of intolerance, the doctrine of persecution, and never his persecutors or the Colony of Massachusetts. Indeed, we shall presently behold him requite their severity, by exposing his life at their request, and for their benefit. It is not strange, then, if ' many hearts were touched with relentings. That great and pious soul, Mr. Winslow, melted and kindly visited me,' says the exile, ' and put a piece of gold into the hands of my wife, for our supply;§ the founder, the legislator, the proprietor, of Rhode Island owed a shelter to the hospitality of an Indian chief, and his wife the means of sustenance to the charity of a stranger. The half-wise Cotton Mather concedes that many judicious persons confessed him to have had the root of the matter in him; and his nearer friends, the immediate witnesses of his actions, declared him, from ' the whole course and tenor of his life and conduct, to have been one of the most disinterested men that ever lived, a most pious and heavenly minded soul.'"‖

Dr. Palfrey, in his History of New England, lately published, takes a less favourable view of Roger Williams' conduct, especially in the controversy which issued in his banishment, than some other historians have done; but he allows him, on the whole, to have possessed great merit. The following paragraph is from his pen :—

" Williams had great virtues, and some of them were of that character which peculiarly wins and attaches. He was eminently courageous, disinterested, and kindhearted. If (in his early days, at least) he belonged to that class of men who had no peace for themselves except in sharp strife with others,—if the *certaminis gaudia*, the joy of quarrel, made an indispensable condition of his satisfaction of mind,—he was incapable of any feeling of malice or vindictiveness towards opponents. Though, in his controversies, he uses strong language, as was his wont on all occasions, a tone

---

* John Cotton's Reply, 2.
† The expression is partly from Gibbon and Sir Henry Vane.
‡ Winthrop and Savage.
§ Williams to Mason.
‖ Callender, 17.

of friendliness is scarcely ever abandoned. Differ and contend he must. For him a stagnant life was not worth living. When he had made a few proselytes to his last novelty, and so far prevailed to have his own way, he would start off on some new track, impelled by his irresistible besetting hunger for excitement and conflict. But with all this he had a sweetness of temper and a constancy of benevolence, that no hard treatment could overcome, and no difficulties or dangers exhaust or discourage."

———◆◆———

JOHN CLARKE.*

1644—1676.

JOHN CLARKE was born in England, (tradition says in Bedfordshire) on the 8th of October, 1609. Where he was educated is not known; but the following clause in his will may give some idea of his learning—"Item, unto my loving friend, Richard Bayley, I give and bequeath my Concordance and Lexicon thereto belonging, written by myself, being the fruit of several years' study: my Hebrew Bible, Buxtorff's and Parsons' Lexicons, Cotton's Concordance, and all the rest of my books." Previous to his coming to this country, he was married to Elizabeth, daughter of John Harges, Esq., of Bedfordshire. He entered the medical profession, and was, for some time, a practising physician in London. Under what circumstances, or in what year precisely, he came to America, I am unable to ascertain; but he seems to have brought with him a strong antipathy to the reigning spirit of the times, and an intense love of religious liberty. He settled in Boston as a medical practitioner; but so much was he disgusted with the tone of public feeling in the Massachusetts Colony, especially as evinced by the banishment of Mr. Wheelwright and Ann Hutchinson, that he proposed to several of his friends to remove with him out of a jurisdiction that was the seat of so much intolerance. His friends listened to his proposal; and it was agreed that he and some others should look out for a place where they might enjoy the blessing of religious freedom. By reason of the extreme heat of the preceding summer, they first went North to a place which is now within the bounds of New Hampshire; but the severity of the next winter there led them, the following spring, to take a Southern direction. They agreed that, while their vessel was passing around Cape Cod, they would cross over, by land, having either Long Island, or Delaware Bay, in view, as a place for settlement. They stopped at Providence, where they found Roger Williams, who fully sympathized in their principles and designs, and was disposed to render them all the aid in his power. He suggested two places to them as worthy of their consideration,—namely, Sowams, now called Barrington, and Aquetneck, now Rhode Island. Mr. Williams accompanied Mr. Clarke and two others of the company to Plymouth, to see whether either of these places was considered as falling within the Plymouth jurisdiction. They were met with great kindness; and, while they were told that Sowams was "the garden of their patent," they were advised to settle at Aquetneck, and were pro-

* Backus' Hist. N. E. III.—Benedict's Hist. Bapt. I.—Callender's Hist. Disc.—Peterson's Hist. R. I.

mised that they should be regarded as "free," and "treated and assisted as loving neighbours."

On their return, March 7, 1638, they incorporated themselves (eighteen in number) as a body politic, and chose William Coddington their chief magistrate. They forthwith purchased Aquetneck of the Indian Sachems, and called it the Isle of Rhodes or Rhode Island. The Indian deed is dated March 24, 1638. The settlement commenced at Pocasset, or Portsmouth, near what is called Common Fence Point, but they soon removed to Newtown, some two miles South. In May, 1639, Mr. Clarke was one of nine who founded Newport.

It seems not to be fully settled when Mr. Clarke became either a preacher or a Baptist; as no record, or even tradition, remains in respect to either his Baptism or Ordination. He conducted religious worship in the Colony until 1641, when they held meetings in two or more separate bodies. He was the Founder and first Pastor of the Baptist Church in Newport, which tradition dates back to 1644, and which was the second Baptist Church established in America. He was also the Physician of the Island for several years.

In 1649, Mr. Clarke was Assistant and Treasurer of the Rhode Island Colony. In July, 1651, he, in company with Mr. Obadiah Holmes and a Mr. Crandall, made a religious visit to one William Witter, a resident of Lynn, near Boston, which, in its results, marked an important epoch in his history. Mr. Witter, by reason of his advanced age, and partial or total blindness, could not undertake so great a journey as to visit the church at Newport. He lived about two miles out of the town; and, the next day after their arrival being Lord's day, they concluded to hold a religious service at his house. Mr. Clarke commenced preaching from Rev. iii. 10— "Because thou hast kept the word of my patience, I also will keep thee from the hour of temptation, which shall come upon all the world to try them that dwell upon the earth;" and, in the midst of his discourse, he had an opportunity, according to his own account, practically to illustrate some of the truths he was endeavouring to set forth. The following description of the scene which ensued, is from his own pen.

Having referred to the fact that he was then engaged in a religious service, he says,—

" Two constables came into the house, who, with their clamorous tongues, made an interruption in my discourse, and more uncivilly disturbed us than the pursuivants of the old English bishops were wont to do, telling us that they were come with authority from the magistrates to apprehend us. I then desired to see the authority by which they thus proceeded; whereupon, they plucked forth their warrant, and one of them, with a trembling hand, (as conscious he might have been better employed,) read it to us; the substance whereof was as followeth:—

" ' By virtue hereof, you are required to go to the house of William Witter, and to search from house to house, for certain erroneous persons, being strangers, and them to apprehend, and in safe custody to keep, and to-morrow morning at eight o'clock, to bring before me.   " ' ROBERT BRIDGES.'

" When he had read the warrant, I told them, Friends, there shall not be, I trust, the least appearance of a resisting of that authority by which you come unto us; yet I tell you that, by virtue hereof, you are not strictly tied. but, if you please, you may suffer us to make an end of what we have begun, so you may be witnesses either to or against the faith and order which we hold. To which they answered they could not. Then said we, notwithstanding the warrant, or anything therein contained, you may. They apprehended us, and carried us away to the ale house or ordinary, where, at dinner, one of them said unto us, Gentlemen, if you be free, I will carry you to the meeting. To whom it was replied, Friend, had we been free thereunto, we had prevented all this; nevertheless, we are in thy hand, and if thou wilt carry us to the meeting, thither we will go. To which he answered, Then will I carry you to the meeting. To this we replied, If thou forcest us into your assembly, then shall we be constrained to declare ourselves that we cannot hold communion with them. The constable answered, That is nothing to me; I have not power to command you to speak when you come there, or to be silent. To this I again replied, Since we have heard the word of salvation by Jesus Christ, we have been taught as those that 'first trusted in Christ,' to be obedient unto Him both by word and deed; wherefore, if we be forced to your meeting, we shall declare our dissent from you both by word and gesture. After all this, when he had consulted with the man of the house, he told us he would carry us to the meeting; so to their meeting we were brought, while they were at their prayers and uncovered; and, at my first stepping over the threshold, I unveiled myself, civilly saluted them, and turned into the seat I was appointed to, put on my hat again, and sat down, opened my book and fell to reading. Mr. Bridges, being troubled, commanded the constable to pluck off our hats, which he did, and where he laid mine, there I let it lie, until their prayers, singing and preaching was over. After this, I stood up and uttered myself in these words following—I desire, as a stranger, to propose a few things to this congregation, hoping, in the proposal thereof, I shall commend myself to your consciences, to be guided by that wisdom that is from above, which, being pure, is also peaceable, gentle, and easy to be entreated; and therewith made a stop, expecting that, if the Prince of Peace had been among them, I should have had a suitable answer of peace from them. Their Pastor answered, We will have no objections against what is delivered. To which I answered, I am not about at present to make objections against what is delivered, but, as by my gesture, at my coming into your assembly, I declared my dissent from you, so, lest that should prove offensive unto some whom I would not offend, I would now, by word of mouth, declare the grounds, which are these: First, from consideration we are strangers each to other, and so strangers to each others' inward standing with respect to God, and so cannot conjoin and act in faith, and what is not of faith is sin. And, in the second place, I could not judge that you are gathered together, and walk according to the visible order of our Lord. Which, when I had declared, Mr. Bridges told me I had done, and spoke that for which I must answer, and so commanded silence. When their meeting was done, the officers carried us again to the ordinary, where being watched over that night, as thieves and robbers, we were the next morning carried before Mr. Bridges, who made our mittimus and sent us to the prison at Boston."

After they had remained in prison about a fortnight, the Court of Assistants sentenced Mr. Clarke to pay a fine of twenty pounds, Mr. Holmes of thirty, and Mr. Crandall of five, or to be publicly whipped; and as they all refused to pay their fines, they were remanded back to prison. Some of Mr. Clarke's friends paid *his* fine, without his consent. Mr. Crandall, against whom nothing was alleged, except that he was found in company with the other two, was released upon his promise of appearing at their next Court; but the time was passed before he was informed of it, and then they exacted his fine of the keeper of the prison. But Mr. Holmes was kept in prison until September, when the sentence of the law was executed upon him with the utmost severity. It is stated in a manuscript of Joseph Jenks,—Governor of Rhode Island from 1727 to 1732,—that " Mr. Holmes was whipped thirty stripes, and in such an unmerciful manner, that in many days, if not some weeks, he could take no rest, but as he lay upon his knees and elbows, not being able to suffer any part of his body to touch the bed whereon he lay."*

* OBADIAH HOLMES was born at Preston, Lancashire, England, about the year 1606; arrived in America about 1639, and continued a communicant with the Congregationalists, first at Salem, and then at Rehoboth, eleven years, when he became a Baptist, and joined the Baptist Church in Newport. After he had recovered from his wounds, inflicted at Boston, he removed his family from Rehoboth to Newport, and, in 1652, the year after Mr. Clarke sailed for England, was invested with the pastoral office, which he held till his death, which occurred in 1682, at the age of seventy-six. He was buried in his own field, where a monument has been erected to his memory. He had eight children, and his posterity are widely spread through several different States. His son, *Obadiah*, was long a Judge in New Jersey, and a preacher

Mr. Clarke is said to have defended himself and his brethren, on the trial, with much ability. But the Governor seems to have listened with little patience to his statements; for he stepped up and told them all that they had denied Infant Baptism, and told Mr. Clarke that he deserved death, and declared that he "would not have such trash brought into his jurisdiction;" and he added, as Mr. Clarke states,—"You go up and down, and secretly insinuate into those that are weak, but you cannot maintain it before our ministers." But before Mr. Clarke had time to reply, the Governor commanded the jailor to take them away. The next morning, Mr. C. availed himself of an opportunity to make the following motion to the Court:

"To the Honourable Court assembled at Boston:—

"Whereas, it pleased this honoured Court, yesterday, to condemn the faith and order which I hold and practise; and, after you had passed your sentence upon me for it, were pleased to express I could not maintain the same against your ministers, and thereupon publicly proffered me a dispute with them: Be pleased, by these few lines, to understand I readily accept it, and therefore desire you to appoint the time when, and the person with whom, in that public place where I was condemned, I might, with freedom, and without molestation of the civil power, dispute that point publicly, where I doubt not, by the strength of Christ, to make it good, out of his last will and testament, unto which nothing is to be added, nor from which nothing is to be diminished. Thus desiring the Father of Lights to shine forth, and by his power to expel the darkness, I remain your well wisher,   "JOHN CLARKE.

"From the prison this
  1st day, 6th mo., 1651.

"This motion, if granted, I desire might be subscribed by the Secretary's hand, as an act of the same Court, by which we were condemned."

The motion was presented, and in due time Mr. Clarke was informed that a disputation was granted, to be held the next week. Mr. C., after some further conference between himself and the magistrates, committed to writing the several positions he proposed to defend, which were no other than the distinctive principles of the Baptist system. But this disputation, which had been anticipated with great interest, was prevented by the payment of Mr. C.'s fine, and his consequent release from prison. Fearing that the failure might be attributed to himself, he immediately sent the following note to the magistrates:—

"Whereas, through the indulgency of tender hearted friends, without my consent, and contrary to my judgment, the sentence and condemnation of the Court at Boston (as is reported) have been fully satisfied on my behalf, and thereupon a warrant hath been procured, by which I am secluded the place of my imprisonment; by reason whereof I see no other call for present but to my habitation, and to those near relations which God hath given me there; yet, lest the cause should hereby suffer, which I profess is Christ's, I would hereby signify that, if yet it should please the honoured magistrates, or General Court of this Colony, to grant my former request, under their Secretary's hand, I shall cheerfully embrace it, and, upon your mention, shall, through the help of God, come from the island to attend it, and hereunto I have subscribed my name.   "JOHN CLARKE.
"11th day 6th mo., 1651."

The above called forth another letter from the magistrates, and a rejoinder from Mr. Clarke, but the disputation never took place.

In 1651, shortly after this event, so characteristic of the times, Mr. Clarke was sent to England, with Roger Williams, to promote the interests of Rhode Island, and particularly to procure a revocation of William Coddington's commission as Governor. Soon after his arrival in

in the Baptist Church at Cohansey. Another of his sons,—John, was a magistrate in Philadelphia at the time of the schism occasioned by Keith. One of his grandsons was living in Newport, in 1770, in the ninety-sixth year of his age.

England, he published a book, giving an account of the New England persecutions, with the following title:—"Ill News from New England, or a Narrative of New England's Persecution; wherein it is declared that while Old England is becoming New, New England is becoming Old; also Four Proposals to Parliament and Four Conclusions, touching the Faith and Order of the Gospel of Christ, out of his Last Will and Testament." This was a quarto, of seventy-six pages, and was answered by Thomas Cobbett, of Lynn.

The more immediate object of the mission to England was accomplished by the annulling of Mr. Coddington's commission, in October, 1652. Though Mr. Clarke's colleague returned to this country in 1654, he himself remained behind in England, as agent for the Colony. The second charter was granted on the 8th of July, 1663, though, in order to obtain it, Mr. C. was obliged to mortgage his estate in Newport. He came home in 1664, and immediately resumed his relations with his church, and his practice of medicine, and continued them till the close of life. The Assembly did not at once pay the expenses to which he had been subjected during his absence, but they ultimately voted him a handsome consideration. A few years after his return, he seems to have been brought, in some way, in conflict with the Quakers; and, in October, 1673, five of the members of his church were excluded from communion for asserting that "the man Christ Jesus was not now in Heaven, nor on earth, nor anywhere else; but that his body was entirely lost."

Mr. Clarke died, resigning his soul to his merciful Redeemer, on the 20th of April, 1676, in the sixty-sixth year of his age.

Mr. Clarke was three times married. His first wife died without issue. His second wife, who was Mrs. Mary Fletcher, died on the 19th of April, 1672, leaving an only daughter, who died at the age of eleven years. His third wife was Mrs. Sarah Davis, who survived him. He was buried, by his own request, between his two wives, in a lot which he gave for a burial ground to the church. He left considerable property in the hands of trustees, empowered to choose their successors,—for the relief of the poor and the education of children, according to instructions given in his will,— namely, "that, in the disposal of that which the Lord hath bestowed upon me, and with which I have now entrusted you and your successors, you shall have special regard and care to provide for those that fear the Lord; and, in all things, and at all times, so to discharge the trust that I have reposed in you, as may be most to the glory of God, and the good and benefit of those for whom it is by me especially intended." His whole estate was appraised at £1080, 12s.

Mr. Clarke left three brothers, *Thomas, Joseph* and *Carew*. From Joseph many of the families by the name of Clarke, in Rhode Island, have sprung.

He left behind him a statement, in manuscript, of his religious opinions, from which it appears that, with the distinctive views of the Baptists he united those which are commonly called Calvinistic.

The Rev. John Callender, the Historian of the First Century of the Colony of Rhode Island, has left the following testimony concerning Mr. Clarke:

"He was a faithful and useful minister, courteous in all the relations of life, and an ornament to his profession, and to the several offices which he sustained. His memory is deserving of lasting honour, for his efforts towards establishing the first government in the world, which gave to all equal civil and religious liberty. To no man is Rhode Island more indebted than to him. He was one of the original projectors of the settlement of the island, and one of its ablest legislators. No character in New England is of purer fame than John Clarke."

THE WIGHTMANS.

VALENTINE WIGHTMAN.   1705—1747.
TIMOTHY WIGHTMAN.   1754—1796.
JOHN GANO WIGHTMAN.   1800—1841.

FROM THE REV. FREDERIC DENISON.

NORWICH, Conn., June 8, 1858.

Rev. and dear Sir: In reply to your inquiry concerning the Wightmans of Groton, Conn., I can only say that, as I know of no person who has gathered a full history of these three worthy fathers, and, as my attention has been turned towards them during the past year, while collecting the Religious Annals of Groton, I have, by advice of friends, consented to forward to you the following memorabilia of them, that have fallen under my notice. In the first two cases, my authorities are family history, private papers, town and church records, ecclesiastical and Associational Minutes, and historical sketches: in the last instance, I am able to add some personal recollections.

VALENTINE WIGHTMAN was a descendant of Edward Wightman, who was burnt for heresy, at Litchfield, in England, in 1612. Of the Wightmans, there came to this country five brothers, all Baptists—two were preachers; two were deacons; one a private member of the church. Valentine was a son of one of these five.

Valentine was born in North Kingston, R. I., in 1681. He removed to Groton, Conn., in 1705,—the year in which the town was incorporated. Probably he was licensed to preach in his native Colony. Upon his removal to Groton, he immediately gathered the few Baptists in the town into a church, and in the same year (1705) was chosen their Pastor. This was the first Baptist Church planted in the Colony of Connecticut, and which, as a mother of churches, still rejoices in her age.

Unfortunately, no sketch of the early life and personal appearance of Mr. Wightman has come down to us: and what is more to be regretted, since the times were peculiarly fruitful of historic incident, all the records of the church for the entire period of his ministry have perished. However, not a few of the fruits of his labours are yet to be found. The strong marks he made on his generation, and the fragmentary records of his deeds, lodged in collateral history, by the circling waves of his influence, enable us to present the man, the preacher, and the Christian builder, in a light worthy of historic mention.

On coming into public life, Valentine evinced the possession of excellent endowments, and creditable attainments. He was soon widely known, and as widely respected for his character and his abilities. With a sound mind in a sound body, and, what is yet more important, a disposition withal to work, and to work for the good of his generation, he necessarily rose to a commanding position, and wielded a truly enviable influence. In fine, he distinguished himself as a preacher, a writer, a disputant, a counsellor, and a builder in Zion.

Mr. Wightman maintained his individuality and his peculiar tenets ; but he was no partisan preacher, no self-sufficient champion of a sect, no bigoted adherent to a school. He was humble, firm, faithful. As a preacher, he was plain, logical, earnest, and sometimes eloquent. As a builder, he was wise, prudent, and skilful. He was an indefatigable labourer, and he laboured to edify rather than to please and captivate. With the numerical increase of his flock, he, as well, sought their culture in all the ways that consisted with the poverty and pressure of his times. He preached in all the adjoining towns. For many years he was the only settled Baptist minister in the Colony.

Through his instrumentality, and in the face of sharp opposition from the Standing Order, Baptist Churches were gathered in Waterford, Lyme, Stonington, and other places. His preaching cost him much unpleasant controversy, and not a little persecution, as, in the matter of parish lines, he preferred the commission given by Christ, to the ecclesiastical laws of Connecticut. In his own town, he was increasingly prospered in his work until the glorious period of the Great Awakening, in which his zeal and labours abounded, and were crowned with a precious harvest.

Valentine's few papers testify to his thorough knowledge of the Scriptures, and his honourable acquaintance with Church History, and the writings of the first Christian Fathers. That he wrote but little is explained by the culture of his times, in connection with the multitude of temporal engagements and hardships belonging to his generation, which narrowed the opportunities for liberal studies, and furnished few incentives for committing his thoughts to paper. He wrote a tract on Church Music, which is reported to have been useful. But the most historic of his efforts is his Debate with the Rev. John Bulkley, of Colchester. This Debate was a famous one : it was the trial of theological strength, previously agreed upon, between the Standing Order, who gave the challenge, and the Dissenters in the Colony. The champions selected on each side were Mr. Bulkley and Mr. Wightman. The Debate opened orally in the meeting house, in Lyme, on the 7th of June, 1727, and continued above seven hours. Multitudes attended, among whom were distinguished clergymen and public officers on both sides—two able men presided as Moderators. The topics discussed were, I. The Subjects of Baptism. II. The Mode of Baptizing. III. The Maintenance of Gospel Ministers. The Debate was continued in writing—each disputant published a book. In this encounter, whether considered in a theological or literary point of view, I do not think that Mr. Wightman suffers by comparison with his gifted and learned antagonist, whom Dr. Chauncy has styled " a first rate genius" and distinguished for " solidity of mind and strength of judgment."

He was married to Susanna Holmes, February 10, 1703.

In 1712, by invitation of Mr. Nicholas Eyres, he visited the city of New York, and continued his visits about two years, preaching at Mr. E.'s house. His labours were blessed. In 1714, he baptized seven men and five women, who afterwards were formed into a church under the ministry of Mr. Eyres. This was the first Baptist Church planted in the State of New York.

Valentine came to his death peacefully, and in honour, on the 9th of June, 1747, at the age of sixty-six, and after a ministry of forty-two years. The people whom he had "fed, according to the integrity of his heart, and guided by the skilfulness of his hands," appropriately mourned his departure. His memory is even yet fresh. And his name will endure on the roll of the fathers that opened the wilderness, and, in the name of the Lord, laid the goodly foundations upon which succeeding generations have joyfully built.

TIMOTHY WIGHTMAN was a son of the Rev. Valentine Wightman, and was born in Groton, Conn., November 20, 1719. Of his early life very little can be ascertained. From the loss of the Church Records up to 1754, it is impossible to state when he professed faith in Christ, or when he was licensed to preach; but, in the year 1754, we find him, as also his wife, in covenant with the church. His first wife was Jane Fish, to whom he was married June 1, 1743: she died March 4, 1745. He was married to his second wife, Mary Stoddard, May 13, 1747: she survived him about twenty years—her death occurred February 19, 1817, in her ninety-second year.

In 1754, Timothy succeeded his father in the pastoral office, though he refused ordination till May 20, 1756. His modesty, coupled with the trials and labours of the office, induced this hesitancy. After the death of his father, the church became somewhat entangled with questions of Church government and spiritual liberty, brought into the body by the numerous seceders from the Standing Order, called Separatists, who had now become Baptists; and the Rev. Daniel Fisk who, for a few years, had been ministering to the church, was unequal to the position in this day of spiritual revolution that followed the Great Awakening, and eventually brought in the day of religious liberty. But when Timothy came to the helm of affairs, with his native Wightman judgment and skill, he brought the old ship into the wind, and sent her again bounding on her original course.

Timothy was a man of medium stature, light and erect frame, black hair and eyes, affable manners, serious deportment, and manly bearing. He was well-nigh a model man;—easy, serious, kind, ingenuous, earnest. Being once called before the County Court as a witness, and a lawyer attempting to criticise him by cross-questioning, the Judge remarked,— "It is not necessary to criticise that man; his veracity and candour are evident in his appearance."

As a preacher, Timothy was much like his father,—plain, fearless, faithful. The period of his ministry reached through the two great upheavals in the history of our country—the Separations induced by the Great

Awakening, that culminated in the establishment of evangelical doctrines and Church independency,—and the Revolution that inaugurated our National Independence: the one was the divinely ordained harbinger of the other. The Separate movement was specially powerful in Eastern Connecticut, in and around Groton; and, in the whole Colony, more than thirty Separate churches were formed. Most of these Separatists finally became Baptists. In the Revolutionary War, Groton bore a heroic and mournful part: her Western Heights, on September 6, 1781, were purpled with the blood of more than eighty patriots, and above thirty more lay mortally wounded. In the midst of these trying scenes Timothy was called to minister, and he ministered with discretion. He stood by the altar of God, and by the rights of his country. He withstood ecclesiastical domination at home, and political tyranny abroad. His church furnished its quota of patriotic blood in defence of the principles of liberty, and Timothy animated his people to honour the right.

Besides some annoyances from the State Church party in the town and surrounding country, Timothy was at one time harassed in his ministrations by the little band of ignorant " Rogerenes," whose religion consisted in denouncing the Sabbath, public prayer, preaching, and all Christian ordinances, as "idolatries," and who came, on the Sabbath, driving their teams, and bringing into the meeting-house splints for baskets, cards and spinning wheels, to disturb the preacher, and to win persecution as the evidence of their saintship. They even boorishly interrupted him and charged him with lying. But he calmly proceeded in his work, and exhorted his people never to return railing for railing, but by true kindness to heap coals of fire on their enemies' heads.

Timothy's ministry was favoured by several notable revivals. In 1764, more than thirty were added to the church—the second Baptist Church in Groton was organized in the year following. In 1775, nearly forty souls were added to the flock—in this year a Baptist Church was gathered in North Groton. In 1784, eighty-four members were brought in. Another revival, in 1786–87, brought an increase from every side.

Near the close of his ministry, Timothy suffered from ill health, and was assisted by his brethren in the ministry in preaching and baptizing. His last sermon was founded upon II. Tim. iv. 6–8, " I am now ready to be offered, and the time of my departure is at hand," &c. The words were prophetic in his lips. After a severe illness of about six weeks, he departed in hope, November 14, 1796, in his seventy-eighth year, and after a ministry of forty-two years,—the exact period of his father's pastorate. A church of above two hundred members, nearly all baptized by his hands, wept over his dead body. The Rev. Reuben Palmer preached his funeral discourse from II. Kings, ii. 12.—" My father, my father," &c. His people laid him down in the church-yard, by the dust of his father, and by the side of the altar he defended and adorned. *Modest, solid worth*, would be a fitting epitaph for the second Pastor of the First Baptist Church planted in Connecticut.

JOHN GANO WIGHTMAN was the youngest son of the Rev. Timothy Wightman, and was born in Groton, Conn., August 16, 1766. His early training was of the best character, and was not lost upon his susceptible and ingenuous nature. To the ordinary advantages of education he added much by his own persevering private efforts. He became hopefully pious, it would seem, in 1797, as, during this year, he was baptized into the fellowship of the church. Such were his gifts and attainments that he was soon licensed to preach. It soon became evident that he was called of God to follow in the foot steps of his father and grandfather in the pastoral office of the ancient church. Being chosen to the office, he accepted ordination, August 13, 1800. He was married to Mercy Clark, January 22, 1789: she died May 29, 1816. His second wife was Bridget Allyn, to whom he was married July 7, 1817. She still survives.

John G. was a man slightly above medium height, of rather light frame, spare in flesh, straight in form, and of goodly personal appearance. There was something in his countenance and bearing to remind one of the old lithograph portraits of Jefferson. His eyes were dark hazel; his hair rather light, worn long and flowing behind, but cut short and combed straight in front, thus concealing a part of his well-formed forehead. His voice was not heavy, but full, clear and pleasant. His manner was easy and engaging. In the matter of dress, all was so neat, plain and becoming as never to excite attention or provoke criticism. In both private and public life he was unostentatious and diligent.

In his preaching, I think, the logical element largely prevailed; though he employed happy illustrations, and sometimes rose to strains of impassioned eloquence. Like Valentine and Timothy, John G. was solid and practical rather than brilliant and fascinating—hence his ministry wrought abiding results. He moved not like a meteor, but like a planet. His ministerial brethren always gave him a high rank in their Councils and Associations. As a presiding officer, he was particularly happy. In executive talents he had few superiors,—being composed, ready, impartial, dignified.

His ministry embraced a comparatively calm period. All outward opposition had now nearly passed away, and the land was rejoicing in religious liberty. Only the impotent group of "Rogerenes" sought to molest the peace of the old church. They published a simple and scandalous little volume entitled "The Battle Axe,"—an undigested conglomerate of base metals. To this attack, John G., with characteristic prudence and coolness, simply replied,—"The Axe will cut farther backwards than forwards,"—which proved true. He was cautious and discreet, but never timid or time-serving.

Not less than ten seasons of revival were experienced under Mr. Wightman's labours, some of which were powerful and wide-spread. The numbers, brought into the church by these revivals, varied from ten to fifty-six. Meanwhile, the church, as a parent stock, was sending out branches; the most prosperous of which was the Third Baptist Church in Groton, organized in 1831.

After the custom of our early Baptist fathers, John G. wrote but little to be carried into the desk; but he never preached without preparation.

His trust was in his memory rather than in his pen; and he believed in enjoying Divine assistance in the pulpit. By a culpable carelessness his papers have been permitted to perish. The only surviving productions of his pen are a Sermon preached on the death of Adams and Jefferson, and Circular Letters prepared for the Associations. The last sermon that I heard him preach,—and I recollect it more distinctly than any discourse I heard for years,—was from Prov. vi. 6–8, "Go to the ant, thou sluggard, consider her ways, and be wise." &c.

For a few years before his death, his health was so feeble as to interrupt his ministrations—still he preached at home, and in various parts of the town, while sufficient strength remained. His last sickness was protracted and painful, but borne with fortitude and resignation. He confidently leaned on the word which, for a lifetime, he had preached to others. As it was my privilege to watch with him in some of his last painful nights, I was enabled to discover how the darkness that borders the grave is, to the man of God, lifted and dispersed by the rays of a heavenly morning. He fell on sleep, quietly, on the 13th of July, 1841, in the seventy-fifth year of his age, and after a ministry of forty-one years. His funeral occasioned a solemn day—many came from adjoining towns to look once more on the venerated countenance—ministers of different denominations wept over his bier, and assisted in the solemnities. A Discourse was preached by the Rev. Erastus Denison, from Matthew xxiv. 45–46—"Who then is a faithful and wise servant," &c. His body was laid down mournfully by the side of his fathers.

John Gano Wightman was worthy to succeed his father Timothy and his grandfather Valentine: and these names are still fresh.

> "For only the actions of the just
> "Smell sweet and blossom in the dust."

I remain your sincere friend and brother,

FREDERIC DENISON.

THE MORGANS.*

ABEL MORGAN, (Senior.) 1711—1722.
ABEL MORGAN, (Junior.) 1734—1785.

ABEL MORGAN, Senior, was born in the year 1637, at a place called Alltgoch, in the parish of Llanwenog, and county of Cardigan, South Wales. He became a preacher at the early age of nineteen, and was ordained at Blaenegwent, in Monmouthshire, where he exercised his ministry for some time. His younger brother, Enoch Morgan, migrated to this country in 1701, and became the third Pastor of the Welsh Tract Church, in Delaware. Abel, having received a favourable account of this country, through his brother and other friends, was induced to follow them hither, and he arrived in America, according to Edwards,

---

* MS. from H. G. Jones, Esq.—Materials towards a History of the Baptists in Jersey, by Morgan Edwards.—Benedict's Hist. Bapt. I.

on the 14th of February, 1711, and took up his residence in Philadelphia. The Baptist Church at Philadelphia was not formally organized as a distinct body until May 15, 1746; and hence the Pastor at Pennepek preached at both places. Mr. Morgan assumed the pastoral care of the church at Pennepek immediately after his arrival in the country. It was regarded a very felicitous circumstance to the Society at Philadelphia that so discreet a minister as Mr. Morgan had come to live among them; for they were in a distracted and unhappy state, and needed his judicious and kindly influence to calm their agitations and restore their harmony. An Irish preacher, named Thomas Selby, and another preacher whose name was John Burrows, had had a severe altercation, and the Irishman had succeeded in shutting Mr. Burrows and his party out of the meeting house. Mr. Morgan's presence and influence soon healed the breach, and Mr. Selby left the town in 1713, and went to Carolina, where he died the same year, though not till he had occasioned much disturbance.

The Records of the Philadelphia Association, during the first thirty years of its existence, are so very meagre that few particulars can be gleaned respecting Mr. Morgan's labours as a minister; and yet there is no doubt that he took an active part in the deliberations of that Body, and was reckoned among its most prominent members. The Minute for 1722 reflects high honour upon him, as being among the earliest of the Baptist advocates for ministerial education. It is as follows:—

"At the Association in the year 1722, it was proposed by the churches to make inquiry among themselves, if they have any young persons hopeful for the ministry, and inclinable for learning; and if they have, to give notice of it to Mr. Abel Morgan, before the 1st of November, that he might recommend such to the Academy, on Mr. Hollis his account." The Mr. Hollis referred to was the celebrated London merchant, who sent donations of books to the Philadelphia Association, and founded the Hollis Professorship in Harvard College.

Mr. Morgan continued in the faithful discharge of his ministerial duties till near the close of life. He died on the 16th of December, 1722, at the age of eighty-five years, and was buried in the grave-yard of the Baptist Church in Philadelphia, where a stone still marks the place of his grave.

Morgan Edwards says that "Mr. Abel Morgan was a great and good man, and is held in dear remembrance by all that knew him."

The following are Mr. Morgan's published works:—A Translation of the Century Confession (the Baptist Confession of Faith) into Welsh. A Concordance of the Holy Scriptures, or a complete Alphabetical Index to the principal words in the Holy Bible, by which any portion of the Scriptures desired, can be immediately found. Compiled carefully and with much labour. By Abel Morgan, Minister of the Gospel for the benefit of the Welsh. This Concordance is a folio volume, and, as its title indicates, is evidently elaborated with much care. The author, however, did not live to see it published; but it was placed in the hands of his brother, Enoch Morgan, who wrote a preface to it, dated February, 1724, and dedicated it to "the Honourable David Lloyd, Esq., Chief Justice of the State of Pennsylvania," who was also a native Welshman. The following is an extract from this Dedicatory Letter:

" In our tongue,—the Welsh,—the deficiency and the great need of such a work have been long felt and ardently desired, not only by our countrymen here, but no less so in the land of our birth, and especially since they have heard that the Author of a *Welsh* Concordance was engaged in its preparation. This, out of the purest love to his countrymen, he ventured upon and accomplished but a short time before his decease. This event, his death, took place December the 16th, in the year 1722, bequeathing this token of his laborious life in the wilderness, in its destitute state, and which now requires the aid of those who are able to carry it through the press, so that it may appear in suitable form for distribution among his beloved countrymen, according to *his* design, and for *their* benefit."

The same Enoch Morgan wrote an Introduction to the work, in which he says of Abel Morgan,—

" He set his mind on compiling a Concordance of the Scriptures, and laboured with unwearied diligence till he had produced and completed the following work, to enable those of imperfect memory and unskilled in scripture knowledge, in obtaining readily the aid thus needed, in comparing scripture with scripture, and thus acquiring enlarged light and knowledge. . . . . The author used every effort in his day to urge all to a proper improvement of their time, setting the example in himself of a devoted, pious life, not in the pulpit alone, but in a chaste and holy conversation, so that he could declare with Paul,—' I am pure from the blood of all men.' In his youth he gave himself to the good work, and he fainted not."

This work was revised and corrected for the press in March, 1730, by another Welshman, named John Cadwallader, who is believed to have been a merchant of some note in Philadelphia.

Besides the two printed works already mentioned, he left several others in manuscript, which were extant as late as 1770.

Mr. Morgan was thrice married. His first wife was Priscilla Powell, of Abergavenny, by whom he had one child, a daughter, who married John Holme, from whom is descended the Rev. John Stanford Holme, a Baptist clergyman of Brooklyn, N. Y. His second wife was Martha Burrows. His third wife was Judith Goading, (a widow,) and daughter of the Rev. Thomas Griffiths, of Welsh Tract. By her he had four children,—three sons and a daughter.

ABEL MORGAN, Jr., was a nephew of the preceding, and was born in Welsh Tract, April 18, 1713. ·He was educated chiefly at an Academy under the care of the Rev. Thomas Evans, in Pencader ; was ordained at Welsh Tract church in the year 1734; became Pastor of the church in Middletown, N. J., in 1738 ; and died there November 24, 1785. He was never married ; and the reason given for it was that such a relation would interfere with due attention to his mother, who lived with him, and whom he regarded with extraordinary filial reverence and affection. He was reputed a man of sound learning and excellent judgment, and was especially distinguished as a skilful disputant. At one time he was engaged in a public discussion on the subject of Baptism, at Kingwood, with the Rev. Samuel Harker, a Presbyterian minister of considerable standing ; and again, in 1743, he had a still more memorable disputation with the celebrated Dr. Samuel Finley, at Cape May, in connection with a powerful revival of religion, in which the labours of Baptist and Presbyterian ministers were, to a great extent, intermingled. It was after this public encounter that Dr. Finley published his well known pamphlet, entitled " A Charitable Plea for the Speechless." Mr. Morgan replied in a pamphlet of a hundred and sixty pages, entitled "Anti-Pedo-Rantism, or Mr. Samuel Finley's Charitable Plea for the Speechless examined and refuted, the Baptism of Believers maintained, and the mode of it by Immersion vindicated." Dr. Finley published a rejoinder, and Mr. Morgan replied to that also, and thus ended the controversy. Morgan Edwards thus concludes his brief account of Mr. Morgan:—

"Mr. Morgan's life and ministry were such, that his people speak of him with veneration and regret to this day. He was not a *custom divine*, nor a *leading-string divine*, but a *Bible divine*. In his last sickness, he sent for the Elders of the church to anoint him with oil, according to the precept, (James v. 14, 15): Elder Crawford attended; but Elder Mott was hindered by sickness; and the healing rite was deferred, for want of *Elders*, in the plural. Perhaps it will be imputed that Mr. Morgan knew not what he sought after. I inquired into the matter, and was assured, by Elder Crawford, (from whom I had the anecdote,) that he was of sound mind and disposing memory. But I needed not to have said so much; for Mr. Morgan practised the rite— one instance was Catalina, wife of Rev. Enoch David, who is yet alive: she had been in a dying way for a long while; but the third day after the salutary unction, she was well and went abroad. I wish all Baptist ministers were of Mr. Morgan's mind; and not allow themselves (like the prodigal brother) to oppose the father's bidding with remonstrances, and not do as they are bid at last. The eight Christian rites stand on the same footing. No argument can be urged for laying aside some, but will operate towards laying aside all. Whoever will read Barclay's Apology will own the justness of this remark. To pick and choose are not fair; neither is it honest to admit the force of an argument in one case, and not in another, of the same nature. O custom! Cruel custom! Tyrant custom! when wilt thou cease to pervert the right ways of the Lord?"

THE CALLENDERS.*

ELISHA CALLENDER. 1718—1738.
JOHN CALLENDER. 1731—1748.

ELISHA CALLENDER was a son of Ellis Callender, who officiated as the principal speaker in the First Baptist Church in Boston, while they were destitute of a Pastor, for about thirty years. The Church, having applied in vain for the services of Mr. William Scréven,† then at Charleston, S. C., gave Mr. Ellis Callender a call to become their Pastor; and he was, accordingly, ordained, in 1708, and continued in the pastoral relation, highly respected and honoured, for more than ten years. He is supposed to have died about the year 1726, not far from the age of eighty.

* Backus' Hist. N. E., III.—Benedict's Hist. Bapt., I.—Boston Evening Post, 1738.— Winchell's Hist. Disc.

† WILLIAM SCREVEN was born in England, about the year 1629. After coming to this country, he settled in the District of Maine, and was one of a small company of Baptists in Kittery, who united at first with the Church in Boston, but in 1682, formed a church by themselves, of which Mr. Screven was recognised as the Elder. In consequence of the violent opposition which they had to encounter from other denominations, they were obliged, in a short time, to disband, and Elder Screven and some of his brethren sought an asylum in the more tranquil regions of the South. He was instrumental of gathering the First Baptist Church in Charleston, S. C., and became its Pastor. He was subsequently invited to return to Boston, to become Pastor of the church there, of which he had formerly been a member, but declined. Late in life, he removed to Georgetown, about sixty miles from Charleston, where he died in peace, in 1713, having reached the age of eighty-four. He is said to have been the original proprietor of the land on which Georgetown is built. During his residence in Maine, he was married to Bridget Cutts, by whom he had eleven children. He is reputed to have been a good English scholar, and eminent for his piety and usefulness. He wrote "An Ornament for Church Members," which was published after his death. Some of his descendants have been highly respectable and influential people in the South.

Elisha Callender, the son, was born in Boston, and was educated at Harvard College, where he received the degree of Bachelor of Arts, in the year 1710. He was baptized and received into the Church, August 10, 1713. On the 21st of May, 1718, he was ordained to the work of the ministry, and became Pastor of the Church with which his father had been connected for nearly fifty years, and towards which, for forty, he had acted the part of a public teacher.

Mr. Callender's ordination was signalized as the occasion of a most friendly demonstration of the Congregationalists and Baptists towards each other,—the more remarkable on account of the different state of things which had existed a few years before. Several of the most prominent Congregational ministers in Boston took part in the Ordination services. The following is the letter missive, addressed to the Church under the care of Dr. Mather and Mr. Webb, requesting their assistance in the Ordination :—

"Honoured and Beloved in the Lord :—
"Considering that there ought to be a holy fellowship maintained among godly Christians, and that it is a duty for us to receive one another, as Christ also received us to the glory of God, notwithstanding some differing persuasions in matters of doubtful disputation; and, although we have not so great a latitude as to the subject of Baptism as the Churches of New England generally have; nevertheless, as to fundamental principles in the doctrine of Christ, both as to the faith and order of the Gospel, we concur with them; being also satisfied that particular churches have power from Christ to choose their own Pastors, and that Elders ought to be ordained in every church, and, having chosen our well-beloved brother, Elisha Callender, to be our Pastor, we entreat you to send your Elders and Messengers to give the Right Hand of Fellowship in his Ordination."

Dr. Cotton Mather preached the Ordination Sermon, which he entitled "Good men united." After speaking of the severities which had been manifested against Christians by the Ruling Power, he says,—

"Cursed the anger, for it is fierce, and the wrath, for it is cruel; good for nothing but only to make divisions in Jacob, and dispersions in Israel. Good men, alas! good men have done such ill things as these; yea, few churches of the Reformation have been wholly clear of these iniquities. New England also has, in some former times, done something of this aspect, which would not now be so well approved of, in which, if the brethren, in whose house we are now convened, met with anything too unbrotherly, they now, with satisfaction, hear us expressing our dislike of every thing which looked like persecution, in the days that have passed over us."

Increase Mather, who was also one of the ordaining council, thus alludes to the circumstance :

"It was a grateful surprise to me. when several of the brethren of the anti-pedobaptist persuasion came to me, desiring that I would give them the Right Hand of Fellowship, in ordaining one whom they had chosen to be their Pastor. I did (as I believe it was my duty) readily consent to what they proposed; considering the young man to be ordained is serious and pious, and of a candid spirit, and has been educated at the College at Cambridge. and that all the brethren with whom I have any acquaintance (I hope the like concerning others of them) are, in the judgment of rational charity, godly persons."

Dr. Benedict states that "the report of this expression of Catholicism in England, induced Thomas Hollis, Esq., a wealthy merchant of the Baptist persuasion, to become one of the most liberal benefactors to Cambridge College, that it ever enjoyed."

Notwithstanding Mr. Callender had but a feeble constitution, he was abundant in labours, not only among his own people, but in other places, in different parts of the Commonwealth. At Springfield, Sutton, Leicester, Marshfield, Salem, and several other towns, he preached frequently, and baptized and admitted to the church a considerable number of persons. His own church was particularly prosperous under his ministry, and scarcely a month passed but that some were added to it.

But, while his prospects of usefulness were the brightest, he was arrested by a disease which, at no distant period, terminated in death. He preached, for the last time, on the 29th of January, 1738, from the text,—" Blessed are all they that put their trust in Him." Having been unable to administer Baptism to several persons who had stood as candidates for that ordinance, he thus wrote in a letter to a friend :—" My indisposition is such, and I am under such methods of cure, as unfits me altogether to attend the ordinance of Baptism to them. I am heartily concerned that it is so with me ; but there is no resisting the Divine Providence." His illness rapidly increased, but he anticipated death without terror, made his will with the utmost composure, and addressed many pertinent and affecting counsels to his friends. Ten days before his death, he said,—" When I look on one hand, I see nothing but sin, guilt, and discouragement ; but, when I look on the other, I see my glorious Saviour, and the merits of his precious blood, which cleanseth from all sin. I cannot say I have such transports of joy as some have had, but, through grace, I can say,—I have gotten the victory over death and the grave." Being asked what word of advice he had for his church, he earnestly replied,—" Away with luke-warmness ; away with such remissness in attending the house of prayer, which has been a discouragement to me; and I have been faulty myself. Live in love and peace, that the God of love and peace may be with you. Improve your time; for your standing in the church will be short; and that is the way to prepare for the inheritance of the saints in light." He died on the 31st of March, 1738, at the age of about fifty, and in the twentieth year of his ministry. His funeral took place on the 4th of April.

The following testimony to his character appeared shortly after his death, in one of the Boston papers :—

" On Friday morning last, after a lingering sickness, deceased the Rev. Mr. Elisha Callender, Minister of the Baptist Church in this town; a gentleman universally beloved, by people of all persuasions, for his charitable and catholic way of thinking. His life was unspotted, and his conversation always affable, religious and truly manly. During his long illness, he was remarkably patient, and, in his last hours, like the blessed above, pacific and entirely serene; his senses good to the last. ' I shall,' said he, 'sleep in Jesus,' and that moment expired, very much lamented by all who knew him."

Mr. Callender was the first native Baptist minister in this country, who had received a collegiate education. The only production of his pen, known to have been published, is a Century Sermon, preached in the year 1720, commemorative of the landing of our Fathers at Plymouth.

JOHN CALLENDER was a nephew of ELISHA CALLENDER, was born in Boston, was educated at Harvard College, on the Hollis foundation ; was graduated in 1723 ; was ordained colleague with Elder Peckham,* as

---

* Mr. WILLIAM PECKHAM was ordained Pastor of the First Baptist Church in Newport, in 1711, and continued to discharge the duties of his office with exemplary fidelity, until the infirmities of age rendered it necessary that he should have an assistant. In May, 1718, a Mr. DANIEL WHITE was received to the fellowship of the Church, and was soon after invited to share the ministerial services with Mr. Peckham; but he proved a troublesome man, and was

Pastor of the Baptist church in Newport, October 13, 1731, and died January 26, 1748, at the age of forty-one. He possessed a vigorous intellect, and was distinguished for his candour and liberality. He collected many papers illustrating the history of the Baptists in this country, which were subsequently used by the Rev. Isaac Backus. He published an Historical Discourse on the Civil and Religious Affairs of the Colony of Rhode Island and Providence Plantations, from the First Settlement in 1638, to the end of the First Century ; also a Sermon at the Ordination of the Rev. Jeremy Condy,* Boston, 1739 ; and a Sermon on the Death of the Rev. Nathaniel Clap, of Newport, 1745.

The following is the inscription upon Mr. Callender's monument :—

" Confident of awaking, here reposeth
JOHN CALLENDER ;
Of very excellent endowments from nature,
And of an accomplished education,
Improved by application to the wide circle
Of the more polite arts and useful sciences.
From motives of conscience and grace
He dedicated himself to the immediate service
Of God.
In which he was distinguished as a shining
And very burning light, by a true and faithful
Ministry of seventeen years, in the First Baptist
Church of Rhode Island, where the purity
And evangelical simplicity of his doctrine, confirmed
And embellished by the virtuous and devout tenor
Of his own life,
Endeared him to his flock, and justly conciliated
The esteem, love, and reverence of all the
Wise, worthy, and good.
Much humanity, benevolence, and charity
Breathed in his conversation, discourses, and writings,
Which were all pertinent, reasonable and useful.
Regretted by all, lamented by his friends, and
Deeply deplored by a wife and numerous issue,
He died,
In the forty-second year of his age,
January 26, 1748 ;
Having struggled through the vale of life
In adversity, much sickness, and pain,
With fortitude, dignity, and elevation of soul,
Worthy of the Philosopher, Christian, and Divine."

the occasion of dividing the church. A new meeting-house was erected for him, in 1724, in which he continued to officiate four years, when, having but a solitary member of his church left, he sold the meeting-house and left the place.

* JEREMY CONDY is believed to have been a descendant of James Condy, who settled at Braintree in 1640, and had three sons. He was graduated at Harvard College in 1726. After preaching a few years in this country, he went to England, and remained there till 1738, when he returned, in consequence of having received proposals to settle over the First Baptist Church in Boston. He arrived in Boston on the 17th of August of that year, but, as the Church had previously engaged the Rev. Edward Upham to supply them until the last of September, no measures were taken with regard to Mr. C's settlement until the 12th of October following, when he was regularly called—eighteen brethren being present—to the pastoral care of the Church. He signified his acceptance of the call on the 24th of December, and was ordained by a Council consisting partly of Baptist, and partly of Pedobaptist, ministers, on the 14th of February, 1739. In his doctrinal views he was reputed to be an Arminian; and, after about four years, a number of his members became so much dissatisfied with him on this account that they withdrew and formed the Second Baptist Church. He resigned his pastoral office in August, 1764, and lived in retirement the rest of his days. He died in 1768, aged fifty-nine years, during twenty-five of which he had been Pastor of the First Church. He was a man of unblemished character, though the church does not appear to have prospered greatly under his ministry. Like his predecessor, he preached and baptized in Springfield, Sutton, and other towns of the Commonwealth. He published a Sermon occasioned by the death of Benjamin Landon, 1747, and a Sermon entitled " Mercy exemplified in the Conduct of a Samaritan."

BENJAMIN GRIFFITHS.*
1722—1768.

BENJAMIN GRIFFITHS was born October 16, 1688, in the parish of Llanllwyni, in the county of Cardigan, South Wales, and was a half brother of Abel and Enoch Morgan. He came to America, with Jenkin Jones† and David Davis, in 1710. He was baptized May 12, 1711, and settled in Montgomery township, then in Philadelphia, but now in Montgomery, County, Pa., in 1720. He was called to the ministry in 1722, but was not ordained until October 23, 1725. He laboured with much success as a Pastor, and was evidently one of the prominent men of the Baptist denomination at that day. His name appears in the Minutes of the Association as early as 1733.

In 1746, he was appointed by the Association "to collect and set in order the accounts" of the several Baptist churches in these Provinces, and to keep a record of the proceedings of the Baptist denomination. He seems to have attended faithfully to this duty; and the work, begun at that early day, when the Minutes of the Association were not printed, is preserved in a large folio volume, the greater part of which forms the first hundred pages of the Century Minutes of the Association, as printed under the direction of the Rev. A. D. Gillette, D. D. But for this valuable compend, kept by Mr. Griffiths, the entire early history of that ancient Body might have been lost. In the year 1749, he prepared, and read an Essay on "the Power and Duty of an Association," which the Association directed to be recorded in their folio volume. He was also appointed to prepare a "Discipline" for the churches.

Mr. Griffiths continued to labour in Montgomery, and the adjoining townships, in which, in the course of time, new churches were organized, and some of which are still in existence. He died at Montgomery, on the 5th of October, 1768, in the eighty-first year of his age. His Funeral Sermon was preached by the Rev. David Thomas,‡ of Virginia, and was published.

---

* Ms. from H. G. Jones, Esq.

† JENKIN JONES was born about 1690, in the parish of Llanfernach, county of Pembroke, Wales, and arrived in this country about 1710. He became the minister of the Church at Pennepek in 1725, though he seems to have had his residence in Philadelphia during the whole period of his connection with it. When the Church at Philadelphia was re-constituted, (May 15, 1746,) he became its Pastor, and continued in that relation during the rest of his life. He died at Philadelphia July 16, 1761, much respected and lamented. He rendered important services, in various ways, not only to his own particular church, but to his denomination, and to the Church at large.

‡ DAVID THOMAS was born at London Tract, Pa., August 16, 1732. He was educated at Hopewell, N. J., under the direction of the Rev. Isaac Eaton, and in 1769, was honoured with the degree of Master of Arts from Brown University. He commenced preaching when he was quite young, and in his twenty-eighth year, removed to Virginia. Having spent about eighteen months in the County of Berkeley, he visited Fauquier County, in the year 1762, and was instrumental in establishing Broad Run Church, of which he afterwards became Pastor. During the early part of his ministry in Virginia, he encountered much opposition, and was frequently assaulted by both individuals and mobs. He travelled extensively, and his preaching commanded great attention. In the latter part of his life he removed to Kentucky. He lived to an advanced age; and, for some time before his death, was nearly blind. "Mr. Thomas is said to have been a man of great distinction in his day. Beside the natural endowments of a vigorous mind, and the advantages of a classical and refined education, he had a melodious and piercing voice, a pathetic address, expressive action, and, above all, a heart filled with love to God and his fellow-men."

Mr. Griffiths was married to Sarah Miles, by whom he had five children,—two sons and three daughters, who were married into the Evans, Coffin, and Roberts families. *Abel Griffiths*, the eldest son, was born at Montgomery, December 23, 1723 ; was baptized April 14, 1744 ; was ordained in 1761; and was settled as Pastor of the Brandywine Church, Chester County, Pa., April 12, of the same year. Here he remained for six years, and then removed to Salem, N. J., where he held a pastoral charge until 1771.

The following is a list of Mr. Griffiths' publications:—Essay on the Power and Duty of an Association, (printed in 1832, in the History of the Philadelphia Baptist Association, by the Rev. H. G. Jones—also in the Century Minutes in 1851.) A Treatise of Church Discipline—two editions. A Vindication of the Doctrine of the Resurrection of the same Body. Answer to a pamphlet entitled "The Divine Right of Infant Baptism. Printed by B. Franklin, 1747.

Morgan Edwards says "Mr. Griffiths was a man of parts, though not eloquent, and had by industry acquired tolerable acquaintance with languages and books." He states also that he was once offered a commission of Justice of the Peace, which, however, he declined ; and, on being asked the reason why he refused such an honour, he replied,—'Men are not to receive from offices, but offices from men—as much as men receive, the others lose, till at last offices come to have no honour at all.'

JOHN COMER.
1725—1734.

FROM THE REV. DAVID BENEDICT, D.D.

PAWTUCKET, R. I., May 16, 1859.

Dear Sir : My estimate of the character of John Comer is such that I am more than willing to do any thing in my power to honour and perpetuate his memory. In compiling the following sketch, I have access to his well known Diary, which is the principal original source of information concerning him.

JOHN COMER, the eldest son of John and Mary Comer, was born in Boston, Aug. 1st, 1704. His father died at Charleston, S. C., as he was on a voyage to England, to visit his relatives, when John was less than two years of age. He was then left to the care of his mother, and grandfather, of the same name.

The mind of this well disposed youth, according to his own recollections, which go back to his earliest years, was wholly bent on study, merely for the sake of it, and without any particular vocation in view ; but, as the family was not in circumstances to support him in his chosen pursuit, at the age of fourteen, he was bound out to a seven years' apprenticeship to learn the glover's trade. For upwards of two years, he submitted quietly to the disposition which his grandfather, who acted as his guardian, had made of him. His master made no complaint of him, except that he "read too much for his business.*"

---

* In Comer's Diary, I find the following statement : "This year I composed a set Discourse from Eccl. xii. 1—Remember now thy Creator," &c. This was at the age of fifteen, while he was an apprentice ; and it evidently shows the bent of his mind at that early age.

Being now in his seventeenth year, by the intercession of Dr. Increase Mather, to whom he applied for his friendly aid, and by the consent of his grandfather, he was released from his apprenticeship, commenced his preparatory studies, and in due time entered the College at Cambridge. His grandfather, dying soon after, left him a legacy of £500. "This," he says, "was to bring me up, and introduce me comfortably in the world, which it did."[*]

After spending some years at Cambridge,—as some of his companions had gone to New Haven, and as living was cheaper there,—by the consent of the Rev. Mr. Webb, who, by his grandfather's will, had become his guardian, he repaired to that institution, where he finished his college course, though I believe he did not graduate on account of ill health. This college then consisted of about fifty students.

Relative to Mr. Comer's experience in the concerns of personal religion, and his change of denominational position, the account may be thus briefly given : His pious propensities in early life have already been stated ; but, not relying on the goodness of his morals, or the soundness of his ancestral creed, he sought, and, after a long course of anxious enquiry, obtained, a satisfactory evidence of his conversion, according to what he believed were the scripture requirements. This was at the age of seventeen. In due time, while a member of the College, he united with the Congregational church in Cambridge, then under the pastoral care of the Rev. Nathaniel Appleton. His membership in this church continued about four years, during all which time, he appears to have had much satisfaction with his spiritual home ; and all his accounts of his Pastor breathe the spirit of filial affection and Christian fellowship ; and the same may be said, by what appears in his Diary, respecting the other ministers of Boston and elsewhere, who took an interest in his welfare, and of the churches under their care, with which he associated, and occasionally communed.[†]

There was one very alarming event which happened to Boston and vicinity in 1721, just at the time of the serious awakening of young Comer, which served to deepen his religious impressions, and increase his fearful apprehensions of being hurried to his grave, without a due preparation for an exchange of worlds. The small-pox, then the terror of mankind, was making a rapid and, to a great extent, fatal progress, among the people, most of whom had no protection against it. Among the victims of this terrible disease, were some of the most intimate friends of young Comer, whose dread of it was so great, that, according to his own representations, it might be literally said of him, in the language of Young,—

"He felt a thousand deaths in fearing one."

After all his precautions, he was soon seized with the loathsome malady, from the effects of which he barely escaped with his life.[‡]

_____

[*] Diary, 1721.

[†] These churches, with their Pastors, in 1723, in addition to Cambridge, were, *in Boston*, the Old North, *Cotton Mather*; the New North, *John Webb*; the New Brick, *William Waldron*. *In Andover, John Barnard.* In this place young Comer occasionally pursued his classical studies. Andover then was a frontier town.
In Newport, R. I., Nathaniel Clap.
In New Haven, Joseph Noyes.

[‡] In the then small population of Boston and vicinity, compared with the present, between eight and nine hundred died of this disease. " The practice of inoculation was *now* set

This assiduous enquirer, and very conscientious man, after an investigation of about two years' continuance, adopted the sentiments of the Baptists on the subject and mode of Baptism, and, according to his Diary, was baptized by the Rev. Elisha Callender, January 31, 1725, and united with the First Baptist Church in Boston, of which Mr. C. was then Pastor. Relative to this transaction, in the old journal before me, I find the following entry :—" Having before waited on Rev. Mr. Appleton, of Cambridge, I discoursed with him on the point of Baptism, together with my resolution—upon which he signified that I might, notwithstanding, maintain my communion with his church—by which I discovered the candour and catholic spirit of the man. He behaved himself the most like a Christian of any of my friends, at that time, upon that account."*

Mr. Comer commenced preaching in 1725, not long after he united with Mr. Callender's church. His first efforts were made with the old Swansea church, which was planted by the famous John Miles, from Wales, in 1663. It was then under the pastoral care of Elder Ephraim Wheaton.† Efforts were made to settle the young and promising preacher, as a colleague with the aged Pastor, but, as the plan failed of success, he repaired to Newport, where, in 1726, he was ordained as Co-pastor with elder William Peckham, in the first church in that town, which bears date, 1644. His ministry here was short but successful; by his influence singing in public worship was there first introduced. He also put in order the old Church Records, which he found in a scattered and neglected condition. The practice of the laying on of hands, (Heb. vi. 2,) as a mode of the initiation of newly baptized members to full fellowship into the church, had hitherto been held in a lax manner, by this ancient community, and Mr. Comer's attempt to have it uniformly observed, was the cause of his dismission from his pastoral charge in 1729. In former ages, this religious rite was a subject of no little discussion and agitation among the Baptists, both in the old country and the new, and sometimes churches were divided on account of differences of opinion respecting it. The Six Principle Baptists, so called, from tenaciously adhering to this number of points laid down in the passage above named, still hold on to this ancient rule of Church Discipline. As a general thing, however, the practice has long been disused among the Baptists, both American and foreign.

Mr. Comer preached, as a supply, for nearly two years, in the Second Baptist Church in Newport, which was founded in 1656. It was then under the pastoral care of Elder Daniel Wightman, from whom Mr. Comer received the imposition of hands, in Gospel Order, according to his judgment and belief.

In 1732, this transitory peacher, whose race was rapid and peculiar, and lamentably short, became the Pastor of a church of his own order in the Southern part of old Rehoboth, near to Swanzea, and about ten miles from

---

up. . . . Dr. Zabdiel Boylston was the chief actor in it—I joined in the *lawfulness* of the practice, though some wrote and printed against it." Comer was preparing to avail himself of the benefit of this new method of prevention, when he found it was too late, and the malady had its natural course. The whole College was dispersed.

* Elsewhere Mr. C. remarks that, at this time he knew of no one of his relatives, who was in the Baptist connection.

† EPHRAIM WHEATON was an Associate Pastor of this Church as early as 1704; and he continued in the faithful discharge of his duties here until his death, which occurred in 1734, at the age of seventy-five. He lived within the bounds of Rehoboth.

Providence, R. I. Here he died of consumption, May 23, 1734, aged twenty-nine years, nine months and twenty-two days. "He was," says Dr. Jackson, "a gentleman of education, piety, and of great success in his profession. During his brief life, he collected a large body of facts, intending, at some future period, to write the history of the American Baptist Churches. His manuscripts he never printed, nor did he, as I learn, ever prepare them for publication. He was even unable to revise them, and they were, of course, left in their original condition. Nevertheless, he made an able and most valuable contribution to Rhode Island History. His papers were probably written about 1729—1731.*

For the historical purposes above named, this industrious man visited most of the churches in New England. He also went as far as Philadelphia, through the Jersies, in a Southern direction. He corresponded, somewhat extensively for that age, with intelligent men in all the Colonies, where those of his own order could be found, as well as in England, Ireland, and Wales, from which regions many of the earliest emigrants, of the Baptist faith, came to this country. In Comer's time, and at a still later period, Pennsylvania and the Jersies were more distinguished than any of the Colonies for the number of their strong men of this creed. Here were found the Joneses, the Morgans, the Mannings, the Smiths, the Harts, and many others. Could this diligent enquirer have lived to make out the history he proposed, from personal interviews, and from historical documents, then easily obtained, and from reliable traditions, in all the Colonies, where the Society had planted their standards, a great amount of labour would have been saved to the historians who succeeded him.

Comer's Diary, to which reference has already often been made, consists of two thin folio manuscript volumes, of about sixty pages each. Most of them are occupied in the relation of passing events, and in them are found many historical facts concerning the affairs of his own people, and also of all the religious denominations in the land, so far as he had any knowledge of them, or intercourse with them, which appears to have been quite extensive and familiar.

"Comer," says Backus, "was very curious and exact in recording the occurrences of his time." This remark is fully verified by looking over the details of the journal in question. Here we find accounts of earthquakes and storms, of wars and rumours of wars among the Indians at home, and the nations abroad: the doings of the Colonial governments; the names and characters of governmental men, especially of those in the Rhode Island Colony, are often met with in this Diary; and, among other things, is a full account of a petition, which was got up by the ministers and lay-members of the Baptist people, with whom Mr. Comer was associated, against the oppressive laws, which were bearing hard on the few of their brethren, who were scattered "up and down," in the adjoining Colony of Connecticut. The chief matter of complaint in this petition was the parish taxes, for the support of the Standing Order. This document, which is transcribed in full, was endorsed by Governor Jenks, in a respectful note to the Colonial Assembly.

* Churches in Rhode Island, pp. 80, 81.

The arrival of the celebrated Dean George Berkeley, at Newport, and some items respecting the popularity of this distinguished visiter, and of the personal interviews which he, in company with others, had with this affable man, are pleasantly related.

Mr. Comer's popularity amongst the ministers and people of different orders is plainly indicated by the frequent entries in his Diary of his correspondence and personal conferences with them. In this way we learn many interesting facts, some painful, some pleasant, respecting men with whom this youthful divine had no ecclesiastical connection. At one time, he informs us that he was invited to the pulpit of the Rev. Mr. Cotton, then the only Congregational clergyman of Providence, which he would gladly have complied with, had not a previous engagement hindered him.

This young minister, during his short race of about nine years after he entered into public service, made his mark unusually high for the time. His name is still had in grateful remembrance in a large religious and literary circle. He left one son and two daughters, and his descendants still survive in Warren, R. I.

Yours respectfully,

DAVID BENEDICT.

EDWARD UPHAM.*

1740—1797.

EDWARD UPHAM was born in Malden, Mass., in the year 1709, and was graduated at Harvard College in 1734. He is supposed to have received the benefit of Mr. Hollis' donation.

In 1727, five persons were baptized by immersion, in West Springfield, by the Rev. Elisha Callender, Pastor of the First Baptist Church in Boston. In 1740, they, with several others who had joined them, were formed into a church, and the Rev. Edward Upham became their Pastor. Though there were persons belonging to this church from different parts of the town, yet most of them were from that part which was afterwards the Second Parish; and that was the principal field of Mr. Upham's ministerial labour. In 1748, he resigned his charge, in consequence of an inadequate support, and removed to Newport, R. I., where he succeeded the Rev. John Callender, as Pastor of the First Baptist Church in that town.

Sometime after Mr. Upham left West Springfield, most of those who had constituted the church of which he had had the care, consented so far to waive their distinctive denominational views as to join with a number of others, of a different communion, to form the Congregational Church, of which the Rev. Sylvanus Griswold† became Pastor. There was a

---

* Benedict's Hist. Bapt., I.—Dr. Lathrop's Autobiography.

† SYLVANUS GRISWOLD, a son of the Rev. George Griswold, (who was graduated at Yale College in 1717, became the Pastor of the Second Congregational Church in Lyme, Conn., and died in 1761,) was born at Lyme about the year 1732; was graduated at Yale College in 1757; and was ordained Pastor of the Second Congregational Church in West Springfield, in Novem-

mutual agreement that while Mr. Griswold should, when desired, conform to the views of the Baptist brethren in respect to the mode of Baptism, they, on the other hand, would receive from him the sacrament of the Lord's Supper.

In 1771, Mr. Upham, having resigned his charge at Newport, returned to reside * on a farm which he owned in his former parish in West Springfield. At the instance of some of the people, he resumed his public labours, and again collected his former charge. As a considerable proportion of them had become members of Mr. Griswold's church, which, at best, was feeble in point of numbers, their secession was sensibly felt. Mr. Upham continued his labours among them till he had passed his eightieth year, from which time he gradually sunk under the infirmities of age. The church, of which he had been Pastor, about that time became extinct. He died at his residence, in Feeding Hills Parish, October, 1797, aged eighty-seven years. His Funeral Sermon was preached by the Rev. Dr. Lathrop, from Job. xlii., 7—"So Job died, being old and full of days."

Mr. Upham was one of the earliest and most zealous friends of Rhode Island College. He was a Trustee and Fellow of that institution from its foundation in 1764 till 1789.

Mr. Upham was married in March, 1740, to Sarah, daughter of Dr. John Leonard, of Feeding Hills. They had six children, five of whom survived him. His eldest son was shot dead, by mistake, while engaged, with a party, in hunting bears, in the night.

Dr. Lathrop has described Mr. Upham to me as a sensible, well educated and liberal minded man. He was an Open Communion Baptist, both in sentiment and in practice. After his return to West Springfield from Newport, he preached several times at private houses in Dr. Lathrop's parish, and introduced the Baptist controversy; and it was understood put in circulation among Dr. Lathrop's people certain pamphlets, designed to vindicate his own views. This led Dr. L. to preach two sermons on the subject, which were afterwards published; but I believe it never disturbed the friendly personal relations that existed between himself and Mr. Upham. I know Dr. Lathrop had a high regard for him, as being. in general, a fair minded and honourable man. I received the impression from him that Mr. Upham's orthodoxy was not of the straitest sect, and would probably not rise above Arminianism. He had the reputation of being a very respectable preacher; and so I think he must have been, from having read some of his manuscript sermons. His style was remarkable for simplicity and perspicuity, and, though very correct, was adapted to the humblest capacity. I believe he used his manuscript in the pulpit, contrary to the common usage of ministers of his denomination at that day.

ber, 1762,—one week after its organization. He continued minister of the parish till 1781, and Pastor of the church till his death, which occurred on the 4th of December, 1819, at the age of eighty-seven.

* Dr. Ezra Stiles, who at that time resided at Newport, has the following entry in his journal, under date, April 19, 1771:—" Rev. E. Upham, with his wife and family, sailed for Connecticut river, removing to Springfield. His congregation and friends accompanied them to the ship with many tears."

EBENEZER KINNERSLEY.

1743—1778.

FROM HORATIO GATES JONES, ESQ.

PHILADELPHIA, April 1, 1859.

My dear Sir: More than a century ago, the name of Ebenezer Kinnersley, of whom you ask me to give you some account, was as well known, especially in all scientific circles in this country, as perhaps any other of which the country could boast; but, in the lapse of years, it has been suffered, even here in the city in which he lived, to pass—I had almost said—into total oblivion. I have endeavoured to gather the few records and authentic traditions of him that remain, and such of them as I suppose are suited to your purpose I will proceed to embody in this communication.

EBENEZER KINNERSLEY was born in the city of Gloucester, England, on the 30th of November, 1711. His father, William Kinnersley, a worthy Baptist minister, migrated to America in 1714, when this son was three years of age, and settled in Lower Dublin, near Philadelphia, where he united with, and officiated as minister to, the Pennepek Baptist Church,— the first permanent Society of that faith in the Province of Pennsylvania. It was in this quiet retired country, on the banks of the beautiful Pennepek Creek, that young Kinnersley's early life was passed—there he pursued his studies under the supervision of a pious father, whose counsels no doubt were instrumental in directing the attention of the young man to the higher concerns of religion; for, on the 6th of September, 1735, about one year after his father's death, he was baptized and united with the Pennepek Church. In 1739, he married Sarah Duffield, and about the same time removed to the city of Philadelphia. The ability which he displayed, and his excellence as a speaker, led the church to call him to the ministry, and, after due trial, he was ordained in 1743; but, owing to delicate health, and other objects of interest that engaged his attention, he never became a Pastor. He was one of the few, in Philadelphia, who had doubts in regard to the character of the preaching which was introduced by Whitefield; nor did he hesitate to enter a solemn protest against it, from the pulpit of the Baptist Church. This happened on the 6th of July, 1740, and the excitement produced by the sermon was so great that he was absolutely forbidden the privilege of communion. For some time, he attended the Episcopal Church, but ere long the difficulty was settled, and, on the 5th of May, 1746, when the Philadelphia Baptist Church was organized as a distinct Society from that at Pennepek, Mr. Kinnersley formed one of the constituent members. He remained in communion with this church as long as he lived.

The year 1746 marked an epoch in his life; for his attention was then first directed to the wonderful and unknown properties of the *Electric Fire*,—as it was then termed; and he was brought into close companionship with Benjamin Franklin. He gave himself up to this department of science with so much zeal that his health failed, and he was compelled to make a voyage to the Bermudas, then a place of frequent resort for invalids, carrying with him his electrical apparatus, to continue his experiments.

About this time Mr. Kinnersley published a pamphlet entitled "A Letter to the Reverend the Ministers of the Baptist Congregations in Pennsylvania and the New Jerseys, containing some Remarks on their Answers to certain Queries, proposed to them at their Annual Association in Philadelphia, September 24, 1746."

Upon Mr. Kinnersley's return to Philadelphia, in 1753, he was chosen Chief Master of the English School in connection with the College. Having served in this capacity two years, he was, on the 11th of July, 1755, unanimously chosen Professor of the English tongue and of Oratory in the College. And so successfully did he perform the duties of his Professorship that, in 1757, he was honoured by the Trustees with the degree of Master of Arts; and, in 1768, he was chosen a member of the American Philosophical Society, which was then composed of the most learned and scientific men in the city. Failing health, however, interfered with the prosecution of his duties, and, on the 17th of October, 1772, he tendered his resignation as Professor, and his connection with the College thereupon ceased. The following extract from the Minutes of the Board of Trustees, under date of February 2, 1773, shows the estimate they had of Professor Kinnersley's usefulness and ability:—

"The College suffers greatly since Mr. Kinnersley left it, for want of a person to teach public speaking, so that the present classes have not those opportunities of learning to declaim and speak, which have been of so much use to their predecessors, and have contributed greatly to aid the credit of the Institution."

After terminating his relation to the College, he made a visit of a few months to the Island of Barbadoes; and, on his return to America, with still enfeebled health, he retired to the country, and there, amid the scenes of his early youth, with the companionship of his faithful wife and sympathizing friends, he passed the few remaining years of his life.

Mr. Kinnersley died on the 4th of July, 1778, in the sixty-eighth year of his age, and was buried at the Lower Dublin (or Pennepek) Baptist Church. He left a widow and two children,—a daughter and a son. The daughter, *Esther*, was born, November 30, 1740, was married to Joseph Shewell, a merchant of Philadelphia, and became the mother of three children. The son, *William*, was born October 29, 1743; was graduated at the College of Philadelphia in 1761; studied Medicine, and settled in Northumberland County; and died (unmarried) in April, 1785, aged forty-two. Mrs. Sarah Kinnersley, the Professor's widow, died November 6, 1801, aged eighty-one years.

Family tradition states that Mr. Kinnersley's personal appearance was dignified, and his manners of the old school; and Mr. Alexander Graydon, in his Memoirs, speaking of his attending the Academy at Philadelphia, says,—"I was, accordingly, introduced by my father to Professor Kinnersley, the Teacher of English, and Professor of Oratory. He was an Anabaptist Clergyman, a large, venerable looking man."

It is impossible now to ascertain for how long a time, or to what extent, Mr. Kinnersley laboured as a minister of the Gospel, though it is known that he retained his connection with the Baptist Church till the close of life. It is certain, however, that he acquired his chief renown, not in the exercise of his ministry, but in his scientific pursuits and discoveries; and, though your request does not contemplate any thing like a history of what he accomplished in this department, I cannot withhold the opinion that, owing to various circumstances, posterity has done him but very meagre justice. That he was intimately associated with Dr. Franklin in some of his most splendid discoveries, and that Franklin himself more than once gratefully acknowledged his aid; that he attracted the attention of many of the most eminent philosophers of his day on both sides of the Atlantic; that he delivered Lectures in Philadelphia, New York, Boston, and Newport, on the great subjects that were then engrossing the attention of the philosophical world, and that these Lectures excited great interest, especially among the more intelligent classes, is proved by evidence the most incontrovertible. The results of a somewhat extended examination on this subject I have embodied in another form; but it could not perhaps legitimately find a place in the "Annals of the American Pulpit." I cannot doubt that it is only justice to give this man a place—little as is now known of him—among the leading spirits of his time.

Very sincerely yours,

HORATIO GATES JONES.

OLIVER HART.*

1746—1795.

OLIVER HART was born of reputable parents, in Warminster, Bucks County, Pa., July 5, 1723. His mind seems to have been early directed to the subject of religion; for he made a public profession of his faith at Southampton, Pa., and was received a member of the Church in that place, in 1741, when he was in his eighteenth year, having been previously baptized by the Rev. Jenkin Jones. He was accustomed, at this time, often to listen to the preaching of Whitefield, the Tennents, and others of that school, by means of which he was not a little encouraged and quickened in his spiritual course.

On the 20th of December, 1746, he was licensed to preach by the church with which he first united; and, on the 18th of October, 1749, was ordained to the work of the Gospel ministry.

As there was, at that time, a loud call for ministers in the Southern Colonies, and the Baptist Church in Charleston, S. C., was vacant, Mr. Hart was induced, immediately after his ordination, to make a visit to that part of the country. He arrived in Charleston on the very day of the Funeral of Mr. Chanler,† Pastor of the church at Ashley River, who had

* Morgan Edwards' Materials towards a History of the Baptists in New Jersey.—Benedict's Hist. Bapt., II.
† ISAAC CHANLER was born at Bristol, England, in 1701; came to Ashley River about 1733; and continued the much esteemed Pastor of that church until he died, November 30, 1749, in

supplied the church at Charleston a part of the time, and who was the only ordained Baptist minister in that region. The Charleston Church had made repeated efforts to obtain a minister both from Europe and the Colonies at the North. Mr. Hart's arrival was, therefore, very gratefully welcomed; and so well were the people satisfied with him and his labours, that they proceeded forthwith to invite him to become their Pastor; and he was, accordingly, installed over them on the 16th of February, 1750.

During the thirty years following, he continued in the faithful and vigorous discharge of his duty, passing through scenes of affliction with great calmness and dignity, uniformly exemplary in his life, and favoured with a large measure of public respect and usefulness. He was useful, not only as a minister, but as a citizen, and especially in connection with the events of the Revolution. In 1775, he was appointed, by the Council of Safety, which then exercised the Executive authority in South Carolina, to travel, in conjunction with the Hon. William H. Drayton and the Rev. William Tennent, into the interior of the State, to enlighten the people in regard to their political interests, and reconcile them to certain Congressional measures of which they were disposed to complain. But, on the approach of the British fleet and army, to which Charleston was surrendered in 1780, he thought proper to leave the city, and seek a more Northern residence. The Baptist church in Hopewell, N. J., being then vacant, sent him a pressing invitation to settle among them as their Pastor; and, he having accepted it, the pastoral relation was duly constituted on the 16th of December of the same year.

Mr. Hart continued the minister of Hopewell during the remainder of his life. For a few years immediately preceding his death, the infirmities of age and the attacks of disease had made such inroads upon his constitution that he was obliged, in a great measure, to decline public service. In the last few months of his life, he raised large quantities of blood, and suffered intense bodily distress; but was uniformly sustained by the consolations and hopes of the Gospel. Just as he was on the eve of his departure, he called upon all around him to help him praise the Lord for what He had done for his soul. Being told that he would soon join the company of saints and angels, he replied "Enough, Enough." He died on the 31st of December, 1795, in the seventy-third year of his age. Two Sermons were preached in reference to his death, one by Dr. Furman, of Charleston, the other by Dr. Rogers, of Philadelphia.

The following is a list of Mr. Hart's publications:—Dancing exploded. A Discourse occasioned by the Death of the Rev. William Tennent, 1777. The Christian Temple. A Circular Letter on Christ's Mediatorial Character. America's Remembrancer. A Gospel Church portrayed.

Mr. Hart was twice married. His first wife was Sarah Brees, by whom he had eight children. His second wife, to whom he was married in 1774,

the forty-ninth year of his age. He was distinguished for both talents and piety. He was the author of a treatise in small quarto, entitled "The Doctrines of Glorious Grace unfolded, defended, and practically improved." He also published a treatise on Original Sin, and a Sermon on the Death of the Rev. William Tilly.

WILLIAM TILLY, above mentioned, was a native of Salisbury, England; came early to this country; and was called to the ministry and ordained by the church in Charleston. He lived on Edisto Island until his death, which occurred on the 14th of April, 1744, in the forty-sixth year of his age. Mr. Chanler, in his Funeral Sermon, represents him as an able and faithful minister, who had honoured religion in his death as well as in his life.

was Ann Sealy, daughter of William Sealy, of Eutaw, and the widow of Charles Grimball, of Charleston. By this marriage he had two children,—both sons. The second Mrs. Hart died on the Island of Wadmalaw, in South Carolina, on the 5th of October, 1813, in the seventy-third year of her age.

The following is an extract from Dr. Furman's Sermon occasioned by Mr. Hart's death :—

"In his person, he was somewhat tall, well-proportioned and of a graceful appearance; of an active, vigorous constitution, before it had been impaired by close application to his studies and by his abundant labours. His countenance was open and manly, his voice clear, harmonious and commanding; the powers of his mind were strong and capacious, and enriched by a fund of useful knowledge; his taste was elegant and refined. Though he had not enjoyed the advantage of a collegiate education, nor indeed much assistance from any personal instructions, such was his application that, by private study, he obtained a considerable acquaintance with classical learning, and explored the fields of science, so that, in the year 1769, the College of Rhode Island, in honour to his literary merit, conferred on him the degree of Master in the Liberal Arts.

"But as a Christian and Divine his character was most conspicuous. No person who heard his pious experimental discourses, or his affectionate, fervent addresses to God in prayer, who beheld the zeal and constancy he manifested in the public exercises of religion, or the disinterestedness, humility, benevolence, charity, devotion and equanimity of temper he discovered on all occasions, in the private walks of life, could, for a moment, doubt of his being not only *truly* but *eminently* religious. He possessed, in a large measure, the moral and social virtues, and had a mind formed for friendship. In all his relative connections, as husband, father, brother, master, he acted with the greatest propriety, and was endeared to those who were connected with him in the tender ties.

"From a part of his diary now in my possession, it appears that he took more than ordinary pains to walk humbly and faithfully with God; to live under impressions of the love of Christ; to walk in the light of the Divine presence; and to improve all his time and opportunities to the noblest purposes of religion and virtue.

"In his religious principles he was a fixed Calvinist, and a consistent, liberal Baptist. The doctrines of *free efficacious grace* were precious to him. Christ Jesus, and Him crucified, in the perfection of his righteousness, the merit of his death, the prevalence of his intercession, and efficacy of his grace, was the foundation of his hope, the source of his joy, and the delightful theme of his preaching.

"His sermons were peculiarly serious, containing a happy assemblage of doctrinal and practical truths, set in an engaging light, and enforced with convincing arguments. For the discussion of doctrinal truths he was more especially eminent, to which also he was prepared by an intimate acquaintance with the Sacred Scriptures, and an extensive reading of the most valuable, both of ancient and modern authors. His eloquence, at least in the middle stages of life, was not of the most popular kind, but perspicuous, manly and flowing,—such as afforded pleasure to persons of true taste, and edification to the serious hearer.

"With these various qualifications for usefulness, he possessed an ardent desire to be as useful as possible. . . . . . . Many owned him as their father in the Gospel. Among these are two distinguished and useful ministers, who survive him, and shine as diffusive lights in the Church.* These were not only awakened under his preaching, but introduced, also, by him, into a course of study for the ministry.

"The formation of a Society in this city to assist pious young men in obtaining education for the public services of the Church, and which has been of use to several, originated with him; and he was a prime mover in that plan for the association of churches, by which so many of our churches are very happily united at the present day. To him, also, in conjunction with his beloved and amiable friends, now, I trust, with God, Rev. Francis Pelot and Mr. David Williams, is that valuable work of public utility, the System of Church Discipline, to be ascribed. His printed sermons have contributed to the general interest of religion, and his extensive regular correspondence has been the means of conveying rational pleasure and religious improvement to many.

"To all which may be added his usefulness as a citizen of America. Prompt in his judgment, ardent in his love of liberty, and rationally jealous for the rights of his country, he took an early and decided part in those measures which led our patriots to successful opposition against the encroachments of arbitrary power, and brought us to possess all the blessings of our happy independence. Yet he did not mix politics

---

* One of these was the Rev. Dr. Stillman of Boston.

with the Gospel, nor desert the duties of his station to pursue them; but, attending to each in its proper place, he gave weight to his political sentiments, by the propriety and uprightness of his conduct; and the influence of it was felt by many."

GARDINER THURSTON.*
1748—1802.

GARDINER THURSTON, a son of Edward and Elizabeth Thurston, was born in Newport, R. I., November 14, 1721. He very early discovered a serious disposition, and being sent to pass some time with some relatives in the country, they were struck with the fact that he was not only attentive to his own private religious duties, but exhorted his youthful associates to remember their Creator, and to cultivate a sense of their dependance on Him. His friends noticed these early developments with much interest, regarding them as a sort of pledge that he was destined to a pious and useful life.

After he returned to Newport, and had been for some time under the ministry of the Rev. Daniel Wightman,† and his colleague, the Rev. Nicholas Eyres,‡ he addressed to them a letter, which is still preserved, expressing a deep sense of his own sinfulness, and unworthiness, and inability to effect his own salvation, and an earnest desire that he might be enabled to rest wholly on the free grace of God, as revealed in the Gospel. Shortly after this letter was written, he supposed that he obtained peace and joy in believing; but did not make a public profession of his faith till the 4th of April, 1741. When the day came in which he was to be examined as a candidate for Baptism, he was in a state of great spiritual darkness, and was much inclined to believe that his previous experience had been nothing better than delusion. When he came to the door of the meeting-house in which the church were assembled to attend to his examination, he was so much oppressed by a sense of his unworthiness, and the apprehension that he had deceived himself, that he turned away, and walked into a burying ground, and sat down upon a rock; and while there, the cloud that had hung over him was dissipated, and he rejoiced again in the confidence of the Divine favour. About sixty years afterwards, when walking in the same burying ground, he stopped, and putting his staff upon the rock, said,—"There I sat down, overwhelmed with distress, while the church were waiting for me to come in, to give them an account of the dealings of God with my soul. Soon after I sat down, I was enabled through rich

* Mass. Bapt. Miss. Mag. I.—Benedict's Hist. Bapt. I. and II.
† DANIEL WIGHTMAN was born in Narragansett, January 2, 1668, and was ordained in 1701, at which time he took the joint care of the Second Church in Newport, with the Rev. Mr. Clark. He continued in this relation till his death, which occurred in 1750. He was greatly respected and beloved.
‡ NICHOLAS EYRES was born at a place called Chipmanslade, Wiltshire, England, August 22, 1691; came to New York about the year 1711; was baptized there three years after; and in September, 1724, was ordained to the Pastorship of the First (or Gold street) Baptist Church, in that city. In October, 1731, he resigned his charge, and became Co-pastor with Mr. Wightman of the Second Church in Newport. He died on the 13th of February, 1759. The inscription on his monument represents him as a man of great intelligence, benevolence, and piety.

grace, to give up myself and all I had into the hands of my blessed Jesus, who immediately dispelled the darkness that covered me, removed my distress, filled me with peace and consolation, and gave me strength to declare what He had done for my soul."

He was received by the church, and baptized by their Pastor, the Rev. Nicholas Eyres. He commenced very soon to take part in social religious exercises. and delivered himself with so much propriety and unction that his brethren began to think of him as adapted to occupy a wider field of Christian usefulness. The church, accordingly, licensed him to preach, in 1748, and requested that he would act as an assistant to their Pastor, the Rev. Mr. Eyres. With this request he complied, preaching once on the Lord's day, and once on one of the secular days of the week; at the same time prosecuting with great zeal the study of Theology, in which he enjoyed the assistance of his venerable friend and ministerial associate.

Mr. Eyres having died suddenly in February, 1759, the church immediately invited Mr. Thurston to the sole pastoral charge. He accepted the invitation, and was, accordingly, constituted their Pastor, by the usual form, on the 29th of April following. Previous to this time, Mr. Thurston had connected a worldly occupation with the duties of the ministry; but he now abandoned the former, with a view to devote himself entirely to the latter.

Mr. Thurston continued regularly to discharge his official duties, until about three years previous to his death. From that time, his bodily infirmities were so great that he did not attempt to preach, though he was still as zealously devoted to the interests of his flock as ever. After a gradual decline, which was marked by the most humble, quiet and trusting spirit, and a full confidence of entering into rest, he died on the 23d of May, 1802, in the eighty-first year of his age. His Funeral Sermon was preached by the Rev. Stephen Gano, D. D., of Providence. The only member of his family that survived him was a daughter. His wife died in 1784.

FROM THE REV. JOSHUA BRADLEY.

St. Paul, Minn., 18th June, 1853.

My dear Sir: I was settled as a colleague with the Rev. Gardiner Thurston, in the pastoral charge of the Second Baptist Church in Newport, in the year 1801. He was then just about eighty years of age, and had been, for some time, obliged to desist from preaching, on account of bodily infirmity. His mind, however, was generally clear, his affections lively, and his interest in all that pertained to the great objects of the ministry was increased rather than diminished by the near prospect of his departure. He was able, also, till near the close of life, to attend public worship on the Sabbath, and to perform some pastoral service in the way of visiting; and it is hardly needful to say that he did every thing in his power to promote the comfort and usefulness of my own ministry.

Mr. Thurston had enjoyed in his day a much more than common degree of popularity as a preacher. Though he had not received a collegiate education, he had a great thirst for knowledge, and never lost any opportunity for acquiring it. He was also the Pastor of the church in which he had been born and educated, and was, moreover, the successor of a man of more than ordinary talents and acquirements; and these circumstances, no doubt, were an additional incentive to his making the most of his opportunities for intellectual culture. I do not mean to intimate that he was a highly educated man; but he had so much general information, and so happy a talent at using it, that he would pass very respectably even in the more cultivated circles.

Mr. Thurston had naturally a good constitution, and, during much the greater part of his life, vigorous health. With a discriminating mind he united a lively imagination and warm sensibilities. He was a model in his domestic relations, always performing every duty in his house promptly and gracefully. He was an attraction in every social circle; for, though he never forgot the dignity of his office, he knew how to unbend in the freedom of a well regulated intercourse. He was a popular man in the community—every one regarded him as a fine example of a tried Christian character,—of a venerable and unsullied old age.

His preaching was eminently scriptural, and he never wished to go beyond " Thus saith the Lord," in establishing any doctrine that he advanced. He was accustomed to write the heads of his sermons, noting down also the proof texts, and then, by meditation, to render the whole train of thought familiar to him, so that, in the delivery, he had no occasion to refer to his manuscript; and generally, I believe, he had no notes before him. He had an excellent voice for the pulpit, and he used it to good purpose. While he was accustomed to make mature preparation for his public services, he evidently depended greatly on Divine aid; it was manifest that, while he spoke out of a warm heart and well furnished mind, he felt most deeply that his sufficiency was of God.

Mr. Thurston always showed himself deeply concerned for the honour of the ministry; and he would never assist in introducing one to the sacred office, who he did not believe possessed the requisite qualifications. He was equally far from expecting any thing like a miraculous call on the one hand, and from dispensing with what he deemed suitable intellectual moral, and religious qualifications on the other; and thus his whole influence went to elevate and purify the ministry. He had a strong conviction that with the character of the Ministry is identified, in no small degree, the character of the Church, at any given period; and that he could not labour more efficiently for the latter, than by directing a due share of his attention to the former.

My venerable friend, though he died when the great modern movement towards the conversion of the world had only begun to be made, yet was most deeply interested in contemplating all those signs of the times, that were beginning then to awaken so much attention in Evangelical Christendom. His heart was thoroughly baptized, even then, with the missionary spirit. He saw the things that we see, only through the medium of faith in the Divine testimony; but this was among the brightest visions of his old age. It was manifest to all who saw him that, to his latest hour, the commanding desire of his heart was that the reign of Christianity might be universal.

Some eighteen months before his death, I called at his house, with several ministers and other Christian friends, all of whom were most deeply impressed with the spirituality of his conversation, and some of them, after leaving him, remarked that they had never witnessed an instance in which the promises of God seemed to be so entirely and unconditionally relied on. A favourite topic of conversation with him was the Christian's victory over death, through the mediation of the Lord Jesus; and, in connection with this, he was accustomed to dwell with great delight on the glorious realities of the future, and especially on the reunion with Christian friends who had gone before him. I had the opportunity of visiting him frequently in his last days, and witnessing the triumphs of grace amidst the decays of nature. He talked to me upon his death-bed with a sweet serenity, and sometimes a glowing fervour, that made me feel as if his eyes were already open upon Heaven. I sat by him when his spirit gently passed away; and, though he was unable to speak in his last moments, there was a serene smile upon his countenance that seemed like a response to the voice from Heaven, saying, "Come up hither."

Faithfully yours,

JOSHUA BRADLEY.

FROM THE REV. BENJAMIN H. PITMAN.

PROVIDENCE, Saratoga County, N. Y.,
August 17, 1851.

My dear Sir: I would gladly refer you, if I could, to some one whose recollections of Gardiner Thurston are more extended than my own; but the generation to which he belonged has so nearly passed away that I scarcely know an individual, now living, who can be supposed to remember so much of him even as I do myself. Though I grew up by the side of him, and his form and countenance, in my early years, were very familiar to me, yet, as I belonged, at that time, to another communion, my personal knowledge of him was not very great; and yet I think I understood very well the general estimation in which he was held in the community. In addition to this, I have had access to some notices of him that were written shortly after his death, which fully confirm all my early impressions.

From the period of my earliest recollection of Mr. Thurston, he was far advanced in years, venerable in appearance, and still more venerable in character. He was a thin, spare man, I should think of about the medium height, and had an intelligent and expressive countenance. He wore an old-fashioned white wig, after the manner of most of the old ministers of that day. Considering his age, he was unusually quick and graceful in his movements, and left the impression upon you that, in his earlier years, he must have been distinguished for agility and personal attraction.

His manners were, in a very high degree, amiable and winning. He mingled with great ease and familiarity in the social circle, and had the faculty of making all around him feel perfectly at home; but he never did any thing, or said any thing, or connived at any thing, that was of even questionable propriety. He never forgot, in any circumstances, his high calling as a minister of Christ; and, though he thought, with the wise man, that "every thing is beautiful in his time," and that "for every thing there is a season," yet his object always seemed to be to leave some really useful impression on the minds of those with whom he conversed. He was a person of a remarkably benevolent disposition, and was always rendered happy by seeing others so.

He was undoubtedly a man of much more than ordinary powers of mind. I should suppose that his predominating faculty was judgment, though he was by no means deficient as a reasoner, and withal was considerably imaginative. But I think few men were his superiors in what is usually called common sense. He discerned intuitively what was fitting, at all times, and on all occasions. There was no tendency in his mind to extremes,—nothing of what, at this day, is called *ultraism*. Hence he had, in a remarkable degree, the respect and confidence of the whole community. His opinion was allowed to have great weight in every circle, and on almost every subject.

As a Preacher he was at once instructive and persuasive. What impressed you most in his preaching was the simple earnestness and deep solemnity which breathed in both his matter and manner. No one who heard him could doubt, for a moment, that he was truly a man of God; that every word that he spake came from his inmost soul; and that he lost sight of every thing else in his preaching, in the one paramount desire to save the souls of those whom he addressed.

He was a zealous friend to revivals of religion, and was privileged to witness more than one during his ministry. Among those in whose conversion and spiritual growth he was supposed to be instrumental, were several who became useful ministers of the Gospel. And there were some in whose minds the good seed was sown, through his instrumentality, but the harvest was not reaped till after he had gone to his rest.

Mr. Thurston was remarkable for the interest he took in young ministers. Several letters which he addressed to one or more of them are still in existence, and they breathe the most intense desire for their spirituality, fidelity, and success. They show his high appreciation of ministerial obligation, and his unyielding purpose to know nothing, as a minister, save Jesus Christ and Him crucified.

I am very truly yours,

BENJAMIN H. PITMAN.

ISAAC BACKUS.*
1751—1806.

ISAAC BACKUS, a son of Samuel and Elizabeth (Tracy) Backus, was born at Norwich, Conn., January 9, 1724. His parents were respectable members of the Congregational Church. His father was a descendant from one of the earliest and most respectable settlers of Norwich, and his mother was of the Winslow family, that came to Plymouth in 1620. Some of his relatives belonged to the denomination called Separates; and his mother, when a widow, with some other of his family connections, was actually imprisoned for holding and promulgating offensive doctrines. It was in the midst of the great excitement that prevailed in connection with the labours of Whitefield, in 1741, that he received his first permanent religious impressions. He united with the Congregational Church in his native town, though not without many misgivings, on account of what he deemed their unreasonable laxity, especially in regard to the admission of members. In the beginning of 1745, he, with a number of others, withdrew from the church, and set up a meeting of their own on the Sabbath, which of course drew upon them the displeasure of the church, and ultimately led to their being suspended from the Communion. The separation proved a permanent one, and Mr. Backus and his associates became identified with the great religious movement of the time, which led to the formation of a large number of Separate or New Light churches.

Soon after a Separate church was formed in Norwich, Mr. Backus was led to devote himself to the preaching of the Gospel. His first sermon was preached to the church of which he was a member, on the 28th of September, 1746, and was received with great favour. For fourteen months following, he was engaged in preaching in various towns in Connecticut, Rhode Island, and Massachusetts. In December, 1747, he commenced his labours in Middleborough, (Titicut Precinct,) and on the 13th of April,

---

* Benedict's Hist. Bapt. II.—Prof. Hovey's Memoirs of the Life and Times of the Rev. Isaac Backus.—MS. from Zechariah Eddy, Esq.

1748, was ordained as Pastor of the church in that place. This church had its origin in a disagreement in respect to the settlement of a minister. The Society was formed in February, 1743, being composed of persons who wished for a clergyman of different religious views from the one who had actually been settled over the parish to which they belonged; and, as they could not obtain a dismission from the church by an ecclesiastical council, after waiting five years, they withdrew, without this sanction, and, in February, 1748, formed a church by themselves. This, however, was not the end of their troubles; for they were still taxed for the support of public worship, or for the building of a new meeting house, in the old parish. Mr. Backus himself was not only taxed, but seized and imprisoned, though he was soon released, without either paying the tax, or coming to any compromise.

In 1749, the subject of Baptism was agitated in the church of which Mr. Backus was Pastor; and several of its members became Baptists, and thus obtained an exemption from the Congregational tax. In August, 1751, Mr. Backus himself was baptized by immersion, by Elder Pierce of Warwick, R. I. For some time afterwards, he held communion with those who had not been thus baptized, but he adopted the principle of Strict Communion after a few years. On the 16th of January, 1756, the members of his church who had become Baptists, formed themselves into a distinct church, and he was installed its Pastor on the 23d of June following, by ministers from Boston and Rehoboth. In this relation he continued till the close of life.

In the year 1772, Mr. Backus was chosen Agent for the Baptist Churches in Massachusetts, in place of Mr. Davis, who had been Pastor of the Second Church in Boston, but had left his charge on account of ill health. This agency, which was designed for the promotion of religious liberty, and especially to secure to the Baptists an exemption from the burdens imposed upon them by law, he executed with great ability, and not altogether without success.

When the Continental Congress met at Philadelphia in 1774, Mr. Backus was sent as an Agent from the Baptist Churches of the Warren Association, to endeavour to enlist some influence in their favour. On his return, he found that a report had preceded him that he had been attempting to break up the union of the Colonies; whereupon, he addressed himself to the Provincial Congress of Massachusetts, on the 9th of December following, and was met in a manner that relieved him from all suspicion. When the Convention, in 1779, took into consideration the Constitution of the State, the subject of the extent of the civil power in connection with religion naturally came up, and, in the course of the discussion, some severe reflections were cast upon the Baptist memorial presented at Philadelphia. Mr. Backus immediately appeared in the columns of the Chronicle, in his own defence, giving a full account of his proceedings as Baptist Agent, and urging reasons for opposing an article in the Bill of Rights of the Constitution of Massachusetts. He strongly repudiated the idea that the civil authority had a right to interfere in matters purely religious; and maintained vigorously and earnestly that all connection between Church and State should be dissolved.

In 1789, Mr. Backus took a journey into Virginia, and North Carolina, which kept him from his people about six months. During this time he preached an hundred and twenty-six sermons, and travelled by land and water more than three thousand miles. This journey was undertaken in consequence of a request from some of the Southern brethren, that they might have, temporarily, the aid of some one of the ministers of the Warren Association, in the wide field of labour which then opened before them.

He was honoured with the Degree of Master of Arts from Brown University in 1797.

For a few months previous to his death, Mr. Backus was laid by from his public labours, in consequence of a paralytic stroke, which deprived him of his speech and the use of his limbs. His reason, however, continued till the last; and, in his expiring moments, he exhibited the triumph of Christian faith. He died on the 20th of November, 1806, in the eighty-third year of his age, and the sixtieth of his ministry.

On the 29th of November, 1749, he was married to Susannah Mason, of Rehoboth, with whom he lived about fifty-one years. His own testimony was, that "she was the greatest earthly blessing which God ever gave him." They had nine children, all of whom became respectable members of society.

The following is a list of Mr. Backus' publications:—A Discourse on the Internal Call to preach the Gospel, 1754. A Sermon on Galatians, iv., 31, 1756. A Sermon on Acts, xiii. 27, 1763. A Letter to Mr. Lord, 1764. A Sermon on Prayer, 1766. A Discourse on Faith, 1767. An Answer to Mr. Fish, 1768. A Sermon on his Mother's Death, 1769. A Second Edition of his Sermon on Gal. iv. 31, with an Answer to Mr. Frothingham, 1770. A Plea for Liberty of Conscience, 1770. Sovereign Grace Vindicated, 1771. A Letter concerning Taxes to support Religious Worship, 1771. A Sermon at the Ordination of Mr. Hunt, 1772. A Reply to Mr. Holly, 1772. A Reply to Mr. Fish, 1773. An Appeal to the Public, in Defence of Religious Liberty, 1773. A Letter on the Decrees, 1773. A History of the Baptists, Vol. I., 1777. Government and Liberty described, 1778. A Discourse on Baptism, 1779. True Policy requires Equal Religious Liberty, 1779. An Appeal to the People of Massachusetts against Arbitrary Power, 1780. Truth is great and will prevail, 1781. The Doctrine of Universal Salvation examined and refuted, 1782. A Door opened for Christian Liberty, 1783. A History of the Baptists, Vol. II., 1784. Godliness excludes Slavery, in Answer to John Cleaveland, 1785. The Testimony of the two Witnesses, 1786. An Address to New England, 1787. An Answer to Remmele on the Atonement, 1787. An Essay on Discipline, 1787. An Answer to Wesley on Election and Perseverance, 1789. On the Support of Gospel Ministers, 1790. An Essay on the Kingdom of God, 1792. A History of the Baptists, Vol. III., 1796. A Second Edition of his Sermon on the Death of his Mother; to which was added a short account of his Wife, who died in 1800. Published in 1803.

FROM THE HON. ZECHARIAH EDDY.

MIDDLEBOROUGH, Mass., May 16, 1852.

Dear Sir: I was well acquainted with the Rev. Isaac Backus, and was contemporary with him twenty-six years. Though we belonged to different denominations, being myself a Congregationalist, I had a high esteem for his character, and consider it a privilege to do any thing I can to perpetuate his memory.

All New England is indebted to Mr. Backus more, I think, than to any other man, for his researches in relation to our early ecclesiastical history. Mr. Bancroft bears the most honourable testimony to his fidelity, and considers his History, as to its facts, more to be depended on than any other of the early Histories of New England. And there is good reason why it should be so; for he sought the truth, like the old philosophers, who said " it was in a well, and long and persevering labour only could bring it up." He went to the fountain head. All our early Records at Plymouth, Taunton, Boston, Essex, Providence, Newport, Hartford, New Haven,—the Records of Courts, Towns, Churches, Ecclesiastical Councils, were thoroughly searched, and he has fully and accurately presented the results of these researches, and brought to light and remembrance many important facts and events, which, probably, would never have gone into our history but for him. His diligence, patience, and perseverance, in this department of labour, are above all praise.

And what renders this the more remarkable is that it was done in the midst of domestic cares, pastoral duties, and, I might almost say, " the care of all the churches." He was often called upon to preach at ordinations, and on other special occasions, and he wrote numerous tracts on the Order of the Churches, and in defence of True Liberty of Conscience. He was also an efficient representative of those who were seeking to enjoy this liberty, before Legislative Bodies and Civil Tribunals, Councils, and Associations. Let any man open his History, and observe the numerous extracts from documents contained in the depositories of towns and churches, in public offices, and printed books of authority, and bear in mind the extent and variety of his other engagements, and he will not doubt that he was one of the most industrious and useful men of his time. In his own day, his labours were certainly appreciated. It is truly wonderful that, amidst the poverty and privations incident to the War of the Revolution, there could have been awakened interest enough to defray the expense of publishing large volumes of History, at the high price which was then demanded for such works. The effect was a rapid increase of light and knowledge, and a rapid increase of churches and communicants.

Mr. Backus was called " Father," not only by his own people, who might well thus honour him, but by almost the entire community; and a Patriarch he was, not only by ecclesiastical powers, but as a Pastor and Divine, and in moral power and weight of well-earned and well-established character.

In regard to ornament of style, and even the arrangement of his materials, it must be acknowledged that he was deficient; but this was well compensated by the authenticity of his facts, the accuracy of his statements, and his just, philosophical and forcible reasonings. His aim evidently was, not so much to produce a classical history, as to establish facts, and make proper deductions from them, which might furnish the future historian of our country with the means of forming a right estimate of the trials to which his brethren were subjected, as well as the views and conduct in which those trials originated. He is a true Congregationalist in doctrine and discipline, except in respect to Baptism and Communion; renders a cordial testimony in favour of John Robinson; and vindicates the Plymouth Colony from all blame in the persecutions experienced by his denomination. He preserves his temper and candour, and vindicates the rights of conscience with great skill and power. He gives several instances of *veto* power claimed by their Pastors, in which such claims were promptly met and put down by the Churches and Courts of law.

Mr. Backus was of a large, robust and muscular frame, made firm, probably, by his early agricultural labours, and by his travels on horseback, the greater part of his life. His large face and head appeared more venerable by reason of his very large wig, an adornment of ministers in the times in which he lived.

I have known him as a Preacher of the Gospel. His sermons were marked by strong good sense, and often striking thought, and were generally of a highly biblical character. Few men make so strong an impression upon their audience by personal appearance as he did. His venerable countenance, his large features, his imposing wig, in which he always appeared in the pulpit, his impressive gravity and deep toned voice, added to the weight of his sentiments, gave him great power over an audience.

It need not be disguised that Mr. Backus partook of the spirit of the Mathers and others, in taking a peculiar interest in what were called "Wonder-working Providences," and in admiration of striking coincidences and extraordinary appearances, bordering hard on the miraculous. Indeed, he himself related an assault of the adversary, in his experience, strongly resembling that which Luther relates as made upon himself, which he returned with his inkstand and all its contents. He was exhorting to constancy in prayer, and regular seasons of private devotion, notwithstanding all the wiles and opposition of Satan, and in that connection related the following case of his own experience:—He retired to his closet at the usual season, and, as he made the attempt to pray, Satan presented himself in bodily form, and frowned upon him in grim opposition. He turned to another side of his closet, and the same forbidding form still frowned upon him. He turned to the third, and then to the fourth, side, and still he had to encounter the same horrible appearance; "and then," he added, "I said to myself, I will pray, if I have to pray *through you*; and I did pray *through* the devil."

I attended a Baptist ordination when I was young, and, during the delivery of the sermon, he sat in the pulpit,—an object not merely of awe, but I may say of absolute terror. In the midst of the service, he groaned in such fearful tones as started me from my seat; and this groan, which was heard distinctly through every part of the house, was repeated three times in the course of the sermon. This, however, was more than sixty years ago, when such things were regarded in a very different light from what they would be now.

Mr. Backus was full of "good works and alms deeds which he did," and "his works do follow" him. I know not that any of the churches which he founded have become extinct. Certainly his own still lives. Notwithstanding his very stinted income, that prudence, industry, and economy, by which he was so much distinguished, and that have since characterized his children and grandchildren, enabled him to leave the family estate unincumbered.

With great respect,
Z. EDDY.

DANIEL MARSHALL*.

1754—1784.

DANIEL MARSHALL was born of respectable and pious parents, in Windsor, Conn., in the year 1706. He was hopefully converted at the age of about twenty, and joined the Congregational church in his native place. Being naturally of an ardent temperament, he became a very zealous Christian, and, before he had been long a member of the church, he was chosen one of its Deacons. This office he held, discharging its duties with great fidelity, for about twenty years. During this time, he was in easy circumstances, and married and lost a wife, by whom he had one son. At the age of thirty-eight, he heard Whitefield preach, caught his glowing spirit, and fully believed, with many others, that the scenes which were then passing betokened the near approach of millenial glory. Not a small number, under the powerful influence of the moment, sold, or gave away, or abandoned, their earthly possessions, and, without purse or scrip, rushed up to the head of the Susquehanna, and settled in a place called Onnaquaggy, among the Mohawk Indians, with a view to their conversion to Christianity. Of this self-denying group was Mr. Marshall. It is not easy to conceive of greater sacrifices than he must have made, in taking his wife and three children from the bosom of civilized society, where they were surrounded with all the comforts of life, to live in a wilderness, in the midst of savages, and exposed to hardships and perils innumerable.

Mr. Marshall addressed himself to his missionary labours, with burning zeal, and not without considerable success. Several of the Indians gave evidence of receiving the Gospel in its power, while others were brought into a thoughtful and inquiring state of mind, which promised a favourable result. But, after residing there about eighteen months, and just as he began to witness the fruits of his labours, the breaking out of war among the savage tribes obliged him to withdraw, and seek another field. He now removed to a place in Pennsylvania, called Conegocheague; and, after a short residence there, took up his abode near Winchester, Va. Here he fell in with a Baptist church, belonging to the Philadelphia Association; and, being led to a particular examination of their faith and order, he became convinced that they were both scriptural, and, accordingly, both himself and his wife were shortly after baptized by immersion, and became members of this church. This occurred about the year 1754.

Mr. Marshall, who had hitherto laboured only as a private teacher and exhorter, was now licensed to preach; and his efforts, in this capacity, were, from the beginning, instrumental of bringing many to serious reflection. In his zeal to prosecute his ministry to the greatest advantage, he passed on from Virginia to a place called Hughwarry, in North Carolina, where large numbers were hopefully converted through his instrumentality. Encouraged by the success which attended his labours, as an itinerant preacher, he proceeded to Abbot's Creek, in the same State, where he

* Memoir by his son, Rev. Abraham Marshall.—Taylor's Lives of Virg. Bapt. Min.—Campbell's Georg. Bapt.

gathered a church, of which he was ordained Pastor, in the fifty-second year of his age, by his brothers-in-law, the Rev. Messrs. Henry Leadbetter and Shubael Stearns.* He seems, however, still to have performed much missionary labour, for it is stated that, "in one of his evangelical journeys into Virginia, he had the singular happiness to baptize Colonel Samuel Harriss, with whom he immediately afterwards made several tours, and preached and planted the Gospel in several places as far as James River." He resigned his charge at Abbot's Creek, after a few years, and, in the hope of increasing his usefulness, went still farther South, and settled on Beaver Creek, in South Carolina. Thence, after having accomplished an important work in gathering a large church, he removed to Horse Creek, about fifteen miles North of Augusta. Here also he laboured, for some time, with great success, and gave an impulse to several minds, which afterwards made themselves powerfully felt in the extension of the Gospel. From this place he occasionally made visits to the State of Georgia; and, on one of these occasions, while engaged in the devotional service at a public meeting, he was seized by a civil officer for preaching in the parish of St. Paul, and forced to give security for his appearance in Augusta, on the Monday following, to answer to the charge. The result of the trial was that he was ordered to come no more *as a preacher* into Georgia; but he simply replied, in the spirit of the Apostle,—"Whether it be right to obey God or man, judge ye." He pursued his course, regardless of this judicial decision, and, on the 1st of January, 1771, removed with his family to Kiokee, Ga., where he spent the remainder of his life. The next spring a church was formed there, which has been distinguished for its efficiency in various respects, and especially for having sent forth several excellent ministers.

The church, which was thus planted and cherished through Mr. Marshall's instrumentality, enjoyed an increasing degree of prosperity, until the commencement of the War of the Revolution, which, everywhere, proved most adverse to the success of evangelical labours. But this excellent man still kept at his work, as far as possible; and, in the midst of the most gloomy and appalling scenes, he was always on the alert to perform, up to the full measure of his ability, the duties of a Christian minister. As he was an open and earnest friend to the American cause, he was once made a prisoner and placed under a strong guard; but, by permission of the

---

* SHUBAEL STEARNS was born in Boston, in the year 1706. He was a subject of the great revival in which Whitefield was so prominent, about the year 1740, and became connected with the body called Separates, in 1745. In 1751, he embraced the views of the Baptists; was immersed by Elder Wait Palmer, at Tolland, Conn.; and, on the 20th of May, of the same year, was ordained to the work of the ministry. After labouring for two or three years in New England, he went to the South, and preached for some time, first, in the Counties of Berkeley and Hampshire, Va., and then proceeded to Guilford County, N. C., where he made his permanent settlement. He commenced his labours here by building a house of worship, and constituting a church of sixteen members; and here he continued, preaching much in the surrounding country, till the close of his life. He died on the 20th of November, 1771. Morgan Edwards writes thus concerning him:—"Mr. Stearns was a man of small stature, but of good natural parts, and sound judgment. Of learning he had but a little share, yet was pretty well acquainted with books. His voice was musical and strong, which he managed in such a manner as, one while, to make soft impressions on the heart, and fetch tears from the eyes in a mechanical way, and anon to shake the very nerves, and throw the animal system into tumults and perturbations. All the Separate Baptists copied after him in tones of voice and actions of body; and some few exceeded him. His character was indisputably good as a man, a Christian, and a preacher. In his eyes was something very penetrating—there seemed to be a meaning in every glance."

officers, he commenced praying and exhorting with so much earnestness that his enemies were soon more than willing to set him at liberty.

Mr. Marshall's zeal in his Master's cause kept him labouring after he was bowed by the infirmities of age, and almost up to the very day of his death. A few months before he died, rising in his pulpit, where he had so long instructed and exhorted his people with tearful solicitude, he said,— "I address you, my dear hearers, with a diffidence which arises from a failure of memory, and a general weakness of body and mind, common to my years; but I recollect he that holds out to the end shall be saved, and am resolved to finish my course in the cause of God." Accordingly, he attended public worship regularly, through a somewhat lingering decline, until the last Sabbath but one previous to his death; he attended family worship until the morning immediately preceding; and, in the near approach of death, he expressed the utmost confidence that he was about to come in possession of an eternal weight of glory. He died on the 2d of November, 1784, in the seventy-eighth year of his age. A Discourse was delivered on the occasion of his death by the Rev. Charles Bussey.

The maiden name of Mr. Marshall's first wife I have not been able to ascertain. His second wife, to whom he was married in 1748, was Martha Stearns, sister of the Rev. Shubael Stearns. The Georgia Analytical Repository, in referring to this lady, says,—"In fact it should not be concealed that his extraordinary success in the ministry is ascribable, in no small degree, to Mrs. Marshall's unwearied and zealous co-operation. Without the shadow of a usurped authority over the other sex, Mrs. Marshall, being a lady of good sense, singular piety, and surprising elocution, has, in countless instances, melted a whole concourse into tears, by her prayers and exhortations." By his second marriage, Mr. Marshall had nine children,—seven sons and two daughters. One of his sons, *Abraham*, was, for many years, a highly respected and useful Baptist minister.

The prominent feature of Mr. Marshall's character, as developed in the history of his life, seems to have been a burning zeal for the salvation of his fellow-men. Without any extraordinary talents, or much intellectual culture, he made himself felt as an element of life and power in every community in which he mingled. It was manifest to all that love to Christ, and love to the souls of men, constituted his ruling passion; and though he might do some things of questionable prudence and propriety, his influence, on the whole, was felt to be at once salutary and powerful. Notwithstanding all the sacrifices that he made for the cause of Christ, he always had enough for the comfortable support of himself and his family, and, at his death, left behind him an estate of considerable value.

JOHN GANO.*

1754—1804.

JOHN GANO was born at Hopewell, N. J., on the 22d of July, 1727. He was of Huguenot extraction. His great grandfather, Francis Gerneaux, escaped from the Island of Guernsey, during the bloody persecution that arose in consequence of the Revocation of the Edict of Nantz. One of his neighbours having been martyred, a faithful servant of his deceased friend informed him that he himself had been doomed to the same fate, and that he was to suffer that very night, at twelve o'clock. Being a gentleman of wealth, and having trustworthy and influential friends around him, he at once secured a vessel, and, having caused his family to be placed on board, he was himself conveyed in a hogshead, to the same retreat, and, before morning, the vessel was not to be seen from the harbour. Mindful of the condition of other persons, at other Protestant settlements, he so managed as to send his boat ashore at several of those places, and by this means his company of emigrants was much enlarged. They sailed for America, and arrived safely at New York; and, after obtaining lands at New Rochelle, they settled there, making that place their adopted home. Mr. Gerneaux died at the extraordinary age of one hundred and three years. Immediately after his abandonment of Guernsey, his property was confiscated; and, when the fact was communicated to him, his reply was,—" I have been expelled from my birth place, and my property has been taken from my family for only one aggression,—*a love for the Bible and its teachings*. Let my name change with changing circumstances :"—and it has ever since been known, as pronounced by the English, GANO.

One of the sons of this religious refugee, named *Stephen*, was married to Ann Walton, by whom he had a large family of children. *His* son, *Daniel*, was married to Sarah Britton, of Staten Island; and these were the parents of the subject of this sketch. They were both eminently pious, and, from his earliest years, he was faithfully instructed in the great principles of religion. His maternal grandmother, who lived to the age of ninety-six, was, during almost her whole life, a devout member of a Baptist church. His mother also was of the same communion; but his father was a Presbyterian. His own predilections were originally for joining a Presbyterian Church; but, not being fully satisfied on the subject of Infant Baptism, he determined to give it a thorough examination, and it turned out that the farther his inquiries extended, the more his doubts increased. There is a tradition that he held a long conversation with one of the Tennents on the subject, at the close of which the venerable Presbyterian minister said to him,—" Dear young man, if the devil cannot destroy your soul, he will endeavour to destroy your comfort and usefulness; and, therefore, do not be always doubting in this matter. If you cannot think as I do, think for yourself." Having become ultimately satisfied

---

* Benedict's Hist. Bapt. I, II.—Collins' Hist. of Kentucky.—MS. from Henry Jackson, D. D.

that the peculiar views of the Baptists are fully sustained by Scripture, and having obtained his father's cordial consent to his joining that denomination, he was, in due time, baptized by immersion, and admitted to the Church in Hopewell, his native place.

Up to this time, he seems to have been occupied upon a farm; but he now began to entertain the idea of becoming a minister of the Gospel. It was not long before his purpose to do so was fixed; and he had begun a course of study preparatory to it. With occasional interruptions, he continued thus engaged for two or three years. Before he was licensed to preach, he took a journey into Virginia, in company with two prominent Baptist clergymen, who went thither, by request, to settle some difficulties which had arisen, in two infant churches. Previous to his return home, a report reached Hopewell that he had, prematurely, and without the usual formality of being approved by the church, commenced preaching in Virginia. He was, accordingly, called to an account for what was deemed a disorderly procedure. He acknowledged that he had " sounded the Gospel to perishing souls in Virginia, whose importunities to hear it he could not resist," but he justified the seeming irregularity, in view of the peculiar circumstances of the case, which he did not think were likely to occur again. The church, after hearing his explanation, appointed a time for him to preach, and to be examined in respect to his qualifications; and, the result having been entirely satisfactory to them, he was regularly set apart to the ministry. Soon after this, he became connected with the church at Morristown, and so numerous were the demands made upon him for public labour, that his studies were not only greatly interrupted, but, for the time, in a great measure, relinquished.

At the next meeting of the Philadelphia Association, there were present messengers from the South, who had come to procure, if possible, a minister of the Gospel to labour among them. As there was no ordained minister, who could conveniently undertake the mission, Mr. Gano was urged to engage in it. He pleaded his youth and inexperience; but the importunity of the messengers, joined to that of his own brethren, finally prevailed over his scruples; and, having been ordained in May, 1754, he set out, shortly after, on his journey Southward. He travelled and preached extensively in the Southern Colonies, and went as far as Charleston, S. C. His account of the first sermon he preached in the pulpit of the Rev. Mr. Hart, of Charleston, is as follows:—

" When I arose to speak, the sight of so brilliant an audience, among whom were twelve ministers, and one of whom was Mr. Whitefield, for a moment brought the fear of man upon me ; but, blessed be the Lord, I was soon relieved from this embarrassment; the thought passed my mind, I had none to fear and obey but the Lord."

On his return to the North, he visited an island, where he was informed there had never been but two sermons preached. The people soon assembled, and he preached to them from these words—" Behold the third time I am ready to come to you, and I will not be burdensome to you." Various incidents occurred, on this missionary tour, illustrative of Mr. Gano's shrewdness, firmness, and devotion to the honour of his Master.

In 1756, Mr. Gano was induced, by repeated solicitations, to make another missionary tour to the South, which occupied him about eight months. In many places, he had the pleasure to find the fruits of his labours during his former visits.   Shortly after his return from this tour, he was invited, by an infant church, which he had been instrumental of planting, in a place called the Jersey Settlement, in North Carolina, to remove thither, and become its Pastor.   Messengers came to Morristown, a distance of several hundred miles, to induce that church, if possible, to give him up.   They, at first, utterly refused, but, subsequently, referred the matter to his own choice; and he, in consideration of the great spiritual destitution that prevailed in the region to which he was called, felt constrained to give an affirmative answer.   He, accordingly, removed to North Carolina, and took charge of the church that had called him.

His connection with this church continued about two years; during which time the number of communicants greatly increased, and he laboured extensively and successfully throughout that whole region.   But, in consequence of the incursions of the Cherokee Indians, in the year 1760, his labours were interrupted, and he found it necessary to leave the country. He, accordingly, returned with his family to New Jersey.   About this time, the First Baptist Church in the city of New York was organized by the Rev. Benjamin Miller,* of Scotch Plains, and the Church in Philadelphia had also just been rendered vacant by the death of the Rev. Jenkin Jones. Mr. Gano preached, for some time, alternately, at both cities; but when the Church in New York was organized, (June 19, 1762,) he became its Pastor, and continued there nearly twenty-six years, excepting the time he was obliged to be absent on account of the war.   During his ministry, the church was eminently prospered, and received, by Baptism, about three hundred members.

Mr. Gano was, for some time, a Chaplain in the War of the Revolution; and, by his earnest prayers and patriotic counsels, did much to encourage his countrymen in their struggle for national freedom.   On the return of Peace, he went back to his accustomed field of labour; but, out of upwards of two hundred members, of which his church consisted at the time of its dispersion, he was able to collect at first but thirty-seven: his congregation, however, rapidly increased, and a revival soon followed, in consequence of which, nearly forty young persons were added to the church, at one time.   In this state of things, when every thing seemed auspicious of continued and increasing usefulness, Mr. Gano formed the purpose of removing to Kentucky, partly on account of being somewhat embarrassed in his worldly circumstances, and partly from a conviction that his usefulness would thereby be increased.   His congregation offered to increase his salary, and presented every inducement they could to detain him; but his purpose had already been formed, and he could not consent to yield it. Accordingly, having disposed of his property, he left New York, and, on the 17th of June, 1787, reached Limestone, Ky., and, shortly after, repaired to Washington, where he remained for some time.   In 1788, he

---

* BENJAMIN MILLER, a native of Scotch Plains, was a wild and reckless youth, but was converted in consequence of a sermon preached by Gilbert Tennent, who encouraged him to enter the ministry.   He was ordained in 1748, and continued Pastor of the church in his native place until 1781, when he died in his sixty-sixth year.   His Funeral Sermon was preached by his friend, Mr. Gano, who said concerning him,—"Never did I esteem a ministering brother so much as I did Mr. Miller, nor feel so sensibly a like bereavement, as that which I sustained by his death."

became Pastor of the Town Fork Church, in the neighbourhood of Lexington, which was connected with the Elkhorn Association.

Mr. Gano, probably, never found the advantage he anticipated, in respect to either comfort or usefulness, from his removal to Kentucky. Still, however, he laboured there with quite encouraging success. In 1798, while he was still actively engaged in the duties of the ministry, he fell from a horse, and fractured his shoulder-blade, in consequence of which he was, for some time, deprived of the use of one of his arms. Before he had recovered from the effects of this casualty, he was suddenly seized in his bed with a paralytic shock, which rendered him almost speechless for nearly a year. He, however, subsequently recovered his speech, and the use of his limbs, so far as to be able to be carried out to meetings, and he preached frequently, especially during the great revival in the West, with remarkable power. He died in 1804, in the seventy-eighth year of his age.

At the close of 1754, or early in 1755,—shortly after his return from his second visit to the South, Mr. Gano was married to Sarah, daughter of John Stites, a highly respectable citizen of Elizabethtown, N. J. She was the sister of the wife of Dr. Manning, the first President of Rhode Island College. They had a number of children, one of whom,—*Stephen*, the second son, became Pastor of a Baptist church in Providence. Not long after his removal to Kentucky, his wife was rendered a cripple by a fall from a horse, and, shortly afterwards, was removed by death. In 1793, he made a visit to North Carolina, where he married, for his second wife, the widow of Capt. Thomas Bryant, and daughter of Colonel Jonathan Hunt, formerly of New Jersey, and one of his old neighbours and friends. She had been baptized by his son, Stephen, three years before, when the father and son visited North Carolina together. The second Mrs. Gano survived her husband.

FROM THE HON. CHARLES S. TODD,
AMBASSADOR FROM THE UNITED STATES TO RUSSIA, &c.

SHELBYVILLE, Ky., June 9, 1857.

Rev. and dear Sir: In reply to your request for some account of the character of the Rev. John Gano, I am obliged to say that my impressions concerning him are very general, and are derived, not from personal intercourse with him, but from having often seen him in my boyhood, and lived in a community in which, for many years, he exercised his ministry. Well do I remember the venerable and imposing appearance which he used to make, as he walked the streets, and how every body respected him, both as a Christian gentleman, and a Minister of the Gospel. But I feel so inadequate to do any thing like justice to his memory that, instead of attempting to embody any recollections and impressions of my own, I take the liberty to transcribe the following account of him, from the pen of the Rev. Dr. Furman, of Charleston, S. C., who had every opportunity of forming a correct judgment of his character and standing:—

"He was, in person, below the middle stature, and, when young, of a slender form; but of a firm, vigorous constitution, well fitted for performing active services with ease, and for suffering labours and privations with constancy. In the more advanced stages of life, his body tended to corpulency; but not to such a degree as to burden or render him inactive. His presence was manly, open and engaging. His voice strong and commanding, yet agreeable and capable of all those inflections which are suited to express either the strong or tender emotions of an intelligent, feeling mind. In mental endowments and acquired abilities he appeared highly respectable; with clear conception and penetrating discernment, he formed, readily, a correct judgment of men and things. His acquaintance with the learned languages and science did not commence till he arrived at manhood, and was obtained chiefly by private instruction; but under the direction of a clerical gentleman, well qualified for the office. To the refinements of learning he did not aspire—his chief object was such a competent acquaintance with its principles as would enable him to apply them with advantage to purposes of general usefulness in religion, and to the most important interests of society; and to this he attained.

" His mind was formed for social intercourse and for friendship. Such was his unaffected humility, candour, and good-will to men, that few, if any, have enjoyed more satisfaction in the company of their friends, or have, in return, afforded them, by their conversation, a higher degree of pleasure and moral improvement.

" His passions were strong, and his sensibility could be easily excited; but so chastened and regulated were they by the meekness of wisdom, that he preserved great composure of spirit, and command of his words and actions, even in times of trial and provocation, when many, who yet might justly rank with the wise and good, would be thrown into a state of perturbation, and hurried into extravagance.

"As a minister of Christ, he shone like a star of the first magnitude in the American Churches, and moved in a widely extended field of action. For this office God had endowed him with a large portion of grace, and with excellent gifts. He *believed*, and therefore *spake*. Having discerned the excellence of Gospel truths, and the importance of eternal realities, he felt their power on his own soul, and, accordingly, he inculcated and urged them on the minds of his hearers, with persuasive eloquence and force. He was not deficient in doctrinal discussion, or what rhetoricians style the demonstrative character of a discourse; but he excelled in the pathetic,—in pungent, forcible addresses to the heart and conscience. The careless and irreverent were suddenly arrested, and stood awed before him; and the insensible were made to feel, while he asserted and maintained the honour of his God, explained the meaning of the Divine law,—showing its purity and justice,—exposed the sinner's guilt,—proved him to be miserable, ruined and inexcusable, and called him to unfeigned, immediate repentance. But he was not less a son of consolation to the mourning sinner, who lamented his offences committed against God,—who felt the plague of a corrupt heart, and longed for salvation; nor did he fail to speak a word of direction, support, and comfort, in due season, to the tried, tempted believer. He knew how to publish the glad tidings of salvation in the Redeemer's name, for the consolation of all who believed in Him, or had discovered their need of his mediation and grace; and to him this was a delightful employment. Success attended his ministrations, and many owned him for their father in the Gospel.

" The doctrines he embraced were those which are contained in the Baptist Confession of Faith, and are commonly styled Calvinistic. But he was of a liberal mind, and esteemed pious men of every denomination. While he maintained, with consistent firmness, the doctrines which he believed to be the truths of God, he was modest in the judgment which he formed of his own opinion, and careful to avoid giving offence, or grieving any good man who differed from him in sentiment. Hence he was cordially esteemed and honoured by the wise and good of all denominations.

"His attachment to his country, as a citizen, was unshaken, in the times which tried men's souls; and, as a Chaplain in the army for a term of years, while excluded from his church and home, he rendered it essential service. Preserving his moral dignity with the purity which becomes a Gospel minister, he commanded respect from the officers; and, by his condescension and kindness, won the affections of the soldiers, inspiring them, by his example, with his own courage and firmness, while toiling with them through military scenes of hardship and danger.

"He lived to a good old age; served his generation according to the will of God; saw his posterity multiplying around him; his country independent, free and happy; the Church of Christ, for which he felt and laboured, advancing. And thus he closed his eyes in peace; his heart expanding with the sublime hope of immortality and heavenly bliss."

That the above is a faithful estimate of the character of this venerable man, I cannot doubt. I am glad to have been even indirectly instrumental in assisting to embalm his memory.

I am, very truly and devotedly,

C. S. TODD.

————◆◆————

NOAH ALDEN.
1755—1797.

FROM THE REV. ABIAL FISHER, D. D.

WEST BOYLSTON, Mass., 18 March, 1859.

My dear Sir: The Rev. Noah Alden, Pastor of the Church in Bellingham, died fifteen years before I began my ministry in that place ; but a son of his was, at that time, a Deacon of the church, and a daughter,—a very intelligent lady, was a member; and there were living there many other persons who knew Mr. Alden well, and who verified all the statements I am about to make to you.

NOAH ALDEN was a descendant, in the third generation, from the venerable John Alden, one of the first settlers of Plymouth. His mother was a lineal descendant from another of the first settlers, by the name of White. He was himself born at Middleborough, Mass., where his father was then settled, on the 30th of May, 1725, and was the youngest of thirteen children. His parents both died while he was yet in his boyhood. His father, possessing means, designed that this son should have a collegiate education, and left property for the purpose : but it was very improperly diverted from its design, in consequence of which Noah was subjected, during his early years, to many deprivations and hardships. When he was about sixteen, he experienced a radical change of character, that gave a new complexion to his life. He early had a desire to engage in the ministry, but his poverty and some other circumstances seemed to forbid his entertaining the idea. Before he was twenty, he was married and removed to Stafford, Conn., where he purchased a farm, and engaged in cultivating it. Both himself and his wife became members of the Congregational Church, and continued in that connection until the year 1753, when, from an examination of the subject of Baptism, to which he was brought by his reflections on having one of his own children baptized, he was led to embrace the views of the Baptists, and united with that denomination. The question whether it was not his duty to preach the Gospel now presented itself to him with still greater urgency than before; and, though the difficulties had by no means diminished, he felt constrained to come to an affirmative decision. Accordingly, on the 5th of June, 1755, he was ordained at Stafford, and became the Pastor of the church in that place. But the support afforded him was so scanty, and his prospect of usefulness so small, that, after labouring with that people about ten years, he thought it his duty to leave them, and seek another settlement. Accordingly, on the 12th of November, 1766, he was installed Pastor of the church in Bellingham, as successor to the Rev. Elnathan Wight.* His ministry here, at its commencement, met with considerable opposition; but his friends were united in his support, and the Lord was with him. He discharged his duties with so much wisdom and kindness that the opposition gradually died away, and he gained not only the respect but affection of all. The church increased under his ministry, and beside occasional additions, there was a revival in 1781 and '82, by which his heart was greatly encouraged.

When the Constitution of the Commonwealth of Massachusetts was formed, Mr. Alden was the delegate from Bellingham to the Convention called for that purpose; and he occupied a conspicuous place in it. He was one of the most able and active friends of religious liberty found in that Body. Although he did not gain all that he desired, he nevertheless gained much; and the friends of the cause for which he exerted himself so vigorously and efficiently, will always owe him a large debt of gratitude. He was also a member of the Convention to which was submitted the Constitution of the United States; and here, as on all public occasions, acquitted himself with great credit.

Mr. Alden was abundant in labours, not only among his own people, but in vacant congregations, and wherever his services were desired. He visited various Associations, attended many Councils, not only for the ordination of ministers, but for the adjustment of difficulties, and always showed himself wise, conscientious and efficient. He was one of four ministers who originally formed the Warren Association, in 1767.

For several months before his death, he had become enfeebled by a partial shock of the palsy. He endured his sufferings with great composure

* ELNATHAN WIGHT was born about the year 1715, at Medfield, Mass.; but, while he was very young, his father removed to Bellingham, where he spent the rest of his life. About the year 1737, the First Baptist Church in Bellingham was formed, and he was one of the constituent members. At the age of about thirty, he came to the conclusion that it was his duty to preach the Gospel; and he, accordingly, spent about four years in preparing for it, chiefly under the instruction of the Rev. John Graham, of Southbury, Conn. Though he was a Baptist, he was, through the influence of Mr. Graham, licensed to preach, early in 1750, by a Congregational Association. In May of that year, he received a call to the Pastorship of the Church in Bellingham; and, having accepted it, he sought ordination from Congregational ministers, but they refused to comply with his request. He was ordained by a Council of Baptist ministers on the 14th of January, 1755, and preached his own Ordination Sermon, which was printed. From this time he continued to discharge his duties to great acceptance till the close of his life. He was suddenly cut off, by dysentery, on the 6th of November, 1761, in the forty-sixth year of his age. He was, especially in the early part of his ministry, an Open Communion Baptist. He was naturally irascible, but had great self-control. He was a diligent student, and generally wrote his sermons, and delivered them with his manuscript before him. He was a man of eminently devout feelings, and his preaching was of a strongly evangelical type.

and patience, and exercised habitually a joyful confidence in the power and grace of his Redeemer. He hailed the approach of death with a serene triumph, choosing rather to depart and be with Christ. He died on the 5th of May, 1797, aged nearly seventy-two; and a large concourse of people attended his funeral in testimony of their affectionate respect for his memory.

Mr. Alden was rather below the middle stature, and in early life spare, but in his latter years he became corpulent; and with this change of physical habit there came a painful difficulty of breathing. His countenance was expressive of great mildness, benevolence, and dignity, and his manners were in a high degree winning and agreeable. Children were his delight, and they were never happier than when they were the objects of his attentions, and caresses. In his own domestic relations he was a model. In all his intercourse with society he studied the things that make for peace, and was always on the alert to arrest or prevent discord. He was for many years one of our most distinguished and honoured ministers, and his name deserves to be held in grateful remembrance.

Very truly yours,

ABIAL FISHER.

JOHN DAVIS.

1756—1809.

FROM THE REV. GEORGE F. ADAMS.

BALTIMORE, Md., March 24, 1859.

My dear Sir: After the most diligent inquiry concerning the venerable man of whom you ask me to give you some account, I am constrained to say that I find the materials too few to enable me to comply with your request in a satisfactory manner. In the following brief sketch you have the substance of all that I have been able to gather concerning him.

JOHN DAVIS was born in Pennepek, Pa., on the 10th of September, 1721. He was called to the ministry, and ordained at Montgomery in the same State, in 1756; and the same year he went to Maryland, and became the Pastor of Winter Run Church, in Harford County. He resided a considerable distance from this church, and, from the abundance of demand, and smallness of supply, of ministerial labour, the Pastor could only minister to the people at distant periods—probably seldom or never oftener than once a month. Nearer home, however, he preached more frequently. The consequence was that converts became more numerous near his residence than at his more distant appointment. Harford finally became the seat of the church; and in 1774 a reorganization took place under that name. Though a Baptist Church had been constituted at Chestnut Ridge, under the ministry of the Rev. Henry Loveall,* as early as 1742, yet,

* HENRY LOVEALL was a native of Cambridge, England; migrated to America in early life; was baptized in New England in 1725,—probably at Newport, R. I.,—for it appears by John Comer's Journal that he was in that town in 1729, and had then begun to preach. He travel-

under the ministry of Mr. Davis, Harford was emphatically the mother Church of the Baptists in Maryland. His labours in the ministry extended not only through many parts of his own county, but to Baltimore City, and into Baltimore and Frederick Counties. He continued in the uninterrupted Pastorship of Harford Church till his death, which occurred in 1809, after a ministry of fifty-three years, and in the eighty-eighth year of his age.

Mr. Davis is represented by those who knew him as a man of most untiring energy, as well as of great piety, enlightened evangelical views, fervent zeal, and consistent character. He travelled much, preaching Christ wherever he went. The woods, the school-room, the barn, the cabin, the parlour, equally with the meeting-house, were all to him places of worship and of labour for Christ's sake. Nor did he fail, as he had opportunity, to preach Christ, like Philip, to the solitary traveller, whom he might meet or overtake on the way. Thus labouring with primitive zeal, he was sometimes called to endure almost primitive persecution. The law indeed guaranteed protection to all denominations; yet there were not wanting " certain lewd fellows of the baser sort " to resort to measures corresponding with their character for the purpose of intimidating him, and, if possible, arresting the progress of the truth which he proclaimed. It is said that even the magistrates lent their influence, on some occasions, to further the objects of those who sought to drive him from his fields of labour.

Several churches, still in a flourishing condition, besides some congregations that have, with the preacher, passed away, owe their origin, under the Divine blessing, to this indefatigable servant of the Lord. Among these we may reckon the First Baptist Church in Baltimore, the " Gunpowder " and " Patapsco " Churches, and probably those at Taney Town and Frederick City. During the ministry of Mr. Davis, Harford Church appears to have been the largest and most flourishing Baptist church in the State. For a few years,—from 1799 to 1803,—he had associated with him in the Pastorship, the Rev. Absalom Butler; and, under their joint labours, there was a continuous revival. The number of members was considerably more than doubled, notwithstanding the drafts that were made upon them for materials to constitute other churches around. Thus was verified the proverb,—" There is that scattereth, and yet increaseth."

Though Mr. Davis has been among the dead for about half a century, it is gratifying to know that he still lives in the memory and affections of many, who, during the latter portion of his life, enjoyed his acquaintance. None speak of him but in terms of respect, reverence, and affection.

Very truly yours,

G. F. ADAMS.

led into the Jerseys, carrying with him the recommendation of several ministers; but he was soon charged with shameful immorality, and it was discovered that his real name was Desolate Baker. He was ordained at Piscataqua, N. J., in 1730; but the discovery of his true character prevented him from officiating there. After occasioning much trouble at Piscataqua, he went to Maryland in 1742, and became, as already stated, the minister of the Chestnut Ridge Church. In 1746, he went to Virginia, and formed the Mill Creek Church, from which he was shortly after excommunicated for his conduct. He then returned to Chestnut Ridge, where he was living in 1772, in the seventy-eighth year of his age.

SAMUEL STILLMAN, D. D.*
1758—1807.

SAMUEL STILLMAN was born in the city of Philadelphia, February 27, (O. S.) 1737. His parents, who were worthy, respectable people, removed to Charleston, S. C., when he was eleven years old; and there, under the direction of a Mr. Rind, a teacher of some celebrity, he received the rudiments of his education. At an early period, both his intellectual and moral developments were such as to give promise of the highest respectability and usefulness.

He seems to have been, occasionally, the subject of religious impressions, in his early childhood; but, for the most part, they proved inoperative and evanescent. After a few years, however, he became deeply impressed with Divine truth, under the preaching of the Rev. Mr. Hart, an excellent Baptist clergyman, on whose ministry he was accustomed to attend; and, at no distant period, he found relief from his convictions and struggles by practically availing himself, as he believed, of the gracious provisions of the Gospel. Shortly after this, he was baptized, and became a member of the church of which Mr. Hart was Pastor.

Having completed his classical education, he gave a year to the study of Theology, under the direction of Mr. Hart; and was then formally recognised, by the church of which he was a member, as a Christian minister. He preached his first sermon on the 17th of February, 1758; was recommended as " an orderly and worthy minister of the Gospel," by the Charleston Association, on the 13th of November following; and, on the 26th of February, 1759, was ordained, in the city of Charleston, to the work of an Evangelist.

His first settlement in the ministry, which occurred shortly after his ordination, was at James Island,—a beautiful place in the immediate neighbourhood of Charleston. On a visit which he made, about this time, to his native city, he formed a matrimonial connection with a Miss Morgan, daughter of a highly respectable merchant, and sister of Dr. John Morgan who was afterwards distinguished as a Surgeon in the Revolution, and as one of the first Professors in the Medical Institution at Philadelphia. She was the mother of fourteen children, only two of whom survived their father.

During this visit which he made at Philadelphia, he was honoured with the degree of Master of Arts from the College in that city; and, in 1761, the same degree was conferred upon him by Harvard University.

From Philadelphia he returned to his charge on James Island; but, after having remained with them only about eighteen months, he became the subject of a violent pulmonary attack, which rendered it necessary for him to seek another climate. Accordingly, he travelled with his family to the North, and fixed himself at Bordentown, N. J., where he continued for two years, supplying two different congregations.

* Memoir prefixed to his Sermons.—Benedict's Hist. Bapt. I & II.—Winchell's Hist. Disc.— MS. from the Rev. Dr. John Pierce.

At the close of this period, he was induced to travel still farther North, and visit New England. His services in the pulpit were everywhere eminently acceptable and useful; and, by request of the Second Baptist Church in Boston, he removed his family thither, and for one year officiated as an Assistant to the Rev. Mr. Bound.* The First Church, being, at that time, vacant, signified their desire to put his services in permanent requisition; and, having accepted a call to settle among them, he was installed in the pastoral office, on the 9th of January, 1765. The liberal spirit for which he was always remarkable, was strikingly exemplified in the fact that the Rev. Dr. Andrew Eliot, minister of a Congregational Church in Boston, took part, by Mr. Stillman's request, in the solemnities of the installation.

As he knew by experience the value of a good education to a Christian minister, he was strongly desirous of increasing the advantages for intellectual culture to candidates for the ministry, especially in his own communion. With a view to this, he lent the most cordial and efficient aid to the interests of Brown University, an institution then in its infancy; and his name appears, in the Act of Incorporation, 1764, in its first list of Trustees. The next year, he was elected one of its Fellows, and held the office till his death. In 1788, the College conferred upon him the degree of Doctor of Divinity. To the prosperity which it enjoyed, in the earlier periods of its history, it may safely be said that Dr. Stillman was one of the principal contributors.

In almost every public effort that was made, whether to bless his neighbourhood, his country, or his race, Dr. Stillman was found more than willing to co-operate; and in turn he received, from the community in which he lived, various and strongly marked testimonies of respect and good-will. The Humane Society of Massachusetts, the Massachusetts Charitable Fire Society, the Boston Dispensary, and the Boston Female Asylum, received, severally, his active and efficient patronage; and of one of them he was honoured with the Presidency at the time of his death. His services were often required on public occasions; and he rarely, if ever, failed to meet the highest expectations. In 1788, he was elected a member for Boston of the Federal Convention,—the only instance in which he ever appeared on the arena of political life; but he quickly showed himself at home in the new field, and distinguished himself alike by his wisdom and his eloquence.

For a considerable time previous to his death, he had earnestly desired the settlement of a colleague, so that, at his decease, his beloved flock should not be left, even temporarily, as sheep without a shepherd. His congregation at length expressed their willingness to co-operate with him for the accomplishment of this favourite object; and the Rev. Joseph Clay, from Georgia, had, with Dr. Stillman's hearty concurrence, received and accepted a call from the church. But, while he was on a visit to the

* JAMES BOUND was a native of England, and, after his arrival in this country, became a member of the First Baptist Church in Boston. Being dissatisfied, however, with the doctrinal views of the Pastor, the Rev. Mr. Condy, he, with six others, seceded, and formed the Second Church, of which Mr. Bound became Pastor. His ministry seems to have been an acceptable and useful one, as the church increased, during his incumbency, from seven to a hundred and twenty members. He died, from the effect of a paralytic shock, in the year 1765.

South, preparing for a removal to his new field of labour, Dr. Stillman was suddenly called to his reward. Notwithstanding his constitution was not at all vigorous, and he had suffered more than a common share of bodily debility through life, yet the interruptions of his labours were by no means frequent, and he outlived all his contemporaries in the ministry, in Boston and its vicinity. He had reached his threescore and ten; and he felt that he was ready to put off his earthly house of this tabernacle. It was only for two Sabbaths previous to his death that he was detained from the sanctuary and the pulpit. On the Wednesday succeeding the last Sabbath, he was suddenly attacked by paralysis, which terminated fatally within about twelve hours. He died on the 12th of March, 1807; and his Funeral was attended on the 17th, when the Rev. Dr. Baldwin, who had long been his neighbour and intimate friend, preached, to an immense and deeply affected assembly, an impressive Discourse on II. Timothy, iv. 7, 8. An appropriate hymn, written by the Rev. Dr. Harris, of Dorchester, with whom Dr. Stillman had been on terms of cordial friendship, was sung on the occasion. The Rev. Dr. John Pierce, of Brookline, who attended the Funeral, writes thus concerning it:—" I have a distinct recollection of the solemnity of the occasion. All the members of the Society appeared with badges of mourning: the women with black bonnets and handkerchiefs. If their Pastor had been removed in the bloom of youth, his people could not have been more deeply affected. The line in the Elegy—

‘ Though the voice tremble while we sing,’—

was not mere poetry—it was a sad reality."

The following is a list of Dr. Stillman's publications:—A Sermon on the Repeal of the Stamp Act, 1766. A Sermon occasioned by the Death of the Author's Mother, Mrs. Mary Stillman, who died in Charleston, S. C., 1768. Four Sermons; the first entitled " Mankind universally apt to trust in their own Righteousness." The second, " The Sinner's best Righteousness proved to be essentially deficient." The third, " Imputed Righteousness one of the Glories of the Gospel." The fourth, " Believers exhorted to continue in their obedience," 1769. A Sermon on the Character of a Good Soldier; delivered before the Ancient and Honourable Artillery Company in Boston, 1770. Young People called upon to consider that for their Conduct here they must be accountable hereafter, at the Judgment Seat of Christ, 1771. Substance of a Sermon delivered at the Ordination of the Rev. Samuel Shepard, in Stratham, N. H., 1771. God's Compassion to the Miserable: a Sermon preached at the desire of Levi Ames, who was executed for Burglary, 1773. The Character of a Foolish Son : a Sermon preached on the Lord's day after the execution of Levi Ames, 1773. A Sermon on the death of the Hon. Samuel Ward, Esq., Member of the Continental Congress from Rhode Island, and delivered before that Body in Philadelphia, 1776. A Sermon delivered on the day of the General Election in Massachusetts, 1779. A Sermon on Charity, preached before the Most Ancient and Honourable Society of Free and Accepted Masons, in Charlestown, 1785. A Speech delivered in the Convention of Massachusetts, on the New Constitution and the Necessity of Amendments thereto, (published in the American Museum, Philadelphia,) 1788. An Oration delivered to the inhabitants of the town of Boston, on the Fourth of July, 1789. Three Sermons on Apostolic Preaching, 1790. A Sermon preached in Providence, R. I., on the death of Nicholas Brown, Esq., 1791. Thoughts on the French Revolution : a Sermon delivered on the day of the Annual Thanksgiving, 1794. A Good Minister of Jesus Christ : a Sermon preached in Boston at the Ordination of the Rev. Mr. Stephen Smith Nelson, 1797. A Sermon delivered at Boston, on the day recommended by the President of the United States for a National Fast, 1799. A Sermon occasioned by the death of George Washington, late Commander-in-Chief of the Armies of the United States of America, 1799. A Sermon on the Opening of the New Baptist Meeting-House in Charlestown, 1801. A Discourse delivered before the Members of the Boston Female Asylum, on the occasion of their First Anniversary, 1801. A Sermon preached at Charlestown, at the Instalment of the Rev. Thomas Waterman * to the Pastoral Care of the Baptist Church and Society in that town, 1802. A Sermon preached in Boston before the Massachusetts Baptist Missionary Society, on the occasion of their First Anniversary, 1803. A Sermon preached in the Tabernacle, Salem, at the Ordination of the Rev. Lucius Bolles to the Pastoral Care of the Baptist Church and Society in that town, 1805. A Sermon preached at the Funeral of the Rev. Hezekiah Smith, D. D., of Haverhill, 1805.

In 1808, an octavo volume of his Sermons was published, consisting of a selection from those printed in his life time, with the addition of eight which had not before appeared.

FROM JAMES LORING, ESQ.

Boston, October 24, 1847.

Rev. and dear Sir : I promised you some account of my venerated and beloved Pastor, the Rev. Dr. Stillman; and I furnish it the more cheerfully, because the remembrance of him is associated with some of the most interesting scenes of my life. Though forty years have now passed since he finished his earthly course, I have a most distinct impression of what he was, and am

---

* THOMAS WATERMAN was born in the city of London, where he received the rudiments of his education. He was subsequently, for some time, at the Dissenting College at Homerton. He was first settled as Pastor of an Independent Congregation in London, but, not long after, became a Baptist, and was baptized by the Rev. Dr. Rippon. He continued his relation to the Independent Church after this change in his views; but,.as he could not conscientiously baptize infants, it was not long before he resigned his charge. He came to the United States about 1802, bringing with him various introductory letters, and, among others, one from Dr. Rippon to Dr. Stillman, which seems to have been of great use to him. At the time of his arrival, the Baptist Church in Charlestown were looking out for a Pastor; and Mr. Waterman, having preached to them with great acceptance, received from them a unanimous call, which, shortly after, he accepted. But, though his prospects of usefulness in that relation were highly flattering, a difficulty soon arose, in connection with his marriage, which proved the occasion of his leaving the church in less than two years after his settlement. He preached but little for several months after this, but was called, in the mean time, to bury his wife. He now, for two or three years, supplied a Society, composed of Baptists and Pedobaptists, in the town of Bow, N. H., and during his residence there formed a second matrimonial connection. For the next two or three years, he preached in Topsham and the vicinity, in Maine. At length, by particular request, he returned to Boston to take charge of the Addison Academy; and, while thus employed, was also engaged, almost constantly, as a supply in different churches in the neighbourhood. The Baptist church at Woburn, being destitute of a Pastor, invited him to remove his school to that place, and supply their pulpit as far as he should be able. He accepted their invitation, and entered with alacrity upon his double duties; but, finding his labours too arduous, he determined to reduce the number of his scholars, and devote more time to the interests of his flock. But just at this time his earthly career was terminated. He died suddenly, of apoplexy, on the 23d of March, 1814. He was an amiable man, an accomplished teacher, and an eloquent preacher.

quite willing to leave on record some of my recollections of him for the benefit of those who may come after me.

As a popular preacher, I greatly doubt whether there was his superior in New England; certainly no other clergyman of his day was so much sought after by distinguished strangers who visited Boston. Among his admirers were the elder President Adams, General Knox, and Governor Hancock, the latter of whom, in the decline of life, was, for a season, a member of his congregation. His doctrine was highly evangelical; and sometimes his rebukes of the general inattention to religion were most pointed and scathing. I remember, on one occasion, a distinguished stranger went to hear him preach, when he so strikingly exhibited the depths of depravity in the human heart, that the gentleman, on retiring, remarked to his friend that the Doctor had really made them all out a set of scoundrels, but had done it so gracefully and eloquently that he did not feel disposed to complain.

It was his custom, in his first prayer, to remember, with special earnestness and tenderness, the sea-faring portion of the community ; and I recollect an instance in which a sailor, happening to be in his church, was so much impressed by this part of the service, that he resolved to hear no other preacher while he remained in the city. A considerable part of the gallery of his meeting-house was occasionally occupied by this class; and they were often so much impressed by the truths which he delivered, as well as by the pathos and power of his manner, that many of them would involuntarily rise up in admiration. His discourses were frequently characterized by sudden bursts of impassioned eloquence, which seemed entirely unpremeditated, and which quite overwhelmed his audience. His manner was always most affectionate, and found its way directly to the hearts of his hearers.

In the intercourse of private life, he was eminently agreeable and useful; and his religious visits among the serious of all denominations were most highly appreciated. He was frequently requested to minister at the sick beds of persons, not of his own congregation, or even his own communion, who were anxious to be counselled in reference to their eternal interests; as there was no clergyman to whom they could so freely impart both their anxieties and their hopes. To the dying sinner, who had no hope, he was accustomed, with great earnestness, to exhibit the freeness and fulness of the Gospel, assuring him that all that he had to do was to believe in the Lord Jesus Christ. To the dying Christian he presented the sweetest consolations of Christianity, and seemed like an angel of mercy sent to open the portals of heavenly bliss.

He was habitually cheerful in his temper, and always ready to testify his kind regard to those with whom he associated. Towards those who regarded themselves as his inferiors he was, in the best sense, condescending, and endeavoured, as far as possible, to relieve them from all feelings of embarrassment. An instance of his condescension occurred in a walk with one of his friends, which has sometimes been erroneously attributed to another individual. A coloured man, whom they met, very politely took off his hat, and bowed to the Doctor, who instantly reciprocated the civility. His friend, unused to such demonstrations, could not help asking why he took off his hat to that black man. " Why," replied Dr. Stillman, " the man made his obeisance to me, and I should be loth to have it said that I had less manners than a negro." There was in his constitution a remarkable blending of moral greatness with all the more gentle and retiring of the Christian virtues.

It was not uncommon for Dr. Stillman, in his preaching, to introduce, by way of illustration, some impressive anecdote; and it was always done with such grace and appropriateness as to produce a great effect upon the hearers. Scarcely a year, in the course of his ministry, elapsed, in which he did not relate the story of Addison's death; and, even after his audience had become familiar with it, they were never weary of hearing it repeated. The story to which I refer, you doubtless remember. Addison, while dying, was informed that a beloved nephew was in the house, and was desirous of seeing him. "Let him come to my bedside," was the reply. He did so, and the venerable man held out his hand, as the youth approached him, and said, "See, my young friend, with what peace a Christian can die."

I have known few men who were more remarkable than Dr. Stillman for Christian fortitude and submission in the hour of trouble. In the compass of two weeks, he was called to bury two of his children, who had reached their maturity. It was indeed an overwhelming stroke; but still he was enabled to endure the affliction quietly, even cheerfully. Well do I remember how the spirit of humble submission, of joyful confidence in God, came out in his ministrations, the first time he appeared before his people after his bereavement. His sermon was founded upon that triumphant declaration of Paul,—"For I reckon that the sufferings of this present time are not worthy to be compared with the glory that shall be revealed in us." His contrast of the afflictions of this world and the blessedness of Heaven was striking beyond measure; and not only what he said, but the manner in which he said it, showed that his faith in the promises was stronger even than parental sensibility, and that he knew what it was to rejoice in tribulation.

Dr. Stillman was indefatigably devoted to the duties of the ministerial office, and in the faithful discharge of them found his highest pleasure. He almost uniformly declined invitations to public festivals, where toasting and the merriment of song were the accompaniments. He also frequently refused invitations to large dinner parties, the object of which was political discussion, rather than intellectual or moral improvement. But, whatever might be the character of the circle into which he was thrown, his behaviour was always characterized by the utmost discretion and dignity; and, though he could enter, with even a keen relish, into the enjoyments of social life, he never for a moment forgot the decorum that belongs to the character of the Christian, and the vocation of the Christian Minister.

His ministry was eminently a successful one. Several revivals of religion, of great interest, attended his faithful labours; and, on these occasions especially, he showed himself a workman that needeth not to be ashamed. The years most signalized for the displays of Divine grace in his congregation were 1804 and 1805. Indeed, so extensive was the religious feeling which then prevailed here, that it was thought expedient to establish a lecture, which was kept up, for a considerable time, on every Lord's day evening. The meetings, on these occasions, were intensely solemn, and so crowded that even the aisles of the house were entirely filled: they were held alternately at the meeting-houses of the First and Second Churches,—the two ministers officiating alternately. So deeply were the multitude impressed with the great realities of religion, that one sermon at a time seemed quite insufficient to meet their demands; and, as there were generally two or three ministers in the pulpit, it was not uncommon for the people to remain sitting after the sermon, till they had heard, from one of the other preachers, at least a brief address. A happy union of effort pervaded the two Societies, during the continuance of the revival; and the two Pastors especially,—Dr. Stillman and Dr. Baldwin, were united in the most cordial and efficient co-operation. Dr. Eckley, of the Old South Church, also, occasionally favoured us with a sermon at this season, and rendered his cheerful testimony to the genuineness of the work. It was the custom, during this extensive revival, to receive inquirers on the subject of religion at the house of the minister, for the purpose of private conversation. Each individual could thus freely make known his feelings, and solicit and receive the appropriate advice. I have often been a witness to the kindness and freedom with which my venerated Pastor would, on these occasions, communicate the most pertinent and excellent instruction, sympathizing with the burdened and distressed conscience on the one hand, and rejoicing with those who gave evidence of faith in the Redeemer on the other. I remember once to have been in his study when several, who were candidates for admission to the church, had expressed their faith and hope in Christ with unwonted freedom and cheerfulness; and so deeply was the good man affected, by their expressions, that he looked round most affectionately upon the little group, and, with a smile of delight, exclaimed,—" What a wonderfully strange thing religion is! How happy it makes us!" To one who said,—" Sir, I was walking in the street, in happy meditation, and my mind was so delightfully elevated that Heaven appeared to be but a little way off," he replied, " Ah, Heaven is not far off, when we feel right."

Dr. Stillman lived but about one year after this revival; and he seems, from this time, to have been impressed with the idea that his ministry was nearly at a close. The last sermon he preached, was from Luke, xxiv. 50, 51, on the Saviour's Ascension. A few hours previous to his death, Dr. Baldwin, who, for sixteen years, had been privileged to enjoy his society and counsel, called upon him, and expressed his deep regret at the prospect of parting. Dr. Stillman, who had not entirely lost the power of speech, articulated, in reply, these impressive words:—" God's government is infinitely perfect." In death, as well as in life, he evinced the living power, the sublimity, and greatness, of Christian faith.

I am, my dear Sir, faithfully yours,
JAMES LORING.

FROM THE REV. WILLIAM JENKS, D. D.

Boston, February 19, 1859.

Rev. and dear Sir: I have recently read again the ' Biographical Sketch' of the late Reverend Dr. Stillman, prefixed to the volume of his Sermons, published soon after his decease, and that with great satisfaction and approbation. I think that I could not desire the alteration of a single sentence. It expresses my own views of his character, in all respects, and of the impression it made on the public mind, as well as on the members of the church under his care, and the religious denomination with which he was immediately connected.

This being the case, I almost despair of adding to the documents you already possess any thing of essential consequence. But such is the reverence with which my recollections of him are associated, and such my feelings of gratitude for the benefits which, as I trust, I derived from his ministry and friendly kindness, that it seems a privilege of which I ought to avail myself, to recall and record his sainted memory.

There was, indeed, in Dr. Stillman, a happy union of the gentleman, the scholar, and the devoted Christian Minister, calculated to obtain and secure, in any well-principled community, both esteem and love. I never heard an individual speak ill of him. And, although a wo be denounced against such, he appears to have escaped. Nevertheless, he was no time-server, but as fearless as he was affectionate, and as discreet as he was faithful. All believed him to be sincere, and he was seen to be earnest, eloquent and prayerful.

The type of Dr. Stillman's piety appeared to me very much like that of Hervey, Watts, Doddridge, and our lamented Payson. It was warm, deep, heartfelt, all-pervading, but scriptural, manly, reasonable. In one of his manuscript volumes he recorded the religious exercises of several of his children, in whose deaths he was greatly afflicted, yet admirably sustained. I have just been reading these narratives, and find them as scrupulous as becomes a faithful Christian Pastor, while they exhibit all the tenderness of a loving parent. In fact, he came near the standard of his Divine Master, who wept over Jerusalem, and at the grave of Lazarus, while yet he could say, ' The cup which my Father hath given me, shall I not drink it ?'

My dear and honoured father was a member, when he removed to Boston, of the Congregational church under the care of the Rev. Mr. Greenough, of Newton. As such he was recommended to Brattle Street Church, then under the Rev. Dr. Thacher. But, living near Dr. Stillman, and becoming attached to him, and also having married for his second wife a member of Mr. Grafton's (Baptist) church, he arranged with Dr. Thacher to be a communicant at Brattle Street, but otherwise an attendant on the preaching of Dr. Stillman. This brought me under his instructions.

During this time, when about eight years old, perhaps, I was seized, abroad, with a fit, and carried home senseless. My father, greatly alarmed, called in successively two of our most eminent physicians, but in vain. He then sent for his friend Dr. Stillman, who came at once, and pouring out his affectionate heart in prayer for the child, he awoke and recovered. Turning to my father, the Doctor remarked, with moistened eyes,—' I never saw so immediate an answer in my life.' You will judge, my dear Sir, if this circumstance, of which I did not hear the particulars until thirty years after, from a brother who was present, would not endear to me Dr. Stillman's memory.

I was called in the family ' the little minister,' and my brother told me the Doctor prayed for my future usefulness. And who but God can tell the connection of his prayer with my own subsequent life ?

Dr. Stillman was by no means an indifferent and silent spectator of public affairs. His religious denomination had, from the beginning, been too much concerned in them for this. Hence he preached, in 1766, on the Repeal of the Stamp Act; in 1770, before the Honourable Artillery Company; at the General Election, in 1779; delivered an Oration on the 4th of July, 1789; preached, in 1794, on the then recent Revolution in France, from which, as an ardent philanthropist, he had hoped much for the cause of human freedom, civil and religious; and, on other public occasions, besides officiating, occasionally, as a Chaplain of the General Court. Yet was he not what would be called a political partisan, but claimed, nevertheless, and never surrendered, the rights of an American citizen,—observing, as I have myself heard him, that ' the complaint against ministers was, not that they preached at times on politics, but that they did not preach the right politics,'—namely, the complainant's own.

With respect to liberal feelings towards good men of other denominations, the Biographical Sketch already referred to has done but justice to Dr. Stillman in saying that ' though, from education and from principle, a Baptist himself, he never believed that the peculiarities of any sect ought to form a separating line, or hinder the union of good men for the advancement of the common cause of the Redeemer. With many such he long lived in habits of undissembled friendship.'—These representations are corroborated by a charge which the Doctor himself gave to the church in Salem, over which he aided in placing the late Rev. Dr. Bolles. To them he said, ' Entertain a liberal mind towards your fellow Christians, who differ from you in some things. Wise and good men do not yet see eye to eye. While you enjoy your own privileges, leave others to the enjoyment of theirs, and fall not out by the way. This mutual candour becomes disciples of the same Divine Master, and is not incompatible with fidelity to your own principles and practices.'

In his person, Dr. Stillman was slender, and very small of size, agile in movement and erect in bearing, in address polite, combining dignity with condescending kindness, so as to maintain rank with the most eminent, though affable with the meanest, and scrupulously neat in his dress; wearing, as in his painted and engraved portrait, a wig, as was in his day common, and a gown, with bands.

And now, dear Sir, commending you anew to the guidance and support of our Heavenly Father, and your labours to his blessing, I remain,

Yours affectionately, and in the best bonds,

WILLIAM JENKS.

SAMUEL HARRISS.*
1759—1795.

SAMUEL HARRISS was born January 12, 1724, in the County of Hanover, Va., but settled in early life in the County of Pittsylvania. Before his conversion, he had a highly respectable position in society, and held the offices of Church-Warden, Sheriff, Justice of the Peace, Burgess for the County, Colonel of the Militia, Captain of the Mayo Fort, and Commissary for the Fort and Army.

It was not till he had reached his thirty-fourth year that his thoughts were directed permanently in a serious channel. The Baptists were, at this time, holding frequent meetings in the neighbourhood in which he lived, and were exciting much attention by the simplicity and earnestness with which they presented Divine truth; and, in his perplexity and distress of mind, he resolved to be present at some of their meetings. It is related of him that, on one occasion, when Joseph and William Murphy, two well known Baptist preachers of that day, were to preach in a particular place, and the people were collecting for the service, Colonel Harriss rode up in full military dress, and said—"What is to be done here, Gentlemen?" "Preaching, Colonel." "Who is to preach?" "The Murphy boys, Sir."† "I believe I will stop and hear them." He accordingly did stop, and seated himself behind a loom in a corner of the room. The truth to which he listened on that occasion deeply affected his mind, and, not long

* Semples' Va. Bapt.—Benedict's Hist. Bapt., II.
† WILLIAM MURPHY was awakened, and hopefully converted, under the ministry of the Rev. Shubael Stearns, and was also baptized by him. He began to preach not long after his conversion, and occupied a somewhat conspicuous place in the ministry. The field of his labours was chiefly in the South Western parts of Virginia, though it extended also into the State of North Carolina. About 1775, he took part in a controversy on the Extent of the Atonement, though he was more distinguished as an earnest and effective preacher than an able polemic. He died in one of the Western States.
JOSEPH MURPHY was a brother of William, and, like him, was baptized by Elder Stearns. After labouring successfully many years in Virginia, he removed to North Carolina, and became Pastor of a Church on Deep Creek, in the County of Surry. He is said to have been the most distinguished minister of the Yadkin Association. His influence extended also very considerably to South Carolina. In 1766, he assisted in forming the Congaree Church, which has since been distinguished for its piety and efficiency. In 1803, he was living, at the age of more than eighty years.

after this, he found joy and peace in believing, and, in 1758, joined the Baptist denomination, being baptized by Elder Daniel Marshall.

From the time of his conversion, it was evident that, if his life were spared, he was destined to do much in aid of the cause of evangelical religion in Virginia. The year after he became connected with the church, he commenced his ministerial course. For seven or eight years, he laboured chiefly in Spottsylvania and the neighbouring counties; and it is somewhat remarkable that, during this time, he had not been authorized by the church of which he was a member to administer the ordinances of Baptism and the Lord's Supper.

In 1769, he was ordained and began to administer the ordinances. The first person he baptized was Mr. James Ireland,* who himself afterwards became distinguished in the Baptist ministry of Virginia. Mr. Ireland thus refers to this circumstance :—" He was a great favourite of the ministers in Virginia, and they had planned it among them that I should be the first person he baptized. He was considered a great man in the things of time and sense, but he shone more conspicuously as a luminary of the Church. He was like another Paul among the Churches. No man was like-minded with him. As the sun in his strength, he passed through the State, displaying the glory of his adorable Master, and spreading his light and heat to the consolation of thousands."

The Rev. John Leland who then lived in Virginia, writes thus :—

" I attended a meeting of the General Committee at Buckingham; after which, I travelled Southward to Pittsylvania, to visit that great man of God, Rev. Samuel Harriss. I had met Mr. Harriss before on the banks of James River, and accompanied him at his meetings through Goochland, Fluvanna, and Louisa, to Orange. At a meeting in Goochland, after preaching was over, Mr. Harriss went into the yard, and sat down in the shade, while the people were weeping in the meeting-house, and telling what God had done for them, in order to be baptized. A gentlewoman addressed Mr. Harriss as follows:—' Mr. Harriss, what do you think all this weeping is for? Are not all those tears like the tears of a crocodile? I believe I could cry as well as any of them, if I chose to act the hypocrite.' On this address, Mr. Harriss drew a dollar out of his pocket, and replied,—' Good woman, I will give you this dollar for a tear,

---

* JAMES IRELAND was born in the city of Edinburgh, in the year 1748. His father designed to give him a liberal education, and he made some proficiency in the Latin language; but he had little relish for study, and withal evinced a somewhat romantic temper, which led his father to try the experiment of sending him to sea. After making several voyages to the Northern seas, he was guilty of some indiscretion, in consequence of which he left his father's house, and came to America. On his arrival in this country, he took charge of a school in the Northern part of Virginia. He was, at this period, utterly regardless of religion, and devoted to every species of frivolity, and did not scruple, in certain circles, to profane the name of God. His conversion was brought about by a remarkable instrumentality. By request of a young man who had sought to make himself useful to him, he undertook to write a composition on " the natural man's dependance for Heaven;" and this was the means of his own conviction. Shortly after, he indulged a hope in the mercy of God through Christ, and almost immediately proceeded to take part in public religious exercises. He had been educated a Presbyterian, and was strongly prepossessed in favour of the Presbyterian views of Baptism; but he ultimately adopted the Baptist views, and was baptized by the Rev. Samuel Harriss, at a meeting of the Separate Baptist Association, held at Sandy Creek, N. C., in 1769. He was now licensed to preach the Gospel, and went forth preaching it with great zeal. But he quickly drew towards him the attention of the civil authorities, was arrested, and, as he would not give security that he would cease preaching, was cast into Culpepper jail, where he suffered the most cruel and shameful indignities. He was instrumental of forming many churches of the Ketockton Association, and, for many years, sustained the relation of Pastor to the Congregations at Buckmarsh, Happy Creek, and Water Lick, in the Counties of Frederick and Shenandoah. In 1802, he baptized, in one of his churches, ninety-three persons,—fifty-two of whom were received in one day. In consequence of injuries sustained by a fall from his horse, and afterwards by the upsetting of his carriage, he was, in the early part of 1806, confined to his bed. Consequent upon this was the dropsy, under which he gradually declined till death put an end to his sufferings, on the 5th of May, 1806. His decline and death were marked by perfect composure and a joyful anticipation of Heaven.

and repeat it ten times;' but the woman shed no tears. In 1787, Colonel Harriss made me a visit, whose coming called out a vast crowd of ministers and people. His eyes,—his every motion, was preaching; but, after he had read his text, his mind was so dark that he could not preach; and of course the lot fell on me. From my house he went down to Spottsylvania, where the work of the Lord, like a mighty torrent, broke out under his ministry."

Mr. Harriss had now become extensively known, as one of the most laborious ministers and effective preachers throughout Virginia. Of the estimation in which he was held by his brethren, long before this, something may be inferred from the fact that, when the General Association strangely decided that the apostolic office was designed to be perpetual, he was unanimously designated to the office. This decision and this appointment were made in the year 1774; but he held the office for only a few months.

Mr. Harriss continued his labours with unabated zeal, until infirmity disabled him for further effort. Some time before his death, he was struck with paralysis, from the effect of which he never recovered; though he was able, even after this, occasionally to do good service for his Master. At length, however, his earthly tabernacle yielded to the combined influence of age and disease, and he went calmly to his rest, after having seen more than threescore and ten years. He died in the year 1795.

Elder Semple, an eminent Baptist minister of Virginia, who knew Mr. Harriss well, writes thus concerning him :—

" His manners were of the most winning sort. He scarcely ever went into a house without exhorting and praying for those he met there. As a doctrinal preacher, his talents were rather below mediocrity; unless at those times when he was highly favoured from above,—then he would sometimes display considerable ingenuity. His excellency consisted chiefly in addressing the heart; and, perhaps, even Whitefield did not surpass him in that respect. When animated himself, he seldom failed to animate his auditory.

. . . . " Being in easy circumstances when he became religious, he devoted not only himself, but almost all his property, to religious objects. He had begun a large new dwelling house, suitable to his former dignity, which, as soon as it was finished, he appropriated to the use of public worship, continuing to live in the old one. After maintaining his family in a very frugal manner, he distributed his surplus income to charitable purposes. . . . . . He was once arrested and carried into Court, as a disturber of the peace. In Court, a Captain Williams vehemently accused him as a vagabond, a heretic, and a mover of sedition everywhere. Mr. Harriss made his defence. But the Court ordered that he should not preach in the county again for the space of twelve months, or be committed to prison. The Colonel told them that he lived two hundred miles thence; and that it was not likely he should disturb them again, in the course of one year. Upon this he was dismissed. From Culpepper he went into Fauquier, and preached at Carter's Run. Thence he crossed the Blue Ridge and preached in Shenandoah. On his return, he called at Capt. Thomas Clanahan's, in the county of Culpepper, where there was a meeting. While certain young ministers were preaching, the word of God began to burn in Colonel Harriss' heart When they finished, he arose and addressed the congregation,—' I partly promised the devil, a few days past, at the Court House, that I would not preach in this county again in the term of a year. But the devil is a perfidious wretch; and covenants with him are not to be kept, and therefore I will preach.' He preached a lively, animating sermon. The Court disturbed him no more.

" On one occasion, in Orange county, he was pulled down as he was preaching, and dragged about by the hair of his head, and sometimes by the leg. His friend rescued him. On another time, he was knocked down by a rude fellow, while he was preaching. But he was not dismayed by these or any other difficulties. To obtain his own consent to undertake a laudable enterprise, it was sufficient for him to know that it was possible. His faith was sufficient to throw mountains into the sea, if they stood in the way. He seems also never to have been appalled by the fear or the shame of man. He could confront the stoutest son of pride.

" When he first began to preach, his soul was so absorbed in the work, that it was difficult for him to attend to the duties of this life. A man owed him a sum of money which he actually stood in need of to defray the expenses of his family. He went to the man, and told him he would be very glad if he would discharge the debt he owed him. To which the man replied that he could not pay him the money. Harriss said, 'I want the money to buy wheat for my family. You have a good crop by you. I had rather have wheat than money.' The man answered,—'I have other uses for my wheat.' 'How then,' said Mr. Harriss, 'do you intend to pay me?' 'I never intend to pay you until you sue me,' replied the debtor. Mr. Harriss left him meditating: 'Good God,' said he to himself, 'what shall I do? Must I leave preaching to attend a law suit? Perhaps a thousand souls will perish in the mean time, for the want of hearing of Jesus. No, I will not. Well, what will you do for yourself? What? I will sue him at the Court of Heaven.'

"Having resolved what to do, he turned aside into a wood, and fell upon his knees, and thus began his suit:—'Oh blessed Jesus, thou eternal God, thou knowest that I need the money which the man owes me, to supply the wants of my family, but he will not pay me without a law-suit. Dear Jesus, shall I quit thy cause, and leave the souls of men to perish? Or wilt thou, in mercy, open some other way of relief?' In this prayer Mr. H. found such tokens of Divine goodness, that, to use his own words, Jesus said unto him,—'Harriss, keep on preaching, and I will become security for the payment.'

"Mr. H., having his debt thus secured, thought it most proper to give the debtor a discharge. Accordingly, he, shortly after, passing by to a meeting, carried a receipt in full to the man's house, and gave it to his servant, desiring him to give it to his master. On his return by the house, after meeting, the man hailed him at his gate, and said,—'Mr. H., what did you mean by the receipt you sent this morning?' Mr. H. replied,—'I meant just as I wrote.' 'Well, but I have not paid you,' answered the debtor. Harriss said,—'True; and I know also that you said you never would, unless the money came at the end of an execution; but, Sir, I sued you in the Court of Heaven, and Jesus has agreed to pay me. I have, therefore, given you a discharge.' This operated so effectually upon the man's conscience that, in a few days, he prepared and sent to Mr. H. wheat enough to discharge the debt.

"A criminal, who had just been pardoned at the gallows, met Mr. Harriss on the road, and showed him the document certifying that he was pardoned. 'Well,' said he, and have you shown it to Jesus?' 'No, Mr. Harriss, I want you to do that for me.' The old man immediately descended from his horse, in the road, and making the man also alight, they both kneeled down. Mr. H. put one hand on the man's head, and with the other held open the pardon. And thus, in behalf of the criminal, returned thanks that he had been pardoned, and prayed for him that he might obtain God's pardon also."

MORGAN EDWARDS.*

1761—1795.

MORGAN EDWARDS was born in Trevethin Parish, Monmouthshire, in the Principality of Wales, on the 9th of May, (O. S.) 1722. He was early placed at school, in a village called Trosnat, in his native parish; and, subsequently, became a member of the Baptist Seminary at Bristol, England, then under the care of the Rev. Mr. Foskett. He commenced preaching when he was in his sixteenth year. Having completed his academical course, he went to Boston in Lincolnshire, where he preached to a small congregation, seven years. From Boston he removed to Cork, Ireland, where he took the pastoral charge of a church, June 1, 1757, and remained nine years. From Cork he returned to England, and preached about twelve months at Rye, in Sussex. During his residence in this latter place, the Rev. Dr. Gill, and other Baptist ministers in London, having received a request from the Baptist Church in Philadelphia to assist them

* Dr. Rippon's Annual Register, No. 12.—Benedict's Hist. Bapt., II.

in obtaining a Pastor, applied to Mr. Edwards as the person more likely than any other within their knowledge, to fill the vacancy in a satisfactory manner. He was disposed to think favourably of the proposal, and, accordingly, soon after, took passage for America, and arrived at Philadelphia on the 23d of May, 1761. He immediately took charge of the church to which he had been sent, and continued to serve them acceptably a number of years.

In 1770, he preached a New Year's Sermon from the text,—"This year thou shalt die." He had, from some unaccountable impulse, taken up the idea that he should die on a particular day, and this, it is said, was intended as his own Funeral Sermon.* But the day passed, and the man still lived, and continued to live for a quarter of a century. This circumstance could not but affect his reputation injuriously. In addition to this, however, he is said to have indulged, occasionally, about this time, in the excessive use of intoxicating drinks. Finding himself somewhat under a cloud, he voluntarily resigned his pastoral charge; though he continued preaching to the people till the settlement of his successor,—an event which he was, to some extent, instrumental in bringing about.

In the year 1772, he removed with his family to Newark, De., and was occupied in preaching in a number of vacant churches till the commencement of the Revolutionary War. He then remained silent until the War was over, owing, doubtless, to the fact that he adhered to the cause of Great Britain, and was justly ranked with the Tories; though it is understood that his Toryism was rather a matter of principle than of action. After the Revolution, he occasionally read Lectures on Divinity, in Philadelphia, and other parts of Pennsylvania; also in New Jersey, Delaware, and New England; but, owing to the unhappy fall already alluded to, he declined ever after to resume the active duties of the ministry.

In 1762, Mr. Edwards was honoured, by the College and Academy of Philadelphia, with the degree of Master of Arts; and, in 1769, received the same testimony of respect from the College of Rhode Island, in which institution he held the office of Fellow, from 1764 to 1789.

Mr. Edwards died at a place then called Pencader, De., on the 28th of January, 1795, in the seventy-third year of his age. His Funeral Sermon was preached by the Rev. Dr. William Rogers, of Philadelphia, on II. Cor. vi. 8—"By honour and dishonour; by evil report and good report; as deceivers and yet true." The text was selected by himself, designed, as was supposed, to have a bearing upon his own peculiar history. The Discourse was not published at the time, but it subsequently appeared in the 12th No. of Dr. Rippon's Annual Register, printed in London.

Mr. Edwards was twice married—first to Mary Nunn, originally of Cork, Ireland, by whom he had several children; and afterwards, to a Mrs. Singleton, of Delaware, whose decease occurred previous to his own. One of his sons was a military officer in the British service.

The following is a list of Mr. Edwards' publications:—A Farewell Discourse delivered at the Baptist Meeting-House in Rye, 1761. A Sermon

---

* It is due to candour to state that some of Mr. Edwards' friends have denied that this was designed as his Funeral Sermon, and a perusal of the Sermon itself would seem to leave the case somewhat doubtful.

preached in the College of Philadelphia, at the Ordination of the Rev. Samuel Jones, with a Narrative of the manner in which the Ordination was conducted, 1763. The Customs of the Primitive Churches, or a set of Propositions relative to the Name, Materials, Constitution, Powers, Officers, Ordinances, &c., of a Church; to which are added their Proofs from Scripture, and Historical Narratives of the manner in which most of them have been reduced to practice. A New Year's Gift: a Sermon, 1770. Materials towards a History of the Baptists in Pennsylvania, both British and German, distinguished into First-day, Keithian, Seventh-day, Tunker, and Rogerene Baptists, 1772. A Treatise on the New Heaven and New Earth. Two Academical Exercises; on the Millenium and Last Novelties, 1788. *Res Sacræ*, a Translation from the Latin, 1788. (This contains an enumeration of all the acts of Public Worship, which the New Testament styles *Offerings* and *Sacrifices;* of which giving money for religious uses is one; and, therefore, according to Mr. E., is to be done in the places of public worship, and with as much devotion as any other part of the service.) Materials towards a History of the Baptists in Jersey; distinguished into First-day Baptists, Seventh-day Baptists, Tuncker Baptists, and Rogerene Baptists, 1792.

Beside various manuscripts, which he gave to his friends, as tokens of personal regard, he left behind him forty-two volumes of Sermons,—twelve Sermons to a volume,—all written in a large and legible character; also, about a dozen quarto volumes, on special subjects.

The following estimate of Mr. Edwards' character and attainments is from the Discourse of Dr. Rogers above referred to :—

"He used to recommend writing sermons at large, but not to take them to the pulpit, if it could possibly be avoided. If not possible, he advised the preacher to write a large, fair hand, and make himself so much master of his subject that a glance, as it were, might take in a whole page. Being a good classic, and a man of peculiar refinement, he was vexed to hear from the pulpit what deserved no attention, and much more to hear *barbarisms;* because, as he used to say, 'they were arguments either of vanity, or insolence, or both; for an American, with an English Grammar in his hand, a learned friend at his elbow, and close application for six months, might make himself master of his mother tongue.'

"The Baptist Churches are much indebted to Mr. Edwards. They will long remember the time and talents he devoted to their best interests, both in Europe and America. Very far was he from a selfish person. When the arrears of his salary, as Pastor of this church, amounted to upwards of £372, and he was put in possession of a house, by the church, till the principal and interest should be paid, he resigned the house, and relinquished a great part of the debt, lest the church should be distressed.

"The College of Rhode Island is also greatly beholden to him for his vigorous exertions, at home and abroad, in raising money for that institution, and for his particular activity in procuring its charter. This he deemed the greatest service he ever did for the honour of the Baptist name. As one of its first sons, I cheerfully make this public testimony of his laudable and well-timed zeal.

"In the first volume of his materials, he proposed a plan for uniting all the Baptists on the Continent in one Body politic, by having the Association of Philadelphia (the centre) incorporated by charter, and by taking one delegate out of each Association into the Corporation; but, finding this impracticable, at that time, he visited the churches from New Hampshire to Georgia, gathering materials towards the history of the whole. Permit me to add that this plan of union, as yet, has not succeeded.

"Mr. Edwards was the moving cause of having the Minutes of the Philadelphia Association printed, which he could not bring to bear for some years, and, therefore, at his own expense, he printed tables, exhibiting the original and annual state of the associating churches.

"There was nothing uncommon in Mr. Edwards' person; but he possessed an original genius. By his travels in England, Ireland, and America, commixing with all sorts of people, and by close application to reading, he had attained a remarkable ease of behaviour in company, and was furnished with something pleasant or informing to say on all occasions. His Greek Testament was his favourite companion, of which he was a complete master; his Hebrew Bible next, but he was not so well versed in the Hebrew as in the Greek language; however, he knew so much of both as authorized him to say, as he often did, that the Greek and Hebrew are the two eyes of a minister, and the translations are but commentaries; because they vary in sense as commentators do. He preferred the ancient British version above any other version that he had read, observing that the idioms of the Welsh fitted those of the Hebrew and Greek like hand and glove.

" Our aged and respectable friend is gone the way of all the earth; but he lived to a good old age, and with the utmost composure closed his eyes on all the things of time. Though he is gone, this is not gone with him; it remains with us that the Baptist interest was ever uppermost with him, and that he laboured more to promote it than to promote his own; and this he did, because he believed it to be the interest of Christ, above any in Christendom. His becoming a Baptist was the effect of previous examination and conviction, having been brought up in the Episcopal Church, for which Church he retained a particular regard during his whole life."

------◆------

DAVID JONES.

1761—1820.

FROM HORATIO GATES JONES, ESQ.

PHILADELPHIA, March 15, 1859.

My dear Sir: The life of my venerable grandfather, particularly as connected with some of the most stirring scenes of the Revolution, was one of no ordinary interest. It might very well form the subject of a narrative that would occupy much more space than you can afford to it; but I shall be able, I think, to give you the more prominent facts and characteristics without exceeding the limit you have prescribed to me.

DAVID JONES, a son of Morgan and Eleanor (Evans) Jones, was born in White Clay Creek Hundred, New Castle County, De., on the 12th of May, 1736, and resided there until 1750, when his parents removed to a place called Ironhill. During his residence at this place, in the year 1758, he was brought to a saving knowledge of the truth, at the age of about twenty-two, and was baptized on the 6th of May, 1758, by the Rev. David Davis. Soon after his Baptism, he went to Hopewell School, under the care of the Rev. Isaac Eaton, A. M., where he remained three years, and, as he himself states, "learned Latin and Greek." His attention was no doubt early drawn to the ministry, but it was not till the year 1761 that he became a licentiate, at the Welsh Tract Church; and the same year he went to Middletown, N. J., to improve himself in Divinity, under the instruction of his relative, the learned Abel Morgan. He preached at various places, but more especially at Freehold, Monmouth County, N. J., until December 12, 1766, when he was ordained Pastor of that Church. He continued in this relation, labouring with great fidelity, until the year 1775. It was during his Pastorate at Freehold that he became strongly impressed with a desire to visit the Indians Northwest of Ohio River; and, having laid the case before the Association of Philadelphia, which met that year (1772) at New York, he received from that Body a certificate of his good standing, with a view to the prosecution of his intended mission.

He had already made one journey to the Ohio, which occupied him about three months. Besides visiting the Indians, he had "views of settling on the East side of the River Ohio; in a province under the care of Messrs. Franklin, Wharton, Baynton, Morgan, and others." His first journey was begun on the 4th of May, 1772, and terminated in August. His second journey commenced October 26, 1772, and ended in April 1773, so that he spent nearly one year in his travels among the Indians. One of his companions, while navigating the Ohio in a canoe from Fort Pitt, was the celebrated George Rogers Clarke. His missionary efforts were directed especially to the Shawnee and Delaware Indians; but they were attended with so little success that he finally abandoned the benevolent enterprise, and returned to his charge at Freehold. He subsequently published an account of his mission,—including both visits,—to the then Western wilderness, and it is full of interesting observations both of the country and its native inhabitants.

Mr. Jones continued his labours in New Jersey without interruption till the commencement of the Revolutionary War, when his great zeal in the cause of independence rendered him so obnoxious to the Tories, who abounded in that part of the State, that even his life was placed in imminent jeopardy. Accordingly, in April, 1775, he removed from Jersey, and settled as Pastor of the Great Valley Baptist Church, Chester County, Pa.

In 1775, the Continental Congress recommended to the Colonies the observance of a day of Fasting and Prayer, in view of the alarming state of affairs; and the recommendation was very extensively heeded. Mr. Jones preached a Sermon on that occasion, before Colonel Dewee's Regiment, entitled "Defensive War in a Just Cause Sinless," which breathed a highly patriotic spirit. It was published and extensively circulated through the Colonies.

In 1776, Mr. Jones received the appointment of Chaplain to a Pennsylvania Regiment under Colonel St. Clair, which was ordered to the Northern Department. He was on duty with St. Clair at Ticonderoga, where, on the 20th of October, 1776, while they were in hourly expectation of the enemy from Crown Point, he delivered a characteristic Address to the Regiment, that served to inspire them with fresh military ardour. He served through two campaigns, under General Gates, and was also Chaplain to a Brigade under General Wayne, in 1777. He was in the battle of Brandywine, on the 11th of September of that year; on the 21st of the same month was at the massacre of Paoli, and narrowly escaped death; and on the 4th of October following, was in the battle of Germantown. He accompanied the army to Whitemarsh and Valley Forge, and was with Wayne in the battle of Monmouth, and in all his subsequent campaigns until the surrender of Cornwallis, at Yorktown, in the autumn of 1781. By his open and untiring efforts in his country's cause, he rendered himself emphatically a marked man, insomuch that General Howe offered a reward for him, and a plan was actually set on foot for his arrest. At the close of the War, he returned to "the Valley," where he bought a farm situated in Easttown township, Chester County, a short distance from the residence of his old Commander, General Wayne.

Here he resumed his labours as a minister of Peace, and they were accompanied with many tokens of the Divine favour.

In 1786, Mr. Jones was called to the pastoral care of the Church in Southampton, Bucks County, Pa. He accepted the call, and remained there till 1792, when he returned to "the Valley" for the residue of his life.

In 1794, he yielded to the request of General Wayne, to accompany him as Chaplain, on his expedition against the Indians in the North Western Territory. At the commencement of the War of 1812, he again entered the army, though he had reached the age of seventy-six,—and served under Generals Brown and Wilkinson, until Peace was restored. From 1812 to 1817, besides performing a considerable amount of professional duty, he made many important contributions to the newspapers of the day, touching the affairs of the State and the nation. A junior Pastor (the Rev. Thomas Roberts) was in the mean time called to "the Valley," who, for many years, during the absence or the illness of the Senior Pastor, performed, either wholly or in part, the duties of the Pastorate. In 1817, he delivered an Address at the Dedication of the Monument erected at Paoli, commemorative of the Americans who were massacred there on the night of the 21st of September, 1777; and this is believed to have been the last public occasion on which he officiated.

But his life was now rapidly drawing to a close, under the influence, not only of old age, but of a complication of maladies that had long been preying upon his constitution. Surrounded with friends whose highest pleasure it was to minister to his comfort, and filled with gratitude in view of the past, and inspired with joyful hope in respect to the future, his strength gradually declined until the 5th of February, 1820, when he entered into his rest, in the eighty-fourth year of his age. A Sermon on occasion of his death was preached by the Rev. Dr. William Rogers, of Philadelphia.

Mr. Jones was married on the 22d of February, 1762, to Anne, daughter of Joseph and Sarah Stilwell, of Middletown, N. J. They had eight children,—five sons and three daughters. The youngest child was my father, the Rev. Horatio Gates Jones, who, I understand, is to form a distinct subject of your work.

Poulson's American Daily Advertiser, of February 10, 1820, after announcing the death of the Rev. David Jones, proceeds thus :—

"In sketching the character of this venerable servant of the Cross, truth requires us to say that he was an eminent man. Throughout the whole of his protracted and eventful life, Mr. Jones was peculiarly distinguished for the warmth of his friendship, the firmness of his patriotism, the sincerity and ardour of his piety, and the faithfulness of his ministry. The vain honours of the world, it is true, are not his, but in another he has ere this received a crown of glory, and heard the joyful welcome,— "Well done, good and faithful servant." In the army of the Revolution, he was a distinguished Chaplain, and was engaged in the same arduous duties during the last war. As a scholar, he was accurate. Possessing a mind of superior texture, he embellished it with the beauties of classical literature, and the riches of general science. The Fellowship of Brown

University, R. I., in the year 1774, as a testimony of respect for his learning and talents, conferred upon him the degree of Master of Arts."

As an illustration of some of my grandfather's peculiar characteristics, I will venture to relate an anecdote or two, communicated by the Rev. George W. Anderson, D. Ph.

On his way to join the Army of the North, he rode from New Brunswick to New York in the stage, in company with a number of gentlemen, all of whom seemed to take a lively interest in the political affairs of the day. Among them was a young lawyer, who was criticising, in no measured terms, the policy and spirit of President Madison. "A weak administration—a miserably weak administration," was the epithet which he applied to the powers that then were. Mr. Jones had sat quietly, taking but little part in the animated discussion. But now he woke up— "Yes Sir," said he, "it is a weak administration,—a miserably weak administration." Some surprise was manifested at this concession from a man of Mr. Jones' well known political principles. "Yes, indeed, a miserably weak administration—if President Madison were half the man he ought to be,"—looking full in the eye of the young lawyer,—"he would have hung, long ago, scores of such confounded Tories as you!" "Sir," said the lawyer, with a great deal of warmth,—"if you were not an old man, you would not say that to me." "Yes, yes, Sir,"—replied Mr. Jones, shaking his head energetically toward the angry youth,—"and if I were not an old man, you would not dare to say that to *me*."

On one occasion, when returning from the Army at the North, during the late War, he stopped in New York City, and was invited to preach in the First Baptist Church. When he rose to commence his sermon, he looked up at the ceiling, and round the house, making a general and careful survey of the building. He then cast a keen, scrutinizing glance over the congregation. The whole of this careful survey occupied a very short time, which, to the expectant assembly, appeared twice the length it really was. Of course every eye was fixed on the tall, venerable form in the pulpit, and all were wondering what would come next.

"It seems to me,"—at length he said, as if satisfied with his survey, "that you have a very nice house here—very neat, and very comfortable, and quite a large and respectable congregation." At this unexpected exordium the attention became more profound. "Things appear very different from what they did when I first came to New York City. I landed here in the morning, and thought I would try if I could find any Baptists. I wandered up and down, looking at the place and at the people, and wondering who of all the people I met might be Baptists. At length I saw an old man, with a red cap on his head, sitting on the porch of a respectable looking house. Ah! thought I, now this is one of the old residents, who knows all about the city, and about every body in it—this is the man to enquire of. I approached him and said—'Good afternoon, Sir—can you tell me where any Baptists live in this city?' 'Hey?'" Here the preacher, in imitation of the action of the deaf old Gothamite, put his hand to his ear, and bent his head in the attitude of a listener. Then raising his voice, as if shouting into the ear of the deaf man, he said,—'Can you tell me, Sir, where I can find any Baptists in this place ?' 'Baptists, Baptists,' said the old man, musing, as if ransacking all the corners of his memory,—' Baptists ! I really don't know as I ever heard of any body of that occupation in these parts !!' "

The attention of the congregation was now wide awake. There were of course many smiling faces, as he thus sketched his first attempt to find Baptists in the City of New York. But soon he turned to his subject, and, in a few minutes, tears were seen in the eyes of half the congregation, and no doubt many good impressions were made by his discourse.

Trusting that the above epitome of the life of my venerable ancestor may be sufficient for your purpose,

I remain, very truly yours,

HORATIO GATES JONES.

———◆◆———

JAMES MANNING, D. D.*

1762—1791.

JAMES MANNING was of Scottish extraction, and was born at Elizabeth-town, N. J., October 22, 1738. His parents, James and Christian Manning, were persons of worth and respectability, and it is inferred, from the interest which he himself exhibited in agricultural pursuits, that his father was a farmer. For his early intellectual and moral training he was indebted chiefly to his parents, in connection with the school in his native village. The precise period at which his mind became permanently interested in religious things is not known; though it *is* known that he made a public profession of his faith in 1758, when he was about twenty years of age.

His immediate preparation for College was made in a school established at Hopewell, N. J., in 1756, by the Rev. Isaac Eaton,† " for the education of youth for the ministry ;"—the first institution of the kind in this country in connection with the Baptist denomination. At the age of about twenty, he became a member of Princeton College, and graduated with the highest honours of his class, in 1762.

Mr. Manning entered the ministry shortly after leaving College, and, probably, without any other preparation than was involved in his college course, together with that amount of theological reading that he was able to connect with it. But, however defective may have been his training,—and it was an evil which he shared in common with most of his brethren at that day,—he possessed, in a high degree, the qualities requi-

---

* Benedict's Hist. Bapt. II.—Memoir by Prof. Goddard.

† ISAAC EATON was a son of Joseph Eaton, of Montgomery; joined Southampton Church, and commenced preaching at an early age. He came to Hopewell in April, 1748, and, on the 29th of November following, was ordained Pastor of the Church in that place. He continued in this relation till July 4, 1772, when he died in the forty-seventh year of his age. His Funeral Sermon was preached by the Rev. Dr. Samuel Jones of Pennepek, who thus briefly portrayed his character :—" The natural endowments of his mind, the improvement of these by the accomplishments of literature, his early and genuine piety, his abilities as a Divine and a Preacher, his extensive knowledge of men and books, his catholicism &c., would afford ample scope to flourish in a Funeral Oration; but it is needless." He received the degree of Master of Arts from three Colleges—the College of New Jersey in 1756; the College of Philadelphia in 1761; and Rhode Island College in 1770.

site to constitute a popular preacher; and hence we find that, from his very earliest appearance in the pulpit, it was confidently predicted that he was destined to be a burning and shining light. He was first settled as Pastor of a Baptist Church in Morristown, N. J. Afterwards, he received an urgent solicitation to take charge of a congregation, belonging to the same denomination, in his native town, which, however, he felt himself obliged to decline. Shortly after this, he travelled extensively in different parts of the country, with a view to enlarge his general knowledge, and particularly to make himself better acquainted with the moral condition of the people.

In 1763, he was married to Margaret Stites, daughter of John and Margaret Stites, of Elizabethtown,—a lady of great excellence of character, who adorned every relation she sustained. They had no children. Mrs. Manning survived her husband many years, and died in Providence, R. I., November 9, 1815, at the age of seventy-five.

After having remained at Morristown somewhat less than a year, he accepted an invitation, near the close of 1763, to become the Pastor of the Baptist Church in Warren, R. I. Shortly after entering on the duties of his pastoral charge, he instituted a Latin school, which seems to have been, if not the germ, at least the harbinger, of Rhode Island College.

Notwithstanding it was only a scanty support that he gathered from his labours here, both as a minister of the Gospel and a teacher of youth, he prosecuted his double vocation with great contentment and alacrity, and was most effectually preparing himself for that wider sphere of usefulness which he was destined to occupy in coming years.

It has been asserted by Morgan Edwards that the College was originally projected by the Philadelphia Association; but, admitting that the conception originated with them, there is little or no doubt that the part which Manning took in relation to it fairly entitles him to the honour of being considered the founder of the institution; and the motive which chiefly influenced him, probably, was, to elevate the intellectual character and standing of the Baptist clergy. In 1763, he proposed to several influential gentlemen of the denomination, assembled at Newport, the establishment of "a Seminary of polite literature, subject to the government of the Baptists." The project having been favourably received by them, he, at their suggestion, presented a plan of the proposed institution, which also met their approval. A charter was granted by the Legislature of the Colony in 1764; and the original Corporation, consisting of both clergymen and laymen, numbered some of the most illustrious names in the Colony, and among them Stephen Hopkins and William Ellery, which afterwards took their place in the brightest constellation of our political horizon. Notwithstanding the charter secures to the Baptists a controlling influence in the College, yet it is by no means an influence inconsistent with the grand principles of universal toleration.

Mr. Manning, who, from the beginning, had been one of the most active and influential members of the Corporation, was appointed, in September, 1765, "President and Professor of languages. and other branches of learning, with full power to act in those capacities, at Warren or elsewhere." In 1766, the College went into operation at Warren, where the first Commencement was held, and a class of seven graduated, in September, 1769. To this class belonged the Rev. Dr. William Rogers, who, in his later years, was Provost of the University of Pennsylvania, and the Hon. James Mitchell Varnum, who figured as an eminent lawyer and patriot, and was a General in the army of the American Revolution.

But, notwithstanding the College commenced its operations at Warren, in consequence no doubt of that being the residence of Mr. Manning, yet, when the question of the erection of a college edifice came to be considered, involving, as was supposed, the ultimate location of the institution, each of the several counties of Newport, Providence, and Kent, put in its claims with Bristol ; and it was not without a patient and protracted hearing, on the part of the Corporation, that they finally, in 1770, decided "that the said edifice be built in the town of Providence, and there be continued forever." They now signified, by a committee, to President Manning, their entire approval of his administration, and their earnest wish that he should remove with the institution to Providence ; and, at the same time, and by the same committee, approached his congregation with the utmost delicacy, with a view to obtain their consent to the proposed arrangement. His separation from his charge having been amicably effected, he removed to Providence, with the other officers of the College, and the undergraduates, in May, 1770 ; and, in the course of that year was erected, chiefly or entirely at the expense of citizens belonging to the town or county of Providence, the first college edifice, now known as University Hall. The first Commencement at Providence was held on the first Wednesday of September, 1770, when a class of only four graduated, among whom was the Hon. Theodore Foster, who was afterwards, for many years, a member of the Senate of the United States.

President Manning now addressed himself to his appropriate duties in connection with the College, with an earnestness and energy not a little quickened by its enlarged accommodations, and by the constantly increasing favour which it found in the eyes of a liberal community. Morgan Edwards, Hezekiah Smith, and some other prominent Baptist clergymen, co-operated with him with great vigour and efficiency ; while many of the more respectable inhabitants of the town, who had never themselves enjoyed the advantages of high intellectual culture, were found more than willing to help forward an enterprise which contemplated the better training of their posterity.

For several years, the College, under its accomplished and devoted President, was constantly growing in respectability and usefulness ; but, in common with some other similar institutions, its prosperity was checked, and its operations altogether suspended, by the Revolutionary War. In 1776, the college edifice was turned into a barrack for the militia, and, afterwards, into a hospital for the French army under command of Rochambeau. From this time till the close of the War, in 1783, the College remained dispersed, and no degrees were conferred until 1786. During this period, President Manning was constantly occupied with the duties of the ministry, and such other social and philanthropic services as the peculiar state of the country gave him an opportunity to perform. On one occasion, he was instrumental of obtaining a reprieve for three men belonging to the regular army, who had been condemned, by a Court Martial, to suffer death. By his earnest entreaties with General Sullivan, the commanding officer in that department, he succeeded in obtaining the order just in time to arrest the execution of the fearful sentence. He rode from the General's house with the utmost speed, and reached the spot with his message of mercy, after the appalling ceremonies, which were to terminate in the discharge of the fatal volley, had begun. The proceedings were instantly stayed, and the crowd who were assembled gave utterance to their joy in no equivocal demonstrations, while the individuals who were to have suffered, were well-nigh paralyzed by the tidings of deliverance.

President Manning had taken a deep interest in the concerns of the country from the commencement of the Revolutionary struggle ; but there is no reason to suppose that the idea of engaging actively in political life had ever occurred to him. In the progress of the conflict, however, his labours were put in requisition, as a politician, and a statesman. The first important civil function that was confided to him, and the exemplary manner in which he discharged it, are thus represented by the venerable John Howland, President of the Rhode Island Historical Society :—

" The repeated calls of the militia, while the enemy remained in this State, (Rhode Island,) operated with peculiar severity; in some districts the ground could not be planted, and in others, the harvest was not reaped in season; the usual abundance of the earth fell short, and he who had the best means of supply, frequently had to divide his store with a suffering neighbour. In addition to this, laws existed in several States, prohibiting the transport of provisions beyond the State boundary. The plea for these restrictions was that there was danger of the enemy being supplied; but the real cause was to retain the provisions for the purpose of furnishing their State's quota of troops, as the War was generally carried on by the energy of the Governments of the individual States. These restrictions came with double weight on the citizens of Rhode Island, as a great part of the State was in possession of the enemy, and the remainder was filled with those who had fled from the islands and the coasts for safety. These restrictions and prohibitions were variously modified, but, under all their variations, which referred chiefly to the mode of executing the law, the grievance was the same. The Governor and Council of War of Rhode Island, wishing to give their language of remonstrance a power of impression which paper could not be made to convey, commissioned Dr. Manning to repair to Connecticut, and represent personally to the Government of that State the peculiar situation of Rhode Island, and to confer with and propose to them a different mode of procedure. The Doctor, in this embassy, obtained all that he desired; the restrictions were removed; and, in addition to this, on his representation of the circumstances of the refugees from the islands, contributions in money or provisions were made in nearly all the parishes in the interior of Connecticut, and forwarded for their relief."

But President Manning was destined to occupy a still more important and responsible post in civil life. In 1786, at a crisis of great depression and alarm, occasioned by the utter failure of the Articles of Confederation, adopted in 1781, to accomplish the ends of Government, he was chosen to represent the State of Rhode Island in the Congress of the United States. The circumstances of his election to that office were somewhat remarkable. Happening to step into the State House one afternoon, from motives of mere curiosity, while the General Assembly was holding its session there, his peculiarly graceful and dignified air could not escape the observation of the members. There was a vacancy in the delegation to Congress, then to be filled ; and no one in particular had been proposed as a candidate. Shortly after President Manning entered the room, and took his seat, Commodore Hopkins, then a member of the assembly, rose and nominated the President as a delegate to Congress; and the vote being taken, it was decisive, it is believed unanimous, in his favour. The Hon. Ashur Robbins, upon whose authority this statement is made, remembered to have heard Commodore Hopkins say that the thought of such a nomination had never occurred to him, until he saw President Manning enter and take his seat on the floor of the Assembly.

As Congress, under the old Confederation, always sat with closed doors, and allowed no report of their proceedings to be published, it is not known to what extent Mr. Manning participated in their debates; it is inferred, however, from his natural readiness as a speaker, from the deep interest which he felt in the state of the country, as well as from the perfect familiarity which he subsequently evinced with the various subjects that came before them, that he must have been not only a deeply interested, but a very active, member of the Body. On one occasion, he was brought into unpleasant collision with one of the delegation,—an impetuous young man, from Georgia. The member referred to had made some offensive allusion to the New England States; and Mr. Manning repelled the attack, and turned the tables upon him by referring to some of the less attractive features of his own State. The young man assumed a threatening tone, and appeared in Congress the next day with his sword by his side, and with an avowed intention of violence upon his antagonist. Such, however, were the demonstrations of the Body that he was glad to lay aside his sword, and before night he apologized to Mr. Manning for his offensive conduct.

On receiving the appointment of Delegate to Congress, Mr. Manning obtained leave from the Corporation to be absent from College from March till September; and, during this period, his place was supplied by the Rev. Perez Fobes, at that time a Congregational minister of Raynham, Mass., and shortly after a Professor in the College. At the expiration of the time for which he had obtained leave of absence, he returned, and entered again with alacrity and zeal upon his accustomed duties.

Dr. Manning was an earnest advocate for the adoption of our present National Constitution, fully believing that on that measure the future well-being of the country was suspended. Being aware that several clergymen of his own denomination were members of the Convention, and that they generally looked upon the proposed Constitution with a jealous eye, he went to Boston with a view to exert whatever influence he could to disarm his brethren of their prejudices, and bring them to act as he fully believed the interests of the nation required. In this effort he was seconded by his intimate friend, Dr. Stillman, who was himself a member of the Body, and two or three other very influential clergymen; but their arguments seem to have availed little with those to whom they were addressed. The question of ratification, however, was finally carried by a majority of nineteen. Just before the final vote, Governor Hancock, the President of the Convention, called upon Dr. Manning to pray; and, though the request took him by surprise, he fell upon his knees, and offered a prayer in which patriotism and piety were most delightfully blended, and which left an extraordinary impression upon the whole Assembly. On his return to Providence, after the Convention had closed its sessions, he met his friends with the warmest gratulations, and could scarcely find language strong enough to express his sense of the importance of the result which had been reached.

It will naturally be inquired whether Dr. Manning, during the period in which he presided over the College, and had so much to do with the affairs of State, wholly intermitted his duties as a Christian minister. So far from this, he seems always to have regarded the ministry as his appropriate calling, and to have been never more in his element than when he was dispensing the consolatory and sanctifying truths of the Gospel to his fellow-creatures. Soon after he removed to Providence, he was invited by the Rev. Samuel Windsor,* then Pastor of the First Baptist Church, to occupy his pulpit a certain Sabbath, on which was dispensed the Sacrament of the Lord's Supper. Mr. Windsor invited Dr. Manning to join with them in the celebration of the ordinance; to which, however, a portion of the church strongly objected, on the ground that they could not recognise the principle of " transient communion." From this there grew up a troublesome controversy in the church, which finally resulted in the secession of a portion of the communicants, with their Pastor, who subsequently identified himself with the dissentients, on other grounds than those upon which the controversy commenced. After Mr. Windsor had retired, the church formally appointed Dr. M. to be their pastor, *pro tempore*, or to use his own language, " until there may be a more full disquisition of this matter, or time to seek other help; at least until time may prove whether it will be consistent with my other engagements, and for the general interest of religion."

From the commencement of his pastoral labours at Providence, the church of which he had the charge experienced a manifest revival, in respect to both its numbers and graces. It was soon found that a larger house of worship was needed, and then it was that the spacious and beautiful edifice was erected, which to this day remains, a noble testimony to the taste and public spirit of the generation that produced it. It was dedicated in May, 1775, and a Sermon preached on the occasion by Dr. Manning, from the text,—" This is none other than the house of God, and this is the gate of Heaven." During a period of about twenty years, he continued the stated minister of that church, preaching not only to the satisfaction, but to the delight, of his hearers; while, at the same time, he discharged his varied and arduous duties in connection with the College, with the most exemplary fidelity. It is wonderful that he could have performed such an amount of labour; and it is only to be accounted for from the fact that he was gifted with a versatility and readiness of mind, which enabled him to preach admirably with but little preparation, and to accommodate himself with great facility to every variety of circumstances.

---

* SAMUEL WINDSOR was a son of the Rev. Samuel Windsor, who was born in Providence, R. I., in 1677; was ordained Pastor of the First Baptist Church in his native place, in 1733, and continued in this relation till his death, which occurred on the 17th of November, 1758. He (the son) was born in Providence, November 1, 1722, and was ordained as his father's successor June 21, 1759. He continued for about ten years in the acceptable discharge of the duties of his office; but, about the year 1770, he requested the church to provide an assistant or successor, as his duty to his family forbade him to perform any longer the amount of service to which he had been accustomed. The Rev. James Manning was accordingly employed, in 1770; but, owing to some difficulty that arose in connection with his introduction there, Mr. Windsor withdrew, with a small portion of the congregation, and formed a new church, at Johnston, a few miles from Providence, to which he subsequently ministered.

Dr. Manning, during the whole of the latter part of his ministry, seems to have been oppressed by the reflection that the interests of his congregation required more attention than he was able to give to them ; and hence he more than once intimated a wish that he might be allowed to resign his pastoral office. Notwithstanding the affections and wishes of his flock would still have detained him, he actually did resign, in 1791, and, on the last Sabbath of April in that year, preached his Farewell Sermon. It was a deeply affecting occasion to both himself and his people ; and it, subsequently, derived a greatly increased interest from the fact that it proved the harbinger of his removal from all earthly scenes. It would seem almost as if he had a presentiment that the time of his departure was at hand ; for he not only relinquished his pastoral charge, but, at the Annual Commencement, in 1790, expressed to the Corporation of the College his wish that they would select some suitable person to succeed him as President. But, before his request had been complied with, they were summoned to follow him to the grave. While he was engaged in family worship, on Sabbath morning, July 24, 1791, he was seized with a fit of apoplexy, which, from the beginning, deprived him, in a great measure, of consciousness, and terminated his life on the succeeding Friday, at the age of fifty-three.

The death of Dr. Manning produced a great sensation throughout the whole community. Not only the congregation who had, for so many years, been edified by his ministerial labours, and the students of the College who had enjoyed his valuable instruction, as well as been the objects of his parental solicitude, and the Corporation, and all who were associated with him in the government of the institution,—not only these, but the whole intelligent portion of the State at large, besides many in every part of the country, felt most deeply that a great man had fallen. On the day succeeding his death, his remains were conveyed from his dwelling to the College Hall, where the Funeral service was performed, by the Rev. Dr. Hitchcock, a Congregational minister in Providence, and one of the Fellows of the College. On the next Sabbath. the Rev. Jonathan Maxcy and the Rev. Perez Fobes, both of them at that time Professors in the College, delivered impressive and eloquent Funeral Discourses to the congregation that had, for so many years, been privileged to sit under his ministry.

The Corporation of the College, in due time, erected a monument over his grave, on which is inscribed a fitting record of his extraordinary talents and worth, and his eminently useful life. In later years, one of his pupils, Nicholas Brown Esq., built, at his own expense, a noble edifice for the use of the University, which he has named in honour of his venerated teacher, MANNING HALL.

FROM THE HON. WILLIAM HUNTER, L.L. D.,
MEMBER OF THE UNITED STATES SENATE, ETC.

PROVIDENCE, January 16, 1848.

My dear Sir: I was a member of the class in Brown University that graduated the year that Dr. Manning died, and of course the last class that enjoyed the full benefit of his instruction. I had great reverence for him as a Man, a Minister, and the President of a College; and am glad to contribute any recollections of him that remain with me, in aid of your design to frame some enduring memorial of his talents and worth.

I may safely say that Dr. Manning inspired his own times with a deep sense of his high qualities as a Scholar, an Orator, a Statesman, a Theologian, and an Educationist. As he died in 1791, there are few of the present generation who can claim to have known him. A general impression of his high excellence remains; but what composed it, now that it has become a matter of tradition, is so indistinctly stated, that it rather irritates than satisfies, the spirit of rational inquiry. His few surviving contemporaries ought, therefore, to retrace what they can remember of him,—not the minute facts that make up biographical detail, but those prominent lines and marks which constitute character. If I understand your request, this is what you wish me to do, and what I shall now attempt.

In the first place, to satisfy a natural and excusable curiosity, I would say that in person, President Manning was not only beyond the ordinary size, but in these "degenerate days," would be deemed bulky, and would have been so regarded in his own days, if he had not known literally how to carry *off* his bulk. His motions and gestures were so easy and graceful that ordinary observers thought not of his immense volume of flesh, and those who criticised, admired the manner by which it was spontaneously wielded. I do not know that he had ever read Hogarth's Analysis of Beauty, but he moved in *his* line of grace. His face was rotund and handsome, his head large, and his countenance intelligent and impressive.

As a Scholar, President Manning was highly respectable. To the immense erudition of President Stiles he could make no pretension. He was bred in Colonial times, at an institution, (Princeton), then and ever since distinguished for thorough scholarship, especially in the department of the classics. Manning certainly delighted to teach both the Roman and Greek classics,— Horace and Cicero being his favourites in the former, and Longinus in the latter. In my time, he never heard recitations in the Mathematics or Natural Philosophy, or in Rhetoric and Criticism, then taught by the study of Blair's Lectures, and Kames' Elements. But he taught Logic, Metaphysics, and Moral Philosophy, and in these he was always at home. Our Logic was that of Watts,—as useful perhaps as any. Our Metaphysics, Locke's Essay on the Human Understanding. He taught Sophomores the former, and Seniors the latter, with apparently equal delight. Our Moral Philosophy was Paley's, then a new work. I think the President never appeared to more advantage than when, after dwelling with all praise on Paley's general merits,—his clearness of style, his aptness of illustration, and his comparative liberality of sentiment, he endeavoured to guard us against the abuses that might result from the indefinite adoption of his doctrine of expediency. He took occasion, too, amply to vindicate our larger notions of religious freedom, our rejection of an Established Church and of privileged orders. His opinions were soundly republican. He regarded freedom as a blessing that could be perpetuated only by an education sound and wide, involving the inculcation upon the rising generation of an enlightened love of order and submission to law.

President Manning has, so far as I know, published no book. It is, therefore, difficult to estimate, or describe him as a writer. He was chiefly an extemporaneous speaker, and for that reason perhaps never wrought out for himself any peculiar model style. In his sermons he was careful in regard to the divisions of his subject, but in his general range of thought he moved with the largest freedom. His periods were shaped by his impulses, and were modulated, if not with the view, certainly with the effect, of increasing the power of his elocution, and of giving swell, depth, tone, to his almost peerless voice.

His admonitory addresses to the students (sometimes made necessary by juvenile excesses) were bursts of indignant and pathetic reprimand. But his rule was mild, and his scheme of administration seemed entirely free from causeless suspicions, and over minute search for petty offences. His imposing presence, his dignity, his impressiveness, were his instruments of government.

It hardly becomes me to speak of him as a Theologian, and yet I could not help observing, in some degree, his course of reading. Gill's Commentaries, the works of Doddridge and Watts, and some of Baxter's, Saurin's, and Tillotson's Sermons were always about him.

His position in Society was eminently desirable. His influence was that of high literary merit rendered easily accessible, of urbane and polished manners inviting intercourse, and of great moral elevation and purity. His election to the old Congress was a spontaneous tribute to his acknowledged worth. So far from soliciting or expecting the appointment, it took him wholly by surprise.

Such, very briefly, is the record, from an old man, in his seventy-fourth year, of feelings and opinions he entertained at sixteen.

I am, Dear Sir, truly yours,

WILLIAM HUNTER.

HEZEKIAH SMITH, D. D.

1763—1805.

FROM THE REV. SAMUEL F. SMITH, D. D.

NEWTON CENTRE, Mass., August 30, 1858.

Rev. and dear Sir: Dr. Hezekiah Smith was the paternal grandfather of my wife ; and thus many facts and incidents of his life, and many an heir loom, have come into my possession. From the materials at my command, I am happy to furnish you such a sketch of him as I suppose the plan of your work contemplates. I ought to say, however, that he seems to have studiously avoided historical notoriety, and suppressed the means, if they ever existed, of any extended posthumous notice. He left no continuous nor even fragmentary record of his life, out of which his biography could be framed, nor would he ever permit a painter to delineate his features on canvass.

HEZEKIAH SMITH was born on Long Island, N. Y., April 21, 1737. He became pious in early life, and joined the Baptist Church in New York city, under the pastoral care of the Rev. John Gano, before he was nineteen years old. He commenced his classical education at the Academy in Hopewell, N. J., one of the earliest Academies founded by the Baptist churches for the education of pious young men for the ministry. From this Academy he entered the College at Princeton, N. J., then under the Presidency of the Rev. Samuel Davies. He graduated in 1762, and received the degree of Master of Arts in course, in 1765.

After leaving College, it was deemed requisite for him to reinvigorate his health, which had become impaired by study, by a tour in the Southern

Provinces. In a single year he travelled four thousand miles, and laid the foundation of lasting friendship with men whose intercourse and correspondence proved a delight to him in his riper years. At Charleston, S. C., he was ordained by several ministers of the Charleston Association, and resided in that Province some time afterwards. He supplied the pulpit of what was then known as the Cashaway Church, near the Pedee River, and preached, as he was able, in other places in the vicinity. His labours were both acceptable and useful. Not intending, however, to make South Carolina his permanent residence, he left in the spring of 1764, and came to New England. He was admitted to preach in several Congregational pulpits, and a Divine blessing attended his ministry. When he first visited Haverhill, the committee of the West parish in the town, which was then destitute of a minister, invited him to preach awhile in their meeting-house. An unusual attention to religion was then prevailing in the parish, and at this juncture he both enjoyed much satisfaction and was eminently useful. But, as the people were not Baptists, they desired, after a time, to settle a minister of their own faith. Hence, after a few months, they instructed their committee to procure a minister whose views of the New Testament were harmonious with their own.

Mr. Smith now resolved to return to New Jersey, where several of his relatives resided. The day was fixed for his departure from the scene of his labours and successes. In the morning, several young persons came to visit him, deeply affected by the prospect of losing their loved and revered teacher, by whose instrumentality they had been brought to believe on the Lord Jesus Christ. They exhibited their ardent affection towards him, and expressed the wish that he would baptize them. Still they found him fixed in his determination. Notwithstanding, they ventured to utter their conviction that he would soon return, and be their minister. He replied,—"If I return, your prayers will bring me back." The same day he proceeded to Boston, and the day following commenced his journey to Providence. But, after he had advanced eighteen or twenty miles, the words were impressed with unusual weight upon his mind,—"Strengthen ye the weak hands, and confirm the feeble knees. Say to them that are of a fearful heart, Be strong, fear not; behold your God will come with vengeance, even God with a recompense; He will come and save you." (Is. xxxv. 3. 4.) Stopping his horse, he mused a while on the occurrence. He soon proceeded, but was shortly after arrested again by the same passage. Yielding to the impulse, he turned his horse, and rode back to Boston. Here he found two persons, sent by his friends in Haverhill to solicit his return. He readily accepted their invitation, and went back the next day to Haverhill, where he was received with many expressions of affection and gratitude.

The first time he preached, after his return, was from Acts x : 29—"Therefore I came unto you without gainsaying, as soon as I was sent for ; I ask, therefore, for what intent ye have sent for me?" The people at once erected a meeting-house for him, and thus commenced the First Baptist Church, in Haverhill, of which he was the honoured, beloved and successful Pastor for forty years. The church was organized May 9, 1765, and Mr. Smith was publicly recognised as the Pastor, November 12, 1766. The ministers who officiated on the occasion were the Rev. John Gano, of New York, Dr. Manning, President of Brown University, and Dr. Stillman, of Boston.

He continued to maintain correspondence with his brethren in South Carolina, and to Mr. Smith, in connection with Oliver Hart and Francis Pelot,* of that State, is to be given the credit of originating a Society in Charleston to aid pious young men studying for the ministry.

His life was now devoted to the care of his church and congregation, and great success crowned his labours. The church acquired, under his ministry, a commanding position and a leading influence in the town, which it has maintained till this day.

Besides his labours at home, he performed very widely the work of a home missionary at his own charges. It was on one of these missionary tours that an occurrence took place which has often been related, and often without being accredited to the true actor in the scene. On a journey into Maine, he arrived weary at a public house, where he sought lodgings for the night. "A gathering crowd soon made him acquainted with the fact that a ball was to take place in the house that evening. Intending soon to seek the retirement of his room, he paid no attention to the gay party near him, but was warming himself by the parlour fire-side, in preparation for repose, when, to his surprise, he was waited upon by a deputation, with the request that he should join in the mirth of the evening. He politely declined; but they urged his acceptance. Again he begged to be excused, and again they insisted on having his company. At length, overcome by their entreaties, he accompanied them to the hall, where the assembly was waiting to commence the dance. His appearance being that of a gentleman, the company were desirous of showing him some marked respect; and united in inviting him to take the most prominent part in the performance. Finding himself, involuntarily, in this predicament, he resolved to make the best of it, and turn the whole affair, if possible, to some moral benefit. So, after having acknowledged, in his own easy and pleasant manner, the attention which had been shown him, he remarked that he had always made it a principle, through life, never to engage in any employment, without having first asked the blessing of God; and he presumed that the courtesy of the company would be farther extended to him, while he engaged in this imperative act of duty. Upon this, he immediately commenced a prayer. The singular turn which was thus given to the anticipated amusement of the evening, produced a remarkable effect. The commanding tones of his voice; his impressive style of supplicatory address; the fervour of his prayer, and the solemn allusions made in it, rivetted first upon himself every eye, and then upon his sentiments every heart, so that, before he closed, many were dissolved in tears.

"Finding, as he ended, the way quite prepared, he began a close and pathetic address to the consciences of his audience, and continued it some

*FRANCIS PELOT, A. M., was born at Norville in Switzerland, March 11, 1720. His parents were Presbyterians. Having received a good education in his native country, he migrated to South Carolina in 1734, and ten years afterwards embraced the principles of the Baptists. Soon after the Eutaw Church was constituted, he was called to be its Pastor, and held the place, with much reputation and usefulness, until his death, in 1774. He possessed an ample fortune and a valuable library, and was a diligent student.

length of time. The result was most happy. Suffice it to say, there was no music or dance there, that evening. The company broke up with pensive thoughts. Many, who, to that hour, had been immersed in the gay and dissipating pleasures of this life, now resolved to break off their sins by righteousness, and seek a more solid and substantial good. A work of grace, of uncommon interest, commenced in the neighbourhood, and, on the return of Mr. Smith in the following year to that region, he had the pleasure of receiving the blessings of many of this same party, who had been raised, through his instrumentality, to a new life, and who were exhibiting, in their deportment, the genuine virtues of the Christian character."

In the year 1775, commenced the struggle of the American Colonies with the mother country. The Baptists had always been the friends of civil and religious freedom, and at this critical period were among the first to pledge their fortunes and lives in its defence. Their Chaplains were among the most prominent and useful in the army, and their spirit and principles were not unappreciated by Washington, as the following letter from the Commander in Chief, addressed to Samuel Harriss. Chairman of the Committee of the United Baptists in Virginia, will testify:—

"While I recollect, with satisfaction, that the religious Society of which you are members, have been, throughout America, uniformly and almost unanimously, the firm friends to civil liberty, and the persevering promoters of our glorious Revolution, I cannot hesitate to believe that they will be faithful supporters of a free, yet efficient general government. Under the pleasing expectation, I rejoice to assure them that they may rely upon my best wishes and endeavours to advance their prosperity.

"GEORGE WASHINGTON.'

In 1776, Mr. Smith received appointment as Chaplain in the American army; and, notwithstanding the tender ties binding him to his flock, he left his people and home, and continued in the army four years. He became the intimate friend of Washington, and possessed the confidence and esteem of the officers and men of the whole army. Repeatedly did he expose his life in battle, and ever was he among the foremost in encouraging the soldiers, and in soothing the sorrows of the wounded and dying. He was the humble, heroic, holy man, who would never compromise his principles in any station, but reproved vice, with a boldness of tone and manner which, contrasting with his gentleness in the approval of virtue, awed the most hardened into respect and fear. Devotion to the interests of the army,— above all, devotion to the God of armies, gave him a superiority of worth and of influence which all admired and confessed. The proofs which he gave of his disinterestedness, were constant and striking. In urging the necessity of pure morals, and dependance on a Divine arm for success in the great enterprise of freedom, he himself was the living example of what he recommended; and, on every occasion, would he sustain the efforts of the patriot 'by his exertions, his sympathies, and his prayers."

After the clouds of war had been dispersed, Mr. Smith returned joyfully to his family and his parish, and to the sacred duties to which he had consecrated his life. In his work at home, and his missionary tours abroad, his time was fully occupied, and the even tenor of life flowed on.

He was also an ardent friend of education, and, in connection with Dr. Manning, used the most strenuous endeavours to secure the establishment and prosperity of Brown University. To obtain funds for its support, he travelled through various parts of the country, at much personal sacrifice. He was eminently fitted for the service, and his efforts were highly successful. He was, at an early period, elected one of the Fellows of the University, and in 1797 received from it the degree of Doctor of Divinity,—an honour not inappropriate to a man of great personal worth, extensive attainments, and a character venerable for age and sanctity.

Dr. Smith was the Pastor of the First Baptist Church, in Haverhill, forty years. As he grew in years, he advanced in every excellence that could adorn the Christian and minister, and gained a deeper hold on all who came within the sphere of his influence. He often expressed the wish that he might not outlive his usefulness, and his desire was graciously fulfilled. He preached, for the last time, among his people, on the Sabbath, from John xii. 24—"Except a corn of wheat fall into the ground and die, it abideth alone; but if it die, it bringeth forth much fruit." The sermon was unusually impressive, and a revival of religion followed, to which it seemed introductory. On the Thursday succeeding, he was seized with paralysis, and spoke no more. His life-work was finished, and its record complete. He lay a week in this condition, and died January 22, 1805, in the sixty-eighth year of his age, and the forty-second of his ministry. A Discourse was preached at his Funeral by Dr. Stillman of Boston, from Acts xiii. 36. His ashes repose in the village graveyard at Haverhill, surrounded by many of his parishioners and the fruits of his ministry.

Dr. Smith was married, shortly after his settlement at Haverhill, to Miss Hepzibah Kimball, of Rowley, Mass,—(some testimony maintains of Boxford, Mass.) They had four children,—*Hezekiah*, who became a farmer, and died a few years since at Northumberland, N. H.; *William*, who was at one time engaged in marine pursuits; *Jonathan Kimball*, who died at my house, in Newton, in October, 1843, aged sixty-eight; and *Rebecca*, who became the wife of the late Thomas Wendall, for many years a highly respected Deacon of Dr. Sharp's Church in Boston. She died, nearly half a century ago, in great peace. Mrs. Smith died on the 9th of December, 1824.

Dr. Smith was a man of commanding presence, large and well proportioned, inspiring respect by his dignity, and winning affection by his affability and grace. His voice was one of unusual compass and power, and his genuine eloquence opened a way for his message. His views of truth were strictly evangelical, and his ministry combined, in due proportions, the doctrinal, the practical, and the experimental. He never wrote his sermons, but uniformly went into his study on Thursday morning, and devoted the residue of the week to careful preparation for the duties of the Sabbath. He left a large number of skeletons of sermons, which supply a general idea of his method; but the life of his ministry is among the treasured things belonging to memory and to God.

Allow me to add an incident or two in Dr. Smith's experience, illustrative of the times in which he lived.

When his influence began to be largely felt in Haverhill and the vicinity, many members of the Standing Order, both clergy and laity, were not a little grieved at the progress of Baptist opinions, and of course looked somewhat coldly upon him, as their exponent and representative. Dr. Smith, however, took it all with meekness and dignity. When days of fasting and prayer were held, with reference to this peculiar state of things, he was often present, as an auditor, in the public assemblies. When less conscientious men annoyed him by petty physical persecution, he possessed his soul in patience. Once, when he was contemplating a missionary tour, his horse was brought to him in the morning, having been denuded, the preceding night, of his mane and tail. "Ah, old fellow," said the good man, "you may as well go back to the pasture till your mane and tail are grown." When a stone was thrown, with evil intent, through his window, and would have done him serious damage, had he been occupying his usual place in his study, he quietly laid it up, as a memorial of God's protecting providence.

The most amusing instance of persecution, which occurred to him, was once when he went to a neighbouring town to preach. The Constable of the town, a weak and inferior looking person, was moved to go, clothed in the majesty of the law, and "warn him out of the place." The little officer, on coming into the presence of one of such commanding person, and bearing all the airs of a consummate gentleman,—on such an errand, was very naturally much confused, and, on opening his mouth to deliver his message, said,—"I warn you—off of God's earth." "My good Sir," said the preacher, "where shall I go?" "Go any where," was the reply; "go to the Isle of Shoals." It may be presumed that the expounder of the law was scarcely aware of the indignity done to the inhabitants of those sea-girt rocks, in placing their geographical position so far out of the ordinary track of navigators. Dr. Smith was of course amazed, but did not feel himself under obligation to undertake so dubious a journey.

I am, my dear Sir, fraternally yours,

S. F. SMITH.

FROM THE REV. LABAN CLARK, D. D.

MIDDLETOWN, Conn., March 1, 1852.

Dear Sir: There are certain incidents in one's life, which, though of no great moment in themselves, yet leave lasting impressions on the mind, and lead to important ultimate results. Such was the slight acquaintance I had with the Rev. Dr. Hezekiah Smith, concerning whom you ask for my recollections.

My parents were born in the vicinity of Haverhill, where he was a settled Pastor, but migrated in early life, with the first settlers, to the Coos country, on the Connecticut River, some time before the Revolutionary War. In their religious views and attachments they were decided Congregationalists; but they entertained a high regard for Dr. Smith, and, in my boyhood, I often heard them speak of him, both as a man and a minister, in terms of high commendation. Dr. Smith occasionally visited that country. I remember hearing him preach in our parish church, when I was about eighteen years of age. The two congregations (Congregational and Baptist) came together; for all were desirous of hearing him. Though I was, at that time, a stranger to the power of religion, I well recollect that I was much interested in the appearance of the man, and highly delighted with his eloquence.

In the fall of 1800, when I was about entering the ministry, I made a visit to my relatives in Haverhill and its vicinity, among whom was my father's youngest sister, a member of Dr. Smith's church. She was a devoted Christian, and, as might be expected, warmly attached to her excellent Pastor. I was gratified to learn from her that the Doctor's fame was as good at home as it was abroad; and that, after a ministry of more than thirty years, his popularity and usefulness among his people remained undiminished. I availed myself of this opportunity of hearing him in his own church. When I arrived at the place of worship, the younger members were just concluding a prayer-meeting; and the house seemed hallowed with the Divine presence. I took my seat, not only as a willing worshipper, but with an earnest desire to learn, if possible, the secret of the great popularity and unusual success of the preacher to whom I was to listen. The Doctor soon entered the pulpit,—a man of venerable appearance and stately form,—robust, but not corpulent; his locks white as wool; his eye-brows retaining their natural dark hue; his face full and fair, bearing almost the flush of youth, and beaming with intelligence and good-will; and his manner grave and dignified, and well befitting the office of an ambassador of God. He commenced the public service, after the usual form, with singing and prayer. The prayer was solemn, devout, comprehensive, and did not exceed six or eight minutes. He then announced his text; and, after a brief introduction, passed on to the exposition, which was clear, concise and full, while his illustrations were uncommonly natural and appropriate. His composition was chaste and manly, and his delivery earnest and impassioned. The sermon occupied about thirty minutes; at the close of which, he went off, for ten minutes more, into a highly impressive exhortation; and then concluded with an affecting prayer of about three minutes. The entire service did not exceed fifty minutes; and the congregation seemed to hang upon his lips, with eager attention, to the last, and left the church with a good relish for more. While I was edified and delighted with the service, I was at no loss as to the secret of the uncommon success which attended his ministry. While he laboured to keep his own heart imbued with the spirit of his Master, he fed, not glutted, his flock with the sincere milk of the word; not exhausting his subject, nor yet the patience of his hearers. I considered him a model preacher; and, during my own ministry of fifty years, I have never lost sight of his admirable manner of conducting the services of the sanctuary.

Dr. Smith's superior talents and accomplishments, his remarkably well balanced character and untiring devotion to his work, undoubtedly placed him among the most prominent ministers of his day. Not by his own communion only, but by all evangelical denominations, he was held in the highest respect while he lived, and was tenderly and reverently mourned for, when his earthly labours were ended.

I am, dear Sir, your most respectful and affectionate brother and fellow-servant in Christ,

LABAN CLARK.

SAMUEL JONES, D. D.*
1763—1814.

SAMUEL JONES was a son of the Rev. Thomas Jones, who was born at Newton, Glamorganshire, South Wales, in 1708; came to America in 1737; was ordained in 1740, the first Pastor of the Baptist Church in Tulpohokin, Pa., which was constituted chiefly of emigrants from Wales,— on the 19th of August, 1738; and died in the year 1788. In the Minutes of the Philadelphia Baptist Association, held at Philadelphia, in October of that year, there appears the following record :—" By a letter from the Church at the Great Valley, we were informed that the Divine Providence has removed, in the year past, that ancient and beloved servant of Christ, Thomas Jones, as we trust, to the Church triumphant."

The subject of this sketch was born on the 14th of January, 1735, at a place called Cefen y Gelli, in Bettus Parish, in Glamorganshire, South Wales, and was brought to this country by his parents, when he was two years old. His father was a man of wealth, and was able to give him the best advantages for education which the country could furnish. Accordingly, he sent him, in due time, to the College of Philadelphia, where he received the degree of Master of Arts, on the 18th of May, 1762. He immediately devoted himself to the work of the ministry, and, on the 2d of January, 1763, was ordained at the College Hall, at the instance of the First Baptist Church in Philadelphia, of which he was a member, and became Pastor of the United Churches of Pennepek and Southampton. In 1770, he resigned the care of the Southampton Church, and devoted himself entirely to that of Pennepek, afterwards called Lower Dublin, from the name of the township in which it was situated. Of this latter church he was Pastor upwards of fifty-one years.

In the autumn of 1763, Mr. Jones repaired, by request, to Newport, R. I., and new modelled a rough draft they had of a charter of incorporation for a College, which, soon after, obtained the legislative sanction. This was the germ of Brown University. He received the Honorary Degree of Master of Arts from the College of Rhode Island, in 1769; and the Honorary Degree of Doctor of Divinity from the College of Pennsylvania, in 1788.

With the work of the ministry Dr. Jones connected that of a teacher of youth; and, in the latter capacity, as well as in the former, he was much distinguished. He was remarkably considerate and judicious in his attentions to young men, especially with reference to their becoming ministers of the Gospel; and not a few who have been useful, and some who have been eminent, in the ministry, were educated under his care.

The Minutes of the Philadelphia Association show that Dr. Jones, during the whole period of his connection with it, was one of its most useful members. Here he is appointed to frame a System of Discipline, and there to compile a Book of Hymns, and again to draw up a Map

* Dr. Staughton's Fun. Serm.—Min. Phil. Assoc.—MSS. from General Duncan and Mrs. Sarah A. Griffith.

representing the various Associations: one year he holds the office of Moderator, and the next writes the Circular Letter to the Churches, and the next performs some other important public service—indeed it is impossible to look through the Minutes without perceiving that he was always one of the master spirits of the Body. Few men could manage more adroitly than he a difficult and involved case; and, sometimes, by a single suggestion, in a deliberative Body, he would bring light out of the thickest darkness, and order out of the wildest confusion. His services were almost always put in requisition at the constitution of churches, and the ordination of ministers, in Pennsylvania and New Jersey.

In the course of his pilgrimage, he was called, several times, to suffer severe affliction. In August, 1778, he lost three lovely children in two weeks; two of whom,—his sons *Thomas* and *Samuel*,—the one thirteen years of age, and the other ten, were laid in the same grave. Being devotedly attached to them, he observed to a Christian mother, after the interment, that he was astonished to find himself able to speak over their grave. In his latter years, he found a source of much comfort and amusement in his grandchildren.

The approach of death occasioned no dismay to this venerable man; for he had been for half a century in the enjoyment of an intelligent and unwavering Christian hope. With the great Apostle he could say,—"I know in whom I have believed." He devoutly recognised God's goodness in having granted him so long a life, and crowned it with such abundant testimonies of his favour. "When alone," said he to a friend, "I tune like a nightingale at the prospect of dying;" and, on another occasion,—"I have now finished my course, and am going to rest." At one time, as he was lying down, greatly exhausted, he said—"See here a picture of a poor man." His mental faculties continued in calm and delightful exercise till the last, though his physical suffering, attendant on the final conflict, was intense. On Monday, the 7th of February, 1814, he closed his own eyes, and, shortly after, sunk into his last slumber. A Sermon, commemorative of his life and character, was preached by the Rev. Dr. Staughton, of Philadelphia, in May following.

Dr. Jones published, beside what has been already referred to, a Sermon entitled "The Doctrine of the Covenant," preached at Pennepek, in 1783, and a Century Sermon, preached at the opening of the Philadelphia Baptist Association, in 1807.

He was married, on the 10th of November, 1764, to Sylvia Spicer, of Cape May County, N. J. They had five children, all of whom died young, with the exception of one daughter, Mrs. Harris, who died January 6, 1856, in the eighty-second year of her age. Mrs. Jones died on the 23d of July, 1802, aged sixty-six years.

FROM GENERAL WILLIAM DUNCAN.

PHILADELPHIA, September 18, 1856.

My Dear Sir: I am quite willing to give you my recollections of the Rev. Dr. Samuel Jones; for though I have seen eighty-four years, the appearance of that venerable man is still vividly in my memory, and his character embalmed in my heart. My particular acquaintance with him commenced as early as

1797, in connection with an exchange of property which I made with him; and, during eight years, in which I resided at Bustleton, a few miles from this city, I was a constant attendant on his ministry. We were often visiters at each others' houses; and I had every opportunity I could desire of seeing and hearing him, both in public and in private.

Dr. Jones was a large, firmly built man,—six feet or more in height, and every way well proportioned. His face was the very image of intelligence and good-nature; which, with the air of dignity that pervaded all his movements, rendered his appearance uncommonly attractive and impressive. His intellect was confessedly of a very superior order; but I think was more distinguished for solid than brilliant qualities. His temper was remarkable for equanimity and kindliness,—for that charity which thinketh no evil; and, though I have sometimes seen him in circumstances which were well fitted to disturb his equanimity, I do not remember ever to have witnessed in him the least sign of anger, or to have seen him even thrown off his guard. These qualities of mind and heart gave him a commanding influence, not only in his denomination, but in society at large. His great knowledge of human nature, together with his firmness, self control, and peaceable and dignified bearing, imparted a weight to his opinions and counsels, which can be claimed for comparatively few clergymen whom I have known.

Dr. Jones had a deservedly high reputation as a preacher. His voice was naturally well suited to public speaking; though, in his latter years, it became somewhat husky and less attractive. His person was commanding, his attitudes in the pulpit simple and natural, and his whole manner such as could not fail to leave the impression that he was deeply interested in the truths which he was delivering. The staple of his discourses was evangelical truth: the great doctrine of Jesus Christ and Him crucified he delighted to present in its various relations; and his grand aim evidently was to bring his hearers under its practical influence. His sermons were not remarkable for splendid rhetoric, nor did they contain elaborate philosophical discussions; but, for vigorous thought, sound common-sense reasoning, and an effective presentation of Divine truth, they certainly held a very high rank. He delivered himself with great freedom, and generally spoke either without any manuscript before him, or from short notes.

It was my privilege to visit this excellent man in his last illness, and to witness the workings of his strong faith, when he was just ready to put on immortality. May our last end be like his, is the fervent prayer of

Your affectionate brother in Christ Jesus,

WILLIAM DUNCAN.

THE BURROWSES.

SILAS BURROWS. 1765—1818.
ROSWELL BURROWS. 1801—1837.

FROM WILLIAM H. POTTER, ESQ.

MYSTIC RIVER, Conn., February 25, 1859.

Dear Sir: Though I regret that some one could not have been found more competent than myself to do justice to those venerable men,—Silas and Roswell Burrows, I will cheerfully furnish you such information concerning them as I have been able to obtain. What I shall communicate has been gathered chiefly from surviving relatives and friends; from manuscripts left by Elder Roswell Burrows ; from the Records of the church they served ; from the Minutes of Public Bodies ; and, I may add, from a residence of some twenty years on a portion of the field they cultivated.

SILAS BURROWS was born at Fort Hill, in Groton, in the year 1741. His father, Amos Burrows, was the fourth in descent from Robert Burrows, one of the three original proprietors of the town. Amos Burrows had been educated a strict Congregationalist ; but, early in the great New-Light Stir, he and his wife,—Mary Rathbone, whom he married in Colchester,—united with others in forming a little church of Separates, who chose Elder Park Avery* to be their Pastor.' With this then despised, but truly pious and heroic, band, they retained their membership during life. Indeed, Mr. Burrows had the approbation of his brethren to conduct meetings, and "improve his gift," which he occasionally did in a humble way, to the edification of his hearers, till his death, which occurred in 1773, in the fifty-eighth year of his age. His wife survived him more than thirty years. Of their nine children, *Amos*, the eldest son, united with the Baptist Church of Groton, was licensed to preach, and finally closed his useful labours in Central New York. His second son, *Silas*,—the subject of this sketch, was married to Mary Smith, daughter of Isaac Smith, of the same town, with whom he lived happily nearly sixty years, and who preceded him to the grave only about two years. He was married, only a few months before his death, to Mrs. Phebe Smith, who survived him.

Mr. Burrows became hopefully pious when he was about twenty-three years of age, during a revival in his neighbourhood, and under the preaching of Elder Reynolds, a New Light Baptist minister from Norwich, who organized a small church near Fort Hill, which was afterwards known as the "Second Baptist Church in Groton." This church made choice of Silas Burrows as their leader ; and he was ordained about the year 1765, and held the office during the long period of fifty-three years. He did not pretend to much learning, but he had unquestionable piety, ardent zeal, and a well balanced mind ; and considerable success attended his labours. There was need of great energy to overcome the opposition, which at once beset the new enterprise on all sides. There were churches of Congregationalists, Separates, and stricter Baptists, around him, who confidently predicted that the movement would prove a failure ; while Infidelity was taking the attitude of open and stern resistance. Still, however, their numbers gradually increased, and they were constantly encouraged by fresh tokens of the Master's presence. The stirring times of the Revolution were approaching, and, like his Baptist brethren elsewhere, Elder Burrows at once boldly espoused the cause of freedom, and saw in that struggle not only the political enfranchisement of the land, but a boon which to him and his oppressed people was still dearer,—freedom to worship God independently of the Civil Power. It is true that the Baptists of Groton were shielded from many embarrassments and annoyances, to which their breth-

* ELDER PARK AVERY was reputed to be an eminently pious man, and was mild and winning in his address, and greatly beloved. He was an intimate friend and counsellor of Elder Silas Burrows, while he lived. He had four sons, and a grandson aged sixteen, in the Fort, at the time of the massacre. Two of his sons, and his grandson, were killed outright. Both of the surviving sons were wounded, one of them losing an eye and part of his skull. The old man staggered under this awful shock, but murmured not, and died in 1797, aged eighty-seven.

ren, in some places, were subjected; but it was rather through the magnanimity of the Congregational ministry than the protection of the law.

Perhaps, in no portion of our country was the patriotism of the people more severely tested, during the War of the Revolution, than in Groton. On that eventful morning when Fort Griswold was captured by the British, in sight of his residence, and forty-two wives became widows in one day, Elder Burrows was neither indifferent nor inactive. He rushed to the Fort to ascertain the fate of his two youthful brothers,—both of whom were members of his household. He found only the hat of one of them. The appalling sight of sixty of his neighbours lying dead in their gore, and thirty others mortally or very dangerously wounded,—from the youth of fifteen to the man of gray hairs, cannot be even faintly portrayed. Elder Burrows did what he could in this trying hour to comfort the mourner, to soothe the wounded, and to point the dying patriot to the Lamb of God. His ministrations in connection with this appalling scene did much to conciliate the favour of the community, not only towards himself, but towards the church of which he had the charge. Indeed, this seems to have been the providential preparation for that extensive revival of religion which followed the next year, the memory of which has come down to us, fragrant with the blessings of many an aged saint, who, in our day, has delighted to detail its glorious results. Meanwhile, his brothers returned to his house, from their weary captivity and confinement in the prison-ship of the enemy, to communicate the small-pox to his family. He removed his wife to a place of safety, and opened his dwelling as a hospital, where, although many had the disease, but one person died of it.

During the revival of 1782–83, several of his children were gathered into the church, and among them *Daniel* and *Roswell*, who afterwards became preachers. *Daniel* subsequently united with the Methodists, and represented his native State in Congress, where, without compromising his character as a servant of God, he faithfully served his country. He died in his native town, in 1858.

The borders of Elder Burrows' church and congregation now became so much extended that they found private houses no longer large enough to accommodate the people. The Pastor's own house had been enlarged and opened expressly for their Sabbath meetings; but they now resolved to build a meeting-house on land given for the purpose by their Pastor. This edifice was soon so far advanced as to make it suitable for public assemblies, though it was many years before it was completed. Soon after its erection, the Groton Conference was organized in it. This Body, which was composed of a score of churches of the same faith and order, was especially dear to Elder Burrows, who ever bore a chief part in its deliberations, until, some twenty years later, it united with another similar Body in forming the Stonington Union Association, which, in turn, held its first session in the same house. In these meetings, the ever watchful eye and warm heart of Father Burrows were felt, in guarding the independency of the churches, checking unholy innovations, cherishing their own mode of worship and form of doctrine, and binding together, in the bonds of love, the then feeble sisterhood of Baptist churches. It would be pleasant to recall the names of the godly ministers who laboured with him, and with whom he was most intimate. Elders Zadoc Darrow,* of Waterford, Jason Lee,† of Lyme, Peter Rogers,‡ of Bozrah, Samuel West, § of New London; and, subsequently, Asa Wilcox, ‖ of Lyme, John Sterry, of Norwich, Joseph Utley,¶ of Hartford, in his own State; and William Northup, Philip Jenkins, and Josiah Wilcox, of Rhode Island, were members of the same old Groton Conference of which Elder Burrows was regarded as the father. Then, in the Stonington Association, were the Wightmans, the Palmers,** the Miners,†† and the Browns,‡‡ with others,—a noble brotherhood, with whom he took sweet counsel, in a day when, without salaries, but not without great sacrifices, these men of God laid the foundation of that prosperity in Zion, which few of their number lived to see, but which we so richly enjoy.

The most considerable revival which occurred under Father Burrows' ministry, whether we regard its number of converts or the period of its continuance, began in January, 1809, and continued eighteen months. After the church had spent a day in Fasting and Prayer, Father Burrows and his son, who was at that time Assistant Pastor, accompanied by their Deacons, commenced visiting from house to house, and holding more frequent meetings in all parts of their parish, and in adjoining towns, as the Providence of God opened the way. While the son was preaching one night, the mighty power of God came down, and souls were born into the Kingdom, almost constantly, for many months. One hundred and thirty

* ZADOC DARROW, Pastor of the First Baptist Church of Waterford, was born December 25, (O. S.) 1728. He was the only son of Ebenezer Darrow, and his mother was a Rogers, a lineal descendant of John Rogers, the Martyr. He was educated an Episcopalian. He was converted under the preaching of Elder Joshua Morse, a famous New Light preacher, and was himself ordained over the Waterford Church in 1769, and continued in the pastoral office till his death in 1827, aged ninety-nine years, having been a minister to the same church almost sixty years. His grandson, the Rev. FRANCIS DARROW, was associated with him in 1809, and continued in the pastoral relation till his death, in 1851, at the age of seventy-one, and in the forty-first year of his ministry. They were both very successful ministers.

† JASON LEE, the second Pastor of the First Baptist Church of East Lyme, was the son of the Rev. Joseph Lee, of Long Island. He was ordained and settled over that church in 1774, and continued in that relation till his death, which occurred in 1810, in the seventieth year of his age, and the thirty-sixth of his Pastorate.

‡ PETER ROGERS was born in New London, Conn., in 1754. His father was Peter Rogers, the fourth in descent from James Rogers, the earliest of the name who came to New England, and who claimed to be a great grandson of John Rogers, the Martyr. Peter Rogers, in the early part of the Revolutionary War, was a famous privateersman. He afterwards entered the army, and won distinction in the Washington Life Guard. In March, 1790, he was ordained Pastor of the Bozrah Baptist Church. His first wife was a Green, but he afterwards married a daughter of Elder Zadoc Darrow, and died in the State of Illinois in 1849, in the ninety-sixth year of his age, and the sixtieth of his ministry.

§ SAMUEL WEST was born in Hopkinton, R. I., October 6, 1766; was converted in 1787; was ordained in 1799; was settled for ten years in New London; and finally finished his useful labours in North Madison, in the seventy-first year of his age, and the thirty-eighth of his ministry.

‖ ASA WILCOX was the son of the Rev. Isaiah Wilcox, of Westerly, R. I. The father died at an advanced age, in 1793. His son, Asa, was ordained in 1798; married Mercy Rathbun, and spent most of his life in Connecticut. He died at Salem, Conn., greatly lamented, in 1834.

¶ JOSEPH UTLEY was a protégé of Elder Silas Burrows, with whose church he united at the age of sixteen. He afterwards became an opposer, but eventually returned to the church, was ordained in Groton, where, for many years, he retained his membership, while itinerating as an Evangelist. He was the chief instrument in a revival of religion in Albany, N. Y., which was the means of establishing the First Baptist Church in that city.

** WAIT PALMER was ordained in 1743; CHRISTOPHER PALMER in 1782; ABEL PALMER in 1785; REUBEN PALMER in 1785; GERSHOM PALMER in 1805; PHINEAS PALMER in 1808.

†† ASHUR MINER was ordained in 1805, and died in 1814; JONATHAN MINER was ordained in 1814.

‡‡ SIMEON BROWN, Pastor of the Second Baptist Church of North Stonington, was ordained the same year with Elder Silas Burrows, and died two years before him. ELEAZAR BROWN, Pastor of the First Baptist Church of North Stonington, was ordained in 1770, and died June 20, 1795.

were baptized into Father Burrows' church, and a large number into Elder Wightman's. The servant of God, though aged, continued to preach till within a few weeks of his death, which did not occur till he had lived to see his church flourishing, and to witness the consummation of his long-cherished hopes and earnest endeavours,—the adoption of a Constitution in Connecticut, securing equal religious privileges to all. Soon after this joyful event, feeling that his warfare was accomplished, he sweetly fell asleep in Jesus, on his birth-day, 1818.

Elder Silas Burrows was a man of marked character. He was energetic and did nothing by halves. He was not hasty in forming opinions, nor did he claim infallibility for them when formed. But he brought all things to the Scripture test, and if, upon a candid and careful examination, any one's conduct or views could not be there sustained, he rejected them without hesitation; and, if occasion required, he openly exposed their fallacy. A striking instance of this occurred in reference to Jemima Wilkinson, who requested liberty to preach in his house, claiming a newer light than had been vouchsafed to others. Not being then aware of her extravagant views, he appointed a meeting for her, at which she boldly and blasphemously set forth her fanatical claims. He heard her through, and then, with the law and the testimony in his hands, he proceeded to unmask her imposture, quoting chapter and verse against her extravagant pretensions, till she could bear it no longer, but, interrupting him, said, in a loud, imperious voice, accompanied by a majestic wave of her hand,—"Silas Burrows, dost thou know with whom thou art contending?" "Oh yes," said he, "with Jemima Wilkinson;" and proceeded to urge home the truth of God against her fanaticism, till she left his presence, never to trouble him again.

In preaching, he placed great reliance on the sensible presence of his Master, and, sometimes, when his feelings were warmed and quickened by a powerful Divine influence, he delivered himself with an energy and pathos that were quite irresistible. But his *forte*, after all, was in prayer. Commencing in simple, trusting strains, he would raise his heart, his eyes, his voice, and his right hand, to Heaven, while his left hand crowned his temple, and, as one object of supplication after another presented itself, it seemed not only to himself but to those who listened as if Heaven and earth had come in actual contact. I hardly need add that the tone of his preaching was clearly and decidedly evangelical. He was eminently faithful in reproving vice, in visiting the sick and sorrowful, and indeed in every department of pastoral duty.

In person he was tall and commanding, and had a mild blue eye, and a stentorian voice, that was, on more than one occasion, distinctly heard in the open air, more than a mile.

ROSWELL BURROWS, a son of Elder Silas Burrows, was born at Fort Hill, in Groton, September 2, 1768. He was an apt scholar, and received a good English education. While yet a youth, he was entered, as a merchant's clerk, with Mr. Daniel Stanton, a friend of the family, living at Guilford, who took a lively interest in his welfare. During his residence here, he came home on a visit, and found himself in the midst of a revival, in the blessings of which he became a sharer. After his return to Guilford, his father wrote to Mr. Stanton to inquire how his son appeared since having professed a change of character, and the answer was that his conversation and conduct would do honour to a minister. Fearing lest his son was in danger of becoming unduly forward, he wrote him a monitory letter on the subject, which gave a shock to the son's sensitive mind, from which it did not soon recover. His fine talent for business, his excellent powers of conversation, his studiousness and exemplary conduct, at this period, rendered him a favourite, wherever he was known.

At the age of twenty-one, he was married to Jerusha Avery, only daughter of Luther Avery, Esq., of Groton, who survived her husband more than a year. They had seven children, all of whom enjoyed excellent advantages for education. Four of his children still survive, one of whom was recently a member of Congress from the State of New York. At the time of his marriage, he was a prosperous merchant in Hopkinton, R. I.; but, at the earnest solicitation of his wife's parents, he soon after settled in his native place, and eventually in the old family homestead, on Fort Hill, where he and several generations of his ancestors found their last resting place. Within a few years after his conversion, it became with him a question of deep interest whether it was not his duty to devote his life to the preaching of the Gospel; but, though he received every encouragement from the older and more prominent members of the church, such was his view of the responsibility of the work, in connection with his constitutional self-distrust, that it was not till the summer of 1801 that he could summon the resolution to carry out his own convictions of duty. In August, 1806, after repeated solicitations from his brethren, he consented to be regularly set apart to the work of the ministry. The church associated him with his father as Pastor, with authority to labour as an Evangelist, at his discretion and the call of Providence. Soon after his ordination, he performed, by appointment of the Groton Union Conference, a missionary tour, of between two and three months, in which he rode about thirteen hundred miles, and preached, most of the time, once or twice daily. His labours on this journey, extending through a portion of the country, which was, at that time, to a great extent, both a natural and moral wilderness, are known to have been attended with a rich blessing. The Report of his tour, which he submitted to the Conference, after his return, was received with great favour, and gave an impulse to the cause of missions among the churches, which has, it is believed, never been lost. And here I may as well say that, like his father, he ever took a deep interest in the prosperity of the Groton Conference, and the Stonington Union Association, which Bodies he often served in an official capacity, at their annual sessions, or as their representative abroad.

Mr. Burrows laboured also occasionally, and very successfully, in Preston,—a town lying a few miles North of Groton. Here a church was organized through his instrumentality, first as a branch of his own church, and afterwards as a distinct Body. He was also the first Baptist minister who laboured with much success at Greenport, L. I.   After the death of his father, his labours were, for a number of years, confined principally to his own people; though he made frequent visits to his children in Western New York, which were always rendered subservient to the objects of his ministry.   For several of the last years of his life, his health being less firm, and his pastoral labours greater, the church, by his request, gave him an assistant.   In this capacity the Rev. E. Denison was employed for one year; but it was not till March, 1833, that a permanent Assistant Pastor was secured.   This was the Rev. Ira R. Steward, whose faithful services greatly lightened the labours of his venerable colleague.   The church was then in the midst of a powerful revival.   In a letter which he addressed to the Editor of the Christian Secretary, about that time, he says,—"Since December, 1809, the Lord has visited this church with seven special revivals; in which time I have had the unspeakable pleasure of formally introducing into the church six hundred and thirty-five."   About ninety were added by Baptism during the year in which this letter was written; and he lived to enjoy yet another season of refreshing in the year 1835.

It appears, from private records left by Mr. Burrows, that, during his ministry of thirty-five years, he preached no less than two thousand, eight hundred and eighty-six times.   Though he was not accustomed to deliver his sermons from a manuscript, he rarely preached without having written at least the plan of his discourse, and not unfrequently much the greater part of all that he delivered.   His sermons were eminently biblical, always lucid, full of evangelical thought, often pungent, often pathetic. He was distinguished for sound judgment and excellent common sense, which made him an admirable counsellor in things temporal as well as spiritual.   In personal appearance he was of medium height, of prepossessing presence, with a grave countenance when in repose, but, when animated in conversation or in the pulpit, his dark blue eye and his every feature reflected the genial warmth within.

Without possessing naturally a very firm constitution, he was rarely visited with severe illness during his life.   In the fall and early in the winter of 1836, his health was uncommonly good, and his labours as constant as in almost any preceding period of his ministry.   But he was now performing his last work.   While on a visit to his daughter in Griswold, in January, 1837, he was thrown from a sleigh, which lamed him in one leg so as to confine him for nearly a fortnight.   About this time, as he stepped out of his house, one very icy morning, he fell upon the corner of the door-stone, and injured himself near the small of his back.   From the effect of this fall he never recovered, but continued gradually to sink, often enduring the severest distress.   About a week before his death, he suffered a severe attack of pleurisy, which he seemed to recognise as the immediate harbinger of dissolution.   He died in the exercise of the most quiet and unqualified submission to the Divine will, on Sabbath morning, May 28, 1837.   On the Tuesday following, the Rev. Daniel Wildman, of New London, delivered an appropriate Funeral Discourse to a large assembly, from Psalm xii. 1.

Allow me to add, in concluding this communication, that, in writing of the Rev. Roswell Burrows, I have availed myself of the substance of some of the statements contained in a biographical notice of him by the Rev. I. R. Steward; and am also indebted to Mrs. Mary Randall for incidents in the life of her father, the Rev. Silas Burrows.

Hoping that the above sketches may avail to your purpose, I am,

My dear Sir, truly yours,

WILLIAM H. POTTER.

----◆◆----

JOHN WALLER.*

, 1768—1802.

JOHN WALLER was born on the 23d of December, 1741, in Spottsylvania County, Va., being a descendant of a family of that name, of high respectability, in England. At a very early age, he manifested an uncommon talent for satire; and this determined his uncle, who was his guardian, to educate him for the Law. He was, accordingly, sent to a Grammar School, and made considerable progress in the Latin and Greek classics; but his uncle's death, and his father's straitened circumstances, in connection with his own unrestrained inclinations for vice, were the occasion of his being prematurely withdrawn from the school, and the idea of his prosecuting the study of the Law being abandoned. He now became addicted to almost every species of vice, and acquired such an ignoble notoriety, by his profaneness, that he was familiarly known by the appellation of *Swearing Jack Waller*,—being thus distinguished from some other persons of the same name. As an illustration of his mischievous tendencies, it is stated that he had once three warrants served on him at the same time, on account of the part which he had in one riotous procedure. He was particularly bitter in his hostility to the Baptists, and was one of the Grand Jury who presented the Rev. Lewis Craig,† for preaching. But, happily, this was overruled for bringing him to a better mind. Mr. Craig, the moment the Jury were dismissed, wishing to say

* Benedict's Hist. Bapt. II.—Taylor's Lives of Virg. Bapt. Min.
† LEWIS CRAIG was a native of Virginia, and belonged to an eminently pious family. He was first awakened under the preaching of the Rev. Samuel Harriss, and, in 1767, when he was about twenty-seven years of age, was baptized, and began to preach. Though not possessed of a cultivated mind, he was a sensible man, had a musical voice, agreeable manners, and earnest piety, and was quite a favourite among the people. He travelled largely, and his preaching was heard with much attention, and produced no inconsiderable effect. The first Baptist church organized between James and Rappahannock Rivers, called Lower Spottsylvania, afterwards Craig's, was the fruit of his labours. This church was constituted in 1767, and three years after, he became its Pastor. He was arrested by the Sheriff of Spottsylvania, and brought before three magistrates, in the yard of the meeting-house,—who bound him, with three others, in the penalty of two thousand pounds, to appear at Court, two days after. They attended, and the Court agreed to liberate them, if they would pledge themselves to preach no more in the county for a twelve-month. On their refusing to comply with this condition, they were sentenced to close confinement in the jail; and there they remained for one month, at the end of which time they were released. In 1771, he was again imprisoned, for a similar cause, and for three months, in the County of Caroline. After his liberation, he continued to labour with his wonted zeal, and the Churches of Tuckahoe, Upper King and Queen, and Upper Essex, in the Dover Association, were placed under his ministry. In 1781, he removed to the West, and settled on Gilbert's Creek, in Lincoln County, where he formed a church, and two years after again removed to within six miles of Lexington, and built up the first Baptist Church in that part of Kentucky, called South Elkhorn. In 1795, he settled in Bracken County, where also he was instrumental of building up a large church. He died after a short illness, in the eighty-seventh year of his age.

something for their benefit, thus addressed them:—"I thank you, Gentlemen of the Grand Jury, for the honour you have done me. While I was wicked and injurious, you took no notice of me, but since I have altered my course of life, and endeavoured to reform my neighbours, you concern yourselves much about me. I shall take the spoiling of my goods joyfully."

These remarks, uttered with great firmness, yet with great meekness, arrested Waller's attention, and suggested to him the idea that there must be a reality in that religion which could produce such effects. From this period he began to attend the Baptist meetings, and to feel, for the first time, a deep anxiety in respect to his salvation. He was, for seven or eight months, overwhelmed with a sense of his exceeding sinfulness, and, during much of the time, was on the borders of despair. Some of his exercises are thus described by himself:—

"I had felt the greatest abhorrence of myself, and began almost to despair of the mercy of God. However, I determined never to rest until it pleased God to show mercy or to cut me off. Under these impressions, I was at a certain place, sitting under preaching. On a sudden, a man exclaimed that he had found mercy, and began to praise God. No mortal can describe the horror with which I was seized at that instant. I began to conclude my damnation was certain. Leaving the meeting, I hastened into a neighbouring wood, and dropped on my knees before God, to beg for mercy. In an instant, I felt my heart melt, and a sweet application of the Redeemer's love to my poor soul. The calm was great, but short."

From this time, he seems to have indulged a hope in the mercy of God through Christ, though it was some time before he had sufficient confidence in the genuineness of his experience to make a public profession of his faith. He was baptized by James Read,* in the year 1767, and he realized from the ordinance a great accession of strength and comfort. He sold property to pay debts which he had contracted by dissipation. Fired by an ardent zeal for the salvation of souls, he began, almost immediately, to preach the Gospel; but his preaching seems, from some cause, to have awakened a powerful opposition.

At length, a church was constituted in Mr. Waller's neighbourhood, and he was ordained its Pastor, on the 20th of June, 1770. He began now to extend his labours, travelling in different directions, and preaching with uncommon power. The first person he baptized was William Webber,† who soon after became a minister. He attracted great attention, everywhere, by the vigour and boldness that characterized his ministra-

---

* JAMES READ was born about the year 1726, and was hopefully converted under the preaching of Elder Daniel Marshall, when he was not far from thirty years of age. When he entered upon the ministry, he could neither read nor write, but, under the instruction of his wife, he was soon able to read the Bible. He travelled extensively, both in Virginia and North Carolina, and preached with great earnestness, and not without very considerable effect He was, at one time, on account of some impropriety of conduct, excluded from Christian fellowship for two or three years; but, subsequently, upon having given evidence of repentance, was restored not only to communion, but to the exercise of his ministerial functions. There seems to have been a strong tendency in his mind to enthusiasm. He died in 1798, in the seventy-second year of his age, having been for more than forty years engaged in the ministry.

† WILLIAM WEBBER was born of respectable parentage, on the 15th of August, 1747. At the age of sixteen, he was apprenticed to a house-joiner. He was baptized when he was in his twenty-third year, and united with the Lower Spottsylvania Church, and a short time after was ordained to the ministry. After being engaged, for several years, in itinerant labours, he accepted the Pastorate of the Dover Church, in 1774, and held it till his death, which occurred on the 29th of February, 1808. In two instances, he was arrested by the civil authority, cast into prison, and subjected to the most cruel treatment, for preaching the Gospel. Elder Semple says that "he was a man of sound and correct judgment, well acquainted with mankind, well versed in the Scriptures, sound in the principles of the Gospel, and ingenious in defending them."

tions, and the Baptists in that region seemed, by common consent, to recognise him as their leader. The following letter, written by him, during an imprisonment of forty-six days, in the County of Middlesex, will give some idea of the trials to which he and his associates in the ministry, were subjected :—

"URBANNA PRISON, Middlesex County, August 12, 1771.

"Dear Brother in the Lord:

"At a meeting which was held at Brother McCain's, in this county, last Saturday, whilst Brother William Webber was addressing the congregation, from James ii. 18, there came running towards him, in a most furious rage, Captain James Montague, a Magistrate of the county, followed by the Parson of the parish, and several others, who seemed greatly exasperated. The Magistrate and another took hold of Brother Webber, and, dragging him from the stage, delivered him, with Brethren Wafford, Robert Ware, Richard Falkner, James Greenwood,* and myself into custody, and commanded that we should be brought before him for trial. Brother Wafford was severely scourged, and Brother Henry Street received one lash from one of the persecutors, who was prevented from proceeding to further violence by his companions—to be short, I may inform you that we were carried before the above mentioned Magistrate, who, with the Parson, and some others, carried us, one by one, into a room, and examined our pockets and wallets for fire-arms, &c., charging us with carrying on a mutiny against the authorities of the land. Finding none, we were asked if we had license to preach in this county; and, learning we had not, it was required of us to give bond and security not to preach any more in the county, which we modestly refused to do; whereupon, after dismissing Brother Wafford with a charge to make his escape out of the county by twelve o'clock the next day, on pain of imprisonment, and dismissing Brother Falkner, the rest of us were delivered to the Sheriff, and sent to close jail, with a charge not to allow us to walk in the air until Court day Blessed be God, the Sheriff and jailor have treated us with as much kindness as could have been expected from strangers. May the Lord reward them for it. Yesterday we had a large number of people to hear us preach; and, among others, many of the great ones of the land, who behaved well, while one of us discoursed on the new birth. We find the Lord gracious and kind to us beyond expression, in our afflictions. We cannot tell how long we shall be kept in bonds: we, therefore, beseech, Dear Brother, that you and the Church supplicate, night and day, for us, our benefactors, and our persecutors.

"I have also to inform you that six of our brethren are confined in Caroline jail,—namely, Brethren Lewis Craig, John Burrus, John Young,† Edward Herndon, James Goodrick, and Bartholomew Cheming. The most dreadful threatenings are raised in the neighbouring counties against the Lord's faithful and humble followers. Excuse haste. Adieu. "JOHN WALLER."

Mr. Waller continued in great favour with his denomination, everywhere attracting much attention as a preacher, until 1775 or 1776, when he formed an intimate acquaintance with a Methodist preacher of some repute by the name of Williams, and, through his influence, became a convert to the Arminian system of doctrine. Knowing that his brethren strongly dissented from these views, he resolved to make a bold effort, at the next meeting of the Association, publicly to maintain them; and, if his brethren were not convinced by his arguments, to submit to an expulsion from their

---

* JAMES GREENWOOD was born about the year 1749, in the lower part of Virginia, and in his twentieth year became a Baptist, and a preacher of the Gospel. At the constitution of the Piscataway Church, Essex County, he became its Pastor, and continued to sustain the relation nearly forty years. He was distinguished for an eminently blameless and consistent Christian life. When he was imprisoned for preaching the Gospel, he still preached from the windows of his cell, and some who were without are said to have wept and believed.

† JOHN YOUNG was born in Caroline County, Va., on the 11th of January, 1739. He was brought up to the occupation of a farmer. About the year 1770, he made a profession of religion, was baptized by the Rev. James Read, and soon commenced preaching the Gospel. He was ordained in 1773; at which time the church, called Read's, in his native county, was constituted, and he became its Pastor. He continued to preach in that vicinity twenty-five years. In 1799, he removed to Amherst, and the next year became Pastor of the Buffalo Church, since called Mount Moriah. He was arrested, in one of his early preaching excursions, and confined in Caroline jail six months, until, by a writ of habeas corpus, he was taken to Williamsburgh. He continued to preach until he was disabled by the infirmities of age. He was distinguished for the purity of his life, and the fidelity and success of his ministrations. He died, in a rapturous frame of mind, on the 16th of April, 1817.

Body. He preached from I Cor. xiii. 11. In his exordium, he stated that, when young and inexperienced in religion, he had fallen in with the Calvinistic plan, but that, becoming more expert in doctrine, or, in the language of his text, when he became a man, he put away these childish notions. He then went at length into the argument; but, as he failed to carry conviction to the minds of any of his brethren, and foresaw what the result of a trial would be, he took the shorter course, and proclaimed himself an Independent Baptist. He immediately set up his standard, and made the most vigorous efforts to attract persons to it, from all quarters,— preaching from house to house, ordaining lay-elders in every neighbour- hood, and establishing what he called camp-meetings; and, by this means, his party gained considerable strength. He kept aloof from his brethren, from whom he separated, until the year 1787, when he returned to them, with suitable concessions, and was formally reinstated in their connection.

In 1787, there commenced a great revival under Mr. Waller's labours, which continued for several years, and extended to all the places in which he exercised his ministry. Of this revival his nephew, Mr. Absalom Waller,* became a subject, and, after a few years, began to preach, and, by his uncle's request, became his successor in the Pastorate. Accord- ingly, Mr. John Waller, on the 8th of November, 1793, took an affection- ate farewell of the churches to which he had ministered, and removed to Abbeville, S. C. This removal is said to have been induced, partly by economical considerations, and partly from the desire of himself and wife to live near a beloved daughter, who had some time before been married to the Rev. Abraham Marshall, of Georgia. He continued his labours, as he had opportunity, after his removal, but without, as it would seem, any signal results. The last sermon he preached was on the death of a young man; and he took occasion to express his confident conviction that it *would be* his last, and fervently prayed that, like Samson, he might slay more by his death than by his life. He continued speaking until his strength failed him, and it was not without difficulty that he was conveyed to his house after the service. Just before his departure, he summoned all his family, black and white, around him, and told them he was anxious to be gone and to be present with Christ, and then warned them to walk in the fear of God, shook hands with all, and, shortly after, with the utmost serenity, breathed his last. He died on the 4th of July, 1802.

The Rev. James B. Taylor, in his "Lives of Virginia Baptist Minis- ters," after giving some particulars of Mr. Waller's death, says:—

"Thus this great man of God conquered the last enemy, and ascended to that rest that remaineth for the people of God. He died in the sixty-second year of his age, having been a minister of God's word for about thirty-five years, and in that time had lain in four different jails, one hundred and thirteen days, besides receiving reproaches, buffetings, stripes, &c. Nor was his labour in vain. While in Virginia, he baptized more than two thousand persons, assisted in the ordination of twenty-seven ministers, and in the constitution of eighteen churches. For many years, he had the ministerial

* ABSALOM WALLER was born in Spottsylvania, Va., in 1772; was hopefully converted when he was nineteen years of age, and was ordained to the ministry about two years after. He took charge of Waller's, County Line, and Bethany Churches, and continued to labour for them many years. His ministry was attended by several powerful revivals, the most exten- sive of which was in 1817–18; but, previous to that time, he had baptized more than fifteen hundred persons. For many years previous to his death, he was afflicted with partial deafness, so as to render it difficult for him to engage in conversation. He died in great peace about the year 1820, and was lamented in death, as he had been esteemed and venerated in life.

care of five churches, for which he preached statedly. As a preacher, his talents were not above mediocrity, but he was certainly a man of very strong mind. His talent for intrigue was equalled by few. This he exercised, sometimes, beyond the innocence of the dove. He was perhaps too emulous to carry his favourite points, especially in Associations; yet it must be owned that such influence as he acquired in this way, he always endeavoured to turn to the glory of God."

JOHN DAVIS.

1769—1772.

FROM HORATIO GATES JONES, Esq.

PHILADELPHIA, January 3, 1859.

My dear Sir : The materials for a sketch of the Rev. John Davis, of whom you ask me to give you some account, are by no means abundant ; but I have had access to all the sources of information concerning him within my knowledge, and I now send you the result of my inquiries, in the hope that it may answer your purpose.

JOHN DAVIS was born at Welsh Tract, Pencader Hundred, New Castle County, De., in the year 1737. His father, the Rev. David Davis, was a native of Pembrokeshire, South Wales, but came to America in 1710, when he was two years of age, and was Pastor of the Welsh Tract Baptist Church, from May 27, 1748, until his death, August 19, 1769. His mother was Rachel Thomas, daughter of the Rev. Elisha Thomas,* second Pastor of the Welsh Tract Church. His parents had three sons and three daughters. Their son *Jonathan* became a Seventh Day Baptist, and was Pastor of the church of that denomination at Cohansey. His son *John* early evinced a taste for literature, and, after preliminary instruction at Hopewell School, under the Rev. Isaac Eaton, he was placed at the College of Philadelphia, where he was graduated in the year 1763. He exercised his gifts in Delaware, and, upon his father's decease, supplied the Welsh Tract Church, where there is scarcely any doubt that he was ordained. The talents which he exhibited caused him to be known abroad ; and, in the spring of 1770, he was called to the Pastorate of the Second Baptist Church of Boston. At this time he was only thirty-three years of age, and the Baptists were suffering from the stringent laws then in force in Massachusetts. As he had come from Delaware and Pennsylvania, where full religious liberty was enjoyed by all denominations, his heart went out in deep sympathy for his oppressed brethren. At the period referred to, the grievances to which the Baptists were subjected were so heavy that the Associations took the matter in hand, and " Committees of Grievances " were appointed, to whom all complaints were made known, and an agent was chosen to represent the sufferings to which the brethren were subjected. Mr. Davis was appointed to this agency, in 1770, and was thus placed in the front rank of his Church. It was finally concluded to petition the Throne on the subject ; for the Act of Assembly,

---

* ELISHA THOMAS was born in the county of Caermarthen, in 1674. He emigrated from Wales with the other original members of the Welsh Tract Church; became its Pastor in 1725; and died on the 7th of November, 1730.

passed in 1757, which was designed to relieve Baptists and Quakers, was rendered almost inoperative by those in power. Mr. Backus said that "no tongue or pen could fully describe all the evils that were perpetrated under it."

Referring to Mr. Davis' sentiments, Mr. Backus, in a letter to the Rev. Dr. Stennett, of London, observes,—"Upon search, he found that our charter gives equal religious liberty as well as theirs; and that what is called the Religious Establishment in this Province, stands only upon some laws made by the Congregationalists to support their way which [have] happened not to be timely discovered by the powers at home, but [which] are really in their nature contrary to our charter. And when they tried to call a Provincial Synod, in 1725, an express was sent from the British Court against it, in which it was declared that their way was not established here. Therefore Mr. Davis judged it to be our duty to strike more directly at the root of our oppressions than we had before done."

Soon after his appointment as agent, he wrote as follows to the Rev. Morgan Edwards, who was his attached friend:

"Boston, September 26, 1770.

"My good friend: I have just time to tell you that when we published our advertisement, Dr. C. pretended to me to be much interested in our affairs, and said he would join us in an Address to the General Court, and a good deal to that purpose. In consequence of which, I called the committee together, when it was agreed to suspend further publication till we had asked the Court to give us a law, and, if they refused, to prosecute the matter with all the spirit we could. I sent for Mr. Smith of Haverhill, who is now in town. We had drawn a petition which we propose presenting as soon as convenient after the Court goes upon business. I waited yesterday on the Lieut. Governor, who said many things to encourage us, and said he would do all he could for us, if we could make our way through the Supreme Court. I asked him whether it would be proper to say *they had no right by charter to establish a religion*, &c.—he told me such a thing might do beyond the water, but not here. I mentioned the evil that our going to England might do. He said he did not think it would do any; for, said he, it is bad as can be already. I have had remarkably kind invitations from one of the Council within these few days; for what reason I know not. I have refused his kindness hitherto; perhaps it may do for something or other at some future time. He happens to be a courtier, and, therefore, not to be depended on. Our religious affairs have been full as well, if not better, than I expected. . . . . JOHN DAVIS."

Mr. Davis, Samuel Stillman, and Hezekiah Smith, drew a petition and presented it to the General Court, which met in the fall of 1770, and styled it "The Petition of the Baptist Committee of Grievances, acting in the name, and by the appointment, of the Baptist Churches, met in Association at Bellingham, in this Province."

The old "certificate law" expired in 1770, and the new one directed that the certificates should be signed by three or more principal members, and should state that the holder thereof was *conscientiously* of the Baptist persuasion.

Mr. Davis, therefore, called the Committee together, and it was resolved not to accept the Act. He was also requested to, and did, reply to some anonymous attacks on the Baptists, which drew from the opposite party a rejoinder full of personal abuse, and designating Mr. Davis, as "a little upstart gentleman," &c. But none of these things moved him, and he retained the esteem and regard of all his suffering brethren.

Dr. Benedict says of him,—" His learning, abilities, and zeal were adequate to any services to which his brethren might call him. Mr. Backus had now begun his History, and had the promise of assistance from this literary companion; but a mysterious Providence saw fit to cut him down almost in the beginning of his course."

Early in 1772, Mr. Davis' health failed, and in July he resigned his pastoral charge, and returned to Delaware, hoping that a milder climate would restore him to his accustomed vigour. And, for a time, the experiment seemed likely to succeed. He very soon set out on a journey for his health, with the Rev. David Jones, then of Freehold, N. J., who was at that time on a missionary visit to the Indians West of the Ohio, and kept a journal of his travels,—from which I make the following extract:—

" We travelled so slow, and could make so little progress over the Alleghany Mountains, that we did not arrive at Redstone until the 17th day of November, [1773.] A few days before me, the Rev. John Davis arrived here, and intended to go with me to Ohio. I was surprised to see him so much reduced in health. We conversed awhile, and I found he would go with me at least as far as Ohio. I endeavoured to dissuade him from his purpose, but could not prevail. . . . . . Mr. Davis and I, in company with some others, set out for the River Ohio, but, by bad, stormy weather and high waters, our journey was so retarded that we did not arrive at the Ohio till Wednesday, the 2d day of December. When we came to the house of Dr. James McMachan, who formerly lived a neighbour to Mr. Davis, the heart of poor Mr. Davis was filled with joy to see his old acquaintance and the River Ohio, after such a tedious journey— but, dear man, his time was short; for, on the 13th day of said month, he departed this life.

" During the time of his illness, he was very submissive to the will of God, and was often heard to say,—' Oh that the fatal blow was struck!' When he drew near his last, he was very delirious. To compose him, I gave him a strong anodyne, which had so much effect that, for about fifteen minutes, he enjoyed his senses, and spoke very rationally, and told me that in a little time he expected to be with Christ. He told me his faith in his Saviour was unshaken. At this time, he made as humble addresses to God as I ever heard drop from mortal lips. Soon after, his delirium returned, and never more remitted. On the Lord's day, about one hour and a half before sunset, this great man took his final departure from this troublesome world, being the 13th day of December, 1772. Mr. Davis, it is well known, was a great scholar, possessed of a good judgment and very retentive memory. He had a great soul, and despised any thing that was little or mercenary. He told me the reason why he left Boston was because he abhorred a dependant life and popularity; that, if God continued him, he intended to settle in this new country, and preach the Gospel of our Saviour freely. His address, in all his religious performances, was sweet and pleasing; his private conversation, informing and engaging, though he was at times a little reserved in company; and, what is above all, I believe he was an humble disciple of our blessed Saviour.

"The remains of this worthy man are interred near a brook, at the North end of the level land, that lies adjacent to Grave Creek. About sixteen feet North of his grave, stands a large black oak tree, on which, with my tomahawk, I cut the day of the month, date of the year, and Mr. Davis' name. . . . . . He was the first white man that died in this part of the country."

Thus died, at the early age of thirty-six years, this noble defender of religious liberty. Dr. Hovey, in his Life of Backus, says,—"Mr. Backus calls him 'the pious and learned Mr. John Davis,' and always refers to his character and conduct with the utmost respect. During the brief period of his ministry, in a place remote from all his early friends, he so discharged the duties of his responsible office as to win the esteem and love of his flock; and he so commended himself to his brethren throughout New England as to be made their agent in affairs which they esteemed of vital interest. His task was soon done, but we have reason to believe it was well done."

As early as 1770, Mr. Davis was a member of the American Philosophical Society.

The following notice of his death appeared in the Pennsylvania Gazette for February 3, 1773:—

"OHIO, (ninety-five miles below Pittsburgh,) December 13, 1772.

"This day died here, after three weeks severe illness. the Rev. JOHN DAVIS, A. M., Fellow of Rhode Island College, and late Pastor of the Second Baptist Church in Boston. The third day following, his corpse was decently interred near the river, in a spot of ground which had been fixed upon for erecting a Baptist meeting-house. His Funeral was attended by the Rev. David Jones, Mr. James McMachan, (at whose house he died,) and several others of his old acquaintances, who are settling in this part of the country. As yet, he has no other Monument than a large and venerable Oak, standing at the head of his grave, with his Name carved on it. Mr. Davis was a Man of fine Parts, an excellent Scholar, and a pretty Speaker.

"Refined his Language, and his reasoning true,
"He pleased only the Discerning Few."

With great regard,
Very sincerely yours,
H. G. JONES.

BURGESS ALLISON, D. D.

1769—1827.

FROM THE REV. HOWARD MALCOM, D. D.,

PRESIDENT OF THE COLLEGE AT LEWISBURGH, PA.

LEWISBURGH, August 18, 1858.

My dear friend : I am glad to comply with your request for a sketch of the late Dr. Allison, and yet I fear that it will be but a meagre view of his life and character that I shall be able to give you. I first knew him in 1817, when I was beginning to preach, and was a member of Dr. Staughton's Theological School. He was loved by us all ; and, though slender and unimposing in appearance, always commanded the highest respect. It gives me pleasure, even at this late day, to pay the tribute to his memory which your request contemplates.

BURGESS ALLISON, a son of Richard and Ruth Allison, was born in Bordentown, N. J., August 17, 1753. His father, who was an eminently pious man, died in 1766; but so happy had been the influence of his example and counsels upon this, his only son, that, from the age of five years, Burgess was under strong religious impressions. He seems, however, to have had no correct views of his character and condition as a sinner, and to have settled down, for the time, with the conviction that he had only to perform a certain round of external duties, in order to become entitled to the blessings of salvation. He prayed, fasted, read the Scriptures, &c., with great punctuality, and seems not to have doubted that he was in the way of life. But, on being placed at a boarding school, he found himself derided by the boys for kneeling in prayer before retiring to bed, and subjected to other petty persecutions. His religion could not stand such a test as this, and he gradually came to enjoy vain company, Sunday excursions, and other improper practices.

He was arrested in this fatal course, by encountering great peril from a violent gust of wind, on one of his Sunday frolics. When the party reached the shore, he and another left their companions, being fully resolved that they would break off from their evil ways, and cast themselves at the feet of Divine mercy. They solemnly announced this intention to their thoughtless associates ; and, from that time, all intimacy with them ceased. But Allison began, as before, to build on a sandy foundation. He became circumspect in all his conduct, and strictly attentive to his external duties. He felt that he needed a Saviour's aid, and that he was quite unable of himself to merit Heaven. But he presumed that Christ would make up what he lacked in himself. He worked for life, but was continually falling under the power of temptation, and began to feel that Christians had something of which he was destitute.

Deep and anxious now were his reflections, and he soon felt that he was under the condemnation of a violated law. His subsequent exercises he thus describes :—"As I was taking a solitary walk, more disturbed in mind than usual, all at once a ray of Divine light broke into my soul, and I was filled with wonder and joy. I beheld in imagination the blessed

Saviour, full of compassion, and ready to receive me, notwithstanding the vileness I now saw in myself. Immediately I cast myself upon Him. I felt emptied of self. The demands of the law I saw to be answered in Him. My feet seemed to be placed on a rock, and a new song put into my mouth. I stood astonished,—so wonderful did the way of salvation through a Redeemer appear, and so utterly different from any views I had ever before experienced."

During the succeeding summer, he continued to enjoy great peace, and resolved to join some church. He set himself to a diligent examination of the New Testament, and, having become "satisfied that the Baptist Church was nearest the primitive constitution," he offered himself as a candidate for communion at Upper Freehold, where he was baptized, October, 1769.

At this time, Bordentown was destitute of the preaching of the Gospel, with the exception of perhaps five or six Sabbaths in a year. This occasioned him deep regret, and it became an object of much interest with him to have religious services regularly established there. There was, however, no one but himself to officiate ; and, being but about sixteen, he shrunk from the attempt. But a sense of duty overcame his timidity. He obtained a room and invited the people to attend. The novelty of the occasion brought out a large number. It was a severe trial. Before him were many of his former associates—most of his audience had known him from infancy—he was but a boy—all conspired to abash and confound him. He, however, proceeded through the usual form of public worship, and expounded a passage of Scripture. This meeting was regularly kept up on Sunday evenings, for about four years. A considerable number of persons were thus hopefully brought to a practical knowledge of the truth, were baptized in the Delaware, and were subsequently formed into a church. Mr. Allison was meanwhile anxiously deliberating whether it was not his duty to give himself permanently to the work of the ministry. When, at length, his Christian friends communicated to him their conviction that such was his duty, he resolved on the measure ; and at once (in 1774) placed himself under the instruction of the Rev. Samuel Jones, D. D., of Lower Dublin, near Philadelphia. Here he received a classical education, and also, to some extent, studied Theology. He prosecuted his studies with great diligence, and, as his mind was strong, and susceptible of high culture, his progress was proportionally rapid.

An admirable feature in Dr. Jones' school was the provision which it made for bringing into successful exercise both the reflective and the rhetorical powers of his pupils. He preached but once on Sunday, and the afternoon was devoted to discussions, by the young ministers, of questions in Theology, cases of conscience, &c., which had been previously given out. His students generally showed, in after life, the value of this discipline.

In 1777, Mr. Allison studied a session or two at Rhode Island College ; and, on his return, became Pastor of the recently formed congregation at Bordentown. As he received from his people little or no pecuniary compensation for his services, he opened a classical boarding school,—his mother acting as matron. This institution rose rapidly in both reputation and numbers, and ultimately brought him an ample fortune. His pupils— numbering generally about one hundred—came not only from almost every State in the Union, but from Lisbon, the West Indies, the Azores, and South America. His Electrical Machine, Orrery, and most of his philo- sophical instruments, were of his own construction,—the Revolutionary War precluding him from importing apparatus.*

In December, 1783, he was married to Mrs. Rhoda Stout, widow of Zephaniah Stout, of Hopewell, N. J.,—a connection that proved pre-emi- nently happy. She at once engaged zealously in the superintendence of the boys out of school, and was universally loved and honoured by them. They never spoke of her but with respect and affection. Such a woman was admirably adapted to aid Mr. A. in his new mode of government; for he had introduced the plan of ruling without a rod. In his hands it proved successful, and no school had better discipline. He was among the first, if not the very first, to try this mode, now so universally approved.

Having rendered himself independent in his worldly circumstances, he retired from his school in 1796, renting his buildings to the Rev. William Staughton, who entered into his labours in the business of instruction.

He now engaged with great zeal in the invention and improvement of sundry machines and implements. Among these were a machine for taking profiles, and a polygraph in which steel pens were used, but especially the steam engine which, for some years, he had endeavoured to apply to navi- gation. But, like his great compeers in such enterprises, he found that these projects wasted his estate. He also suffered some heavy losses by endorsements, and still more by the discovery of a flaw in his title to twenty thousand acres of land in Kentucky. But the heaviest blow was the removal of his noble wife by death. In these most trying circum- stances, his piety shone out with new lustre. Instead of deep dejection or querulous regret, he manifested a calm and all-sustaining confidence in God. He would say,—" My Heavenly Father knows best what my interest requires, and why should I desire to take the direction of my affairs out of his hands?" He often, in subsequent years, remarked that he had learned more true wisdom in the brief period of his adversity than in all the prosperous years of his life.

In October, 1801, he repurchased the Academy buildings in Borden- town, and resumed his school with a large patronage. Dr. Staughton had removed to Burlington, and the pulpit, thus made vacant, was again tendered to Mr. Allison, and accepted. But the failure of his health soon compelled him again to relinquish these labours.

For some years, he now enjoyed relaxation from the burdens of care, and gave himself assiduously to theological studies, in which he had the advantage of one of the finest libraries in the country at that time. His religious feelings became more fervent, and his whole demeanour more impressive. He was much in prayer, especially ejaculatory prayer, even in company, and in the midst of business. Adversity had chastened him; and a faith, strong and steady, infused into his heart, and spread over his life, a most delightful tranquillity.

*His ingenuity, as well as patriotism, was exerted, about this time, in preparing kegs contain- ing explosive substances, which were floated down the Delaware, for the destruction of the British men-of-war, at anchor there.

In 1816, he was elected Chaplain to the House of Representatives in Congress, and continued in that office for several years. He then was appointed Chaplain at the Navy Yard in Washington, in which office he died, February 20, 1827, having reached the venerable age of seventy-four.

As a preacher, Dr. Allison may be said to have lacked fluency, though his discourses always indicated good sense, a well furnished mind, and an evangelical spirit. He was an eminently wise man, and this rendered him a most acceptable and useful counsellor. In all ecclesiastical meetings, he was honoured and trusted, and his influence ever tended to love and zeal. As a teacher of youth, he had few, if any, superiors. His reputation in this respect procured him invitations to the Presidency of three several Colleges, all of which he declined. He possessed great mechanical ingenuity, and was no mean connoisseur in some of the fine arts. He was an adept particularly in music and painting, in both which he took great delight as recreations, and spent some hours almost daily. At an early period, he was elected a member of the American Philosophical Society, and was long one of its Secretaries. He kept up an extensive foreign correspondence, and wrote much for magazines and newspapers. On the formation of the Baptist Board of Foreign Missions, he was chosen one of its Vice Presidents. Indeed, I may safely say that few men have lived a longer, better, happier and holier life than Burgess Allison.

Dr. Allison had seven children,—four sons and three daughters. A son and a daughter died in early childhood—the others were all married and had families. Three of them,—two sons and a daughter, died many years since; and a son and a daughter still survive.

The following notice of Dr. Allison was written by Morgan Edwards in 1789:—

"Mr. Allison is a slender built man, and neither tall nor of firm constitution, yet approaches towards an universal genius beyond any of my acquaintance. His stated preaching shows his skill in Divinity. The Academy he opened in 1778 gives him daily opportunities of displaying mastership in the liberal arts and sciences, and ancient and modern languages; several foreign youths deem his seminary their *Alma Mater;* foreigners prefer him for a tutor, because of his acquaintance with the French, Spanish, Portuguese, &c. The Academy is well furnished with books, globes, glasses, and other pieces of apparatus for experiments in Natural Philosophy, Astronomy, Geography, Optics, Hydrostatics, &c. Some of the said pieces are of his own fabrication. He is now preparing materials for an Orrery, on an improved plan. He is not a stranger to the Muses and Graces; for he is an adept in Music, Drawing, Painting, Katoptrics, &c. He has two curious and well finished chandeliers in his parlour, which show the maker, whenever he stands before them. He is as remarkable a mechanic as he is an artist and philosopher: the lathe, the plane, the hammer, the chisel, the graver, &c., have displayed his skill in the use of tools. His accomplishments have given him a name and a place in our Philosophical Society, and in that distinguished by the name of *Rumsey*, and in the Society for promoting Agriculture and Home Manufactures."

Yours with affectionate respect,

HOWARD MALCOM.

LEWIS LUNSFORD.
1770—1793.

FROM THE REV. JAMES B. TAYLOR, D. D.

RICHMOND, December 13, 1848.

Dear Sir: LEWIS LUNSFORD, concerning whom you inquire, may justly be reckoned among the more distinguished ministers of the Baptist denomination. He was born in Stafford County, Va., about the year 1753. His parents were poor, and, from earliest infancy, he was accustomed to the hardships peculiar to his condition in life. Though possessing a mind of superior order, the ample stores of knowledge were not, in childhood, placed within his reach. He was destined, however, with his powers consecrated to the cause of Christ, to be the instrument of extensive good to his fellow-men. At what time his conversion took place, cannot, with precision, now be determined. It must, however, have occurred at an early period, as there is reason to believe he had commenced the preaching of the Gospel, when he was not more than seventeen years old. The instrumentality of his conversion is attributed to Elder William Fristoe,* and by him he was baptized.

Having united himself with the Potomac Church, now called Hartwood, he began immediately to proclaim salvation through the blood of atonement. It was perceived by all that he possessed remarkable talents, and crowds attended his ministry from every direction. His extreme youth, united with the fluency and pungency of his address, excited astonishment. He was familiarly called "the wonderful boy," and it is justly a matter of surprise that, amidst so many flattering attentions as he received, he was not ruined.

A few years after his entrance into the ministry, he left his native county, and extended his influence through all the counties of the Northern Neck of Virginia. In Westmoreland, Northumberland, and Lancaster especially, did the Lord make his ministrations effectual, and believers were daily added to the Church. Several churches were gathered as the fruit of his toils; the most prominent of which are Nomini, Moratico, and Wicomico. When the Moratico Church was constituted, in the year 1778,

* WILLIAM FRISTOE was born in Stafford County, Va., in the year 1742. His parents belonged to the Established Church, but were not particularly interested in religious things. In his fourteenth year, when he was watching with a sick and dying man, a word that was dropped by a Scotch Presbyterian, who was sitting up with him, went to his heart, and awakened deep solicitude in respect to his own salvation. At length, after a protracted struggle with himself, his mind became composed, and his heart fixed upon the gracious promises of the Gospel; and, soon after this, when he was not far from the age of nineteen, he was licensed to preach by the Chapawansick Church, of which, in due time, he was called to take the pastoral care. He, however, travelled extensively, and was instrumental of forming many other churches. He also, at different periods, supplied several churches regularly, among which were those of Brentown, Hartwood, Grove, and Rockhill. On removing to the County of Shenandoah, he resigned all but one, and that he retained till the year before his death. After his settlement in Shenandoah, he took charge of Ebenezer, Buckmarsh, Bethel, Zion, and Salem, in their destitution, and gave them up successively, whenever Pastors could be obtained. In the year 1809, he published a work entitled "The History of the Ketockton Baptist Association." He died, after a short illness, at his residence in Shenandoah County, on the 14th of August, 1828, having reached his eighty-sixth year. Without having enjoyed the advantages of an early education, he had, by care and industry, acquired much general knowledge, and was an acceptable and useful preacher of the Gospel.

he was unanimously chosen its Pastor. This relation he sustained as long as he lived. It is proper here to state that he was never ordained by the imposition of hands, as he entertained the sentiment that there was nothing necessary to constitute a valid ordination, but the call of some church to the work of a Pastor or an Evangelist. Many of his brethren, at that time, considered his course objectionable, in reference to this subject; they were, however, disposed to make it a matter of forbearance, they loved him still, and co-operated with him in every good work.

I have already intimated that he was distinguished for his natural talents; he was also a diligent student, and acquired a large fund of useful knowledge. In the early part of his ministry, when compelled to labour during the week, whilst he preached on Lord's day, he was accustomed to occupy a large portion of the night in reading by fire-light. When he settled in the Northern Neck, he supplied himself with a small but valuable collection of books, and employed all the time he could abstract from active ministerial labour, in the cultivation of his intellectual powers. His memory was most retentive. The stores of knowledge which he had accumulated were always at hand, and so well arranged that, when necessary, he could bring them forth, and use them for the instruction of his auditors. In ability to make extensive and accurate quotations from good authors, few excelled him. He possessed, also, a very considerable taste for the study of Medicine, and read the most approved works on that subject. His medical attainments were so considerable that his services as a physician were frequently solicited by families residing at a distance. The following reference to his talents as a minister is furnished by Elder J. P. Jeter, Pastor of the First Baptist Church, Richmond, and, for several years, Pastor of the Moratico and Wicomico churches, in the Northern Neck.

" Lunsford was unquestionably endowed with superior genius. Destitute of literary acquirements, residing in an isolated and obscure part of the country, having access to few books, and few enlightened ministers, he rose, by native vigour of intellect and dint of application, to real distinction. For this distinction he was not indebted to the gloom by which he was surrounded. He would have been distinguished in any age, or any country. I have conversed with several intelligent gentlemen, who were intimately acquainted with him, and who concur in the opinion that his pulpit talents were of the first order. His conceptions were clear, quick and sublime ; his style, though far from being polished, was lucid, copious and strong, and his gestures were natural and impassioned."

The following anecdote was related by a living clergyman of high standing, who belongs to a different denomination of Christians ʳ ᵢn that to which Lunsford belonged. Dr. Samuel Stanhope Smith, ᵢ Princeton, N. J., had engaged to preach in the neighbourhood of his appointment: through courtesy to Dr. S., Lunsford declined preaching, and repaired with all his congregation to hear the Doctor's sermon. Dr. S., having heard the fame of Lunsford, earnestly pressed him to preach. Lunsford, yielding to his importunity, preached, after Smith had delivered his discourse. Dr. Smith afterwards remarked,—" I had heard much of Lunsford's preaching, and was prepared to hear a great sermon, but the one-half had not been told me."

Although this distinguished man was taken from the field of labour in the vigour of his days, few have accomplished more than he did for the extension of the Redeemer's Kingdom. He was in various respects useful. As a Pastor, he was affectionate and faithful. He delighted to contribute to the relief of those who were in suffering circumstances. Being qualified to administer in sickness, he attended the calls of distress which met his ear, and uniformly without compensation. Mr. Semple says of him,—" From the time he settled in the Northern Neck, and indeed from the time he began to preach there, he gradually increased in favour with the people. He had two remarkable revivals of religion within the bounds of his church—the one about the time of the constitution of the church, and the other commenced in the year 1788, and had scarcely subsided at his death, in 1793. During these revivals, he was uncommonly lively and engaged. He preached almost incessantly; and, by his acquaintances, after the last revival, it was thought that he made a rapid advance both in wisdom and warmth, especially the latter, from which he never receded, during his residence on earth."

" If Lunsford were now living," says Elder Jeter, " he would be an advocate for the benevolent institutions by which the age is distinguished. The Moratico Church Book contains an order, made during his Pastorate, and doubtless by his influence, for making collections to aid the College in Providence, R. I., now Brown University. He was a man of enlarged views and feelings. He corresponded with Isaac Backus, of New England, and Dr. Rippon, of London. With the Presbyterian ministers of his neighbourhood he maintained the most intimate and friendly intercourse. He appears to have possessed a catholic spirit towards all Christian denominations."

The early part of Lunsford's ministry was in the midst of perilous times. No power of mind or extent of attainments; no piety, zeal, or faithfulness, was sufficient to shield from the assaults of persecution. Elder Semple, referring to Lunsford's early visits to the Northern Neck, says,—" Here, as in most other places where the Baptists preached, they cried out that some new doctrine was started ; that the Church was in danger. Mr. L. was accounted worthy to share a part of this opposition. A clergyman appointed a day to preach against the Anabaptists. Crowds attended to hear him. He told stories about Jack of Leyden and Cromwell's Roundheads; but he could not, by such tales, stop the Gospel current, now swelling to a torrent. When Mr. L. preached again in those parts, they attacked him by more weighty arguments. A constable was sent with a warrant to arrest him. The constable, with more politeness than is usual on such occasions, waited until Mr. Lunsford had preached. His fascinating powers palsied the constable's hand. He would not, he said, serve a warrant on so good a man. Another man took it, went tremblingly and served it. Mr. Lunsford obeyed the summons, and appeared before a magistrate. He held him in a recognizance to appear at Court. The Court determined that he had been guilty of a breach of good behaviour, and that he must give security or go to prison. He was advised to give security, under the expectation of obtaining license to preach. He tried, but could not. He often regretted that he had taken this step, and was sorry that he had not gone to prison. This took place in Richmond County.

"After the repeal of the law for establishing one sect to the exclusion of the rest, a banditti attended Mr. Lunsford's meeting-house, with sticks and staves, to attack him. Just as he was about to begin to preach, they approached him for the attack. His irreligious friends, contrary to his wish, determined to defend him. This produced a great uproar and some skirmishes. Mr. Lunsford retired to a house. The persecutors pursued him. He shut himself up, and they were not hardy enough to break in to him. One of them desired to have the privilege of conversing with Mr. L., with a view of convincing him. He was let in, and did converse. When he came out, he wore a new face. His party asked him the result. 'You had better,' said he, 'converse with him yourselves.'"

I quote still further from Elder Semple in reference to Mr. Lunsford's last hours:—"This great, this good, this almost inimitable, man, died when about forty years of age. He lived in a sickly climate, and had frequent bilious attacks. They were sometimes very severe. For two or three years before his death, he laboured under repeated indispositions, even when travelling about. His manly soul would never permit him to shrink from the work, so long as he had strength to lift up his voice. Sometimes, after going to bed, as being too ill to preach, prompted by his seraphic spirit, he would rise again, after some other person had preached, and deal out the bread of life to the hungry sons and daughters of Zion.

"The Dover Association for the year 1793 was held at Glebe Landing Meeting-House, in Middlesex County. This was nearly opposite to Mr. Lunsford's, and, the river emptied, not more than fifteen or eighteen miles from his house. Although just rising from a bilious attack, he would not stay from a place where his heart delighted to be, and where he had the best ground to believe he could do good. He went, and appeared so much better, that he made extensive appointments to preach in the lower parts of Virginia. He was chosen to preach on Sunday, and he did preach indeed. On Tuesday, he came up to King and Queen, and preached at Bruington Meeting-House, from these words,—'Therefore, let us not sleep as do others, but let us watch and be sober.' It was an awakening discourse, worthy of this masterly workman. On that day, he took cold, and grew worse. He, however, preached his last sermon, the next day evening, observing, when he began,—'It may be improper for me to attempt to preach at this time; but, as long as I have any strength remaining, I wish to preach the Gospel of Christ; and I will very gladly spend and be spent for you.' He then preached his last sermon from—'Therefore, being justified by faith, we have peace with God through our Lord Jesus Christ.' He continued to grow worse, until, having arrived at Mr. Gregory's, in Essex, he took his bed, from whence he was carried to his grave. In his sickness he was remarkably silent; having very little to say which he could avoid. He was fond of joining in prayer; and sometimes exerted his now relaxed mind, in making remarks worthy of such a man. He expressed some anxiety at the thought of leaving his helpless family, but appeared quite resigned to the will of Heaven. On the 26th of October, 1793, he fell asleep in the arms of Jesus, aged about forty years."

The Rev. Henry Toler* preached two Funeral Sermons for him :—One at the place of his death ; another at Mr. Lunsford's Meeting-House in Lancaster County, called Kilmarnock. These two Sermons were printed in a pamphlet, and annexed to them were two handsome elegies, written by ladies of his church.

Mr. Lunsford was twice married : by his first marriage he had one child ; by his second, three.

I am, Dear Sir, faithfully yours,

JAMES B. TAYLOR.

---◆◆---

JOHN WILLIAMS.
1770—1795.

FROM THE REV. JAMES B. TAYLOR, D. D.

RICHMOND, December 15, 1848.

Dear Sir : I regret to say that the materials for any thing like a satisfactory sketch of Elder John Williams, of this State, cannot now be obtained. In the brief notices which follow, you have the result of a pretty thorough inquiry, which I have instituted in respect to him.

JOHN WILLIAMS was born in Hanover County, in the year 1747. His parents, though not wealthy, were in comfortable circumstances, and availed themselves of the opportunities they enjoyed, to give their son a liberal education. At what time he left Hanover is not known ; but, in 1769, he was engaged in the capacity of Sheriff in Lunenburg County. About this period, the right hand of the Lord was gloriously displayed, in various parts of Virginia, and many yielded to the sway of the King of saints. It was at this time that Mr. Williams' attention was first directed to the subject of religion ; and, having himself been brought to the feet of Christ, he began at once to tell others of the value of a Saviour. Being extensively acquainted in the county, in discharging his duties as Sheriff, he had a favourable opportunity of doing good to many. Nor did he neglect it. He warned his fellow men to turn from sin's deceitful ways, notwithstanding he had not then made a public profession of his faith in Christ. He was not baptized until February, 1770, six months after his conversion.

---

* HENRY TOLER was a native of King and Queen County, Va., where he lived till he reached manhood. He received his first religious impressions under the ministry of Elder John Courtney, and in due time became a member of the Upper College Church, and shortly after began to speak in public. After this, through the kindness of a wealthy and benevolent friend, he went to Pennsylvania, and became a member of the celebrated School, then conducted by Dr. Samuel Jones; and here he remained, greatly to his advantage, for about three years. He then returned to his native county, was ordained shortly after, and addressed himself with great zeal and energy to the work upon which his eye and his heart had so long been fixed. Having preached with much acceptance in the County of King George, in 1783 he consented to settle there ; though, after two or three years, he removed into the County of Westmoreland, where he exercised his ministry with great success, at the same time travelling extensively in the upper counties, and in the Northern Neck, as well as between the York and Rappahannock Rivers. He was, however, obliged, for want of an adequate support, to leave this place, and he purchased a farm in Fairfax County, but, finding himself unable to pay for it, he relinquished his title, and removed West of the Blue Ridge. Thence he emigrated to Kentucky, and became Pastor of a church in Versailles, which position he occupied at the time of his death. He died in March, 1824.

He continued to prosecute the work of the ministry, as a licentiate, with the diligence and perseverance of one who knew the value of the Gospel, and who earnestly desired the salvation of sinners. At length, the number of disciples had so far increased, that it was thought expedient to form a new church in the County of Lunenburg, to be known by the name of Meherrin. The church was constituted November 27, 1771; and, after a short time, they invited Elder Williams to become their Pastor; which invitation he accepted. In December, 1772, he was publicly set apart by imposition of hands. He appears, while labouring for this church, to have been eminently useful. At the Association in 1774, it was ascertained, from the report of the churches, that the church at Meherrin had received, during the previous year, a larger number than any other represented at that meeting. Such was the increase, during his ministry, that five or six churches were formed from the Meherrin Church, in the counties of Lunenburg, Mecklenburg, and Charlotte. In 1785, he removed his membership to Sandy Creek Church, Charlotte, and became their Pastor. This relation he sustained as long as he lived. He consented, also, in 1786, to serve the Blue Stone Church, Mecklenburg County. They were supplied by him about eight years, until the removal of Elder William Richards* into their immediate vicinity; when he tendered his resignation. It ought here to be mentioned that, immediately after Mr. Williams' conversion to God, he began to preach in a destitute neighbourhood of Mecklenburg County, and was successful in the formation of a church called Allen's Creek. Here, for twenty years, as frequently as possible, and with much success, he preached the Gospel. Many coloured persons were brought to a knowledge of the truth, and added to this church.

The influence of this servant of Christ was not to be confined within these limits. He early distinguished himself as one who felt deeply for the general interests of the Redeemer's Kingdom. He was a regular attendant of the meetings of the General Association, which continued in existence until 1783; and, afterwards, when the General Committee was organized, he never failed to be present. Many of the most important subjects were discussed at these meetings. and there is satisfactory evidence that he was one of the leading spirits in those deliberations. Any scheme which promised to promote the welfare of man, he was not only willing to approve, but to aid in its accomplishment.

Among the important objects which engaged his attention may be mentioned the cause of religious liberty. When he entered the ministry, the Church of England was established by law, and dissenters were deprived

---

* WILLIAM RICHARDS was born in Essex County, Va., of highly respectable parents, in the year 1763. At the age of eighteen, he became hopefully pious, through the instrumentality of the Baptists, but joined a Baptist Church in 1781. Soon after this, he commenced preaching the Gospel, but his first efforts were regarded as rather unpromising. Having laboured, for some time, in North Carolina, he removed, in 1794, to Mecklenburg County, Va., where he spent the remainder of his life. The same year that he removed, he was chosen Pastor of Blue Stone (now Bethel) Church. In 1799, a revival took place in connection with his labours, that resulted in the accession to the church of more than one hundred members. The year previous, he consented to serve the Sandy Creek Church, Charlotte County, and in 1802 an interesting revival commenced there also, which continued for eighteen months. His labours were extended to different parts of Mecklenburg, Lunenburg, and Charlotte, for many years, though his attention was chiefly given to the Bethel Church, which was near his residence. He died, after having been disabled, by bodily infirmity, for pastoral labour, several years, on the 13th of July, 1837, in the seventy-fourth year of his age. He was an eminently consistent and devout Christian, and a highly evangelical, acceptable and useful preacher.

of many privileges enjoyed by Episcopalians. As Non-conformists, they were exposed to the loss of personal liberty, and to the endurance of many severe sufferings. The Baptists had sore experience of these grievances. Elder Williams was, in the meetings of the General Association and General Committee, one of the most unbending champions in opposing these proscriptions, and employed his influence to encourage his brethren to resist, by all scriptural means, those unhallowed, though legalized, oppressions. At the meeting of the General Association, in 1775, a Resolution was adopted, authorizing memorials to be prepared and circulated throughout the Colony, praying the General Assembly of Virginia that the Church Establishment might be abolished, and that religion might be allowed to stand upon its own basis. Elder Williams, with two others, were deputed to wait on the Legislature with these petitions. At several times was he appointed on a similar mission. Nor were his efforts, with those of his brethren, vain,—for he lived to see one of the warmest wishes of his heart gratified in the entire prostration of ecclesiastical tyranny.

The interests of education also found in him an efficient patron. He had no idea of having learning divorced from piety. The subject of education, it is well known, was favourably received, and plans adopted for its promotion by the Baptists of the last century. In 1793, it was committed by the General Committee to John Williams and Thomas Read, who reported the following plan:—that fourteen Trustees be appointed, all of whom shall be Baptists ; that these, at their first meeting, appoint seven from the other denominations ; and that the whole twenty-one then form a plan and make arrangements for executing it. Why this scheme failed is not distinctly known ; but it is evident that the brethren of that day not only contemplated the establishment of a Seminary of learning, but actually adopted the incipient measures for carrying their wishes into execution. The following extract from a paper, presented by Elder Williams, indicates his own feelings, and the progress which had been made in the cause of education :—" Two Seminaries of learning are proposed in our State,—one on each side of James River. We have sufficient encouragement from our learned brethren in the North that we shall not want for able, skilful teachers. This will also require very diligent efforts and liberal contributions. And if we, in this, as we ought in every thing, act with a single eye to the glory of God, and the advancement of the Redeemer's interest, then shall we have sufficient grounds to hope we shall meet with the approbation of Heaven."

Another subject in which this excellent man felt a deep and lively interest, was the preparation of a History of the Virginia Baptist Churches,— in reference to which Elder Semple writes thus : — " The compilation of a History of the Virginia Baptists having been committed wholly to the hands of Mr. Williams, after Mr. Leland's removal, he had made no inconsiderable progress in collecting documents, when, in consequence of the decline of his health, he found himself under the necessity of resigning his trust. This he did, in a letter to the General Committee, in 1794. The Committee received his resignation, and resolved to decline it for the present." A few years previous, he himself thus refers to this subject : — " It is thought very expedient to form or compile a History of the Baptized Churches in Virginia,—their rise, progress, hindrances, remarkable events and occurrences, chief instruments, present condition, &c. Our General Committee have taken up the matter, and appointed ministers in the various districts to collect materials, who find it very necessary to claim the exertions and assistance of the several churches, ministers, and other individuals. We desire every circumstance to be presented as clearly as possible, and with candour and truth."

Elder Williams was a man of no ordinary strength of intellect. This is indicated by such written documents as were left by him, and the concurrent testimony of those who knew and still survive him. He was much devoted to reading, and his attainments were by no means inconsiderable. Especially on theological subjects was his knowledge enlarged and profound. As a public speaker, Elder Semple thus describes him :— " His talents, if not equal to any, were certainly very little inferior to those of the first grade. His appearance in the pulpit was noble and majestic, yet humble and affectionate. In the beginning of his discourses, he was doctrinal and somewhat methodical; often very deep, even to the astonishment of his hearers—towards the close, and indeed sometimes throughout his sermon, he was exceedingly animated. His exhortations were often incomparable."

From the Minutes of Associations to which he belonged, and other sources, it appears that, in his religious sentiments, he was a moderate Calvinist. It is intimated by some who knew him that he was favourable to Open Communion. If this were his sentiment, it was not carried into practice. Nor did he fail, on all suitable occasions, to vindicate the exclusive propriety of Believers' Baptism. Mr. Patillo, a Presbyterian minister of some celebrity, having preached in his vicinity a discourse on the subject of Baptism, a reply of considerable merit was prepared by Mr. Williams. This reply he intended to put to the press, had the discourse itself been published. A brief extract from the preface will indicate the spirit with which the work was undertaken :—" I hope I have sufficiently demonstrated to my countrymen, for a series of years, that I am not overbearing on others, or bigotted to those of my principles which are not essential to salvation. I have universally endeavoured to promote a catholic spirit, with peace and concord, in the Israel of God. But, nevertheless, I am set for the defence of the Gospel ; and, as such, circumstances often occur, that require me to contend for the faith and order of Christ's Church."

Mr. Williams laboured diligently, wherever he had opportunity, for the salvation of souls ; and his heart was set upon the promotion of the great interests of the Redeemer's Kingdom. Immediately previous to the Declaration of Independence, while the American army were encamped in the lower part of Virginia, permission to preach to the soldiers was obtained from the Legislature, and he gladly engaged in the work. Had he lived in the present day, none can question that he would heartily unite in those efforts which are intended to send among the nations the unsearchable riches of Christ.

Elder Williams was not permitted to live to old age. A quotation from Elder Semple will give all the particulars, which may be interesting, in respect to the latter part of his days :—" Being very corpulent, at an Association in 1793, he accidentally fell by the turning of a step, as he was passing out, of a door, and became, for a year or two, a cripple, being under the necessity of going on crutches. Notwithstanding this, he would still go in a carriage to the meeting, and preach, sitting in a chair in the pulpit. During several of the last years of his life, he was afflicted with a very painful disease. Under his severe suffering he was not only patient, but, when he could have any mitigation of his pain, he was also cheerful. About ten days before his death, he was attacked by a pleurisy, from which no medicine could give him relief. His work was finished, and, April 30th, 1795, he fell asleep.

" Nothing very remarkable occurred in connection with the closing scene. He told his wife that it was a matter of indifference with him whether he lived or died: he had committed this to God, who would do right. He said he felt some anxiety for his numerous family ; but that these also he was willing to trust in the hands of a Gracious Providence."

In January, 1768, Elder Williams was married to Miss Frances Hughes, of Powhattan county, by whom he had fourteen children ; of whom eleven were living at the time of his death ; and, of these, four professed religion and were baptized.

I am, dear Sir, very truly yours,

JAMES B. TAYLOR.

CHARLES THOMPSON.
1770—1803.

FROM THE REV. ABIAL FISHER, D. D.

WEST BOYLSTON, Mass., March 24, 1859.

My dear Sir: Of the Rev. Charles Thompson, the subject of your inquiry, I had all the opportunities of information that could be furnished by my having the pastoral charge, for several years, of the same church which he served, having access to both the Town and Church Records, and being in intimate relations with his descendants and many others who had personal knowledge of him. You may, therefore, rely upon the statements which I am about to make concerning him as perfectly authentic.

CHARLES THOMPSON was born in Amwell, N. J., April 14, 1748. As Dr. Manning came from New Jersey, and commenced the College at Warren, R. I., which is now Brown University at Providence, Mr. Thompson came with him, or soon after him, for the purpose of obtaining an education. He was a member of the first class in that institution, graduating in 1769, and delivering the Valedictory Oration. Before he graduated, he had commenced preaching, and in the autumn of 1770 was called to preach at Warren as a candidate for settlement. In March following, he received a call to become the Pastor of that church, and, having accepted it, was, in due time, inducted into the pastoral office. He continued, for some time, to discharge his duties in this relation, much to the satisfaction of his people. But, early in the War of the Revolution, he was appointed a Chaplain in the American army, and continued to hold the place for about three years. At the time of the burning of the meeting-house in Warren, by the British soldiery, he was there with his family, who, until that time, had made Warren their home. He was taken and carried to Newport, and confined there in a guard-ship, from which he was released in about a month, but by what means he never knew. After this, he removed his family to Ashford, Conn., where they remained for some time, and meanwhile he was occupied in preaching at Pomfret, and other places in that neighbourhood. The First Baptist Church in Swansea, Mass.,—only three miles from Warren, where he had been previously settled, being now vacant, invited him to become their Pastor; and he accepted the call, and entered upon his labours there in the fall of 1779. The Church at Warren having been broken up and scattered by the burning of their meeting-house and parsonage, and the destruction of much of their property, and being unable, in consequence, to maintain public worship by themselves, proposed to unite with the people of Swansea in supporting their minister, and enjoying the benefit of his labours—and their proposal was acceded to. Mr. Thompson's preaching here was attended with a manifest blessing, almost immediately, so that, within a few months, seventy-five persons were baptized and added to the Church. About 1789, there was another extensive revival, which brought into the church about fifty new members; and in 1801, another, of still greater extent, that resulted in the admission to the church of about one hundred.

After a ministry of twenty-three years in Swansea, Mr. Thompson found his support so scanty that he felt obliged to ask for the dissolution of his pastoral relation. He accepted an invitation to settle in Charlton, Worcester County, Mass., in the beginning of 1803, with every prospect of a comfort-able support and a useful ministry. But, even before his removal to Charlton, he was attacked with hemorrhage of the lungs, which proved the harbinger of a rapid consumption, that terminated his life on the 4th of May following. He died in the full confidence of passing to a better world.

Mr. Thompson was tall, spare, and of a fine figure. The expression of his countenance was indicative at once of a vigorous intellect, and an amiable disposition. He placed a high value upon time, and improved all his hours to good purpose. In his family, and in the church, he was a model at once of kindness and firmness. As a preacher he held a very high rank. He had a voice of great compass, and its tones were at once sweet and commanding. He had great depth and tenderness of feeling, and often wept with his people, while he occasionally addressed them in a voice of thunder. His sermons were carefully studied, and sometimes written, but his manuscript was never seen in the pulpit, and his language was generally such as was supplied to him at the moment. He had a deep sense of his responsi-bility, and feared not to proclaim, in all fidelity, the whole counsel of God.

For several years, Mr. Thompson received young men under his care, with a view to direct their education. He was fully master of every thing he attempted to teach. Indeed he may be regarded as having been an accomplished scholar, as well as a devout Christian, and an able and suc-cessful preacher. When he died, it might well be said,—" A great man is fallen in Israel."   Very faithfully yours,

                                                    ABIAL FISHER.

SAMUEL SHEPARD, M. D.*
1770—1815.

SAMUEL SHEPARD was born in Salisbury, Mass., on the 22d of June, 1739. His father, Israel Shepard, was born in England, in 1685. After he went to reside in Salisbury, he was married to Mary True, and they became the parents of ten children, the youngest of whom was the subject of this sketch.

His intellect, in its earliest developments, showed a much more than ordinary degree of strength; and his power of committing to memory was almost unrivalled. When a mere lad, he was stationed in a watch-tower, in the neighbourhood, to report the approach of the Indians. His father's house stood on the main road, leading from Newburyport to Portsmouth,— two miles from the mouth of the Merrimack. That point of land, on the East side of the river, was in those days a favourite resort for the Indians, and said to be visited occasionally, even to this day, by a remnant of the Penobscot tribe.

At the age of sixteen, he was employed as a clerk in a store at South Hampton, N. H., and, soon after, taught a school in the same place. He studied Medicine, and settled as a practising physician at Brentwood, N. H., where he soon became distinguished in his profession. A Miss Rachel Thurber, an excellent and zealous Baptist lady, who resided in the neigh-bourhood,—having removed thither, some years before, from Rehoboth, Mass.,—had distributed among the families of her acquaintance a consid-erable number of copies of Norcott's work on Baptism; and one of these happened to fall into the hands of Dr. Shepard at the house of one of his patients. On glancing at it casually, he was induced to read it through; and the result was that, though he had always been a Congregationalist, he adopted heartily the views which this book maintained, and became a decided Baptist. In June, 1770, he was baptized by the Rev. Hezekiah Smith, of Haverhill, and, shortly after, began to preach. On the 18th of July following, he, with thirteen others, united to form a Baptist Church in Stratham. On the 2d of May, 1771, another church, consisting of thirteen members, was constituted at Brentwood; and, on the next day, another still, consisting of sixteen members, at Nottingham. These three churches unitedly called Dr. Shepard to become their Pastor. He accepted the call, and was ordained at Stratham, on the 25th of September, 1771; on which occasion Dr. Stillman of Boston preached, Dr. Smith of Haver-hill gave the Charge, and Dr. Manning of Providence, the Right Hand of Fellowship.

Dr. Shepard was, until the time of his death, one of the most active and honoured ministers of his denomination. He had not only an uncommonly vigorous mind, but great power of physical endurance, and his labours were so widely extended that he might almost be said to have lived the life of an itinerant. And, in addition to his duties as a minister, he con-

---

* Benedict's Hist. Bapt., I.—MSS. from Rev. Dr. E. E. Cummings and Mrs. U. S. Riddle.

tinued his practice, to some extent, as a physician; as his medical skill was so highly appreciated that the community in which he lived were not willing to dispense with his services in that capacity. The following letter, which he addressed to the Rev. Isaac Backus, in 1781, furnishes some idea of the extent of his early labours :—

"I rejoice, Sir, to hear that, in the midst of judgment, God is remembering mercy, and calling in his elect from East to West. You have refreshed my mind with good news from the West and South, and, in return, I will inform you of good news from the North and East. Some hundreds of souls are hopefully converted in the counties of Rockingham, Strafford, and Grafton, in New Hampshire, within a year past. In the last journey I made before my beloved wife was taken from me, I baptized seventy-two men, women, and some that may properly be called children, who confessed with their mouths the salvation God had wrought in their hearts, to good satisfaction. Meredith, in Strafford, has a church gathered the year past, consisting of between sixty and seventy members. I baptized forty-three, in that town, in one day, and such a solemn weeping of the multitude on the shore I never before saw. The ordinance of Baptism appeared to carry universal conviction through them, even to a man. The wife, when she saw her husband going forward, began to weep, to think she was not worthy to go with him; in like manner, the husband the wife, the parent the child, the children the parent; that the lamentation and weeping methinks may be compared to the inhabitants of Hadadrimmon, in the Valley of Maegiddon. Canterbury, in Rockingham County, has two Baptist Churches, gathered in the year past: one in the parish of Northfield—the number I cannot tell, but it is considerably large. I baptized thirty-one there, and a number have been baptized since by others. The other is in the parish of Loudon, in said Canterbury, containing above one hundred members. Another church, of about fifty members, is gathered in Chichester; another in Bennington, consisting of a goodly number, and one in Hubbardston,—all three in Strafford County. Two churches in Grafton County,—one in Holderness, the other in Rumney. The church in Rumney had one Haines* ordained last August, much to the satisfaction of the people. All these seven churches have been gathered, in about a year past. One church was gathered last fall in Wells, over which Brother Nathaniel Lord,† late of Berwick, is ordained. There appears to be a general increase of the Baptist principles, through all the Eastern parts of New England."

We find the following notice of Dr Shepard in the Life of Governor Plummer :—

"In 1777, by the influence of the labours of Dr. Shepard, a flourishing church was gathered at Epping. Governor Plummer's father had joined this church, and his son attended this meeting. In less than seven years after Dr. Shepard's ordination, his church had become the largest ever collected under one Pastor in New England. He had a meeting-house built in Epping, Brentwood, and Stratham, and preached successively in each. Through a wide spread region of country, he was followed and admired by a multitude, and everywhere revivals and conversions attested the power of his preaching. Among others, Governor Plummer, then in his twentieth year, attended these meetings, and became a convert. He was baptized by Dr. Shepard in May, 1779, in company with twenty others, in the river, at Nottingham."

Dr. Shepard's plan of church extension was to furnish branch churches to the one of which he was the Pastor. These branches were supplied with ministers; but Brentwood was their Jerusalem to which they used frequently to repair. There Dr. Shepard resided, like a Bishop in the midst of his Diocese. In his active days, he was accustomed to visit all these churches, making a circuit of about two hundred miles; and they all looked up to him with grateful and reverential regard. The general spirit with which he prosecuted his work, may be inferred from the following extract from a manuscript record of his views and feelings, made by himself, about five years before his death :—

* Cotton Haines, who was not long after ejected from the fellowship of the Baptists.
† Nathaniel Lord was born in 1754; was ordained Pastor of the Church in Wells, Me., in 1780; resigned his charge, and became Pastor of the Second Church in Berwick, Me., in 1804; and died in 1832. He was a devoted minister, and rendered important service to the Baptist denomination in Maine, especially at an early period.

"I have thought my work, for about thirty-five years past, has been to warn sinners to flee from the wrath to come; to alarm those who are at ease in Zion, and dwell in their ceiled houses, shunning the Cross of Christ, holding a form of godliness and denying the power; and to endeavour to feed those who appeared to be the sheep and lambs of Christ, with the sincere milk of the word, according to my ability. My work has often been my wages. It has at times been in my mouth sweet as honey, and bitter as gall in my belly. Persecutions and trials have awaited me many years; but, through all these things, I have been supported thus far. But alas, such is my ignorance, I am at times fearful to proceed, lest I should darken counsel with words without knowledge, or should give the Ark of the Covenant a wrong touch. The truth contained in the Scriptures is the key of true knowledge, which reveals the settled counsel of God, the only foundation of hope."

Dr. Shepard died at Brentwood, on the 4th of November, 1815, aged seventy-seven years.

The following is a list of Dr. Shepard's publications:—A Scriptural Inquiry respecting the Ordinance of Water Baptism. A Reply to several Answers, in defence of this Inquiry. A Scriptural Inquiry concerning what the Friends or Quakers call Spiritual Baptism; being an Answer to a work published by Moses Brown, of Providence, R. I. The Principle of Universal Salvation examined and tried by the Law and the Testimony. An Examination of Elias Smith's two Pamphlets, respecting Original Sin, the Death Adam was to die the day he eat of the Forbidden Fruit, and the Final Annihilation of the Wicked.

The following anecdotes have been communicated to me by Mrs. Riddle, a grand-daughter of Dr. Shepard, as illustrative of some of his characteristics:—

"He used to tell a story which he was accustomed to apply to men who attempted to dodge difficulties by assuming neutral ground. He said that a certain farmer was in the habit of riding on the tongue of the cart as a place of safety,—being out of the way of both the cart and oxen. This was all very well till the team came to a rough piece of ground, when the oxen became restive, kicked the farmer off, and the wheels ran over him.

"On a visit he made at Meredith, at a certain time, he baptized forty-four persons in one day, and preached from the words—'Wilt thou go?'—which Isaac's servant addressed to Rebecca, to persuade her to become his master's wife. As he was approaching the close of the sermon, he began to apply the subject, with great earnestness and pathos, to the impenitent portion of his audience, and, as he uttered the words of his text—'Wilt thou go?'—in a most expostulatory tone, a man in the congregation, believing himself converted at the moment, arose and said,—'Yes, I will go.' The preacher instantly closed the book and sat down. On being asked why he so abruptly terminated his discourse, his reply was,—'Why the match was made.'

"He was a man of extraordinary presence, and could, almost by a look, exert great power over other minds. On one occasion, he was called to visit a suffering woman, a member of his church, whose husband, wealthy but penurious, did not allow his family necessary comforts. After calling for different things, and being told there were none in the house, Dr. Shepard rose upon his feet, indignantly stamped upon the floor, and said,— 'Mr,—do you go at once and tackle your horse, and purchase the articles, and a tea-kettle.' The man started, as if electrified with terror, and obeyed the command, to the great comfort of his sick wife.

"The Rev. Elias Smith, when he was quite a young man, paid a visit to Dr. Shepard, at Brentwood, of which he gives the following account :— 'He received us kindly—so we tarried with him over night. He was naturally a cheerful man, and, after we had partaken of his hospitality, he told a story, which he wished me always to remember, lest I should be too much lifted up, on account of the notice taken of me by the brethren and elders. He said that a certain Indian, having to cross a river in his canoe, thought to save the labour of paddling, by raising a large bush in the bow of his boat. When launched upon the tide, the wind blew so hard that it upset the canoe, and he was obliged to reach the shore by swimming, while his boat floated down the stream. People saw his difficulty, and asked him, after he had reached the land, why he did not come in his canoe, instead of swimming to the shore. 'Oh, said the Indian, 'me carry too much bush.' 'Now,' said Dr. Shepard, 'you are young, and just set out in the world, and you will do well, if you do not carry too much bush.'"

Dr. Shepard, according to the testimony of those who remember him in his later years, was a large and well proportioned man, with dark eyes and flowing locks, and a mild yet commanding expression of countenance.

He was married three times, and had fifteen children, several of whom have occupied important posts of usefulness. His first wife was Elizabeth Hill, of Portsmouth, N. H.; his second was Ursula Pinkham, of Madbury, N. H.; and his third, Mrs. Lydia Thacher, of Concord, Mass.

EDMUND BOTSFORD.*

1771—1819.

EDMUND BOTSFORD was born at Woburn, Bedfordshire, England, in the year 1745. At the age of seven years, he had lost both his father and his mother; though the lack of parental guardianship was very happily supplied by his being placed under the care of an excellent aunt, who sent him to board with a lady, an intimate friend of his mother, with whom he attended a Baptist meeting. At this early age, he was frequently the subject of strong religious impressions, which were occasioned or deepened by reading Bunyan's works, and other serious books, and especially by a remarkable dream which he had in his eighth or ninth year.

After this, however, he lost his interest in religious things, and became irregular in his habits, so that his friends well-nigh despaired of both his respectability and usefulness. He wished to go to sea, but, not having the opportunity, he enlisted as a common soldier; and, in this capacity, was

* Georg. Bapt.—MS. from Rev. Dr. Mallary.

subjected to many perilous adventures and severe hardships. At the age of twenty, he sailed for Charleston, S. C., where he arrived in January, 1766.

Finding himself now a stranger in a strange land, and having to encounter some serious difficulties in his new situation, his early religious impressions began to return upon him, and at length his distress became so great as to attract the notice of the members of the family in which he lived. At the suggestion of one of them, he went, on a certain Sabbath, to hear the Rev. Oliver Hart, an excellent Baptist minister, of Charleston; and it was under his faithful preaching, as he believed, that he first obtained spiritual light, and was enabled to devote himself to the service and glory of God. He was baptized on the 13th of March, 1767.

After continuing, for some time, in secular pursuits, Mr. Botsford became impressed with the idea that he was called to devote himself to the Gospel ministry; and, accordingly, he was licensed to preach by the Baptist Church in Charleston, in February, 1771. His immediate preparation for the ministry was made under the direction of his Pastor, the Rev. Mr. Hart. In referring to the commencement of his ministry, in connection with some previous events of his life, he says,—"So I have been groom, footman, painter, carpenter, and soldier, and have now commenced preacher."

Mr. Botsford continued with Mr. Hart till the following June, when, having been presented by some of his friends with necessary clothing, together with a horse, saddle, and bridle, he left Charleston, and travelled to Eutaw, where he remained with the Rev. Mr. Pelot till the end of July. There were a few Baptists, constituting a branch of the Eutaw Church, and residing near Tuckaseeking,—a settlement about forty miles from Savannah, Ga., whose minister, the Rev. Mr. Stirk,* had then recently died; and, hearing of Mr. Botsford, they invited him to come over and help them. He accepted their invitation, and preached his first sermon to them on the 27th of June, 1771. His labours were highly acceptable, and he agreed to remain with them one year. He did not, however, confine his ministry to this place, but preached extensively in contiguous regions, both in Georgia and South Carolina.

In 1772, he enlarged still more the field of his labours, travelling and preaching almost incessantly. He visited Augusta, Kiokee, and several other places on the frontiers of Georgia and South Carolina. At the close of this year, he concluded to leave Tuckaseeking, and preached his Farewell Sermon, though he continued, for some time after, to favour the neighbourhood with his occasional services.

* BENJAMIN STIRK was a native of Leeds, Yorkshire, England. He was taken by Mr. Whitefield under his patronage, and was employed by him, in some capacity, at his Orphan House, in Georgia, as early as 1760. He was educated a Presbyterian, but became a Baptist in 1763. He remained at the Orphan House about four years after this, and then, in consequence of his marriage, removed to a plantation in the neighbourhood of Goshen, about eighteen miles from Savannah. As there was no Baptist church in that vicinity, he united with the Church at Eutaw, S. C., distant from his residence about twenty-five miles. He soon commenced preaching,—holding one meeting in his own house, and another at Tuckaseeking, and occasionally officiating at Eutaw. As he was on his way to the latter place, he fell from his horse into the water, and received an injury, of which, after languishing for some time, he died in 1770. He was a man of good talents, and considerable cultivation, and was especially distinguished for his piety and zeal. He was a benefactor of Rhode Island College.

The Church in Charleston, hearing of the success of Mr. Botsford's ministry, determined to call him to ordination. He was, accordingly, ordained on the 14th of March, 1773,—Oliver Hart and Francis Pelot officiating on the occasion. He began to administer the ordinance of Baptism, shortly after, and, by the middle of November following, had baptized forty-five. He travelled so much, during this year, that, he says, "some used to call me the flying preacher."

For some time after he left Tuckaseeking, he seems to have had no particular place of residence; but, in May, 1774, he purchased some land, and built him a house on Brier Creek, in Burke County, Ga. About this time, he received between three and four hundred pounds sterling from the estate of his brother in England, recently deceased, which enabled him to live comfortably, though he had but a poor compensation for his services as a minister. From this place he sallied forth in various directions, preaching the Gospel with great fervour and success through the whole surrounding country.

Mr. Botsford continued to be thus employed till the spring of 1779, when he was driven from his home, and from the State, by the horrors of the Revolutionary War. Such was the haste in which they were compelled to make their escape, that they were only able to take with them two horses and a cart, containing a bed, a blanket, and a sheet. The property which he had received, a short time before, from his brother's estate, was all sacrificed in his precipitate flight. He was, for a while, a Chaplain in the army, but at what period of the Revolution does not appear.

On leaving his home in Georgia, he directed his course to Virginia, and for some time laboured in different places in that State with much acceptance. Early in the year 1782, he accepted a call to the pastoral charge of the West Neck Church, in South Carolina, which he had previously served as a temporary supply; and he took up his residence near the Pedee, on a tract of land presented to him by a generous friend, and in a dwelling erected for him by the church. He retained his connection with this church about fifteen years, and was the means of gathering in a considerable number to its membership. Whilst residing on the Pedee, during several successive years, he visited the city of Charleston, and, by his zealous and timely labours, was instrumental in reviving there the Baptist interest, which had become much weakened and depressed by the trying events of the Revolutionary War. During his visit to Charleston, in 1785, he commenced the practice of preaching to children, and continued it in his subsequent visits, until the church was supplied with a stated Pastor. Several of these children afterwards became hopeful subjects of a spiritual renovation, and exemplary members of the Baptist Church.

In February, 1797, Mr. Botsford removed to Georgetown, S. C., and took the oversight of the Baptist church in that place, where he remained, the object of peculiar respect and affection, as long as he lived.

During the last fifteen or sixteen years of his life, Mr. Botsford suffered much from bodily disease. His principal complaint was an affection of the nerves, called 'Tic-Douloureux,' which, though seated principally in one side of his head, subjected his whole frame to the most distressing paroxysms, varying in duration from half a minute to several minutes. In whatever position he was when they seized him, he became fixed as a statue, and remained so till they passed off. Sometimes, for weeks at a time, they recurred in quick succession, rendering it difficult for him to eat, drink or sleep; and so slight a movement as some particular contraction of the lip, would sometimes appear to bring them on. "He was," says one of his particular friends, "a kind and affectionate preacher, and when engaged in his subject, used considerable action. Many, many times have I seen him, when preaching, seized with one of those dreadful paroxysms, when his hand was up or extended, and his head stretched forward with earnestness; and there he would stand till it passed off,—the only perceptible movement a sudden start, extending or lifting the hand a little. He became so accustomed to the agony that it did not disturb his train of thought, and he would resume the discourse where he had been stopped. I have known him thus arrested several times in one exercise; but he would not withhold his hand as long as he could speak." In a letter to a Christian brother, Mr. Botsford thus alludes to one of these attacks:— "Last Lord's day, in the midst of my discourse, I was struck so violently that I was obliged to desist from speaking, and could not, for some minutes, dismiss the congregation, who were all attention. Who knows but some sudden stroke may unawares send me to Heaven! Surely I ought to live each day looking for my change."

This terrible disease continued to prey upon his constitution till it terminated in death. He died at Georgetown, on the 25th of December, 1819, in the seventy-fifth year of his age. His Funeral Sermon was preached by the Rev. Dr. Furman of Charleston.

Mr. Botsford rendered good service to the cause of religion with his pen. His principal production was The Spiritual Voyage,—an Allegory in which the Christian's life, embracing his various trials, conflicts, comforts, victories, &c., are happily illustrated under the similitude of a sea-voyage. This little work has passed through many editions, and is embraced in the list of books issued by the American Baptist Publication Society, at Philadelphia. He also published Sambo and Toney: A Dialogue between two Servants. Republished by the American Tract Society.

Mr. Botsford was married four times. In 1773, he was married in Augusta, Ga., to Susanna Nun, who was a native of Cork, Ireland, but had lived in America from her childhood. She died March 9, 1790, aged thirty-nine years. By this marriage he had six living children—Mary, the eldest daughter, was married to the late Thomas Park, LL. D., for many years Professor of the Learned Languages in South Carolina College, and died in 1828, in the fifty-fourth year of her age. In 1791, he was married to his second wife, who was a Mrs. Catharine Evans, and who died in 1796. By this marriage he had one daughter, who is still living, (1858,) a pious and honoured widow in South Carolina. In 1799, he was married to his third wife, Mrs. Ann Deliesseline, by whom he had two children— she died in 1801. In December, 1803, he was married to his fourth wife, Mrs. Hannah Goff, who survived her husband a few years, and perished, with several others, in a terrible storm, which raged along the sea coast in Georgia, in or about the year 1822.

FROM THE REV. CHARLES D. MALLARY, D. D.

ALBANY, Ga., November 18, 1857.

Rev. and Dear Sir: I had the pleasure of receiving your recent communication, in which you express a desire that I should furnish something that may aid you in illustrating the character of the Rev. Edmund Botsford. I will endeavour to comply with your request. As he died several years before I came to the South to reside, I had not the privilege of a personal acquaintance with him, and never so much as saw him; but the recollections of one of his granddaughters, who was my first wife, and that of several other relatives and intimate friends, together with the use with which I was favoured of his manuscripts and most of his private correspondence, when, some twenty-six years ago, I prepared a Memoir of his life, supplied me with pretty ample means of forming a just estimate of his character. I think I knew him well. He was one of the Fathers of the Baptist denomination in the Southern States, and was truly an admirable character. Though not a person of great genius or extensive learning, yet he was a man of such sterling integrity and worth; so rich in the experience of Divine things; he passed through such a variety of interesting scenes, and aided so considerably in nourishing the infant cause of piety in our land, that he deserves to be held in lasting remembrance.

He possessed an active mind, warm affections, sanguine temperament, and fine social qualities. In conversation he was animated and instructive: he had at his command a rich fund of anecdote, and his manner of narrating events was peculiarly happy. There was about him a touch of English bluntness, so blended, however, with hearty, unaffected kindness, as to produce pleasure rather than dislike. His personal appearance was in his favour: he was, if I rightly remember what was said of him, of medium size and stature, (perhaps slightly less as to stature,) erect in his carriage, active in his movements, and neat in his apparel. He lived in the days of short pantaloons and silver knee-buckles; and I think I have heard it said that his appearance, in the antique costume of those times, was quite agreeable.

He was a man of unquestioned piety. His long life of useful and self-denying labours; his ardent love for souls and the Kingdom of Christ; his peculiar attachment to the Word of God, and his habitual conformity to its Divine requirements; his patient acquiescence in the will of God in times of severe bereavement and suffering; the savoury Christian sentiments which adorned his conversation, and breathed sweetly through his epistolary correspondence; all went to show that he was truly a man of God, endowed, in no ordinary measure, with the graces of the Holy Spirit. In his last days, he was quite remarkable for his habit of devotion. Suffering much from protracted illness, he used to pass many sleepless nights, and many solitary days, in which he could neither read nor write. On such occasions he would spend whole hours in prayer for his friends, presenting their cases separately and minutely to the Throne of Grace; and these devout exercises greatly refreshed his own soul.

He had a certain nobleness of spirit and bearing, which one could not easily overlook. He once said of himself, and no doubt truly,—"I do not remember ever to have considered myself poor, even when I had not a half-penny in the world. I somehow thought myself a gentleman born; and whether I had money or not, I had much the same feeling; yet I do not remember that I ever despised any body, except for base actions."

Mr. Botsford had a great aversion to every thing like impertinent curiosity. If he could have found out any thing relating even to one inimical to him, by questioning a youth, a servant, or any one; or by glancing at an open letter which might be thrown in his way; it would not even have occurred to him to avail himself of any such opportunity. "Guard," says he, "against inquiring into family secrets."

Though he was often straitened in his pecuniary affairs, he seems to have maintained an habitual confidence in God's providential care. "I do not remember," says he, "that I was ever in my life the least uneasy in respect to my poverty. I never knew what it was to be afraid of coming to want, and I do not remember ever being but one whole day without food: that was in Scotland. Distrusting Providence for food and raiment is a sin I have not to account for, either when single or married."

He was never corrupted by the love of money. "He had less of covetousness in his disposition," says a friend, who knew him well, "than almost any man I ever knew." He was often generous beyond his means. When he had but a penny in the world, he would give a beggar half. He would never see a person in distress without relieving him, if in his power. He seldom, if ever, shed tears, when receiving benefactions from others, but he frequently did so, when giving to the poor.

He was faithful in his reproofs, and had a happy talent of reminding his brethren of their faults in a way the least likely to give offence. To a young Christian brother he thus writes:—"When I think or hear of your doing wrong, I will scold you; and if you do not like it, I will give you up a while, and let out at you again. You shall hear of your faults from me as long as I live." And yet he as freely and honestly invited the reproofs of others. "Do, my brother," says he to a pious friend, "pray for me, and do not spare me in any point, where you think a hint will be of service. I promise you I will receive it kindly, and try to benefit by it." That same brother had occasion to reprove him for unbecoming lightness of conduct; and what a noble Christian response the admonition drew from him:—"I forget if I ever returned you thanks for the hint—if not, I do now most sincerely; and, at the same time, beg you will, my brother, for my sake, but more especially for the sake of the cause of God, continue to use freedom with me." And more than twenty years afterwards, and but a short time before his death, he calls up the circumstance again, with grateful emotions:—"Many a time your brotherly admonition has met me full in the face; yes, my brother, to this day I feel thankful to you and to God for it."

During Mr. Botsford's ministry, much preaching was done in open fields and in forests. Ministers were not over nice about their pulpits. It is said that, on one occasion, Mr. Botsford ascended a barrel, and when he had made some progress in his sermon, either in consequence of some radical defect in the barrel, or the vehement emphasis of the foot, (an oratorical embellishment which some of our zealous fathers well understood,) all at once the head of the barrel gave way, and the preacher went down with it. It does not appear, however, that he was diverted from his upright posture, or that the misfortune essentially deranged the thread of his discourse.

I may mention in this connection another somewhat ludicrous incident that occurred, (perhaps about the period of the Revolution,) while Mr. Botsford was preaching. The congregation was assembled in a grove, or perhaps an open field. During the progress of the sermon, one of the distant outside hearers became quite drowsy. At length he began to nod. A large surly goat, that was nibbling grass hard by, happened to notice the sleeper; and interpreted the nodding of his head as a challenge for battle. There was no flinching in his goatish nature; and, after having gone through the usual preliminaries of advancing and receding a few times,—the nodder continuing to repeat the challenge,—he at length darted forward with fury and laid the sleeper low. Many of the congregation smiled; and the preacher who was so situated as to be obliged to witness the whole transaction, could not find it in his heart to reprove them. It was one of those incidents that sometimes occur, reminding us how intimately the indescribably ludicrous is occasionally blended with the solemn and sacred, and that whilst many things are providentially permitted for the special trial of the Christian's faith, other things are permitted, as it might seem, for the special trial of the Christian's gravity.

Mr. Botsford frequently used notes in preaching,—sometimes pretty copious ones. But he was never a *reader* of sermons. Referring to some of his young brethren, who were in the habit of reading their discourses, he thus writes to a friend:—"It surely never was the design of our Master that his servants should *read* the Gospel, when he said 'Go, preach.' Do you say, Dr. Stillman writes all his sermons? But Dr. Stillman does not read his sermons. I mean not to object against writing, but reading. I hope you will use your influence to persuade young gentlemen to lay aside their crutches by degrees." At a certain time, however, it appears that Mr. Botsford himself depended too much upon his crutches, and thereby subjected himself to some little disappointment and mortification. He had prepared himself "handsomely," as he thought, for an Education Sermon. When the day arrived, the weather was rainy; the man whose business it was to raise the tunes did not come; and at this he was a little damped. After reaching the pulpit, he found that he had left his spectacles at home: he sent his son for them, and in the mean time commenced by prayer. When his son returned, he had brought the wrong spectacles. He was now in a sad dilemma—however, he made out to read his text, (Gal. vi. 10,) hobbled along as well as he could, sweating profusely, and his heart in dreadful palpitation. He was glad when he was done, and wound up by saying what he thought was the best thing he had said that day—"I am sorry, truly sorry, so good an institution has not a better advocate." "Is it not a shame," he says, when referring to the incident, "an old soldier should be so foiled? What a poor, worthless, proud, ignorant wretch am I!"

Mr. Botsford sustained a very interesting and endeared relation to some of the most excellent and useful men of the denomination. The Rev. Oliver Hart, of precious memory, was his spiritual father; that truly wise, godly, and eminent servant of Jesus Christ, the late Richard Furman, was one of his bosom counsellors and friends; and the Rev. William B. Johnson, still living in South Carolina, honoured for his years, wisdom, and useful service, was in a sense a spiritual son, for whose happiness he felt a most intense and affectionate interest. Some of his letters addressed to Mr. Johnson, when an irreligious young man, and also subsequent to his conversion and entrance upon the Christian ministry, are amongst the most faithful and interesting letters of the kind that I have ever met with.

And this naturally leads me to speak of one of Mr. Botsford's striking and useful gifts,—the talent for letter-writing. His letters were indeed truly charming;—simple, easy, picturesque, pious, abounding, as occasion required, with pungent appeals, faithful reproofs, paternal counsel, scriptural instruction, and the most tender condolence. His kind native bluntness was pretty sure of a place, often mingled with a touch of chastened wit and playful humour. Whilst preparing the sketch of Mr. Botsford's life, already alluded to, I had an opportunity of knowing with what great care his letters were preserved by surviving acquaintances, as precious, fragrant memorials of his affectionate and faithful friendship.

I must not omit to say that this excellent man took a lively interest in the instruction of the coloured people. Besides composing a little book adapted to their condition, he took much pains to instruct them from the pulpit in discourses suited to their capacity, and also in private conversation. "I was once told," said he, "You are a pretty good negro preacher. I suppose the meaning was, preacher *to* negroes. Really were my labours blessed to them, I should feel thankful, and could be well content to preach wholly to them."

But I must close my communication,—already extended to an unreasonable length. I will only add that the Sermon, preached by Dr. Furman on the occasion of Mr. Botsford's death, contains an estimate of his character that fully justifies all the praise I have bestowed upon him.

I remain yours, dear Sir,
With sentiments of Christian respect and affection,
C. D. MALLARY.

WILLIAM ROGERS, D. D.*
1771—1824.

WILLIAM ROGERS, the second son of William and Sarah Rogers, was born in Newport, R. I., July 22, (O. S.) 1751. His parents were highly respectable persons, and worthy members of a Baptist Church in that town. They were careful to conduct the education of their son upon truly Christian principles. The effect of this was that his mind early became awake to the importance of religion, though it was not till he had reached the age of nineteen that he believed himself the subject of a radical spiritual change.

At the age of twelve, he was placed under the care of the Rev. Aaron Hutchinson, a Congregational minister of Grafton, Mass., with a view to fit for College. Having gone through his preparatory course, he joined the Freshman class in Rhode Island College, (then at Warren,) September, 1765, being only fourteen years of age. He was admitted to the degree of Bachelor of Arts in 1769. The next year, 1770, he made a public profession of religion, was baptized by the Rev. Gardiner Thurston, Pastor of the Second Baptist Church in Newport, and was received as a member of that church, by prayer and the imposition of hands. His reading from this time was chiefly on theological subjects, though he still indulged, to some extent, his taste for scientific studies. It does not appear at what time his purpose for entering the ministry was definitely formed; but, in August, 1771, he was called and licensed to preach, by the church of which he was a member. In December following, in consequence of earnest solicitations, he removed from Newport, where he was Principal of an Academy, to Philadelphia, and continued preaching on probation till March, 1772, when he received a unanimous call to take the charge of the Baptist Church in that city. He accepted the call, and was ordained on the 31st of May following. The Sermon on the occasion was preached by the Rev. Isaac Eaton, from the words—"And who is sufficient for these things?" It proved to be the last sermon that Mr. Eaton ever preached, while the text was the first upon which Mr. Rogers ever preached. He resigned his pastoral charge in March, 1775, but continued his labours among them, as a supply, till June following.

The General Assembly of Pennsylvania, having, in March, 1776, voted three battalions of foot for the defence of their Province, appointed Mr.

* Amer. Bapt. Mag., 1824.—MS. from Dr. Rogers' daughter, Miss Eliza J. Rogers.

Rogers to be the sole Chaplain of the said forces.   In June, 1778, he was promoted to a Brigade Chaplaincy in the Continental army, which office he continued to hold till June, 1781, when he retired from military service altogether.   About this time, he received invitations from three very important churches,—and what is somewhat remarkable, of as many different denominations,—in different parts of the country, to settle in the ministry; but he declined them all, choosing rather to supply destitute churches, as he might find occasion or opportunity, in the city and vicinity of Philadelphia.

In March, 1789, he was appointed Professor of English and Oratory in the College and Academy of Philadelphia; and, in April, 1792, was elected to the same office in the University of Pennsylvania.

In July, 1790, he was honoured with the degree of Doctor of Divinity by the University of Pennsylvania; having received the degree of Master of Arts from Yale College, in 1780, and from the College of New Jersey in 1786.

On the death of the Rev. Mr. Ustick, Pastor of the First Baptist Church in Philadelphia,—which occurred in April, 1803, he was invited to become the stated supply of the vacant pulpit.   This invitation he accepted, and continued his services there until February, 1805.

In January, 1812, he resigned his Professorship in the University of Pennsylvania, in consequence of some dissatisfaction with the proceedings of the Trustees.

In May, 1813, he received a call from the church in Newark, N. J., to become their Pastor; in consequence of which, he visited them, but finally declined the proffered settlement.

In 1816 and 1817, he was elected a member of the General Assembly of the State of Pennsylvania, by the county of Philadelphia, and served in that capacity.

His last years were spent in dignified retirement, and in the diligent cultivation of pious and devout feelings.   He died in Philadelphia, April 7, 1824, aged seventy-three years.   The First Baptist Church of Philadelphia, as a testimony of their regard and veneration, erected a handsome monument to his memory.

Dr. Rogers was connected with many of the important benevolent movements of his day.   In 1790, he was chosen one of the Vice Presidents of the Pennsylvania Society for promoting the Gradual Abolition of Slavery; in 1794, a member of the Maryland Society for the same object; in 1797, one of the Vice Presidents of the Philadelphia Society for alleviating the miseries of Public Prisons; in 1802, one of the Correspondents and Editors of the London Evangelical Magazine; in 1805, Chaplain to the Philadelphia Militia Legion; in 1816, Senior Chaplain of the New England Society of Philadelphia; in 1819, Vice President of the Religious Historical Society of Philadelphia, &c., &c.

The following is a list of Dr. Rogers' publications:—A Circular Letter on Justification, 1785; (reprinted in London, 1786.)   An Introductory Prayer at the request of the Pennsylvania Society of Cincinnati, 1787. An Oration at the request of the same Society, 1789.   A Sermon on the Death of the Rev. Oliver Hart, Hopewell, N. J., 1796.   An Introductory

Prayer, occasioned by the Death of General Washington, 1800. A Circular Letter on Christian Missions. Various Moral, Religious and Political Essays in newspapers and different magazines.

Dr. Rogers was married to Hannah Gardner, daughter of William Gardner of Philadelphia, June 29, 1773. They had four children,—all of them sons,—only one of whom lived to maturity. Mrs. Rogers died in Philadelphia, October 10, 1793, of Yellow Fever, at the age of forty. On the 15th of January, 1795, Dr. Rogers was married to Susannah Marsh, daughter of Joseph Marsh, of Philadelphia. By this marriage he had five children,—four daughters and one son. His widow, a lady highly distinguished for her accomplishments and virtues, died at Bristol, R. I., November 8, 1849, aged eighty-eight years. Two daughters only now (1858) survive.

Dr. Rogers was undoubtedly one of the most influential of the Baptist clergymen of his day in this country. He was in intimate relations with many of the prominent actors of the Revolution, as well as of the generation succeeding, and was also extensively known, and highly respected in Great Britain. Among his foreign correspondents he numbered such men as Rippon, Pearce, Carey, Marshman, &c. The late Albert Gallatin, shortly before his death, is said to have referred to his acquaintance with him with great pleasure, and to have expressed a very high estimate of his character and accomplishments.

FROM THE REV. DANIEL SHARP, D. D.

Boston, December 7, 1850.

Rev, and dear Sir: I regret my inability to give you such a sketch of the character of the late Rev. William Rogers, D. D., as might be due to him, and worthy of a place in your proposed work.

It is true I was a student in Theology, in Philadelphia, some forty-three years ago; but disparity of age, and some other circumstances, over which I had no control, prevented my acquaintance with him from becoming as intimate as might have been desirable to me.

Having mingled much in what is called good society, Dr. Rogers was much more than ordinarily refined in his manners and habits. There was something not only pleasant but highly venerable in his appearance. I have no doubt, from what I saw and heard of him, that he commanded the respect of all his acquaintance, and won the affection of those who were privileged to be near to him. I believe he was a person of a truly catholic spirit. Without surrendering his principles to any one, he had words of truth and kindness for all.

But it was (I have been told by one who well and tenderly knows) in the circle of his family that the light and beauty of his character shone in mildest and brightest radiance. He was almost worshipped, certainly he was greatly loved, reverenced and confided in, by his wife and children.

As he occupied a Professor's chair, in the University of Pennsylvania, and had no pastoral charge, I seldom heard him preach. But the following description of him, as a preacher, which was from the pen of one who knew him well, and esteemed him highly, I think you may receive as accurate:—

" As a Gospel Minister, his characteristics were of the best kind; for he was a *plain* preacher,—he exhibited the truth and taught it as he had received it of God. His style and language evinced this; for while he avoided commonplace and low phraseology, still, knowing the Gospel was designed for persons of every grade of intellectual capacity, he meant to be understood, and therefore presented Divine truth in such a style and manner as was acceptable to the hearer of taste and acquirement, and at the same time instructive to the plain unlettered Christian. In the best sense of the word, Dr. Rogers was a powerful preacher—he testified to the truth like a witness for God, being deeply impressed with its reality and importance. In his manner he was earnest, but not boisterous and declamatory; his cadence and emphasis belonged to his theme, and the richest evidence was exhibited that he believed and felt what he spake. Dr. Rogers was a *profitable* preacher. Systematic Theology had long engaged his attention; his subjects were well chosen, and his Sermons, clearly arranged and well digested, did not fail to interest the hearer; and, being a man of faith and prayer, and much in the habit of cherishing a sense of dependance on the Holy Spirit, his discourses were listened to by religious persons of different denominations with satisfaction and benefit. With an extensive knowledge of human nature, and a deep conviction of the original sin and depravity of man, he kept back nothing designedly, that might be profitable to his hearers. He knew when and how to point the artillery of Divine truth at the obdurate heart and stupid conscience of the sinner, and when, ' in strains as soft as angels use,' to proclaim peace to the awakened and anxious soul. He avoided a dry metaphysical mode of sermonizing on the one hand, and on the other that careless kind of preaching, which is connected with no thoughtfulness, no study, and no preparation for the duties of the pulpit. The feeling, spiritual, ardent and correct course was his choice; and, acquainted with the best helps, a great reader, and blessed with a retentive memory, it is not strange that attentive Christians retired from his preaching, edified, delighted and built up in the truths of our holy religion. He possessed the happy talent of exhibiting the essential truths of the Gospel with such clearness of illustration and scriptural connection, as to remove doubts from the mind of the anxious believer, when perplexed with the plausible and confident assertions of the advocates of popular errors, and, by showing the intimate and necessary connection between each doctrine of the Gospel and the whole scheme of grace, he was instrumental in leading many a wandering and doubting Christian back to the simplicity which they first found in Christ Jesus.

"It is proper to observe that Dr. Rogers was a highly *evangelical* preacher. What are called the doctrines of the Reformation, such as were believed and preached by a Watts, a Doddridge, and a multitude of able advocates of virtue and religion, were ably and constantly defended by him. The doctrines of repentance towards God and faith in Jesus Christ as the only Saviour, the necessity of the influences of the Holy Spirit to convince, enlighten and save, and the obligation of all men to believe the Gospel, formed the grand features of his preaching. It has been remarked by those most conversant with him, that, in illustrating these great and saving truths, more particularly towards the close of his long and useful life, he seemed to regain the ardour of youthful feeling; and the zeal and solemnity with which he spake of them, evinced that they were deeply rooted in his mind. But, notwithstanding his attachment to evangelical principles, Dr. Rogers was truly the *liberal Christian;* for he loved all good men; and, at one period of his life, he was invited, by churches of three different denominations, to settle in the ministry."

Hoping that this extract, in connection with what I have myself written, may give your readers a tolerably correct idea of the venerable man of whom you have asked my recollections, I am ever, my dear Sir,

Truly yours,

DANIEL SHARP.

JOB SEAMANS.*

1772—1830.

JOB SEAMANS was born at Rehoboth, Mass., on the 24th of May, 1748. His father, Charles Seamans, was a farmer; was born in the year 1700, and died at the age of seventy one, a highly esteemed Deacon of the Baptist Church in Sackville, in the Province of New Brunswick. His mother, Mrs. Hannah Seamans, died at the age of eighty-nine years, at the residence of her son, in New London, N. H., on the 19th of March, 1798. Both his parents were persons of an excellent religious character.

When he was about a year and a half old, his father sold his farm in Rehoboth, and purchased one in Swansea, in the same neighbourhood, where he lived until the son was about five years old. He then removed to Providence, R. I., where he remained about ten years, and, during the greater part of the time, this son attended school, though, owing to the incompetency or unfaithfulness of his teacher, he made but little improvement. The family then migrated to New Brunswick, and took up their residence in a place called Sackville, in the County of Cumberland, in that Province. Here the father carried on a farm; and his son Job became a labourer upon it. The young man seems to have been rather precocious in some of his developments. He took the lead among those who were considerably older than himself, in all scenes of gaiety and merriment; and, though his regard for the good opinion of his fellow-men kept him from gross vices, he had not the fear of God before his eyes to deter him from those sins which were tolerated by the more decent part of the community.

From early childhood, he remembered to have had, at times, fearful apprehensions of death and judgment: but that which first awakened his conscience in any high degree, was the reading of Robert Russell's Seven Sermons. In the summer of 1766, when he was eighteen years of age, one of his companions, who afterwards became a zealous preacher of the Gospel, was converted, and began at once publicly to exhort men to repent. An unusual attention to religion now commenced in the neighbourhood; but young Seamans looked upon it, not only without complacency, but with strong aversion; though he flattered himself that it was one of those New Light excitements that would quickly die away. As it continued, however, from summer to autumn and from autumn to winter, without any perceptible abatement, he began to feel considerable uneasiness; and, on listening one evening to a discourse from his young friend, already referred to, who had, by this time, become a preacher,—on the text,—"Incline your ear and come unto me, hear and your souls shall live,"—he became the subject of distressing convictions, and resolved that, thenceforward, he would make religion his chief concern; though he seems, at this time, to have had no just view of the Gospel plan of salvation. In August, 1767, from listening to the preaching of Elder Windsor, of Rhode Island, and to the

* Benedict's Hist. Bapt., I.—MS. from Dr. E. E. Cummings.

relation of the Christian experience of several of his young companions, he evidently gained a much deeper sense of his entire dependance on the grace of God, than he had had before. In this state of mind, he went to see the ordinance of Baptism administered to some of his youthful associates; though, from a deep feeling of unworthiness, he only followed at a distance, and was absorbed in meditation upon what seemed to him the hopelessness of his prospects. But, as he walked along under this fearful burden of anxiety and distress, he imagined that he saw, with his bodily eyes, the Saviour, in the act of being crucified for his redemption; but, though this scene overwhelmed him, and left an impression upon his mind that remained vivid till the close of life, instead of melting him into penitence, it seems, by some strange process, to have only nourished a spirit of despair. He still had to pass through a protracted scene of conflict before he was enabled heartily to bow to the requirements of the Gospel. The change, when it occurred, was emphatically a change from darkness to light; old things had passed away, and all things had become new.

Shortly after this, Mr. Seamans related his experience to the church in Sackville, and was baptized. He felt, at once, a strong conviction that it was his duty to preach the Gospel; though he was, at the same time, greatly oppressed by a sense of his incompetency to the work. For some time, he was painfully embarrassed on the subject; but, at length, his scruples so far yielded that he determined to give himself to the ministry. He commenced his public labours while he was yet in New Brunswick; but it would seem that, shortly after, and probably in consequence of his father's death, he, with the family, returned to New England; for, in the year 1772, we find him supplying the Church in North Attleborough, Mass., and, on the 15th of December, 1773, he was ordained as its Pastor. The Sermon at his Ordination was preached by the Rev. Isaac Backus of Middleborough, and the Charge was delivered by the Rev. James Manning, first President of Rhode Island College.

Mr. Seamans' connection with this church continued about fourteen years, during which time he witnessed two powerful revivals as the fruit of his ministry. His labours, however, were not confined to his own people: he made frequent preaching excursions in the surrounding country, and there was scarcely a town in the region where his voice was not sometimes heard in proclaiming the offer of salvation. During his residence in Attleborough, he baptized more than a hundred persons.

But the field of Mr. Seamans' most important labours was New London, N. H. He was attracted thither by the spiritual desolation of the region, the country being then but very sparsely settled, and the few people who were there being entirely destitute of the means of religious instruction. He preached his first sermon in New Hampshire on the 17th of June, 1787; and, on the Sunday following, preached, for the first time, in New London; but it was not until February of the next year that he could be said to have become identified with that people. His preaching seemed at once to be attended with a blessing; and he soon had the pleasure of baptizing five persons, who, with seven from other churches, including the Pastor and his wife, were constituted a church in October, 1788. He was regularly installed as the Pastor of this church by an Ecclesiastical Council, convened for the purpose, on the 21st of January, 1789, on which occasion the Rev. Amos Wood,* of Weare, preached the Sermon, and the Rev. Thomas Baldwin, of Canaan, gave the Charge. The public exercises were held in an unfinished meeting-house,—there being no pews to sit in, nor even floors to stand upon ; but, notwithstanding the poor accommodations, and the inclement season, there was a very large and deeply interested audience.

Mr. Seamans' ministry here continued for upwards of thirty-seven years,—until the infirmities of age led him to resign his charge. He died among the people whom he had so long served, on the 4th of October, 1830, in the eighty-third year of his age.

Mr. Seamans' salary, on his settlement at New London, was fixed at forty pounds, lawful money ; to be paid in corn and grain, with the exception of three pounds, which he was to receive in cash. In addition to this, as the first settled minister of the place, he had what was called "the ministerial lot." His life was attended with at least the usual degree of vicissitude, and there were times when he found a formidable opposition arrayed against him. During his Pastorate in New London, there were three extensive revivals,—in the years 1792, 1809, and 1818. In the first, about one hundred were added to the church ; in the second, forty ; in the third, eighty-three. During his connection with this church, he baptized, in New London and the neighbouring towns, two hundred and twenty-seven ; and in the last revival during his ministry, when he was too feeble to administer the ordinance, forty-seven were baptized by another minister, making in all two hundred and seventy-four. The whole number supposed to have been converted under his ministry, most of whom were baptized by him also, was three hundred and seventy-nine. Three of them afterwards became ministers of the Gospel.

FROM THE REV. E. E. CUMMINGS, D. D.

CONCORD, February 8, 1858.

My dear Sir : My acquaintance with the Rev. Job Seamans was limited, as the infirmities of age compelled him to retire from the active duties of the ministry before I entered upon them. The first time I saw him was at the installation of his successor in the pastoral office, among the people with whom he had so long lived and laboured. I was, at that time, deeply impressed with a feeling of veneration for this aged servant of Christ, when, at the close of the service, I saw him moving among the retiring congregation, like a father among his children, giving to each one a word of paternal greeting. He was greatly beloved by the younger ministry, who, though not permitted to labour with him, were indulged the privilege of witnessing the sublime and heavenly composure that marked the closing part of his eminently useful life.

He was a man of about medium stature, with rather coarse features and light complexion, and in advanced life had a very commanding and venerable appearance.

That he was a man of sincere, ardent and uniform piety, no one who knew him could ever doubt. He made it manifest, by all his conduct, that he possessed true love for the Saviour and his Church, and earnest desires for

* AMOS WOOD was graduated at the College of Rhode Island, in 1786 ; was ordained Pastor of the Baptist Church in Weare, N. H., in 1787; and continued in that relation until his death. He was a respectable and useful minister, and the church, during his connection with it, was in a flourishing condition.

the salvation of sinners. In the family, in social life, in the pulpit, in the discipline of the church, he evinced great coolness, self-control, and wisdom. Perhaps I may say that his distinguishing characteristics were a ready and almost intuitive perception of the workings of human nature, and a high degree of practical common sense in meeting those developments. Hence he made few blunders, and always secured the confidence of those with whom he had intercourse. He was a man of great industry—having a large family, and receiving only a small salary, he was obliged to perform no little labour on the farm. He deeply lamented that all his time and energies could not be given to the ministry. Yet, whether he were called to farming or tent-making, to study, or preaching, or visiting, he went cheerfully to the duty, and laboured in it to the extent of his ability. Few men enter the study more earnestly, or apply themselves with more enthusiasm or success, than he did. He gave himself to study that his profiting might appear unto all. As a preacher, he was uniformly acceptable, seldom rising to a high degree of eloquence, yet always serious, instructive, earnest, and often making direct and pungent appeals to the heart and conscience. He never wrote a sermon; yet his manner of treating many texts, as exhibited in his own written memoranda, still extant, shows that he had a mind of more than common clearness and vigour. His views of doctrine and duty were discriminating and well-defined. In early life, he embraced what is commonly called the doctrine of limited atonement, as set forth by Dr. Gill; but he, subsequently, held, substantially, the views of that subject, which were entertained by Andrew Fuller.

I will only add, in the language of another, — "The best monument of Elder Seamans is the enterprising and thriving town, in whose grave-yard his remains have long since mouldered away. His long ministry there was no insignificant element, among others, that have ministered to the temporal and spiritual prosperity of the people and church of New-London."

Yours fraternally,
E. E. CUMMINGS.

JOHN TAYLOR.

1772—1833.

FROM THE REV. JAMES E. WELCH.

HICKORY GROVE, Warren county, Mo.,
July 7, 1854.

My dear Sir: In compliance with your request, I send you the following sketch of the life and character of the Rev. John Taylor, an eminent Baptist clergyman, with whom I had the privilege of an acquaintance during the latter years of his life.

JOHN TAYLOR was born in Fauquier county, Va., in the year 1752. He was a great grandson of John Taylor, who, with two brothers,—Argyle and William, emigrated from England to Virginia, in 1650. He was a son of Lazarus and Anna (Bradford) Taylor—his maternal grandfather was a native of Scotland, his maternal grandmother, of France. While he was growing up, he was compelled to labour hard for the support of his father's family, which had been rendered dependant upon him by his father's improvident or dissolute habits. His early education was, of course, much neglected. Before the Revolutionary War, his father removed, with his young and growing family, to the west of the Blue Ridge, and settled near the Shenandoah River, in Frederick county, Va. When John was about seventeen years of age, the Rev. William Marshall,* an uncle of the late Chief Justice Marshall, came through that fertile country on a preaching tour ; and while Marshall, standing on a stump, was discoursing of the awful scenes of the judgment, he uttered this fearful exclamation— " Oh rocks, fall on me ; oh mountains, cover me from the face of Him that sitteth on the throne, and from the wrath of the Lamb ; for the great day of his wrath is come, and who shall be able to stand ?" " I felt," said Taylor, " the whole sentence dart through my soul." He, however, soon after, lost the vivid impressions then made upon his mind, and relapsed into his former general habit of indifference ; though he had repeated warnings of conscience, and his mind was ill at ease. Under the fervent and solemn addresses of two young preachers, who lived near his father's residence, he was again awakened to a deep sense of his guilt and danger ; and, soon afterwards, in a lonely, uninhabited mountain, kneeling beneath an overhanging rock, was enabled to apprehend the fulness and grace of Christ, and to rejoice in the hope of the glory of God.

He was baptized by James Ireland, and united with the Baptist Church at South River, of which Ireland was then Pastor, in the twentieth year of his age. He soon began to feel a strong desire to communicate what he felt and knew of the Saviour, to his fellow-men ; and, when attending the social meetings of the neighbourhood, would aid in conducting the public services, and thus, in a few months, he came to be known as a public speaker in the region in which he lived.

He says himself,—" Although I was twenty years old, my lack of information filled me with dismay. My boyhood was such, even in stature, that, in a strange place, I was taken to be about sixteen years old—in one place it was said that my head came but little above the pulpit." About four years after he had been licensed to preach, he was ordained, as an itinerant, at South River. For a number of years, he, in company with Joseph Redding,† another Baptist minister, continued to range through the

---

* WILLIAM MARSHALL was born in the Northern Neck, Va., in the year 1735. In early life, he was remarkable for his devotion to fashionable amusements; but, in 1768, he was awakened, under the ministry of those who were then called New Lights, and, after a season of deep distress, became the subject of a hopeful renovation. This occurred in the county of Fauquier. He soon joined the Baptists, and commenced preaching, to the great surprise of those who had known his previous history and habits. His earnest and impressive appeals gave so much offence that he was actually seized, and an attempt was made to imprison him, but he was released through the interposition of his brother, Col. Thomas Marshall. He continued to preach for some time, and with great success, in the county of Fauquier, but, afterwards, visited the county of Shenandoah, where his labours were equally successful. At length he became the Pastor of Happy Creek Church, though this connection continued but a short time. In 1780, he removed to Kentucky, and settled in what is now Shelby county, and, shortly after, was interrupted in his labours, for a considerable time, by a fall from a horse. During this period of confinement, he devoted himself to study, and was afterwards more instructive and systematic in his pulpit efforts. He died in 1808, in the seventy-third year of his age.

† JOSEPH REDDING was born in Fauquier County, Va., in the year 1750. He was left an orphan in early life, and, with six or seven other children, was thrown upon the care of an uncle In consequence of this bereavement, they received but little education, though they were brought up in strict conformity to the Episcopal Church. Joseph was hopefully converted, under circumstances of peculiar interest, was baptized by immersion in 1771, and, almost immediately after, commenced preaching. Having laboured for two years in his native State, he removed to South Carolina, where he remained, preaching with much success, until 1779, when he finally settled in Kentucky. There he became a prominent man,—at first connected with the Elkhorn District, but afterwards a leader in the Licking Association. He died in December, 1815.

mountains, washed by the waters of the Shenandoah, Potomac, Monongahela, and Green Brier Rivers, and even into the wilds of Kentucky,
preaching the Gospel and organizing churches, where no messenger of
salvation had ever penetrated before. Their lives were often in danger
from the mountain snows, and still more, perhaps, from the ruthless tomahawk. In this hazardous work they laboured with pleasure, and were
greatly blessed in their labours ; and, as they passed from mountain to
valley, they would sing

> "On these mountains let me labour,
> "In these vallies let me tell
> "How He died, the blessed Saviour,
> "To redeem a world from hell."

In 1782, he was married to Elizabeth, daughter of Philemon and Nanny
(Cave) Kavanaugh,—a young lady of a respectable family, and a member
of the Baptist Church. About the same time, an uncle of his died, who
left him sole heir to his property, which was valued at about three thousand
dollars. This was altogether unexpected to him, and was the more welcome because it came at a time when he needed it most. Soon after this,
he considered it his duty to remove to Kentucky; and, accordingly, he
took passage at Redstone, (now Brownsville,) for a place then called Bear-
grass, (now Louisville ;) the whole country on the Ohio River between
Wheeling and Louisville being entirely unsettled, and travelling being
attended with great jeopardy. This was about the close of the year 1783.
Within a few days after his arrival, he left Louisville for Craig's Station,
in Lincoln County, Ky,—a distance of eighty miles ; though it was now
mid-winter. This was a most perilous journey; and it required, on the
part of both himself and his wife, an indomitable strength of purpose.
Accustomed, from early childhood, to range over and around the spurs of
the Alleghany Mountains, he was prepared, by habit, to meet and brave
the dangers of the river and the wilderness, while his piety taught him to
trust for protection to that God who holds the waters as in the hollow of
his hand, and can bid the wild beasts, and more savage men, to touch not
his anointed, and do his servant no harm.

There was a Baptist Church at Craig's Station, in Lincoln County,
called Gilbert's Creek, the members of which had emigrated from Virginia
to Kentucky, with Lewis Craig, their Pastor. Just before Taylor arrived
in Kentucky, Craig, with a number of others, had left Gilbert's Creek,
and settled on the North side of the Kentucky River, and established a
church at South Elkhorn, six miles South of Lexington. This church was
favoured, in no small degree, with the labours of William Hickman, Senior,*

---

* WILLIAM HICKMAN, Senior, was born about the year 1746, in one of the counties South
of James River, Va. He was hopefully converted in consequence of listening to sermons
delivered by certain Baptist ministers from the windows of the jail, in the County of Chesterfield. Soon after making a profession of religion, he visited Kentucky, and there, in 1776,
commenced preaching. On his return to Virginia, he preached with great effect, especially in
the Southern part of Chesterfield County, where, in 1778, he was instrumental in founding the
Skinquarter Church. In 1781, the church called Tomahawk also secured his services, and he
laboured among them for three years. In 1784, he became a permanent resident of Kentucky.
Here he submitted to great sacrifices and perils for the sake of carrying the Gospel to the scattered population in those frontier settlements. He was, for many years, Pastor of the church
known by the name of the "Forks of Elkhorn," and in this church alone baptized more than
five hundred persons He was twice married, had a number of children, one of whom, *William*,
became a respectable Baptist minister in Kentucky. He (the father) lived to an advanced age,
and at fourscore years had almost his full vigour. Elder Taylor writes thus concerning him :—

who lived in this neighbourhood. After a residence of seven months in Lincoln County, Taylor followed Craig to the North side of the River, and settled in what is now Woodford County, and, in August, 1784, united in membership with the South Elkhorn Baptist Church, then under the pastoral charge of Lewis Craig, who had aided in his ordination in Virginia.

In 1785, a church was formed at Clear Creek, of which Mr. Taylor, and three other preachers, who had moved into that neighbourhood, became members. Some time the next winter, Mr. T., much to his surprise, was chosen Pastor of the Church; and though, at first, he declined the call, on the ground that there were three ministering brethren in the church older than himself, two of whom had already sustained the pastoral relation, yet, when it came to be urged upon him, as a matter of unquestionable duty, he finally consented to accept the place, and was installed after the usual mode. His introduction to the pastoral office marked the commencement of a powerful revival of religion, and proved auspicious of the greatly increased prosperity of the church. In consequence, however, of different views of the subject of Church Discipline, the harmony of the church began at length to be disturbed, and Mr. T., after a ministry of about three years,—during which he baptized an hundred persons,—was led to resign his pastoral charge. Though this measure was at first strongly objected to by a portion of the church, they became reconciled to it, upon his giving them the assurance that though, sustaining no longer the pastoral relation, he should continue to serve them with as much alacrity and fidelity as ever. This he actually did; and, not long after, a revival of great power commenced, which brought large numbers into the church, and was marked by many very signal instances of conversion.

But scarcely had this revival passed away, before evil surmisings and jealousies arose among the members of the church, which presented a sad contrast to the scenes which had then lately been witnessed. This, in connection with some other circumstances, suggested to Mr. Taylor the idea of seeking another residence. Though he had originally possessed fifteen hundred acres of land in that neighbourhood, he had disposed of it to one friend after another, till only about four hundred remained to him; and he felt the importance of making some better provision for his increasing family. As there was an eligible opening on the Ohio River, near the mouth of the Great Miami, in Boone County, he purchased nearly three thousand acres, in different tracts, in that region, and removed thither, with his family, in April, 1795, nearly eleven years after he had settled on Clear Creek.

The summer before his removal to the Ohio River, while on a visit there, he was present at the constitution of a small church, called "The Baptist Church of Christ at Bullittsburg." To this church he transferred his membership; and though he was immediately requested to take the pastoral charge of it, he peremptorily declined the proposal, while yet he cordially proffered them any ministerial service which he might be able to perform. At this period he seems to have had little enjoyment in his

"His preaching is in a plain and solemn style, and the sound of it like that of thunder at a distance; but, when in his best gears, his sound is like thunder at home, and operates with prodigious force on the consciences of his hearers—his mode of speaking is so slow that the hearer at times gets ahead of him in the subject."

ministry, partly because there were so few people around him for his influence to act upon, and partly because the prospect was at best a very distant one, of his condition in this respect being materially improved. He, however, addressed himself, with characteristic enterprise, to the work of felling the forest and cultivating the earth; and, after a few months, the settlement was enlarged by very considerable emigrations from Virginia, as well as from different parts of Kentucky. The church soon numbered not less than sixty members; and, though it received few or no additions from the world, and there seemed a suspension of the converting influences of the Holy Spirit, in respect to the surrounding population, the utmost harmony and good-will prevailed among the members. This state of things continued, without interruption, for several years.

In the Spring of 1800, Mr. Taylor, having heard from a friend of an extensive revival of religion at the mouth of the Kentucky River, made a journey thither, intending not only to mingle in the scenes of the revival, but to settle the boundaries of a tract of land in Gallatin County, which he had purchased some time before. He attended a meeting at the house of his friend, and preached, but he had little comfort in the exercise, and went on his way, to meet his secular engagement, with a heavy heart. The land which he went to survey had been surveyed about forty years before for a Colonel Byrd, and, being one of the highest bluffs on the river, it was called Mount Byrd. From this place, he went to visit the Clear Creek Church, and spent a Sabbath with them, and preached a sermon, suited not less to his own gloomy feelings, than to their depressed condition. On his return to Bullittsburg, he was not a little distressed to find that professing Christians there were becoming lamentably conformed to the world, and that some of them were indulging freely in scenes of mirth and frivolity, to the great dishonour and injury of religion. This state of things, however, was quickly succeeded by a revival that continued about a year, and resulted in an addition to the church of an hundred and twelve new members. The whole number of communicants, at this time, was about two hundred.

As the church at Bullittsburg had now several preachers connected with it, and as the climate had proved unfavourable to the health of his family, Mr. Taylor, after a residence there of seven years, moved, in the spring of 1802, to Mount Byrd, some sixty or seventy miles distant,—where, as I have already stated, he had a considerable tract of land. He now, with his family, became connected with the Corn Creek Church, which was about four miles from his residence, and, as he was already well known to most of the members, was almost immediately called to take the pastoral charge of it. This, however, he declined to do, while yet, as on former occasions, he expressed his willingness to serve them, in the general capacity of a minister, to the extent of his ability.

Mr. Taylor now entered afresh on the work of cutting down trees, and enclosing lots, and doing whatever else was needful for a comfortable settlement; and his wife and children co-operated with him most vigorously in the new enterprise. Providence smiled on their industry, the change of climate proved favourable to their health, and they were soon in possession of a pleasant and commodious home. Though the church was well satisfied with his ministrations, its numbers were very small, and its growth, by no means, rapid, as there were not more than fifty families in the entire settlement. But, before he had been long there, several circumstances occurred, to disappoint his hopes and mar his enjoyment. A fine barn which he had just built, and filled with choice grain, was struck with lightning and burnt, occasioning him a loss of at least a thousand dollars. Two of his children were taken from him by death. And, to crown all, a powerful prejudice had sprung up against him in the church, and the surrounding community, on account of his endeavouring to bring the discipline of the church to bear upon a member for having become a Freemason. These and other circumstances connected with them, he interpreted as a providential intimation that it was his duty to seek yet another home; and, accordingly, in March, 1815, after living at Mount Byrd thirteen years, and labouring with the Corn Creek Church, during that period, (though without any marked success,) he left the place, and went to live at the Forks of Elkhorn.

Here he became connected with the Big Spring Church, in Woodford County, about five miles distant from his residence, and then under the pastoral care of the Rev. Silas M. Noel. Just before this, Judge D——, an influential member of this church, had published a pamphlet, containing a vigorous defence of Arminianism. Mr. Taylor, while entertaining great respect for the author of the pamphlet, felt constrained to secure some public expression of disapprobation in respect to it; and, though his movements on the subject were embarrassed, and to a great extent resisted, in the church, yet no less than three Baptist Associations ultimately passed judgment against it.

As a church was now about to be constituted at Frankfort, Mr. Taylor, partly from its being more convenient to him, and partly from the want of sympathy with him, on the part of the Big Spring Church, in regard to the offensive pamphlet, resolved to identify himself with the new enterprise; and, accordingly, he took his letter of dismission from Big Spring in January, 1816, after being a member there about ten months. He seems, however, to have felt little at home in the Frankfort Church; and, after about two years, he joined with a number of his brethren in forming yet another church within the Forks of Elkhorn—this church was called "the Baptist Church of Christ on Black Run," and was constituted in January, 1816.

Mr. Taylor was immediately called to the pastoral charge of the Black Run Church, but, on stating to them his objections to serving them in that relation, and his willingness to preach to them, as a stated supply, once a month, and administer ordinances, they readily yielded to his proposal. His labours proved highly acceptable, and the church increased, from year to year, under his ministry. His strength gradually declined during his last years, though he continued to labour up to the full measure of his ability. He died in the year 1833, in the eighty-fourth year of his age. He had several children, one of whom entered the ministry, and, after labouring some years in Kentucky, removed to Illinois, and died on Apple Creek, several years ago.

John Taylor was one of the most industrious of men, in both his secular and sacred callings. He could not tolerate idleness under any circumstances; and hence, in his seventy-fifth year, when unable to ride much on horseback, (his usual mode of travel,) he prepared for the press a work, forming a duodecimo volume of almost three hundred pages, entitled, "A History of Ten Baptist Churches, of which the Author has been successively a member; in which will be seen something of a Journal of the Author's Life for more than fifty years. Also a Comment on some parts of Scripture, in which the Author takes the liberty to differ from other Expositors." I have witnessed his persevering industry, when travelling with him to and from Associations in Kentucky,—six or eight of which, lying between the Kentucky and Ohio Rivers, he usually visited every year.

Another prominent trait of his character was punctuality, especially in his ministerial engagements. He said himself,—" I have been in the ministry just about fifty-four years; and, of the many thousands of meetings I have appointed, I do not recollect that worldly business ever detained me from one of them; and I have been a man of such uninterrupted health, that I do not think I have disappointed half as many meetings in my life as I have been preaching years." Nor could he be easily diverted from what he considered the path of duty. When once his mind was fully made up, he carried out his convictions with such unyielding tenacity, as to render himself liable, in the estimation of some, to the charge of obstinacy. He was, undoubtedly, a man of strong prejudices. He was once bitterly opposed to the missionary cause, and prepared a pamphlet entitled " Thoughts on Missions," which no persuasion of his friends could induce him to withhold from the press, notwithstanding it contained palpable mistakes. I saw him at the Long Run Association, in 1830, at New Castle, Ky., when I expressed a desire to have some conversation with him relative to that pamphlet; but he replied,—" Oh, Brother James, I hope you do not doubt that I *believed* I was telling the truth, when I wrote that thing." I answered,—" How could you ? " and he replied,—" Oh, never mind, let it sleep in silence; " and his whole manner showed that he regretted he had ever written it. Wherever he became attached, his friendship was ardent; and, on the other hand, whoever should offend him, might expect to feel the weight of his displeasure; and yet he was famed for his success in reconciling contending parties, and usually so directed his efforts as to be regarded the friend of both. I recollect an instance of this, in 1805, when contention ran high in the Elkhorn Association, for several days, and was terminated by a vote, which induced several of the oldest ministers to withdraw. On Sabbath, John Taylor took for his text,—" Let Reuben live " (Deut. xxxiii. 8); and, from the fact that Reuben was the oldest son of Jacob, he pleaded with the younger ministers of the Association not to rejoice over their elder brethren, because they were in the minority; and, although it did not heal the breach, it acted, for a time, like oil upon the troubled waters. There was, undoubtedly, something of eccentricity about him. He would often arise to preach, without a moment's study, whenever prompted by any unexpected or exciting circumstance. He once met Jacob Creath, Sen., and James Suggett, (if my memory serves me,) at the Forks of Elkhorn, on the Sabbath, when, as was usual on such occasions, they determined to have two services before dismissing the congregation. Suggett preached, and then he and Taylor urged Creath to preach, which he refusing to do, Taylor arose at once and took for his text,—"Pray ye the Lord of the harvest that he would send forth *labourers* into his harvest." With this text, he soon entered the harvest fields of Virginia, and began to describe the kind of "labourers" the Virginia farmers wanted—"not *gentlemen*, who, when asked to cut a swarth, would plead various excuses—not men to lie about under the shade—such hands always had their wages docked; but they wanted *labourers*,—men who were willing to bear the burden and heat of the day," &c., &c. As soon as Taylor closed his sermon, Creath arose, and made an apology to the audience for his inactivity.

I saw this aged brother at the meeting of the Elkhorn Association, at the Big Spring Church, near Frankfort, in 1832. He was a member of the Body; and yet he took his place on the front seat of the gallery. The Moderator, observing him, said,—"Come down, Brother Taylor, and sit with us;" but he promptly replied,—"I am a free man, Brother Moderator," and kept his seat. He was low of stature, muscular, had broad shoulders and a broad face, high cheek bones and heavy eye brows, overhanging a pair of light and small, but expressive, eyes. He was plain, and by no means particular, in his apparel, and rather reserved in conversation, though, at times, he seemed to enjoy a dry joke upon his brethren.

His death was peaceful and tranquil, and he has left behind him a name worthy of enduring remembrance.

Very sincerely yours,

JAMES E. WELCH.

------◆◆------

WILLIAM WILLIAMS.*

1773—1823.

WILLIAM WILLIAMS, a son of John and Ann (White) Williams, was born in Hilltown, Bucks County, Pa., in the year 1752. His father emigrated from Wales to this country, and was obliged to work his passage over as a sailor, having no other means of paying for it. He settled in Bucks County as a farmer, where he accumulated a handsome property, and spent the remainder of his days. The son,—the subject of this sketch, was fitted for College at Hopewell, N. J., at a somewhat celebrated school taught by the Rev. Isaac Eaton. He entered the institution which is now Brown University,—then situated at Warren, R. I., one year in advance, in 1766, and graduated with the first class in 1769. In the autumn following, he was married to Patience, daughter of Colonel Nathan Miller, of Warren. On the 29th of September, 1771, he was baptized by the Rev. Charles Thompson, of the same place, and admitted to the communion of the church under his pastoral care. On the 18th of April, 1773, he was licensed, by the Warren Church, as a preacher of the Gospel.

* MSS. from his daughter,—Miss Williams, from Rev. Gideon Cole, and Professor Gammell.

For several years after leaving College, he was engaged chiefly in teaching. He commenced preaching at Wrentham as early as November, 1773, and shortly after removed his family thither, by request of the church, though not to assume the pastoral charge. In March, 1775, the church invited him to become their Pastor, and he accepted the invitation,—but his ordination did not take place till the 3d of July, 1776.

About the time of his settlement at Wrentham, he opened an Academy, which attained to high distinction among the literary institutions of that day. He is supposed to have had under his care nearly two hundred youth, about eighty of whom he fitted for his Alma Mater, and not a few became distinguished in literary and professional life. He also conducted the theological studies of several young men, with a view to their entering the ministry.

Mr. Williams continued to be engaged as both teacher and preacher till almost the close of his life. In May, 1823, he began to exhibit decisive symptoms of consumption, and it was quickly found that the disease was too deeply seated to yield to medical treatment. He preached his last sermon at his own house, after he had become so ill as to be unable to go to the usual place of worship. At one time it was thought that there was some reason to hope for his recovery; but he seemed rather desirous to depart, and could hardly be reconciled to the idea of surviving his usefulness. He died on the 22d of September, 1823, aged about seventy-one years.

Mrs. Williams died of apoplexy, on the 17th of June, 1803. In February, 1804, he was married to Mrs. Dolly Hancock, of Wrentham, daughter of a Mr. Titus. He was the father of seven children, all of whom, except the eldest and the youngest, still (1859) survive.

Mr. Williams was a Fellow of Brown University, from 1789 to 1818. In 1777, when the College building was occupied as a barrack for Militia, and afterwards as a hospital for French troops, the library was removed to the country, and placed in the keeping of Mr. Williams.

FROM THE REV. ABIAL FISHER, D. D.

WEST BOYLSTON, March 22, 1859.

My dear Sir: I did not know the Rev. William Williams, of Wrentham, till he was far advanced in life, but I was well acquainted with his general character and standing, both as a teacher and a minister of the Gospel. He is especially worthy of notice as having been one of the first graduates of the College of Rhode Island, now Brown University, and as having contributed not a little to the intellectual improvement of the Baptist denomination in New England.

As respects his personal appearance, he was of about the middle size, quite spare, and, when I knew him in old age, somewhat inclined to stoop—his complexion was ruddy, and his nose somewhat prominent. His manners were easy and agreeable, and his powers of conversation such as to render him quite attractive. His talents and acquirements were highly respectable. His services as a teacher commanded great respect, not only in but out of his denomination. Among his pupils were the late Hon. David R. Williams, Governor of South Carolina, and the Hon. Tristam Burgess, LL.D., late Professor of Oratory and Belles Lettres in Brown University, and for many years a distinguished Representative in Congress. He could not be regarded as a highly popular preacher, though he was strongly evangelical in his doctrines, and succeeded in keeping his church in a quiet and orderly state. He was not a man greatly to attract or impress the multitude in any way, but, by a steady course of enlightened and Christian activity, he accomplished an amount of good for his denomination, which fairly entitles him to a place among its more distinguished benefactors. He diffused a spirit of improvement, a love of intellectual culture, throughout the circle in which he moved, and no doubt his influence will continue, and find new channels through which to flow down to posterity, long after the last of his surviving contemporaries shall have passed away.

Very truly yours,
ABIAL FISHER.

RICHARD FURMAN, D. D.*
1773—1825.

RICHARD FURMAN was born at Æsopus, in the then Province of New York, in the year 1755. In his early childhood, his father removed with his family to South Carolina, and, after spending some time on the sea coast, settled at the High Hills of Santee. His father was a person of more than ordinary intelligence for that day : he followed the profession of a Surveyor, and also held the office of Prothonotary in the place where he lived. He attended carefully to the education of his son, instructing him not only in the common English branches, and the Mathematics, but especially in the Sacred Scriptures. Under a judicious and evangelical training, the mind of the son gradually opened, giving early promise of an earnest and useful Christian life.

On account of the uncommon maturity of his intellectual and Christian character, he was brought forward, by the church of which he was a member, to preach the Gospel, at the early age of eighteen. After some probationary exercises in his own church, he began gradually to extend the sphere of his labours, making it an object to preach in the most destitute places. There were large portions of South Carolina, which, at that period, were altogether without the means of religious instruction; and, in these desolate regions particularly, his influence was widely and deeply felt. Through his instrumentality, many churches were now established, which were afterwards embodied in the Charleston Association. Though he was a mere youth, such were the attractions of his character and eloquence, that he commanded the respect and affection of all classes, from childhood to venerable age.

Like most of the Baptist ministers of that day, Mr. Furman was a decided Whig, and entered, with all his heart, into the cause of American Independence. As the British army had invaded South Carolina, thus not only interrupting the exercise of his ministry, but rendering it hazardous for him to remain there, he retired, with his family, into North Carolina and Virginia; and, in this retreat, continued not only to fulfill the duties of a

* Dr. Brantly's Fun. Serm.—MS. from Rev. Dr. W. B. Johnson.

Minister, but to exemplify the character of a Patriot.   Here, by his fervid
eloquence, as well as his lofty patriotism, he attracted the attention of
some of the most distinguished advocates of the Revolution, among whom
was Patrick Henry.

After the danger had passed away, he returned to his former residence,
at Statesburg, S. C., where he remained as the Pastor of a church until
the year 1787, when he accepted an invitation to take the pastoral charge
of the Baptist Church in Charleston.   Here he laboured with great zeal,
fidelity, and acceptance, to the close of life.

He received, at various times, high testimonies of public respect and confidence.   He was one of the members of the Convention that framed the
Constitution of South Carolina.   He was appointed, by the Revolution
Society, in connection with the Society of Cincinnati, to deliver a Discourse
commemorative of Washington, and, at a later period, another, commemorative of Hamilton.   In 1800, he received the degree of Doctor of Divinity
from Brown University, having received the degree of Master of Arts from
the same institution, in 1792.   He was President of the First Baptist
Convention for the United States, held in Philadelphia, in 1814.

Dr. Furman was blessed with an uncommonly vigorous constitution, and,
during nearly his whole life, with excellent health.   At length, however,
his health began to decline, and it was apparent to both himself and his
friends that the silver cord must quickly be loosed.   His last Sermon was
founded on the text,—"And Enoch walked with God, and was not, for
God took him."   It was a noble effort, worthy of one who was standing at
the portals of Heaven; but it left him in a state of great physical exhaust-
ion, that told but too plainly that the time of his departure was at hand.
In the progress of his disease, he had intense bodily suffering, but he
exhibited a uniformly serene and patient spirit.   The last time he visited
the house of God, he heard a sermon, from one of his brethren, on some
of the plainest and simplest points of the Christian faith; and he remarked
respecting it,—"These are blessed truths on which we may live and die."
As he was making his passage through the dark valley, he said to some of
his friends who stood around him,—"I am a dying man, but my trust is in
the Redeemer: I preach Christ to you dying, as I have attempted to while
living."   The moment before he expired, he requested that the twenty-
third Psalm should be read; and, before the reading of it was concluded,
his heart had ceased to beat.   He died on the 25th of August, 1825, aged
seventy years.   The Funeral Discourse was preached by the Rev. William A. McDowell, of the Presbyterian Church.   Another Sermon, commemorative of his life and character, was subsequently preached by the
Rev. Dr. Brantly, and was published.

Dr. Furman published Rewards of Grace conferred on Christ's Faithful
People: A Sermon delivered in Charleston, on occasion of the Death of
the Rev. Oliver Hart, 1796; an Oration delivered at the Charleston
Orphan House before the Intendant and Wardens of the city, the Board
of Commissioners, and a large Assembly of the Benefactors of the Institution, 1796; Humble Submission to Divine Sovereignty, the Duty of a
Bereaved Nation: A Sermon commemorative of General Washington,
1800; and a Sermon on the death of the Rev. Edmund Botsford, 1819.

One of Dr. Furman's sons has been settled, for many years, as a Baptist minister, in his native State.

FROM THE REV. WILLIAM B. JOHNSON, D. D.

EDGEFIELD COURT HOUSE, S. C., May 27, 1848.

My dear Sir: My acquaintance with the Rev. Dr. Furman began when I was a boy, and I well remember the deep and solemn impression which his grave and minister-like appearance made upon my mind, young as I then was;—an impression which was deepened by a more intimate knowledge of his character. As we never lived in the same town or neighbourhood, after I entered the ministry, nor indeed before, with the exception of a few months which I spent in his family, when going to school,—I saw him but seldom, except in the meetings of the general organizations of the denomination; so that my opportunities for observing him continuously were not ample. His deportment, however, was so uniform that his life presented a series of good deeds, without very numerous incidents of striking variety. His regular habits, his conscientious regard for duty, made him observe, with more than ordinary faithfulness, the precepts of his Divine Master. So that, though of Adam's race, he was, by common consent, regarded as not exceeded by any, as a consistent, uniform and exemplary person, in a community of from twenty to thirty thousand, of whom not a few were upright professors of religion in different denominations.

As a man, Dr. Furman was most kind and benevolent. In his family, he was a pattern of conjugal and parental tenderness. To the poor he was sympathizing and beneficent. To the sick, a physician of both soul and body. He was the former by his profession, and to become the latter, he bestowed much attention upon the science of medicine. To this he was led by the benevolence of his heart, from seeing the necessities of the numerous poor in the city, whose streets and lanes he threaded in his pastoral visits. During the sickly season, in Charleston, sometimes visited by that awful scourge of the sea-ports,—*the Yellow Fever*, Dr. Furman remained firm at his post, and, like an angel of mercy, was found at the bedside of the sick and the dying. In one of the most fatal seasons of this epidemic, he had more than thirty patients, of whom he lost none; and, to the honour of this philanthropist, be it said, these acts of kindness were performed *without money and without price*. In the exercise of the same benevolence, which led to these acts, his manner was to take with him, when he travelled, his lancet and medicines; and, not unfrequently, was it his privilege to minister, on these journeys, to the relief of the sick, especially in the General meetings of the denomination, when some sudden attack of disease upon one or other of the members called into requisition his skill and his kindness.

Dr. Furman was the firm friend of true freedom and of equal rights. As a member of the Convention of this State, in the year 1790, he took part in the deliberations of that Body, assembled to form the Constitution. When the article, which prohibits ministers of the Gospel from admission into the Legislative, Judicial and Executive offices, came up for discussion, he opposed it on the ground of its violating the *right* of the people to elect whom they pleased, and of the ministry to fill any office to which the people should elect them. He repudiated the principle of disfranchising a class of citizens, on the ground of their consecration to a holy office.

As a Christian, the bearing of Dr. Furman was pre-eminently that of a man of God, who set the Lord always before him, ordering his conversation aright, and acting under the solemn conviction,—"*Thou God seest me.*" The religion of this good and great man was truly a spiritual, practical religion, under whose influence he was careful to maintain good works, thus letting his light shine before others, with no false or doubtful lustre. Indeed, so eminent was he for exemplary piety and holy living, that the whole city held him in veneration. The ungodly stood abashed in his sight, and the profligate carefully hid his iniquities from his view. A member of a bachanalian party once said to his fellows in debauch,—" Suppose Rev. Mr. —— should enter the room, would you be restrained?" "No," was the reply. The names of other ministers of the city were mentioned, with the like inquiry, and with the like negative. Last of all, Dr. Furman's name was mentioned in the same way, when the universal exclamation was—" Yes, *Dr. Furman* would restrain us—we could not stand *his* presence." It was no unfrequent remark that, if good works could save a man, the good works of Dr. Furman would assuredly secure *him* admission into Heaven.

As a *Minister of Jesus Christ*, the *tout ensemble* of Dr. Furman was more solemn and imposing than that of any other man whom I have ever beheld. When *he* arose to speak in Church-meeting, Association, Convention, or any other assembly, all eyes were turned upon him, with profound attention, and reverential awe. In the services of the sacred desk, such was the appropriate solemnity of his manner, that the audience *felt* themselves to be in the presence of a man of God, who had " studied to show himself approved unto God, a workman that needed not to be ashamed, rightly dividing the word of truth."

As an *Orator* of the grave character, Dr. Furman was pre-eminent. In his preaching, he intermingled doctrine and practice, experimental religion and pathetic appeal. I remember hearing him, more than forty years ago, preach from the text,—" I am set for the defence of the Gospel "—it was truly a masterly effort. Never shall I forget his solemn, impressive countenance, his dignified manner, his clear statements of the Gospel doctrine and precepts, his unanswerable arguments in support of the Gospel's claim to a Divine origin, the lofty sentiments that he poured forth, the immovable firmness with which he maintained his position, and the commanding eloquence with which he enforced the whole argument. Another discourse, two or three years before, is fresh in my memory, from the text,—" They shall ask the way to Zion, with their faces thitherward, saying, come and let us join ourselves to the Lord in a perpetual covenant that shall not be forgotten." In this discourse there was much pathos. The audience was deeply moved. Indeed, the Doctor seemed to reign over them with irresistible influence, melting their hearts into the tenderest frame, and happily preparing them for the Sacramental table.

In the administration of Baptism, and the Lord's Supper, his manner was of the happiest kind; more especially in the latter, when directing the faith of the communicants to their suffering, crucified Lord. Deeply affected himself with the remembrance of the scenes of Calvary, he failed not, by their recital, to affect the communicants. Their abhorrence of sin, which had nailed their Great Head to the Cross, was deepened, whilst their gratitude for his condescension, in delivering them from guilt and condemnation, by such sufferings, was heightened, and their love inflamed.

As the Presiding Officer of an Ecclesiastical Body, his administration was in keeping with all the other parts of his character. Intimately acquainted with parliamentary rule, he conducted the movements, and preserved the decorum, of the Body, with ease, propriety, and dignity. Indeed, his very appearance preserved order. The points presented in ordinary business, or in queries from the Churches, which were of difficult solution, met at his hands an easy explanation, so that the facilities of the Body were equal to the exigencies,—a privilege and blessing of no small importance.

The gift of such a man to the denomination, for the period that Dr. Furman lived, was a gracious ordering of Divine Providence, and it is with melancholy pleasure that I present, for the "Annals of the American Pulpit," this tribute of respect to the memory of so good and great a man.

Affectionately yours,

WILLIAM BULLEIN JOHNSON.

—————◆◆—————

THOMAS USTICK.*

1774—1803.

THOMAS USTICK was born in the city of New York, on the 30th of August, 1753. His grandfather, Thomas Ustick, was a native of Cornwall, England, came to this country in early life, and purchased a tract of land near Schooley's Mountain, N. J., known by the name of Copper Mines. His father, Stephen Ustick, the eldest son of Thomas, was a respectable architect in New York, and, with the other members of the family, belonged to the Episcopal Church. His mother's maiden name was Jane Ruland—she was a sister of the Rev. Luke Ruland, many years Pastor of the Baptist Church at Patchogue, Long Island, and was herself a member of the Baptist Church. His father died at Port Au Prince.

Thomas was early placed under the care, and in the family, of his uncle, William Ustick, a hardware dealer, in New York; and, until he was thirteen years of age, he was employed in his uncle's business. During this time, he became acquainted with several families connected with the First Baptist Church, then under the pastoral care of the Rev. John Gano. In company with some of these, he was accustomed to attend a weekly prayer meeting, where his first enduring religious impressions were supposed to have been received. His general deportment was so consistent and serious that, on one occasion, he was asked to lead the devotions of the meeting; and, after hesitating a few moments, he resolved to comply; and the effort served greatly to deepen his own impressions, and to carry him forward towards the decisive point of an unreserved dedication of himself to God. He was but little more than thirteen years of age, when he was baptized, on a profession of his faith, by the Rev. Mr. Gano. In reading the Hymn to be sung on the occasion, Mr. Gano so changed it that it read,—

" His honour is engaged to save
" The *youngest* of his sheep."

Young Ustick, as he leaned on his Pastor's arm, looked him in the face, and said,—" Why did you not read the word as it is,—' the *meanest* of his sheep;' for truly so I am."

The young man had serious obstacles to encounter in becoming a member of the Baptist Church. His uncle, with whom he lived, was a decided Episcopalian, and could not give his consent that he should connect himself with any other than the Episcopal communion; and he even meditated

* Benedict's Hist. Bapt. I.—Bapt. Mem., 1844.—MS. from Miss S. M. Ustick.

the purpose of confining him to his chamber, during the day on which he was baptized. The nephew, however, succeeded in following out his conscientious convictions, and the uncle—notwithstanding that one act of disobedience (and it is said to have been a solitary one)—never withdrew from him, in any degree, his confidence and affection.

Having now accomplished his desire in becoming a member of the Baptist Church, he soon expressed a wish that he might be permitted to become a minister of the Gospel. Accordingly, after due consideration of the subject on the part of his friends, it was arranged that he should be put in the way of making the requisite preparation for the ministry. Shortly after this, he was admitted a student in the Academy at Warren, R. I., of which the Rev. James Manning was then Principal. This Academy was soon incorporated as a College, and removed to Providence—young Ustick, in due time, became a member of the College, and graduated in the year 1771.

In 1772, Mr. Ustick was married to Hannah, youngest daughter of John Whittier, a bell-founder, of Fairfield, Conn. They had thirteen children, most of whom reached mature years, and became professors of religion and useful members of society. One of them only, an unmarried daughter, now (1855) survives. Mrs. Ustick died in March, 1837, in her eighty-sixth year.

For some time after his graduation and marriage, he was engaged, in the city of New York, in teaching a school, at the same time prosecuting his studies with reference to the ministry. In 1774, he received the degree of Master of Arts, and, about the same time, was licensed to preach, by the church with which he originally connected himself.

In 1775, when there was a prospect that the city of New York would be taken and occupied by the British troops, Mr. Ustick retired, with his family, to Fairfield, Conn., and spent some time with his wife's relatives, who resided there. He was, however, very soon employed in preaching to the neighbouring church of Stamford; and, when he closed his labours there, they gave him a letter, certifying that "his conduct was in character with his calling, and that he had given such general satisfaction in his public labours as proved the Apostle's declaration, who, after saying Christ had ascended on high, added 'and hath given *gifts* unto men.'"

In 1776, he removed to Ashford, Conn., by an invitation from the church in that place, and laboured there, and in the surrounding region, with very considerable success. The next year, he was solemnly ordained to the ministry, by the Rev. Dr. Manning, Rev. Job Seamans of Attleborough, and Rev. William Williams of Wrentham.

In 1779, he removed to Grafton, Mass., where he remained in the faithful and successful discharge of his duties nearly three years.

In October, 1781, the incipient step was taken towards his removal to Philadelphia. Dr. Manning, being on a visit to that city, and finding the church there destitute, cordially recommended his friend and pupil as a suitable person to fill the vacancy. Mr. Ustick was, accordingly, invited, by the church, to visit them, with a view to their hearing him as a candidate. After spending a winter with them, they gave him a unanimous call to become their Pastor. He accepted the call, and removed his family, shortly after, from Grafton to Philadelphia, where he lived and preached the Gospel for twenty-one years. His settlement here was attended by some circumstances of peculiar difficulty. His immediate predecessor was the Rev. Elhanan Winchester, who had received the doctrine of Universal salvation, and preached it with considerable effect. He established another congregation, and drew off a large number of the church to which he had previously ministered; and it was only by a suit at law that those who remained were confirmed in the right of possessing their meeting-house. In consequence of these unpropitious circumstances, he had but a small congregation, at the commencement of his ministry; but, by the blessing of God upon his labours, the number of his hearers increased, and the tone of religious feeling and action among them was greatly elevated.

In 1793, when the Yellow Fever occasioned such almost unprecedented desolation in Philadelphia, and the inhabitants were flying, panic-struck, in every direction, one of Mr. Ustick's friends,—a highly respectable gentleman in Bucks County, requested him and his family to occupy a house in the country, which he had made ready for their use; but, as his eldest daughter was, about that time, attacked by the disease, and, as he could not feel willing to submit to a separation of the family, under such circumstances, he concluded to remain at his post, and keep them with him, trusting to God's preserving care and goodness. During that time of peril and dismay, he devoted himself, without any regard to his own safety, to the sick and dying,—the great and good Dr. Rush being his companion in labour and in sorrow; and both himself and his family were mercifully spared, though several of his children were violently attacked by the disease.

In 1801, a pulmonary complaint fastened upon him, which was followed by a gradual decline of strength. In 1802, an epidemic fever prevailed in the city, in consequence of which, he removed his family to Burlington, N. J.; and, though his health was then much reduced, he occasionally officiated for Dr. Staughton, who was then the Pastor of a church there. His last sermon to that people was from Paul's benediction,—'' The grace of our Lord Jesus Christ be with you all, Amen;'' and it was prepared under the conviction that he should preach to them no more. From that time his disease made rapid progress, and, in March following, confined him entirely to his room. The night before he died, being fully sensible of the approaching change, he said to his son—'' The Lord is my shield and buckler.'' He passed away in perfect peace, on the 18th of April, 1803, aged about fifty years. An appropriate Funeral Discourse was preached by the Rev. Dr. William Rogers, from the text,—'' Our friend Lazarus sleepeth.''

FROM GENERAL WILLIAM DUNCAN.

PHILADELPHIA, September 18, 1856.

My dear Sir: It gives me pleasure to answer your inquiries concerning the Rev. Thomas Ustick, as I knew him intimately, and had a high appreciation of his character. When I came to this city to reside, I found him here, the Pastor of the First Baptist Church; and, in 1792, he married me to a lady

who, though not then a communicant in his church, was one of his stated
hearers; and, from that time till his death, we attended half of the time his
ministry, and half of the time that of Dr. Sproat and Dr. Green, of the Arch
Street (Presbyterian) Church. I knew him so well that I can speak of him,
in both his public and private relations, without any embarrassment.

Mr. Ustick was a man of about the middle size, had a well proportioned
frame, and fine expressive countenance, showing a sedate and thoughtful
mind, with the utmost gentleness and kindliness of spirit. And his face was
but a faithful expression of his character. With highly respectable talents,
and an excellent education, he combined a most lovely and loving temper,
which could not fail to make him a favourite wherever he was known. He
was an extremely modest man, and, instead of seeking to occupy high places,
was always disposed to keep himself in the back ground, unless urged forward by an imperious call of duty. In his private intercourse, he was most
considerate and obliging; and in his pastoral duties, while nothing could
exceed his tenderness, nothing was suffered to interfere with his fidelity.
He evidently watched for souls as one that must give an account. His preaching, though not the most stirring and animated, was always edifying and
acceptable. His voice was not distinguished for strength or compass, but
was of a bland and pleasant tone, and loud enough to fill any ordinary place
of worship. His discourses were not mere rhapsodies, or the unstudied
effusions of the moment, but were evidently premeditated, and arranged with
devout care, though, I think nothing beyond the outline was ordinarily written. His general influence in the community was that of an intelligent,
godly and earnest Christian minister. His death occasioned deep lamentation,
much beyond his own immediate circle.

Very sincerely, your friend and brother in
Christian fellowship,
WILLIAM DUNCAN.

ABRAHAM MARSHALL.

1774—1819.

FROM THE REV. A. E. MARSHALL,
PROFESSOR IN MARSHALL COLLEGE.

GRIFFIN, GA., May 25, 1859.

My dear Sir: I am happy to aid your proposed effort to commemorate
my venerable grandfather. Most of his contemporaries are gone; but
there remain authentic records and family traditions concerning him,
amply sufficient to supply the material for such a sketch as you desire.

ABRAHAM MARSHALL was born in Windsor, Conn., on the 23d of
April, 1748. Although born under a New England sky, it was not
allotted to him to be reared in so genial a clime; but he left the home of
his nativity, and the refinements of the highest social life, to accompany
his father, during the tender years of childhood and youth, in his various
perigrinations, as a missionary to the Mohawk Indians in Pennsylvania,
and as an evangelist to the scattered inhabitants of Virginia, North and
South Carolina, and Georgia. Thus, at the same time that he became a
witness of the self-denial and heroic zeal of his father, his constitution

became hardened by the active life to which he was subjected, so that, to a good old age, he was able to undergo a vast amount of physical labour. Riding on horseback became his usual mode of travelling; and twice in this way did he perform the long journey from Georgia to Connecticut and back. In these excursions, so exhilarating to the feelings, and so conducive to health, it would appear, from his diary, that he never lost an opportunity of preaching. He was in stature low, but remarkable for strength and agility. Indeed, after he had entered the ministry, he appears to have still indulged a passion for running and wrestling. It is related of him, that he was once bathing with a number of others in a river, and an Irishman, who made one of the party, and who could not swim, leaped on to his back as soon as he made his plunge into the deep stream. In order to save his life, he sank to the bottom, until his companion was compelled to relax his hold to prevent suffocation.

He was the subject of early religious impressions; but it was not until he had reached his twentieth year that he made an open profession of religion, and united himself with the Baptist Church at Kiokee, Columbia County, Ga.,—the first Baptist Church constituted in the State. Soon after this, he began his labours as a licentiate, and, in his twenty-seventh year, was ordained as an Evangelist. At the death of his father, in 1784, he succeeded to the pastoral care of the church at Kiokee,—a relation which he held until his own death, in 1819.

His education was, in early life, confined to about forty days instruction in what is known in Georgia as an " old field school ;" but his manliness of character, his native good sense, his all but perfect acquaintance with the avenues to the human heart, his familiarity with the Bible, his splendid bugle-like voice, and his unquenchable zeal in his Master's service, supplied, in a great measure, this lack, and rendered him acceptable as a preacher amid the refinement of cities, and to churches holding other doctrines than his own. Whilst preaching to a Congregational church in the town of Simsbury, Conn., where there was a very crowded audience, the galleries gave way, from the unusual pressure, and he was forced to resort to what, with him, was very common—preaching in the open air. But he had enough of the art of the orator to turn the consternation that ensued to a good account, and thus made a powerful impression on the hearers.

It falls to the lot of but few ministers, especially those whose advantages for education are so limited, to attain the fame of Abraham Marshall. His labours were not confined to a single city or town, to any one County or State, still less to a single church; but, of the two thousand whom he baptized, some were in Connecticut,—the land of his nativity ; many were in Georgia, his principal field of labour ; and not a few were scattered over the intervening States. It may not be assuming too much to say that it was owing, in no small degree, to a few zealous labourers in the early settlement of Georgia,—Abraham Marshall among the number,—that such seed was planted, as produced the surprising result which we now behold in the Baptist denomination.

But it is not as a minister only that Mr. Marshall must be viewed. He was, when necessity required, a soldier in our Revolution, and fought in the battle at Augusta. He was also a delegate to the State Convention, when the Constitution was formed. He was prominent among the friends of Education in the State; was a Trustee of the State University; and, in the Baptist State Convention, he appears prominent as a promoter of education amongst the denomination of his choice.

At the age of forty-four, he married Miss Ann Waller, daughter of the Rev. John Waller, of Spottsylvania County, Va., by whom he had four sons;—one of whom (*Jabez*) became a minister, who succeeded him as Pastor of the famous Kiokee Church. Thus, for nearly fifty years, was that church under the pastoral charge of a Marshall. Nor has the race of Marshalls, as preachers, yet become extinct—a fourth, in the order of generation, still lives to hold up Christ crucified; and, if the prayers of a dying mother be heard, and her consecrated offer be accepted, a fifth,—a lovely child of two and a half summers, will yet stand on the walls of Zion. A College in Griffin bears the name of Marshall.

At the ripe age of seventy-three, this servant of God was called to put on immortality. His last sermon was preached to his beloved charge at Kiokee, the Sabbath before he died. Among his last words, were these—" I have.fought a good fight; I have finished my course; I have kept the faith; henceforth there is laid up for me a crown of righteousness, which the Lord, the righteous Judge, will give me at that day."

His method of preaching was extemporaneous. He, indeed, made copious skeletons, many of which were included in the biography which was written by his son. Only one of his sermons was ever published—the text was " The iron did swim." It was preached before the Faculty and Students of the State University.

Hoping that the above may answer the purpose contemplated by your request.

I am very truly yours,
A. E. MARSHALL.

FROM THE REV. JURIAH HARRISS.

Appling, Columbia County, Ga.,
March 21, 1859.

Dear Sir: I have received your letter, asking for my recollections of the late Rev. Abraham Marshall, and am glad of an opportunity to render my testimony in honour of that truly venerable man. I became acquainted with him, first, in February, 1807, when I came into his immediate neighbourhood to reside. About that time, he performed the ceremony of marriage for me, and I always lived within a short distance from his dwelling, and a still shorter distance from his church, until his death, which was about a dozen years. This gave me an opportunity not only of hearing him in public, but of frequent personal intercourse with him, of observing him in various circumstances and relations, and, in short, of forming an intelligent opinion of his character.

Mr. Marshall, when I first knew him, was a man of decidedly fine personal appearance. He was rather low in stature,—not more than five feet, eight or nine inches, of a square frame, and a full habit, without being corpulent. When he was dressed in his fine suit of black broadcloth, with his long, white-topped boots, after a fashion that still lingered at that day, his appearance was really imposing. Though his early education was quite limited, his mind was naturally of a superior order, and, by the aid of a good library, he ultimately attained to a very considerable degree of mental culture. His dispositions were amiable and benevolent, and his manners affable and winning—indeed he may be said to have been an accomplished man, of the old school. He had a good knowledge of men and things, and had a large fund of anecdotes at command, which he could put in requisition to illustrate almost any subject, and which served greatly to enliven his conversation. I heard him preach pretty constantly from 1807-to 1819; and my honest conviction is that—take him all in all—I have not known his superior. I do not remember ever to have heard him preach what I would call an indifferent sermon. His voice was one of great power, melody, and flexibility—it could pass from the highest to the lowest note in the twinkling of an eye, and with the most graceful facility. In nothing, perhaps, was he more remarkable than the power of description. He would portray the glories of Heaven with such matchless force and beauty, that his hearers could scarcely remain upon their seats; and then he would depict the miseries of the lost in such terrible, burning language, as almost to make the hair stand erect upon your head. Dr. Gill and Dr. Doddridge were, I suppose, his favourite theological authors; for he quoted from them more frequently than from any others; but his quotations—no matter who the author might be—were always made with great ease,—thus illustrating the remarkable power and readiness of his memory. And he was an eminently successful as well as popular preacher—large numbers were baptized, and admitted to the church, under his ministry. He had great influence among his brethren, and, as an illustration of their regard for his character, I may mention that, from the time I first knew him until his death, he was always the Moderator of the Georgia Association. Indeed he commanded great attention, and occupied a wide space, in his day; and his name is still fragrant much beyond the limits of his own denomination.

Very truly yours,
JURIAH HARRISS.

—————◆◆—————

JOHN HASTINGS.*
1775—1811.

JOHN HASTINGS was born in Suffield, Conn., in the year 1743. His father was Joseph Hastings, who was a farmer, and for some time a member of the First Congregational Church in Suffield. Soon after the "Great Awakening" commenced, (about 1742,) he (the father) seceded from that church, and united with others in forming a Separate church, in the Western part of the town, of which he was himself subsequently ordained Pastor; but how long he continued in that relation is not known. It appears, however, from Backus' History, that he, with several other preachers in the Separate connection, were baptized by immersion, in 1752; but it does not appear that he changed his ecclesiastical relations for several years afterwards. In 1763, he was one of a number to organize the First Baptist Church of Suffield. As he had been Pastor of the Separate church, so he was regarded Pastor of the new Baptist church, though there is no evidence that he ever received ordination or installation as a Baptist clergyman. He was, at this time, sixty-six years of age; but he was sole

* Backus' Hist. N. E.—MSS. from Rev. E. Andrews and Rev. G. Robins.

Pastor until 1775, when his son John was ordained, as Associate Pastor. After the settlement of his son, he travelled abroad, preaching in various places, until near the time of his death; and was instrumental, by this means, of doing much to advance the interests of his denomination. He died in 1785, aged eighty-two years.

John Hastings, the son, was, during the earlier part of his life, not only a neglecter, but a contemner of religion. For several years after he had a family of his own, he lived in his father's house, and was rendered, by his infidelity, so forgetful even of filial respect, that he made his preaching a subject of ridicule. He was, however, a good singer, and used to lead the singing in his father's church; but he always made it a point to leave the place of worship before the sermon. He used to play the violin, for dancing parties, and would often tell his companions in gaiety that his father had always predicted that he would become a preacher, and that they must make up their minds to hear preaching from him instead of fiddling. The same gift that made him the centre of attraction in the convivial circle, afterwards rendered him no less attractive in the religious circle. The event which was chiefly instrumental in bringing him to serious reflection, was connected immediately with his marriage. He was married, in his early manhood, to Rachel Remmington, of Suffield; and, when he commenced housekeeping, he thought it his duty, according to the custom of that day, with strange inconsistency, to institute family worship. He found himself, however, utterly incompetent to the service; and, as he occupied part of his father's house, he made a compromise with his conscience, by going with his wife into his father's apartment, at the appointed hour, and hearing him read and pray. The old man told John and Rachel that that would never do—that, as they had become a distinct family, so they must have worship by themselves; and that he could not countenance their coming into his room to share in the devotions. This prohibition and admonition lodged an arrow of conviction in John's heart, and he found no peace until he had become a penitent at the foot of the Cross, and there erected a domestic altar. The exact period of his conversion is not known; but in 1775 he had become a minister of the Gospel, and, as has been already intimated, was ordained, in that year, as Co-pastor with his father, of the First Baptist Church in Suffield. After his father's death, in 1785, he continued in sole charge of the church until his own death, which occurred on the 17th of March, 1811, at the age of sixty-eight. During the thirty-six years that his ministry continued, he travelled extensively in different parts of the country, and was instrumental in gathering a large number of churches. His own church greatly increased in numbers and strength, and became one of the largest and most efficient Baptist churches in Connecticut. It is said that, during his whole ministry, he baptized about eleven hundred persons.

Mr. Hastings became prematurely an old man, so that, for several years previous to his death, his pulpit was supplied by other ministers, among whom was the Rev. Caleb Green.* He died in great peace of mind, and

* CALEB GREEN was born in Newport, R. I., in the year 1767, and early became a member of the Baptist Church in his native town. Though his advantages for school education were but limited, his father's house was the resort of many ministers and other persons of intelligence and piety, from whose conversation, especially on religious and theological subjects, he derived

is held in grateful remembrance throughout the region in which he exercised his ministry.

FROM THE REV. DANIEL WALDO.

SYRACUSE, February 19, 1858.

My dear friend: I ought to be able to tell you something about Elder Hastings; for he was my neighbour for eighteen years, and my relations with him were always of the most agreeable and fraternal kind. Though we belonged to different denominations, that circumstance never in the least interfered with our social and Christian intercourse, and indeed the points of difference between us we rarely conversed upon, and never but in the most kindly spirit.

In private life, Elder Hastings was highly and deservedly esteemed. He was a man of an amiable temper, and of a pleasant and cordial manner; and while he was always ready, in social intercourse, to bear his part in the conversation, he was no less ready to listen to others, and always seemed grateful for any information they might communicate. He had had, I think, nothing more than a common education, and his general knowledge was not very extensive; but he had naturally a mind of more than ordinary capacity, and was capable, either in or out of the pulpit, of making a vigorous effort. He was especially a diligent student of the Bible; and I remember his once saying that there was no passage in it upon which his mind was not so definitely made up that he felt ready to preach upon it. This, doubtless, was more than most of his brethren would be able to say; but it showed at least a consciousness of what was undoubtedly true,—that he was much devoted to the study of the Scriptures.

Elder Hastings' preaching was of a strongly evangelical tone, the type of his Theology being, I think, pretty high Calvinism. He had a manly and pleasant voice, which he modulated to very good purpose, and manifested that interest in his subject and his audience, that rarely fails to produce an effect. He never, I believe, preached even from short notes, and I doubt whether he ever wrote a sermon; still, his thoughts were generally well expressed, and quite consecutive, though I sometimes thought that a little more premeditation would have rendered his discourses somewhat shorter. I suppose him to have been one of the most popular, as well as successful, preachers of his denomination in Connecticut, during the period in which he lived.

Elder Hastings was a very decided Baptist, and yet it gives me pleasure to say that I never saw any thing in him to indicate an unfair, sectarian spirit. With the Rev. Mr. Gay, the minister of the First Congregational Parish, to whom he was a still nearer neighbour than to myself, he was always on the

great advantage. On arriving at manhood, he was licensed to preach by the church of which he was a member, and was immediately after chosen its Pastor. He, however, owing to some peculiar circumstances, felt obliged to divide his time between his pastoral and secular duties,—being at the same time a busy merchant and an earnest preacher. He was a zealous politician of the Jefferson school, and was not only the representative of his town in the State Legislature, but occupied the Speaker's chair in that Body. Through his whole life, he was the uncompromising enemy of slavery, and exerted himself to the utmost for its abolition. In 1809, he removed to Suffield, and at first officiated for the Mother Church, but soon became Pastor of the Second. Here he remained, giving his undivided attention to the ministry, during a period of six years. He then became Pastor of the neighbouring church of Westfield, Mass., and, at a later period, of the church in Waterford, N. Y. During the latter part of his life, he enlisted with great zeal in the cause of Anti-Masonry. His last ten years were years of much bodily debility. The last time that he left his house was the day of the Presidential Election, in 1840; and, when he had deposited his vote, he felt that his last act as a citizen was performed. His death, which took place shortly after, was marked by the utmost composure, and his attention seemed fastened upon the mysterious process of dissolution, even up to the point of taking note of his last pulsation. He possessed an uncommonly vigorous mind, and an indomitable strength of purpose.

most friendly terms, and, so far as I know, enjoyed the respect and confidence of the whole neighbourhood.

In his person, he was fully the medium height and size, and stooped a little in his gait. His whole personal bearing was that of a plain but dignified man.

Yours affectionately,

DANIEL WALDO.

JOHN LELAND.*
1775—1841.

JOHN LELAND was born of Congregational parents, in Grafton, Mass., on the 14th of May, 1754. He evinced an early fondness for learning, though he enjoyed no other advantages than were furnished by the common schools. The minister of the town urged his father to give him a collegiate education, with a view to his becoming a minister; the physician of the place was equally desirous that he should become a medical practitioner; and he himself had formed the purpose of being a lawyer; but his father designed that he should remain with him, as the support of his declining years. Though he was, by no means, free from serious reflection, and occasionally even suffered deep remorse, during his childhood and early youth, he seems to have yielded, to some extent, to vicious indulgences, until he reached the age of eighteen, when he became deeply impressed with the importance of eternal realities. For the next fifteen months, his mind was in an unsettled, and much of the time agitated, state; and the record that he has left of his exercises shows that he was disposed to deal with himself with great honesty and fidelity. It was during this period that he became acquainted with Elhanan Winchester, then a young Baptist (afterwards a Universalist) preacher, whose influence probably assisted to give a direction to his mind favourable to the distinctive views of the Baptists. On the 1st of June, 1774, he was baptized at Northbridge, with seven others, by Elder Noah Alden, of Bellingham. On the 20th of the same month,—there being no preacher at the meeting in Grafton, to which he had gone,—he felt constrained to say a few words himself; and, finding that he had an unexpected freedom of utterance, he continued to speak, with comfort to himself, and to the edification of his hearers, for half an hour. He now formed the purpose of devoting himself to the ministry, and, from that time, preached in the neighbouring towns, whenever he was requested. In the autumn of that year, he joined Bellingham Church, (for until then he had belonged to no church,) and, "about six months after," he says, "that church gave me a license to do that which I had been doing for a year before."

In October, 1775, he made a journey to Virginia, and did not return till about the beginning of the next summer. On the 30th of September, 1776, he was married to Sally Devine, of Hopkinton, Mass., and immediately started with her for Virginia, where he had previously found, as he

* Autobiography, &c.

thought, an advantageous field for labour. At Mount Poney, in Culpepper, he joined the church, and engaged to preach there every alternate Sabbath. In August, he was ordained, by request of the church, without the imposition of the hands of a Presbytery; and, as this was a departure from the usage of the Virginia churches, they generally withheld from him their fellowship. He remained in Culpepper but a short time, as difficulties, with which he was more or less connected, sprung up in the church, and he was glad to seek another field. He removed now to the County of Orange, and laboured abundantly, but, for some time, without much apparent success. He, however, very soon commenced his preaching tours in different parts of the State, and extending sometimes much beyond the State, in which his labours were instrumental often of gathering large numbers into the church. In 1784, he travelled Northward as far as Philadelphia, where he remained six weeks. As he went in company with Mr. Winchester, who, meanwhile, had become a Universalist, he was suspected of holding the same views with his fellow-traveller, and, therefore, was not invited to preach in the Baptist meeting-house in Philadelphia; but he preached in the Hall of the University, and in private houses, and, as the number of his hearers increased, he appointed meetings in the street, which were very largely attended; and, as a result of his labours here, he baptized four persons in the Schuylkill.

In June, 1787, he was ordained by the laying on of hands, by means of which he was brought into fraternal relations with the Baptist ministers in the State generally. In 1788, he laboured constantly in a revival, extending through several counties, and baptized three hundred persons. In 1790, he made a journey to New England, to visit his friends, and was absent about four months, during which time he baptized thirty-two. The winter following, he made his arrangements to remove to New England for a permanent home; having baptized seven hundred persons during his residence in Virginia, and having, at that time, charge of two large churches, one in the County of Orange, the other in the County of Louisa. On the last of March, 1791, he embarked with his family at Fredericksburg, and, after a most perilous voyage, in which all hope of making land was, for a time, abandoned, the vessel arrived at New London, Conn. Having remained there a couple of months, he went with his family to Sunderland, Mass., and thence to Conway, in the same neighbourhood, where his father and some of his early acquaintance were living, and where he determined to make a temporary residence. Here his family remained about eight months, while he was himself occupied chiefly in travelling, with a view to find a place which might be their permanent home. In February, 1792, he removed his family to Cheshire, Mass., where he spent a considerable part of his remaining days.

Elder Leland made a visit to his old friends in Virginia, in the summer of 1797, and was absent from home about six months. In 1800, he made a tour of four months, travelling Southward as far as Bedford, N. Y., and Eastward into Rhode Island and Massachusetts. In November, 1801, occurred the event of his life, which perhaps has contributed as much to his celebrity as any other,—the affair of the Mammoth Cheese. He went to Washington City to present an immense cheese to Mr. Jefferson, as a present from his people at Cheshire, and a testimony of their approbation of his politics. It was made from curds, furnished, on a particular day, by the dairy-women of the town, and weighed fourteen hundred and fifty pounds. The Elder presented it in behalf of his people, as a "pepper-corn" of their esteem for the Democratic President. Referring to this event, he says,—"Notwithstanding my trust, I preached all the way there, and on my return. I had large congregations, led in part by curiosity to hear the Mammoth Priest, as I was called."

In March, 1804, he removed into Dutchess County, N. Y.; but returned to Cheshire in 1806. At the close of 1813 and the beginning of 1814, he made another visit to Virginia, and remained in the State eighty days, during which time he travelled seven hundred miles, and preached more than seventy times. In the autumn, after his return home, he sold his place in Cheshire with a view to removing into the Western part of New York, where his children were settled, but his object was defeated by the breaking of his leg shortly after; and he purchased a place at New Ashford, where he lived for more than sixteen years; but, in November, 1831, he returned to Cheshire.

In 1819, Elder Leland wrote a brief narrative of his life, from which the following is an extract:—

"Since I began to preach, in 1774, I have travelled distances which, together, would form a girdle nearly sufficient to go round the terraqueous globe three times. The number of sermons which I have preached is not far from eight thousand. The number of persons whom I have baptized is one thousand, two hundred and seventy-eight. The number of Baptist ministers whom I have personally known is nine hundred and sixty-two. Those of them whom I have heard preach, in number, make three hundred and three. Those who have died, (whose deaths I have heard of,) amount to three hundred. The number that have visited me at my house is two hundred and seven. The pamphlets which I have written, that have been published, are about thirty.

"I am now in the decline of life, having lived nearly two-thirds of a century. When Jacob had lived twice as long, his days had been few and evil Looking over the foregoing narrative, there is proof enough of imperfection; and yet what I have written is the best part of my life. A history seven times as large might be written of my errors in judgment, incorrectness of behaviour, and baseness of heart. My only hope of acceptance with God is in the blood and righteousness of Jesus Christ. And when I come to Christ for pardon, I come as an old gray-headed sinner; in the language of the Publican,—'God be merciful to me a sinner.'"

On the 10th of November, 1831, he writes thus:—

"My age and decays admonish me that the time of my departure is not far distant. When I die, I neither desire nor deserve any funeral pomp. If my friends think best to rear a little monument over my body, 'Here lies the body of JOHN LELAND, who laboured —— to promote piety, and vindicate the civil and religious rights of all men,' is the sentence which I wish to be engraved upon it."

Elder Leland continued to prosecute his ministerial labours till near the close of his life. On the 5th of October, 1837, he was afflicted by the death of his wife, in whom he had found a most efficient and admirable helper, during a large part of his pilgrimage. Shortly after her death, he removed to the house of his son-in-law, Mr. James Greene, in Lanes-borough, where he resided most of the time till his death. In the summer of 1838, he made a journey to Utica, and its vicinity, (the residence of his eldest son,) and was absent several weeks. In the winter of 1840–41, he was induced, by some considerations, to remove back, for a few weeks, to Cheshire, to the house of Mr. Chapman. His last sermon was preached at North Adams, on the evening of the 8th of January, 1841, from I John

ii. 20, 27. After the service, he went to the house of a Mr. Darling, and appeared as well and cheerful as usual. Soon after he retired to his chamber, the family were alarmed by an unusual noise, and Mr. D., on going to the room, found him prostrate on the floor. It was apparent, at once, that he was seriously ill; but, being placed in a bed, he was able, during the night, to get a little rest. He continued until the evening of the 14th, suffering little, except from laborious breathing, but making many strikingly characteristic demonstrations,—and then passed away so quietly that it was impossible to fix the moment of his departure. His remains were conveyed to Cheshire for interment; and a Funeral Discourse was delivered by the Rev. John Alden, from Rev. xiv, 13.

Elder Leland was among the most prolific writers of his denomination in this country, at least during the period in which he lived. His productions, which consist of Occasional Sermons and Addresses, and Essays on a great variety of subjects, moral, religious, and political, were published, in a large octavo volume, together with his Autobiography, and additional notices of his life by Miss L. F. Greene, of Lanesborough, in 1845.

FROM THE HON. G. N. BRIGGS, LL. D.,
GOVERNOR OF THE STATE OF MASSACHUSETTS.

PITTSFIELD, Mass., April 15, 1857.

Dear Sir: The first personal recollection I have of Elder John Leland dates back to 1803 or 1804; when he lodged a night at the house of my father in Manchester, Vt. He had started on a missionary tour to Canada, on horseback. In the morning, after he left, he called at a house about a mile on his way to deliver a message to the family from their brother in Cheshire. The woman of the house came to the door, and, on learning who she was, he said,—"Madam, your brother in Cheshire wished me to call and tell you that his family are well." As he was turning his horse, she inquired his name—"You may call me Mr. John," said he, "and I stayed at Capt. B.'s last night;" and rode on. Some of the family were very soon at Capt. B.'s to ask who the odd stranger was. On hearing, they were much disappointed and surprised that so noted a man had dodged them so successfully. On his return from Canada, he preached in the neighbourhood, to the great delight of the people. I was a small boy, but I distinctly remember his person and manner.

Three or four years before he died, Mrs. Briggs and myself spent an afternoon with him, and his aged and worthy wife. They had then lived together more than sixty years. They lived entirely by themselves. "As to numbers and family," said he, "we are just where we started in life." They had ten children, and I think he told me they were all then living; and what was most remarkable, he said they had never had a death in their house. Their house was an humble, but convenient, dwelling, a mile from the village of Cheshire. The inside was a beautiful specimen of the antique, of convenience, neatness and taste,—a model from which modern and more fashionable houses could have taken useful lessons. He was then eighty-five, and she eighty-three, years old. To me it was an afternoon of rare interest, enjoyment, and instruction. When the tea hour approached, the good old mother went about getting tea, in the style and manner of her own time. She kneaded and baked her nice short cake, and cooked her steak in the same room where we sat. When supper was on the table, nothing about her person indicated that she had been cook, and nothing in the room showed that that simple and tasteful repast had been prepared there. In due time, the venerable form of that aged minister bent over the table, as he implored the blessing of Heaven, and we sat down. In the fulness of my heart, I said to him,—"Sir, I never sat down to a table with more pleasure than I do to this." With patriarchal dignity and simplicity, he instantly replied,—"You never sat down to a table where you were more welcome."

In the course of the afternoon, he spoke of many of the incidents of his long life. When he was twenty-one years of age, the only books in his father's house, and that he had ever read, were the Bible, Bunyan's Pilgrim's Progress, and Doddridge's Rise and Progress of Religion in the soul. He said he had been charged with being an enemy to education; but it was not so—he was a friend to education, and always had been. "Education," said he, "has but one enemy in the world; and that is ignorance." He believed the history of the Christian world would show that learning with clergymen had too often been made to take the place of piety, and those spiritual gifts and qualifications, which he deemed essential to one who entered upon the sacred duties of the Gospel ministry. A clergyman could not have too much learning, if it was made subordinate, and especially auxiliary, to those higher spiritual endowments which he considered indispensable, and without which no man had a right to assume to be a minister of the Gospel. From the time he began to feel the need of education, he had had a strong desire to read, and he had read every thing that came within his reach. "Once," said he, "I had a discussion with a Jew as to a passage in the Hebrew Bible; and I went on foot four miles through a wilderness to get a Hebrew Bible to settle the question."

Soon after his conversion, the minister of the parish to which his father belonged preached at his father's house. He was a pious and excellent man. After he had finished his sermon, and taken his seat, he observed that if any one present wished to make any remarks on the subject of the sermon, or any other religious topic, there was then an opportunity, and he should be very happy to hear him. He said that, through the sermon, he had been impressed with the idea that the minister had mistaken the import of the text, and that he ought to give his own views of its true meaning. But it seemed that it would be presumption in a mere boy, in his tow frock and trowsers, with his leather apron on, and in his own father's house,—the neighbours all there, and in the presence of the venerable clergyman, with his great wig on, to call in question the correctness of the minister's interpretation of the Scripture. After waiting some time,—no one else rising, and the invitation being repeated in a kind and familiar manner, he found himself on his feet, and, in the best and most respectful way he could, gave his views as to the true meaning of the text, and resumed his seat. During the few moments of silence which followed, he said he was exceedingly depressed, and felt as though he had been guilty of inexcusable presumption.

Very soon the minister rose, and expressed his satisfaction that the young man had so clearly and properly stated his views of the text upon which he had been commenting; and, though they differed materially from his own, he was not then prepared to say that the young man was not right. He should endeavour carefully to review his own construction of the passage, and try to find out the truth. The friendly and paternal manner of his minister somewhat quieted the perturbation of his own mind, but for a good while he was oppressed with the idea that he had been quite too forward for one of his years.

In the course of the afternoon, I told him that I had recently seen in the public prints an extract from an Eulogy delivered by J. S. Barbour, of Virginia, upon the character of James Madison; that Barbour had said that the credit of adopting the Constitution of the United States properly belonged to a Baptist clergyman, formerly of Virginia, by the name of Leland; and he reached his conclusion in this way—he said that if Madison had not been in the Virginia Convention, the Constitution would not have been ratified by that State; and, as the approval of nine States was required to give effect to this instrument, and as Virginia was the ninth State, if it had been rejected by her, the Constitution would have failed; and that it was by Elder Leland's influence that Madison was elected to that Convention.

He replied that Barbour had given him too much credit; but he supposed he knew to what he referred. He then gave this history of the matter:—Soon after the Convention, which framed the Constitution of the United States, had finished their work, and submitted it to the people for their action, two strong and active parties were formed in the State of Virginia, on the subject of its adoption. The State was nearly equally divided. One party was opposed to its adoption, unless certain amendments, which they maintained that the safety of the people required, should be incorporated into it, before it was ratified by them. At the head of this great party stood Patrick Henry, the Orator of the Revolution, and one of Virginia's favourite sons. The other party agreed with what their opponents said as to the character and necessity of the amendments proposed; but they contended that the people would have the power, and could as well incorporate those amendments into their Constitution after its adoption as before; that it was a great crisis in the affairs of the country, and if the Constitution, then presented to the people by the Convention, should be rejected by them, such would be the state of the public mind, that there was little or no reason to believe that another would be agreed upon by a future Convention; and, in such an event,—so much to be dreaded,—the hopes of constitutional liberty and a confederated and free Republic would be lost. At the head of this party stood James Madison. The strength of the two parties was to be tested by the election of County Delegates to the State Convention. That Convention would have to adopt or reject the Constitution. Mr. Madison was named as the candidate in favour of its adoption for the County of Orange, in which he resided. Elder Leland, also, at that time, lived in the County of Orange, and his sympathies, he said, were with Henry and his party. He was named as the candidate opposed to the adoption, and in opposition to Mr. Madison. Orange was a strong Baptist County; and his friends had an undoubting confidence in his election. Though reluctant to be a candidate, he yielded to the solicitations of the opponents of the Constitution, and accepted the nomination.

For three months after the members of the Convention at Philadelphia had completed their labours, and returned to their homes, Mr. Madison, with John Jay and Alexander Hamilton, had remained in that city for the purpose of preparing those political articles that now constitute *The Federalist*. This gave the party opposed to Madison, with Henry at their head, the start of him, in canvassing the State in his absence. At length, when Mr. Madison was about ready to return to Virginia, a public meeting was appointed in the County of Orange, at which the candidates for the Convention,—Madison on the one side, and Leland on the other,—were to address the people from the stump. Up to that time he had but a partial personal acquaintance with Mr. Madison, but he had a high respect for his talents, his candour, and the uprightness and purity of his private character. On his way home from Philadelphia, Mr. Madison went some distance out of his direct road to call upon him. After the ordinary salutations, Mr. Madison began to apologize for troubling him with a call at that time; but he assured Mr. M. that no apology was necessary—" I know your errand here," said he, " it is to talk with me about the Constitution. I am glad to see you, and to have an opportunity of learning your views on the subject." Mr. Madison spent half a day with him, and fully and unreservedly communicated to him his opinions upon the great matters which were then agitating the people of the State and the Confederacy.

They then separated to meet again very soon, as opposing candidates before the electors, on the stump. The day came, and they met, and with them nearly all the voters in the County of Orange, to hear their candidates respectively discuss the important questions upon which the people of Virginia were so soon to act. "Mr. Madison," said the venerable man, "first took the stump, which was a hogshead of tobacco, standing on one end. For two hours, he addressed his fellow-citizens in a calm, candid and statesman-like manner, arguing his side of the case, and fairly meeting and replying to the arguments, which had been put forth by his opponents, in the general canvass of the State. Though Mr. Madison was not particularly a pleasing or eloquent speaker, the people listened with respectful attention. He left the hogshead, and my friends called for me. I took it——and went in for Mr. Madison; and he was elected without difficulty. This," said he, " is, I suppose, what Mr. Barbour alluded to." A noble Christian Patriot! That single act, with the motives which prompted it, and the consequences which followed it, entitle him to the respect of mankind.

After Elder Leland came to Massachusetts, he kept up a correspondence with Mr. Madison for many years. He said he had given to his friends all Mr. Madison's letters, except one, and that he showed to me. One opinion, I remember, was expressed in it, which seems singular enough to those acquainted with the present condition of the revenues of this Government, and shows how very limited and incorrect were the views of the public men of that day, as to the future sources of revenue for the United States. He said it was not probable that the duties derived from imports would ever be sufficient to defray the expenses of the Government.

For candour, integrity, and intelligence, he placed Mr. Madison before any of our statesmen whom he had ever known. As a public debater, he said he had one trait which he had never witnessed in any other man—after stating, in the clearest manner, the positions and arguments of his opponent, if that opponent had omitted any thing that would strengthen his side of the case, he would add it, and then proceed to meet and answer the whole.

When in Virginia, he was in the habit, occasionally, of preaching at the house of a widow lady, who had a son who had been an officer in the Revolutionary War. After the War closed, he came home, and became both a drunkard and an infidel. He was displeased at the meetings being held at his mother's house, and gave out threats that if Leland came there again to preach, he would kill him. His threats, however, were disregarded; and, after that, when another meeting was being held, this Captain came home drunk, and during sermon time. He made his way through the people in one of the rooms, and seized his sword, which hung on the wall, drew it from the scabbard, and rushed towards the preacher. No one interposed to arrest him, until he got almost within reach of the object of his malice, " when, instantly," said the old gentleman, " a pair of arms were thrown around him from behind, and they held him as firm as a vice, until he was disarmed by others, and secured." Turning his bright blue eye, and pointing his finger, towards his aged wife, whose arms hung down by her side, he said,—" Those are the arms which arrested and held the madman. The men present seemed to be stupified by the daring act of the desperado."

While I was at his house, I inquired of him about a remarkable noise, which I had, when a boy, heard that he and his family had been annoyed by, when they lived in Virginia. He gave this account of it:—His family, at the time, consisted of himself, wife, and four children. One evening, all the family being together, their attention was attracted by a noise, which very much resembled the faint groans of a person in pain. It was distinct, and repeated at intervals of a few seconds. It seemed to be under the sill of the window, and between the clap-boards and the ceiling. They paid very little attention to it, and in a short time it ceased. But, afterwards, it returned in the same way—sometimes every night, and sometimes not so frequently, and always in the same place, and of the same character. It continued for some months. He said it excited their curiosity, and annoyed them, but they were not alarmed by it. During its continuance, they had the siding and casing removed from the place where it appeared to be, but found nothing to account for it; and the sound continued the same. He consulted his friends, especially some of his ministerial brethren, about it. I think he said it was never heard by any except himself and his family; but it was heard by them when he was absent from home. Mrs. Leland said that often, when she was alone with the children, and while they were playing about the room, and nothing being said, it would come, and they would leave their play, and gather about her person. They had a place fifty or sixty rods from the house, by the side of a brook, where the family did their washing. One day, while she was at that place, it met her there precisely as it had in the house.

After the noise had been heard at brief intervals for, I think, six or eight months, they removed their lodgings to quite an opposite and distant part of the house; but it continued as usual, for some time, in its old locality. One night, after they had retired, they observed, by the sound, that it had left the spot from which it had previously proceeded, and seemed to be advancing, in a direct line, towards their bed, and was becoming constantly louder and more distinct. At each interval, it advanced towards them, and gathered strength and fulness, until it entered the room where they were, and approached the bed, and came along on the front side of the bed, when the groan became deep and appalling. "Then," said he, "for the first time since it began I felt the emotion of fear; I turned upon my face, and if I ever prayed in my life, I prayed then. I asked the Lord to deliver me and my family from that annoyance, and that, if it were a message from Heaven, it might be explained to us, and depart; that if it were an evil spirit, permitted to disturb and disquiet me and my family, it might be rebuked, and sent away; or if there was any thing for me to do, to make it depart, I might be instructed what it was, so that I could do it." This exercise restored his tranquillity of mind, and he resumed his usual position in the bed. Then, he said, it uttered a groan too loud and startling to be imitated by the human voice. The next groan was not so loud, and it had receded a step or two from the front of the bed, near his face. It continued to recede in the direction from which it came, and grew less and less, until it reached its old station, when it died away to the faintest sound, and entirely and forever ceased.

No explanation was ever found. "I have given you," said he, "a simple and true history of the facts, and you can form your own opinion. I give none." His wife confirmed all he said. I think I can say that I never knew a person less given to the marvellous than Elder Leland.

Forty years ago, a very intelligent physician in this county became pious. He had long known Elder Leland. One day he met him on the highway, leisurely driving along a horse that he called Billy. They both stopped, and, after some conversation, the Doctor told him that he should be glad to have his views upon two or three points of religious doctrine. First, as to the Sovereignty of God. This was with Elder Leland a favourite theme, and one in which his head and his heart had been engaged for sixty years. He proceeded, and occupied several minutes in repeating appropriate passages of Scripture, and commenting upon them in a most lucid and able manner, until the Doctor said that he was entirely satisfied with those views. "Now," said he, "please let me know what you think of the free agency of man." With no less authority from Scripture, and no less potency of reason, he made this point equally satisfactory. "Now, Elder," said the Doctor,—"one more solution, and I shall be entirely satisfied—will you tell me how you reconcile these two great and important truths." "Doctor," said he, "there was once a mother, who, while busy with her needle, was teaching her little daughter to read. The child at length came to a hard word, and asked her mother what it was. 'Spell it, my child,' said she. The child made an effort, but did not succeed. 'Mother,' said she, 'I can't spell it.' 'Let me see it then.' She handed her the book, and the mother, after puzzling over it for some time, returned it to the child, and said,—'Skip it then.'" "Get up, Billy," said the Elder, and drove along, leaving the Doctor to skip the word, or ponder over it, as he pleased.

I once heard him say in a sermon that, in the course of his life, he had not unfrequently heard preachers,—generally young men, propose to prove the sovereignty of God, and the free agency of man, and then to show the harmony between them. "At the last point," said he, "I always dropped my head; for, though they always did it to their own satisfaction, they rarely satisfied any of their hearers. And what is more remarkable,—no two of them ever came out in the same place with their demonstrations."

He said he had some ten or twelve sermons that were quite distinct, and did not run into each other. When he had preached them, he took new texts, relied on the bad memories of his hearers, and got along in the best way he could. "But," said he, "if I take my text in Genesis, my conclusion carries me forward to the third chapter of John: if I start in Revelations, I must go back, and end my sermon in the same third chapter of John." I do not think I ever heard him preach a sermon in which this remark was not illustrated and verified—when the great truth uttered by the Saviour to Nicodemus, was not, in terms, proclaimed to and enforced upon his hearers.

When in Virginia, he had an appointment to preach at the house of a planter, in a distant part of the State. Not being able to reach the place on Saturday night, early on Sunday morning he rose and pursued his journey. Coming to a plantation, which he judged to be near his destination, he rode up to the door, and inquired of a lady how far it was to Mr. such a one's. "This is his plantation," said she. "Then," replied the Elder, "I have an appointment here to-day." "Why," said the lady, "then you are the great Elder Leland, are you?" "Instantly," said he, "the Devil patted me on the back, and said, "you are the great Leland, are ye?" That, he said, was the first time the idea of being a great preacher ever entered his mind. He had always wished and striven to be a powerful and a useful preacher, but never before had the thought beset him of being a great preacher.

More than forty years ago, I heard him preach one evening from this text,— "I will now turn aside, and see this great sight, why the bush is not burned." It was a discourse of great power and impressiveness. Nearly every word was made a distinct head. *I*—Religion is a personal matter. *Will*—The will is involved, and must be active and decided. *Now*—Its importance demands immediate attention, and precedence of all things else. *Turn aside*—The business and cares of life must be laid by, and the whole attention, for the time, be given to the one thing needful. *And see*—It demands inquiry and investigation—consequences of vast importance depend on a right decision. *This great sight, why the bush is not burnt*—The burning, yet unconsumed, bush, represented the union of the Divine and human natures in the person of the Saviour; and the great fact of the incarnation involving the destiny of the soul, and of the race, demands the profoundest investigation of man. He spoke an hour and three-quarters; but there was no flagging of interest in the hearers, and their silent and breathless attention continued till the sound of the last word died upon his lips. He preached some of his most interesting discourses, when, as he said, he took an Old Testament text, and preached a New Testament Sermon. This was emphatically one of that class.

His preaching had none of the charms either of a refined oratory or a cultivated rhetoric; but there were times when, his great Christian heart being filled with his all-inspiring theme, I have heard him appeal to an audience with a pathos and power that I have never known to be exceeded in the desk. He had a gesture of great significance and effect, when he was deeply interested. It was that of swinging his hand, half closed, from his mouth the whole length of his arm; and it had the appearance of throwing his words broadcast over the congregation. I have rarely heard a person speak of hearing him preach, who has not alluded to that remarkable and impressive gesture. He used no swelling or high-sounding words, but spoke plain, good, John Bunyan Saxon. His prayers were all and always prayers,—direct, earnest and short. Sometimes, after a sermon in which he had been greatly moved himself, he literally agonized in prayer.

Many years ago, I heard him preach in Pittsfield, to a large congregation, when his text was from that chapter of the Acts in which the history of Philip and the Eunuch is given. His subject included that narrative, and involved the question of Baptism. He read on till he came to the question, put by the Eunuch to Philip,—" See here is water, what doth hinder me to be baptized. And Philip said, " if thou believest with all thine heart, thou mayest." And then read, " Philip and the Eunuch went up the broad alley of the meeting-house, and Philip put his hand in a basin of water, and laid it on the Eunuch's head, and baptized him, and they came out of the meeting-house, and the Eunuch went on his way rejoicing." " Stop, Leland," said he, " you don't read right?" and beginning again,—" And they went down both into the water, both Philip and the Eunuch. Ah, that's it," and went on with the narrative; and he finished his sermon with no other allusion to the subject.

On another occasion, he gave an account of his own Baptism, when he was a child. The minister came to his father's house to baptize him. When he learned the fact, he fled, and resolved not to be taken back. But the hired girl pursued, overtook, and recaptured him. He, however, had fallen on his face, and his nose bled, so that it was some time before he was in a condition to receive the baptismal water; and he reluctantly submitted at last. And to show that children had no voluntary part in their Baptism, he said he believed the little saints very generally showed all the resistance in their power. In the course of about thirty of the last years of his life, I heard him preach a great many times, and I believe these were the only two occasions, except at Baptisms, where it was his custom to repeat appropriate passages of Scripture, when going into and coming out of the water, that I ever heard him speak about the subjects or mode of Baptism. In the pulpit he declared his own doctrines and opinions boldly and fearlessly, and sustained them with ability; but he never denounced those who differed from him, or treated their opinions with disrespect. Quite early in life, he eschewed polemic discussions with those who differed with him on the doctrines of religion, as being altogether unprofitable.

He had a pleasant and often amusing humour, sometimes highly satirical, but never acrid.

In his person, Elder Leland was tall, muscular and commanding. Age had slightly bent him, in the later years of his life, but that added to his patriarchal venerableness. He had a noble head; a high, expanded and slightly retreating forehead; a nose a little aquiline, and a bright, beautiful, sparkling blue eye, which eighty-seven years had not dimmed. The expression of his eye, especially in the pulpit, was electrical.

In his manners and personal intercourse he was plain, courteous and dignified. Without the outward polish and veneering of the artificial, he had all the elements and bearing of the real, gentleman. He was bland and kind to all. No man could approach him with a rude familiarity.

Politically, he belonged to the old Republican party. And when this party, in 1824, split into four parts, each supporting its own candidate for the Presidency, he fell in with the Jackson party. Many thought he intermeddled too much in politics for a clergyman; though it is probable that that opinion prevailed most among those who did not belong to the same party with himself. That he was a real friend to the religious and political rights of man, I am sure, no one who ever knew him, can doubt for a moment. It is a fact in respect to him worthy of record, that he discouraged the efforts of his friends to secure his political advancement, or invest him, in any way, with civil authority. Once indeed, in 1811, he consented to be a member of the Legislature, from the town of Cheshire, but it was in the hope that he might be instrumental in securing their legitimate rights to the religious sects of Massachusetts, who did not belong to what was then called "the Standing Order" in the State. He hoped to abate the rigour of existing laws, and lived to see the great principle of what Roger Williams aptly called "Soul Liberty," firmly and forever established in the Commonwealth which gave him birth.

The last time I saw him was in November, 1840, a few days after the election of General Harrison to the Presidency of the United States. I drove up to the public house in Cheshire, just as he had entered his carriage to drive away. After the compliments of the day, he said pleasantly, "Well, you have beat us in the Presidential election—General Harrison is chosen by the people. I yield to the will of the majority constitutionally expressed. It is the duty of all good citizens to do so. I hope his administration will be a good one, and that it will promote the best interests of the country. We are all alike interested to have it so." He then bid me good bye, and I looked upon his venerable person for the last time. His last words to me were those of a true patriot. Such he was.

Respectfully yours,
G. N. BRIGGS.

FROM THE REV. B. T. WELCH, D. D.

NEWTON CORNERS, December 6, 1855.

Dear Sir: I knew the celebrated John Leland intimately, from the commencement of my ministry in Albany; and the first, and last, and every intervening, time that I met him, he impressed me greatly by his eccentricity. On his first visit to my house, I introduced him to my wife, and, as he took her hand and shook it with great apparent cordiality, his first salutation was,— "Well, Madam, that is a sort of hand that I like—it is a good, honest, industrious hand—I know from the feeling of it, that it is well acquainted with domestic duties." After this, he became very familiar in my family, and would, sometimes, when he came, make his way first into the kitchen, light his pipe, and, after taking a whiff or two, without having spoken a word, would say,—"And how is the family?" And then he would go on talking with great fluency, and in his usual eccentric manner.

John Leland's personal appearance was decidedly imposing. He had an uncommonly fine face, a prominent Roman nose, a piercing eye, well-formed and expressive mouth, and altogether he was a model of a fine commanding person. And his intellectual developments corresponded well with his personal appearance. With all his eccentricities, which were almost boundless, and some of them very undesirable, he possessed some very noble traits. He was blunt, often beyond measure, and yet he had a kind and warm heart. His shrewdness was proverbial; and he often exhibited it, in public as well as in private, in a way that would not only provoke a smile, but occasion great amusement. The world is full of anecdotes concerning him; and one or two of them, the authenticity of which, I believe, is unquestionable, I will give you, as furnishing the best illustration of his character.

During the early part of his ministry, as you are aware, the Congregationalists were the " Standing Order " in New England,—the privileged denomination, to the support of which all, unless availing themselves of a special provision to the contrary, were obliged to contribute. Of course the Baptists, in common with some other denominations, looked upon this as a somewhat oppressive exaction. John Leland, in travelling about on his preaching excursions, was accustomed, occasionally, to preach to a small congregation of Baptists, who, for want of a better place of worship, occupied a school-house. One of the Congregational brethren in the neighbourhood told one of the Baptist brethren that Mr. Leland did not preach extempore, but wrote his sermons, and committed them to memory,—which the Baptist of course denied. The Congregationalist then proposed to him that if Mr. L. would preach on a text that should be given to him at the commencement of the service, he would secure for his use the Congregational meeting-house; and the Baptist, after consulting Mr. L., assured him that the requisition should be complied with. Accordingly, the meeting-house was opened, and, as Mr. L. was about to ascend the pulpit stairs, a little piece of paper was put into his hands, indicating the place where the text that he was to preach upon was to be found. He did not open the paper until he rose to begin his sermon; then he opened it leisurely, stating that he did not know what the text was, but that they should quickly see; and, on turning to it in the Bible, he found it to read thus—"And Balaam saddled his ass,"—and, as he announced it, he said that if he had searched the Bible through, he could not have found a text more appropriate. " It brings to our view," said he, " three things,—a *prophet*, an *ass*, and a *saddle*. Balaam, the prophet, who loved the wages of unrighteousness,— and he well represents the class who oppress their fellow-men (otherwise the Congregationalists); the ass, a patient bearer of grievous burdens, represents those who are oppressed by them; and the saddle is the unrighteous exaction that is made of these down-trodden denominations;" and the result was that he preached a sermon that even those who liked the doctrine the least, were obliged to acknowledge, furnished evidence of his remarkable promptness, shrewdness, and pungency.

On another of his circuits, he happened to be in a place where the minister had not long before lost his wife, and had married another, as his people, especially the ladies, generally thought, a little prematurely; and it was agreed to refer the matter to Mr. Leland's judgment. After having heard a full statement of the facts and the complaints in the case, he said very calmly,—" It is evident from the rule which the Apostle has laid down in the seventh chapter of the First Epistle to the Corinthians, that the husband is ' free ' to marry as soon as his wife dies; but, as a matter of decency, perhaps he had better wait at least till she is buried."

That which, probably, interfered more than any thing else with his usefulness as a minister, was his almost mad devotion to politics. He was a very prince among the democrats of his day; and some would doubtless say that he magnified his office as a politician at the expense of lowering it as a Christian minister. On one occasion, when he preached in my pulpit, he took for his text that expression of the Saviour,—"The cup that my Father hath given me, shall I not drink it?"—and he went on through the greater part of his discourse in such a tone of spirituality and evangelical fervour, as led me to think it was impossible that he should descend from such a height to any thing so low as party politics. But I was disappointed after all. By some association that occurred to him, he was carried, in the twinkling of an eye, from the scenes of Calvary to the War of 1812; and, though he afterwards tried to recover himself, by closing in an evangelical strain, the audience had experienced too severe a shock to have the effect of it only momentary. His sermons always showed the workings of a vigorous and original mind, which, with more of culture and less of eccentricity, might have left a bold mark in any of the walks of professional or public usefulness. I do not mean, however, that his mind was uncultivated; for I remember that he seemed familiar with the British poets, and with some of the classics in the English translations, and sometimes he made striking allusions to them in his sermons; but I suppose he never had more than the common advantages of education.

In his prayers, I do not recollect any thing of eccentricity—on the contrary, he seemed to be deeply serious and devout in all his approaches to a Throne of Grace. And I always found him ready to converse on religious subjects, and especially on matters of Christian experience; and I feel bound to say that, while there was much about him that I could not but regret, he left upon my mind a strong impression that he was a truly devout and godly man.

Yours sincerely,

B. T. WELCH.

JOSEPH COOK.*
1776—1790.

JOSEPH COOK was born of pious parents in the city of Bath, England, and was hopefully converted, at an early period of his life, under the preaching of Whitefield, at the Chapel of the late Countess of Huntingdon, in his native city. Whitefield's attention seems to have been particularly drawn to him as a youth of much promise, and he sometimes asked him to ride with him, that he might have an opportunity of conversing with him on religious subjects. Lady Huntingdon also became specially interested in him; and, when he was in his nineteenth year, she sent him to her College, at Trevecka, in Brecknockshire, in South Wales. Here he was a diligent and successful student; and, by his kind and gentle spirit as well as his pious and exemplary walk, he endeared himself greatly to both his Tutors and fellow-students. While pursuing his studies, he occasionally went forth into the neighbouring villages to exercise his gifts in preaching the Gospel; and his labours in this way were always highly acceptable.

In September, 1771, Lady Huntingdon received an anonymous letter, requesting her to send a minister to Margate, in the Island of Thanet,

* Rippon's Register.—Benedict's Hist. Bapt., II.

which was represented to be a very dissolute place. She, accordingly, selected for the mission Mr. William Aldridge, one of her senior students, and gave him liberty to associate with himself any other student whom he might think best suited to such a work. He fixed upon Mr. Cook, who readily consented to accompany him. After making the requisite preparation, they proceeded to the place designated as their field of labour; and, as they were entire strangers, they commenced preaching in the open air. Not a small number came to hear them, and several were supposed to be savingly benefitted; while they gradually extended their labours to other places on the Island.

About this time, many persons in Dover, having become dissatisfied with Mr. Wesley's doctrine and ministers, and left his meeting, applied to these two young itinerants to come and labour among them. They accepted the invitation; and Aldridge preached there, for the first time, on Sabbath day, in the market place, but met with great opposition. The persons who had invited them, then procured the use of a Presbyterian house of worship, which, for some time, had not been occupied; and there the two continued to preach as long as they remained in Dover. It was now arranged that they should supply Margate and Dover, preaching alternately in both places. Mr. Cook's first sermon at Dover awakened great interest, not merely from its earnest, evangelical tone, but from its being delivered extempore,—a mode of preaching to which the people there had never been accustomed. The two continued to supply for some time at Dover, and occasionally also at Deal and Falkstone, and, at the latter place particularly, their preaching was attended with a signal blessing.

Two years after, Lady Huntingdon, having been informed that there were many favourable openings for the preaching of the Gospel in North America, resolved on forming a mission for that part of the world; and, with this view, called in the students from all parts of the country to the College of Wales, spread the case before them, and requested that they would seek the Divine guidance in respect to it, and that as many as thought it their duty to embark in the enterprise, would signify it. Mr. Cook and several others offered themselves for this service, and shortly after went to London, and, in the presence of many thousands, in the Tabernacle, Tottenham Court Road Chapel, and elsewhere, made a statement of their views of the proposed work, which was printed. After taking an affecting farewell of their friends, they embarked for America with the Rev. Mr. (afterwards Dr.) Percy; but, as the ship was detained in the Downs by a contrary wind, Mr. Cook availed himself of the opportunity to pay a farewell visit to his friends at Dover; and, the next Sabbath, several of his fellow-students also, who were coming with him to America, went thither to preach. A sudden and favourable change of the wind having taken place at night, the ship sailed, and they were all left behind. Two of them now wholly gave up the idea of coming; but Mr. Cook, with the rest, resolved to persevere, and actually came by the first opportunity.

On their arrival in this country, they considered themselves authorized to preach, on their general plan, as they had done in England; and hence they travelled about, preaching among different denominations, as they found opportunity. Though they seem to have been generally regarded as belonging to the Episcopal Church, and were themselves apparently not unwilling to keep up that idea, yet it soon became manifest that their sympathies were increasingly with the Baptists; and it came out at length that they had received a leaning in that direction from the influence of a young man who had embraced those views in Lady Huntingdon's Seminary. Mr. Cook, however, seemed less disposed than the rest to mingle with the Baptists, though he ultimately became a Baptist, while they, with a single exception, joined other denominations.

Soon after his arrival in this country, Mr. Cook was married to Elizabeth Bullein, of Baptist parents then deceased, at the village of Dorchester about eighteen miles from Charleston. Here, probably in consequence of this connection, he determined to settle. The congregation to which he preached was of a very mixed character—the greater part of them were professedly Episcopalians; a number were the children of the members of a Baptist Church, then extinct, which had once flourished under the ministry of the Rev. Isaac Chanler; and the rest were the remnants of an Independent congregation. With the latter Mr. Cook seems to have formed his closest connection, preaching, ordinarily, in the place of worship they had been accustomed to occupy.

Though the Church of England, at the commencement of the Revolution, was the Established Church in South Carolina, some of the other denominations began to associate with the idea of civil independence the kindred idea of equal religious rights; and hence, early in 1776, an invitation was given to ministers and churches of various denominations,—originating, it is understood, with the Baptists,—to meet at the High Hills of Santee, at the seat of the Baptist Church there, to consult in regard to their general interests. To this meeting Mr. Cook came; and, the business being concluded, he remained till the next week. As the Sacrament of the Lord's Supper was to be celebrated on the ensuing Sabbath, religious services were held, according to the usage of that period, on the two preceding days; and on Saturday Mr. Cook was invited to preach. Just before the service was to commence, he took aside the Rev. Mr. Hart of Charleston, who had staid to assist in the solemnity, and the Rev. Mr. (afterwards Dr.) Furman, then Pastor of the Church at Santee, and very young in the ministry, and acknowledged to them that he had for some time had increasing convictions in favour of the distinctive views of the Baptists, but had resisted them at the expense of his own peace of mind; that he had then recently examined the whole subject with great care, resolved to accept and submit to whatever might appear to be the truth and the will of God; and that, as the result of this examination, the previous tendencies of his mind had been fully confirmed. He stated that the address of Ananias to Paul, —"And now, why tarriest thou? arise and be baptized, and wash away thy sins, calling upon the name of the Lord," had been brought home to his mind with great power, and suggested to him the importance of being baptized without delay, especially as a favourable opportunity then offered. "I have only to add, Gentlemen," continued he, "that I should be glad of your advice, whether to embrace the ordinance immediately, or defer it to be administered among the people where I live; and if I submit to it immediately, seeing my sentiments and intention have been hitherto unknown to the public, whether it would be proper to make Ananias' address to St. Paul, just now mentioned, and from which I have felt so much conviction, the subject of the discourse I am about to deliver, and just in the light I now behold it, as it applies to myself. This I confess is the dictate of my own mind; but I would not wish to act unadvisedly."

Having heard his statements, the ministers were both of opinion that there was no reason why the ordinance should not be administered to him at once, and that it was highly proper that he should preach on the subject which he had proposed. He, accordingly, did preach upon it; and, the next day, after having satisfied the church of his acquaintance with experimental religion, he was baptized by Mr. Furman, the Pastor. They then began immediately to contemplate his ordination; and, within a few days, he was actually ordained by Mr. Hart and Mr. Furman.

The Church in Euhaw, having become vacant by the death of the Rev. Francis Pelot, invited Mr. Cook to become their Pastor. He accepted the invitation, and preached there without interruption for some time; but, in consequence of the invasion of the State, the imminent danger incident to his situation, near the sea-coast, and the distress and losses to which he had already been subjected, he removed into the interior, and remained there till the close of the War. He did not, however, find a place of safety; for he suffered severely in the ravages of the State by the troops under Lord Cornwallis, and other commanders; so that, when he returned to his residence at Euhaw, at the commencement of the Peace, he was actually reduced to poverty. Previous to his leaving Euhaw, he had lost his first wife, and married a second. There were some circumstances attending this marriage, which gave pain to his friends, and which subsequently occasioned him much regret.

The church of which Mr. Cook was Pastor had become considerably reduced before he took charge of it; and when he returned to it, after the suspension of his labours occasioned by the War, it had become almost extinct. But, on resuming his ministry there, he seems to have been greatly quickened, and proportionally blessed in his work. The Church gradually increased in numbers, spirituality, and influence; and, during the last five years of his life, he admitted, by Baptism, seventy-eight new members, some of whom were persons of great respectability.

In September, 1790, he addressed a letter to Dr. Rippon, of London, in which, after giving an account of the Baptist Negro Church in Savannah, he writes as follows:—

"My sphere of action is great, having two congregations to regard, at a considerable distance from each other, exclusive of this where I reside; as, also, friendly visits to pay to sister Churches and Societies of other denominations, who are destitute of ministers, frequently riding under a scorching sun, with a fever, twenty miles in a morning, and then preach afterwards. Our brethren in England have scarcely an idea of what hardships we struggle with, who travel to propagate the Gospel. I have been in a very poor state of health for two months; but it has not prevented an attention to the duties of my station. O, what a blessing is health! We cannot be too thankful for it."

But Mr. Cook had now almost reached the end of his journey. The feeble state of health to which he refers, as having been of two months' standing, had commenced with a dry cough, a stricture of the breast, and great lassitude, immediately after preaching, on a very sultry day, to a

congregation about twenty miles from his residence. About two weeks
before his death, he preached his last sermon from Eph. i. 6, when he
was so feeble that serious apprehensions were entertained that he would
not be able to go through the service. It was delivered under the full
impression that it was the last sermon his people would ever hear from
him ; and he distinctly stated this, and concluded a very pathetic train of
remark by bidding them a solemn and affectionate farewell. On the Tuesday following, his symptoms became more decidedly alarming ; and, from
this time, both himself and his friends were convinced that the hour of
his departure was near at hand. He evinced great tranquillity of spirit,
during his remaining days, though he said that he had not those intense
joys which he had sometimes experienced. He died on the next Sabbath,
September 26, 1790, in the forty-first year of his age, and his remains
were interred the same evening, immediately after the administration of
the Lord's Supper, when a very tender Address was delivered, at the grave,
to a deeply affected audience, by the Rev. Dr. Holcombe. The Funeral
Sermon was preached, some time afterwards, by the Rev. Dr. Furman of
Charleston, from II. Timothy i. 12 ;—a text which Mr. Cook had himself
designated for the occasion.

Mr. Cook left a widow, and one son by his first marriage,—then about
fifteen years of age. His widow survived him but a few weeks, being cut
off by a short and severe illness. The son, *Joseph B.*, was graduated at
Brown University in 1797, became a Baptist minister, and succeeded Dr.
Holcombe in the same church of which his father had been Pastor. Here
he continued until 1804, when the Euhaw Church was divided, and the
Beaufort Church was formed from it, with the pastoral care of which Mr.
Cook was immediately invested.

The following is an extract from a letter written by an intimate friend
of Mr. Cook, to the Rev. Dr. Rippon, shortly after his decease :—

" Mr. Cook was of a middle stature, and slender make, but had acquired a degree
of corpulency a few years before his death. His mental powers were good, and had
received improvement by an acquaintance with the liberal arts and sciences, though
his education had not been completed. His conversation was free and engaging. As
a preacher, he was zealous, orthodox and experimental. He spoke with animation
and much fervour, though his talent lay so much in the persuasive, that, at the end
of his sermon, he frequently left the audience in tears. He was taken from his labours
at a time when his character had arisen to considerable eminence, and a spacious field
of usefulness was opening all around him, and at a time when he was greatly endeared
to his people."

BENJAMIN FOSTER, D. D.*
1776—1798.

BENJAMIN FOSTER was born in Danvers, Mass., on the 12th of June, 1750. His parents were respectable members of the Congregational Church. From early childhood, he exhibited a remarkably tender and conscientious spirit, though it was not till he had nearly reached manhood, that he gained evidence, satisfactory to himself, of his having been renewed in the temper of his mind. While a mere youth, his temptations to utter blasphemous expressions were sometimes so strong, as he related to some Christian friends, that he actually held his lips with his hand to keep himself from falling into so terrible a sin.

He spent his early years at the public school in his native town; and, at the age of about twenty, became a member of Yale College. Here he distinguished himself no less by his exemplary life, than by his diligence and success in the various branches of study. He took his first degree in the year 1774. Shortly before this, several tracts relative to the Proper Subjects of Baptism, and also to the Scriptural Mode of administering the ordinance, having made their appearance, and excited considerable attention, this was selected as a subject for discussion at one of the exercises in the College. Mr. Foster was appointed to defend the doctrine of the Pedobaptists; and, in order to prepare himself for the discussion, he went into an extended and thorough examination of the whole subject. The result disappointed both himself and others; for, when the day for discussion arrived, he avowed himself a decided convert to the doctrine that those only who profess faith in Christ are legitimate subjects for Baptism, and that immersion is the only valid mode of administering the ordinance. In short, he had become a thorough Baptist, and so he continued till the close of his life.

Shortly after his graduation, he joined the Baptist Church in Boston, under the care of the Rev. Dr. Stillman, who also directed his studies in Theology. · On the 23d of October, 1776, he was ordained Pastor of the Baptist Church in Leicester, Mass., then vacant by the death of the Rev. Thomas Green.† During his residence here, he published a tract, entitled " The Washing of Regeneration, or the Divine Right of Immersion," in answer to a Treatise on the subject of Baptism, by the Rev. Joseph Fish. And, soon after, he published another pamphlet, entitled " Primitive Baptism defined in a Letter to the Rev. Mr. John Cleveland." Both these publications were marked by a vigorous intellect and a Christian spirit. He continued at Leicester until 1782, when he was induced to ask a dis-

---

* Benedict's Hist. Bapt., I.—Mass. Bapt. Miss. Mag., III.—Worcester Hist. Mag. II.

† THOMAS GREEN was a native of Malden, Mass., and was an early settler of the plantation, called by the natives *Towtaid*, and by the English Strawberry-bank, now Leicester. His first dwelling was formed under a shelving rock, which stretched, a natural roof, over his cabin. By communicating with the Indians, he acquired their knowledge of roots and herbs; and this, together with the science he derived from a few books, and the action of a vigorous mind, made him a skilful physician. He became Pastor of the Baptist Church in Leicester, on its first formation, and continued, highly respected and eminently useful, in this relation, until his death, which took place, on the 25th of October, 1778, at the age of seventy-three.

mission from his people, for want of an adequate support; after which, he preached about two years in his native place. In January, 1785, he commenced preaching to the First Baptist Church in Newport, R. I., and, on the 5th of June following, was installed as their Pastor. Here he had the satisfaction to find that his sphere of usefulness was much enlarged, and his means of improvement greatly increased.

In the year 1788, he paid a visit to the First Baptist Church in the city of New York, by their request; and, after preaching to them a short time, received a unanimous call to become their Pastor. On his return to Newport, he laid the matter before his church, and, while they were desirous of retaining him, and expressed a high appreciation of his services, they were unwilling to oppose any obstacle to his leaving them, if he thought the proposed change would be the means of extending his usefulness. Accordingly, he accepted the call, and, in the autumn of that year, removed to New York, and took charge of that church, and remained in connection with it as long as he lived.

In 1792, he received the degree of Doctor of Divinity from the College of Rhode Island. He is said to have had this honour conferred upon him, in consideration of the talent and learning which he had evinced in a work entitled "A Dissertation on the Seventy Weeks of Daniel; the particular and exact fulfilment of which Prophecy is considered and proved." This work was published in 1787, during his residence at Newport.

Dr. Foster, from the commencement of his career as a minister of the Gospel, was distinguished for diligence and zeal in his work. Nor did these qualities decline as he advanced in life; for, during his last twelve or fourteen years, he was accustomed to preach from four to six sermons a week. But the Yellow Fever, which accomplished such a work of desolation in New York, in the summer and autumn of 1798, put an end to his ministry and his life. The fearful malady had made its appearance, and several of his friends had been numbered among its victims. He was frequent and faithful in his visits to them, and, while almost all around him were panic-struck, *he* feared no danger, as long as he met it in the path of duty. The disease, however, at length, attacked him with great virulence, and, after suffering a few days, he expired on the 26th of August, 1798, in the forty-ninth year of his age.

Dr. Foster was twice married, and, in each case, was blessed with a pious and excellent companion. His first wife, who was Elizabeth, daughter of the Rev. Thomas Green, of Leicester, died, August 19, 1793; and his second, who was Martha, daughter of James Bingham, of New York, died July 27, 1798,—one day less than a month previous to his own death.

Dr. Benedict, in his History of the Baptists, says;—

"Dr. Foster, as a Scholar, particularly in the Greek, Hebrew, and Chaldean languages, has left few superiors. As a Divine, he was strictly Calvinistic, and full on the doctrine of salvation by free grace. As a Preacher, he was indefatigable. In private life, he was innocent as a child, and harmless as a dove, fulfilling all the duties of life with the greatest punctuality. The following inscription on a handsome marble over his grave, in the Baptist burying-ground in New York, written by an eminent Presbyterian clergyman of that city, is an encomium justly due to his memory:—"As a Scholar and Divine, he excelled; as a Preacher, he was eminent; as a Christian, he shone conspicuously; in his Piety he was fervent; the Church was comforted by his life, and it now laments his death."

CALEB BLOOD.*
1776—1814.

CALEB BLOOD was born in Charlton, Worcester County, Mass., on the 18th of August, 1754. At the age of twenty-one, he became hopefully pious, having, as it is said, received his first serious impressions amidst the gaieties of the ball-room. Shortly after this, becoming deeply impressed with a sense of the moral and spiritual wants of the world, he resolved to devote himself to the ministry; and, in about eighteen months from the time of his hopeful conversion, he commenced preaching,—having been licensed, as is believed, by the Church at Charlton, then under the pastoral care of the Rev. Nathaniel Green.

Mr. Blood, after preaching in a number of places, visited Marlow, N. H., in the autumn of 1777, where he received ordination, probably as an Evangelist. He remained here about two years, and then removed to Weston, Mass., and supplied a Baptist Church in that place a year and a half. At this time, there was an extensive revival of religion in the neighbouring town of Newton, and a considerable number of its subjects were baptized by immersion. In the summer of 1780, a Baptist church was constituted there, which, in the space of fourteen months, increased to seventy members. Of this infant church Mr. Blood became the Pastor in 1781; and here he continued labouring with great fidelity for more than seven years.

In January, 1788, notwithstanding the strong attachment that existed between him and his church at Newton, he felt constrained to yield to the request of several brethren from Shaftsbury, Vt., to take charge of the Baptist Church in that town. He, accordingly, removed thither, and was eminently useful, not only in the place in which he lived, but in the whole surrounding country. Several revivals of religion took place under his ministry; and one especially of great power, in the winter of 1798–99, which resulted in the addition of about a hundred and seventy-five to his church, among whom were several of his own children. The church, when he took charge of it, consisted of a hundred and twenty-five members—when he left it, of three hundred and fifty-five.

When the University of Vermont was established, in 1791, Mr Blood was appointed one of the Trustees, and he held the office as long as he remained in the State. In 1792, by appointment of the Legislature, he preached the Annual Election Sermon.

Besides a great amount of labour, which Mr. Blood volunteered to perform, in the destitute region in which he lived, in the autumn of 1804 he performed a missionary tour of three months, under an appointment of the Shaftsbury Association, into the Northwesterly parts of the State of New York, and the adjacent Province of Upper Canada. His labours are said to have been highly useful, in many places, in " setting in order the things that were wanting," and in " strengthening others that were ready to die."

* Mass. Miss. Mag., 1814.—Benedict's Hist. Bapt., I.—Maine Bapt.—Hist. Shaftsb. Assoc.

During his connection with the Shaftsbury Association, he was regarded as one of its most able and influential members. He wrote the Circular Letter of the Association in 1789, and in 1796; the former of which was considered by his brethren as exhibiting a very clear and comprehensive view of the great principles of Church Government. He had also an important agency in framing the Constitution or Plan of the Association, both in 1789 and 1806. In the early discussion of the subject of Free-masonry in this Body, he took a very decided stand against the institution, in which he found vigorous coadjutors in Messrs. Barber,* Webb,† and others of his brethren of the Association.

In April, 1807, after having spent nearly twenty of the best years of his life in Vermont, he resigned his pastoral charge, and accepted a call to the Third Baptist Church in Boston. Here he laboured with good acceptance for nearly three years—from September, 1807 till June, 1810. During this period, he experienced some very severe afflictions. A blow which he accidentally received in the face, so affected his whole system that, though the wound seemed trifling, it often occasioned him great pain; and, at one time, in consequence of taking cold in the part affected, a fever ensued, which had well-nigh proved fatal. This, with some other trials, served greatly to depress his spirits.

After resigning his charge in Boston in 1810, he accepted a call from the First Church and Society in Portland, Me., where he continued during the remainder of his life. Though he had now begun to feel the infirmities of age, he laboured in this new field with much acceptance, and not without a good degree of success. His labours had never been more highly

* EDWARD BARBER was born in Exeter, R. I., on the 23d of September, 1768. He made a profession of religion at the age of eighteen, and soon began to "improve his gift" in public speaking. He was licensed to preach by the Church in Berlin, N. Y., under the care of the Rev. Justus Hull, and was ordained as Pastor of the Bottskill Baptist Church, at Union Village, in the same State, on the 25th of September, 1794,—the sermon on the occasion being preached by the Rev. Caleb Blood. Previous to his settlement, the church had been greatly distracted, by reason of the unworthy conduct, and consequent exclusion from the ministry, of his predecessor; but it revived at once under his ministrations, and one hundred were added to it during the first six years of his Pastorate. His ministry continued forty years, and was an eminently prosperous one, as was indicated by the fact that his church, at the time of his death, numbered upwards of five hundred members. He died of apoplexy, at his residence in Greenwich, on the 1st of July, 1834, in the sixty-sixth year of his age. He was distinguished as a Preacher, a Pastor, and a Counsellor.

JUSTUS HULL, above mentioned, was born in Reading, Conn., July 26, 1755, but, when quite young, removed with his parents into the region which, in after life, was to be the field of his ministerial labours. His mind was directed to the subject of religion as early as 1773 or 1774; but it is supposed that he did not make a public profession until 1778, and that he commenced preaching the same year. He rendered some service in the army, at the taking of Burgoyne, in 1777; and the tradition is that, but for his having commenced preaching the next year, he would have had the command of a brigade of militia. For several years, he preached as an itinerant, travelling, not only in New England, but as far South as Virginia. He was ordained Pastor of the Church at Berlin, or Little Hoosick, on the 23d of February, 1785. After a faithful and fruitful ministry, of more than fifty-five years, he died on the 20th of May, 1833, in the seventy-eighth year of his age. He had enjoyed but small advantages for education, but had naturally a strong mind, and was a devout and earnest Christian.

† ISAAC WEBB commenced his ministerial career at Brandon, Vt., where he was ordained on the 24th of September, 1789. In 1793, he became the Pastor of the First Baptist Church in Pittstown, Rensselaer County, N. Y. Here he remained till 1802, though his Pastorate seems to have continued only till 1799. From 1803 to 1811, he was Pastor of the Church in Troy; and from 1812 to 1816, of the Church in Albany. In 1817, he was Pastor of the Church in Hoosick. Though he was engaged during a great part of his life in mercantile pursuits, he continued to preach occasionally till he was disabled by the infirmities of age. He died at Lansingburgh, N. Y., on the 20th of February, 1842. He was a very active and useful member of the Shaftsbury Association.

appreciated by his people, than when they were forced to the conviction that they must soon be deprived of them.

For nearly two months before his death, Mr. Blood was unable to walk to the meeting-house, though it was but a very short distance from his dwelling. But his zeal for the honour of his Master and the salvation of his people suffered no abatement ; and he not only continued to preach, but his preaching grew in earnestness and interest with his bodily infirmities and sufferings. On the 19th of February, 1814, he was attacked more violently, and from that time he continued to sink until the 6th of March, when he peacefully finished his course. During his last days, his mind was completely absorbed in spiritual contemplations, and he seemed to forget every thing in the one great desire that ministers might be faithful, souls saved, and his Master glorified. His Funeral was attended by a large concourse of people, of all denominations, and an appropriate and impressive Sermon, from Job v. 17, was delivered on the occasion, by the Rev. Sylvanus Boardman, of North Yarmouth.

Mr. Blood left behind him a widow and two children.

Mr. Blood published Historical Facts, recorded for the benefit of Youth. Reprinted, 1822.

FROM THE HON. HEMAN LINCOLN.

BOSTON, June 21, 1858.

Rev. and dear Sir: Agreeably to your request, I have endeavoured to revive some of my impressions of the person and character of the Rev. Caleb Blood, regretting only that, owing to the lapse of time and the unfaithfulness of my memory, they are not as full and particular as I could wish.

My acquaintance with Mr. Blood commenced in 1807, on the occasion of his settlement in Boston as Pastor of the Charles Street Baptist Church, then lately constituted. He was its first Pastor. I remember him as a man of grave and dignified demeanour, well becoming a Minister of the Gospel of Christ, but never degenerating into an unpleasant stiffness of manners.

In the pulpit he was direct, plain and forcible. His conceptions of truth were distinct, earnestly held, and earnestly put forth. He was ever accustomed to give special prominence to the great doctrine of Salvation by Grace— " Christ and Him crucified " was the theme on which he delighted to dwell. He was eminently a Biblical preacher. Naturally of strong intellectual powers, he had devoted them to the acquisition of Bible truth. The Bible had been the study of his life. He was in truth an able expositor, to whom might worthily be applied that high commendation,—" Mighty in the Scriptures." His expositions were a rich spiritual repast.

In doctrine he was decidedly and strongly Calvinistic—indeed he was inclined to favour some of the distinctive views of the celebrated Baptist divine, Dr. Gill. He was still ready, however, to assert his independence, if occasion called for it, pleasantly apostrophizing,—" Well, Father Gill, I am glad I am not obliged to believe with you in every thing."

As a Pastor, he was both affectionate and faithful, and was revered and loved by all who consorted with him, but especially by his more spiritual church-members. He was always seeking to maintain proper discipline in the church. He was decidedly averse to disorder and noisy excitement. He would sometimes revert pleasantly to an incident that occurred in the earlier part of his ministry. Attending a meeting marked with excitement and zeal, but, as he thought, " not according to knowledge," a good woman, at the close, came to him, with uplifted hands, exclaiming,—"O, Mr. Blood, did you ever see such a meeting before?" "No," he promptly replied, "and I hope I never shall again." In common personal intercourse he had the tact to make himself both agreeable and instructive. Although favoured with but very limited advantages of education in early life, yet, from long and intimate association with men and things, he had treasured up much and varied information, which he was not backward to communicate to others.

He died not far from the age of sixty, having accomplished much in the Master's service, and, as I doubt not, had many souls given to him as the fruit of his toils.

The foregoing is a very brief and imperfect sketch of some of the marked features in the character of a good minister of former times.

I am, Reverend and dear Sir,

Very respectfully, your obedient servant,

HEMAN LINCOLN.

JOHN PITMAN.*

1777—1822.

JOHN PITMAN, the son of William and Mary (Blower) Pitman, was born in Boston, April 26, 1751. When he was about thirteen years of age, his father removed to Beaufort, S. C., where he was engaged in mercantile pursuits, and for nearly a year had this son for a clerk. His parents had taught him to reverence the Bible, and attend church on the Sabbath; though it does not appear that any very decisive religious impressions were made upon his mind at that period. While he was in Carolina, he was, on some occasion, exposed to imminent danger, and was the subject of a remarkable deliverance; and, though his conscience was at that time somewhat awakened, he quickly relapsed into his accustomed lethargy.

In 1765, he returned to Boston, and, his mother being now a widow, with several young children, he was apprenticed to learn the business of a rope-maker. Here he cast off all the restraints of his early education, became dissolute and profane, and was even marked for his rapid progress in vice, during a period of about four years. Sometime in the year 1769, he was brought to serious reflection, and resolved to change his course and turn to the Lord. But, not being enlightened in regard to the gracious provisions of the Gospel, he set himself upon a course of self-righteous effort, by means of which he hoped to merit the Divine favour. He prayed three times a day, strictly observed the Sabbath, and fasted from Saturday till Sunday night; but, amidst all his pharisaical observances, his pride kept him from revealing the state of his mind to any individual. Sometimes he would yield to the temptation to sinful indulgence, and then would think to atone for it by increasing his measure of self-denial; but he at length became convinced that he had found no true peace to his conscience. Under these circumstances, he addressed a letter to Dr. Still-

* Amer. Bapt. Mag, 1822.—MS. from Hon. John Pitman.

man, the Pastor of the First Baptist Church in Boston, informing him of the state of his mind, and requesting from him appropriate counsel and instruction—to which the Doctor returned the following answer:—

"I have just received yours and read it. I have not the pleasure of being acquainted with you, but shall be glad if it will suit you to come to my house to-morrow after the afternoon service, when I shall be ready to converse with you upon those things which are of infinite importance. Believe me to be your real friend and soul's well wisher, "SAMUEL STILLMAN."

He, accordingly, visited Dr. Stillman the next day, and opened to him the secret history of his mind during a period of nearly two years, and was much assisted and relieved by the Doctor's evangelical instructions. He continued to visit him frequently, and, after about two months, experienced a delightful change in his feelings, which he was encouraged to believe marked the transition from an unregenerate to a regenerate state. Having informed Dr. S. that his views of the subject of Baptism were in harmony with his own, he soon after appeared before the church, and gave a relation of his Christian experience, which they approved. On the 24th of February, 1771, he was baptized, and on the 7th of March following was received as a member of the church. Subsequently to this, he was the subject of sore temptation, and was greatly oppressed with spiritual gloom; but meditation upon the sufferings of Christ melted him into a state of godly sorrow, which was followed by the return of peace and joy. It was a considerable time before his mind settled into a state of uniform tranquillity.

Mr. Pitman's hopeful conversion took place but a short time before the breaking out of the War of the Revolution. Though he gave the most satisfactory evidence of the genuineness of his Christian hope, he felt it his duty, afterwards, as he had done before, to maintain and defend the rights of his country. When the British soldiers fired on the citizens of Boston, on the 5th of March, 1770, he was not far from one of the persons who was shot, and was one of those who mounted guard on that memorable night. He remained in Boston till the passage of the " Boston Port Bill," 1774, which, occasioning a general suspension of business, led to his removal to Philadelphia. In 1776, he joined a volunteer company, consisting principally of Quakers belonging to Philadelphia, commanded by Captain Joseph Copperthwait, which formed a part of the first battalion of Pennsylvania Militia, under the command of Colonel Dickinson. They marched for Elizabethtown, N. J., on the 10th of July, and arrived on the 18th; and, the next day, at Elizabethtown Point, relieved the Jersey Militia, the enemy being in sight on Staten Island. During this tour, and on other occasions, he evinced great natural as well as Christian firmness, and showed that his patriotism was tempered and directed by his piety.

From the time of his removal to Philadelphia until 1777,—about three years—Mr. Pitman was engaged in his secular business. The precise time when he began to preach is not known; but it *is* known that he preached at different places in New Jersey as early as April, 1777. The presumption is that, after he left Dr. Stillman's church, he united with some church in Philadelphia, by which he was approved as a preacher of the Gospel.

On the 12th of October, 1777, he received a call from the Baptist Church in Upper Freehold, N. J., which he accepted. On the 21st of September, 1778, he was married to Rebecca, daughter of Richard Cox, of that place. He continued to preach to this church till April 10, 1780, when he removed near to Allentown, N. J. From this time he preached occasionally in the towns of Cranbury, Jacobstown, Hopewell, Penepek, Upper Freehold, and Bordentown, until the next spring, when he returned to Philadelphia. His labours in these several places are said to have been highly acceptable to the people, and apparently attended with the Divine blessing.

On his removal to Philadelphia, on the 12th of April, 1781, he found it necessary, for the support of his family, to return to his former business. The First Baptist Church was, about this time, not a little distracted, in consequence of the avowal of the doctrine of Universal Salvation by the Rev. Mr. Winchester, its Pastor, and the exclusion from church fellowship of all who had embraced his views. After Mr. W.'s removal, Mr. Pitman acted as Pastor to this church from September till January following, (1782,) when the Rev. Mr. Ustick, from New England, succeeded to the Pastorate. Mr. P. remained in Philadelphia, at this time, for about three years, and, in connection with his secular business, exercised his ministry, as he found occasion or opportunity, in Philadelphia and its vicinity, and sometimes also among his friends in New Jersey.

On the 20th of May, 1784, he left Philadelphia, and arrived in Providence, R. I., on the 28th. From the church then called Penepek, he was dismissed to the Baptist Church in Providence, and joined it in July following. Here he was received with much favour; and, though he was engaged with his brother in different kinds of secular business, he preached occasionally, and devoted no small part of his time to the study of Theology. In September, 1785, he was appointed Steward of the College of Rhode Island, and held the place one year, during the greater part of which he supplied the Congregational Church in Attleborough, Mass. In October, 1786, he was invited by the Baptist Church in Warren, R. I., to become their Pastor; and, after resigning his office in the College, he removed thither, and commenced his labours among them. Here he continued till July, 1790, when he returned to Providence, and re-united with the Baptist Church there. His preaching in Warren was greatly blessed, and the utmost harmony subsisted between him and the church. During his residence there, he received a call from the Baptist Church in Salem, Pa., to settle among them,—which, however, he thought it his duty to decline. He continued to supply the Warren pulpit frequently, after his removal to Providence, until the 20th of March, 1791, when he accepted a call from the Baptist Church in Pawtuxet, R. I.

In the year 1792, Mr. Pitman suffered severe affliction. His wife, after a short but severe illness, died early in the month of February. Her infant daughter had died a few days previous; and a servant girl in his family, about the same time, having gone into the cellar for some water, fell into the well, and was drowned. Their corpses were carried to the Baptist meeting-house, where, after an appropriate sermon by Dr. Maxcy, from Romans xiii. 11, they were interred in one grave. Though he felt the stroke most deeply, he behaved under it with the most exemplary Christian fortitude. Owing to the peculiar circumstances of his family, he thought it his duty to form another matrimonial connection at an early day; and, accordingly, on the 5th of September following, he was married to Mrs. Susannah Greene, of Providence.

Mr. Pitman continued to reside at Providence,—preaching regularly on the Sabbath at Pawtuxet, until the 30th of April, 1797, when he commenced preaching to the Baptist Church in Rehoboth, Mass., (First Precinct.) Here he continued his labours, with a slight interruption, till the close of his life. The church gradually increased under his ministry; and, in the year 1820, thirty-seven were added as the fruit of a revival.

In April, 1815, Mr. Pitman, in consequence of embarrassment in his worldly circumstances, and the inability of the people to whom he ministered to provide for his support, removed to Salem, Mass., and thence successively to Malden and Medford. In each of the two latter places he undertook to resume his former secular business, but without much success. In consequence of some favourable change in his former concerns, he removed back to Rehoboth, on the 2d of May, 1816, and again officiated as Pastor of that Church.

From this period he laboured on, in the enjoyment of his accustomed health, and with great zeal and fidelity, till near the close of life. On the Sabbath immediately preceding his death, he preached with so much fervour and impressiveness that one of his audience expressed the opinion that it was well worthy to be his last effort in the pulpit. On the evening of the 22d of July, 1822, he was attacked with apoplexy, of which he died two days after, in the seventy-second year of his age. A few minutes after he was taken, he remarked,—" I shall die and not live ; " and, immediately after, sunk into a lethargy from which he never awoke. An appropriate Discourse was delivered at his Funeral by the Rev. William Rogers, D. D., of Philadelphia, from II. Cor. v. 1.

Mr. Pitman had six children,—one son and five daughters,—all by the first marriage. The son, the Hon. John Pitman, of Providence, has long been distinguished in civil life, being Judge of the District Court of the United States for the District of Rhode Island. The second Mrs. Pitman survived her husband several years.

Judge Pitman, in reply to certain inquiries which I addressed to him concerning his father, pays the following tribute to his memory:

" He was a man of remarkable firmness, and of great courage, physical and moral. As a father and husband, he was most affectionate and indulgent. In all his dealings with his fellow-men, he evinced the strictest integrity. As a Christian, he was most exemplary and devout, discharging his various duties with conscientious exactness. His preaching was addressed more to the understanding than the passions—he was much in the habit of expounding Divine truth, by comparing Scripture with Scripture; and I remember to have heard a gentleman of much intelligence and learning say that he was the best expounder of the Bible to whom he had ever listened. But he still often appealed successfully to the feelings, especially on such themes as the love of God in the gift of his Son, and the grace and condescension of the Saviour. He did not ' shun to declare the whole counsel of God,' and, 'knowing the terror of the Lord,' he endeavoured to 'persuade men.'

" For the last six years of his life, he was entirely devoted to the study and preaching of the Gospel to the Church in Seekonk, and I have heard him say, during this latter period, that it was the happiest portion of his life. He had saved enough from the wreck of his property to enable him to live, with some assistance derived from his people, so that he was delivered from nearly all secular cares, and was free to devote himself entirely to the discharge of his ministerial duties, and to his immediate preparation for Heaven."

In my early life, I used occasionally to hear Mr. Pitman preach " in an upper room" in my native place, and, after half a century, I still retain a vivid impression of his appearance and manner. I recollect that his delivery was calm and solemn, and, though I was not capable of forming a judgment of the matter of his discourse, my impression is that he was most acceptable to the most intelligent and serious portion of his audience. Other Baptist ministers often preached in the neighbourhood, but I think the announcement of Mr. Pitman secured the best, if not the largest, audience.

FROM THE REV. BENJAMIN H. PITMAN.

Albany, April 19, 1858.

My dear Sir: I suppose the Rev. John Pitman, of Providence, and myself were remotely connected, but the relationship was so distant that we never recognised it; though, as my native place was Newport, and my early religious connection was with the Baptist denomination, I had a pretty good opportunity of forming a correct judgment of his character. He was certainly a man of great worth and dignity, and, in my opinion, justly entitled to a place among the more distinguished Baptist ministers of his day.

Mr. Pitman was not quite of the medium height, but was firmly built, and had rather more than the ordinary degree of flesh. His face was round, his expression calm and dignified, his hair, as far back as I remember him, white, and his whole appearance singularly impressive. His original powers of mind were, I think, considerably above the medium; though it was for solid rather than brilliant qualities that he was distinguished. His excellent judgment rendered him a wise counsellor; and this, combined with his kindly disposition, eminently fitted him for a peace-maker. While he always maintained a gravity suitable to his character as a minister, he was as far as possible from any thing austere or forbidding, and ever showed an interest in the happiness of those around him. He was one of the most hospitable of men, and whoever visited him, whether friends or strangers, were sure to feel that they were welcome guests. He had a large heart and an open hand; and I have heard that his rule in giving was always to take counsel of his first generous impulse, and not wait for the more sober calculations of interest and prudence. Acting upon this principle, it was acknowledged, on all hands, that he gave, up to the full measure of his ability.

Mr. Pitman had always so much to do with secular business that he could not have been a very close student; and yet his preaching was always characterized by well-digested and well-arranged thought, expressed in a simple and perspicuous manner. He had a good voice for public speaking,—sufficiently loud to fill a large house, and yet bland and agreeable. His manner was not particularly impassioned, but it was dignified and solemn, and natural withal, and made you feel that he possessed the true spirit of an ambassador of God. His views of Divine truth were nearly of the same type with those of Dr. Gill—some might say, verging a little towards Antinomianism; and yet I do not think there was any thing in his preaching to relax the sense of moral obligation. He loved to feel himself a debtor to Divine grace, and he strove to make the same impression on the minds and hearts of his hearers.

He always impressed me as an eminently devout and godly man. I remember once standing with him before the door of the Baptist church in Providence, when a blind man, who was passing, asked him how he was. He said, in reply, "I thank God, I am well; I have peace of conscience, and, I trust, a good hope of a better life." It was said in all simplicity, and without the semblance of any thing like boasting; and I think it might be taken as a faithful index to his Christian character.

Truly yours,
BENJAMIN H. PITMAN.

LEWIS RICHARDS.

1777—1832.

FROM THE REV. GEORGE F. ADAMS.

BALTIMORE, March 29, 1859.

My dear Sir : Agreeably to your request, I send you the following brief sketch of the life and character of the late Rev. Lewis Richards. For the facts stated, I am indebted in part to Benedict's History of the Baptists, also to the Records of the Church of which he was so long Pastor, and to the personal recollections of a number of his old friends still living in this city, with whom I have conversed freely in respect to him.

LEWIS RICHARDS was born in the year 1752, in the parish of Llanbardarn vowr, Cardiganshire, South Wales. He made a public profession of religion at the age of nineteen, and joined a Society of Independents, and shortly after became acquainted with Lady Huntingdon, and studied for a short time at the College which she had endowed. He then embarked for America, with several of his fellow-students, with a view to prosecute his studies at the famous Orphan House in Georgia. He was baptized by the Rev. Richard Furman, at the High Hills of Santee, S. C., in 1777, and was ordained, the same year, in Charleston, by the Rev. Messrs. Oliver Hart and Joseph Cook. After travelling about a year in different parts of South Carolina and Georgia, he removed to Northampton County, Va., on the Eastern Shore of the Chesapeake Bay. From that place he removed to this city in 1784, and became the Pastor of the First Baptist Church in Baltimore, immediately after it was constituted.

Mr. Richards continued alone in the Pastorship till 1815, when the Rev. E. J. Reis was elected Co-pastor. In 1818, he resigned his pastoral charge, but continued his connection as a member of the church till the close of his life. He died on the 1st of February, 1832, in the eightieth year of his age.

Physically, Mr. Richards was a well-made man,—about five feet, four inches in height, and of prepossessing appearance. He was not distinguished either for learning or eloquence, but he possessed, in an eminent degree, the respect and affection, not only of the members of his church, but of his fellow-citizens generally, for his meekness of spirit, his unaffected piety, and his untiring devotion to his Master's service. His charity was literally that "which seeketh not her own, is not easily provoked, thinketh no evil." During the early part of his ministry, he not only filled his own pulpit with credit to himself, and acceptance to his people, but he travelled and preached much in places at considerable distance from home. The churches at Frederick and Taney Town especially were often favoured with his labours. To this division of his ministrations may probably be ascribed the fact that he was not more eminently successful in his own congregation. The statistics of the church show that, during his thirty years Pastorate, the number of members increased from eleven to only a hundred and sixty-four. His doctrinal sentiments were decidedly Calvinistic, without, however, the least approach to Antinomianism. He was eminently practical both in his preaching and his living. Of him it may be said as emphatically as of almost any man with whose history I have been acquainted,—"Mark the perfect man, and behold the upright, for the end of that man is peace."

Mr. Richards was twice married. His first marriage, which took place shortly after his settlement in Baltimore, was to Miss Ann Mathews, of Accomac County, Va. She was related to the Custis family, so well known and highly honoured in that patriotic State. By this marriage, he had six or seven children, of whom five,—three sons and two daughters, reached maturity, and were married. One of his sons, *John Custis*, "used the office of Deacon well," ("being found blameless,") for many years, in the church of which his father had been Pastor. Mrs. Richards died on the 21st of May, 1797. His second wife, to whom he was married in 1806, was Angelica Collins, of Jefferson County, Va. She died on the 2d of June, 1815. By this marriage there were no children.

Very truly yours,
G. F. ADAMS.

AMBROSE DUDLEY.

1778—1823.

FROM THE REV. JAMES E. WELCH.

Hickory Grove, Warren County, Mo.,
December 13, 1858.

Rev. and dear Sir: I am happy to say that my knowledge of the life and character of the Rev. Ambrose Dudley is such that I am able to furnish you a sketch of him, which I believe you may rely on as entirely authentic. He baptized both my parents, at Bryan's Station, in 1789. My recollections of him, though it is many years since he has passed away, are still perfectly distinct, and I have little fear that I shall mistake in describing him to you.

AMBROSE DUDLEY was born not far from Fredericksburg in Spott-sylvania County, Va., in 1750; and, of course, at the commencement of the Revolutionary War, was in the vigour of early manhood. Possessed, as he was, of an ardent love of freedom, he engaged with all the zeal of '76, for the emancipation of his down-trodden country.

Being a man full six feet high; of fine personal appearance; unusually active, intelligent and decided, he was readily commissioned as a Captain in the Continental army. When he left home to engage in the service of his country, he had never made the great truths of the Bible a subject of candid and prayerful examination. It is believed, however, that the scenes of carnage and death through which he passed, first gave a serious direction to his thoughts; and from becoming deeply impressed with the uncertainty of life, he became yet more deeply impressed with his ruined condition as a sinner, being brought to feel that he had been all his life in an attitude of rebellion against an infinitely higher power than the King of England,— even the King of Kings, and Lord of Lords.

This conviction of his sinfulness was succeeded by a truly penitent and contrite spirit, associated with joy and peace in believing. He was, at this time, in command of his company, and stationed at Williamsburg; and, notwithstanding his circumstances seemed most adverse both to the culture of religion, and to a public profession of it, he had too much firmness of purpose to yield to the influence of circumstances in so momentous a concern. He therefore publicly declared himself on the Lord's side, by being baptized at Williamsburg; and, if I mistake not, it was done in the presence of the company he commanded, and of some of his fellow officers of the army.

While devout Cornelius was praying to God, the Disposer of events was preparing Peter to " preach among the Gentiles the unsearchable riches of Christ :" so, while the church in his native county was earnestly beseech-ing the Great Head of the Church, that He would remember them in their destitute condition, and send them a Pastor, Ambrose Dudley was con-verted in camp, was baptized, and shortly after left the army and returned home. When, however, he " essayed to join himself to the disciples," those who had known him from early life could scarcely " believe that he was a disciple ;" for when he left home he was not only openly immoral, but it was understood that he was inclined to infidel opinions. He, how-ever, soon convinced them that he had indeed passed from death unto life. Shortly after, he united with the church, and at the same time intimated to them his ardent desire to devote himself to the Gospel ministry. They received him with open arms, regarding him as a special gift from God in answer to their prayers. Nor were they disappointed ; for his earliest efforts gave promise of that high degree of usefulness which attended and crowned his whole ministry.

After labouring in the Gospel, for several years, with great acceptance, in his native State, he removed to Kentucky in 1785, and settled near Bryan's Station, in the vicinity of Lexington; nor did he change his place of residence, after that, till he was taken to the " house appointed for all living."

Few men have ever laboured in the West with greater success than he. The Church at Bryan's Station, which was organized under his ministry in 1786, had two hundred and nineteen members in 1793. In the great revival, which swept over that part of the State in 1803, I saw him baptize, on one occasion, fifty-eight persons at David's Fork ; and the following Sabbath he baptized sixty-eight at Bryan's Station, only six miles distant.

He was domestic in his habits, and very fond of his family, and his home ; and hence never travelled extensively. His labours were principally within the bounds of the Elkhorn Association ; and I think I may safely say, without disparaging other excellent men, that there never was, in that large and intelligent Body, one whose influence was wider and more powerful than was that of Ambrose Dudley. He was their presiding officer for many years, and the first man in all that region who had moral courage enough to tell the churches plainly from the pulpit that God hath " ordained that they which preach the Gospel should live of the Gospel." As a preacher, he was zealous, dignified and solemn. No one who heard him could doubt that he was deeply impressed with the truths which he delivered, and that the great object at which he constantly aimed, was not to gain the applause of his hearers, but to save their souls.

His manners and general habits seemed to indicate that he was born to exercise authority. The very glance of his piercing eye was often enough to awe into silence. In his personal appearance he was unusually erect and neat, so that when a stranger in Lexington asked where he might be found, he was told to walk down the street, and the first man he met having on a superfine black coat, without a single mote upon it, would be Ambrose Dudley. And but few men have ever lived and died in the ministry, who " kept their garments more unspotted from the world." He was, in his religious views, a thorough Calvinist ; and, whenever he thought truth or duty was involved, he showed the most unbending firmness. He was remarkably punctual to his engagements, and never failed of fulfilling one, unless he was prevented by sickness, or some other cause beyond his control. Whenever it was known that he had made an appointment to preach, the common saying was, " Rain or shine, Brother Dudley will be there."

In family discipline he was very decided. He never spoke but once. In political matters he took but little interest, nor had he much to do with the affairs of the world beyond the limits of his own plantation.

He was a man of God, whose praise is in all the churches throughout the region in which he lived. He " died, at the horns of the altar," in the year 1823.

Believe me your brother in Christ,

JAMES E. WELCH.

ISAAC CASE.*

1780—1852.

ISAAC CASE was born at Rehoboth, Bristol County, Mass., on the 25th of February, 1761. Though his early religious advantages were few, his thoughts seem to have been seriously directed to the concerns of his soul, while he was yet a mere child. When he was about nine years old, a profane and wicked boy, with whom he had been associated, was suddenly killed. He could not but inquire what had become of the soul of that bad boy; for he had read in the Bible that "the Lord will not hold him guiltless that taketh his name in vain;" and this led him to ask what would have probably been his own condition, if he had been taken away in a similar manner. The result was that his mind became burdened with anxiety in regard to his salvation; and this continued, in a greater or less degree, till he was about eighteen years old. At this time his solicitude became much more intense, and for three weeks he was well-nigh ready to despair of the mercy of God. At length, in listening to a sermon, the tumult of his mind subsided into a state of unwonted tranquillity, which he at first mistook for evidence of the departure of the Holy Spirit from his soul; but, after a short time, the happy change in his views and feelings led him to hope that the Spirit had actually performed an effectual work upon his heart. All his hopes of salvation now centered in the Cross of Christ. This was in the year 1779. In the course of this year, he made a public profession of his faith, and united with the Baptist Church in the neighbouring town of Dighton.

Soon after this change in Mr. Case's views and feelings, he began to feel a strong desire to do what he could to bring about a similar change in others; and here originated the thought, which was quickly matured into a purpose, of becoming a minister of the Gospel. Accordingly, in 1780, when he was about nineteen, he received the approbation of the church of which he was a member, to go forth as a candidate for the Christian ministry. In 1783, he was ordained as an Evangelist, and, in October of that year, went to Maine, and entered upon his work there, without expecting any pecuniary compensation.

His first preaching was at Brunswick. Here he found not only a prevailing indifference to religion, but not a little prejudice against those doctrines which he regarded as fundamental in the Christian system, and which he felt constrained to make most prominent in his preaching; and the state of things altogether was such as to give little promise of success to his labours. After remaining there a short time, hearing that there was an unusual interest in religion on the Island of Sabasdegan, belonging to Harpswell, he repaired thither; and the first sermon that he preached produced a visible and powerful effect. Numbers were hopefully converted, and among them two brothers, who became useful ministers in Baptist Churches. A revival of great power here took place in connection with his labours, and the great concern of salvation became the all-engrossing theme in almost every family. Having laboured about three months in that region, and preached in nearly all the settlements, and administered

* Hist. Maine Bapt.—Dr. Thurston's Fun. Serm.—MS. from Rev. Dr. A. Wilson.

Baptism to many of the converts, he was impressed with the idea that he ought to go still farther East. This impression was much strengthened by the fact that, on his way to Thomaston, he met two persons going from that place to the place of his then recent sojourn, to request him to "come over and help" them. On arriving at Thomaston, he was further encouraged by finding that a few pious persons were spending the day in fasting and prayer, in the prospect of his visit. Several were awakened under his first sermon; and this proved the beginning of a very extensive and powerful revival. In the space of a few months, he baptized seventy-eight persons. In May, 1784, a church was organized,—the first ever established in the place, and he became its Pastor, and continued in that relation eight years. He was chiefly instrumental in establishing the Baptist churches in Bowdoinham, East Brunswick, and several other places. Indeed his labours were widely extended in that part of Maine, and in almost every place in which he preached, some were hopefully converted through his instrumentality.

In 1792, he gathered the Baptists in what is now called East Winthrop and Readfield into a church, which was then known as the Baptist Church in Winthrop; and which was subsequently enlarged by accessions from the Western parts of Augusta and Hallowell. In 1793, they erected a house of worship in the Southeastern part of Readfield, as the place which would accommodate the greater number of the members, and changed the name to the Baptist Church in Readfield. He resigned his charge of the Church at Thomaston to become the Pastor of this; and here he laboured with comfort and usefulness for about eight years.

In 1800, Mr. Case again resigned his pastoral charge with a view to being employed as a missionary. And in this capacity he *was* employed, with unwearied diligence and great efficiency, until the infirmities of age rendered him incapable of continued exertion. There are comparatively few towns, especially in the Eastern part of Maine, that have not enjoyed the benefit of his labours. Of the number of churches he was instrumental in establishing, and the number of converts to whom he administered the ordinance of Baptism, he kept no account; but he supposed the latter to have been more than a thousand. He made several visits also to the Provinces of New Brunswick and Nova Scotia, where he laboured with his accustomed diligence, and not without visible tokens of success. At length, however, he began to feel the palsying hand of age, and was obliged gradually to withdraw from active service. But his interest in the cause to which he had been so long devoted, survived his ability to labour for it, and continued to call forth his earnest prayers, as long as the power of thought and utterance remained to him. He died at Readfield, November 3, 1852, in the ninety-second year of his age, and the seventy-second of his ministry. His Funeral Sermon was preached by the Rev. David Thurston, D. D., late Pastor of the Congregational Church in Winthrop, Me.

Mr. Case was married to a daughter of the Rev. Elisha Snow,* of Thomaston. They had several children, and one of the sons became a physician.

---

* ELISHA SNOW commenced preaching at Thomaston in 1784; was ordained, as an Evangelist, at Harpswell, in 1790; and was Pastor of the Church at Thomaston from 1794 to 1821. He travelled much and aided many destitute churches. He had the reputation of being a strong-minded man, and a very strong Calvinist.

FROM THE REV. ADAM WILSON, D. D.

PARIS, Me., March 10, 1857.

Dear Sir: My first attendance at a Baptist Association was forty years ago last September. The people, their customs, and the preaching, were all new to me—the ministers were all strangers. Among the ministers I noticed a *marked* man. He was not distinguished by any thing in his physical appearance. He was of about a medium size, and in all his physical developments much like other men. But his countenance wore the marks of habitual devotion. Yet it was a devotion without gloom. He appeared to *enjoy* religion. Progress, and praise, and love to Christ, and defence of the Gospel, seemed to be the happy elements of his every day life. He was sparing in his words, and never spoke but that he seemed to have an object to accomplish. His general mien and bearing bespoke the reign of peace within. That man was the Rev. Isaac Case, of Readfield.

He was not, I think, at that time, the Pastor of any church; but was known, loved and honoured in all our churches within the territory that now constitutes the State of Maine. More than thirty years before that time, he had aided in the organization of several of the first of our churches, in all that part of the State, East of the Saco River. He was Clerk of the first Association in the State, in 1787. The Minutes of the Association were never printed. The manuscript remained long in the possession of Mr. Case, as a relic of antiquity.

When he came to Maine, he was a young man, only about twenty years old, and without a family. He gave his time and all his energies to the work of the ministry, without any salary from any quarter, and wherever Providence opened a door. Afterwards, when he became the head of a family, he was a missionary in the employ of a Missionary Society, whose head-quarters were in Boston, and whose officers were such men as Stillman, Baldwin, and Sharp. He was careful and economical in the management of his worldly affairs; and this led some prejudiced observers to accuse him of worldliness. But I never heard that the most prejudiced ever suspected him of dishonesty. What might appear to superficial observers as evidence of a worldly spirit, appeared to more discerning men as nothing more than a careful observance of that scriptural precept,—" Provide things honest in the sight of all men." Even among good men there are few who so fully acknowledge God in all their temporal affairs. In him the words of our Lord were both illustrated and verified—" Seek ye first the Kingdom of God and his righteousness, [the things right in his sight,] and all these things [all needful temporal things] shall be added unto you." He was never rich, but was always blessed with a competence. Paul could scarcely with more confidence proclaim himself " willing to live honestly."

Among a portion of the community, Christian ministers are often suspected of insincerity. Those men who have only a vague and very inoperative belief in the reality of " things not seen," appear to find it difficult to comprehend the power of such motives as come up from a living faith in the unseen things of the Gospel. They are slow to understand how any minister can be actuated by other than selfish motives. Mr. Case succeeded, beyond most men, in overcoming this prejudice. The following anecdote will show something of the extent to which even scoffers were convinced of his sincerity.

In one of his missionary tours, his road led through a forest of some twenty miles, with only one opening about midway that distance. Here were two farm houses on opposite sides of the road. Mr. Case reached this opening about sunset, and sought and found entertainment for the night. He applied for accommodations simply as a traveller, and not as a minister. But he was not the man whose ministerial character could be hid. His host guessed he was a minister, and communicated his conjecture to his neighbour, who was a scoffer at religion, and of course a bitter enemy of what he ignorantly termed the Christian Priesthood. This man, prompted partly by his enmity to the Gospel, and partly by his Yankee curiosity, quickened by a residence in a forest, hastened into the presence of the traveller, to try him with all manner of questions. Here was just the opportunity he desired. He did not know that this stranger was a minister, and so could excuse himself from an intention of personal rudeness, while he poured all sorts of abuse and sarcasm on the ministry.

At length, wearied in the greatness of his way, he paused as if some new idea had just found its way into his mind, and said that there was one minister that he had often heard of, though he had never seen him, who, he thought was an exception to the general rule. From all that he could learn, he thought that man was sincere. His name was Isaac Case. In relating this anecdote, Mr. Case said that up to that moment he had remained quiet in his own mind; but then he was troubled. He could bear censure, but could not endure flattery.

Mr. Case was always the devoted minister of Christ, whether in public or in private. I have travelled in his company in strange places, and, however far removed from home influence, or secluded from the public eye, he was uniformly the same devout and God-fearing man.

With little of the learning of the schools, and without any unusual natural endowment, by his earnest piety and good common sense he made himself agreeable to the most learned of his brethren. His example shows what these two qualities will do, in making one both acceptable and useful. Everywhere, among our churches, his memory is blessed. "He was a good man, and full of the Holy Ghost, and much people were added to the Lord."

Yours respectfully,

ADAM WILSON.

———◆◆———

THOMAS BALDWIN, D. D.*
1782—1826.

THOMAS BALDWIN, the only son of Thomas and Mary Baldwin, was born in Bozrah, Conn., December 23, 1753. His father was attached to the military service, and rose to some distinction in the then Colonial army. His mother's family was distinguished for talent; and she herself possessed not only a vigorous intellect, but an elevated piety. He was remarkable in childhood for serenity of temper, love of justice, and a taste for reading. His leisure was all sacredly devoted to the cultivation of his mind; and while he was yet quite a youth, he had acquired a considerable stock of valuable, though miscellaneous, information.

When he was about sixteen years of age, his father having died some time before, his mother was married, a second time, to a Mr. Eames, and removed to Canaan, N. H. He removed with the family, and lived there several years.

---

* Memoir by Rev. Daniel Chessman.—Mass. Bapt. Miss. Mag., V.

On the 22d of September, 1775, at the age of twenty-two, he was married to Ruth Huntington, of Norwich, Conn., with whom he lived most happily till her death,—February 11, 1812. They had six children, only one of whom survived the father. He was subsequently married to Margaret Duncan, of Haverhill, Mass., who survived him many years.

Before he was thirty years of age, he was chosen to represent the town of Canaan in the State Legislature; and, as he was repeatedly re-elected to this office, it is presumed that he discharged its duties in a manner to satisfy his constituents.

Though never chargeable with open vice, he was, during his youth, fond of amusement and gaiety, and little disposed to admit any serious thoughts concerning the future. In the autumn of 1777, he lost his first-born child under circumstances peculiarly afflictive; and the effect of this was to induce the resolution that he would make religion his grand concern. It was not, however, till the year 1780 that he was brought, as he believed, to understand and acquiesce in the gracious constitution of the Gospel; and the change which he then experienced he referred, immediately, to the instrumentality of two Baptist preachers, who came to labour temporarily in the neighbourhood in which he lived.

He had been educated among Pedobaptists; but his mind became, about this time, not a little agitated on the subject of Baptism, and he finally reached a result very different from what he had expected, and even hoped,— namely, a conviction that the views in which he had been trained were unscriptural, and that, if he would follow his Lord fully, he must follow Him into the water. He knew that this would be most unwelcome intelligence to many of his friends, as indeed it proved to be; but he determined that no earthly consideration should prevent him from carrying out his conscientious convictions; and, accordingly, in the latter part of the year 1781, he was baptized by immersion, by the Rev. Elisha Ransom,* then of Woodstock, Vt.

Previous to the change in his feelings on the subject of religion, he had determined to devote himself to the legal profession, and had actually commenced his studies with reference to it; but his mind now took a different direction, and he came soon to abandon the purpose altogether. He began first to exhort in public meetings; and in August, 1782, he became, in the technical sense, a preacher. In the spring of 1783, the church (for a Baptist church was now established in Canaan) proposed to him to receive ordination: he consented to the proposal, but declined being installed over that particular church, though it was understood that he would perform the duties of a Pastor as long as he might find it convenient to remain with them. A Council was accordingly convened in Canaan, on the 11th of June, 1783, when he was ordained to the work of an Evangelist, the Sermon on the occasion being preached by the Rev. Samuel Shepard, of Brentwood, N. H.

Here he continued to labour seven years. He had no stipulated salary, and all that he received did not average more than forty dollars a year.

---

* Rev. ELISHA RANSOM planted the Church in Woodstock, in 1780, having removed thither a little before from Sutton, Mass. He remained there about twenty years, and the church increased greatly under his ministry.

Though he was generally at home on the Sabbath, he spent a considerable part of almost every week in travelling and preaching in destitute places. Sometimes he made journeys of more than a hundred miles, and that, too, through a wilderness, and in midwinter, and depending almost entirely on the charity of those among whom he might happen to fall; but so great was his zeal to preach the Gospel to the poor, that he accounted no sacrifice great by means of which he might accomplish his end.

Towards the close of the winter of 1789–90, the Baptist Church in Sturbridge, Mass., understanding that Mr. Baldwin had never been formally settled as Pastor of the church in Canaan, applied to him to visit them as a candidate for settlement. About the same time, he received a similar request from the church in Hampton, Conn. He determined that it was his duty at least to visit these places; and, after he had set out on his journey, early in the next summer, he was met by a similar invitation from the Second Baptist Church in Boston. After stopping a little at Sturbridge and Hampton, and receiving from both churches a unanimous call to become their Pastor, he proceeded to Boston, and, by request of the church there, preached to them his first sermon, on the 4th of July, 1790. He continued to supply the pulpit a few Sabbaths; and, as the effect of his labours, there was very soon a greatly increased attention to religion, especially among the young. On the 22d of August, the Church and Society voted him a unanimous call to settle among them; and, on the 18th of September, he returned an affirmative answer.

He was installed on the 11th of November following, the services being performed in the meeting-house of the Rev. Dr. Eliot, (Congregational,) which was kindly offered for the purpose. The Sermon was preached by the Rev. Dr. Stillman, from II. Cor. iv. 7.

Mr. Baldwin proved himself fully adequate to the important field into which he was now introduced. The revival, which was in progress at the time of his settlement, continued about two years, and, in the year 1791, about seventy were added to the church. In 1797, the congregation had so much increased that it was found necessary to enlarge their place of worship; and though the additional accommodations thus secured, were very considerable, they were almost immediately taken up, so that the house was as full as before the enlargement was made. In the spring of 1803, another revival of great power commenced in the church, which continued nearly two years and a half, during which the number received to communion was two hundred and twelve.

In 1794, he received the degree of Master of Arts from Brown University; and, in 1803, the degree of Doctor of Divinity from Union College.

In September, 1803, Dr. Baldwin, by appointment of the Baptist Missionary Society of Massachusetts, became the editor of a periodical work, under the title of the Massachusetts Baptist Missionary Magazine. Until the year 1817, he continued its sole editor; from that time till his death, he was its senior editor. This work was, for many years, the only religious periodical in the Baptist denomination in this country; and it was undoubtedly a most efficient auxiliary to the prosperity of the denomination.

Dr. Baldwin acquired no small degree of reputation as a controversial writer on Baptism and Communion. His first work, in connection with this controversy, entitled "Open Communion examined," was published in 1789, at the request of the Woodstock Association, while he resided in New Hampshire. The second was published in 1794, and was an answer to a pamphlet, entitled "A Friendly Letter," addressed to the author. In 1806, these were republished in a volume, with an Appendix, containing a Reply to Peter Edwards' "Candid Reasons," &c., together with additional remarks on some tracts and sermons which had then lately appeared on the subject. In 1810, he published what has been considered his most important work, entitled "A series of Letters, in which the distinguishing sentiments of the Baptists are explained and vindicated, in answer to a late publication by the Rev. Samuel Worcester, A. M., addressed to the author, entitled Serious and Candid Letters." This is a volume of about two hundred and fifty pages. The celebrated Andrew Fuller is said to have pronounced it the ablest discussion of the question he had ever met with. The last of his works on this subject was a short Essay on John's Baptism, published in 1820.

In 1802, he delivered the Annual Sermon on the day of the General Election. It was received with much more than common favour, as was indicated by the fact that it passed through three editions.

About seven years before his death, he had a slight attack of paralysis; from which, however, his physical system soon recovered, though he always believed that his mind had received an injury from it that was not to be repaired. As early as 1822, it became manifest to his friends that his intellectual vigour was rapidly declining, though the strength and fervour of his devout affections continued unabated. During the last year of his life, the change became still more marked, and he was himself deeply impressed with the conviction that his end was near. Towards the close of August, 1826, he left Boston to attend the Commencement at Waterville College, Me. On his way, he passed the Sabbath at Hallowell, and preached twice, apparently under the full impression that he was just finishing his earthly labours. The next day (29th of August) he proceeded to Waterville, and spent the afternoon in walking over the College grounds, and examining the condition of the institution. He retired to rest about nine o'clock, apparently slept well for an hour, then heaved a deep groan, and in the twinkling of an eye was dead. His remains were taken to Boston, and a Sermon at his interment was delivered by the Rev. Daniel Sharp, from Acts xi. 24. "He was a good man."

Dr. Baldwin received various testimonies of public respect and confidence. He was chosen a Trustee of Brown University in 1807, and at the time of his decease had been for several years the Senior Fellow. Of Waterville College he was a Trustee from its first organization. Of most of the benevolent institutions of Boston he was an active Manager, and of several of them a Presiding officer. At the time of his death, he was President of the Baptist Board of Managers for Foreign Missions, and one of the Trustees of the Columbian College, in the District of Columbia. He was a member of the Convention for amending the Constitution of

Massachusetts, in 1821, and took part in many of the discussions, acquitting himself with great credit.

Beside the several works already noticed, Dr. Baldwin published the following:—A Tract entitled "The Backslider." A Catechism. This had passed through six editions in 1826. A Sermon delivered at Bridgewater at the Ordination of the Rev. David A. Leonard, 1794. A Thanksgiving Sermon, 1795. A Sermon delivered at a Quarterly Meeting of several Churches for Special Prayer, 1799. A Sermon delivered at Boston at the Ordination of the Rev. William Collier, 1799. A Sermon on the Death of Washington, 1799. An Approved Workman in the Gospel Ministry: a Sermon delivered at Templeton at the Installation of the Rev. Elisha Andrews, 1800. A Sermon delivered at the Interment of Lieut. Governor Samuel Phillips, 1802. A Sermon delivered at Barnstable at the Installation of the Rev. John Peak,* 1802. A Sermon delivered at the Dedication of the new Meeting House in Bellingham, 1802. A Sermon delivered at the Installation of the Rev. Elisha Williams, Beverly, 1803. The Eternal Purpose of God the Foundation of Effectual Calling: A Sermon delivered before the First Baptist Society in Boston, 1804. A Sermon delivered in the Baptist Meeting House, Gold Street, New York, at the Ordination of the Rev. Jeremiah Chaplain, 1804. A Sermon delivered before the Baptist Missionary Society of Massachusetts, 1804. The Happiness of a People illustrated: A Sermon delivered before the Second Baptist Society in Boston, on the day of Annual Thanksgiving, 1804. A Sermon delivered at the Ordination of the Rev. Daniel Merrill, at Sedgwick, Me., 1805. A Discourse delivered before the Boston Female Asylum on their Sixth Anniversary, 1806. The Peaceful Reflections and Glorious Prospects of the Departing Saint: A Discourse delivered at the Interment of the Rev. Samuel Stillman, D. D., 1807. A Discourse delivered before the Ancient and Honourable Company in Boston, being the Anniversary of their Election of Officers, 1807. The Dangerous Influence of Vicious Example: A Sermon delivered in the Second Baptist Meeting House in Boston, 1809. A Discourse delivered at the Opening of the new Meeting House belonging to the Second Baptist Church and Society in Boston, 1811. The Supreme Deity of Christ illustrated: A Discourse delivered before the Second Baptist Church and Congregation in Boston, with an Appendix, containing Remarks on the terms "Only Begotten Son of God," &c., 1812. The Knowledge of the Lord filling the Earth: A Sermon delivered in Boston, before the Massachusetts Bible Society, 1812. Heirs of Grace: A Sermon delivered at Charlestown, occasioned by the death of Mrs. Abigail Collier,

---

* JOHN PEAK was born in Walpole, N. H., September 26, 1761. When he was three years old, his parents removed to Claremont, where, as the country was new, there was no school, though the deficiency was well supplied in respect to himself by the watchful and faithful care of his mother. In consequence of repeated attacks of rheumatic fever that settled in one of his hips, he early became a cripple, and, being thus rendered unable to labour on the farm, he was, in 1778, apprenticed to a tailor. In the summer of 1785, he was hopefully converted under the preaching of Dr. Baldwin, by whom also he was baptized in September following. In 1787, he removed to Woodstock, and was shortly after licensed by the church in that place as a candidate for the ministry. On the 18th of June, 1788, he was ordained first Pastor of the Church in Windsor, Vt. He was subsequently the Pastor of various other churches, as Deerfield and Newtown, in New Hampshire; Woburn, Barnstable, and Newburyport, in Massachusetts; and, during his ministry, he baptized more than a thousand persons. In the spring of 1828, he retired from the work of a Pastor, and soon after removed to Boston, where he resided until his death, which occurred on the 9th of April, 1842. He was distinguished for good sense, an amiable and cheerful disposition, and an unswerving Christian integrity.

wife of the Rev. William Collier, Pastor of the Baptist Church in said
town, 1813. The Christian Ministry: A Sermon delivered in the First
Baptist Meeting House in Boston, at the Installation of the Rev. James
M. Winchell, 1814. Missionary Exertions encouraged: A Sermon delivered in Sansom Street Meeting House, Philadelphia, before the General
Convention of the Baptist denomination in the United States, 1817. A
Sermon delivered at Cambridge, at the Opening of a new Meeting-House,
and the Constitution of a Baptist Church in that place, 1817. The Danger
of living without the Fear of God: A Discourse on Robbery, Piracy, and
Murder, in which Duelling and Suicide are particularly considered: Delivered in Boston, the Lord's Day following the Execution of the Pirates,
1819. A Sermon delivered at the Funeral of the Rev. James M. Winchell, A. M., late Pastor of the First Baptist Church in Boston, 1820.
The Duty of Parents to Children: A Sermon delivered in the Meeting-
House of the Second Baptist Church and Society in Boston, 1822. A
Discourse delivered in the Second Baptist Meeting-House in Boston; with
an Appendix, containing Historical Sketches of the Church and Society,
from their Commencement to the Present Time, 1824.

FROM THE REV. FRANCIS WAYLAND, D. D.
PRESIDENT OF BROWN UNIVERSITY.

PROVIDENCE, September 20, 1850.

My dear Sir: I cheerfully comply with your request for some notices of the
character of my venerated friend, the late Dr. Baldwin, though, in doing so,
I must avail myself of some sketches that I wrote shortly after his death,
when my recollections of his peculiar traits were far more vivid than they are
now. I had a good opportunity of knowing him, having lived in the same
house with him eighteen months, and had him for a neighbour from the time
of my settlement in Boston till his death; and it gives me pleasure to do any
thing I can in aid of an effort to honour his memory.

The history of a man's life is the only sure evidence of his ability. What
a man has done we hold to be proof positive of his power. Judged by this
standard, Dr. Baldwin will be ranked among the eminent men of his profession
in this country. To say nothing of his publications, some of which are certainly of a high order, it is evident that no man, not highly gifted of nature,
could ever, under his circumstances, have acquired so extensive an influence,
and retained it to the last, entire and undiminished. Men do not confide their
interests into the hands of another, unless he be abler than themselves. And
he who, for so long a time, united the suffrages of all, could only have
retained them by giving repeated proofs of undoubted native pre-eminence.

And this consideration will be more striking, if we recollect the circumstances under which Dr. Baldwin entered the ministry in Boston. His opportunities for improvement, either by reading or intellectual association, had
been limited. He had read little; he had seen little; but God had given him
the ability to think. He was of an age at which the intellectual habits of
most men are formed. They are too wise to learn, and too much attached to
the habits of their early education to mend them. Hence, too, frequently, to
men of this age, a change of location is the end of usefulness. But not so
with my venerable friend. The change was a great one, but he was equal to
it. He looked upon the relations of society in the light of common sense and
truth. He perceived what was required in the situation which he had entered.
He saw what he wanted; and, in the strength of a mind competent to dictate

terms to itself, he resolved to supply it. He threw aside what was unsuitable
to his present station. He performed with his full ability what that station
required; and soon found what he who honestly does his duty will always
find, that he was competent to the work which Providence had assigned him.

The prominent trait in Dr. Baldwin's intellectual character was vigorous
and manly discrimination. His imagination was not luxuriant, nor had his
taste acquired that accuracy, which is only the result of an early acquaintance
with the classics. Hence he succeeded best in a train of ratiocination, especially if it were one which led to an urgent appeal to the conscience. Hence
his style is remarkable more for perspicuity than grace. It is clear and forcible, but not ornate; and it gains nothing when the author attempts to adorn
it. When relying on his reasoning power, he is strong; but when attempting
to indulge his imagination, the critic might sometimes say, in good nature,
Bonus Homerus dormitat.

In public life, Dr. Baldwin combined, in a rare degree, unbending rectitude
with unsophisticated kindness of heart. In the discharge of his duty, he
never knew fear. He was naturally above anything like timidity; and
religious principle had still more effectually taught him to do right, "uncar-
ing consequences."   And yet no man could have more carefully avoided
unnecessarily injuring the feelings of the most insignificant human being. He
rigidly obeyed the command,—"Speak evil of no man." In company or at
home, he either spoke kindly or was silent. Whilst true to a hair's breadth
to the principles which he believed, he gave full credit to the honesty and the
rectitude of those from whom he differed. Hence was it that he so often
obtained the blessing of a peace-maker. Hence he retained to the last the
entire confidence of men of the most conflicting opinions, and even came off
from the arena of theological controversy, rich in the esteem of those whom
his argument failed to convince.

But it was in the retirement of domestic life, as the husband, the father,
and the friend, that you beheld him clothed in the most endearing attributes.
It was here that he shed around him the bland and attractive lustre of
finished moral excellence. His disposition was, in a pre-eminent degree,
charitable, kind and benevolent. To know him at home was to venerate and
love him. Always self-possessed and always dignified, yet always instructing
and always cheerful, no one could long be unhappy beneath his hospitable
roof. I can truly say that, during the four years in which I was in the habit
of seeing him daily, I cannot remember a single instance in which he betrayed
a temper inconsistent with the Christian profession.

The character of his piety corresponded, as might be expected, with the
type of his mind. It was visible in the firm adherence to truth, and the conscientious practice of what he believed to be his duty. This was, at the same
time, blended with fervent charity and ardent love for souls. He was a sincere believer in the doctrines of the Reformation, and his daily life was conformed to a high standard of Christian virtue. If any feature of his piety
was more prominent than another, it was meek, child-like humility. This
was seen in every walk of life, and everywhere did it add a new charm to his
other excellent endowments.

As a preacher, he stood among the most eminent of his time, in the denomination of which he was so long the distinguished ornament. He published
more than thirty sermons, preached on particular occasions, and all of them
are worthy of attentive perusal. In all of them may be discovered the traces
of strong and accurate reflection, or of fervent and deeply affecting piety.
Sometimes they are remarkable for acute and original argument, and at others
for tender and overflowing feeling. Whatever was his subject, he always left
upon his audience the conviction of his own sincere and earnest solicitude for

their everlasting good. His expostulations with the young were, in a remarkable degree, affectionate, parental and pathetic. Very frequently, on such occasions, he was melted even to tears.

His manner in the pulpit was dignified, simple and unaffected. He rarely wrote his sermons in full; and not generally, at least in the better part of his life, did he even furnish himself with a copious skeleton. His preparation most commonly consisted in studious reflection upon his subject, and writing merely the leading divisions. To this method he had been earliest accustomed, and in this he was probably more generally successful. Some of his ablest printed sermons were preached in this manner, and never written till after their delivery. Though far from being prejudiced against the use of notes, he was fully, and doubtless very truly, aware that, in New England at least, there is as much danger to be apprehended from too great a reliance on writing, as there is from not writing at all.

In person Dr. Baldwin was rather above the usual size, firmly and strongly built, and, towards the close of his life, slightly inclined to corpulency. His countenance was dignified, mild and engaging, and his hair, in his latter years perfectly white, rendered his whole appearance in the highest degree venerable. His habits were temperate and regular, without being formal or ascetic. Hence it will be readily imagined that he uniformly left upon every one the impression of old age in its loveliest and most interesting aspect, and Christianity in its mildest and most attractive exhibition.

I am, Rev. and dear Sir,

Yours very truly,

FRANCIS WAYLAND.

HENRY HOLCOMBE, D. D.*

1784—1824.

HENRY HOLCOMBE, son of Grimes and Elizabeth Holcombe, was born in Prince Edward County, Va., September 22, 1762. While he was yet a child, his father removed with his family to South Carolina. His opportunities for early improvement were exceedingly limited, and " at eleven years of age," (to use his own words,) " he completed all the education he ever received from a living preceptor." His mind, however, was of an inquisitive turn, panting for knowledge of every kind; and there was nothing on which he dwelt with such intense admiration as the number and grandeur of the heavenly bodies.

He was a mere stripling at the commencement of the Revolutionary War; but he was not too young to be deeply impressed with a sense of wrong done to his country, or to feel the stirrings of a lofty patriotism. Accordingly, when he had yet scarcely emerged from boyhood, he entered the army, and so much of both courage and discretion did he evince, that he was quickly raised to an important post of authority. It was during the period of his connection with the army that his mind became first deeply impressed with religious truth. Here, amidst the temptations of a camp, and the intense excitement incident to a contest for liberty, he

* Baptist Chronicle.—Georg. Bapt.—MS. from his daughter, Mrs. Hoff.

renounced the world as a supreme portion, and entered with vigour and resolution upon the service of a new Master. He was in his twenty-second year when he made a public profession of religion. His own account of it is as follows:—

" In conversing with my father, he informed me that I was baptized in my infancy, and said I was a Presbyterian. Asking on what passages of Scripture the peculiar tenets of that denomination were founded, he took up the Bible, and kindly endeavoured to satisfy me on those points. But, to his painful disappointment, we could find nothing that seemed to me in favour of baptizing infants, nor for governing a Gospel Church, otherwise than by the suffrages of its members. To pass softly over this tender ground, the result of my serious and reiterated inquiries into the materials, ordinances, and government of the Apostolic Churches, was the full conviction that, to follow the dictates of my conscience, I must be a Baptist; and, not conferring with flesh and blood, I rode near twenty miles to propose myself as a candidate for admission into a Baptist church."

Immediately after his Baptism, he received a license to preach according to the forms of the Baptist denomination, and forthwith commenced his work with great energy and fervour. The Church at Pike Creek, S. C., soon invited him to become their Pastor; and, accordingly, on the 11th of September, 1785, he was duly placed over them in the Lord. His labours, for some time, seem to have been attended with an uncommon blessing, and not a few were hopefully converted to God through his instrumentality.

In April, 1786, he was married to Frances, youngest daughter of Robert Tanner, of North Carolina; and, in the following June, she, together with her brother and mother, were among twenty-six persons to whom he administered Baptism. In August of the same year, he baptized seventeen more, among whom was his own father, who had proved more docile under the teachings of the son than the son did under those of the father. Up to this time his clerical services were rendered without any pecuniary compensation.

It was no small testimony of the confidence of his fellow-citizens that they appointed him to represent them in the Convention of South Carolina, held in Charleston, for ratifying the Constitution of the United States.

Not long after this, he was invited to take charge of the Baptist Church at Euhaw; and, having accepted their invitation, he removed thither in February 1791. He preached statedly at this place, May River, and St. Helena. As the climate here proved unfavourable to the health of his family, he removed hence, in 1795, to Beaufort, still, however, retaining his previous pastoral relations. At Beaufort the state of religion was, at that time, exceedingly low, and the Baptist denomination had few, if any, representatives there. By his unwearied efforts, a commodious Baptist meeting-house was erected, and not a few, both men and women, made a profession of their faith, and received the ordinance of Baptism at his hands.

In 1795, a few Baptists in Savannah undertook to erect a house of worship; but, the next year, while it was yet in an unfinished state, they rented it to the Presbyterians, whose church edifice had recently been destroyed by fire. In 1799, a little before the expiration of the term for which it was rented, the pew-holders in this building invited Mr. Holcombe to come and dispense to them the Gospel, upon an annual salary of two thousand dollars ; and he accepted their invitation. He had a congregation composed partly of Baptists and partly of Presbyterians, and his labours seem to have been equally acceptable to both. This state of things, however, continued but a short time, as the Baptists, early in 1800, conceived it to be their duty to have a distinct organization of their own ; and, accordingly, Mr. Holcombe, with his wife and ten others, entered into a covenant that they would " endeavour to keep house for the Lord, as soon as the necessary arrangements could be made." The church was regularly constituted, on the 26th of November, 1800.

During Mr. Holcombe's residence in Savannah, his labours were various and abundant. He was far from being satisfied with the ordinary routine of pastoral service. In 1801, he had the chief agency in establishing the Savannah Female Asylum,—an institution which has since united the energies and charities of Christians of different communions, and has diffused an immense amount of blessing among the wretched and destitute. He conducted a Magazine devoted to literature and religion, entitled the " Georgia Analytical Repository." He published an earnest Address to the friends of religion in Georgia, designed to convince them that a Christian profession does not in any degree interfere with the obligations of the citizen. He directed public attention to the extreme severity of the penal code, as it then existed in Georgia,—taking occasion to do this from the fact that a man was executed for the crime of stealing a gun ; and the State Penitentiary is said to have originated, in a measure, in his philanthropic efforts.

Mr. Holcombe's vigorous opposition to infidelity, theatrical amusements, and other things which he regarded of evil tendency, rendered him any thing but a favourite with the profligate and profane ; and it was several times the occasion of his life's being in imminent jeopardy. Two instances of cowardly attack, and somewhat remarkable providential deliverance, are thus related by himself :—

"A well dressed fellow, who assumed the style and manner of a gentleman, endeavoured to get me out of my house, after midnight, under the pretence of wanting me to perform a marriage ceremony. And had I not happened to hear the clock strike twelve just before the knock at my door, I might have believed him in the assertion that it was but a little past ten o'clock, and been led into the snare of my adversaries. He said his name was Clarke; that the parties to be married were respectable strangers, had been disappointed in not obtaining their marriage license sooner, had to sail next morning, were very desirous of being married by me, and that he would give me immediately a fee of fifty dollars. But, on peremptorily refusing from an upper window to come down stairs, on any consideration, at so unseasonable an hour, this Judas, who had before expressed himself with the greatest politeness, overwhelmed me with a torrent of the bitterest curses; and swore by his God that if I opened my mouth to call the guard, he would break every window in my house. From this unsuccessful stratagem they had recourse to violence. Returning, according to my well known custom, about nine o'clock in the evening, from the meeting of a Society of which I was a member, with a small son at each of my hands, a musket was snapped at my breast, and the fire rolled so near me that, in throwing out my hand in the dark, I laid hold on a bayonet. But God being pleased, at this critical moment, to make my heart like adamant, I exerted a loud authoritative voice in a few interrogations, which so alarmed the two cowardly assassins, whom I perceived before me with fixed bayonets, that they sneaked away, as if expecting every moment to be seized, *begging ten thousand pardons*, and with tremulous voices apologizing for their dastardly attempt on my life."

Mr. Holcombe was in the conference of Baptist ministers, which resolved to found the Mount Enon Academy, in 1804, and which adopted a constitution, as a Missionary Society, in 1806. In both these objects he took a deep interest, and he laboured for both with no inconsiderable zeal and success.

While on a preaching tour in the up-country, he allowed himself, on a very warm day, immediately after preaching, to drink freely of cold water. The effect of this had well-nigh been instantaneous death. He, however, so far recovered as to proceed on his journey homeward; and at Mount Enon he attempted to preach, but fainted in the pulpit. On his return to Savannah, he resumed his accustomed labours, but was quickly prostrated by a violent fever, which kept him confined about two months. In 1808, he again attended a meeting of the General Committee at Mount Enon, and, in 1809, went to Augusta, and assisted in the ordination of the Rev. (afterwards Dr.) William T. Brantly. In 1810, owing probably to an excess of labour, he experienced another severe and protracted illness; and, while he had yet only partially recovered, he resigned his pastoral charge at Savannah, and retired to Mount Enon, to give himself an opportunity to recruit his debilitated system.

In 1810, he was honoured with the degree of Doctor of Divinity from Brown University.

As soon as it became known that Dr. Holcombe was without charge, attempts were made in different quarters to secure his ministerial services. He was recalled to Beaufort, shortly after invited to Boston with a view to settlement, and then called to the First Baptist Church in Philadelphia. To this latter call he returned an affirmative answer.

Dr. Holcombe reached his new field of labour, after a stormy and perilous passage by sea, in January, 1812. Here, as in other places, he laboured with exemplary diligence. His views differed from those of some of his brethren in respect to the prosecution of the missionary enterprize, and his life was not altogether undisturbed by controversy. He died on the 22d of May, 1824, after an illness of only a week, in the sixty-second year of his age. His last words told of the peace and triumph of his spirit.

Dr. Holcombe was the father of ten children,—seven sons and three daughters. Three of his sons died in infancy, and four sons with the three daughters survived him. His elder sons were engaged in commercial pursuits, and the youngest was a practising physician. Mrs. Holcombe died at Philadelphia, October 20, 1827.

The following are Dr. Holcombe's publications:—A Discourse on the Sovereignty and Unchangeableness of the Deity, 1790. A Sermon on Isaiah liii. 1; containing a Brief Illustration and Defence of the Doctrines commonly called Calvinistic. Preached before the Charleston Association of Baptist Churches, 1791. A Sermon occasioned by the Death of Mr. Charles Bealer, who cheerfully resigned his soul to God, in the fifty-fifth year of his age, 1793. A Sermon occasioned by the Death of Lieutenant General George Washington, late President of the United States of America, who was born February 11, 1732, in Virginia, and died December 14, 1799, on Mount Vernon, his favourite seat, in his native country. First delivered in the Baptist Church, Savannah, Ga., and now published at the request of the Honourable City Council, 1800. The First Fruits, in a series of Letters, 1812. The whole Truth relating to the Controversy betwixt the American Baptists, 1820.

FROM THE HON. JOSEPH R. CHANDLER.

PHILADELPHIA, January 25, 1849.

Rev. and dear Sir: Dr. Holcombe is one of the friends of my earlier days, whose memory I still cherish with an affectionate and reverential regard. It gives me pleasure, therefore, to comply with your request, in giving you my impressions of his character.

He was in a high degree a positive man: he had fixed views, and could not relinquish them from motives of mere expediency. He had the ability to enforce these views, and, as there was nothing selfish in the composition of his mind, it was not strange that a vast number should follow his teaching. Of course, many who stood upon the general platform of the Baptist Church, dissented from him; but such a man, whether his sphere be politics or religion, is sure to be surrounded by hearty, devoted friends. And Dr. Holcombe, while he had the respect of all Christians who knew him, either personally or by his writings, was cherished by a very large congregation of admiring hearers, with an affection which no man of yielding or negative character can ever hope to enjoy.

Dr. Holcombe's earnestness in whatever he deemed right in itself and profitable to others, manifested itself in his professional relations with his congregation, to whom he preached with exceeding plainness; shunning not to declare what he considered the whole counsel of God, whatever might be the effect of that truth upon himself or others.

His style of address, though plain, was impressive; and his discourses, without being marked by evidence of art, or of that labour which is apparent in the sermons of many, showed a clear understanding of the subject he discussed. They were intended to be eminently practical: he loved especially to show how the doctrines of Christianity affected, restrained and influenced the practice of Christians. And he was careful, while he persuaded men to virtue, to present to them those great vital principles upon which virtue, to be stable, must be based.

Dr. Holcombe did not seek controversy. The relations in which he stood to some of the public efforts of his own denomination, brought him into occasional collision; and he used his pen and the press in the defence of what seemed to him right, and the exposure of what he considered wrong, in such cases, with the same zeal and efficiency that always distinguished the exercise of his powers whenever they were called into action. He was a forceful, pungent writer, seizing upon the strong points of the question at issue, and presenting them in the clearest light. Of course a Christian divine, like Dr. Holcombe, would not violate gentlemanly proprieties in any discussion; but if his assailants did, they and others were soon made sensible of the error.

In 1822, Dr. Holcombe openly proclaimed from his pulpit the belief to which he had attained, that War is inconsistent with the doctrines and requirements of Christianity, and that it was time for Christian Men, Christian Associations, and Christian Nations, to proclaim such a principle, and illustrate it by their example.

This was a startling subject, and for a time it created some uneasiness among the members of his church, many of whom had, like himself, shared in the toils and sacrifices of a military life in defending the Declaration of the Nation's Independence. And, at that juncture, the peculiar aspect of the Presidential canvass rendered the new Peace doctrines not altogether palatable to a portion of the community. Dr. H., however, preached openly what he considered the truth. But he paused on the truth. He did not denounce those who could not see as he saw. He persuaded a large proportion of the church, and many of the congregation, to become members of a Peace Society; but he never allowed a difference of opinion on that subject to work between him and his people any diminution of affection or intercourse.

Dr. Holcombe was a Christian patriot. In his early life he presented to his country those services which she most needed, and which he then believed it his duty to offer. In later years, with maturer intellect, he thought it his duty to serve his country by hastening the fulfilment of the Gospel promises of Peace on earth. And however men may have differed from him in these views, there was none to impeach his motives, to doubt his sincerity, or to suspect that his advocacy of Peace was less the effect of a well conducted inquiry than the love of quiet which age begets. Those who knew him knew well that the wonted fire of youth animated his latest years, and that he was as impulsive for good at sixty as at twenty-one. Not a feeling influenced his patriotism in the Revolutionary army, that was not acknowledged in his latest ministry. He loved his country, and always sought and prayed for her honour. One anecdote will illustrate both his feelings and his judgment.

While sitting with some friends, chiefly officers with himself of the Pennsylvania Peace Society, a gentleman came into the parlour, who, in answer to an inquiry of " What is the news "—mentioned a report that a Spanish sloop-of-war had met one of the smaller vessels of the United States' Navy, and, after the Spanish officer had used some indecorous language, he fired into the American vessel. " Ah," exclaimed Dr. Holcombe, with great earnestness, " and what did the American Commander do ?" " The papers say," answered the informant, " that the American Commander, seeing that his vessel was much smaller than the assailant, sent word to the Spanish Captain that he should consider himself a prisoner of war." " Did he ?" asked Dr. H. with a look of contempt, mingled with a little anger,—" did an American do that ?" And he rose from his chair,—his almost gigantic form dilating with the idea of insult to his country,—" Did he do that ? I would have sunk the Spaniard to the bottom of the ocean. That is," continued the good man, as he looked round and saw a little surprise settle on the faces of a part of his auditors, or as the impulse of the Patriot gave way to the judgment of the Christian,— " that is, I would, if I were not a man of Peace."

While Dr. Holcombe lived, he illustrated the beauty of every doctrine he professed and preached. His life was one great self-denial,—that is, it was a self-denial, unless it were his pleasure to give all he obtained, and to give up all he might have obtained, for the benefit of others. And when he closed his labours with his life, then first his friends knew how much of self he devoted to others.

To give abundantly from a great abundance is good, and the blessings of those who are the recipients must reward the charity. But that charity which deprives the giver of the means of many comforts, which bestows all to-day upon the needy, and looks that to-morrow shall bring its own supply,—that charity is indeed an illustration of the doctrines of the great Master of Christianity, and denotes a faith in the promises of his Gospel.

With assurances of hearty wishes for your health and happiness, I am, Rev. Sir,

Your friend and servant,

JOSEPH R. CHANDLER.

JOSEPH GRAFTON.*
1784—1836.

JOSEPH GRAFTON was born in Newport, R. I., June 9, 1757. His parents were natives of Salem, Mass., and were honest and industrious people. His father, William Grafton, was a mariner, and, for several years, commanded a vessel in the West India trade. At the age of about fifty, he relinquished the sea, removed to Providence, and devoted himself to the business of sail-making. His son Joseph was, at this time, about ten years old.

The advantages for education in Providence were then quite limited; and the father of young Grafton, with his moderate means, was able to keep his son at school only till he was about fourteen. Having been taught only the elementary branches, he was now initiated into his father's business; and, as this occupation brought him into frequent contact with sailors, he soon began to show himself an imitator of their vices. His mother, who was a serious woman, often catechized and instructed her children; but her efforts seem not to have permanently impressed his mind. Though he sometimes had momentary apprehensions in regard to the issue of a sinful life, he continued in the main indifferent to religion until he had reached his eighteenth year.

About this time,—in the latter part of 1774 and the beginning of 1775, an extensive revival of religion prevailed in Providence, chiefly in the Congregational Church, under the pastoral care of the Rev. Joseph Snow, and in the Baptist Church, then in charge of the Rev. (afterwards Dr.) James Manning. The former of these churches, Mr. Grafton, with his parents, usually attended. When the revival had been in progress some months, he was aroused to a deep sense of his sinfulness, and his need of an interest in the great salvation; and, after two or three weeks of extreme anxiety and distress, his mind became not only tranquil but joyful, and he found himself adoring the wisdom and goodness of God in every thing around him, even before it occurred to him that he had been the subject of any spiritual change. Having given himself sufficient time to test the character of his own feelings, he united with the Congregational Church in Providence, which was of a somewhat mixed character, many of the members, being, to a great extent, Baptist in their opinions, but choosing this church on account of not being prepared to subscribe to the doctrine of Strict Communion. Before taking this step, however, he examined the Scriptures in respect to Baptism, and came to the conclusion that immersion is the only mode, and believers the only legitimate subjects, of that ordinance. And thus he was baptized.

It became now a serious question with Mr. Grafton in what way he could best serve the Master to whose honour he had consecrated himself. The War of the Revolution was just commencing, and most of the young men around him became connected with the army; but *he* only performed his quota of military duty, when called upon. By this means he was pre-

---

* Mem. by Dr. Smith.—Fun. Serm. by Dr. Sharp.

served from many temptations to which he would otherwise have been exposed, and which might possibly have given a different ultimate direction to his life. Amidst all the excitement of the times, the great question that was constantly urging itself upon his conscience, was, what the Lord would have him to do ; and when the thought occurred to him that *possibly* it might be his duty, at some future time, to preach the Gospel, he felt entirely disinclined to it, on the ground that neither his abilities nor acquisitions were adequate to so responsible an office. Still, however, his mind was not at rest; and he became at length so deeply impressed with the idea that it was his duty to enter the ministry, that he was actually meditating the incipient steps for qualifying himself ; but, as unexpected obstacles were now thrown in his way, he regarded this, for the time, as a decisive indication of Providence that his duty lay in a different direction. The consequence of this, in connection with the unpropitious state of things that existed around him, was, that his mind seemed to lose, in a great degree, its spiritual sensibility, and to settle too much upon the objects and interests of the world.

Under these circumstances, he was married, on the 12th of December, 1779, to a daughter of Capt. Barnard Eddy, who died while he was on his way to join the Northern army, in the year 1776. This event seemed to have fixed his lot in a private station for life. But, shortly after this, the subject of his entering the ministry was again urged upon his consideration by the Deacons of the church with which he was connected, and they finally induced him to consent to the appointment of a meeting of the church, that he might preach before them, and give them an opportunity to judge of his qualifications. The result of this effort was that the church decided at once that it was his duty to preach, and gave him their approbation in so doing. He was, however, reluctant to yield to their judgment, and compounded the matter by preaching occasionally, and at the same time attending to his secular business.

While he was in this indecisive state of mind, he was overtaken with a succession of severe afflictions. In May, 1783, he lost the eldest of his two children, and, a few weeks after, the other followed ; and both were followed by their mother, a person of great excellence, within less than a year afterwards. Even these events do not seem to have roused him from the state of spiritual languor into which he had previously fallen; and God had still further trials in store for him. In July, 1784, he was seized with bleeding at the lungs ; and such was the violence of the attack as to leave but little hope of his recovery. In this state he severely reproached himself for having been so unwilling to listen to the Providence of God, calling him, as he then believed, to devote himself to the ministry. Contrary to his own expectations and those of his friends, he gradually recovered his health, and immediately surrendered himself to the claims which he believed the Church, and the Head of the Church, made upon him.

Having now received from the church to which he belonged a full license to preach, he devoted himself, thenceforth, entirely to the work of the ministry. He laboured at first, for some time, at a place called Rehoboth Neck. Afterwards, he preached by invitation at Plainfield, Conn., to a congregation of Separates, where he continued fifteen months. During his residence with this church, his mind became exercised on the terms of communion; and the result of his inquiries was a full conviction that he had hitherto stood on unscriptural ground. In the year 1787, he asked a dismission from the church with which, for twelve years, he had been connected, and joined the First Baptist Church in Providence.

Having thus changed his ecclesiastical relations, he immediately received an invitation to preach to the Baptist church in Hampton, Conn., where he laboured several months. During his stay, there existed a more than ordinary attention to religion among the people, and they twice formally invited him to settle over them; but he thought proper to decline the invitation.

The Baptist Church in Newton, Mass., being rendered vacant by the removal of the Rev. Caleb Blood, solicited Mr. Grafton to preach to them as a candidate; and, after hearing him a suitable time, they invited him to become their Pastor. He accepted their call, and was ordained on the 18th of June, 1788,—the sermon on the occasion being preached by the Rev. Mr. Stanford of Providence. He addressed himself now, with great vigour, not only to his public labours but to his private studies; and he was not a little facilitated in the latter by having access to two or three excellent libraries in the neighbourhood.

Here Mr. Grafton continued to labour with untiring zeal, and with encouraging success, for nearly half a century. The church was favoured with frequent revivals of religion during his ministry, and seems to have had a sound and vigorous growth. The whole number admitted to the communion during the period of his Pastorship was five hundred and fifty-four.

Mr. Grafton received numerous testimonies of the high estimation in which he was held by his brethren and the public at large. He was Vice-President of the Massachusetts Baptist Missionary Society, from 1815 to 1825, and, after the death of Dr. Baldwin, President. He was appointed on the Committee of the Evangelical Tract Society, in 1817, and was Trustee of the same from 1823 to 1829. In the early history of the Baptist General Convention for Foreign Missions, he was one of the Committee for the Northern section of the Union to examine candidates for missionary labour. He was Vice-President of the Baptist Foreign Missionary Society for Boston and vicinity, being elected several times, successively, for the space of three years each, from the year 1819. In 1826, he was elected President of the Board of Trustees of the Newton Theological Institution. He was President, successively, of the Norfolk County Foreign Missionary Society, and of the Middlesex and Norfolk County Missionary Society. He preached the Annual Sermon of the Warren Association at Middleborough in 1799, and of the Boston Association in 1815, and was Moderator of the latter in 1822 and 1826.

Mr. Grafton was thrice married. He was married to his second wife, whose maiden name was Sally Robinson, not far from the time of his settlement at Newton. She had seven children, and died on the 15th of June, 1804, aged forty-one. His third wife—Hannah Parker—died on the 26th of January, 1835, aged seventy-three.

Mr. Grafton was, for many years previous to his death, subject to severe nervous attacks, which, in connection with the growing infirmities of age, led him often to look forward to the close of his labours. In July, 1835, he requested his church to release him from the responsibilities of the pastoral office, that they might avail themselves of the labours of a young and vigorous minister, who might more effectually serve their spiritual interests. This proposed arrangement, accordingly, took effect; and another minister was soon after settled, though Mr. Grafton's occasional services were always thankfully accepted. During the winter of 1835–36, he was confined to his chamber by illness; but he recovered with the opening of summer, so as to be able to visit his friends, both in and out of his congregation. The Church and Society had been engaged in building a new house of worship; and, as it was nearly ready for occupancy, it was arranged that, on the third Sabbath in December, they should take their leave of the old house, and that their venerable Pastor should preach on the occasion. But it turned out that the last public service in the house was the Funeral service of the Pastor himself. He had, for some time, been uncommonly vigorous in both mind and body. The first two Sabbaths in December he spent in Roxbury, preaching twice on each Sabbath. He was not as well as usual when he left Roxbury, and, on reaching home, became seriously ill, though he seems not at once to have apprehended a fatal issue. He lingered about two days, partly in an unconscious state, and partly in the exercise of an intelligent and serene confidence in his Redeemer, and died on the 16th of December, 1836, aged seventy-nine years. His Funeral Sermon was preached by the Rev. Dr. Sharp of Boston, and was afterwards published, in connection with a Memoir of Mr. Grafton's life.

The following is a list of Mr. Grafton's publications:—A Sermon occasioned by the Death of Jonathan Shepard, James Ward, and Michael Bright, who died of small-pox, 1792. A Sermon on the Death of his daughter, Miss Sally Grafton, 1802. A Sermon occasioned by the Death of Mr. Samuel Richardson, 1804. A Sermon exhibiting the Origin, Progress, and Present State of the Baptist Church and Society in Newton, 1830.

Besides the above, Mr. Grafton printed a few shorter pieces, as Letters, Brief Addresses, &c.

FROM PROFESSOR WILLIAM GAMMELL,
OF BROWN UNIVERSITY.

PROVIDENCE, January 20, 1855.

My dear Sir: From the year 1811 to 1828, my father, the Rev. William Gammell,* was settled as a Baptist minister in the town of Medfield, Mass. The clergymen of his denomination who were settled nearest to him,—though at distances which seemed by no means inconsiderable,—with whose names

---

* WILLIAM GAMMELL was born in Boston, January 9, 1786. His parents were Unitarians, and were connected with the Federal Street Congregational Church. In 1805, he was baptized by Dr. Stillman, and united with the First Baptist Church in Boston. His academical education was at the Boston schools, and his theological under the direction of the Rev. William Williams, of Wrentham. His first engagement for supplying a pulpit was at Bellingham, Mass., where he was ordained in 1809. The next year, he removed to Medfield, where he continued the Pastor of a prosperous church, gathered from several adjoining towns, till August, 1823, when he removed to Newport, R. I., and became the Pastor of the Second Baptist Church in that town. Here he continued, growing in reputation and usefulness, until the 30th of May, 1827, when he died, suddenly, of apoplexy, in his forty-second year. In 1817, he received the

and persons my boyhood was most familiar, were Rev. William Williams of Wrentham, Rev. Abial Fisher of Bellingham, Rev. Charles Train of Framingham, and Rev. Joseph Grafton of Newton. I recall them all as they appeared at my father's house—the outlines of their persons and manners still linger with singular vividness in my imagination. They were all pious and intelligent men, who, in an humble sphere, laboured with unremitting zeal in the ministry of the Gospel. Two of them at least had been educated at College—Mr. Train having graduated at Cambridge, in 1805, and Mr. Williams at the College of Rhode Island, in 1769,—the first class that appears on the College Catalogue. They were all earnest friends of a high education, uncompromising advocates of entire religious freedom, and, according to their ability, in their respective spheres, they were zealous promoters of every interest of society and of the Church of Christ. The period in question was that in which the Societies of the Baptist denomination for promoting Domestic and Foreign Missions, and Ministerial Education, had their origin. Most of the meetings of these neighbouring clergymen with which I was familiar in boyhood, were probably designed to advance these interests of their humble communion. They were occasions of unusual interest to the younger members of the minister's family, to whom these well known and respected visiters appeared to stand in the familiar relation of grandsires and uncles, according to their several ages. I well remember the warm personal regard, and the reciprocal sympathy in each others' fortunes, which they always manifested, and also how much their conversation, to which I was often an eager listener, turned upon the trials which they experienced in consequence of the unfriendly public sentiment which existed around them.

From this little circle of excellent Christian ministers, no single form, after that of my own father, comes back to my memory with a distinctness so marked and life-like as that of my father's venerated friend, Rev. Joseph Grafton, of Newton. He was, I think, next to Mr. Williams, the oldest of them all; but he was also, without exception, the sprightliest and wittiest in his conversation, and on this account, the most interesting family visiter in the estimation of the children. In dress he was extremely neat, and in person perhaps somewhat below the average stature; but of a firm, compact frame, and unusually flexible, easy and quick in all his movements. He had long resided at Newton, near Boston, and had there a larger acquaintance and a freer intercourse with both ministers and laymen of other denominations than would have been practicable even for his social and genial nature in the severer and less intelligent neighbourhood of Medfield and its border towns. His eye was dark and unusually expressive, and in its quick flashes, whether in the pulpit or at the fireside, there beamed forth a deep, spiritual intelligence and sincerity; while the tones of his musical and well modulated voice did not fail to enlist the attention of all who heard him speak, whether in public or in private. His conversation, though I think not copious, abounded in anecdote, as I presume his preaching did also. I doubt not those who knew him well could relate many an interesting incident, touching his method of playing with words and thoughts, and of illustrating the peculiarities of individual character, or embodying the maxims of wisdom and the doctrines of religion. His education must have been limited, but his experience in the world had given him a large acquaintance with human nature, and taught him how to interpret its mysteries, conciliate its prejudices, and display its motives in the light of religious truth. His reading, too, though not extensive, must have

honorary degree of Master of Arts from Brown University, and in 1820 was elected to its Board of Trustees. He published a Sermon delivered on the death of a parishioner, and contributed largely to some of the periodicals of his day. He was a highly acceptable preacher, and an earnest friend of every object connected with the extension of Christianity.

been among good books; for his language was pure and without pretension, and his general style of discourse such as could seldom be secured by an acquaintance only with the theological standards of that day. How he would now be ranked as a preacher or as an intellectual man I am wholly unable to form an opinion. I recall him only as he appeared at a period of my life, when my judgments of men were immature, and my standards of character wholly unformed. I associate his image with that of my father, as one of the most venerable in the circle of his clerical brethren and friends, and one whose sympathies he largely shared, and whose counsels he often sought. I seldom saw him after my own childhood had passed away; but he remains most distinctly in my memory, as one of those who gave me my earliest conception of the character of a Christian minister, in which were gracefully blended good breeding without worldliness, wit without levity, sincere piety without austerity. I remain, my dear Sir, with much regard,

Very respectfully yours,

WILLIAM GAMMELL.

FROM THE REV. SAMUEL F. SMITH, D. D.

NEWTON CENTRE, Mass., April 10, 1855.

Rev. and dear Sir: About five years subsequent to the death of the Rev. Mr. Grafton, Pastor of the First Baptist Church in Newton, I came to the Pastorate of the same church, and continued to fulfil its duties for twelve and a half years. From my earliest intercourse with the people, I found that the memory of the revered old man, who had led parents, and children, and children's children, to Heaven, was exceedingly fragrant. Scarcely a day passed in my parochial visits, on which I did not hear some agreeable recollection of him. The aged delighted to live over again the scenes of *his* early ministry, and *their* early Christian experience, and gave me, from day to day, accounts of the methods of his preaching and his pastoral labours, or anecdotes illustrative of his character and spirit. The fathers and the mothers spoke, as eye and ear had witnessed; and the children narrated what they had heard and loved to hear of the venerated friend of his people, from their cradles upward. Many anecdotes, which exhibit the good man in the unembarrassed freeness of an affectionate and cheerful life, I have heard from several independent sources, but always substantially the same. These anecdotes I prized as indices of the social and intellectual character of the man, in some respects superior to any set discourse, weighing and registering his mental power and friendly spirit. I do not think that I can better fall in with the spirit of your request than by detailing a few of these anecdotes, illustrative of different points of Mr. Grafton's character.

His preaching was often characterized by great aptness, and sometimes by expressions that would excite a smile. He once preached the Annual Sermon before the old Massachusetts Baptist Missionary Society, and took for his text, Matthew xvii. 26, 27. At the close of his sermon, as there was to be a collection in aid of the funds of the Society, he said,—"And now let every gentleman feel in his pocket, and every lady in her purse, and see if there be not there a piece of money, as there was in the mouth of Peter's fish." The archness and naiveté with which this was said, produced general gratification, and secured a handsome donation to the funds of the Society.

In preaching a Charity Sermon, he once remarked that some persons are always ready to give when they are asked; but they are governed by impure motives, hoping for some sort of recompense. He said they were willing to cast their bread upon the waters, but they were careful to have a string tied to it, that they might be secure of drawing it back.

He spent little time in his study, but a great deal in pastoral visitation. There was scarcely a day when he did not ride abroad to see some of his parishioners. Much of his preparation for the pulpit was conducted in his chaise. Sometimes, when riding with a familiar friend, he has been observed not only talking out the plans of his sermons, but actually gesticulating, as if preaching them in his pulpit.

In the old meeting-house, the ancient square pews were generally furnished with one or two chairs, besides the permanent seats around the sides. On the Sabbath noon,—most of the families remaining during the intermission, and bringing their lunch with them,—the box of provisions was placed in a chair in the middle, and all the family helped themselves. Father G. uniformly remained also, but brought no refreshment with him. He went round, however, from pew to pew, taking a piece of pie here, and of cake there, and an apple from another place, and going on, eating and conversing with his parishioners, like another Oberlin, among his Alpine flock. At a suitable opportunity, all having had time enough, he used to say,—" Come, friends, it is time to go to the prayer-meeting;" and thus, in this simple and primitive way, the good old man went in and out among his people, as a good shepherd, knowing his sheep and known of them.

He was very social in his disposition, and greatly enjoyed the companionship of friends. On Saturday evening he had been conversing with a number in his parlour, until eight o'clock, when he pleasantly remarked, alluding to the members of the Theological Institution, that he had now a learned congregation to preach to, and must withdraw to his study to prepare for the Sabbath. He was absent only about twenty minutes, when, yielding to the strong temptation below, he came running down again, and spent the residue of the evening in friendly chat.

On a certain occasion, an exchange of pulpits had been arranged by him with the Rev. Dr. Sharp; but, at the last moment, the plan was unavoidably broken up. When Mr. Grafton appeared before his congregation, he explained the circumstances as an apology for his want of preparation, adding,—" In music, every tune is either a *sharp* or a flat; and I am afraid you will have a flat to-day;"—playing upon the name of Dr. Sharp. After this he proceeded with his sermon.

He seemed to delight, by an innocent pleasantry, to awaken expectations which he designed, by some artful turn of expression, to disappoint. Thus, in preaching upon Paul's "thorn in the flesh," he stated at considerable length the opinion of several commentators as to the question what the thorn might be. To close up all, he added,—" And now, my hearers, you may perhaps wish to know what is the opinion of your minister; and I will tell you—when Paul tells me."

He was a great friend to singing-schools, promoting them, when they were established in his parish, by all his influence, often going into the school and showing his interest by some kind remarks. One winter, when a dancing school in the place drew away the attention of the young people, he pleasantly imputed the prevention of the singing-school by such means to Satanic agency, and remarked that "John, the Baptist, lost his head by dancing."

On one occasion the Rev. Mr. B——, the Junior Pastor of the First Congregational Church, was called upon to immerse three candidates, who could not be satisfied with any other Baptism. After the Baptism of the first, Father Grafton stepped down to the administrator, and "instructed him in the way of the Lord more perfectly." At the close of the ceremony, the assembly were beginning to disperse, without singing, praying, or parting blessing. Father Grafton, with his characteristic aptness, took off his hat and exclaimed, in allusion to the ordinance just witnessed, and expressing his joy in the event,—"Lord, it is done as thou hast commanded, and yet there is room;"—after which he pronounced the Apostolic benediction.

He had a deep sense of unworthiness, and keenly felt the little kindnesses which were shown to him. Being once at the house of a friend in cold weather, and a fire having been kindled in his chamber for his comfort,—on entering the room, he walked across it several times with evident emotion, and then, speaking of the fire, remarked,—"I am not deserving of this."

The late Dr. Benjamin Shurtleff of Boston was informed by a friend that probably Father Grafton, in the latter part of his life, was in needy circumstances, and that a benefaction would prove very acceptable to him. Dr. Shurtleff, soon after, meeting the venerable minister in Washington Street, Boston, called to him, inviting him to his chaise, where they conversed for a considerable time. At parting, Dr. S. put into the hand of Mr. Grafton a roll of bank-notes, saying,—"Perhaps you may find a use for them." Father G., looking up with one of his arch smiles, replied in a way expressing at the same time his gratitude and true wit,—"When I get home I shall tell my Master."

Being once at a public dinner, where he was much annoyed by a young gentleman opposite him, who scarcely uttered a sentence without some profane oath attached to it, he rose in his place, and exclaimed,—"Mr. President." When the President had rapped upon the table with his knife, producing silence, and calling the attention of the guests, Mr. Grafton said,—"Sir, I move you that no person at the table have permission to utter a profane oath, except my friend, the Rev. Dr. Homer." Such was the mutual intimacy of the two clergymen, and so well established was the character of Dr. Homer for piety, that no offence was taken, and the well merited reproof had its designed effect.

Within the circle of his knowledge was a person distinguished by a penurious spirit. He was gaining wealth by degrees, and seemed resolved to let nothing go out of his hands, particularly for any charitable or religious use. On a certain time, the store of this person was broken open and robbed of a considerable amount. The next day, Father Grafton called to condole with the man in regard to his loss, and, in his witty method, remarked,—"What the Lord did'nt get, the devil did."

A clergyman of another denomination, for a long time, manifested a great curiosity to know what salary Father Grafton received from his people; but the old gentleman had his own reasons for refusing to gratify him. On one occasion, he took the liberty to ask him the question directly; to which he answered, regarding at the same time the good name of his people, and alluding to the scantiness of his support,—"My people give me all they are able, and I take all I can get."

When he came to the decline of life, he was not unconscious of the ravages of time upon him. Even in those respects in which persons are not so readily sensible of their own decay, he felt that what he might not perceive himself was perceptible by others. Dr. Homer once asked him pleasantly,—"Brother Grafton, what is the reason that there are now no old people, as there used to be? Where are the old people?" Mr. G. perceived the hallucination of his venerable friend, and replied,—"Brother Homer, ask the young people; they will tell you."

But there is no end to the anecdotes which I might relate concerning Father Grafton. The above probably are sufficient for your purpose.

With best wishes for your success in perpetuating, among this and later generations, the memory of those whom God honoured in earlier days, as the means of adding stars to Christ's crown, I remain, my dear Sir,

Very affectionately yours,

S. F. SMITH.

STEPHEN GANO.*

1786—1828.

STEPHEN GANO was the third son of the Rev. John and Sarah (Stites) Gano, and was born in the city of New-York, on the 25th of December, 1762,—his father being at that time Pastor of the Gold Street Baptist Church. His early advantages for education were the best which his father was able to command. It was fully intended that he should take the regular course at the College of Rhode Island, of which his uncle, the Rev. Dr. Manning, was then President; but, in consequence of the troubles which the Revolutionary War brought with it, his father found it impossible to carry out this purpose; and, as the best thing he could do for his son, then thirteen years of age, placed him under the care of his maternal uncle, Dr. Stites, to be educated for the medical profession, while he himself entered the army as a Chaplain. The son, having at length made honourable proficiency in his studies, and being also very anxious to enter the public service, received the appointment of Surgeon. His mother, who had been the principal agent in procuring the appointment for him, having buckled on his regimentals, said to him, as they parted, (concealing her tears,) " My son, may God preserve your life and your patriotism—the one may be sacrificed in retaking and preserving the home of your childhood : but never let me hear that you have forfeited the birth right of a freeman."

Young Gano was at that time nineteen years old. He continued in the service of his country about two years, and then retired to settle as a Physician in Tappan, now Orangetown, Rockland County, N, Y.,—having been married, on the 25th of October, 1782, to Cornelia, daughter of Capt. Josiah Vavasor, an officer in the English Navy, then a resident of New York city. In 1783, one year after his marriage, he became hopefully pious, and soon after was impressed with the idea that it was his duty to preach the Gospel. On the 2d of August, 1786, he was ordained in the Gold Street Church, by his father, Dr. Manning, and some other clergymen. His first ministerial labours he performed in the character of a missionary on the Hudson ; and wherever he went, his preaching awakened a deep interest. He was, successively, for some time, the Pastor of the Baptist Church at Hillsdale and at Hudson. At the latter place he lost his wife by death, after she had become the mother of two sons and two daughters. On the 4th of August, 1789, he was married at Stamford, Conn., to Polly, daughter of Colonel Tallmadge, father of the late Colonel James Tallmadge of the city of New York. By this marriage there were three daughters and one son.

In 1792, Dr. Gano received a unanimous invitation to the Pastorate of the First Baptist Church in Providence, R. I.,—the oldest Baptist Church in America. This call he accepted, and here, in the faithful and acceptable discharge of his ministerial duties, he spent the remainder of his life. His church was one of the largest in the country, and few enjoyed more fre-

---

* Memoir in connection with the list of members of the First Baptist Church in Providence.— Dr. Sharp's Fun. Serm.—MS. from Rev. Henry Jackson, D. D.

quent or powerful revivals. The years which were signalized by the largest additions to its communion, were 1793 and '94, 1801, '05, '06, '08, '12, '16, and '20. In this last year, the number added by Baptism was one hundred and forty-seven, making the whole number of communicants six hundred and forty-eight.

In 1797, Dr. Gano was again afflicted by the death of his wife. On the 18th of July, 1799, he was marrried a third time to Mary, daughter of Professor Joseph Brown, of Brown University. She was spared to him but a very short time, and died, leaving one daughter. On the 8th of October, 1801, he was married to Mrs. Joanna Latting, of Hillsdale, N. Y., who survived him many years. In each of his wives he found a companion eminently suited to his tastes, and an efficient auxiliary to his usefulness. At his death, he left six daughters, four of whom have married clergymen : namely, the Rev. John Holroyd,* the Rev. Peter Ludlow, the Rev. David Benedict, D. D., and the Rev. Henry Jackson, D. D.

Dr. Gano was an invalid during several of his last years ; but he continued to preach until within about three months of his death. His disease proved to be a dropsy of the chest, and was attended with the most acute physical suffering. But his confidence in his Redeemer was so strong as to disarm death of terror, and to enable him to even greet its approach with a joyful welcome. On the 18th of August, 1828, just after he had stated that his sky was without a cloud, he passed gently away, with a cheerful smile upon his countenance, which lingered after the spirit was gone. The event was immediately made known by the tolling of the city bells, and the children who had just assembled in the several schools, were permitted, out of respect to his memory, to retire. His Funeral was attended on the third day after, by an immense concourse, and with every demonstration of affectionate respect. A Sermon appropriate to the occasion was preached by the Rev. Dr. Sharp of Boston.

Dr. Gano received the honorary degree of Master of Arts from Brown University, in 1800. Though he usually bore the title of *Doctor*, it was only in reference to his having been in the medical profession. He was one of the Overseers of Brown University from 1794 till his death.

Dr. Gano published a Sermon on the death of Washington, 1800 ; a Sermon at the Ordination of Mr. Joshua Bradley, Newport, 1801 ; a Sermon at the Funeral of the Rev. Gardiner Thurston, Newport, 1802 ; a Sermon entitled " The Christian Crowned," occasioned by the death of the Rev. Joseph Snow, Congregational minister of Providence ; a Sermon at the Ordination of Mr. Peter Ludlow, delivered in the Second Baptist Church in Providence, 1823 ; and a Sermon on the Divinity of Christ, 1827.

---

* JOHN HOLROYD was born in Providence, R. I,, in May, 1783. He was graduated at Brown University in 1802. He was educated for the legal profession, but in 1830 became a clergyman, and was ordained Pastor of the Baptist Church in Cheraw, S. C., in March of that year. In August, 1831, he was installed Pastor of the Baptist Church in Danvers, Mass., and continued in this relation till his death, which occurred on the 8th of November, 1837, while on a visit to his friends in Providence. He was an accomplished Scholar, an earnest Christian, and a highly acceptable and useful Preacher.

FROM THE REV. HENRY JACKSON, D. D.

NEWPORT, R. I., April 7, 1856.

My dear Sir: In reply to your letter of inquiry concerning my venerable father-in-law, the late Dr. Gano, I will cheerfully give you the impressions of his character which I derived from a long and intimate acquaintance with him.

Dr. Gano officiated at my father's marriage in 1794. From that period until his death, our family mansion was situated in close proximity to the spacious and venerable edifice in which he preached. My own birth occurring in 1798, and my education having been obtained at our own schools and University in Providence, and our family always worshipping under his ministry, and in due time becoming connected, as I did, with his family by marriage, you will easily understand how his memory is intertwined with the most cherished recollections of my childhood, youth, and early manhood. Let me say then that my whole impression of Dr. Gano, as a Man, a Christian, and a Minister, has been, from the time that I was capable of appreciating him, most favourable; and had I no other evidence than his character furnished of the truth and power of Christianity, I could never question it.

While yet a child, I was often so deeply moved in my feelings, under his preaching, that I was unable to maintain my accustomed composure; and again and again was almost persuaded to become a Christian. What Henry Clay once said to me of his emotions under the ministry of the elder Gano, at Lexington, Ky., I can affirm of my own, under that of the son at Providence:—" He was," said he, " a remarkably fervent preacher, and distinguished for a simple and effective manner. And of all the preachers I ever listened to, he made me feel the most that religion was a Divine reality. I never felt so religious under any one's preaching as under his."

Dr. Gano certainly possessed many qualities to render his preaching both attractive and impressive. He had a fine commanding figure, being more than six feet in stature, and every way well proportioned. His voice was full, sonorous, and altogether agreeable. His manner was perfectly artless and unstudied. He had great command of language, and could speak with fluency and appropriateness, with little or no premeditation. His discourses were eminently experimental, and were adapted to edify Christians, while they abounded in direct and earnest appeals to the careless and ungodly. He always preached from a plan, but seldom had a written sermon in the pulpit. Once, during a religious controversy, in 1820, that deeply affected his as well as other churches, I was present when, in his prayer, he besought the Lord that he would give him strength to read what he had written for that occasion. He was so accustomed to the other style of address that he seemed to consider it almost sacrilege to occupy the hour in any other manner.

Dr. Gano combined a sound practical judgment, a power of discriminating character, and a uniform self-command, which gave great weight to his counsels, and rendered him a most useful member of various ecclesiastical bodies. During nineteen consecutive years, he presided at the meetings of the Warren Association. And the " impression of his character," as a friend has written, " upon the younger ministry around him was indeed a most happy one; for they saw in him the rare combination of strict integrity in maintaining his own opinions with great enlargedness of heart regarding those who differed from him. He was always courteous without compromising truth, and zealous without bigotry. Of the liberality which arises from indifference to religious sentiment he knew nothing; of that which springs from Christian love, which embraces in spiritual friendship ' all who hold the Head, even Christ,' he possessed an ample measure. Dignified without affectation, and manly without sternness, his meekness most distinguished him, and his gentleness made him great. His fortitude and firmness were equal to his strength; and his unceremonious encounter of all that is laborious and fatiguing in a minister's travels and official pursuits, was an admirable example for the younger and often over-cautious sons of the ministry. Punctuality and dispatch were among the first lessons of his business creed, and nothing but insurmountable impediments occasioned any hindrance or delay." I may add that he was remarkable for Christian sociability and hospitality. Never did the poor of the flock, or of the ministry, meet a more cordial welcome than he uniformly gave them. The influence of his philanthropy was felt in every direction. He was never weary in serving his generation.

I remember many incidents illustrative of Dr. Gano's character, a few of which I will detail, being able personally to vouch for their authenticity. I have heard him allude to "a peculiarity of his nature," as he termed it,—his utter abhorrence of all ardent spirits from his birth. When, at the age of four years, he was suffering severely from small pox, milk punch was recommended; and, when he was urged by his mother to take it lest he should die, he said that his mother afterwards told him that his answer was,—"Then I will die." And he added,—"Amidst all the trials, hardships, and perils of my changing life, since that time, I have retained that same dislike of all ardent spirits; and, when I consider how many able and learned men have bowed with disgrace, and in ruin, to this vice, I bless God for having given me such a repugnance."

I remember his alluding to an incident of his youth, as having been partly instrumental of his conversion; and, in connection with it, he observed that we should mark and ponder such occurrences for our spiritual advantage. "Being on my way," said he, "to my new home, my uncle's residence,—my father accompanying me,—we called on my father's mother, who was eminently pious, and had reached more than fourscore years; and, on her first seeing me, she bade me kneel beside her, and then gently placing her aged hand on my youthful head, she prayed fervently for my salvation. And directly after, looking upon me, she said, 'Stephen, the Lord designs thee for a minister of the everlasting Gospel: be thou faithful unto death, and He will give thee a crown of life.'"

He had great faith in the efficacy of prayer, and used to refer most gratefully to some signal instances of it in his own experience. On one occasion, during a very severe drought, he prayed in such a manner that some of the younger portion of his audience, on leaving the church, remarked one to another,—"We must hasten home; for, after such a prayer, the rain will overtake us." And so it came to pass—the rain came pouring down in less than an hour.

In an early part of his ministry at Providence, an influential member of the church had become strongly opposed to his continuance there. This had occasioned Dr. Gano great anxiety. One night the gentleman found himself unable to rest; and early in the morning hastened to his minister to make known to him his feelings; and, on reaching the house, the outer door being open, he entered, passed through the hall, and proceeded to the inner room, where he beheld the family at prayer. The Doctor said afterwards that his mind was unusually drawn out in supplication that the Lord would either subdue the opposition, or make his way clear to depart. And so fervent and childlike was he in his petitions, that the mind of his visitor was most tenderly affected, and, at the close of the prayer, he went immediately up to the Doctor, grasped his hand most affectionately, assured him of his friendly feelings, and said,—"I'll go heart and hand for you as my Pastor." And for years after that, the Pastor and his family, by a cordial and urgent invitation, dined at that gentleman's house every Tuesday.

Two children in his house had been at variance. The father, who had watched the scene with a painful interest, brought the case of these little ones before the Lord in family prayer; and the result was that, at the close, they rushed into each others' arms, each having no longer any disposition to quarrel with the other.

His manner of treating hopeful converts was peculiarly kind and encouraging. I shall never forget the Monday prior to the commencement of my Junior year in College, when, having taken a walk to the hills that overlook the city from the East, that I might enjoy the splendid scenery, and especially the going down of the sun, I met this venerable man and thus addressed him:—" These heavens, and these objects of nature around me all seem to be in harmony with their Maker's will; and I trust that I, too, am reconciled to God through Christ;" and, as he looked upon me with the deepest interest,— speaking evidently out of the fulness of a father's heart, he said,—" I bid you a hearty welcome, my son, into the Kingdom of God." On another occasion, when two of his own children, while on a visit to a neighbouring town, had hopefully experienced God's grace in their conversion, and he had gone thither to rejoice with them, he preached in the evening to a large congregation from these words:—" Go home to thy friends, and tell them how great things the Lord hath done for thee, and hath had compassion on thee."

His decision never failed him, when he was confident of being right. The question of laying on of hands upon members when received into the Church being agitated, and he believing that this was an Ordination, rather than a Church act, utterly refused to yield to the opposition, though his resolute persistence had almost occasioned his removal. His advice to a minister, who was anxious to change his location, is well worthy of being preserved:— " You may knock," said he, " at a door, and if it opens, you may enter it; but do not lean against it with such pressure that it opens by your strength; for in such a case you may go out like Abraham, not knowing whither, but, unlike him, without the hand that leads us, in the right way, to the city of habitation." In his letters to his friends, however brief, he was sure to embody some testimony in honour of his Master; so that even his letters and notes of business witnessed to the upward tendency of his thoughts and feelings. He regarded the office of a minister as peculiarly sacred, and always regretted to see its influence in any degree neutralized by an unnecessary devotion to secular engagements. Early one morning he was, with one of his children, passing the door of a minister, who had for years made the ministry subordinate and subservient to his secular business, and who was then sitting by his shop window, watching the Doctor's motion. As the Doctor turned his carriage, as if intending to stop at his house, the other, evidently feeling that some apology was necessary for his course, said,— " Well, Doctor, we read that in old time they sat at the receipt of custom." " Yes, yes," was the reply, " and we also read,—' They arose and left all and followed Him,' " and then proceeded on his way.

Such are my recollections and impressions of this eminent minister of the Gospel. I am sure there are many still living who would fully endorse my estimate of his character and usefulness, and in whose hearts his memory is most gratefully embalmed.

I remain, Rev. and dear Sir,

Your friend and brother in Christ Jesus,

HENRY JACKSON.

FROM THE HON. JAMES TALLMADGE, LL. D.

CLINTON POINT, Dutchess County, N. Y.,
September 27, 1848.

Rev. and dear Sir: I was well acquainted with Dr. Stephen Gano from my boyhood till his decease. During the four years of my collegiate term in Brown University, I resided in his family; and my intercourse with him was always of the most intimate and agreeable kind.

Dr. Gano was admitted, on all hands, to hold a high rank among the ministers of his denomination. He devoted himself with great assiduity to the duties of his profession. Wednesday and Saturday he gave scrupulously to the work of preparation for the duties of the Sabbath and other appointed services. It was his custom, in preparing his sermon, to note, on a small piece of paper, his text and the general divisions of his discourse, with references to passages of Scripture and other illustrations of his subject. This memorandum, placed in the book before him, was a sufficient guide to his thoughts; and it enabled him to speak with great promptness and fluency.

His personal appearance was prepossessing, his voice manly, his articulation distinct, and his diction clear and impressive. His preaching was in turn doctrinal, practical, and experimental. His exhortations were often exceedingly earnest and pathetic, and, in the application of his discourse, it was not uncommon for a portion of his audience to be melted into tears.

The administration of the ordinance of Baptism by immersion, in connection with the singing of a hymn at the water, according to the usage of the Baptist Church, afforded a fine opportunity for an effective display of his powers. His eloquence on these occasions was often greatly admired.

Dr. Gano was very diligent and faithful in the performance of his pastoral duties. He had a talent that qualified him peculiarly for that kind of intercourse; and this, together with his acknowledged sterling integrity,—could not fail to secure to him, in a high degree, the confidence and affection of his people.

In private life, he was amiable, cheerful, social, and generous beyond his means. He was a most agreeable companion, and would often, in the freedom of familiar intercourse, relate many interesting incidents of his early years. He was a favourite among his friends, and had a high standing, both as a man and a minister, in the estimation of the public.

I am, with great respect, yours truly,
JAMES TALLMADGE.

FROM THE REV. DANIEL WALDO.

SYRACUSE, March 1, 1858.

My dear Friend: I had the pleasure of an acquaintance with the Rev. Dr. Gano, of Providence, during a period of about five years—from 1815 to 1820. I was residing at that time in Greenwich, R. I.; and, as some of his friends, who, I believe, were also members of his church, lived there, he occasionally came to visit them, and it was my privilege to share his visits. I also frequently visited him at his own house in Providence, and met him on various public and private occasions, and once or twice, during my stay in Greenwich, we exchanged pulpits. It would perhaps be too much to say that I was in very intimate relations with him, and yet I think I knew him well enough to express an opinion of his general character, without much danger of mistake.

I should not suppose that he was distinguished for what is commonly called genius, or for any extraordinary intellectual culture; and yet his mind seemed to be one remarkably well adapted to active usefulness. The members of his church, which was one of the largest and most flourishing Baptist churches in the land, and withal embodied a great degree of intelligence and influence, were, I believe, well satisfied with his ministrations, and when he died, sincerely mourned the loss of them. His heart was evidently deeply imbued with the spirit of the Gospel, and he determined to know nothing, as a Christian minister, save Jesus Christ and Him crucified. Though he was honestly and strongly attached to the peculiarities of the Baptist denomination, he was far from identifying Christianity with those peculiarities, and wherever he recognized the image of the Saviour, there he acknowledged the claim upon his sympathy and brotherly affection. His reliance for success in his labours was not upon his own might or power, but upon the Truth and Spirit of God; and while he was diligent in his work, he never failed to render due honour to that Divine agency in which, after all, is the main spring of all ministerial success.

Dr. Gano was considerably above the common size, and his personal appearance was altogether commanding. He was amiable and sociable in his private intercourse, and was, I believe, generally a favourite among those who knew him well. I remember he used to amuse himself with fishing on his visits at Greenwich, and, if I mistake not, he was more than ordinarily expert in the use of the hook. I think I never heard him preach more than once, and the impression which both his matter and manner left upon my mind has nearly faded from it, except that I well remember that he spoke with one of the most Stentorian voices to which I ever listened. On the whole, it may safely be said that he ranked among the leading Baptist ministers of this country, during the period of his ministry.

Affectionately yours,
DANIEL WALDO.

WILLIAM ELLIOT.*

1786—1830.

WILLIAM ELLIOT, the second son of John and Sarah Elliot, was born in Bradford, Mass., December 1, (O. S.) 1748; though his father removed with his family to Mason, N. H., as early as 1766. His parents were members of the Congregational Church, and, through the influence of his mother especially, his mind took a serious direction, when he was not more than eight or nine years old, though he did not find the joy and peace in believing until he had arrived at his majority. The following is his own record of his experience, at the time when he believed the radical change passed upon him :—

"Oh the joy, the sweet consolation that filled my soul! I thought I could never praise God enough. When morning came, I arose, and went out to see the glory of God in his handiwork. As I viewed the heavens and the earth with delight, I thought I never saw such a morning before. But, on a sudden, these words suggested themselves to me—'Can God be just, and you out of hell?' The question appeared hard to answer; for I had seen, the night before, the justice of God most clearly in my eternal

* MS. Autobiography.—MSS. from his son,—Rev. Jesse Elliot, and Rev. Benjamin S. Lane.

ruin. Soon his justice appeared exceedingly clear, and these words dropped into my heart with power—'I am satisfied with Christ;' and this turned my mind into the New Testament. Then was brought to view a new scene. Oh the love of God in the gift of his Son! The love of Jesus in undertaking the great work of Mediator! His life, death, and resurrection so filled my mind and increased my joy that such a day I never had before. I now saw that salvation was of the Lord, and grace might reign, through righteousness, unto eternal life by Jesus Christ our Lord. I was brought to believe in the doctrine of Election; for I saw that God would not work without purposing or designing to work. I saw that this was all of God, and felt willing that He should have all the glory. I longed that others might taste and see the goodness and grace of God."

Soon after he experienced this change, he united with the Congregational Church in Mason, N. H., but subsequently removed his relation to the Church in New Ipswich, then under the pastoral care of the Rev. Stephen Farrar,* and continued his membership here until he united with the Baptists.

In September, 1772, he was married to Dorothy, daughter of the Rev. Nathaniel Merrill,† of Nottingham West, N. H.; by whom he had six children, all of whom, to use his own language, were "christened," before he renounced Infant Baptism.

Mr. Elliot, when he was approaching the age of forty, began to have doubts on the subject of Infant Baptism; and those doubts were finally matured into a full conviction that it was not warranted by the Word of God. He now left the Congregational Church of which he was a member, was baptized by immersion, and shortly after commenced preaching the Gospel in the Baptist connection. Through his instrumentality, the Baptist Church in Mason, N. H., was organized, of seven members, in 1786; and he was ordained as its Pastor in 1788,—the Rev. Mr. Grafton, of Newton, Mass., and two other ministers taking part in his ordination. Not only did that church increase rapidly under his ministry, but the Baptist churches in New Ipswich, Jaffrey, Wilton, Milford, and Hollis, in New Hampshire, and Townsend in Massachusetts, owe their origin and early growth, in a great measure, to his vigorous and persevering efforts. The compensation which he received for his labours, as a minister, was very slight, and it was only by training his children to the severest industry and economy, that he was able to maintain his numerous family, and devote his whole time to the appropriate duties of the ministry.

His wife died in June, 1785, and, in March, 1787, he was married to Rebecca, daughter of Oliver Hildreth of Townsend, Mass.,—by whom he had twelve children,—eight sons and four daughters. After having been a true helper to him in the Gospel for upwards of forty years, she died on the 18th of October, 1828.

Mr. Elliot survived his second wife less than two years, and died in the triumph of faith, on the 4th of June, 1830. He had been confined to his

* STEPHEN FARRAR was born at Lincoln, Mass., October 22, 1738; was graduated at Harvard College in 1755; was ordained Pastor of the Congregational Church in New Ipswich, N. H., October 23, 1760; and died June 23, 1809.

† NATHANIEL MERRILL was born at Newbury, Mass., in 1713; was graduated at Harvard College in 1732; was ordained Pastor of the Congregational Church in Nottingham West, November 23, 1737; and died in 1796, aged eighty-three.

room, and, most of the time, to his bed, for about five years. During this long season of decline, he evinced the most serene submission to the Divine will, and, by his faithful conversations and fervent prayers, in his sick chamber, was instrumental of strengthening the faith of believers, and bringing some who had been neglectful of their salvation to reflection and repentance.

Mr. Elliot died on the same farm to which his father's family removed when they left Bradford. In his early manhood, he held an honourable position in society, and was elected by the town in which he lived to several different civil offices. But, after he entered the ministry, he abandoned all participation in civil matters, and devoted himself exclusively to the interests of Christ's Kingdom.

In 1820, he was chosen to preside at a Fourth of July celebration; but, on learning that toasts were to be drank, and guns fired, he politely declined the proffered honour. He never wore badges of mourning for deceased friends. When it was customary to use spirituous liquors at Funerals, he refused to sanction the practice. He sympathized strongly in some respects with the Friends, notwithstanding he differed widely from them in doctrinal views.

In the autumn before his death, when confined by sickness, one of his sons preached in his presence from the words,—"Behold what manner of love the Father hath bestowed upon us, that we should be called the sons of God." The tone of the sermon was strongly evangelical; and, after the congregation had retired, the venerable man called his son to him and said,—"My son, I charge you, rather than relinquish the doctrine which you have now preached, to die at the stake."

Two of Mr. Elliot's sons have become ministers of the Gospel. *Joseph* studied medicine for some time; received the honorary degree of Bachelor of Arts, from the University of Vermont, in 1813; entered the ministry at an early age, and was ordained in Hinsdale, N. H., in May, 1809. He has united with the office of a minister that of a teacher of youth; but is now (1858) laid aside from labour by bodily infirmity. *Jesse* is now Pastor of a church in Stockton, Chautauque County, N. Y. *Israel* was graduated at the University of Vermont in 1813, was Principal of an Academy in Cavendish, Vt., one year, and in Chester, Vt.. for about the same time, being engaged meanwhile in the study of the Law, and died in August, 1815.

FROM THE REV. JOHN PARKHURST.

CHELMSFORD, Mass., March 25, 1858.

Dear Sir: You ask me for some personal recollections, illustrative of the character of the Rev. William Elliot. I can say a few things of him, as I lived near him several years, sometimes heard him preach, was often at his house, and occasionally with him on journeys.

When I first became acquainted with him, which was about forty-five years ago, he was not far from sixty-five years of age. He was of medium height, florid complexion, and his gray locks, hanging in natural curls upon the collar of his coat, gave him an appearance exceedingly venerable. His countenance, which was often lighted up with a benignant smile, was indicative of a calm temperament, of a love of right, and of a fixed determination to *do* right in all things. Christians loved him because he loved the truth: the world respected him for the consistency of his daily walk. I think I never knew a man so evangelical in his sentiments, and so clear and decided in exhibiting them, who, at the same time, enjoyed, in so high a degree, a good report among them that are without.

Although he was not talkative, he was sociable. He could converse sensibly upon agricultural, mechanical and national affairs; but his chosen theme was the Gospel of Jesus Christ. From whatever point he surveyed it, it awakened his admiration, thanksgiving, and joy. His countenance seemed to shine, like that of Moses, with a Heavenly radiance, while he talked about the glories of Immanuel and the blessings of his people.

His sermons, if I may judge from the few I heard, were original, interesting, and highly instructive. He adopted, as we should say in these days, not the topical, but the textual, method. He seldom, if ever, made out a discourse on a single virtue, or a single doctrine, but mingled doctrine with Christian exercises, and urged obedience from evangelical motives. He delighted in unfolding the types of the Old Testament, and in expounding the parables of the New. In his manner he was solemn and affectionate, and no one who heard him could resist the conviction that his inmost soul went along with every word that he uttered. His views of doctrine were obtained from a prayerful and diligent study of the Bible; and perhaps it is sufficient to say that they harmonized with those of the late Andrew Fuller. I remember distinctly that he once said, when we were conversing about that able divine, that "he never read after a man"—to use his own expression—"whose writings he liked so well." The doctrine of Election was a theme on which he delighted to dwell, both in preaching and in conversation; yet he held it in connection with the sentiment that the sinner is accountable to God, and justly condemned for his impenitence. He had no fellowship with the doctrine that the man who does not love our Lord Jesus Christ is so much of a machine as not to be blameworthy. He was a man of great conscientiousness. At the time he obtained his hope of salvation through Jesus Christ, he was paying the customary attentions of his day to the young woman whom he subsequently married. She remained in a state of impenitence. And now a severe conflict arose in his mind. To marry an unbeliever seemed evidently wrong; and yet, inasmuch as he was virtually pledged to her before his own conversion, he felt that it was his duty to take her and leave the event with God. And it may be interesting to add that she subsequently found peace in believing, and became no small help to him in the ways of the Lord.

His first religious connection was with the Pedobaptists. But, as he read the Bible, he became satisfied that Christians, and Christians only, are the seed of Abraham; and the peace of his soul was greatly disturbed until he was baptized on the profession of his own faith. At this time it was his expectation to continue in the Pedobaptist Church. But, after the lapse of a few months, the text in Galatians ii. 18—"If I build again the things that I destroyed, I make myself a transgressor"—so affected his mind that he felt constrained to withdraw from the church with which he had been connected, and join the Baptist communion.

When he first began to preach, there was a certain Dr. G. in his neighbourhood, who would not allow that he was called to the work of the ministry, seeing he was a man of limited education, unless he could preach from a text given him at the very hour at which his meeting was appointed. Mr. Elliot, who had entered the ministry with great diffidence, and who was willing to get rid of the responsibility of the sacred office, if he could honestly do so, consented to submit his call to the test proposed by Dr. G. A meeting was appointed in the week time. Information was spread in relation to it. The hour arrived; the people came together; and the text was given him,—which was "A golden bell and a pomegranate, a golden bell and a pomegranate, upon the hem of the robe round about." Exodus xxviii. 34. He looked at it awhile, and could see nothing in it. He read the opening hymn, and while the people were singing, he looked at it again; but, not discovering a single idea which he could hold up before the assembly, he began to think he must confess that he had no call to the work of the ministry. However, he thought he would go as far as he could. So, when the hymn was sung, he said "Let us pray." In this exercise he enjoyed, in an unusual degree, the aid of the Holy Spirit. During the singing of the second hymn, he was constantly revolving his text in his mind, but no ray of light seemed to fall upon it. In this state of embarrassment, he saw nothing before him but the announcement, so mortifying to his friends, and so gratifying to the Doctor, that he had been deceived in the notion that he was called to preach. But he had been assisted thus far in the meeting, and it still seemed right and proper that he should go as far as he could—so he would read the text; and then if he had nothing to say from it, he would make his confession. He read the passage—impenetrable darkness still rested upon it; but it was not time to stop until, according to custom, he had read it a second time. And now, suddenly, light bursts upon his soul. The text seems full of the Gospel. The golden bell suggests its precious sound among the people, awakening, directing, comforting the souls of men. The pomegranate suggests the fruits of the Holy Spirit. The High Priest's robe points to the righteousness of Christ. He finds enough to say. He preaches an evangelical discourse—he preaches with an unwonted fluency; and the question seems to be settled in every mind that he is called of God to preach the Gospel.

When he was about the age of five and thirty, he was called to part with his first wife. As she lay dying, he was walking the room in great anguish of spirit. His six children were losing one of the best of mothers. He wrung his hands in sorrow—his tears flowed freely. At length a friend, standing by her bed, said, "She is gone." He was well-nigh overwhelmed with the affliction. But he told me that in about two minutes he heard distinctly what seemed like the flapping of wings over him, and the ascending sound grew fainter and fainter till it was lost in the distance. In a moment, the current of his grief was checked; his mind became calm; and he could cheerfully resign the companion of his bosom to the charge of angels to be borne to the Heavenly Paradise.

Confined to his bed for a long season in his last sickness, he was manifestly sustained by Heavenly consolations. I remember particularly what joy was depicted in his countenance when he told me of the meditations he had had on the attributes of the Most High. His holiness, his grace, his wisdom, and his power were sustaining and enrapturing themes. One of his acquaintance who called on him in those days, and who had heard of the sweet serenity of his spirit, said to him, as he approached his bed,—"You enjoy yourself very well, don't you?" "Oh no," was his reply, "I don't enjoy *myself* at all, but I never enjoyed the *Lord* so well in my life." One of his Deacons told me that he called on him, I think on the day of his death, when his lips gave utterance to these striking words,—"Oh the joy of my soul!"

Yours with respect,
JOHN PARKHURST.

AARON LELAND.

1786—1833.

FROM THE REV. IRA PEARSON.

UDLOW, Vt., November 11, 1857.

Rev. and dear Sir: The result of my inquiries in respect to the history of the late Rev. Aaron Leland, Lieutenant Governor of the State of Vermont, I am happy to contribute in aid of your work, commemorative of the worthies who have gone before us. The materials for my sketch have been gathered from different sources, but I believe you may rely on their perfect authenticity.

AARON LELAND, a descendant from Henry Leland, the Pilgrim father of the Leland family in America, was born in Holliston, Mass., on the 28th of May, 1761. He possessed no greater advantages of education, than were furnished by the common schools in Massachusetts, before the Revolution; but, being of a naturally vigorous and inquisitive mind, he availed himself of all the means of self-culture within his reach, and thus grew up with much more than an ordinary share of intelligence. He became a member of the Baptist Church in 1785, and, shortly after, received license to preach from the church in Bellingham. About this time, he received a letter from fifteen persons, living in Chester, Vt., none of whom were communicants in the Baptist Church, requesting him to come and labour among them as a minister. In compliance with this request, he took a journey thither, after a few months; but he found every thing so unpromising for both comfort and usefulness that he could not easily reconcile himself to the idea of continuing among them. But, after some time, he found his mind deeply impressed with this passage of Scripture,—" The Lord hath much people in this city;" and, under the influence of reflections induced by these words, he soon made up his mind to remain there. After a few weeks' sojourn among them, he returned to his friends in Massachusetts; and not many months after went back to Chester with a view to make it his permanent residence,—having previously been ordained by the Church in Bellingham.

In 1789, he had the happiness of seeing a small church gathered, which consisted of only ten members, including himself. This little body travelled on in great harmony, experiencing a gradual increase, but no remarkable revival, for ten years. But, in 1799, a revival of great power commenced, which not only spread throughout Chester, but extended to several of the neighbouring towns. At the close of this work, the church had become so numerous that it was thought proper that it should be divided; and, accordingly, on the 31st of August, 1803, four churches were set off from the original body, which were situated respectively in Andover, Grafton, Weathersfield, and Cavendish.

At an early period in his ministry, Mr. Leland went to Jamaica,—a distance of twenty miles, by marked trees, and administered the ordinance of Baptism to such as were prepared to receive it, and afterwards made frequent visits there, and organized a church, of which Calvin Howard, father of the Rev. Leland Howard, of Rutland, Vt., became the first Deacon. Through his instrumentality, other Churches in that neighbourhood also were formed, and the process went on until the Baptists had a permanent footing throughout the whole surrounding country. It was not uncommon for him, during the early years of his ministry, to go from fourteen to twenty miles through the wilderness to attend a Funeral.

When Mr. Leland commenced his ministry, few of his parishioners were in any better worldly circumstances than himself; and it would not have been easy, even if it had been in accordance with the usage of the day, in that part of the country, to have raised for him a competent support. He commenced, therefore, without any stated salary, and continued in the same way till the close of life. All that he received for his services was contributed voluntarily. His parishioners occasionally laboured for him on his farm, and contributed something to assist him to hire a constant labourer; but he was obliged, after all, to depend for the support of his family chiefly on his own exertions.

Mr. Leland did not scruple to take an active part in civil life. In his politics he was of the Jefferson school, and his opinions were deliberately and maturely formed, and held with great firmness. Besides being frequently elected to different offices in the town, he was chosen, in 1801, to represent the town in the Legislature, and was re-elected to the same office for nine successive years. During three years, he was Speaker of the House; four years, he was a Councillor; five years, he was chosen Lieutenant Governor by the people; and eighteen years, he was one of the Assistant Justices of the County Court. In 1828, he was proposed as a candidate for Governor; but, as the claims of that high station seemed to him incompatible with the duties of the Christian ministry, and as he considered the obligations which he owed to his Master as a minister, paramount to all considerations of political interest, he caused his name to be withdrawn from the canvass.

But, notwithstanding Mr. Leland had so much to do with civil affairs, he laboured much and very successfully in his appropriate calling as a Christian minister; as was evinced, not only by the prosperity of his own church, but by the number of flourishing churches which he was instrumental in establishing. He had high qualifications for a popular and effective preacher. He had a noble figure; a mind of a powerful cast, that perceived quickly and compared easily; a voice of vast compass, but smooth and mellow; great facility at utterance, and great fervour of spirit; clear but impassioned, he would carry with him the multitude irresistibly. He possessed great tenderness of spirit,—often melting down in his prayers and sermons, and usually melting his congregation with him. He spoke extempore without any apparent effort, and, so far as I know, during his whole ministry, never made use of written discourses. He was often put in requisition for lectures on public occasions, and, I believe, never failed to acquit himself most creditably. He had great influence among his brethren, and commanded their high respect, as was evident from their almost uniformly making him the Moderator of their meetings. He was a wise and safe counsellor, always bringing to his aid the best light he was able to command, and forming his judgment with a discreet reference to all the circumstances of the case. He was a man of decidedly liberal views—his heart, and, as far as practicable, his hand also, was in every project or enterprise designed to bless either the Church or the world. When the cause of Temperance came up, he enlisted in it most vigorously, giving not only his example, but his name, and the whole weight of his influence, to the cause of Total Abstinence. He was also an earnest friend to the cause of Ministerial Education: though he believed that the first qualification for the ministry was the grace of the Holy Spirit, he was also deeply impressed with the importance of a proper degree of intellectual culture, in order to the most successful discharge of the duties of the sacred office; and he was ever ready to lend his countenance and aid to any judicious measures for the furtherance of that cause. Indeed, I may say, in general, that he was distinguished for a large measure of Christian public spirit.

In his private intercourse, he was a most agreeable companion, highly instructive, often amusing, and capable, at a proper time, of relishing or relating a humorous anecdote. I remember one that used to excite no little merriment, of which he was partly the subject,—the other party concerned being a neighbour of his, by the name of Hugh Henry, who was also far from having any aversion to a joke. On a Saturday evening, a young man, who was entirely penniless, called at Mr. Leland's house, and asked for supper and lodging. It being inconvenient, for some reason, to the Parson to accommodate him, he sent him to his neighbour Henry, assuring him that *he* would take good care of him; "though," said he, " he will refuse you at first; but you must stick to him, and you will certainly succeed." The young man called, agreeably to the direction, and was refused. "I was told," said he, "that you would refuse to keep me, unless I stuck to you; and that I am resolved to do." "Who told you that?" said Mr. Henry. "A large man," answered he, "living over there,"— pointing to the house from which he had just come. "Well," said Henry, "if Parson Leland sent you here, you must stay, I suppose; and what would you like for your supper?" "Oh, any thing that is convenient, for I have no money to pay for it." "But what would you choose, if you had money?" "Well, to be honest, I should like a good warm supper, if I had the means of paying for it; for I have taken but little food to-day." A warm supper was, accordingly, provided, to which the young man paid his best respects; nor was he allowed to leave the next morning, till he had done justice to a good breakfast. The young fellow was going to try his fortune in the Western wilderness. He had a small dog with him; and just before he was ready to start,—it being near meeting time,—Mr. Henry suggested to his guest that his dog was not a proper one to go into the wilderness with, and that he had a neighbour who had a large dog, which would make great havoc among the wild animals in the woods, and which he ought, by all means, to secure. "He would like," said he, "to exchange him for a small one; but he will probably refuse at first, and perhaps rudely tell you to go about your business, and that he does not swap dogs on Sunday, and the like; but, if you stick to him, you will get the dog." The young man called at the Parson's house, just as he was starting for meeting, and informed him that he had come to swap dogs. And the answer which he received was an almost literal fulfilment of Mr. Henry's prediction. "Well I was told," said the fellow, "that you would make such excuses; but I was also told that if I stuck to you, I should get your dog; and that, Sir, you may rest assured I shall do;" and he actually accompanied the Parson till he got to the door steps of the meeting-house. As it was now evident that he was determined to make good his word, there seemed to be no alternative for Mr. Leland but to yield to his importunity, or to go into the house of worship, disputing about a dog; and he, finally, as the only way of making his escape, said to him,—"Go and take the dog, and be off in a hurry, and never trouble me again in this way." Mr. Henry outlived Mr. Leland a few years; but they both lie buried in the same grave-yard in Chester, and their graves are not far from each other.

Mr. Leland's useful and eventful life was terminated just at the close of a very interesting revival of religion in his congregation. For many months preceding his death, he had been labouring in that revival with all the energies of his body and mind, and had been privileged to witness results which occasioned him unspeakable joy. The last time he administered the ordinance of Baptism, was about four weeks previous to his death. He was then in very feeble health; and, as he stood on the bank, a physician who was near observed to him that he looked more fit to go to bed than to go into the water. His answer was,—"I will go." When he had baptized the last of some eight or ten candidates, he came out of the water, and, lifting up his hands, exclaimed,—"O Lord, it is enough: 'now lettest thou thy servant depart in peace; for mine eyes have seen thy salvation.'" From this time he gradually declined, until, at the call of his Master, he entered into his rest. He died on the 25th of August, 1833.

Mr. Leland's first marriage was to a lady in Holliston, who died after they had been married about two years. His second wife was a Widow Rockwood, who had two children by a previous marriage. His third and last wife was Miss Sally Webb, of Rockingham, Vt.. who survived him several years. He had no child by either marriage.

Mr. Leland was one of the Fellows of Middlebury College from 1800 till his death. He was honoured with the degree of Master of Arts from that College in 1814, and he received the same degree from Brown University in 1815.

I am, with much regard, yours truly,

IRA PEARSON.

JOHN STANFORD, D. D.*
1786—1834.

JOHN STANFORD, the only son of William and Mary Stanford, was born at Wandsworth, in Surrey, England, October 20, 1754. When he was in his tenth year, his uncle, George Stanford, to whom he stood heir at law, took charge of his education, and placed him at a respectable school. Though he was sadly neglected, and even harshly treated, by his teachers, he made very respectable progress in his studies, and, at the age of sixteen, directed his attention to Medicine. About a year after this, (March, 1772,) in consequence of the death of his father, he returned home to live with his widowed mother, continuing his medical studies privately, as he had opportunity.

Mr. Stanford was born and educated in the bosom of the Episcopal Church; and he seems, during his early youth, to have entertained strong prejudices against all who belonged to any other communion. He was, at this period, occasionally, the subject of some serious impressions, and was uniformly correct in his external deportment; and, according to his own account, was reposing on the merit of his own good deeds as the foundation of his hope of Heaven. Hearing that a Confirmation was to be held, at a certain time, by the Bishop, at Lambeth, five miles from London, he resolved, with the consent of his uncle, who was not a religious man, to avail himself of the opportunity to be confirmed; and, accordingly, that rite was administered to him; and, from that time, he supposed that, whatever change was necessary to salvation, he had been the subject of it.

Some time after this, a young man, by the name of Hooper, who had been his classmate, and had experienced, as he believed, a radical change of character, under the ministry of the celebrated William Romaine, paid him a visit, with a view to endeavour, by the Divine blessing, to give a different direction to his thoughts and feelings on the subject of religion. This visit led to a very close intimacy, and to a correspondence, from which Mr. Stanford thought he derived the most important benefit. Not satisfied with the ministry in his native town, he embraced every opportunity to go to London, and listen to the preaching of the venerable Romaine, by which he found himself greatly edified and comforted. At length word was carried to his uncle that he had become "strangely religious," and intimate with Dissenters; which so exasperated him that, from that time till his uncle's death, which occurred shortly after, there was no intercourse of any kind between them. When his will came to be examined, after his death, it was found that he had left his property to an indifferent person, bequeathing no more to the nephew than was necessary to answer the requisition of the law.

Scarcely had this disappointment occurred, when he was overtaken by another and greater affliction in the death of his mother, just as she was on the eve of forming a second matrimonial connection. This devolved upon him the charge of three young sisters; and his trouble did not end here;

* Sommers' Biog.—MS. from his son,—Thomas N. Stanford, Esq.

for a near relative took possession of his mother's property, under pretext of the indebtedness of his deceased father to him, so that they were left not only orphans but destitute. He was, however, sustained by the consciousness of having done what he believed was right, and he had confidence, even in his darkest hours, that the Lord would provide. Having occasion to go to London, two or three weeks after this, to settle his mother's affairs, Mr. Naylor, the attorney whom he consulted, who was a religious man and manifested a generous sympathy in his afflictions, informed him of an opportunity of taking a boarding-school in the neighbourhood of his country-house, and engaged to incur whatever pecuniary responsibility might be involved. Mr. Stanford gratefully accepted the offer, and removed to Hammersmith, where he found himself very favourably situated in respect to both comfort and usefulness.

As he had been educated in the Church of England, he had never, up to this time, felt any scruple in regard to any of its doctrines or usages. His friend Hooper seems to have been the first to suggest a doubt to him on the subject of Baptism ; and, in consequence of this, he was led into an examination which resulted, much to his own surprise, in a full conviction that there is no valid Baptism except that which is administered by immersion, and on a personal and intelligent profession of faith on the part of the subject. In consequence of this, he felt himself called upon to change his ecclesiastical relations. Accordingly, he was shortly after received into the communion of a Baptist Church in London, of which the Rev. Benjamin Wallin, a minister of great worth and considerable note, was Pastor. This step, so far from being popular, occasioned great coolness on the part of many of his friends ; but he was sustained by a conscious integrity, having no doubt that he was walking in the way of God's commandments.

It was through the instrumentality of Mr. Stanford that a Baptist church was formed in Hammersmith ; and he was called to take the pastoral charge of it. The call being accepted, he was regularly ordained,— several ministers taking part in the service, among whom was the celebrated Abraham Booth. This occurred in the year 1781.

Mr. Stanford's situation at Hammersmith did not prove in all respects agreeable to him ; and he, finally, after much deliberation and prayer, resolved to come to the United States. He, accordingly, left England, January 7, 1786, and, after a very tempestuous and protracted voyage, arrived at Norfolk, Va., on the 16th of April, where he met a very hospitable reception, and, for a short time, engaged in teaching the children of a few wealthy families. Having received an invitation from some gentlemen of respectability in New York, to whom he had forwarded letters of introduction, to visit that city, he went thither in November, and, in the course of the following month, opened an Academy, which soon rose to great respectability, and enjoyed an extensive patronage.

The next year, (1787,) the Rev. Dr. Manning, first President of Brown University, having resigned the charge of the Baptist Church in Providence, Mr. Stanford was repeatedly invited to spend a year with them ; and, though the pecuniary compensation which was offered him was much less than he then received, while the labour required would be much more than he performed, in connection with his school, he still thought it his duty, after mature reflection, to accept the invitation. Accordingly, he removed to Providence, and entered upon his pastoral duties with great alacrity. During the first nine months of his residence there, part of his time he employed in writing a History of the church with which he was thus temporarily connected,—a church to which there is attached a peculiar interest, from the fact of its being the oldest church in the State, and the oldest Baptist Church in America. This History was afterwards printed in England, and has since been incorporated with Benedict's History of the Baptists.

Mr. Stanford had not been long at Providence before he was elected a Trustee of Brown University, and, at the Annual Commencement in 1788, he was honoured with the degree of Master of Arts. As there was no Theological department connected with the College, and he was desirous of elevating the character of the ministry in his denomination, he received into his study a small class of theological students whom he instructed gratuitously. His labours, at this time, were abundant, not only among the people whom he had more immediately in charge, but among the poor, for whom, without respect to denominational peculiarities, he felt the liveliest interest. Though his engagement was only for a year, he was induced, by the urgent solicitations of the church, and of a numerous circle of friends, to continue three months beyond the stipulated period. His sojourn in Providence seems to have been equally agreeable to himself and the people, and his ministry was crowned with a large measure of success.

In November, 1789, he returned to New York, and resumed his former employment as a teacher of youth, at the same time preaching the Gospel as he had opportunity. But a severe mental affliction, shortly after this, overtook him. A dark cloud settled over his mind—the tempter assaulted him with his impious suggestions, insomuch that he was left even to doubt the Divine authority of the Scriptures. For a considerable time he rarely attempted to preach, and even his secret devotions seemed to have become a mere formality. On a certain Sabbath, when his mind had begun to emerge from this gloomy state, he heard a discourse from the Rev. Dr. John M. Mason, on the text,—"He hath sent me to bind up the broken-hearted;" which was the means of putting to flight all his doubts, and bringing him to rest once more, with joyful confidence, in the promises of the Gospel. It was five months from the beginning to the end of this season of spiritual depression.

No sooner was he relieved from this overwhelming burden, than his bodily health, which had suffered not a little, was materially recruited, and he returned to his duties with increased interest and zeal. In August, 1791, he was requested, by a large number of young men of different denominations, to deliver a course of Sabbath Evening Lectures. He cheerfully complied with their request, and the Introductory Lecture, on "the Utility of the Gospel to support the mind, under the Sufferings of human life," was published.

On the 16th of June, 1790, he was married to Sarah, daughter of Abraham Ten Eyck, who, at the time of his death, was an officer in the Custom House, and a Vestryman of Trinity Church.

In 1794, Mr. Stanford purchased a lot in Fair (now Fulton) Street, and erected upon it a building, which he occupied both as an Academy, and a Lecture-room. This building was opened with an appropriate Discourse, on the 27th of February, 1795. As most of his hearers had no stated place of worship, he consented, at their request, to hold three services on each Sabbath; and the result was that, within a few months, a number of persons who believed themselves to have been savingly benefitted by his ministry, were baptized and formed into a church of which he became the Pastor. The next year, the newly constituted church and its Pastor were cordially received into the fellowship of the " Association of ministers and representatives of churches " assembled at Pleasant Valley.

In the spring and summer of 1798, Mr. Stanford suffered not a little from bodily indisposition, as well as mental depression, though his labours were not altogether interrupted. On the 5th of August, he was taken severely ill, and the disease was soon ascertained to be the Yellow Fever. For several days, his life was despaired of, and, at one time, the hearse stood two hours before his door, waiting for his body to become a corpse. Most unexpectedly, however, the malady at length yielded, and he gradually regained his health. His wife, in the mean time, was attacked with the disease, and though, for a day or two, she seemed convalescent, yet she had a sudden relapse, which proved the immediate harbinger of death. But, amidst all these afflictions, he was enabled to sustain himself with great fortitude and submission. His four children had been previously removed to another part of the city; and he was himself removed as soon as he had recovered strength enough to endure it. He returned to his own house in the early part of October, and found that it had been invaded and plundered by thieves; and every object on which his eye rested, seemed to deepen his sense of desolation. He betook himself, however, to his covenant-keeping God, and God was his refuge and strength in that season of calamity. On the 28th of October, he re-opened his place of worship with an appropriate Discourse, and on the 1st of November, resumed his academical labours, with only five scholars, owing to the unwillingness of parents to send their children into a part of the city in which the pestilence had just been making its most terrible ravages.

In the early part of the year 1809, he was invited to take charge of at least two literary institutions in different States; but he thought it his duty to decline both invitations. His constitution had by no means recovered from the shock which it had received the preceding year; and, in the month of August, he took a house in Greenwich, in the hope that his health would be benefitted by the purer air which he would there breathe; but, scarcely had a single month elapsed before the Yellow Fever again made its appearance, and the inhabitants were flying in all directions. As his own place of worship was now almost entirely deserted, he accepted an invitation from a friend at Mount Pleasant to come with his family and remain with him during the season of danger. This invitation he gratefully accepted, and, during his visit there, enjoyed the best opportunity for study, and had an ample field for usefulness. His labours were attended with a manifest blessing, and so highly was he esteemed by the people at

Mount Pleasant, that they gave him two invitations to become their Pastor.

In the month of August, 1801, he made another visit to Mount Pleasant, and, in his absence, there occurred a fire which totally destroyed his place of worship,—a house which he had built at his own private expense. A very generous contribution was made by the citizens to compensate his loss ; and this, with other considerations strengthened his determination to devote the residue of his life to the moral and religious benefit of the city. Meanwhile, his congregation having dispersed, and many of them become connected with other churches, he did not think it best to attempt to continue a church organization. His Academy still flourished, and his Sabbaths were generally spent in rendering aid to his brethren in the city and neighbourhood.

In 1803, he suffered greatly from bodily debility ; but still he commenced and continued two services in different parts of the city, both of which were well attended. In August, the Fever again made its appearance, and he found a refuge once more for himself and his family at Mount Pleasant, where they remained till the latter part of October. As soon as circumstances would permit, he re-opened his Academy and resumed his evening Lectures.

In the summer of 1806, he received a unanimous call to take the pastoral charge of the Church in Burlington, N. J. ; but, after having visited the people, and had their call under consideration for about three months, he felt constrained to return to it a negative answer. It seems to have been strongly impressed upon his mind that there was still an important work for him to do in the city of New York ; and that he could not listen to an invitation to go elsewhere without opposing the will of Providence.

In 1807, the Bethel Church in Broome Street, which had been, for several years, in a declining state, requested his services in the way of supply as often as his other engagements would permit : he complied with their request, and his labours were attended with a signal blessing. In March, 1808, he preached, for the first time, in the New York Alms House, to an audience composed of persons labouring under almost every species of infirmity and malady. This was the commencement of a career of self-denying and beneficent action, which was to render his memory fragrant with coming generations ; though a few years were still destined to elapse before he should become engrossed in the prosecution of his great mission. In the early part of 1811, a regular Sabbath morning service was commenced in the Alms House, and the Rev. Ezra Stiles Ely began his labours as Chaplain of the place. In January, 1813, Mr. Stanford was associated with him in the Chaplaincy ; both of them being employed by " the Society for Preaching the Gospel to the Poor in the City Hospital and Alms House." Mr. Ely resigned the place in June, and from that time Mr. Stanford held the office alone. He now relinquished his Academy, after having been engaged in teaching nearly thirty-six years, that he might devote himself entirely to these labours of Christian benevolence.

The history of Mr. Stanford's life from this time would be little else than a record of an uninterrupted succession of efforts, in behalf of degraded, unfortunate, or outcast humanity. The field of his labours ultimately embraced the State's Prison, Bridewell, the Magdalen House, the Orphan Asylum, the Debtors' Prison, the Penitentiary, the Lunatic Asylum, Blackwell's Island, the Marine Hospital, and the City Hospital. In connection with all these institutions he performed a vast amount of laborious service; and to multitudes of the wretched inmates he was instrumental of dispensing the richest blessings. And while he was thus moving about, from day to day, in circles of destitution and misery, his pen was often employed in producing tracts and larger works, which not only served as important auxiliaries to his benevolent mission, but contributed to extend and perpetuate his good influence.

Mr. Stanford rendered important service to his denomination as a Theological Teacher. At various periods, he superintended the studies of young men in their preparation for the ministry, and in 1811 he had a class of eight. His course of Theological Lectures are said to have been highly appreciated by those who had the privilege of hearing them.

In 1829, Mr. Stanford was honoured with the degree of Doctor of Divinity from Union College.

In 1831, his health perceptibly declined, and his public services were performed not without much difficulty. And his ability to labour from that time was constantly diminishing. On the first day of the year 1834, one hundred and fifty children, dressed in the uniform costume of the New York Orphan Asylum, under the direction of their teachers and superintendant, appeared before the door of the venerable patriarch, to offer him their congratulations and good wishes. He immediately presented himself, and addressed them in a few tender and appropriate words, that went to their inmost hearts. They then sung a beautiful hymn, adapted to the occasion, after which they marched up to him in order, and received from him the customary New Year's gift, as the last token of his kindness. The scene was one of the most touching and impressive that can be imagined.

In a fortnight from this time he had gone to his rest. He declined gradually, but continued occasionally to use his pen, till within about six hours of his death. He died in the utmost tranquillity, on the 14th of January, 1834. Two days after, he was followed to the grave by an immense procession, including more than seventy clergymen of various denominations, and headed by about two hundred orphan children. The services were performed by the Rev. Dr. Brownlee of the Reformed Dutch Church, the Rev. Dr. Spencer H. Cone of the Baptist Church, and the Rev. Dr. Milnor of the Episcopal Church.

Dr. Stanford was the father of four children, two of whom survived him, and one,—*Thomas N.*, for many years a highly respectable bookseller in New York, still (1853) survives.

Dr. Stanford published An Address on the Burning of the Orphan House, Philadelphia, 1822; An Address on laying the Corner Stone of the Orphan House, Greenwich, 1823; A Discourse delivered in the New York City Hospital, 1824; A Discourse on Opening the New House of Correction for Juvenile Delinquents, 1826; The Aged Christian's Companion, containing a variety of Essays, adapted to the Improvement, Consolation, and Encouragement of persons advanced in life, 1829. This last is an octavo volume, and has passed to a second edition.

FROM THE REV. CHARLES G. SOMMERS, D. D.

New York, May 14, 1853.

Dear Sir: When I went to reside in New York, a little more than forty years ago, the Rev. Dr. Stanford, concerning whom you inquire, was teaching a school in what is now Fulton Street; and circumstances very soon brought me into somewhat intimate relations with him. From that time to the close of his life, I had the opportunity of observing him much in his daily walks, and of tracing his signally philanthropic career. Indeed, I used to feel myself to some extent under his direction; and, often, at his bidding, visited the State's Prison, the Alms House, and Debtor's Jail, and sometimes attended criminals to the gallows, whom he had followed with his counsels and prayers up to the last scene, parting with them only in time to avoid a spectacle from which his sensitive nature instinctively shrank. After his death, it devolved upon me to write his biography, which was published in an octavo volume.

Dr. Stanford had some fine natural qualifications for the office of a preacher. In his person, he was not above the middle height, but was firmly and symmetrically built, and had a countenance strongly marked with dignity. He had a fine large eye that was expressive of deep and strong thought. His movements were easy and graceful, and indicated—what was really the fact—that his social position in life had always been highly respectable. His voice was one of remarkable power and melody: there is not an edifice in America, I venture to say, so large, but that he could fill it without much effort. He was accustomed to arrange his thoughts for the pulpit on paper, and to make himself master of his subject, committing the outline, thus prepared, to memory, and then to preach without any manuscript before him, so that his preaching had the appearance of being extemporaneous. He spoke deliberately, but was never at a loss for words. His sermons were remarkable for sharp, pithy expressions; and, sometimes, in the exuberance of his wit, a remark would escape him that would cause a smile to pass over his audience, though it was evidently on his part entirely undesigned. His theology was thoroughly Calvinistic; and his preaching was probably more doctrinal than that of most of his brethren. No matter what might be his subject, he always seemed perfectly at home; and he never left it at the option of his audience whether to listen to him or not. His gesture was not very abundant, but it always had a meaning, and produced an effect. His sermons were short, generally ranging from thirty to thirty-five minutes; but within these limits he always contrived to bring a very fair and complete presentation of his subject. His prayers were characterized by an awful solemnity. They seemed perfectly unstudied,—the simple outpouring of the heart at the Throne of infinite purity.

Dr. Stanford was a most agreeable companion, and was always acceptable, as well in general as in Christian society. He could not be called a *great* talker, but he was eminently a *good* talker—he always talked to the purpose; talked to enlighten and benefit his fellow-men; and many of his remarks were strikingly original. He had a great fund of good-humour, and he knew how to use it without abusing it. Without any attempt to put himself forward, he was the life of almost every company into which he was thrown. He was a man of large sympathies, so that denominational lines, as far as respected his Christian intercourse, became to him a matter of little moment. I once said to him,—"Father Stanford, where have you been to-day?" "Oh," said he, "I have been spending the day among our Episcopal brethren." "But," said I, "why do you not confine yourself more to those of your own communion?" "Because," said he, "to tell the truth, I am a sort of universal lover—that is, I love to mingle with all good men."

Dr. Stanford was a man of great sagacity and forecast—he had studied human nature carefully and to good purpose. He possessed also the most unbending integrity—nothing could induce him to vary a hair from his honest convictions of what was true and right; and he expected the same of others; and if he did not find it, he knew how to administer a withering rebuke. I was sometimes unfortunate enough to take ground, on some small matters, which he thought untenable, and he was sure to meet me with "Charles, that will not do."

As a member of a deliberative body, he was always prudent and judicious, and his opinion was greatly relied on, though it was not very frequently, and never unnecessarily, expressed. As a writer, he was characterized by excellent sense, and force and directness of thought, rather than by the graces of composition.

But what distinguished Dr. Stanford far more than anything else, was his abundant, self-denying and philanthropic labours. To give any adequate idea of these would require a volume. He had a vigorous constitution, and he tasked it to the utmost, in fulfilling his mission as a Christian minister. I do not believe that Whitefield himself performed a greater amount of ministerial labour than he. He was at home wherever there was suffering to be relieved, or ignorance to be enlightened, or wanderers to be reclaimed to the path of virtue and holiness; and there was no sacrifice which he did not deem light, if it were necessary to accomplish the benevolent purposes for which he lived. He enjoyed a high reputation among the wise and good during his life-time; and few men die whose memories are more deeply embalmed in the grateful remembrance of their generation.

Very faithfully yours,

CHARLES G. SOMMERS.

ANDREW MARSHALL.*

1786†—1856.

FROM THE REV. J. P. TUSTIN, D. D.

CHARLESTON, S. C., January 15, 1859.

Rev. and dear Sir: My ecclesiastical connection with Andrew Marshall and his church placed me, for several years, in constant communication with him. Having also to act as a legal security to meet the municipal ordinances of Savannah and the State of Georgia, with regard to coloured preachers, I had much to do in matters of counsel and discipline in his Church. The sources of information relative to the following memoir have been often attested by communication with the older members of the Georgia Historical Society, and with many of the oldest and most respectable citizens of that State. I am happy to be able to give you these

---

* This sketch was solicited from the Rev. Dr. Tustin, under an impression that Mr. Marshall had died previous to the period that forms the limit to this work; and the contrary was not discovered until after the sketch had been written and forwarded to me. The very remarkable interest that pertains to the sketch, will, I trust, be a sufficient apology for my allowing it to form an exception to a general rule.

† Marshall, in a brief autobiography, says that he became a member of the Baptist Church in 1785, and *soon after* was licensed to preach; but nothing further can be ascertained on the subject. The extract from his autobiography has been sent to me by I. K. Tefft, Esq., since Dr. Tustin s sketch was written.

memorabilia of one of the most remarkable coloured men who have appeared in our modern times.

ANDREW MARSHALL, late Pastor of the First African Baptist Church in Savannah, Ga., has deservedly become a celebrity in the Annals of the American Church. During the last quarter of a century, his name gradually attracted public attention, until at length it was known in distant parts of the country, and even across the Atlantic.

Several of the most lively sketches of him which appeared, were given by authors whose works are current in various languages. Among these, is the account of Sir Charles Lyell, in his volumes published after his second scientific tour in the United States. Miss Frederika Bremer, in her American tours, has presented a striking portraiture of him. Within the last few years of his life, almost every intelligent stranger who might be visiting Savannah, was likely to seek out or to hear this venerable preacher; and the sketches thus frequently produced were widely circulated by the religious press of various denominations; and some of the leading secular papers in Northern cities had occasionally contributed to spread his fame.

The most noteworthy fact which made Mr. Marshall so celebrated in his later years, was his reputed great age. During his visit through the Northern States in the summer and fall of 1856, the last year of his life, the previously received version of his extreme age was extensively repeated, and has not been discredited. Some years previous to that time, I had, as a tribute to the cause of Science, attempted to collect and to sift the evidence about this story, which, if only apocryphal, would mislead persons engaged in ethnological and historical researches. Literary and scientific gentlemen had frequently made reference to Mr. Marshall, as an important physical phenomenon.

With no wish to detract from a story of popular interest, but nevertheless with a strong desire to arrive at perfect accuracy, I sought all the sources available to myself for testing the question of Mr. Marshall's age. Three several lines of investigation were followed, which partly tended at first to fix his age from ten to fifteen years below what was commonly assigned to him, and claimed by himself.

One of these lines of investigation was in the personal recollections of the late Hon. John Macpherson Berrien, so well known as U. S. Senator, and Attorney General of the United States. Judge Berrien was educated for the Bar by Judge Clay, of Bryan County, Ga., by whom Andrew Marshall was owned as a slave, while Mr. Berrien was a member of the family. Mr. Berrien was born, August 23, 1781, and, after graduating at Princeton, commenced the practice of law in Georgia at the age of eighteen years, which was near the time when Mr. Marshall began his efforts at preaching.

With his great name for integrity and accuracy, Judge Berrien would not be considered likely to give countenance to any opinion which was unsupported by valid evidence. His recollections of Andrew Marshall's appearance could hardly be reconciled with the account which must have made him a person of fifty years of age when Mr. Berrien first knew him as a coachman. But it was at most a matter of *impression* with Mr. Berrien, that Andrew was at that period not more than a middle-aged man. Judge Berrien's impression can be accounted for by the fact that this remarkable African always carried his age so remarkably well, even at a century.

The late venerable Mr. Miller, familiarly known in Georgia as " Cotton Miller," from his having been the person who sent the first bale of cotton to Savannah for shipment, was also of the opinion that Mr. Marshall's age should have been placed several years below what was commonly assigned to him, and by him.

Guided by such cautious and accurate men, who thus seemed to discredit a popular and universally received version, it fell to my lot, some years ago, while acting as one of the Secretaries of the Georgia Historical Society, to examine Mr. Marshall more closely than ever, as to his personal history, and to compare the results of these interrogatories with other collateral evidence. Being charged with the duty, in behalf of the literary representative and grandson of General Nathaniel Greene, of the Revolutionary army, of identifying the spot where that hero was buried in Savannah, I found Andrew Marshall to be a most useful adviser, on points which put at once his veracity and his accuracy of recollection to the closest tests. Some of his statements as to his age at the time of General Greene's death, which occurred in 1786, at first seemed to confirm the impressions of Judge Berrien and Mr. Miller, already referred to. On a review, however, of that case, it appears that these interrogatories were conducted too much in the manner of a cross-examination by a special pleader; and Mr. Marshall's confusion of mind or apparent inaccuracy as to dates, could be sufficiently explained by his want of familiarity with the published literary chronicles of the times in question.

It is, therefore, a concession which is now cheerfully made, that the doubts which I once published as to Mr. Marshall's being truly a living centenarian, may not be justified. No one who intimately knew the venerable subject of this sketch would suspect him of wishing to deceive, in any important matter. The only abatement which any one would feel, arises from the well known propensity of coloured people in all parts of the Southern States to make themselves older than they really are, after they reach to some advanced period. The deference accorded to age; the freedom from labour which aged servants enjoy; and the consideration received from those of their own race—these are among the inducements which lead aged Africans to over-estimate their years, sometimes by a very considerable difference.

It is possible that Mr. Marshall may have been deceived, not only in regard to his years, but also as to some other facts in his history. And yet it is proper to remember that his means of knowing were better than any others possessed. It must be allowed that his statements were not questioned by the oldest and most respectable citizens of his own city and region, and gentlemen now living can certify to more than fifty years' knowledge of him.

If any other question besides his age should be raised as to his accuracy or competency of opinion concerning himself, it would be as to the amount of his African blood. In his conformation and general appearance, he would probably pass for a true mulatto. But some scientific gentlemen, accustomed to the refined tests which the hair and other criteria of physiology seem to have settled in ethnological researches, have formed a decided opinion that Mr. Marshall was more of an African than would follow from a white father and a black mother.

His own account, so often repeated, and so widely known and believed, in lower Georgia, will now be mainly followed. He always referred his birth to the year 1755, being the time of General Braddock's defeat by the French and Indians. This he said, had, from his early recollections, determined the year of his nativity. As informed by his mother, who was an unmixed negress, his father was an Englishman acting as an overseer in South Carolina, where Andrew was born. The father left for England, where he died, not long after the birth of the child. It was always asserted by Andrew that he had been entitled to his freedom from his birth, as his father had arranged with a mulatto person by the name of Pendavis, before going to England, that the negro mother and two children which she had borne him, were to be provided for, and the children educated, and that, upon his return, the father would secure their freedom. His premature death becoming known, the mulatto overseer managed to enforce a claim against the estate of the father, and the mother and children were seized and sold as slaves. Andrew was sold to John Houston, then Colonial Governor of Georgia, who died when Andrew was about twenty-one years of age.

Andrew Marshall was twice married; the first time, at sixteen years of age. By his two marriages he had twenty children, only one of whom now survives. He was separated from his first wife after the death of Governor Houston, by whom he had been bequeathed his freedom on account of having, at one time, saved his master's life. The executors, however, failed to carry out the will, and Andrew was again sold, being then parted from his first wife. He evaded the decision by running away, and was sold while at large, becoming then the property of Judge Clay, as already mentioned.

While in the service of Judge Clay, he accompanied his master, who several times visited the Northern States, in the capacity of a member of Congress, and perhaps on some other occasions also. In these visits, Andrew's position as coachman enabled him frequently to see General Washington, of whom he was fond of relating several striking incidents. At a later period, General Washington visited Savannah, and Andrew was honoured with the appointment of body servant to the President. He was constantly near the General's person during his brief stay in the city, acting as his driver, and waiting upon him at a public dinner. Andrew said that Washington was uniformly grave and serious, and that he was never seen to smile during his whole visit, though he was always calm and pleasant.

The congruity of Mr. Marshall's recollections seems to be verified, especially in regard to his age, in connection with the opening period of the Revolutionary War. The embargo having taken effect at Savannah, fifteen merchants of that city agreed to give him a purse of two hundred and twenty-five dollars, on condition that he should carry word to a number of

American vessels lying in a bay, on the lower seaboard, and destined for Savannah. In this achievement he was successful. The vessels were enabled to escape to Spanish protection, before the courier, previously sent, had informed the fleet of their danger.

Mr. Marshall was an eye-witness of many of the stirring events which occurred in Savannah and its vicinity, during the Revolutionary War. He was a trustworthy servant, especially when honoured with any unusual promotion and responsibility. Even in the last war with England, he was employed, for a period of six weeks, by officers of the Government or the army, on some important business, and for this he refused any compensation, as he always claimed to be a true American, and cheerfully shared in the toils and sufferings of the white population, though never with any unseemly pretensions on his part.

He had distinct personal recollections of General Nathaniel Greene. His account of that hero's early death agrees with the traditions which have been carefully attested by gentlemen familiar with historical reseaches. General Greene, immediately after the war, was rewarded with valuable grants of land near Savannah, to which he repaired with his family, in 1785. Owing either to some disputed title, or to rancour and envy at the hero's valuable possessions, he was not allowed to enjoy them long. He was exposed to so much personal danger that he was obliged to ride armed with pistols, in going to and from his plantation near the city, and he could travel only in full daytime. Thus exposed in the midst of the summer's heat, he was suddenly smitten with inflammation of the brain, and died on the 19th of June, 1786. Andrew Marshall could recall all these events with the distinctness of an eye-witness. His account of the hero's Funeral, in Savannah, is the only apparently faithful picture which can now be furnished, whether from written chronicles or from personal traditions. He described the surprise, grief, and indignation of the people of the city, at the early and untoward death of General Greene, and their willing mind but ineffectual desires to stand up for his honour and defence. The town and region around were summoned to the Funeral, and tubs of punch and barrels of biscuit were placed along the road near the cemetery, to refresh the wearied multitude. Andrew declared that he could pace off the distance from the gate of the old cemetery on South Broad Street, to within half a dozen steps of the spot where the General was buried. But his aid in verifying this locality had been too long deferred, when an invesgation was attempted a few years ago, especially as it was then established by sufficient evidence that the remains of General Greene had previously been exhumed, and removed to a spot which cannot now be identified.

Mr. Marshall's force of character seemed to have been chiefly expended on worldly interests, until he was about fifty years of age. He evinced, even to the last, a lively sympathy in the welfare of the country, and was especially careful to maintain the cause of law and order in the social relations by which he was surrounded in his own city and vicinity. Not far from the time of his conversion, he also acquired his emancipation. He was at that time owned as a slave by Mr. Bolton, whose family name is honourably known among the merchant princes of Savannah. The father of Mr. Bolton had been the special friend of the Countess of Huntingdon while she was patronizing Mr. Whitefield's mission in Savannah, and the Orphan House at Beulah. The Bolton name is associated by marriage with the family of the late Rev. William Jay, of Bath, in England. The business partner of Mr. Bolton was the late venerable Mr. Richard Richardson, who purchased Andrew, and, with the view of effecting his emancipation, advanced him two hundred dollars, in order to purchase himself. With his previous earnings, and with diligence and economy, under the encouragement of his master, he saved enough to pay for himself and his whole family, then consisting of his wife and four children, his wife's father, and his own step-father.

Shortly after his conversion, he began to preach; and in 1806 he became Pastor of the Second Baptist Church in Savannah, which was a coloured Church, in distinction from the First or the White Baptist Church, then recently formed by the distinguished Henry Holcombe, D. D., who afterwards died as Pastor of the First Baptist Church in Philadelphia. About a thousand coloured members then belonged to Mr. Marshall's church; and subsequently the number increased to some three thousand, when it was thought best to divide them. Accordingly, the coloured church was formed, which sometime afterwards purchased the old house of worship which the White Baptist Church vacated when they built their new brick meeting-house, under the Pastorship of the late Rev. Henry O. Wyer,* and which now forms a part of the large house of worship known as the First Baptist Church in Savannah. The church which Mr. Marshall thus formed, took the name of the First African Baptist Church, and he remained its Pastor till the day of his death.

During the long period of his ministry, Mr. Marshall was careful to preserve tolerably good memorials of his ministerial acts. His mere recollections seemed nearly as accurate as if they had been written and publicly certified. He had baptized about thirty-eight hundred persons; and he supposed that over four thousand had professed to be converted under his ministry. His personal influence extended over the plantations through several counties around Savannah; and the planters were generally satisfied with the beneficial effects of his labours. He was often sent for

---

* HENRY O. WYER was a native of Massachusetts, was graduated at the Columbian College, in the District of Columbia, at the age of about twenty-one, and soon after removed to Savannah, and became Pastor of the Baptist Church in that city. He was ordained there, in the year 1824, by a Presbytery consisting of the late Rev. Dr. Brantly, then of Augusta, Ga., and the Rev. (afterwards President) Shannon, of Liberty County, in the same State. The church with which he became connected, had long been in an exceedingly depressed state; but, under the influence of his faithful and acceptable ministry, it began soon to revive, and, as the fruit of a revival which took place in 1827, it received to its communion about one hundred persons. He continued in the active discharge of his duties at Savannah until 1833, when he was compelled by ill health to resign his charge. He spent two years, leading the life of a valetudinarian, preaching as his strength allowed, but accepting no permanent situation. During this period, several of the most prominent churches in the denomination were offered to him, but he felt constrained to decline them. In 1843, when the Rev. Dr. Binney went to Burmah, he accepted the call to the Savannah Baptist Church for one year. Subsequently, he took the temporary charge of a Second Baptist Church in Savannah, which was constituted in 1847, and retained this position about two years. His health was too infirm to admit of regular labour. His death occurred in Alexandria, Va., in April, 1857, when he was fifty-five years of age. He was married, in 1825, to a sister of Lieutenant Harstene, the gallant Commander of the Arctic, which went in quest of Captain E. K. Kane. His widow survives him. He left two sons, one of whom is an honoured Baptist minister in Virginia, the other is a practitioner of medicine. Mr. W. was an uncommonly effective preacher—though his feeble health rarely allowed him to make very mature preparation for the pulpit, his fine elocution, and noble presence, and warm heart were always a pledge of his being listened to with attention and interest.

to preach and to perform Funeral services, at great distances; and such visits were often urged by the planters, and the white people at large, as well as by the blacks.

Whenever he visited any of the larger cities, his appearance in public ministrations was greeted by great multitudes. He occasionally preached in Augusta, Macon and Milledgeville, as well as in Charleston, and even as far off as in New Orleans. On some occasions his audiences were composed, in large part, of the most respectable white people : and the Legislature of Georgia, at one time, gave him a hearing in an entire body. The winter before he died, he visited Augusta, and conducted a protracted meeting, which resulted in the addition of over three hundred and fifty persons to the coloured church in that city. With all these immense results to his ministry, Mr. Marshall preserved a strict and salutary discipline—at least, such was the constant effort and rule of his proceedings. He was jealous of mere animal excitements; and generally unfriendly even to protracted meetings in his own church, or in others where he officiated. He relied upon the appointed and ordinary means of grace; and in his own church, there were seldom any efforts used beyond special prayer and the faithful ministrations of the Word. He, however, was so deeply interested in the Temperance cause, that he encouraged, among his people, those methods of organization for this object, which are somewhat kindred to the plan of the Odd Fellows. There were also Societies among his flock for mutual benefit; and in these ways, the poor and the infirm, especially among the free people of colour, who had no legal masters to care for them in their old age were greatly benefitted. Mr. Marshall was so strong in his opposition to drunkenness that no coloured person would, by this indulgence, willingly incur his censure. There is no doubt that, in this respect, he accomplished much for the cause of virtue among the blacks, and thus for the public welfare generally.

The superiority of Mr. Marshall's character and talents especially appears in the methodical manner in which he conducted his own business, as well as in the discipline of his church. Long after he became a preacher, he had but a small and precarious support from any pecuniary rewards for his ministry. He supported himself and his family as a drayman; but his great capacity soon asserted itself, even in respect to his material means of prosperity. He conducted the portage and draying business on a considerable scale, at one period, having owned a number of drays and teams, and even the slaves who drove them. He owned the large brick dwelling house in which he had lived for many years previous to his death; and was at one time rated in property as high as twenty-five thousand dollars, though this was probably too high an estimate. His property was diminished very considerably in his latter years. With his increasing infirmities he began to fear that he might yet be scarcely saved from the necessity of out-door duties; and that he might have to give up the easy carriage and horse which he had so long enjoyed. He related that, on one occasion, he had advanced twenty-five hundred dollars to purchase a family of twelve persons, to prevent their separation, and that he never received back the money, except a mere trifle, which he had thus paid.

His church, however, were abundantly able and willing to provide for him; and though they did not pay him a fixed salary, they made regular contributions, which amounted to a handsome sum annually, and which, in any extremity, could doubtless have been increased by several hundred dollars. Prominent native citizens were always among his tried friends; and some of the most respectable gentlemen in Savannah, of different denominations, acted as Trustees for his church, to protect their real estate and other property.

Mr. Marshall possessed elements which would of necessity have made him a leading character anywhere. His Anglo-Saxon temperament made him superior to his African race. His strength of character showed itself in his indomitable perseverance, his calm self-possession, his practical sagacity, and a discretion which never failed him. Withal, he had a genial and even humorous temper; and his countenance bore the finest lines of expression. He was entirely free from superstition, and gave no countenance to marvellous relations of experience, even in a work of grace. He could penetrate beneath disguises, and few men, white or black, of any age, could surpass him in reading human character.

The deference which he always showed for the laws and institutions of the country, was combined with a high measure of self-respect, and frequently with a decision and inflexibility which might be taken advantage of by unprincipled white persons. There was a period of about two years,—from 1819 to 1821,—when Mr. Marshall became somewhat unpopular with the white people of his own denomination, on account of his extreme views of Theology, which at first bordered on Antinomianism, and at length receded to the opposite extreme of Sacramentalism in Baptism, as held by Alexander Campbell. During that time, and while engaged in his secular avocations, he had violated the laws, by contraband dealings with negroes. He had made purchases from slaves having no tickets with leave to trade and sell; and, though many white people had laid the foundation of large success in business before, as others have since, by contraband trade with blacks, advantage was taken of Mr. Marshall's inadvertency, and happening together with his temporary unpopularity, he was prosecuted and sentenced to be publicly whipped in the market-place. The kindness of his former master, Mr. Richardson, and the feelings of many of the best citizens, would not allow him to suffer; and personal witnesses of the scene, yet living, can attest that the whipping was only a semblance,—the constable receiving instructions not to scratch his skin or to draw blood,—his old master also being at his side to see that these precautions were faithfully and humanely observed.

While Mr. Marshall was unvarying in his deference to white people, and was never distrusted for any disloyalty to the public peace; and while he was decided in asserting the necessity and advantages of the present institutions in the South, he yet never hesitated to make a firm and respectful declaration of the rights of conscience in matters of religion. He sometimes alluded to his celebrated uncle, the Rev. Andrew Bryan,* who was a

---

* ANDREW BRYAN was a slave belonging to the Hon. Jonathan Bryan, a distinguished patriot of the Revolution, who died in 1788. Andrew, the founder of the First Coloured Church in Savannah, was his favourite servant, and was allowed many privileges. He was at one time arrested and whipped,—it is supposed for holding religious meetings with his members

coloured preacher of nearly as great reputation as ever Andrew Marshall possessed, and who died at an extremely great age, as Pastor of the Coloured Church in Savannah. In one of the turbulent outbreaks of religious bigotry among the baser sort of people, which happened before the demoralizing effects of the Revolutionary War had been followed by better morals and manners, this old preacher, Andrew Bryan, was silenced from preaching; and, upon his assuming again to preach, he was publicly whipped. But, after this flagellation, he declared that he could not stop preaching, even if at the cost of a martyr's sufferings. This old man seemed ever to have been the model for a true preacher, with Andrew Marshall; and when he died, his nephew and successor caused a beautiful mural tablet to be raised in his church, and another large tablet of marble over his grave, in which were recited the events of his life, not omitting the whipping and the persecution he had endured for righteousness' sake. The monument will probably long remain in the coloured cemetery at Savannah.

The bent and tone of Mr. Marshall's mind, was of the old Calvinistic order. His clear intellect was equal to the best distinctions in Theology; and though he was rather too fond of sometimes saying in public that he never had a day's learning in his life, yet he had much of the discipline which every superior mind acquires and asserts for itself, by the very necessity and outgrowth of self-education; for every mind that is truly educated, when we look at the last analysis, educates itself.

He owned a considerable number of books; and among those evidently the most used, were Dr. Gill's Commentaries. In his treatment of a subject in some of his pulpit performances, there was observable the grasp of a mind which would be deservedly called great. Very often, indeed, he intermingled incidents of his personal experience, and then would seem to run into a rambling style; but even these discursive qualities served to keep alive the attention of his simple flock. But a man who could make some of the high mental efforts which Andrew Marshall at times displayed, would be pronounced as fully equal to any subject which he would find occasion to meet, if allowed opportunity for preparation.

The tones of his voice seemed rather to make his preaching of the conversational order; while yet there was really a unity of plan and a purpose, and a progress, in the whole deliverance. In his large house of worship, the soft tones of his voice would reach the farthest corner, and penetrate every ear. He never used notes in preaching; but his self-possession never failed him. His voice was so deep, sonorous and tender, that its capacity for the expression of pathos was unsurpassed. In his Scripture readings, and in reciting hymns, his power was always felt. His

at night,—but his master interceded for him, and the matter being examined by several leading citizens, and there being no evidence that the slaves were plotting mischief or insurrection, the result was that Andrew obtained permission from the Chief Justice to continue to preach during the day time, but not at night. He died on the 6th of October, 1812, in the ninety-sixth year of his age. Several Addresses were delivered at his Funeral, and among them one by the Rev. Dr. Kollock. The following is part of the inscription upon his monument:—" He has done more good among the poor slaves than all the learned Doctors in America. He was imprisoned for the Gospel, and, without any ceremony, whipped. But, while under the lash, he told his persecutors he rejoiced not only to be whipped, but he was willing to suffer death for the cause of Christ. . . . He was an honour to human nature, an ornament to religion, and friend to mankind. His memory is still precious in the minds of the living."

favourite hymns and selections of Scripture were sometimes pronounced with such effect, that the most highly educated and discriminating persons would never forget the impression of such readings.

His appearance was commanding, though he was neither stout nor tall, compared with the average of well formed men. His African skin and hair were compensated by a face of intelligence superior to the limitations of race. His hair was of the clearest white, and though truly African, it rose in unwonted profusion, giving him the presence of a venerable patriarch. His teeth were sound and beautifully clear; his sight and hearing as good to the last as in middle life; and his lower limbs only began seriously to fail him on reaching his one hundredth year. In some of his glowing pulpit efforts, his face and whole person were irradiated with intelligence; and one could not hear him at such times without feeling himself within the influence of a superior mind.

In the last year of Mr. Marshall's life, it became an object of extreme desire with him to erect a new and better house of worship for the church which he felt he soon must leave. The old house, being built of wood, had become much dilapidated, and the city ordinance would not allow another wooden building to be erected on that spot, which was really an eligible one. Feeling the importance of his cause, after making some progress in Savannah and its vicinity, Mr. Marshall resolved upon another journey to the North, which he had frequently visited in the days, and in the presence, of Washington. He was accompanied by his wife, and he hoped also to receive some benefit by consulting physicians there, for his infirmities, which neither nature nor medicine could much longer resist. He was respectfully received by some of the most prominent of the New York clergy, of various denominations. He preached with acceptance in several of the Baptist pulpits,—among them, in Dr. Cone's and Dr. Magoon's—and in those of other denominations, one of which was that of Dr. Krebs; and very soon he received in that city about six hundred dollars for his object.

But his race was run. He was soon admonished to return home at once, if he wished to see his own people again, and to die among them. Extremely weak, and every day becoming more unwell, he reached Richmond in his journey by land; and thence he could proceed no farther. Having a letter to the Rev. B. Manly, Jr., President of the Richmond Female College, he desired his direction to some place where he could stay. Mr. Manly promptly and cheerfully provided for him at his own house, where the old man lingered for more than a month, evincing the same gracious affections, and the same superior traits of character, which had crowned and graced his life for so many years. Here, on the 8th of December, 1856, he breathed his last. His remains were carefully conveyed to Savannah, where his Funeral took place, on Sabbath, the 14th of the same month. The demonstrations of interest, on this last solemn occasion of his earthly history, were unequalled by any thing of the kind in that city or region, where a coloured person was concerned. An immense procession of about a mile long, with fifty-eight carriages, either loaned by families in the city to their servants or other coloured friends, or occupied, as in many instances, by respectable white people themselves, followed him from his church to his grave. His Funeral Sermon was preached by the Rev. Thomas Rambaut,

Pastor of the First Baptist church in Savannah. Not more than two or three Funerals, whether civil or military, and those of the most distinguished citizens of the place, have witnessed so large a collection of people, in the course of the present century, in that city, as followed to their last resting place, the remains of the centenarian, Andrew Marshall.

Yours respectfully,
J. P. TUSTIN.

FROM THE REV. JOHN M. KREBS, D. D.

NEW YORK, June 4, 1859.

My dear Sir: You ask me for my recollections of the Rev. Andrew Marshall, the Centenarian Coloured Preacher, of Savannah.

On a certain Lord's day, in May, 1855, I was in Savannah, on my way to the General Assembly. After preaching in the morning for the late Rev. Dr. Preston, then the Pastor of the Independent Presbyterian Church, I attended in the afternoon, in company with a respected Ruling Elder of the First Presbyterian Church, and several other Christian friends, who were lodging at the same hotel with me, the worship in the African Baptist Church, which was under the pastoral care of Mr. Marshall, celebrated for his great age, his protracted evangelical labours, and his genuine Christian eloquence. On entering the Church, which was a neat substantial structure, accommodating, as I supposed, from eight hundred to a thousand persons, we were conducted to the pews reserved for white visiters, in the middle tier, (immediately in front of the pulpit,) which were occupied by some twenty or twenty-five white persons. The house was crowded in every part with coloured people, whose neat and appropriate dress and decorous behaviour could not be surpassed by any congregation. It happened to be their Communion service, and the exercises were just beginning with a hymn, which was nobly read by the Pastor, and nobly sung by the people. The venerable minister was seated under the pulpit, only a few feet from us. His locks were gray with age, but his form was apparently hale and robust, though the furrows were in his cheeks. As he rose to offer prayer, he steadied himself upon his cane, while gradually he attained an erect position, every feature and every limb trembling, it may be not more with the weight of years than with powerful emotion. The prayer, uttered with clear articulation and with a strong voice, was somewhat long, but it was rich with Christian thought and feeling, appropriate in expression, and attracting the sympathy of the worshippers. The aged man of God proceeded with an address bearing upon the special service in which we were engaged. He made a modest remark in reference to his own illiteracy; but, although there was here and there a quaintness and homeliness of expression, neither out of place nor out of taste,—which, nevertheless, I could not here repeat without exciting a smile, it was not for a moment deficient in force or devotion, nor left any other impression than that of deep and tender solemnity. And if the preacher modestly estimated his own ability, it was clear to his hearers that he was "a man of one book," mighty in the Scriptures, and taught of God. The subject of his address was the indispensable importance of the death of Christ, and the astonishing results which it accomplished. There might occasionally seem to be, to a very fastidious critic, a slight incoherence or fragmentary observation; but it was not so; there was a clear, full, consistent vein of thought running throughout the whole.

I do not attempt to give more than a specimen of his utterance. Referring to the promise of the Saviour's coming couched in the declaration,—"As often as ye eat this bread and drink this cup, ye do show the Lord's death till He come," he said: "My beloved brethren, when I read this promise, my poor trembling heart sometimes sinks within me. The Lord shall be revealed in all the grace and glory of the Redeemer and the King; but these aged eyes of mine will not continue their sight until that day. I am a hundred years old, and these tottering limbs of mine shall be laid in the dust long ere that bright vision shall gladden the face of his redeemed people. But I check myself and rebuke my impatient fear. Do I not read in his sure promise that, though I sleep in the dust of the earth, I shall lose nothing of the perfect grace that is to be brought to us at the revelation of Jesus Christ, even because *He* shall lose nothing of all that the Father hath given Him, for He shall raise it up at the last day. My dead body shall arise in the vigour and immortality wherein it shall be fashioned like the glorified body of Jesus. And these dull ears shall hear the archangel's trump, and these dim eyes shall see the King in his glory, as clearly and to as good advantage as any that shall be alive and remain upon the earth to hail that glorious appearing of the great God and our Saviour Jesus Christ!" Could any thing have been more inspiriting, more adapted to rouse up the faith and hope of the believer?

Again, in allusion to the plotting of the great adversary to destroy Christ, he said:—"At last he succeeded. He was nailed to his cross in agony and shame. Satan had bruised his heel, and thought that he had crushed his head. The fool! It was his own head that was broken then, and he has been a fool ever since; and the proof of all his wicked madness and folly in compassing the death of Christ became apparent. It was Christ that triumphed then, and spoiled the spoiler. The thief was rescued from the kingdom of darkness. The Heathen Centurion acknowledged the Son of God. His death multiplied his disciples. The thousands of Pentecost bowed before the salvation of the cross. Myriads upon myriads, that no man can number, have been delivered from the kingdom of Satan, and translated into the Kingdom of God's dear Son. That great salvation has made its way through the world; its blessed fruits are gathered abundantly on these Western shores. Our skins are dark, but our souls are washed white in the blood of the Lamb. Nor is He the propitiation for our sins only. My brethren, the time was in this city, and through this Southern country, when you would scarcely ever see the face of our white masters in a house of prayer; but how is it now? How many of those to whom we are subject in the flesh, have recognised our common Master in Heaven, and *they are our masters no longer.* They are fellow-heirs with us of the grace of life. They sit with us at the same table of our common Lord. They are our friends, our brethren, our guardians, our fathers; and we are travelling together to that blessed land where we shall dwell together in the presence of Jesus Christ, their Lord and ours."

Who could but be affected with such stirring Gospel eloquence ; and my only regret was this—when the old man was surrounded by the Deacons, some ten in number,—a body of fine looking men,—the most of them intensely black, to receive from him the elements for distribution, I felt a pang, because I supposed the Baptist principle of Close Communion would exclude me from sharing in that feast of love. But this apprehension was quickly dissipated. Before proceeding to distribute, the aged servant of God announced that that was not a Baptist table, but Christ's table, and that all who loved Him were welcome there. And when the bread and wine were handed round, first to the white occupants of the pews, all of whom appeared to be communicants in Presbyterian, Congregationalist, Baptist, Dutch Reformed, Methodist, and perhaps Episcopal, Churches, and then to the six hundred coloured communicants,—as devout and tender as any congregation I ever saw,—I declare to you that never did I administer these emblems of my Saviour's love, nor never did I receive them from the hands of other ministers of Christ, with whatsoever canonical or apostolical authority ordained, with greater joy than I received them, that day, from the trembling hands of that poor, bowed down, weeping *negro* minister of Jesus Christ.

The service continued about two hours and a half, consisting variously of hymns, prayers, reading the Scriptures, and exhortation; and it was all conducted by Mr. Marshall. But it was not long, nor tedious. It was refreshment by the way, and food and strength for many days. And when, at the close, as the assembly orderly broke up, yet seeming loth to part with each other, I went forward to introduce myself to this aged father, I could rejoice, as speaking through tears, with steady, cheerful voice and happy heart, we exchanged the mutual prayer that it might be ours, with all the Israel of God, at our next probable meeting, to sit down together with Abraham, Isaac and Jacob, in the kingdom of God, at the marriage supper, when the Lamb Himself shall preside.

This, however, was not our last interview. Among the respectful friends who gathered around him, was the Captain of a Philadelphia Steamer, regularly plying between that city and Savannah, who seconded my invitation to the venerable man to visit the North, by heartily offering him a free passage in his ship, both coming and going. I encouraged him to expect some help in building a larger and more commodious church, which his congregation were then projecting. About two years afterward, he made the visit. He spent some months in this city, lodging with a respectable, religious family, of his own race, but freely welcomed to the tables and pulpits of the brethren whose acquaintance he made, (among whom was the family of a noble-hearted and wealthy Georgian, then residing here,) who provided for his support while here, and for his getting about from place to place,—for, of course, he was too feeble to walk, or even to travel alone in omnibuses. Perhaps the long journey, and the change of climate and habits, contributed to bring upon him a disorder from which he never recovered. He preached once for me, to a very large concourse of people, whom the occasion attracted. The subject of his sermon was the fierce demoniac who had his dwelling among the tombs, out of whom Christ cast the unclean spirit by which he was possessed. Applying it to his own history, he described his own early life, as a careless sinner, until the grace of God visited and rescued him from the power of Satan, and led him from step to step until he became a preacher of the Gospel. He detailed many interesting incidents of the Revolutionary War, including the siege of Savannah, and his own career as a servant, and his journeys as an express-rider, bearing dispatches from officers of the army to and fro between various military stations, and eventually the purchase of the freedom of himself and his family, and his acquisition, and then the loss, of property. These incidents were wrought into his discourse, not as mere narrative, but as illustrations of the ways of Providence toward him. The sermon was richly evangelical and experimental. But it had not the glow and copiousness, nor perhaps the stricter connection, which would have characterized it, but for the evident pressure of increasing infirmity and unusual disorder of his bodily system. The audience, however, was deeply interested, and responded to his appeal for aid to rebuild his church, with a generous collection. But he did not live to accomplish his object. Returning homeward by easy overland travel, his illness increased upon him, and he died on the way at Richmond.

He had but little learning—hardly any beyond the knowledge of his Bible. But he was shrewd, intelligent, and fervent in spirit, unpresuming, but zealous, and useful among his own people, and greatly respected by all. The following account of his " trial," which I received from the lips of Dr. Preston, may be repeated in this connection.

There was, and perhaps still is, a law of Georgia, which requires that a coloured preacher shall procure a recommendation from three reputable citizens *of his own denomination,* and, upon it, obtain a license from the County Court, before exercising his office. Mr. Marshall applied to Dr. Preston for a testimonial, which the Doctor informed him would be useless, inasmuch as he was a Presbyterian and Marshall a Baptist. For some reason,—most likely because he did not clearly understand the law,—Mr. Marshall proceeded to preach without the license. Some officious person caused him to be indicted. When the day of trial came, it appeared that, in his ignorance of the method of proceeding, he had retained no counsel for his defence. Several of the lawyers, in their kindness towards him, solicited one of the most eminent of their brethren, Mr. Macalester, (afterwards Judge Macalester of California,) to appear for him, as he was incompetent to plead his own cause. Mr. Macalester immediately undertook the case, which looked very hopeless indeed. The prosecution proved the offence fully. At the proper time for introducing his witnesses, Mr. Macalester, observing Dr. Preston in the Court, called him to testify. On the Doctor's entrance upon the witnesses' stand, the presiding Judge interposed, inquiring of the counsel for the defence what he expected to prove by Dr. Preston? The reply was " that Andrew Marshall was qualified to preach the Gospel." " That," said the Court, " is not the question; the accused may be never so well qualified *theologically;* but he is indicted for preaching without the *legal* qualification prescribed by the statute." A little argument took place, which resulted, as a matter of course, in the Judge's decision to exclude the witness. Mr. Macalester immediately called another well-known citizen to the stand, when the previous scene was repeated. The counsel offered a third, equally prominent witness, who was also rejected for irrelevancy. Meanwhile, the attention of the Jury was fastened on this series of overtures, which was just what the astute counsel designed. On " summing up," he made an ingenious and eloquent speech in defence,—particularly and plausibly arguing " the very embarrassing and disadvantageous predicament in which his poor client was placed by the " *remarkable ruling* " of the Court, which, on his offering, on behalf of the accused, the testimony of several of the most respectable witnesses that the city could furnish, had refused even to let them be sworn!" The prosecuting attorney made a few brief comments on the law and the testimony, and clearly established the guilt of the accused preacher in his breach of the law of the State. The Judge as pointedly charged the Jury against him, for the fact was undeniable. The Jury retired, and in a very little time returned with a verdict of " not guilty!" The Court gravely received it—the clerk quietly smiled while he recorded it— and the spectators a little more audibly tittered in token of their satisfaction. The prisoner was discharged, and the Jury dismissed. As they came out of the box, some person present inquired of one of them, " how it was possible for them to bring in such a verdict in the face of the law and the fact, and their own oath." " Easily enough," replied the juror; " you will never catch a Georgian Jury convicting any man of crime for preaching the Gospel."

Whatever may be the opinion to be entertained of the justification of the Jury, it is evident that they had a good deal more of the spirit of toleration than the Jewish Sanhedrim, who scourged Apostles and forbade them to speak any more in the name of Jesus. *Patriotism* triumphed when Patrick Henry plead its cause against the sordid claim of " John Hook, hoarsely brawling through the rejoicing American camp, ' beef, beef, beef!' " And here, likewise, while we have been *amused* by some pleasant descriptions of the ludicrous practice in the rural courts of the Southwest, we may, perhaps, *learn* something from this example of a staid, conservative Southern Jury going in strongly for " the higher law."

I am very truly yours,
JOHN M. KREBS.

THOMAS B. MONTANYE.*
1787—1829.

THOMAS B. MONTANYE was born in the city of New York, in the year
1769. His father, Benjamin Montanye, was a respectable and active member of the Reformed Dutch Church in that city. The son, at the age of
about seventeen, to the great grief of his father, departed from the faith
in which he had been educated, so far as Baptism is concerned, and joined
the Baptist Church, at that time under the pastoral care of the Rev. John
Gano. Shortly after, one of his sisters followed his example; and this
served greatly to aggravate the father's grief. But, being himself led to
a fresh examination of the subject, he ultimately reposed in the same
views to which his children had led the way, and united himself with the
same church of which they had already become members.

Sometime after this change of his ecclesiastical relations, he (the father)
was called to the ministry, and, with a few others, originated the Church
in Oliver Street, New York, for many years under the pastoral care of the
Rev. Spencer H. Cone, D. D., and one of the most numerous of the Baptist denomination in the United States. Having served this church for
some time, he took charge of the Church in Deer Park, Orange County,
N. Y., where he laboured with great success till his death, which occurred
in the eighty-third year of his age.

Mr. Thomas B. Montanye was ordained in the year 1788, when he was
only nineteen years of age, Pastor of the Baptist Church in Warwick, N.
Y. Here he laboured for more than twelve years with great fidelity and
success. He extended his labours also into the surrounding country;
and, wherever he preached, was listened to with great interest, and often
with deep solemnity, and his preaching was followed with many permanently happy results. The church at Warwick, previous to his settlement
there, had been in a very depressed state: not only had spiritual religion
among the professed followers of Christ greatly waned, but ignorance,
profaneness and infidelity seemed to hold an almost undisputed triumph on
every side. But Mr. Montanye, nothing discouraged by adverse appearances, addressed himself to his work with a degree of energy and perseverance which even the strongholds of sin could not withstand. During one
year of his ministry here, more than a hundred and fifty were added to
the church, as the fruit of his labours.

Mr. Montanye's distinguished abilities and success as a preacher rendered him an object of attraction to distant churches and Associations.
On a visit to the Philadelphia Association, in the year 1800, he officiated
for the Church in Southampton, Bucks County, Pa., then destitute of a
Pastor. The next year, he received and accepted a call to the Pastorship
of that church. On entering this new field of labour, he was brought into
intimate association with several of the most distinguished Baptist clergymen in America; and, though he was at this time but little more than
thirty years of age, and withal was very youthful in his appearance, yet

* MS. from H. G. Jones, Esq.

such was his reputation for both talents and piety, that the ablest and oldest members of the Association never failed to listen to him with respect and deference. His services soon came to be sought at Ordinations, distant Associations, Councils, and especially at Religious Anniversaries, which were very numerously attended; and so powerful was his voice that, on these last mentioned occasions, he would easily make himself heard by several thousands. During his connection with the Philadelphia Association, some very grave and perplexing matters of controversy came before that Body, which brought men of high talents and standing in fierce conflict with each other. From the year 1816 to the year 1828, these matters were agitated, without much intermission. Mr. Montanye took and held his position with great firmness and dignity, and, though constrained to oppose many of his long cherished friends, he accounted even that a light matter, inasmuch as it was necessary to his keeping a conscience void of offence.

Mr. Montanye was distinguished for his patriotism; and, when the War of 1812 with Great Britain broke out, he was on the alert for the defence of his country. Having received a Chaplain's commission, he sallied forth to the camp on the banks of the Delaware. His clerical labours there proved highly acceptable and salutary. On one occasion, particularly, he had an opportunity of exhibiting his fortitude and conscientiousness in a way that attracted special notice. A general drill and review of the army had been ordered for the morning of the Sabbath, at the same hour when preaching had hitherto been the "order of the day." He told his friends that this military exercise must not take place at the hour of public worship. He then proceeded to the quarters of the General in command, and stated to him, in a very dignified and courteous manner, that he held a commission from his country, and also from his God; that, by virtue of his latter commission, *he* was superior in command on the Sabbath to any of the military; that the general order for a review would interfere with orders from a higher source; and that, consequently, the review *could* not and *must* not take place. The General heard the Chaplain with surprise, but with respectful attention; and the result was that "after-orders" were issued, and the review was postponed.

Mr. Montanye had a vigorous constitution, and generally enjoyed firm health; and though he had laboured long and diligently in his Master's cause, his friends confidently believed, until his last illness commenced, that the end of his earthly labours was still comparatively distant. On his return from a meeting of the Warwick Association, in June, 1829, he suffered an attack of the jaundice. In July, the disease rapidly increased, but, in August, he obtained some relief, so that he was able to engage several times in his accustomed public duties. In September, he stood in his pulpit for the last time, on which occasion he preached a Funeral Sermon. From that day, his decline was rapid, and it soon became apparent that his days of active service were numbered. To a brother in the ministry, who now visited him, he expressed the strongest confidence that he was destined to a happy immortality. He mentioned three reasons why it would be desirable to him to live longer—one was that he might do something more for the benefit of his family; another, that the affairs of others, entrusted to his care, might be finally adjusted; and the third and most important, that he might see the churches around him supplied with sound, pious and faithful ministers. On this latter point he continued to express great anxiety as long as he lived. "It fills me with gloom," said he, "to see some of our pulpits occupied by Sciolists, who offer the Saviour to sinners apparently with as little concern as a merchant would offer his wares for sale." On one occasion, when his disorder seemed to assume a more favourable aspect, he remarked that he could scarcely calculate on long life. "My course," he said, "has been a rapid one; I was early in sin, and in that I run a mad career; was called early to embrace the Saviour; commenced my ministerial course early; and have preached perhaps oftener since I have been engaged in the ministry than almost any other man; therefore I may expect that my life will be not greatly protracted." While conversing with a friend on his prospects for eternity, he remarked,—"My dependance is not upon any thing I have done,—neither my moral deportment; nor my faithfulness in the discharge of domestic or relative duties; nor in my abundant preaching; but I go to the footstool of mercy as a poor, unworthy sinner, resting my whole salvation on the merits of the Lord Jesus Christ; and I feel a firm persuasion that his work in my soul has long since been performed." His friend remarked to him that it was not probable he would meet the Philadelphia Association, then near at hand, and which he had attended twenty-eight years in succession. After a moment's reflection, he said,—"If I am not there, I shall be"——pointing upwards, as though he would have said,—"I shall be in Heaven." After a violent paroxysm, he exclaimed,—"Tell me, my soul, can this be death?" On the day previous to his dissolution, his friend, already referred to, left him; and, in parting, he said,—"Farewell in Christ Jesus; you can fare well no where else." He died, on the morning of the Lord's day, September 27, 1829. In the full possession of his faculties, he exclaimed,—"I die, I die," and instantly the vital spark was extinguished.

On the ensuing Monday, his remains were deposited in the cemetery of the Baptist Church at Northampton, attended by twelve ministers of the Baptist and Presbyterian Churches, and an immense crowd of sympathizing friends. An appropriate discourse was delivered by the Rev. Joseph Matthias, from the Epistle to the Philippians, i. 21. The Philadelphia Baptist Association assembled a few days after his death, and testified their deep sense of the excellence of their departed brother's character, and of the loss which they had sustained in his removal. The Rev. Dr. Staughton, by request of the Association, delivered a Commemorative Discourse, from II. Tim. iv. 7.

When Mr. Montanye's will was opened, it was found to contain the following Epitaph, which, agreeably to his direction, was inscribed on his tombstone:

Here lies interred
The mortal man,
ELDER THOMAS B. MONTANYE,
Born in the city of New York, January 29, 1769;
Baptized by Elder John Gano, 1786;
Licensed 1787; ordained 1788;
Pastor of Warwick Church, N. Y., 12 years and 6 months.

Moved to Pennsylvania 1801;
Pastor of Southampton Church till death,
a term of [blank to be filled
as God may lengthen out my days.]
Whole time in the ministry
[to be filled.]
The chief of sinners and the least of saints.

The following testimony was rendered concerning him by the Rev. Horatio Gates Jones, D. D., Mr. Montanye's intimate friend :—

Under his ministry "many were translated from the state of nature to the state of grace, and many were advanced to a higher state of holiness. The bad were made good, and the good were made better. His prayers were an effusion of the most lively, melting expressions of his ardent love to God—' from the abundance of his heart his life spake.' His soul took wing for Heaven, and enrapt the souls of his audience with him. In his sermons there was a rare union of argument and persuasion to convince the mind and gain the heart. It was not easy to resist the power of his discourse, without abjuring reason and warring with Divine Revelation. In speaking, he possessed an admirable felicity and copiousness. In his style there was a *noble negligence*,—his great mind not deigning to stoop to the affected eloquence of words. He had not the advantage of an academical education; but, by the Divine blessing on his strong mind, and uncommon dexterity and diligence, he far surpassed in sacred knowledge many who bore the highest collegiate honours. His voice was firm, of full volume, and rather melodious than otherwise—its charm consisted in the fulness of its note, the ease and variety of its inflection, the fine effect of its emphasis, the graceful facility with which it attuned itself to every emotion, and its power to range through the whole domain of human passion. from the deep and tragic half whisper of horror to the wildest exclamation of overwhelming surprise. In persuasion, it was soft and gentle as the zephyrs of spring; while, in rousing the slumbering sinner, the winter's storm that roars along the troubled ocean, was not more awfully sublime.

"If we view our distinguished brother in the social circle, it must be granted that all who knew him were delighted with his urbanity. His natural abilities and endowments invariably commanded respect—his reasoning faculty was prompt and acute; his memory uncommonly tenacious; and his conversation highly agreeable. To place religion in a morose habit of mind was remote from his practice, his judgment, and his temper But his conversation, even when taking in things of a different nature, was yet, in a greater or less degree, of religious tendency; and when he conversed directly on religious subjects, he frequently spake with such decided relish as left it impossible for any one to doubt that his utterances were from the seated temper and habit of his soul."

ELISHA ANDREWS.

1787—1840.

FROM THE REV. ERASTUS ANDREWS.

SUFFIELD. Conn., 29th January, 1859.

My dear Sir : I cheerfully comply with your request for a sketch of my venerated father ; and I will endeavour to perform the delicate task you have assigned me, with all impartiality and fidelity.

ELISHA ANDREWS, a son of Isaac Andrews, was born at Middletown, Conn., September 29, 1768. When he was about twelve years of age, his parents removed to the State of Vermont; and he accompanied them. His father had previously been a sea-faring man, but, as he had had somewhat more than a common education, he afterwards supported his family by teaching a school, and practising the art of Surveying. The fact that the father was so much engaged in teaching was favourable to the improvement of the son ; as it gave him the opportunity of pursuing his studies under his father's instruction, almost constantly, during several of his early years. He acquired knowledge with remarkable facility, in after life, without the aid of a teacher; and this is supposed to have been owing, in a great measure, to his father's peculiar mode of instruction. In giving the pupil a book, he would endeavour to impress him with the idea that it would even be disgraceful for him to ask for help to enable him to understand the most difficult part of it. He used to say,—"If you cannot conquer Pike's Arithmetic, how can you expect to be able to combat the evils of life?" Elisha, while yet a boy, had become master of the art of Surveying, had dipped a little into Latin, and was competent to teach all that was required in the district schools of that day; and at the age of sixteen or seventeen he left home, and went into the State of New York, where he spent several years, partly as a Teacher, and partly as a Surveyor. His home at this time was with an aunt,—a person of an excellent Christian character, who resided in Galway, Saratoga County, then comparatively a new country. In after life, he was heard to say that his first permanent religious impressions were produced by some remarks from this pious woman, occasioned by the sudden death of a neighbour. He was now thoroughly awakened to a sense of his condition as a sinner, but, after a severe and somewhat protracted inward struggle, he was brought, as he believed, to a cordial compliance with the terms of the Gospel. The great change which then took place in his views and feelings he thus describes :—"While walking alone in the woods one day, there seemed to be a conversation carried on between Christ and my own soul, in which I was led to see the sufficiency of that atonement that had been made, and the condescension and grace of that Saviour who had offered Himself a sacrifice for sin." From this time he went on the Christian course rejoicing; and his path became brighter until it terminated in glory. Shortly after his hopeful conversion, he was baptized by Elder Joseph Cornell,* and united with the Baptist Church in Galway.

My father now felt an irrepressible desire to warn others of the danger from which he had himself escaped; and he seems very soon to have formed the purpose of devoting himself to the ministry. An incident

---

* JOSEPH CORNELL, a son of Elisha Cornell, was born at Swansea, Mass., February 11, 1747, and continued to live with his father until he was about twenty-five years of age. He was then married to Mary Mason, and removed to Lanesborough, Mass., where he settled in business, and remained till the year 1780, when he was ordained to the work of the ministry,— having made a profession of his faith and been baptized some twelve years before. Immediately after his ordination, he removed to Manchester, Vt., then a frontier settlement, where there was a "Baptist Conference," which had invited him to come and labour among them. Shortly after the commencement of his ministry, a church was constituted there, of which he became the first Pastor. After remaining at Manchester about fourteen years, during which many tokens of the Divine favour attended his ministry, he accepted an invitation, in 1794, to take the pastoral charge of the Second Baptist Church in Galway, N. Y., then recently constituted. Here he continued, labouring faithfully and successfully, five years, and then resigned his charge, and commenced a series of missionary labours, under the patronage of the Massachusetts Missionary Society, which he continued for three years,—ranging through Middle and Western New York, and Upper Canada. In 1802, his health having become impaired, he went to Providence, R. I., for the sake of recruiting it. For about a year, he supplied the Congregational Church in that place, then vacant by the death of the Rev. Mr. Snow; and then the Second Baptist Church in Providence being formed, he became its Pastor. After remaining in Providence about ten years, he returned to Galway and resumed his relations with his former charge. Having laboured here about nine years, he engaged again as a missionary, under the Hamilton Baptist Missionary Society, and continued thus employed till his death, which occurred at Galway, on the 26th of July, 1826, in the eightieth year of his age, and the forty-sixth of his ministry. He died without a moment's warning. He was distinguished for a discriminating mind, a sound judgment, an earnest piety, and an effective ministry.

occurred in connection with his beginning to preach that was somewhat illustrative of the spirit of the times. A strong prejudice existed at that time, among the Baptists, against ministerial education; and, as my father was a great lover of books, this was urged as an objection against him, when it was known that he felt called to the work of preaching the Gospel. He had a cousin, (a Mr. M.,) a young man about his own age, who did not love books well enough to incur the displeasure of those even who were the least tolerant of a passion for learning, and who also thought it his duty to preach. A meeting was appointed by the church to hear Mr. M. "improve his gifts," with a view to his being licensed as a preacher. After the usual introductory exercises, Mr. M. named a text—but that was absolutely as far as he could go—the attempt proved an entire failure. To relieve the church from its momentary embarrassment, one of the Deacons inquired if Brother Andrews would not like to speak to them on that occasion. My father consented to do so, took the text which had proved an overmatch for his cousin, and delivered what turned out to be a very acceptable discourse. Whereupon, a meeting was appointed the next week for my father to preach; but, on that occasion, he succeeded but little better than his cousin had done before, finding himself obliged to stop before he had finished the introduction of his sermon. M., in his turn, now took the stand, and made a very successful effort. This so balanced the case as to leave the church just where they began,—in favour of licensing M., and opposed to my father's becoming a preacher, on the ground that he was bent upon being a student. M. became a minister, was useful in his vocation, and lived to a good old age. My father, about this time, left Galway, to visit his parents in Vermont, and on his way called on a minister in Granville, Washington County, who, having heard his story, detained him a few days, and put him to the exercise of his gifts among his people. The result was that, when he was about leaving the place to proceed on his journey, the minister said to him,—"Go, and preach as you go; and I will see that your license is forthcoming in due season."

From this time, he "improved his gifts" wherever Providence opened a door, but was still engaged in teaching and surveying, and he spent at least one season in assisting his father in clearing land, building a log-house, and doing other work incident to commencing on a new farm. Thus his time was occupied from the age of nineteen, when he first attempted to preach, until his ordination as Pastor of the Church in Fairfax, Vt., which occurred in 1793. He was ordained in the open air, in front of a log-house, about two miles north of the spot on which the Baptist meeting-house now stands.

On the 9th of January, 1792, he was married to Wealthy Ann Lathrop, whose parents, like his own, had emigrated from Connecticut to Vermont, just at the close of the War of the Revolution. She was eminently suited to the place she was called to fill. His love of study, his frequent absences from home, and the meagre salary of a Baptist minister at that day, made it quite necessary that his wife should assume much of the care and labour of providing for the family, and that she should practise the utmost economy and industry, both of which she possessed in an eminent degree.

My father continued at Fairfax till the winter of 1795–96, when he removed to Hopkinton, N. H. Here he remained a year or more, and then transferred his residence to Nottingham West, (now Hudson,) in the same State. Early in the year 1800, he accepted an invitation to the pastoral charge of the Baptist Church in Templeton, Mass. Here was the field of his widest as well as most protracted usefulness. At that time, there were but few Baptist churches in the country; and the church of which he now became Pastor was composed of members residing in some twelve or fifteen different towns. For a period of fourteen years, he met regular appointments at Holden, a distance of twenty miles; at Barre, a distance of twelve or fourteen miles; and at Athol, a distance of ten or twelve miles; seldom passing and repassing without appointments for occasional preaching at intermediate stations. He visited Holden each month for fourteen years, never failing but once on account of ill health. In a few instances he was prevented from reaching his destined point by violent storms or deep snows, for which the region about the Wachusett Mountain is proverbial. He was equally regular and punctual, though less frequent, in his visits to Barre and Athol. In most of the towns in which the members of his church originally resided, Baptist churches have since been formed, and in nearly or quite every case, were to be found among the constituent members some who had received Baptism at his hands, and who acknowledged him as the instrument of their conversion. At least twelve churches now exist on the ground over which his pastoral labours extended during the first ten years of his residence in Templeton; and he is still remembered in that whole region as the Apostle of the Baptists.

It would seem, from the very laborious life which my father led, that he would have but little time for the improvement of his mind. But, with such an intense love of knowledge and such facility of acquiring it as he possessed, it seemed as if no obstacle could essentially impede his intellectual progress. It was no uncommon thing for him to be seen, while riding horseback, with a book, perhaps the Greek Testament, in his hand, eagerly devouring its contents. And when he found it necessary to hasten the pace of his steed, he would pocket the book, and would very soon become so absorbed in some subject that was occupying his thoughts, that he would pass a familiar friend without recognizing him, or even being aware that he was meeting any one.

Before his settlement in Templeton, he had acquired so much knowledge of the Greek as to have no difficulty in reading or translating it; though his pronunciation of the language, owing to the fact of his being entirely self-taught, was somewhat defective. Some time after this, he became acquainted with the Rev. Dr. Murdock, then Pastor of the Congregational Church in Princeton, who kindly offered to aid him in the study of the Hebrew. As his duties led him through Princeton frequently, he availed himself of the proffered assistance, and ultimately became a very respectable Hebrew scholar. He acquired so much knowledge of the German also as to read it with great ease. Indeed, his love of books seemed to be without a limit. So regardless did it often render him of surrounding circumstances, that, if, while he was making a pastoral visit, he happened to meet with a book that interested him, he would actually forget that he was not in his own study, and would keep on reading, ignoring all that might be said to him, until either he had finished the book, or was interrupted by something too positive and decided for him to withstand. It was always hard to draw him into conversation when he had an interesting book in hand, except by starting some theological question,· and then he was all ear—his mind was sure to kindle at the introduction of such a topic; and he would with great ease hold the attention of the company until he had given his views of it in a lucid and impressive manner. Indeed, he had great materials for conversation, and great facility at using them. When not absorbed in study, he was cheerful and social—he had a large share of ready wit, and his retentive memory furnished him with a rich fund of anecdote, which he always knew how to employ to the best advantage. But, though he could exercise his wit, and not only enjoy but provoke a hearty laugh at the proper time, he never indulged or tolerated the least departure from a serious and reverent demeanour in the pulpit. There, it was manifest to all who heard him that he was absorbed by the great truths on which he dwelt, and that all his utterances were from a heart deeply impressed with eternal realities.

At the commencement of the War of 1812, my father took sides with the Federalists. This was so rare a thing among the Baptists that it created alienation among his people, and finally led to his dismissal. His Federalism, however, consisted not so much in sympathy with the measures proposed or the principles adopted by that party in general, as in a decided opposition to war. He was an advocate of those principles afterwards embodied in the constitution of the American Peace Society: and these views of war led him to feel that a better way of adjusting existing difficulties with Great Britain might be adopted, and bloodshed avoided. The Church and Society were about equally divided; and, as the excitement was great, and the opposition of some of the leading members of the church very decided, he deemed it expedient to ask for the dissolution of his pastoral relation,—which was, accordingly, granted on the 17th of March, 1813. For the two following years, as the church had no Pastor, and he continued to reside in the place, he preached to them a part of the time, still visiting the towns in the neighbourhood, as he had previously done. This was doubtless the most severe trial of his life. He had no love for excitement or contention, but shrunk from every thing of the kind, as far as duty would allow; though no man stood firmer than he to his own deliberate and conscientious convictions. But, notwithstanding the hostility generated by this state of things was very intense, no sooner had the occasion of it ceased in the closing of the War than the conflicting parties were again at peace. Mutual confessions and forgiveness restored the love of former years; so that my father and his old opposers at Templeton died in the most kindly relations with each other.

In February, 1816, my father removed his family to Hinsdale, N. H. The only church then in that town was a small Baptist church,—a Congregational church, which had previously existed there, having become extinct. The people at large, without regard to sect or party, united in his support. This arrangement continued for several years,—he occupying the old Congregational meeting-house, and the Baptist meeting-house in the North part of the town, in proportion as money was raised North or South. After a few years, however, the Congregational interest revived, and the church was reorganized, and they needed for their own use the meeting-house in the South part of the town ; and, as the Baptist place of worship was remote from his place of residence,—for these and other causes, he ceased to preach in Hinsdale for the time, and commenced travelling and preaching abroad. He had at least three several appointments, from the Massachusetts Baptist Missionary Society, to travel in the new and destitute parts of the State of New York. Probably many Baptists yet live who recollect him as a pioneer missionary in all the region West of Lake Champlain, about 1821 and 1822.

He spent considerable time, during the years 1823 and 1824, among the churches which had sprung up on the field of his former labours, especially those of Princeton and Leominster. In 1825, the church at Templeton gave him a united and earnest invitation to return to them as their Pastor. But, as he had a comfortable home at Hinsdale, and was beginning to feel the weight of years, he declined resuming the pastoral relation to them, though he yielded to their wishes so far as to preach to them half or three quarters of the time, until 1831. During this period, the church at Templeton was favoured with an extensive revival ; and my father was instrumental of gathering a church at South Gardiner, which was a colony from the Templeton Church.

Several of the last years of his active life, he supplied the church at Hinsdale a part of the time. The portion of time not occupied at Templeton was spent at Hinsdale—indeed he was regarded as the senior Pastor of the Hinsdale church till the close of his life. That people were greatly blessed under his ministrations, and numerous individuals rise up there to call him blessed.

In January, 1833, he was attacked with paralysis, which deprived him of the use of his right hand. This was a great affliction, as it not only laid him aside from preaching for several months, but wholly prevented the use of his pen, which he seemed to regard as the greatest of all deprivations. So deeply did he feel the loss of the privilege of writing, that, at the age of sixty-three, he attempted to learn to write with his left hand, and actually succeeded so far as to be able to write legibly. This was, however, hardly accomplished, when, in June, 1834, he had a second shock, which deprived him of the use of his left hand, and so paralyzed his tongue as to make it hard for him to converse. After his first shock, he was able to preach, as the spring opened, and the weather became warm, and actually did supply the church in Royalston for several months. When unable to get into or out of his carriage, he would be helped in, ride sixteen miles, be helped out, and up the pulpit stairs, and would then preach, as those who heard him thought, as well as at any previous period of his life. But after the second attack, he was never able to speak very intelligibly, though his mind remained clear till the last. During the last months of his life, the church had been in the habit of holding their business meetings at his house, as he could not go out, and as their young Pastor wished for the benefit of his counsel. On the Saturday before his death, they held such a meeting, in connection with a preparatory conference at his house, in which he took part. On the Sabbath, they adjourned from the meeting-house to his room to hold their Sacrament. He assisted in the breaking of bread ; gave out the hymn ; pitched the tune ; and sung with the church at the close. But his appearance was such as to lead several, when they departed, to remark,—"Father Andrews has communed with us for the last time on earth." During Monday his health continued as usual, and after tea he related to my mother what he had read in the papers that day, talked about the affairs of the church, in reference especially to some interesting questions that existed among them at that time, and closed by observing that his work was done, and he could give them no more advice. He soon complained of feeling weary, and laid himself down upon the bed, and within an hour passed to his final rest, without a struggle or a groan. He died on the 3d of February, 1840, in the seventy-second year of his age.

During his protracted confinement, he suffered but little bodily pain, but he was so helpless as to be quite dependant on those around him. His mind was always clear—he could reason as strongly on any point of Theology an hour before his death as ever. His passion for books never abated—he read and re-read almost every thing that came within his reach ; and, during his last seven years, he probably accomplished more in this way than most clergymen do in a lifetime.

My father received the Honorary degree of Master of Arts, from Brown University, in 1803.

As a writer, he was known chiefly among those of his own denomination, and as a defender of their faith. He published a small volume entitled " The Moral Tendencies of Universalism ; " also a Review of " Winchester's Dialogues on Universal Restoration." These were followed by a work entitled "A Vindication of the distinguishing sentiments of the Baptists, against the writings of Messrs. Cowles, Miller, and Edwards." These were all issued from the press of Manning and Loring of Boston, as early as 1805. In 1810, he published "A Brief Reply to James Bickerstaff's Short Epistle to the Baptists." At a later period, he put forth two other pamphlets—one, a Review of one of John Wesley's tracts on Falling from Grace, in which he defends the doctrine of the Final Perseverance of the Saints,—the other, Strictures on the Rev. Mr. Brooks' Essay on Terms of Communion. The latter was printed in 1823. He also contributed many articles to the Christian Watchman, chiefly on the Unitarian controversy, over the signature of " Gimel." He had prepared for the press a " Bible Dictionary ; " also a work entitled " *Racovicus*, or the Rational Christian : Dialogues on the Unitarian Controversy ; " but these were not published.

My father's family consisted of eight children,—five sons and three daughters. The eldest son, *Elisha, Jr.*, entered Brown University in 1815, but, in consequence of the failure of his health, was obliged to leave before the close of his Senior year, and did not receive his degree until 1821. Most of his time from 1819, when he left College, till his death, was spent in Louisiana, whither he went with his wife to engage in teaching. He was ordained as an Evangelist, but never settled as a Pastor. His talents, acquirements, and piety gave promise of great usefulness ; but consumption early marked him as a victim. When he left New England, no one expected him ever to return ; but he did live to travel from Louisiana to New England and back several times, and to accomplish a great amount of labour, both as a teacher and an itinerant preacher. He died at Jackson, La., November 10, 1827. Another son, *Thomas L.*, went to Louisiana to assist his brother in an Academy at St. Francisville, in 1819, but subsequently entered the profession of the Law, and continued to be engaged in it, at the South, for many years. A year or two before his death, he removed to Illinois, that he might have the opportunity to manumit several slaves. He had, in his boyhood, been thought to be pious ; but, after he became a man, he believed that his experience had been delusive, and therefore ceased to walk with the church. In the winter of 1844–45, while attending the Court in Louisiana, there was a work of grace in Clinton, his old home, and he became a rejoicing convert, and at once renewed his connection with the church, and resolved to abandon his profession and preach the Gospel. Soon after his return to Illinois his wife died, and in August following he died himself.

Hoping that the above outline of the life of my honoured father may answer the purpose for which you have requested it,

I am very fraternally yours,

ERASTUS ANDREWS.

FROM THE REV. ABIAL FISHER, D. D.

WEST BOYLSTON, Mass., January 27, 1859.

My dear Sir: The Rev. Elisha Andrews was in the vigour of life during the first quarter of the present century; and I may safely say that he had a high standing among the ministers of the Baptist denomination in New England. He was in the enjoyment of good health, and had the capacity for labour and the power of endurance in an uncommon degree. He was of about the middle height, and thick set, without any thing very strongly marked in his personal appearance. I should say that he might be called a grave man, and yet I believe his intimate friends always found him sociable and communicative.

Mr. Andrews had not the advantages of a collegiate education; but he possessed a mind of great natural vigour and inquisitiveness, and neglected no opportunity for enlarging the stock of his knowledge. By diligent and persevering application,—turning every moment to the best account, he made himself well acquainted with the Latin and Greek languages, and more especially with the science of Theology. Though in labours he was more abundant than almost any of his brethren, there were few of them who attained to the same measure of mental culture with himself. Besides performing, with great fidelity, the duties which he owed to his own flock, he was in such repute as a preacher that he was often called to officiate on public occasions abroad; and in this way he became very widely known, and, wherever known, was highly respected. He was as far as possible from any thing like self-display—not only did he never court observation, but he always chose to avoid it as far as would consist with his highest usefulness. His sermons were framed, not to draw forth the admiration, but to promote the spiritual growth, the enduring, substantial benefit, of his hearers. I heard him preach for the first time at an Association about fifty years ago, and he managed his subject with a master's hand; and, notwithstanding the long period that has since elapsed, so distinct, well digested and striking were his thoughts, that many of them remain vividly in my mind to this day. It was a marked characteristic of his preaching that it supplied a great deal of material for reflection. His dis-

courses were highly logical in their structure, and deeply serious and evangelical in their tone; and neither the head nor the heart of the attentive hearer
could fail to be benefitted by them. His published works show that his mind
was decidedly of a high order, and some of them very·happily evince his fine
talent for argumentation. He had great influence throughout the whole region
in which he lived; and, though almost twenty years have passed since he went
to his grave, his memory is still fragrant in many hearts.

Yours fraternally,
ABIAL FISHER.

FROM THE REV. JOHN M. GRAVES.

Boston, January 1, 1859.

Dear Sir: My earliest impressions in relation to the late Rev. Elisha Andrews
were those of very high respect. I was then a youth in my teens—I had great
regard for religion and its ministers, and I looked upon him as the very embodi-
ment of goodness and sanctity. After I entered the ministry, I became somewhat familiarly acquainted with him, and my respect now ripened into
reverence and love. He was, I should think, at that time, in the prime of life.
He never seemed to care much about his dress, or personal appearance, or even
the conventional rules of social life. Without any thing of studied refinement, he had still a natural ease and grace that made him sufficiently at home
in any circle. He was not prodigal of words, but he used them with great
care, and often with great power. Nothing ever escaped his lips that involved
the slightest departure from truth, or justice, or delicacy. He had the reputation of being a rigid disciplinarian in his family; but his discipline was
administered, not with harsh words, but with the utmost calmness and consideration, and not unfrequently with tears.

Mr. Andrews was thoroughly grounded in the great truths of the Gospel,
and was always ready for their illustration and defence. He had evidently a
great love for the pulpit, as he had excellent natural and acquired qualifications for it. His manner was free from the least tendency to extravagance—it
was calm and self-possessed, while yet there was a simple earnestness about it
that left no one in doubt that he was speaking from his inmost convictions.
He aimed to accomplish the great end of the ministry, not so much by exhortation or pathetic appeal as by bringing God's truth home to the understanding and conscience in all its life, and power, and legitimate relations, though he
sometimes became so much affected by the tender and solemn thoughts which
he was endeavouring to impress on others, that his emotions would become
well-nigh overwhelming. I remember one instance in particular when, with
his usually mild, calm utterance, he portrayed the sufferings of the Saviour,—
the tears flowing down his cheeks most freely, but no sign of faltering either
in his voice or manner. Whenever he addressed men on the great concern of
their salvation, he seemed to forget every thing else in the all-absorbing desire
that his words might go with a Divine power to the heart. It seemed to me as if
his thoughts were always dwelling upon some evangelical theme; and when he
felt that he had, in some good degree, mastered it, it was his highest delight
to bring it in contact with the minds of others.

The great object of Mr. Andrews' ministry evidently was, not so much to
excite as to instruct—he thought it much more important to sow the good seed
of the Kingdom in good soil, than to sway with his breath the stocks and plants
before him. I have no doubt that much of the seed which he sowed with so
much skill and fidelity, has sprung up, under the culture of others, and is
now bearing fruit.

I am truly yours,
JOHN M. GRAVES.

JOHN TRIPP.*
1787—1847.

JOHN TRIPP was born in Dartmouth, (now Fairhaven,) Mass., March 25, 1761. He is supposed to have been a descendant, on his father's side, from John Tripp, an associate of Roger Williams, and an assistant in the government of Rhode Island. His mother was a daughter of Capt. Jethro Delano, and granddaughter of the Delano who was active in King Philip's War. When he was eight years old, his parents removed to Rochester, adjoining Fairhaven; and, at the age of sixteen, he entered the military service for one month, and spent the time at Narragansett. For several years, he followed the coasting trade, in small vessels, between Massachusetts and Connecticut, and was several times chased, and once or twice near being captured, by British ships of war.

He early evinced a love of learning, amounting almost to a passion, but he had little opportunity to gratify it. In the summer of 1782, being then twenty-one years of age, he resided for six weeks in the family of the Rev. Dr. Samuel West, the Congregational minister of Dartmouth, and, having here acquired some knowledge of English Grammar, he engaged, shortly after, in teaching a school on Martha's Vineyard. While he was thus occupied, he divided whatever leisure he could command between studying human science and the Scriptures. By his own efforts and the assistance of friends, he procured some Latin and Greek books, and commenced the study of those languages.

On the 2d of September, 1784, he was married to Jedidah, daughter of Harlock Smith, of Edgarton, with whom he lived, in great affection, upwards of fifty years. She died in May, 1835.

After his marriage, he had better opportunities for the cultivation of his mind, which he diligently improved by studying not only the languages, but almost every branch that belongs to a course of liberal education. These studies he pursued, in after years, in connection with the labours of the ministry.

At the age of about eleven, he became deeply interested in the subject of religion, as a personal matter, but he suffered not a little for the want of adequate religious instruction. After struggling with many difficulties for some time, his mind seemed to repose joyfully in the provisions of the Gospel, as far as he understood them, and, two years after, when he was about thirteen, he was baptized by the Rev. Ebenezer Hinds,† of Middleborough, and admitted to the Church. For several years after this, he seems to have had little Christian enjoyment, owing. as he himself states, to his being too prone to compromise his Christian obligations in his intercourse with the world. The celebrated dark day that occurred in May, 1780, was

* Zion's Advocate, 1847.—Christian Review, 1849.
† EBENEZER HINDS began to preach stately at Middleborough in 1756, and became the Pastor of the church there about a year after. He continued in this relation not far from forty years, and died at Cape Cod about the year 1812, at the age of ninety. He retained his mental and bodily powers in a remarkable degree. But two or three years before his death, he was accustomed to take long journeys on horseback, visiting his friends, and often preaching in the places where they lived.

the occasion of awakening him to a sense of his spiritual declension, and of recovering him ultimately to the more faithful discharge of his duty.

Soon after he made a profession of his faith, his mind was much exercised on the subject of devoting his life to the preaching of the Gospel; but the purpose, if he had gone so far as to form it, was suffered to slumber during the years of coldness and wandering that succeeded. But, after he had experienced the quickening already referred to, the idea of becoming a minister of the Gospel revived in his mind, and his studies from this time received a corresponding direction. While he resided on Martha's Vineyard, there was a Baptist Church there, which was destitute of stated preaching; and he volunteered such efforts as he was able to make to supply the deficiency. At length, in September, 1787, he accepted an invitation from the Pastor of the Third Baptist Church in Middleborough to preach in his pulpit; and here, properly speaking, commenced his ministry.

He remained on Martha's Vineyard until the next season after he was licensed, and then visited a new Society in Carver, and in December, 1788, removed to that place. The Church in Carver was organized in July, 1791, and he was ordained as its Pastor in September of the same year.

During the earlier years of his ministry, his preaching was attended with little visible success, in consequence of which his mind was deeply and painfully exercised. About 1793, the desire of his heart was granted in an extensive revival in connection with his labours, that in a short time increased the membership of his church from fifteen to fifty.

During his residence at Carver, he was greatly straitened for the means of support, and sometimes found it difficult to obtain even the necessaries of life. He had, in the mean time, invitations to several more eligible places, but he declined them from a full conviction that the church of which he had the care would suffer by his removal. But his health at length began to decline under the heavy burdens that were imposed upon him, and he found it necessary to intermit his labours. As there was no prospect of any improvement in his worldly circumstances, while he remained at Carver, he concluded to remove to Middleborough, where he had previously preached a part of the time. Here he was somewhat better cared for, though what he received was by no means adequate to the wants of a rising family. Hence, in June, 1797, he journeyed into Maine, partly to visit his wife's parents, who had removed to New Sharon, and partly to look for a place of settlement. In September of that year, after he had returned from his journey, he received an invitation from the Church in Hebron, Me., to become their Pastor. This invitation he thought it his duty to accept, though the separation from his people was an occasion of deep mutual regret. He left Middleborough on the 27th of June, 1798, and reached Hebron on the 3d of the next month, being then thirty-seven years of age.

Mr. Tripp's labours in this new field were intense and manifold, and though there was not much fruit immediately apparent, yet, at no very distant period, he began to have the evidence that his labours were not in vain. The years 1802, 1808, 1817, 1824, 1830, 1831–32, and 1839, were specially favoured as seasons of refreshing among his people. During this whole period he was, from time to time, performing missionary tours, not only in different parts of Maine, but in New Hampshire and Vermont; and he performed an amount of service in this way which it is not easy to estimate.

In 1840, Mr. Tripp, having become too infirm to perform all the duties of the Pastorate, was relieved by the settlement of a colleague. He continued to preach, however, one-half or one-fourth of the time while he lived. Indeed, for the last year of his life, he was the only Pastor. During the winter of 1846–47, he was kept at home chiefly by his inability to endure the cold, but in April he began to preach again, and preached nearly every Sabbath until July. He died on Thursday evening, September 16, 1847, after an illness of two or three weeks, aged eighty-six and a half years. His end was eminently peaceful. His Funeral was attended on the Sabbath following, when a Discourse appropriate to the occasion was preached by the Rev. Dr. Adam Wilson.

Mr. Tripp published a Tract on Baptism, a Discourse on the Inspiration of the Scriptures, one on the Perseverance of the Saints, one on the Two Witnesses mentioned in Revelation, and several other Sermons, and a small volume against Universalism.

Mr. Tripp was the father of eight children,—five sons and three daughters. Two of the sons graduated at Waterville College, and are Baptist ministers.

FROM THE REV. ADAM WILSON, D. D.

WATERVILLE, March 15, 1859.

My dear Sir: I could have wished that it had fallen to the lot of some one more competent than myself, to perform the service you have requested of me, and yet such recollections as I am able to command of the venerable man of whom you have asked me to write, I cheerfully put at your disposal.

In the spring of 1815, I became a student at Hebron Academy, and an attendant on the ministry of Mr. Tripp, who was then about fifty-four years old. With a slender physical constitution and a feeble voice, he was still able so to meet the wants of the whole community that no other meeting was held in that vicinity. About ten years before that time, Hebron Academy had been chartered and endowed by the Legislature of Massachusetts. Mr. Tripp had been the firm friend of the institution from its origin. He was able to read the New Testament in the original, and he had science enough to create a keen taste for such studies. He loved the society and conversation of literary men. His improvements were such as to secure for him, somewhat late in life, the degree of Master of Arts from Waterville College.

Mr. Tripp gave his time and strength to the work of the ministry, and looked to his people, under Providence, for his daily bread. His course in this respect differed from that of most Baptist ministers in this vicinity. One of his contemporaries and intimate associates in the ministry, who had owned and cultivated a farm, said, near the close of his life,—"If I had my life to live over again, I would do less for my own support, and would depend more upon my people. Brother Tripp, in this matter, has taken the wise course."

A prominent feature of Mr. Tripp's preaching was care to give the true meaning of his text. It was evident that he had carefully considered what ideas in relation to his text were already in the minds of his people. When he found occasion to displace their ideas by those of a sounder interpretation, he proceeded with so much caution, and candour, and kindness, that he seldom failed of accomplishing his object. A sermon preached in 1816 may be taken as a specimen of this care and success. The text was Math. xxi. 44—" Whosoever shall fall on this stone, shall be broken; but, on whomsoever it shall fall, it will grind him to powder." Many of his people had been accustomed to understand the first part of this text to mean,—" Whoever, conscious of his sin and ruin, shall fall, poor and helpless, on Christ, shall be broken in heart, and broken off from sin, and so shall become a new creature in Christ. Mr. Tripp regarded the sentiment thus educed from this passage as true and very important. But he thought it was not taught in the text. He understood this part of the text to refer to persons who mistake their way. Many are in criminal darkness, and so stumble at that great "stone of stumbling and rock of offence." The closing part of his text he applied to persecutors, admonishing them that if they persevere in their hopeless work, they will arouse "the wrath of the Lamb," and then "He will grind them to powder."

The effect of Mr. Tripp's preaching upon the minds of his hearers soon became apparent. When he first came to Hebron, some of his people were inclined to Dr. Gill's views of the atonement. His own views were nearly the same with those of Andrew Fuller. Though he never disguised or withheld them, he uniformly presented them with so much prudence and kindness, and so fortified them by the testimonies of Scripture, that the opposite doctrine gradually died out of his church; and even while it lingered in the minds of a few of the older members, it was never brought out in any way to disturb the peace of the church.

It was a remark of the late Dr. Payson, of Portland, that the primitive preachers of Christianity seem to have succeeded better than modern ministers in convincing the world of their sincerity. In this respect Mr. Tripp may be classed with primitive preachers. Men often opposed the doctrines he preached, but seldom called in question the sincerity of the preacher. In the whole town where he laboured for so many years, it might be difficult to find two men, who would venture a doubt as to his believing what he professed. And what is still more remarkable,—it was very much so while he was living. The careless, the caviller, the skeptic, the worldling, would all say,—" We do not doubt he is sincere in his work."

It is a remark that most persons may verify by their own experience, that we sometimes feel an interest in a sermon while we are hearing it, but when it is closed, its influence soon passes away. It is very much so with the whole ministry of some men. While they are living, they seem to exert an influence; but they leave behind them no marks on the community in which they have laboured. But the influence of the first Pastor of the Church in Hebron was of an abiding nature. Perhaps the reason was, because he made Christ so prominent in his ministry. He preached Christ, in all his fulness and glory, as the way, the truth and the life.

Mr. Tripp was an occasional correspondent of Zion's Advocate, through a period of eighteen years. And his articles always breathed a truly benevolent spirit, and an earnest desire to promote the cause of Christ. He was a friend to humanity—yet he was not impracticable in his efforts to do good. The possible, the attainable, was what he sought. The one great purpose of his life was to serve Christ and do good to mankind. In pursuing this object, under the guidance of his Divine Master, he put in motion influences that are still in benign operation, and will continue to be so for generations to come.

Very truly yours,
ADAM WILSON.

HENRY SMALLEY.*
1788—1839.

HENRY SMALLEY was born in Piscataway, Middlesex County, N. J., on the 23d of October, 1765. His father was a Baptist, and his mother an Episcopalian. He was the subject of religious impressions in early life, and, at the age of about sixteen, was admitted by Baptism to the communion of the Piscataway Baptist Church, by the Rev. Reune Runyon.† He resolved, contrary to the prevailing usage of his denomination at that period, to acquire a collegiate education, with a view to entering the ministry; and, accordingly, after the requisite preparation, he became a member of Queen's College, New Brunswick. Subsequently, however, he transferred his relation to the College of New Jersey, at Princeton, where he graduated under the Presidency of Dr. Witherspoon, in 1786.

In 1788, having, in the mean time, accomplished his immediate preparation for the ministry, he was licensed to preach the Gospel by the Piscataway Baptist Church. In 1790, he began to preach for the Cohansey Baptist Church, Cumberland County, N. J.; and, on the 8th of November of the same year, was ordained Pastor of that church by the Rev. Dr. Samuel Jones, and the Rev. Mr. Miller, an aged itinerant Baptist minister. In this charge he continued forty-nine years,—until he was removed by death.

In 1794, Mr. Smalley was married to Hannah Fox,—an amiable, pious and intelligent person, who proved herself every way qualified for the station to which she was introduced. She died on the 11th of February, 1836; and, about two years after, he was married to Mrs. Elizabeth Armstrong, an excellent woman, whose tender ministrations soothed his last hours.

Mr. Smalley's ministry was, on the whole, a highly prosperous one. He baptized five hundred and thirty persons, who were admitted to the communion of his own Church, besides a considerable number who connected themselves with other Baptist Churches in the neighbourhood, which were destitute of stated Pastors. While the growth of his church was, for the most part, gradual, there were several revivals which brought considerable accessions to it, the largest numbers being fifty-four, fifty-five, and fifty-seven.

The labours of Mr. Smalley were numerous and various. Besides his stated preaching, attending the weekly prayer meetings, and his pastoral visitations, he had frequent catechetical exercises for the children, youth,

---

* Bapt. Mem. V.

† REUNE RUNYON was of French extraction,—the son of a gentleman of the same name, and was born at Piscataway, March 29, 1741; was called to the ministry in the church in his native place, in March, 1771; was ordained at Morristown in March, 1772, where he continued till April 13, 1780, and then returned to Piscataway. In 1783, he took the pastoral charge of the church there, in which relation he continued till his death, which occurred, after a lingering illness, on the 21st of November, 1811. He was a highly acceptable and useful minister. Morgan Edwards, in his Materials for a History of the Baptists of New York, pays him this rather equivocal compliment:—"He is remarkable for dexterity in administering Baptism—On June 30, 1786, a gentleman held his watch in his hand, till he had baptized thirty in fifty-eight minutes."

and even persons of mature years, in his congregation. For this purpose, in addition to their local meetings, they assembled once a quarter in the meeting-house. But he had a vigorous constitution, and his health continued adequate to his manifold labours, until about the time of the death of his first wife,—an affliction which he felt most deeply, and from the effect of which he never fully recovered.

On the occasion of last meeting his people for Divine worship, he stated to them distinctly that his voice would never again be heard within the walls of their common earthly sanctuary; and this proved a prophetic announcement. From that time, his bodily infirmities greatly increased. His mind, which, during nearly the whole of his Christian life, had been eminently clear and peaceful, now became shrouded in darkness. For a season, he was tempted to believe that his Heavenly Father had forsaken him. But, at length, deliverance came; and, for a week before his death, he dwelt constantly upon the Mount. Having gathered his family around him, and exhorted them to put their trust in their Redeemer, he bade them farewell. His death occurred on the 11th of February, 1839, in the seventy-fourth year of his age.

FROM THE REV. G. S. WEBB, D. D.

New Brunswick, N. J., April 10, 1858.

My dear Sir: I came into this State to labour in 1821, and soon afterwards made the acquaintance of the Rev. Mr. Smalley, who was then past the meridian of life. But, as we were a hundred miles apart, our intercourse was not frequent, nor my opportunities of forming a judgment of his character such as to render me a very competent witness concerning him. What I do know I cheerfully communicate, especially as his contemporaries have so nearly all passed away, that I should be at a loss to whom to refer you for more ample information.

Mr. Smalley was of medium height; rather stout, compact, firm, but not corpulent; and altogether fitted for great endurance. His hair and eyes were dark, and his countenance remarkably grave. His whole appearance was eminently befitting his character as an ambassador of God.

I think I never heard him preach but twice. His manner in the pulpit was calm, deliberate, solemn; more in the style of the compassionate judge pronouncing sentence against the culprit, than of the popular orator. He was not one of that class of preachers who would be likely to be run after by the multitude, though he would be listened to with much interest by the intelligent and reflecting. No one could hear him without being impressed with the idea that his heart went into all his utterances, and no one could hear him with attention without being convinced that he was "a scribe well instructed," "rightly dividing the word of truth."

Mr. Smalley had the reputation of being an excellent Pastor, and of enjoying in a high degree the affection and confidence of his people. He had an admirable facility at preserving harmony in his congregation, and of nipping in the bud every thing like strife or discord. His influence over his people was so silent and unostentatious that they scarcely knew that it was exerted at all, and yet it was decided and powerful. And it was felt, too, much beyond the bounds of his immediate charge. His excellent judgment and eminently peace-making spirit were often put in requisition to settle difficulties in other congregations; and the same qualities rendered him an exceedingly useful member of deliberative bodies.

I am inclined to regard Mr. Smalley as having belonged to a class of minis
ters, who are rarely appreciated, especially by their contemporaries, according to their deserts. He was sound in the faith, in charity, in patience; a
pattern of good works; never in haste, and yet never faltering; like the diligent husbandman, rising early and retiring late, sowing his seed beside all
waters, and leaving at the end of his days many broad acres well cultivated,—
a good inheritance to those who come after him.

Your brother in our common Lord,
G. S. WEBB.

JESSE MERCER, D D.*

1788—1841.

The paternal great-grandfather of Jesse Mercer, emigrated from Scotland to Virginia, about the close of the seventeenth century. His son, the
grandfather of Jesse, removed from Virginia to North Carolina, and
thence to what is now Wilkes County, Ga. Silas, the father of Jesse,
was born in North Carolina, February, 1745. He was educated in the
Episcopal Church, and was taught to regard its Liturgy and forms with
the utmost reverence ; but, as he grew up, his mind underwent a gradual
change, and finally reposed in the system of doctrine and discipline held
by the Baptists. He was immersed in the year 1775 ; and, before he left
the stream, ascended a log, and delivered an exhortation to the spectators.
Shortly after this, he received a formal license to preach. When the Revolutionary War came on, he fled for safety to Halifax County in his native
State ; and, during a six years' residence there, he preached upon an average
oftener than once a day. At the close of the War, he returned to his
former residence in Georgia, where he continued his pious and useful
labours during the rest of his life. He died in the fifty-second year of his
age. Besides several smaller pieces, he wrote a pamphlet of sixty-eight
pages, entitled "Tyranny exposed, and True Liberty discovered."

JESSE MERCER was born in Halifax County, N. C., December 16, 1769,
being the eldest of eight children. He was a remarkably bright, amiable
and conscientious boy ; and, though he showed a good deal of quiet humour,
and was very far from manifesting the spirit of a recluse, he had no relish
for anything coarse, or boisterous, or irreverent. His early opportunities
for education were very limited ; and it is doubtful whether he had ever
been sent to school, previous to the return of his father to Georgia from
North Carolina. From early childhood, he was the subject of serious
impressions ; and, from the age of about fourteen or fifteen till he had
reached his eighteenth year, there was no intermission of his anxiety in
respect to his salvation. Of the change which at length passed upon him,
he has left the following account :—

"While on the verge of despair, I was walking alone along a narrow path in the
woods, poring over my helpless case, and saying to myself—Wo is me ! Wo, wo is me !
for I am undone forever! I would I were a beast of the field ! At length, I found

* Mem. by Dr. Mallary.

myself standing, with my eyes steadfastly fixed on a small oak that grew by the path-side, and earnestly wishing that I could be like the little oak when it died and crumbled to dust. At that moment, light broke into my soul, and I believed in Christ for myself, and not another, and went on my way rejoicing."

He made a relation of his experience to the Phillips' Mill Church, on the 7th of July, 1787, and was immediately after baptized by his father, being then in his eighteenth year.

Shortly after he connected himself with the church, he began to feel an earnest desire to address his fellow-men in respect to their immortal interests; and his first efforts in this way, which were of an hortatory kind, were characterized by so much judgment and feeling as to give promise, in the view of those who witnessed them, of extensive usefulness in the Church. He soon began to preach, and, though the exact time when he received a formal license cannot now be ascertained, yet it is known that he preached to great acceptance, and had the entire approbation of his brethren generally.

On the 31st of January, 1788, being then in his nineteenth year, he was married to Sabrina, daughter of Joel Chivers, and, at the time of their marriage, step-daughter of Oftnial Weaver, of Wilkes County. Though she was poor in this world's goods, she was distinguished for prudence, industry, and piety, and was every way fitted to be a helper to him in his work. Such a helper she proved to be during a period of nearly forty years.

On the 7th of November, 1789, he was solemnly set apart by ordination to the work of the ministry, his father being one of the officiating ministers; and, notwithstanding his extreme youth, he received a call about the same time to take the pastoral charge of the church called Hutton's Fork, (now Sardis,) in Wilkes County. He accepted the call, and continued there in the faithful discharge of his duties, more than twenty years. He was now very diligent in the cultivation of his mind, and availed himself of an opportunity to study the learned languages, under the instruction of the Rev. Mr. Springer, a Presbyterian clergyman, with whom he formed an intimate and enduring friendship. He subsequently prosecuted his studies still further at an Academy that was established in his father's neighbourhood, whither he returned after an absence of two years, in order to avail himself of its advantages. His academic course, after all, was rather limited, though it laid a foundation for more extended improvements in after life.

In 1793, the field of Mr. Mercer's labours was enlarged by his acceptance of the Pastorship of the Church at Indian Creek, (or Bethany,) in Oglethorpe County, to the vicinity of which he removed in the ensuing winter. But, in 1796, his father having died in August of that year, he returned to the place where his father had resided, for the purpose of administering on the estate, and otherwise assisting the bereaved family. At the same time, he became the Preceptor of the Salem Academy. He also succeeded his father in the charge of the Phillips' Mill, Powelton, and Bethesda Churches, to all of which he was highly acceptable. He continued at his father's place for several years, until he had settled the business of the estate; and then removed to the Fork of the Little River in Green County, where he settled on a small farm, which, however, he did not allow to interfere with his ministerial duties. About this time, he directed the studies of several young men in their preparation for the ministry; but his services in this way were rendered gratuitously.

The field occupied by Mr. Mercer between the years 1796 and 1827 was one of the most important in the State of Georgia,—the churches which he served being in the midst of a dense population, and embracing a considerable amount of intelligence and refinement. The Sardis Church, originally called Hutton's Fork,—the first of which he had the charge, he left in 1817. With the Phillips' Mill Church he retained his connection till 1835; with the church at Bethesda until 1827; and with the Powelton church till 1826. Of this latter church Governor Rabun was, for many years, a distinguished member. In 1818, a church was constituted in Eatonton, Putnam County, of which Mr. Mercer took charge in January, 1820, and continued its Pastor till the close of 1826. In 1824, the Baptist State Convention (then denominated the General Association) held its sessions at Eatonton, on which occasion Mr. Mercer preached a Missionary Sermon, that was followed by a very liberal collection from the congregation. His connection with these several churches was the means of quickening them to a higher sense of Christian obligation, of building them up in faith and holiness, and, in nearly every case, of adding largely to their numbers. In addition to his stated labours, he performed much occasional service in other places, and rarely, if ever, made a journey, which he did not render directly subservient to the general interests of religion and the prosperity of some particular church. One means of usefulness which he highly valued, was keeping on hand an assortment of religious books, which he carried with him on his numerous preaching tours, and disposed of among his brethren, as he had opportunity.

Finding a great want of Hymn Books for the use of the rapidly increasing churches, he compiled a small work called "The Cluster." It had passed through three editions before 1817, and has been published several times since. It has had a wide circulation in Georgia, and several of the adjacent States.

Mr. Mercer took a deep interest in the civil affairs of the country, and did not hesitate to speak, or write, or act, in relation to them, as he thought his duty required; though he never suffered himself to be entangled in the strife of politics. In 1798, he was a member of the Convention which was held to amend the State Constitution. About the year 1816, he was a candidate for the office of Senator in the State Legislature; but, fortunately, (as he himself afterwards thought,) was unsuccessful. In 1833, it was proposed by some of his friends that he should be brought forward as a candidate for Governor; and he was subsequently named as a suitable person to be chosen one of the Presidential Electors; but, in each case, he peremptorily declined the honour. In the year last named, certain amendments to the State Constitution had been agreed upon by a Convention appointed by the Legislature, and were submitted to the people for approval or rejection. Mr. Mercer, being greatly dissatisfied with the amendments, published the reasons of his dissent from them, for which he was censured with some degree of severity. He, however, justified himself on the ground of a strong conviction of duty; and maintained that, though a minister has no right to meddle with the every day politics of the country, he *has* a right to be heard on great constitutional questions as truly as any other man.

In 1826, Mr. Mercer attended the General Convention in Philadelphia, and did not return till the month of September. When he had reached Andersonville, Pendleton District, S. C., his wife, who accompanied him, was seized with a violent fever, and died after a few days' confinement, in the fifty-fifth year of her age. Though he felt the loss most deeply, he submitted to it with an humble and trusting resignation. She was the mother of two children.

At the close of 1826, or early in 1827, Mr. Mercer took up his residence in Washington, Wilkes County, under circumstances highly creditable to his disinterestedness. When he had determined to give up most of the churches with which he was connected, and provide for himself a more settled residence, he was earnestly requested, by a committee appointed for the purpose, to make his permanent settlement among the people at Powelton, and assured that competent provision should be made for his support. But, notwithstanding his worldly interest, and especially his strong personal attachments, would have inclined him to listen to their proposal, so strong was his conviction that there was an important work which he was called to perform in Washington, that he felt constrained to return a negative answer to the Powelton brethren, and to plant himself in what seemed in many respects the more unpromising field. He had, for nearly forty years, been in the habit of preaching at Washington, generally on week days, about once a month. There were a few scattered Baptists in the village and the surrounding country; but not enough to justify the organization of a church, until 1827. At the close of that year, a church was constituted, and in January, 1828, Mr. Mercer became its Pastor. He continued in this relation till the close of life. The church grew rapidly in numbers, liberality, and zeal, under his ministry, until it became, in proportion to its numerical strength, one of the most effective churches in the State.

On the 11th of December, 1827, Mr. Mercer was united in marriage to Mrs. Nancy Simmons, widow of Capt. A. Simmons, and then residing in Washington. By this marriage he obtained a considerable addition to his worldly property, while he gained a companion of great Christian liberality and worth, and every way suited to be a fellow-helper in carrying out the objects for which he lived.

In 1833, the Christian Index, a religious periodical, which had for some years been edited by the Rev. W. T. Brantly, at Philadelphia, was transferred to Mr. Mercer. This brought him into a new sphere of labour and responsibility, and occasioned him considerable pecuniary loss; while he felt himself less at home than in almost any other position he had occupied. Though his habits were not decidedly literary, and he could scarcely be considered a highly accomplished writer, he conducted the work with excellent judgment, and rendered it specially useful as a means of defending and sustaining the benevolent operations of the day.

In 1835, he was honoured with the degree of Doctor of Divinity, from Brown University.

For a long series of years, his name and influence were identified with most of the prominent operations of the Georgia Association. He was present at its formation in 1784; shortly after his connection with the Church, he appeared as its delegate; and, from that time till 1839, when he was prevented by illness, he never failed to be present at its annual meetings. From 1795 till 1816, he generally officiated as Clerk of the Body—at the session of the last named year, he was chosen Moderator, and held the office, by re-election, till 1839.

He had an important connection with another Association of a more general character, known as the "Baptist Convention of the State of Georgia;" which, from a small beginning in 1822, gradually grew into a great benevolent institution, which has accomplished, in various ways, a mighty amount of good. Of this Convention Dr. Mercer was regularly chosen Moderator, till the session of 1841, when his impaired health and domestic afflictions prevented his attendance.

Dr. Mercer lost no opportunity of manifesting his interest in the cause of education. When the project of establishing a College in the District of Columbia was first started, he was disposed to give to it all his influence. His name was enrolled among the original Trustees of the institution; and, amidst its protracted embarrassments, his zeal for the promotion of its interests never faltered. In 1834, he delivered a Sermon before the Convention, entitled "Knowledge indispensable to a minister of God," which contained a vigorous argument in favour of an educated ministry, and which was afterwards published and extensively circulated.

He was no less devoted to the cause of Missions than of Education. In May, 1815, when the "Powelton Baptist Society for Foreign Missions" was formed, he became its President. In 1816, was formed "The Mission Board of the Georgia Association," of which Dr. Mercer was always a member, and, from 1830 to 1841, was uniformly its President. His pecuniary contributions to missionary objects were regulated by a high standard of Christian liberality.

Though he was occasionally the subject of bodily infirmity, yet, during his long ministry, he was rarely obliged to suspend his labours for any considerable time. But, at length, neither he nor his friends could resist the conviction that the infirmities of age were gathering upon him. At the annual session of the Georgia Association in 1839, he was prevented from being present by a severe illness; and, though he was able, after a few weeks, to resume, in some degree, his accustomed labours, he never afterwards recovered the point of health from which he had fallen. In May, 1841, he was afflicted by the death of his wife, who had some time before been stricken down by palsy. Early in June following, he preached his last sermon, with uncommon freedom and unction. Towards the close of the month, he went, in great feebleness, to Penfield, with a view of spending a few weeks with his friends, and attending the College Commencement, and the annual meeting of the Board of Trustees. He remained in Penfield till the beginning of August, and then journeyed on to the Indian Springs in Butts County, hoping to derive some benefit from the water. For a few days, there seemed to be some slight improvement of his health, but the force of his disease remained unbroken. On the last

Sabbath in August, he attended public service at the Springs, and, in the evening of the same day, accompanied a friend to his residence, some eight miles distant, with an intention of prosecuting his journey as far as Walton, Monroe County, where some of his relatives resided. It turned out that he went to the house of this friend (Mr. Carter, a brother minister) to die. He languished till the 6th of September, and then, in a state of perfect calmness, and in full possession of his reason, sunk into the arms of death. His remains were taken to Penfield, and interred in the public burying ground. The Funeral Sermon was preached at Washington, by Elder C. F. Sturgis, who had, for a time, been associated with him in the pastoral charge of the church. His death called forth many public demonstrations of affectionate respect and deep sorrow.

The following is a list of Dr. Mercer's principal writings:—A Circular Letter of the Georgia Association, 1801. A Circular Letter on Discipline, 1806. A Circular Letter on the Invalidity of Pedobaptist Administration of Ordinances, 1811. A Circular Letter on Various Christian Duties, 1816. A Discourse on the Death of Governor Rabun, 1819. A Circular of the Georgia Association, on the Unity and Dependance of the Churches, 1822. An Exposition of the First Seventeen Verses of the Twelfth Chapter of Revelation, 1825. A Dissertation on the Prerequisites to Ordination, 1829. Scripture Meaning of Ordination, 1830. Ten Letters on the Atonement, 1830. A Circular Letter of the Baptist State Convention, 1831. Resemblances and Differences between Church Authority and that of an Association, 1833. An Essay on the Lord's Supper, 1833. A Sermon entitled "Knowledge indispensable to a Minister of God," 1834. A History of the Georgia Association, 1836. A Review of a certain Report on Church and Associational Difficulties, 1837. A Sermon on the Importance of Ministerial Union, 1838. A Sermon on the Excellency of the Knowledge of Christ, 1839. An Essay entitled "The Cause of Missionary Societies, the Cause of God," 1839. An Essay on Forgiveness of Sins, 1841. "Hear what the Spirit saith to the Churches," three Nos., 1841.

FROM THE REV. ADIEL SHERWOOD, D. D.

Cape Girardeau, Mo., June 8, 1858.

My dear Sir: My acquaintance with Dr. Mercer began in February, 1819, and our interviews, lasting three and four days generally at Associations, meetings of the Executive Committee of the State Convention, and others of a religious character, were some six to a dozen in almost every year till 1841,—a period of over twenty years. We frequently lodged at the same house, and occupied the same bed. We also made long tours of preaching together, and in 1823 visited the Mission Station at Valley Towns, N. C.,—absent over a month. He wrote me over fifty letters. So far as I recollect, we never disagreed on the subjects discussed in our religious bodies, except that he regarded me *too zealous* in urging incipient measures towards the University which now bears his name, and on the Temperance question. The Doctors, excellent in administering calomel, had advised him to take a little brandy for a chronic complaint, and, though he took very small doses occasionally, was so conscientious that he would not subscribe to the pledge, yet really a friend to the cause. But he threw their prescriptions overboard,—was in better health, and established a Temperance paper.

In his youth he was tall, slender and awkward, but when about fifty was moderately corpulent, weighing over two hundred pounds, having, by much intercourse with society, softened the manners contracted in border neighbourhoods and in times of war. There was something commanding in his appearance. When in the pulpit, arguing some favourite point, he was truly dignified; for he was at home, and seemed like a king on his throne. Mingling with the people, his bearing was marked by kindliness on his part, and by great respect on that of those around him. You felt that you were in the presence of a great man. Some men of intellect, and some of mere wealth, regard themselves as a head and shoulders above all others—not so Jesse Mercer: he seemed not aware of any superiority. He had no tact nor taste for popular favour, though he was a useful member of the Convention which revised the Constitution in '98. He was urged to be a candidate for Governor, but would not listen to the proposal, regarding the ministerial office more honourable than that of President of the United States.

The prominent trait in his pulpit performances was *originality*—originating thoughts of weighty import in his own way, that made an indelible impression,—an impression that continues to this day, after the lapse of so many years: not quaint and odd, but full of force and power, and sometimes with great eloquence. He did not understand the Logic of the Schools, but he went behind their rules, and not unfrequently convinced and overpowered by his new views and ponderous arguments. His *manner* was not graceful but forcible. But you forgot his manner in the rich intellectual feast served up for you, as does the hungry man the oaken table or trencher that holds his meal. In some of his rich discourses, you conceived of a boy from an eminence throwing large bars of gold all around, without much regularity or order; but they fell with power because of their intrinsic weight.

He used to lament over his poor qualifications as a Pastor in his visits: he could not suggest topics for discourse, and so carry on conversation as to render his calls agreeable and useful.

There was great punctuality in meeting his appointments, and in his engagements in secular concerns. He refused to aid in ordaining men who were involved in debt, regarding it as an obstacle in the path of usefulness and a stumbling-block. His honesty and integrity were above suspicion. The ministry was not a mere profession,—it was his meat and drink to proclaim the glad tidings, whether he was compensated or not: necessity was laid upon him to preach the Gospel.

Some regarded him hyper-Calvinistic in his system of doctrine, but he loved Fuller more than Calvin, and followed the Bible more than either. His liberality in contributing to all objects that were presented, whether connected with his own denomination or not, was proved almost daily for many of his later years. He aided the Presbyterians in Washington in their school with a princely donation. His house was the home of ministers and pious persons of all denominations.

A public life of over half a century,—(for he was ordained prior to his twentieth year,) a life of great circumspection, and piety, and usefulness, free from stain, with great and commanding talents, could not fail to win the confidence and respect of those to whom he was known; and there was not a county in the State where he was not known and respected. He had some adversaries, it is true, in the latter part of his life; and some relations by marriage interested in his estate; but these could not weaken the confidence with which he held tens of thousands. Some drew the sage inference that his meek and quiet spirit were assumed to gain popularity; but such reports carried their own refutation. Without fear of the charge of partiality, it may be safely said that there was no minister in the State, who was more highly respected by all Christian persuasions, and none whose death was more deeply deplored.

This feeble tribute to his memory and exalted character has been written under peculiarly hurried circumstances, and with a mind wandering on other pressing engagements. Justice is not done him; but I will not longer hold you in suspense.

Very respectfully yours,
ADIEL SHERWOOD.

ANDREW BROADDUS.*
1789—1848.

The family of Broaddus in Virginia is of Welsh origin, and is descended from Edward Broaddus, who first settled on Gwyn's Island in James River, and removed in 1715 to the lower end of Caroline County, Va. John Broaddus, a son of Edward, was the father of Andrew, the subject of this sketch. He was a man of vigorous intellect; was, by occupation, first a teacher, and then a farmer; was a zealous member of the Episcopal Church; and was actively engaged in the struggle for our National Independence. He was married to a Miss Pryor, said to have been a lineal descendant of Pocahontas.

ANDREW BROADDUS, the youngest son of his parents, was born at the family residence, in Caroline County, November 4, 1770. He was early distinguished for his thirst for knowledge, and for the facility with which he acquired it; and his father fully intended that he should be a minister in the Episcopal Church. His opportunities for early culture were extremely limited,—the whole period in which he had the advantages of a school of any kind being only nine months. He, however, contrived to make up for this deficiency by reading and studying in private; and, as his father was an intelligent man, he probably received some assistance from him.

In the neighbourhood in which he lived, the Baptists had become quite numerous, and Andrew's elder brother, contrary to the wishes of his father, had become one of them. So much was the father opposed to their denominational peculiarities, that he forbade his son's attending their meetings; though Andrew's predilections in their favour were not at all diminished by this prohibition. Whether the father subsequently yielded, or the son felt constrained to disregard parental authority, does not appear; but, on the 28th of May, 1789, he was baptized by Elder Theodoric Noel, a very devout and earnest Baptist minister, and connected himself with Upper King and Queen Church, then the only Baptist church in that vicinity. He was now between eighteen and nineteen years of age.

Shortly after his Baptism, he was called upon to exhort at the neighbouring meeting; and he obeyed the call. His first regular sermon was preached on the 24th of December, 1789, at the house of a Mrs. Lowrie, in Caroline County. Though his advantages for education had been so

---

* Jeter's Memoir.—Obituary notices.—MS. from Rev. Dr. Ryland.

very limited, and he had no theological instruction whatever, he had a mind of much more than ordinary capacity, and an impressive and graceful elocution; so that his earliest attempts at preaching were received with much more than common favour. His youthful appearance also added not a little to the effect of his public services. He was ordained to the ministry at Upper King and Queen Meeting House, on the 16th of October, 1791, by Elders Theodoric Noel and R. B. Semple.

The field of Elder Broaddus' ministrations was composed mainly of the Counties of Caroline, King and Queen, and King William,—among the oldest and most respectable counties in the State. He first settled in the upper end of Caroline County, and performed the duties of the Pastorate in Burrus' (now Carmel) Church, and in County Line. Successively, and for different periods, he ministered to the churches of Bethel, Salem, Upper King and Queen, Beulah, Mangohic, Upper Zion, and some others.

In 1817, he entertained the design of migrating to the State of Kentucky; and, that he might form an intelligent judgment on the subject, made a tour on horseback, in company with a young relative, through the central portions of that State. Though he was, in many respects, well pleased with both the country and the people, and was urged by his brethren to settle among them, and withal was offered the Presidency of Hopkinsville Academy, then a flourishing institution, he relinquished the idea of changing his residence.

In 1821, Mr. Broaddus removed to Richmond, and became Assistant Pastor with the Rev. John Courtney,* in the First Baptist Church. Here his ministry was highly acceptable; but, owing to domestic afflictions and pecuniary embarrassments, it continued for only six months. Except for this brief period, he never lived beyond the limits of his native county, and the adjoining County of King and Queen.

In 1832, Mr. Broaddus was chosen to supply the place of the lamented Dr. Semple, as Moderator of the Dover Association, then the largest Association of Baptist Churches in the United States. This office he retained,—except in 1839, when he was absent,—until 1841, when, by his own request, he was excused from further service.

In 1843, the Trustees of the Columbian College, in the District of Columbia, conferred upon him the degree of Doctor of Divinity, which, however, he respectfully declined.

Though not possessed of a vigorous constitution, Mr. Broaddus, owing no doubt very much to his prudent and abstemious habits, lived to a good old age. Early in the autumn of 1848, it became apparent that he was gradually wasting under the influence of a chronic diarrhœa. He con-

* JOHN COURTNEY was born in the County of King and Queen, Va., about the year 1744. His parents were members of the Church of England, in which, of course, he was himself educated His father dying when he was young, and the estate, according to law, descending to the eldest son, John was bound, as soon as his age would allow it, to the trade of a carpenter. From this time nothing is known of him until, having reached mature years, he makes his appearance as a Baptist preacher. After the close of the War of the Revolution, during part of which he served as a soldier, he removed to Richmond, where, besides labouring "with his own hands," he served the Baptist Church in that city, either as sole or senior Pastor, for a period of more than forty years. His ministry was characterized by great fidelity, zeal, and affection. During the last four years of his life, such was his bodily infirmity that he rarely attempted to preach, though he continued to labour in private, according to his ability, and was a bright example of patience, fortitude, and heavenly-mindedness. He died on the 18th of December, 1824.

tinued, however, to preach, even after he had become considerably enfeebled. His last sermon was delivered a few weeks before his death, in the First African Baptist Church in Richmond, and was regarded as an uncommonly happy effort. In the early part of his last illness, he was somewhat inclined to spiritual despondency, but, as his end drew nigh, no cloud intervened between him and the Sun of Righteousness. When asked, as the death struggle approached, what was the state of his mind, his answer was "Calmly relying on Christ." On another occasion, after having been engaged in silent meditation, he characteristically remarked,—"The angels are instructing me how to conduct myself in glory." The last word he was heard to whisper was "Happy! Happy! Happy!" He died on the 1st of December, 1848, aged seventy-eight years; and was buried in the grave-yard of the Salem meeting-house, where he had for many years faithfully preached the Gospel.

Few ministers were more frequently solicited to settle over other and more important congregations than Mr. Broaddus. He was either invited to accept the pastoral charge, or was corresponded with on the subject of accepting it, by the following Churches:—The First Church in Boston, in 1811 and 1812, to supply the vacancy occasioned by the death of Dr. Stillman; the First Church in Philadelphia, in 1811, to supply the place of Dr. Staughton; the First Church in Baltimore, in 1819; the New Market Street Church in Philadelphia, in 1819; the Sansom Street Church in Philadelphia, in 1824; the First Church in Philadelphia, again in 1825; the Norfolk Church, in 1826; the First Church in the City of New York, in 1832; the First Church in Richmond, in 1833; not to mention several other places of minor importance.

Mr. Broaddus was married to Fanny, daughter of Col. John Temple, of Caroline, about the year 1793. By this marriage he had several children. Mrs. B. died in 1804 or 1805. He was afterwards married to Lucy, daughter of Dr. Robert Honeyman, a gentleman of high intelligence and respectability. By this marriage he had no children. Some time after the death of his second wife, he was married to her sister, then Mrs. Jane C. Broaddus, the widow of his nephew. This marriage was, on several accounts, an occasion of great trouble to him. By it he had several children, one of whom, bearing his own name, became a minister of the Gospel, and proved a great comfort to his father in his latter days. In 1843, Mr. Broaddus was married to Caroline W. Boulware, of Newtown, King and Queen County. She had only one child,—a son, who was but three or four years old at the time of his father's death.

Mr. Broaddus wrote somewhat extensively for the press, and many of his productions are in good repute, both in and out of his denomination. He early published an octavo volume, entitled "History of the Bible." At a later period, he issued a Catechism intended for children, which has passed through many editions, and been extensively circulated by the American Baptist Publication Society. At the request of the Dover Association, he drew up a Form of Church Discipline, which was printed and circulated among its Churches by that Body. He also prepared the Dover Selection of Hymns, which, after a short time, was followed by the Virginia Selection,—a large volume containing a greater variety of

Hymns, and better adapted to the necessities of the Churches. Beside these, he published many Circular Letters, Essays, Addresses, Sermons, Controversial articles, &c., most of which were republished in 1852, in connection with a Memoir of his life.

FROM THE REV. R. RYLAND, D. D.

RICHMOND, Va., December 29, 1854.

Rev. and dear Sir: At your request, I will give you a brief sketch of the character of the Rev. Andrew Broaddus.

I had known him for about thirty years previously to his death, as intimately as the disparity of our ages, and the remoteness of our localities, would allow. During the first year of this acquaintance, I was an inmate of his family, and a participant in his instructions. At periods not widely separated, I enjoyed his society in the private circle, and his ministerial teachings, up to the close of his life. My opportunities for judging of his character, therefore, have been ample, while my relations to him have not been so intimate as to obscure my judgment, and tempt me to give too high a colouring to the portrait.

As a Man, Mr. Broaddus was not above the ordinary stature; slightly inclining in his person, but graceful in his carriage, and self-possessed in his bearing. His face was intellectual rather than commanding in its expression, and from his soft blue eyes shone out a benignity that invited approach and disarmed prejudice. He was very neat in his dress, and by many was regarded as fastidious in his tastes. Without any disposition to satire, he was a critical observer of manners, and though far from exacting respect,—indeed, he was generally annoyed by formal attentions,—was yet keenly alive to the delicate offices of friendship that were cheerfully awarded to him. In the social circle he was generally expected to take the lead in conversation; but seemed so unambitious of the honour as to require to be drawn out before he could be made interesting. Whether it was owing to the state of his nervous system, or to his natural temperament, he was at times impatient of prolonged interviews, became fidgety in his manners, and excited a smile by his little peculiarities.

But it is as an orator that the public mind is likely to feel the deepest interest in him. After hearing a great number of speakers, both on sacred and secular subjects, I have formed the conclusion that Mr. Broaddus, during the days of his meridian strength, and in his happiest efforts, was the most perfect orator that I have ever known. For the last fifteen years of his life, there was a manifest decline in his intellectual efforts. The maturity of his knowledge, and his nice discrimination of truth, added to his humble piety, always rendered him interesting. But the vivacity, the pathos, the magic power of his eloquence, had measurably departed. Hundreds of persons who have heard him discourse within this period have been disappointed. He has not sustained the reputation which he had previously established. Even before that period, there was another, and a still more fruitful source of disappointment to his occasional hearers. When strangers listened to his exhibitions of the Gospel, it was generally on some extraordinary occasion,—some anniversary that called together a large concourse of people. Expectation was raised, curiosity was excited, and that was precisely the time for him to falter. His nervous diffidence frequently gained so complete a mastery over him as to fill him with a real *horror* of preaching. Often, on such occasions, have the united and urgent entreaties of his most cherished friends failed to get him on the stand. And when, by such solicitations, he was prevailed on to preach, often has his timidity so far neutralized his power, that those who

knew him well would not judge him by that effort, and those who did not
know him formed an erroneous conception of his mental ability. When,
however, he did rise superior to this constitutional infirmity, and shake off all
the trammels of despondency and fear, those who hung on his lips soon felt
themselves under the influence of a master spirit. There was such aptness
of illustration, such delicacy and correctness of taste, such a flow of generous
sympathy, and withal so much transparent simplicity, in his eloquence, that
it at once riveted the attention, and moved the heart.

His discourses were rich in instruction. His first aim evidently was to be
understood by the feeblest capacity. Even a child could scarcely fail to comprehend his general trains of thought. If he was ever tedious, it was easy
to perceive that it proceeded from an amiable desire to be understood by all.
Possessed of a sprightly imagination, he employed it to elucidate and enforce
Divine truth, rather than to excite the admiration of the vulgar intellect.
His sermons were not moral essays, nor were they stately orations, neither
were they distinguished by artistic structure and symmetry of parts. They
were chiefly expository of the sacred writings. He always possessed sufficient
unity of plan to indicate the purpose, or to suggest the title, of a discourse;
but his genius hated to be cramped by scholastic rules. He explained his text
in a most able manner, and then deduced from it such general doctrines as
would naturally present themselves to a cultivated mind. Throughout his
discourse, he introduced passages of Scripture in such a manner as to reflect
new light on *them*, while they were made to contribute to his main design.
He was a close student of the Bible, and was uncommonly felicitous in commenting upon it. He had a native talent for painting and poetry, and those
who heard him could easily detect it. He made them see things so vividly
that they often felt as if they were not hearing a description, but beholding
the very objects, in living colours, spread out before the eye.

Another trait in his oratory was that it was natural. He had unquestionably a genius for every work that demands refined taste for its execution; but
he cultivated that genius by varied and long continued study, and thus
reached the highest of all rhetorical attainments,—the art of concealing art.
He seemed to divest himself of the formal air often assumed in the pulpit;
discoursed in a conversational tone, as with a party of select friends, awakened the attention even of those who were not especially interested in the
subject, and made them feel that they were personally concerned. He looked
into the eyes of the assembly with such an individualizing yet meek penetra-
tion, that each hearer fancied himself as much addressed as if he were the
entire audience. I have frequently heard, from half a dozen persons who sat
in different parts of the house, the remark, at the close of a meeting,—"Mr.
Broaddus preached his whole sermon to *me*." And this insulating effect was
not owing so much to the substance as to the manner of his address. He was
not a close, searching, severe, exclusive sort of preacher, as to his doctrines.
His tendency was to encourage, to soothe, to allure. He sought out the
sincere but desponding believer, and, by a lucid exhibition of the system of
Divine mercy, and a nice analysis of the character of the true Christian, gave
him a basis for consolation. But it was his natural manner that brought him
into immediate contact with his hearers, annihilating all formality. *He* was
stripped of the veil of an artificial delivery, and *they* forgot the publicity of
the occasion by reason of the directness of the appeal. The nearness of the
relation that he sustained to his auditory explains in part his bashfulness in
early ministerial life. In several of the early years of his public career, he sat
in his chair to preach. Having gathered his neighbours around him, he occupied the evening in religious exercises. He read select portions of Scripture,
and expounded them in a familiar style. As the congregations increased, and

his confidence became more firm, he began his remarks in that posture, and rose to his feet, when he felt the kindlings of his theme. This early custom probably had some influence on his talent for exposition. It certainly contributed also to the confirmation of the speaker in the natural manner. It must not be inferred from this statement that his style was coarse, or that his gestures were inelegant, or that his general appearance was devoid of seriousness. The contrary was emphatically true. His style was always chaste,—sometimes rising to the beautiful. His gesticulation was appropriate, easy and impressive, never violent, over-wrought or pompous. His manner, though remote from sanctimoniousness, was anything but flippant. His voice had nothing of the whine,—nothing of the affected solemnity of tone about it. It was musical, flexible and capacious. His whole carriage in the pulpit was mild and graceful, without his seeming either to aim at it, or to be conscious of it. In a word, it was natural—it was such as good sense, unaffected piety, and cultivated taste would spontaneously produce.

Another trait of his oratory was his skill in the pathetic. He knew well how to touch the delicate chords of passion in the human heart, but he did not abuse his skill by constant exercise. The main body of his discourse was didactic. He gave the sense of the text, developed the doctrine, enforced the practical duty. But, occasionally, he unsealed the fountains of feeling in the soul. Often have I felt the thrill of his eloquence, and witnessed its melting power on an audience. It came unexpectedly, without any parade, and his hearers resigned themselves up to his control. The most touching parts of his sermons were the episodes. He seemed to have just discovered a new track of thought, and for a moment to luxuriate in its freshness and fertility. His hearers willingly left the main road with him, and sympathized intensely in all his emotions. They knew that he had a right to their hearts, and that he would not abuse his privilege. His sermons were not one uniformly sustained appeal to the passions. He attacked them obliquely. Having first convinced the judgment, he found a ready avenue to the affections, and thus influenced the will. Hence it often happened that a single sentence produced a subduing effect. All that was said before was but a preparation for that one sentence. A moderate charge of gunpowder will more effectually cleave a rock, if, by deep boring, you introduce the explosive agent far into its bosom, than ten times the quantity kindled on its surface. Mr. Broaddus knew exactly when to touch the passions; and, unless he perceived that the mind was prepared, he was careful not to attempt the delicate task. When he did attempt it, he rarely failed.

An important question may here be propounded—Was his ministry successful in winning souls to Christ? I am happy to answer in the affirmative. He laboured in the cause for more than half a century, probably for sixty years. His congregations were always large, his churches prosperous, and though his ministry was better adapted to edify than to awaken, many persons were converted through his instrumentality. Still I am free to acknowledge that his success was not commensurate with his talents. Men of less piety, of less learning, and of less original acuteness, have often been more effective. And why? Because they possessed more courage and energy. The great interests of the church and of the world require decision and perseverance. To be eminently successful in any noble enterprise, we must throw ourselves into it—body, soul and spirit;—must derive new motives to activity from the very difficulties that oppose us; and, confident of the strength of our faculties when guided by truth and animated with love, we must anticipate and labour for large results. "Attempt great things, expect great things." This venerable brother yielded too much to timidity. He needed some one to push him onward. He was frequently absent from the great Baptist Anniversaries, where his counsels would have been valuable, and his labours highly appreciated. This was not occasioned by an unsocial temper, nor by indolence, nor by any hostility or even indifference to the objects that claimed attention, but by a morbid sensibility that shrunk from exposure. Could he have gone to these meetings, and seen and heard every thing, while he himself remained silent and invisible, I think he would have attended them. But his deservedly high standing always put him in requisition, and he was driven to the alternative of either taking a prominent part, or resisting the importunities of beloved friends. To avoid this, I doubt not, he often sought and found some reason for remaining at home. The same disposition discovered itself in his regular pastoral engagements. He seemed to court obscurity, to cherish no desire to be a leader. So depressed in spirit at times as to fancy that any sort of a preacher would be more acceptable and useful than himself, he would put him up as a substitute in his own pulpit. This extreme reluctance to perform the offices of his profession was caused, partly by nervous debility, and partly by the peculiar texture of his mind. Far be it from me to intimate any censure against so excellent a man. Fidelity to truth only requires me to say that he would have been more effective, had he possessed either less exquisiteness of mind, or more strength of body. The union of fine sensibility and of a disordered nervous system rendered him too liable to be disconcerted, and poorly adapted him to elbow his way through the rough world. As a disciplinarian, he was deficient,—not from any imperfection in his own standard of rectitude, nor from any delinquency in his own conduct, but from the want of authority. He had not the heart to inflict a wound on the feelings of a child, or even to retort when his own feelings were unjustly wounded. His intellectual apparatus was thrown out of order by incidents that ordinary men would have scarcely noticed. And when to this temperament was added a prolonged series of domestic afflictions that cannot here be mentioned,—afflictions that would have appalled the stoutest heart, that quickened into acute and protracted agony his sensitive nature, the wonder is that he was not overwhelmed. Nothing but high moral principle,—a stern conviction of duty, and a noble desire to please God and profit men, could have so long and so honourably sustained him in his pastoral labours.

As an Author, Mr. Broaddus deserves the grateful remembrance of the Christian public. The works by which he is perhaps best known are his Bible History and two Hymn Books, the one called the Dover Selection, the other the Virginia Selection. He was a frequent contributor to the religious literature of the day, by writing for the Herald and other periodicals, articles that were always read with eagerness. His principal controversial essays were called out by the opinions of Mr. Alexander Campbell. Over the signature of Paulinus, he wrote several able Letters on the subject of Divine Influence. He afterwards published an examination of Mr. Campbell's Theory of Baptismal Regeneration. As a writer, his style is easy and accurate—as a controvertist, he is mild, argumentative and ingenious. He seems to be free from ambition,—to write for the sake of truth rather than of victory, and to be anxious not to magnify the difference between the sides of the controversy. If he does not convince his opponent, he is so courteous as to conciliate his personal esteem, and to soften the asperity of the contest.

Mr. Broaddus was a close observer and an ardent admirer of the beautiful in nature and in art. Deriving much of his happiness from such studies, he has left, in the specimens of painting and poetry with which he amused himself in his leisure hours, ample indications of what his genius could have effected, had it been devoted to these pursuits.

Affectionately yours,

ROBERT RYLAND.

JONATHAN MAXCY, D. D.*
1790—1820.

JONATHAN MAXCY was born in Attleborough, Mass., September 2, 1768. His great-grandfather, the earliest of his ancestors of whom any thing is now known, was Alexander Maxcy, who removed from Gloucester to Attleborough about 1721. His grandfather, Josiah Maxcy, was held in great esteem by the community in which he lived, and was, for a long time, a member of the Legislature of the Colony. His father, Levi Maxcy, was also a person of great worth and respectability; and his mother, whose maiden name was Ruth Newell, is represented as having been distinguished alike for a vigorous intellect, and an earnest, consistent piety.

The subject of this sketch evinced, in his early boyhood, an uncommon intellectual precocity, and especially a remarkable talent at public speaking; in consequence of which, his parents resolved to give him the advantages of a collegiate course. Having gone through with his preparatory studies in an Academy under the direction of the Rev. William Williams, of Wrentham, he entered Brown University in 1783, at the age of fifteen. His course as an undergraduate was marked by most exemplary deportment, great diligence, and singular versatility; but for nothing, perhaps, was he so much distinguished as fine writing. He had the highest honour in his class, at his graduation, in 1787, and delivered on that occasion a Poem, entitled "the Prospects of America," and the Valedictory Oration.

Notwithstanding his extreme youth, the Corporation of the College immediately appointed him a Tutor; and in this office he continued for four years, discharging its duties with great ability, and to universal acceptance.

About this time, his mind seems to have taken a decidedly religious direction, and he became a member of the First Baptist Church, then under the pastoral care of the Rev. Dr. Manning. He was licensed to preach by that church, April 1, 1790; and Dr. Manning having vacated the pulpit by the resignation of his charge, Mr. Maxcy was invited, in the mean time, to occupy it as a supply. Having preached for several months to great acceptance, during which time he had gained a high reputation for pulpit oratory, the congregation invited him to become their Pastor; and, having accepted their call, he was set apart to the pastoral office, on the 8th of September, 1791. The Sermon on the occasion was preached by the Rev. Dr. Stillman of Boston; and several other distinguished clergymen from a distance took part in the exercises. On the same day, he was elected both a Trustee and Professor of Divinity in the College.

In the new relations into which he was now brought, especially as a minister of the Gospel, he quickly proved himself "a burning and shining light;" and his fame as a preacher reached far and wide. It was but a short time, however, that he continued in this sphere of labour; for the sudden death of Dr. Manning, which occurred July 24, 1791, vacated the office of President of the College, and Mr. Maxcy was shortly after appointed his successor. He accepted the appointment, and on the 8th of September, 1792,

* Benedict's Hist. Bapt. I.—Mem. by Prof. Elton.

resigned his pastoral charge, and was inducted into the Presidential chair. The appointment was an exceedingly popular one; and, at the Commencement succeeding his inauguration, there was an illumination of the College, and a transparency placed in the Attic story, exhibiting " JONATHAN MAXCY, PRESIDENT, TWENTY-FOUR YEARS OLD."

In this highly responsible office he fulfilled the highest expectations of the most sanguine of his friends. The College, though without the advantage of legislative patronage, grew rapidly in public favour, and the name of the President, as had been that of his distinguished predecessor, was identified with its constantly advancing reputation. He was often called to officiate on important public occasions; and his efforts were always such as to do honour to himself and the institution over which he presided. Such was the appreciation of his talents and acquirements, that in 1801, when he was only thirty-three years old, the degree of Doctor of Divinity was conferred upon him by Harvard College.

In 1802, he was elected successor of the second Jonathan Edwards, in the Presidency of Union College. He accepted the appointment, and held the office with great reputation for two years; though it may reasonably be doubted whether, during this period, he attained the same degree of public favour which had marked his previous course as President of Brown University.

In 1804, the South Carolina College. at Columbia, having been established, Dr. Maxcy was chosen its first President; and, in the hope that a Southern climate might prove more congenial to his delicate constitution, he accepted the appointment. Over this institution he continued to preside, with almost unprecedented popularity, until his death, which occurred June 4, 1820, at the age of fifty-two. His brilliant and attractive powers made him extensively known, not only in the State, but through the whole Southern country; and there are many still living in that region, who can never speak of his powers of eloquence but with a kindling enthusiasm.

Dr. Maxcy was married to Susan, daughter of Commodore Esek Hopkins of Providence,—whose name is intimately associated with the history of the Revolution. The union was a most felicitous one. Besides several daughters, they had four sons,—all liberally educated. One of them was the Hon. Virgil Maxcy, who, during his life, occupied several important places of public trust, and was killed by the explosion of a gun, on board the United States' Steam Ship Princeton, February 28, 1844.

The following is a list of Dr. Maxcy's publications:—A Funeral Sermon occasioned by the Death of the Rev. James Manning, D. D., President of Rhode Island College. Delivered in the Baptist Meeting-House in Providence, 1791. An Address delivered to the Graduates of Rhode Island College at Commencement, 1794. An Oration delivered before the Providence Association of Mechanics and Manufacturers, 1795. An Oration delivered in the Baptist Meeting-House in Providence, at the Celebration of the Nineteenth Anniversary of American Independence, 1795. The Existence of God demonstrated from the Works of Creation: A Sermon preached in the Rev. Dr. Hitchcock's Meeting-House in Providence, 1795. A Sermon preached at the Dedication of the Meeting-House belonging to the Catholic Baptist Society in Cumberland. A Discourse designed to explain the Doctrine of Atonement. In two parts. Delivered in the Chapel of Rhode Island College, 1796. A Sermon preached in Boston, at the Annual Convention of the Warren Association, in the Rev. Dr. Stillman's Meeting-House, 1797. An Address delivered to the Graduates of Rhode Island College, at the Anniversary Commencement, in the Baptist Meeting-House in Providence, 1798. A Sermon delivered in the Baptist Meeting-House at Providence, on Lord's day afternoon, occasioned by the death of Welcome Arnold, Esq., 1798. An Oration delivered in the First Congregational Meeting-House in Providence, on the Fourth of July, 1799. A Sermon delivered in the Chapel of Rhode Island College, to the Senior Class, on the Sunday preceding the Anniversary Commencement, 1800. Reason of the Christian's Triumph: A Sermon delivered in the Baptist Meeting-House in Providence, occasioned by the Death of Mrs. Mary Gano, Consort of the Rev. Stephen Gano, 1800. An Address delivered to the Candidates for the Baccalaureate of Rhode Island College, at the Anniversary Commencement, 1801. An Address delivered to the Graduates of Rhode Island College, at the Public Commencement, 1802. A Sermon preached in the Baptist Meeting-House in Providence, before the Female Charitable Society, 1802. A Sermon preached at the High Hills of Santee, before the Charleston Baptist Association, at their Annual Meeting, 1812. An Anniversary Sermon delivered in the Presbyterian Meeting-House in Columbia, on the day previous to the Commencement of the South Carolina College, 1816. An Address delivered to the candidates for the Baccalaureate in the South Carolina College, 1816. An Introductory Lecture to a Course on the Philosophical Principles of Rhetoric and Criticism; designed for the Senior Class of the South Carolina College, and delivered in the Public Chapel, 1817. A Funeral Sermon delivered in the Representatives' Chamber, before both Branches of the Legislature of the State of South Carolina, 1819. A Discourse delivered in the Chapel of South Carolina College, at the request of the inhabitants of Columbia, on the Fourth of July, 1819. A Funeral Sermon, occasioned by the Death of Mr. John Sampson Bambo, a Member of the Junior Class in the South Carolina College, who was unfortunately drowned in the Congaree River, near Columbia. Delivered in the College Chapel, 1819.

These several publications were gathered, in 1844, in a volume entitled " The Literary Remains of the Rev. Jonathan Maxcy, D. D. With a Memoir of his Life, by Romeo Elton, D. D."

FROM THE HON. TRISTAM BURGES,
CHIEF JUSTICE OF THE SUPREME COURT OF RHODE ISLAND.

WATCHEMOKET FARM, (near Providence,) June 8, 1848.

Rev. and dear Sir: It is not possible for me to produce a portrait of Jonathan Maxcy which shall do justice to the great original. 1 saw him as an Instructer, presiding over a scientific and literary institution, and as a Minister, proclaiming the glorious truths of the Gospel; but I was then a pupil, who, but a little before, had exchanged the use of the plough and the sickle for books, and knew little of what the high offices which Dr. Maxcy held required of him. If I could remember so as to tell how his administration

of these offices affected me, I should draw a picture that would be characterized by surpassing beauty and power; but it is so long since I sat under his
instruction, that the bright vision which then astonished and delighted me,
has in a great degree faded from my recollection. Nevertheless, I well remember that no man could have been more popular in the College than President
Maxcy. I never heard so much as a whisper against him. He was universally
loved as a parent, and admired and revered as a great and good man. Though
he was less than the medium stature, there was in his countenance and manners a dignity that seemed to raise him above the ordinary level; and withal
he had so much benignity and affability as well as intelligence, as to captivate
every person with whom he conversed. Though I cannot now convey to you
an adequate idea of all his exalted traits of character, I can at least show
you what, in the year 1796, were the sentiments and feelings of the whole College respecting him as President of that institution.

I graduated at Providence College at the Commencement in September of
that year; and it so happened that the Valedictory Oration and Addresses,
in the public exercises, were, by the authority of College, assigned to me. I
shall say no more of this performance than that it was so much in accordance
with the views and feelings of the whole College, that I was unanimously
called upon to furnish a copy for the press. The little pamphlet, containing
the Oration and Addresses, now lies before me; and though that day, so dear
to my memory, was more than fifty years ago, and almost all those who bore
a part in its exercises, have passed out of time, and he whom I then addressed
in the flesh now sleeps far off in the warm bosom of the South Carolina Hills,
yet this little faithful page has kept, and now brings back to my eye, and
recalls to my memory, what we all then thought and felt concerning our venerated and beloved President. It may be deemed egotism in me to attempt to
weave my little Address into any biography of President Maxcy; but, in doing
this, all may be assured that I shall indulge no mean ambition, or any other
desire than merely to do justice to the merits and the memory of a scholar
and teacher, so deserving and distinguished.

ADDRESS TO THE PRESIDENT.

"*Reverend Sir:*

" We know that you are persuaded that custom alone does not give birth to
this Address. We claim the privilege of telling the world how we feel obliged.
Gratitude can not be refused this small indulgence. On this occasion, should
we attempt to narrate the merits of our benefactor, modesty might raise a
suspicion of adulation, envy would deduce our panegyric from the partiality
of our hearts; while the world would inform us that the science, knowledge,
and philanthropy of the man who has obliged us, are now become themes of
common conversation. We can, therefore, express our gratitude only; and
ardently wish that others, in pursuit of science, may have the same director
who has guided our steps.

" Yes; if ever our souls, in the silent moments of devotion, have dared to
heave a wishing sigh to Heaven for a single favour on ourselves,—often, when
we behold his face no more, often shall that wish be repeated for the health
and felicity of him whom generations yet unborn shall learn to call their
benefactor. The world shall join in our devotion; a prayer so benevolent
must ascend grateful to the ear of Heaven; and the immortal spirit of the
great Manning, the immaculate companion of the LAMB, shall, with a smile
of gratulation, behold you still the father of his orphan seminary."

This address was pronounced on the stage, before a crowded audience, in
the very large Baptist meeting-house in Providence, so that every word must
have reached every ear in that vast multitude; and I fully believe that every

heart in the whole assembly beat in unison with that of the speaker; and would have confirmed the truth and the justice of the whole Address by one loud and united Amen.

It remains to say a few words concerning Dr. Maxcy as a Minister of Christ. For although his duties in the College called for most of his time, yet, without neglecting them, he found more or less leisure to devote to the composition of discourses for the pulpit.

President Maxcy was born an Orator; and though, when I knew him, his native genius had been improved by assiduous culture, yet, had he never sat at the feet of Manning, but continued in his paternal fields to follow the plough and feed his cattle, he would have been as truly one of Nature's Orators, as Burns, in the same condition, was one of Nature's Poets. His voice would have been heard in school-meetings, in church-meetings, and town-meetings; and those little republics would have been moved by his eloquence and directed by his counsels.

When this great man appeared as the Fourth of July Orator at Providence, as he did on one occasion, he attracted a degree of attention almost unprecedented. His theme was the Principles and the Events of the American Revolution; and his audience consisted chiefly of those who had passed through that long and terrible conflict which gave to our nation its independence. Not to mention any other part of his Oration, all of which was admirable, I will recall one out of many brilliant coruscations, containing the divine fire, the heaven-born electricity, of pure eloquence. When, with a glow of patriotism, the orator exclaimed,—" Should our enemy again return to our shores, he will find every plain a Marathon, every defile a Thermopylæ,''—it was then that I felt, as I doubt not all felt, the cold shudder, the electric shock, which always reaches one, when the orator strikes out the true, the divine flash of eloquence.

Enough, however, and perhaps too much of this; for it was of his sacred eloquence that I intended to say a few words. He wrote his sermons, and laid his notes before him on the desk; but, in the delivery, he seemed never to use them. He appeared perfectly at home in the pulpit, as if born only to preach the Gospel. He was not like the great Baptist of Gallilee,—" the voice of one *crying* in the wilderness," yet, like that Divine precursor of the Redeemer, he preached to men to " prepare the way of the Lord;" he preached repentance and works meet for repentance; he preached love to God and love to man,—the great moral law of the universe,—the golden, everlasting chain, which binds each individual to every other, and all to the Throne of the Eternal.

He did not cry aloud. His voice was neither loud nor high, yet his utterance was so perfectly distinct that every word reached every ear with its melody, and he melted every heart with his fervid and overpowering pathos. His preaching was not like the fire, nor like the earthquake, nor like the mighty wind exhibited to the vision of Elijah on the summit of the Mount, but it was indeed the still small voice, heard from the Lord by the Prophet, while sitting at its base. He seemed to be, as he truly was, a messenger sent by his Divine Master with glad tidings of great joy.

Every one who hears of a distinguished man, wishes to know something of his personal appearance. I have never seen a portrait of Dr. Maxcy; and it is many years since I looked upon him; and yet so deeply are his features and expression engraven on my memory, that I am confident I could distinguish his face among thousands. His countenance was grave and dignified, but so tempered with benignity that those who only casually saw him were constrained to regard him as a model of benevolence and goodness. I believe he seldom, if ever, laughed; but he often smiled; and his smile was delightful. All who saw him wished to hear him; and those who heard him once, were sure to wish to hear him again. It was impossible to behold his face without feeling assured that a highly gifted and finely regulated soul looked out upon the beholders from those interesting features.

I have thought, and now fully believe, that if Dr. Maxcy had lived in the age and country of the great Italian school of artists, when and where the exigences of the art required some one to sit as a model before the painter, they would have selected him as the model for their consecrated portraits of Him, who, when on earth, "spake as never man spake;" and some Raphael or Michael Angelo would have placed on the canvass the living lineaments of a minister of Christ, whose countenance, it always seemed to me, was no unapt representation of that of his Divine Master.

I might have said, at the beginning of this letter, that I had never seen a biography of Dr. Maxcy; but, since the above sketch was written, there has been placed in my hands by a friend a copy of "The Literary Remains" of that eminent man, by Doctor Elton. It is a highly meritorious work, honourable to the gifted author, and a rich contribution to American literature. Nevertheless, I rejoice that I had finished my own sketch before I saw this book; because I now know that all I have written concerning this extraordinary man is drawn from my own remembered perceptions of his excellence, and, like the faithful testimony of an eye-witness to some great collection of splendid events, carries with it more evidence of correctness than can be found in any of the most careful and exact accounts, drawn from mere tradition. Professor Elton has done well, eminently well; but how much higher must have been the inspiration he would have felt, had he seen, as others saw, and heard as others heard, Jonathan Maxcy.

I am, Rev. and dear Sir, with the highest respect,

Your obedient servant,

TRISTAM BURGES.

FROM THE REV. GARDINER B. PERRY, D. D.

EAST BRADFORD, Mass., July 18, 1848.

My dear Sir: I am happy to comply with your request, for some recollections of the late President Maxcy. Several considerations, beside a great willingness to meet your wishes, conspire to render this a pleasant service to me. I know not how far what I may write will suit the object you have in view, but I will endeavour to record those circumstances which seem to me best adapted to illustrate the character of that great and venerable man.

The place of Dr. Maxcy's birth was but a few miles from the residence of my father. Our families were somewhat acquainted. From early life I had some knowledge of his history, and the estimation in which he was held by the literary and religious world. My own personal acquaintance with him commenced when I became a member of Brown University, in 1800; and it became more intimate, perhaps I should say familiar, when he removed to Union College. At that time, my father yielded to his wishes to have me accompany him, and I was put under his special care, and became virtually a member of his family. In person, he was below the middle size, and rather thin in flesh. But his face was lighted up with a fine intellectual expression, which chiefly occupied the eye and engrossed the attention of those about him. The mind emphatically made the man. The principle involved in that expression, so far as it concerned the outward person, was, with the exception of the late Aaron Burr, more fully illustrated in him than in any other individual whom I ever met. He was well proportioned in his form, dignified in his appearance, and impressive in his manners. A remarkable harmony prevailed between the movements of his person and the workings of his mind and heart. Every motion without seemed but an expression of what was working within. He wore a three-cornered cocked hat, and on all public occasions appeared in a silk cassock and bands. His complexion was light and somewhat sallow; though a slight freshness never failed to diffuse itself over his cheek, when he was moved by any of the gentler feelings. His forehead was high and open; his eye a mellow pleasant blue; and the whole contour of his head and face, though not altogether filling up the idea of physical beauty, certainly afforded a striking image of mental power and high moral feeling.

Dr. Maxcy was rather uncommonly domestic in his feelings; and no man took a livelier interest than he in whatever concerned the welfare of his family. His children, at the time I was most with him, were young,—the oldest probably not exceeding ten or twelve years. These he encouraged to visit him morning and evening in his study, where he cultivated the most delightful familiarity with them, and expressed the deepest interest in every indication of intellectual or moral improvement. I noticed that, in conversing with them, he ordinarily used the same forms of expression as when speaking with persons of mature age; and his reason for doing so was that he supposed that, by this means, they would sooner become acquainted with the language of books, and thus be enabled to advance more rapidly in their studies.

Dr. Maxcy was exclusively devoted to the duties of his office, and to his studies. He was never, so far as I know, involved in any secular business beyond the common concerns of his family. He was remarkable for diligent and persevering labour. His habit, in respect to any science with which he wished to become acquainted, was to select the best system within his reach, and study it thoroughly till it had become firmly fixed in his mind, and then, as he wished to extend his investigations, to read other authors on those particular parts which seemed to him worthy of further attention. Few departments of knowledge could be named into which he did not extend his inquiries, and with which he had not become so familiar as to enable him to hold an instructive conversation. Two distinguished lawyers, of one of the Middle States, after having incidentally held a protracted discussion with him on the law of *entail*, (he being entirely unknown to them,) came to the conclusion that he was probably a Judge in one of the higher Courts of the United States. Dr. Maxcy supposed that, with a proper training of the mind, most books might be gone through in a much shorter time than is usually devoted to them, and so a much greater amount of knowledge be obtained in a given period. His sermons were composed with the utmost rapidity, and yet when composed, they seemed to be graven on the tablet of his memory, as with a pen of iron and the point of a diamond. If he had occasion, as he sometimes had, to write out a discourse after he had delivered it, there would be found not only the same arrangement and the same general train of thought, but nearly all the same language.

While Dr. Maxcy was an excellent general scholar, he had made himself specially familiar with the branches which he was accustomed to teach. The manner in which the classes regarded his attainments in History may be illustrated by a remark which was made by one of the students in coming from the lecture-room,—namely, that he believed the doctrine of metempsychosis must be true; for, unless the President had himself, in some form, lived in Athens, where the events recorded in our lesson occurred, he never could have been so intimately acquainted with the characters and lives of the men, nor with the general temper of the people he had been describing to us. This thorough knowledge of the various branches in his department, in connection with a remarkable facility of communication, rendered him an uncommonly interesting teacher. His questions were shaped in such a manner as to save the student, who had the least knowledge of the lesson, from the embarrassment consequent on an entire inability to answer, and, at the same time, to leave the best informed with the conviction that there were still other things connected with the subject which it would be useful for them to learn. His mode of teaching was eminently fitted to promote the spirit of inquiry; and the students left the lecture-room, talking over the subject of the recitation, and, after reaching their rooms, often studied their lessons more thoroughly than they had before they left them. A system of questions drawn up after his manner, would be an invaluable help to the youth of the present day; and, perhaps, not more valuable to the youth than helpful to the great body of instructers.

Dr. Maxcy took great pains to cultivate a taste for composition. As a means of doing this, he was accustomed to recommend to the students to read over, two or three times, some well composed piece, and then, having laid the book aside, to write out the same thoughts in the best attainable language. The work which, above all others, he advised to be used, was the Spectator; and next to that the Rambler. He was also desirous that the young men should accustom themselves to extemporaneous speaking, and encouraged those institutions which were fitted to help them in this exercise. For a considerable time, I was connected with an association formed at his suggestion, the only business of which was to speak on subjects proposed by the presiding officer after the members had assembled. Our habit was to meet at sunset, each day, when other exercises did not interfere, and spend a half hour or more together, as we might find convenient. Our instructions from the President were carefully to avoid irrelevant speaking, or attempting to maintain by sophistry an untruth, or giving any plausibility to error, or suggesting any apology for crime.

Allow me here to mention a little incident that may serve to illustrate his habit of turning the most trifling circumstance to good account in the way of communicating instruction. I happened, on a certain occasion, just in the dusk of evening, to be sitting with him at the entrance of his dwelling, when he was illustrating some of the doctrines of the ancient philosophers. Mr. (now the Rev. Dr.) Jacob Brodhead, then a Tutor in College,—a man whom we held in high estimation, passed by; and Dr. Maxcy, observing him, remarked humorously that the members of Union College were better off than the youth of Athens, under one of the most distinguished teachers of ancient times,—as much better as a *Broad-Head* was superior to *wide* or *crooked shoulders*—alluding of course to old Plato. From this he proceeded to show, by various historical facts, how little dependance can be put on the etymological meaning of ancient names, and the ludicrous mistakes, if not hurtful errors, into which many, for want of due caution on this point, have fallen.

Dr. Maxcy manifested much of a devotional spirit. His mind was eminently fruitful in serious and devout reflections. It was true of him, in a spiritual sense, that "the cloud returned after the rain." In his prayers there was always an unction and impressiveness that left you without any doubt that the Spirit was helping him. I had occasion, on a certain day, to call at his study, a short time before evening prayers at the chapel; and I found him deeply interested in a remark which a little son of his, perhaps four or five years old, had just made to him. The little fellow came running into the study, and, with an expression of great earnestness, said,—"Father, the prayers are ringing, the prayers are ringing—why do you not make haste? You will get marked and fined, if you do not go quick." The language, the looks, and the earnestness of the child he described in a manner and tone to which none but a parent could have been adequate. It was evident, however, in a moment, from the change of his countenance, that a serious thought had passed over him; and he went on to remark that the language of the child was a forcible illustration of the passage in which Paul speaks of the outward form of religion as only " sounding brass and a tinkling cymbal;"—too true a description, he said, of many prayers, and he greatly feared of many of his own; and he then added, with deep feeling, that he earnestly desired to keep his mind habitually impressed with the consideration that where the heart is not in the worship of God, forms avail nothing.

Dr. Maxcy's manner in the pulpit was characterized by great simplicity, ease, and earnestness. His style of preaching altogether was eminently fitted to produce solemn reflection and deep self-communion, and thus lead to the best practical results. There was nothing, however, in his public performances, that was of a particularly exciting or agitating character. Every thing was serene, symmetrical, impressive. He attempted to imitate no one, and caught no one's peculiarities. Destitute of all pretension, he was evidently just what his Creator intended he should be; and every one felt, in listening to him, that if he were any thing else than what he was, it would be at the expense of disobeying the impulses of his own nature.

I cannot close this communication without saying that I have ever entertained a deep sense of my obligation to Dr. Maxcy,—not only for the important instruction which I received from him, but for his watchful care over me, at a period when " dangers stand thick around us." Mrs. Maxcy, so far as I know, is still living, highly esteemed by the community around her, and greatly blessed in the worthy characters of a family she has been instrumental of rearing. Though years have passed away since I have had the privilege of seeing her or her children, they are still the subjects of my grateful and affectionate recollections.

I am, dear Sir, very truly yours,
In the bonds of the Gospel,
GARDINER B. PERRY.

ROBERT BAYLOR SEMPLE.*
1790—1831.

ROBERT BAYLOR SEMPLE, the youngest son of John and Elizabeth (Walker) Semple, was born at Rose Mount, King and Queen County, Va., January 20, 1769. His father, who was the son of very wealthy parents, emigrated from Scotland to this country in early life, was a lawyer by profession, and a gentleman of high respectability. He died when his son Robert was only twelve months old; and, in consequence of having become security on behalf of several of his friends for a large amount, nearly his whole estate was required to meet the claims of creditors, and his wife and four children were left nearly penniless.

Mrs. Semple was warmly attached to the Episcopal Church,—then the Established Church of Virginia, and trained her children to a strict observance of its forms of worship. To this training, Robert, in after life, referred the fact that his conscience had been kept tender and wakeful, and he had been preserved from skeptical tendencies.

* Taylor's Va. Bapt.—MS. from Dr. Ryland.

At an early age, he was placed at school, first with a Mr. Taylor, and afterwards with the Rev. Peter Nelson,* known throughout Lower Virginia as one of the most distinguished teachers in the State. When Mr. Nelson removed to the Forks of Hanover, and established an Academy, knowing, as he did, the depressed circumstances of Mrs. Semple's family, and her inability to meet the expenses of Robert's education, and observing withal that he was a youth of great promise, he kindly tendered to him his board and tuition free of expense. Robert studied Latin and Greek under the instruction of Mr. Nelson, and at the age of sixteen had made such proficiency as to become a very competent assistant teacher in the Academy.

Having completed his academical course, he was recommended by his tutor and benefactor as well qualified to be a teacher, and he obtained a situation in a private family. Here he commenced the study of Law; and, being placed in circumstances of great temptation, he began insensibly to yield, and then sought to hush the clamours of conscience by the cavils of infidelity. Hence ensued a conflict which rendered him much of the time unhappy. About this time, the Baptists in that region were especially active and earnest in their efforts to promote evangelical and experimental religion. Among them was one aged man, whom Mr. Semple, regarding as a thorough fanatic, often encountered in argument, endeavouring to convince him that he had fallen into a foolish delusion. It turned out, however, that the old man, being thoroughly acquainted with the Scriptures, was too strong for his opponent; and it was not long before Mr. Semple, as the result of an examination of the Bible and of his own heart, acknowledged himself a ruined sinner, and expressed an humble hope of acceptance through the merits of his Redeemer. Though his prejudices against the Baptists had before been strong, he was brought now to cast in his lot with them, and was accordingly baptized in December, 1789, by Elder Theodorick Noel, and joined the Upper King and Queen Church.

With this change of feeling and of character originated a corresponding change of purpose in respect to his profession—he resolved to give up the study of Law, and devote himself to the Christian Ministry. His first attempt at preaching, which was made within a few days after he became a member of the church, was by no means a successful one; but, though conscious of his failure, it did not at all discourage him. For several months, he laboured in the neighbourhoods adjacent to his own home, with great zeal. In 1790, Bruington Church was constituted in King and Queen, and Mr. Semple was unanimously called to take the pastoral charge of it. On the 20th of September of this year, he was regularly examined and ordained to the work of the ministry, by Elders Robert Ware, Theo-

---

* PETER NELSON was a native of Hanover County, Va., and was graduated at William and Mary College, after which he returned to his native county, and, within a few years, joined the Episcopal Church, and was ordained to the work of the ministry. He established himself permanently at Wingfield, where he became the head of an Academy, at which many who afterwards rose to eminence were, at least in part, educated. About the year 1807, his wife became deeply anxious in regard to her spiritual interests, and was desirous of joining a Baptist church; but he earnestly and peremptorily resisted her wishes. Afterwards, however, he was led to an examination of the Scripture doctrine of Baptism, which resulted in a change of his own views on the subject, in consequence of which he was baptized by immersion, by Elder Broaddus, about the year 1808 or '09, after having been an Episcopal clergyman for upwards of twenty years. He died on the 15th of February, 1827.

dorick Noel, and Iveson Lewis.* He continued to sustain the pastoral relation to Bruington Church as long as he lived,—a period of forty years.

On the 1st of March, 1793, he was married to Mary Ann, daughter of Colonel Thomas Loury, of Caroline County,—an estimable young lady, who had, a few months before, attached herself to the Baptist Church. They were both without property, and felt the importance of practising a rigid economy, in order that he might, without embarrassment, prosecute the duties of his office. After two or three removals, they ultimately settled in King and Queen, on a farm called Mordington. Here they spent the greater part of their lives; and, by teaching a school and cultivating a farm, he soon placed himself in comfortable circumstances, and, before the close of life, had acquired considerable property.

Elder Semple had not been long in the ministry, before he attained a high reputation among all classes. Notwithstanding his necessary confinement in school, he travelled extensively in Lower Virginia, preaching the Gospel and confirming the disciples; though his regular ministrations were confined to King and Queen, and King William Counties. He was instrumental also of nursing and raising to a vigorous maturity several infant churches, which had been founded before he entered the ministry.

Elder Semple was identified with some of the earliest efforts of the Baptist denomination in this country, especially in Virginia, to send the Gospel among the Heathen. He was a member of the first meeting of the Baptist General Convention, and uniformly attended afterwards as long as he lived. From the origin of the Richmond Foreign and Domestic Mission Society, (afterwards the Virginia Baptist Missionary Society,) he lost no opportunity to promote its interests; and for a series of years he presided at its annual meetings. He was also usually the Moderator of the General Association of Virginia, for supplying the destitute parts of the State, and was President of its Board of Managers. He was also an earnest friend to the Colonization Society, regarding it in the triple light of a source of rich blessings to the slaves themselves, to the American nation, and to the savage tribes of Africa. The interests of education lay very near his heart. When the Columbian College, in the District of Columbia, became so deeply involved in debt that its existence as a Baptist College was seriously imperilled, the eyes of the Board were directed to him as the most suitable person to take charge of its financial concerns; and, at a great personal sacrifice, he accepted the appointment, and removed to Washington City, in July, 1827. He entered upon the new and difficult duties

* Iveson Lewis was a son of John Lewis, whose father, Zachary Lewis, emigrated to this country from Wales, in 1692, and settled in King and Queen County, Va. Here Iveson was born on the 4th of March, 1741, and here he lived and died. He was educated in the Church of England, and continued in that connection many years, but was subsequently converted, as he believed, under the preaching of John Waller, and was immersed and united with the Baptist Church about the year 1770. He commenced preaching shortly after, and in 1775 constituted the Church called Matthews, in the county of that name, and continued to visit them, in the capacity of Pastor, once a month, for many years, at a distance of about fifty miles. He also organized two churches in the County of Gloucester, about the year 1790, and sustained a sort of pastoral relation to them for a considerable time. Advancing age compelled him at length to discontinue his ministrations to these distant churches, and to confine his labours to those in his more immediate neighbourhood, in King and Queen, and Middlesex Counties, where he was regularly engaged until December, 1814. He died in the exercise of a triumphant faith, on the 5th of January, 1815.

now devolved upon him, with great discretion and energy; though it pleased Infinite Wisdom that he should not live to accomplish the work.

As an Author, he had considerable reputation, especially in his own denomination. In 1809, he published a Catechism for the use of children, which met with much favour. In 1810, he published the History of Virginia Baptists, with several biographical notices appended, which has generally been considered his most important work. He was also the author of a Memoir of Elder Straughan, and of various Circular Letters from the Dover Association. He also published Letters to Alexander Campbell, which, however, in the opinion of some, were not among his most felicitous productions.

Mr. Semple received many testimonies of public confidence and respect. As early as the year 1805, he was invited to the Presidency of Transylvania University, but declined the invitation. In 1820, he was elected President of the Baptist Triennial Convention, and continued to hold the office till the time of his death. In 1814, the degree of Master of Arts was conferred upon him by Brown University. In 1824, he was honoured with the degree of Doctor of Divinity from the same institution; and in 1826, he had a repetition of the honour from the College of William and Mary; but in both cases he declined it from conscientious considerations.

Mr. Semple suffered severe trials, but they were mostly of a domestic character. The place of his residence was exceedingly unhealthy, and his family was often visited with protracted and dangerous illness. Of twelve children, only four were living at the time of his death. From 1825 to 1827, his house was little else than a hospital; and, though his own life and health were mercifully spared, most of his family were very seriously ill, and two of his children carried in quick succession to the grave.

When he left King and Queen County in 1827, he remained a while in Washington, and then took up his abode in Fredericksburg. With the management of the concerns of the College on the one hand, and the care of the Bruington Church on the other, he found it necessary to be almost constantly journeying in opposite directions; and this, with the great amount of care and responsibility that rested upon him, proved too great a burden for his already decaying constitution. In the year 1831, his health became perceptibly impaired. In the course of that year an extensive revival of religion took place in the church at Bruington, and he was permitted to see, in the month of September, more than one hundred admitted to the ordinance of Baptism, and become members of the church of which he had so long been the Pastor. His last visit to Bruington was made about three weeks before his death. On his return home, he suffered not a little from travelling in extremely inclement weather; and it was soon apparent that he was seized with a serious illness, though his family flattered themselves that it was nothing more than a severe type of the prevailing influenza. It turned out to be a violent fever, which had a fatal termination in just one week from its commencement. He predicted, from the beginning, that it would prove to be his last illness; and so deeply was he impressed with this thought that it was the opinion of his physician that the remedies administered were in a great measure neutralized from the influence which his mind exercised over his body. His mind continued perfectly tranquil during his whole illness; and one of his last expressions was,—"I can depart in peace." He died on Sunday morning, December 25, 1831. The Funeral Sermon was preached by the Rev. Andrew Broaddus; and two or three other Discourses, commemorative of his character and services, were delivered in different places.

FROM THE REV. ROBERT RYLAND, D. D.

RICHMOND, Va., December 30, 1854.

Rev. and dear Sir: I take pleasure in complying with your request for a brief sketch of the character of the Rev. Robert B. Semple. I knew him from my earliest childhood; was awakened to the importance of Divine truth under his labours; was baptized, encouraged to study for the ministry, and ordained to the office of an Evangelist, by him; and have been a careful observer of the effects of his life on the morals of a wide community, and on the prosperity of our churches throughout Eastern Virginia. I mention these circumstances to enable you to judge of my opportunities for forming a correct estimate of his character.

In contemplating his ministerial character, nothing comes to me more forcibly than his great perseverance. I have known many men of equal, perhaps superior, abilities, who fell far short of his usefulness, because they wanted his decision. He was deliberate in forming his conclusions, but, when formed, he acted upon them. He felt that the ground on which he stood was solid, and he, therefore, stood erect and fearless. His course through life was consequently not an irregular one, vacillating from one extreme of doctrine to another, now manifesting an excessive zeal, and now settled down into a frigid insensibility; but it was uniform, steady, dignified. You always found him the same man. Human energy is often wasted because it is applied to some point, for a short time, with great vehemence, and then diverted from that to another before the first is accomplished. Such was not the manner of Mr. Semple. He never abandoned a project because it proved to be difficult or unpopular, but went right on, until a fair experiment had convinced him what was expedient. Hence it was that he acquired so much weight of character in the community. Every person confided in the soundness of his judgment, and in the energy with which he executed his purposes. If he had appointments to fulfil, he suffered no impediment, which mortal enterprise could overcome, to interfere with them. His congregations would go out to hear him in cold and rainy weather, because they were sure of *his* attendance. He was one of your practical men, that set themselves to work in good earnest, and from the same fixed point never decline until their aim is accomplished. It ought to be set down also to his credit that he was constitutionally indolent. His physical nature seems to have been changed by the force of principle. Whatever of activity he displayed was the result, not of natural temperament, but of grace Divine, urging him forward against the current of his feelings;—the effect of holy, ardent love, prompting him to spend and be spent for the salvation of souls. Many men are endued with a restless temper, that makes them energetic by starts. Their motions are rapid, but uncertain and eccentric. Their zeal is blazing, but misguided and injudicious. They rarely effect much good. But this man's energy was steady and efficient. His zeal was uniform and salutary, because guided by a sound judgment, and directed to a hallowed end.

Another quality by which he was distinguished was his intimate acquaintance with the human heart. This was one of the chief sources of his greatness and usefulness. He applied his mind more to the study of this than to books. If he addressed the unconverted, they were often astonished at his perfect insight into their feelings. Like the woman of Samaria, they were constrained to say,— " He told me all things that ever I did." He described them so faithfully that they found no way of escape, and had to confess that they were the very sinners whom he had described. If he spoke to Christians, he seemed to know their trials, their secret exercises, their besetting infirmities. He expatiated on them more correctly than they could have done themselves. And he was well skilled to apply a remedy suited to their spiritual diseases; to administer comfort to the depressed, caution to the unguarded, and reproof to the disobedient. He aimed his darts not over the heads of men, but at their consciences, and they felt their point. He abhorred the disposition which prompts some to attempt great things, merely to attract the stare of the ignorant. The useful was preferred by him to the ornamental, and the homely phrase that all would understand, was selected to convey his thoughts, rather than the classic one which would be understood only by the learned.

His preaching was distinguished also for its practical tendency. He scarcely ever preached without showing his hearers what were their duties, and urging them with motives to their fulfilment. It is true he laid the basis of these duties in the Cross of Jesus Christ, and gave them their just value, as the effects, not the causes, of salvation. But then he insisted on them, as the indispensable evidences of discipleship, and as being " good and profitable unto men." He found it necessary, as a Pastor, again and again, to urge the brethren to a holy life, because they were far more apt to learn the doctrines of religion than to comply with its injunctions.

Another prominent trait in his character was gravity. The form of his head, the strongly marked features of his face, the contemplative moods to which his mind was habituated, and, above all, the air of unaffected sanctity that spread itself over his whole deportment, tended to inspire with awe those who came into his presence. It was this that gave him such a power of discipline in his family and in his church, and imparted such weight to his opinions and decisions as the Moderator of deliberative assemblies. It required a man of more than ordinary nerve to oppose his views,—much more to oppose them in a rancorous or obstinate spirit. A trifling incident will serve to illustrate the force of Mr. Semple's character in this respect. There was once a sale of household and farming utensils near his residence; and, wishing to purchase some articles, he attended on the day appointed. Among the things put up to the highest bidder was a *fiddle*, but not a single bid was made for it, notwithstanding the earnest efforts of the auctioneer. Knowing that a certain gentleman present wished to purchase the instrument, the conductor of the sale afterwards inquired why he had not made a bid for it. He confessed that he was awed by the presence of the holy man, and then added, with vehemence,— " Robert B. Semple is the only person I ever saw in my life, that I was afraid of!" This austerity of manner was however greatly softened on a more intimate acquaintance, and by a sweet smile that occasionally played on his countenance. Few men ever had a deeper or more active benevolence towards their fellow-creatures, or put forth more disinterested and sustained efforts for their highest good.

I will only add that no man probably felt a deeper interest than he in the general welfare of Zion. While the disciples are classed into so many little families, there is danger lest they feel an undue solicitude, each for his own family, and disregard the common cause. Mr. Semple felt a deep interest in the prosperity of his own denomination, but he had also a heart to pray and to labour for the progress of the Gospel in every part of the world. He could have said with Paul,—" Besides those things that are without, that which cometh upon me daily, the care of all the churches.'' Indeed, as his reputation advanced, he was oftener put in requisition to preach in distant neighbourhoods, than was agreeable to his own people. Wherever he sojourned, there he went to work, as if he had been among his own charge. And, on this account, he was looked up to by all the churches as a kind of Apostle; was often called upon to decide controversies, and adjust difficulties. One of his favourite themes in the pulpit was the duty of brotherly love. His soul was oppressed by the schisms which have, in some instances, distracted and rent our churches. To the variant parties his private and public counsels were excellent. If, however, he, at any time, displayed an authoritative spirit, it was while preaching on this subject. He had little patience for the senseless quarrels of those who profess to be disciples of the Prince of Peace, and children of the God of love. In fine, as a public teacher of religion, he was deservedly eminent. He was always appropriate. The variety of his sentiments, the originality of his manner, the solid, earnest, and devout constitution of his mind, made him profitable to all classes of hearers.

Mr. Semple was of ordinary stature, rather inclined to corpulency,—of strongly marked features, expressive of profound thought. His head was large, and indicated deep devotional feeling. He was of fair complexion, deep blue eyes, thin beard, small eye-brows, projecting forehead, dark but not black hair, gradually thinning and whitening with age. His walk was perhaps his most striking peculiarity. It was *waddling*, usually hurried, and suggested to the observer that he was going *somewhere*, and for some *definite object*. Indeed there was something in his whole bearing calculated to impress,—something of patriarchal dignity, not assumed, but natural, that inspired reverence, and that would have prompted a stranger, seeing him in the midst of an assembly of great men, to ask *who he was*. Withal he was, in private life, and among his own people, loved as well as venerated. He could condescend to the poor, without seeming to feel it to be condescension, and could always have a kind word or a sportive gesture for children, without a tincture of levity.

Very fraternally yours,
ROBERT RYLAND.

ABEL WOODS.*
1790—1850.

ABEL WOODS, a son of Samuel and Abigail Woods, was born in Princeton, Mass., August 15, 1765. His father was a very intelligent farmer, and both his parents were highly respected members of the Congregational Church. He lost his mother in his early childhood; but his father instructed him carefully in the great principles of religion, and, besides giving him the advantages of a common school, devoted many of the winter evenings to assisting him in his studies. In 1783, when he was about eighteen years of age, he became deeply concerned in respect to his immortal interests. After having been for a long time in darkness, from not having had right views, as he afterwards believed, of the Gospel plan of salvation, he at length emerged from it into a state of tranquillity and

* Dr. Kendrick's Fun. Serm.—MS. from Rev. Alvah Woods, D. D.

joyful hope. Almost immediately he became impressed with the idea that it was his duty to devote himself to the Christian ministry; and this idea having at length grown into a full conviction, he began to direct his efforts to this object.

Notwithstanding he had been educated a Pedobaptist, doubts seem to have arisen in his mind, at an early period, in respect to the validity of Infant Baptism, and also of Baptism by Sprinkling; and the result of a somewhat extended and earnest inquiry on the subject was a conviction that Baptism could be legitimately administered only by immersion, and only to believers. In 1786, at the age of twenty-one, he was admitted to the Baptist Church in Leicester, Mass. He still continued to labour on his father's farm, while he devoted all his leisure hours to study in preparation for the ministry. It would appear that he subsequently regretted not having taken a more extended course. He says, in a brief sketch of his life which he left, alluding to this period,—"Deeply sensible of my ignorance and unworthiness, I should have commenced academical studies, but for the bad advice of a Baptist minister,—advice which I shall lament having followed, so long as I live."

In 1790, he began to preach stately in the towns of Princeton and Holden, and his labours seemed to be attended with a blessing. He was subsequently invited to settle as Pastor in Dublin, and Alstead, N. H., and Cavendish, Vt., in which latter place, he preached about a year. At length, he visited Shoreham, Vt., where his labours seemed to be eminently useful. Here a church was soon gathered, and he was ordained, and set apart as its Pastor, in February, 1795.

Mr. Woods remained Pastor of the Church at Shoreham fifteen years; during which time there were three revivals, each of which brought a considerable accession to the church. His labours were, by no means, confined to his own immediate congregation, but he often went abroad, as a public man, and bore an important part in various Benevolent Associations, and in organizing a system of effort for the spread of the Gospel. Owing to peculiar circumstances, and much to the regret of his people, he resigned his charge in 1810; and immediately after spent about a year in missionary labour, chiefly under the direction of the Vermont Missionary Society. In 1811, he settled at Panton, Vt., and subsequently laboured in Addison, Granville, and Hubbardston, until the year 1826. In these several places, especially in Addison, large numbers were gathered into the church, as the result of his labour. In October, 1826, he removed to Essex, N. Y., on Lake Champlain, where he remained, labouring most of the time as Pastor, until 1837. At that time, being sensible that the infirmities of age were gradually coming upon him, he felt admonished to withdraw from the active duties of the ministry; and, accordingly, he left Essex, and took up his residence with his son-in-law, the Rev. Alanson L. Covell, then minister of the First Baptist Church in Albany. Here he remained about a year and a half, when the death of Mr. Covell rendered another removal of the family desirable, and it was determined that they should make their future home at Hamilton, N. Y. He selected this spot, partly on account of its pleasant situation, but especially from its being the seat of the Baptist Literary and Theological Institution, in which he felt a deep interest, and to which he had been a liberal contributor. He took up his residence here in the spring of 1838, and never made another remove till he was summoned to his long home.

Mr. Woods retained both his intellectual and physical powers, without much perceptible abatement, to extreme old age. He took a deep interest in passing events, especially as they were connected with the progress of the Kingdom of Christ. It had long been his prayer that he might be spared a lingering sickness at last; and that when there was no more of active service for him to perform in his Master's cause, if it were God's will, he might be called to his rest. And this desire of his heart was granted. During the week previous to his death, he was slightly ill, but not in such a degree as to interrupt materially his ordinary employments. On Saturday he seemed better, and, on retiring to rest at evening, dispensed with the little medicine which he had taken for a few of the preceding days. In the course of the night, his disease which had before seemed so light, took a sudden and fatal turn, and, after a few hours, the earthly tabernacle had become a clod. He died August 11, 1850. His Funeral Sermon was preached by the Rev. A. C. Kendrick, D. D., and was published.

In December, 1792, Mr. Woods was married to Mary Smith, of Clarendon, Vt., who, a few months before, had joined the Baptist Church. She was a lady of great excellence, and happily adapted to fill the station of a minister's wife. She died nearly three years before her husband. They had six children, three of whom died long before their parents; and of the other three who survived them, the eldest is Dr. Alvah Woods, late President of Alabama University; the second is the widow of the late Rev. A. L. Covell;* and the youngest is the wife of the Rev. Dr. Pattison, Professor of Theology at Newton, Mass.

FROM THE REV. LEONARD WOODS, D. D.
PROFESSOR IN THE ANDOVER THEOLOGICAL SEMINARY.

ANDOVER, January 21, 1852.

My dear Sir: You ask me for my recollections of my beloved brother, the Rev. Abel Woods. He was several years older than myself, but I have a distinct recollection of some of the most interesting scenes of his early life. At the time when his mind was first seriously directed to the subject of religion, the Congregational Church in Princeton was very deficient in the spirit of piety, and exerted apparently but little of truly Christian influence. But

---

* ALANSON L. COVELL, the only son and youngest child of the Rev. Lemuel Covell, was born in Pittstown, N. Y., January 20, 1804. From early childhood, he evinced great liveliness of temper, as well as high and generous aspirations. At the age of nineteen, he united with the Baptist Church in Charlotte, Vt., and shortly after commenced preaching. In 1828, he became the Pastor of a Church in Addison, Vt., and was married shortly after. After labouring here, as well as with some other churches, for about two years, he removed, in February, 1831, to Whitesborough, N. Y., where he remained for five years, labouring with great acceptance and success. In 1835, he received a unanimous invitation to become the Pastor of the First Baptist Church in Albany, and, having accepted it, took up his residence there in January, 1836. In the autumn of that year, he took a prominent part in the organization of the American and Foreign Bible Society, and delivered a discourse in reference to it, which was highly approved and widely circulated. He died at Albany, after an illness of seven months, on the 20th of September, 1837, in the thirty-fourth year of his age. He was an eminently devout and godly man, but was subject to great spiritual conflicts. His whole character was one of uncommon attraction. His death was deeply mourned by all who had witnessed the sweetness and purity of his spirit, or his exemplary and devoted life.

there was a little company of devout Baptists, who lived in a neighbourhood in the South part of Princeton, and the North part of Holden. Among these Christians, my brother found those who could sympathize with his feelings, and could afford him the Christian aid and counsel which he needed, and which, through the blessing of God, proved the means of his hopeful conversion and his subsequent growth in grace. He had a youthful friend, who was intimately associated with him in his religious duties. That friend was Sylvanus Haynes,* afterwards well known as a minister in the Baptist churches. He was accustomed, at stated times, to meet with my brother for conversation and prayer, in a retired place in a grove during the summer, and at each other's houses during the winter. I was then about ten years old. I knew the object of their meetings; and I well remember how kind and pleasant their demeanour was towards each other, and towards all around them; how cheerful and happy they appeared, and how earnest they were to get knowledge, particularly on the subject of religion. And I remember that their appearance led me to think how excellent religion is, and how desirable to obtain it in early life.

When my brother told our father, who was a member of the Congregational Church, that he was desirous to join the Baptist Church, our father gave his free consent. I was present when my brother was admitted to Baptism by immersion. It was on the Sabbath, and the assembly was too large to be accommodated in a private house. They resorted, therefore, to a large barn, then empty. I sat on a high beam, near the middle of the building, and there, after a solemn sermon, I heard the examination of my brother, as to his religious knowledge and experience. After which, I went to a small river, and witnessed the Baptism.

My brother soon cherished a desire to preach the Gospel; and, for two or three years, he was engaged in such reading and such exercises as he thought best suited to fit him for the sacred work. He became familiar with Doddridge's Rise and Progress, some of Edwards' works, and other pious books, making the Word of God his chief study.

While he remained at home, he was my companion, day and night. Though he was a very affectionate brother, he was very sparing in his conversation with me on the subject of religion. But some of his remarks were distinctly and permanently impressed on my memory. He said to me repeatedly, and very kindly,—"Leonard, I hope you will be a Christian." Sometimes he said,—"I *expect* you will be a Christian." No advice or warning could have touched my heart so much as to know that my brother hoped and expected that I should become a Christian. Once he came home from a religious meeting, later than common, and when he came to bed with me, he merely said,—"I hope, Leonard, that God is converting some of your mates." This single remark took strong hold of my childish feelings, and such a manner of treating the subject of religion,—such brevity and simplicity of remark, joined with humbleness of mind, and the spirit of love, distinguished him through life.

* SYLVANUS HAYNES, son of Joseph Haynes, was born at Princeton, Mass., February 22, 1768. At the age of about fourteen, he became hopefully pious; at the age of seventeen, he began to have scruples on the subject of Baptism; and in July, 1786, when he was in his nineteenth year, he was baptized by immersion. He commenced preaching in March, 1789, and for about a year exercised his ministry in his native place. In March, 1790, he removed to Middletown, Vt. In July, 1791, he received ordination, and took the pastoral care of the church in that place. In August, 1791, he was married to Louisa Gardner, a member of the Middletown Church. After a successful ministry at Middletown, he removed, in October, 1817, to Elbridge, in the same State, where also a rich blessing attended his labours. His wife died in March 1825, and in January, 1826, he was married to Mary Coman, of Cheshire, Mass. He died on the 30th of December following, after a short illness. He was greatly esteemed, both as a Christian and a minister.

His preaching was exceedingly plain and scriptural, and his prayers free and fervent. But in all his performances he manifested devout *reverence*. It could not be otherwise; for pious reverence and awe belonged to the settled habit of his mind. He happily employed his strong and manly intellect in such a manner as to make the truths of Revelation intelligible to common people, and even to children. His preaching abounded in anecdotes; but they were pertinent and instructive, though evidently carried to excess.

He had a brief and striking way of answering objections. When a man who did not believe the doctrine of the Saints' Perseverance, said,—"What if David had died after his fall, before his repentance," he answered,—"What if the angels who were carrying Elijah to Heaven, had let him slip out of their hands?"

My brother, being the first ordained minister settled in the town of Shoreham, was entitled to the bounty land set apart by the laws of the State, as the property of the first minister. By vote of the town, this land was his; and he occupied it, and made improvements on it for several years. At length it was claimed by a majority of the inhabitants; and, after an expensive lawsuit, it was, with manifest injustice, taken from him. He was thus embarrassed, and involved in a heavy debt. There was, however, a way in which he could evade his obligation to pay the unjust debt. Some of his friends advised him to resort to means which were of doubtful propriety, though not condemned by the laws of the State. Here came the trial of his moral principle. Though the temptation was strong, he overcame it. He determined to avoid whatever would be likely to discredit his character and calling, and to proceed with perfect fairness and honour, however great the losses and difficulties to which he might be subjected. And many a time did he afterwards refer with heartfelt satisfaction to the sound principle which had guided his conduct, devoutly ascribing his deliverance from that temptation to the timely help of Divine grace.

My brother was conscientiously wedded to the principle of Close Communion, so far as relates to the Lord's Supper. But, in every thing else, he had cordial fellowship with other Christians, both publicly and privately. His feelings were most kind and fraternal towards all the followers of Christ, and he delighted to reciprocate with them all the offices of Christian love. He told me that he was as really united in heart with Christians of other denominations, and enjoyed as serene and happy communion with them, as with those of his own.

In this connection permit me to mention what took place during my last visit to him, more than five years since. In the village of Hamilton, where he lived, there was a Baptist church, and a Presbyterian church, and the Lord's Supper was to be administered in both of them in the afternoon, instead of the common Sunday service. I had preached in the Baptist church in the morning, and was to administer the Sacrament in the Presbyterian church in the afternoon. At noon, my brother told me that he intended to go with me to the Presbyterian church. I said to him that I should be glad to have him with me, and should be much gratified if he would assist me in administering the Lord's Supper. "I have no objection," he replied; he went and sat with me at the Sacramental table. After I had introduced the service, and administered the bread, I requested him to address the church and to lead in the next prayer. This he did, giving to the members an affectionate and faithful exhortation, and then offering up, with great fervency, the usual thanksgiving and supplication before the distribution of the cup. In the whole service there was nothing to show that he was a Baptist, except that, while he joined with us *in heart* in commemorating the death of Christ, he did not outwardly partake of the bread and wine. He had a large and

loving heart, and he embraced in cordial fellowship all who bore the image of
the meek and lowly Jesus.

Under the repeated bereavements which were allotted to him. and under all
his other trials, some of which were very severe, he manifested a subdued
and quiet spirit.   While his heart was bleeding under Divine chastisement, he
found relief in prayer, and, with filial confidence, yielded himself to the will
of his Father in Heaven.

In my brother's religious life, there was a long succession of clouds and
darkness, intermixed with great serenity and joy.   My impression is that he
attached too much importance to particular frames of mind, and thought too
little of the habitual course of his life.   He had a clear and often a distressing view of his inward corruptions, and his shortcomings in duty; and, in
consequence of this, he trusted less and less in himself, and more and more in
his Saviour.   He spoke of it as a wonder of free and sovereign grace that a
sinner like him should be saved.   His letters were characterized by a fraternal and devotional spirit.   He always spoke of his success with all lowliness
and meekness, and of his humble hope that, through boundless grace, he
should be admitted to the rest which remaineth for the people of God.

Yours, with hearty love and esteem,

L. WOODS.

DANIEL WILDMAN.*
1791—1849.

DANIEL WILDMAN was born in Danbury, Conn., on the 10th of December, 1764.   He was a son of Capt. Daniel Wildman, whose grandfather,
Abram Wildman, emigrated from the North of England to this country in
or about the year 1683, and settled in Danbury, where the family have
since resided.

The father of the subject of this sketch gave him the advantages of a
good common education, and his proficiency was highly creditable to both
his industry and his talents.   But he early discovered a somewhat way-
ward disposition, which occasioned his father great anxiety, and drew from
him many serious admonitions, which were not altogether without effect,
though they seem to have done little more than embarrass him in his sinful
course.   At the age of twenty, his mind was powerfully wrought upon in
respect to his salvation, and for several months he kept aloof from all
scenes of gaiety, and devoted much of his time to serious reflection; but,
not finding the comfort which he had expected, he resisted, and finally succeeded to a great extent in banishing, his religious impressions.   The next
two years he spent in utter carelessness, with the exception of brief interruptions from the involuntary workings of conscience; but, at the end of
that period, when he was about twenty-two years of age, a more deep and
decisive work was commenced in his heart, which, at no distant period,
resulted in his indulging the hope that he had been born from above.   His
views of his own utter unworthiness, and of the infinite grace and excellence of the Gospel, were, at this period, intense and well-nigh overwhelm-

* MSS. from his son,—Rev. N. Wildman, and Rev. G. Robins.

ing; and the record of these exercises, which he made shortly after, and which still remains, shows that his Christian life must have been very thorough in its beginning.

Several years passed after this change in Mr. Wildman's character before he devoted himself to the Christian ministry; and, during a part of the time, he was occupied in teaching a school. He was licensed to preach by the Church in Danbury, in 1791, when he was about twenty-seven years of age. He commenced his labours at Plymouth, Conn. Here he continued until 1796, when he removed to Wolcott, where he was ordained, and remained two years. In 1798, he removed to Bristol, and commenced preaching to a few people, in a chamber, in his own house; but, in the progress of his labours here, a meeting-house was built, and the church greatly enlarged and strengthened. In 1804, he removed to Middletown, Upper Houses, where his labours were attended by a considerable revival of religion. In 1805, he divided his labours between Middletown and the First Church in Suffield; and at this period he is said to have been at the zenith of his power. In 1806, he returned to Bristol, where he laboured some ten or twelve years longer; thence removed to Stratfield, where he laboured some two or three years; and thence to Bristol again; though, subsequently to this, he spent some portion of his time with the Stratfield Church. In the year 1820, he preached half of the time in Carmel, N. Y., and baptized, during the year, about three hundred persons. After this, he spent a few years in Licking County, O., but in 1826 returned to Connecticut, and was settled over the Church in New London for about three years, in one of which the church received about seventy to its communion. After this, he laboured successively with the church in Russell, Mass.; with the church in Meriden, Conn.; with the First Church in Norwich; and finally with the Church in Andover.

The last years of his life were spent in the family of his son, who resided at Lebanon; and, though he was so blind that he was unable to read, he continued to preach occasionally at Lebanon and elsewhere until he was eighty years old. His last sermon was especially rich in evangelical truth, and was delivered with great pathos. His last illness was brief, and attended with little suffering. For some time before his death, he was frequently heard to preach regular and pathetic discourses in his sleep. He died at his son's residence at Lebanon on the 21st of February, 1849, aged eighty-five.

Mr. Wildman was married on the 15th of August, 1791, to Mary Weed, of Plymouth, Conn. They had ten children, seven of whom reached maturity, and made a public profession of religion. One of them, the Rev. Nathan Wildman, is now (1858) the Pastor of the Baptist Church in Plainville, Conn. Mrs. Wildman died in April, 1816.

FROM THE REV. GURDON ROBINS.

HARTFORD, Conn., April 9, 1858.

My dear Sir: I was well acquainted with the Rev. Daniel Wildman, and am happy to render you any aid in my power, to enable you to give a faithful representation of him; though the circumstances in which I write forbid my attempting any minute delineation of his character. I will only give you my impressions concerning him as a preacher.

And I can truly say that I regarded him as among the very best preachers of his day, to whom I was accustomed to listen. His discourses were evidently framed, not to please the ear, but to enlighten the understanding, to move the conscience, to subdue and purify the heart. They were distinguished for clear and consecutive thought and logical accuracy, as well as for forcible and pungent appeal, and sometimes for a subduing pathos. It was evidently his delight to preach Christ and Him crucified; and it was his privilege to see many gathered into the church as the fruit of his labours. His personal appearance was favourable to the general effect of his preaching. His figure was commanding, and his features prominent, and not prepossessing, when in repose; but when lighted up by some great evangelical theme, his face would sometimes glow with such effulgence that it would remind you of Moses coming down from the Mount.

He was present at a ministers' meeting in Hartford County, on one occasion, after he was very far advanced in years. He had listened the whole day to the exercises of the occasion, which consisted partly in the discussion of some important topics in Theology. There was a rule that there should be a sermon, at the close of the exercises, in the evening; and it fell to my lot to preach; but as my health was not good, and I was desirous of hearing this venerable father on the very important subjects which had been under discussion, I prevailed upon him to take my place. On his consenting to my request, he said, with a characteristic smile,—" Well, I will try to tell the boys how the matter stands." He preached a sermon nearly two hours long, which was an epitome of the entire body of Divinity, and throughout which he spoke with perfect ease and freedom, showing that he spoke at once from a well furnished mind and a well regulated heart. At the close, a most hearty responsive Amen went up from every part of the house. This was the last sermon which I ever heard from him, and the impression which it made upon my mind still remains vivid.

Accept the assurance of my fraternal regard.

GURDON ROBINS.

FROM THE REV. DANIEL WALDO.

SYRACUSE, March 3, 1858.

My dear Sir: I doubt not there are many persons who can tell you more about the Rev. Daniel Wildman than I can; but what I remember concerning him it gives me pleasure to communicate. My acquaintance with him was limited to a few months in 1806 or 1807, which he spent in Suffield, Conn. He was regarded, at that time, as one of the lights of his denomination; and he was there by request of the Rev. Mr. Hastings, minister of the Baptist Church in the First Parish of the town; and, though my residence and parish were two miles West of that, I early made his acquaintance, and often met him, and sometimes heard him preach, while he was in that neighbourhood. He attracted very considerable attention from persons of all classes, and had, no doubt deservedly, the reputation of being much more than an ordinary man.

In person, as I remember him, he was rather above the middle size, of symmetrical proportions, and of a countenance expressive of thought, intelligence, and firmness. His movements were free and easy, and his whole air that of a man who felt that he realized that human life was designed for higher purposes than mere animal or even intellectual indulgence. He seemed to be truly earnest in his Master's work. He preached very often during his stay in our neighbourhood, and his preaching was largely attended, not only by persons belonging to his own communion, but by other denominations. His manner in the pulpit was simple and natural, and much more cultivated than that of the Baptist clergy generally in his day. And the same was true of his discourses. Though not written, they were evidently well premeditated, and showed a disciplined and logical mind. His text was the true index to his subject, and his object seemed to be to bring out the very meaning of the Spirit in the most perspicuous, and at the same time the most forcible, manner he could. His voice was not remarkable for compass, but was pleasant and sufficiently varied in its inflexions to give effect to whatever sentiment he wished to convey. The matter of his discourses was intensely evangelical; and this no doubt was one secret of the interest which his preaching awakened.

In private intercourse Mr. Wildman was familiar and agreeable, yet always sufficiently dignified. He was understood to hold some peculiar views in regard to God's covenant of grace with men; and when he preached for me, I gave him a text which was designed to develop them; but his discourse was throughout in strict accordance with the accredited orthodoxy of New England.

The above is all that I remember concerning him, that would be likely to be to your purpose; and even that you must take with all the allowance to be made for a man who lacks but a few months of having completed his ninety-sixth year.

Truly yours,
DANIEL WALDO.

WILLIAM BATCHELDER.

1792—1818.

FROM MISS ELIZABETH P. PEABODY.

BOSTON, September 5, 1854.

My dear Sir: I have not forgotten my promise, but it was not until yesterday that I could find a moment to see Mr. Batchelder's daughter, whom I wished to hear talk of her father again, and repeat those anecdotes by which she illustrates a character, whose delineation, as it seems to me, would form one of the most interesting chapters in your work, and one from which most important instruction may be derived for the profession. For it shows that the original apostolic fervour, single-heartedness, and many-sided activity, with utter self-abnegation, is possible in this age of the world.

If any man was ever made of porcelain clay, it was Mr. Batchelder. His personal beauty was very great. It was the common remark of those conversant with the great works of art of the sixteenth century, that he recalled one of the master pieces that represented the Saviour; and, in going among the hills and woods of Maine and New Hampshire, where he laboured so assiduously and ardently for the best years of his life, the old people, who never saw a work of art, will tell you that Mr. Batchelder's countenance seemed like that of the blessed Jesus! His hair and eyes were of the colour of Daniel Webster's, with whom he was connected

by the Batchelder blood; but his head was higher and lighter, and his
neck longer, and, on account of frequent nervous headaches, brought on by
the slightest colds, he allowed his beautiful black hair to grow long, which
fell in close ringlets in his neck, nearly to his shoulders.

I remember once going into the Boston Athenæum with his daughter,
when Cole's picture of Christ sitting comforted after the temptation, was
on exhibition, and she was transfixed before it with great expression of
emotion. As soon as she found her voice, she said to me,—"That head
and countenance are exactly like father's."

But his fine temperament of body, and his brilliant qualities which
would have made him the greatest ornament of life, were wholly unaccom-
panied with that sickly, sentimental exaction of others, which often
weakens the manliness of men of this fine order of genius, and leaves
them to live a life of complaint and querulousness. Mr. Batchelder, with
all his sensibility, always appeared as a Power.

I will begin by showing the beautiful wild stock of nature, on which was
engrafted this rare scion of Heavenly Grace.

WILLIAM BATCHELDER, a son of Ebenezer and Susanna (Crosley)
Batchelder, was born in Boston, March 25, 1768. His father was one of
seven brothers,—all Deacons in Congregational churches. His maternal
grandfather was Deacon of Church Green, then called the New South,
where, afterwards, Dr. Kirkland, Mr. Thacher, Dr. Greenwood, and Dr.
Young successively ministered.

His parents were wealthy, but both of them died within a week of each
other, in 1781, leaving William thirteen years of age. The estate was left
to be settled by a neighbour and intimate friend, who was made executor
of the estate, and guardian of the children, by his father. A destructive
fire, immediately after, laid waste the estates of both Mr. Batchelder and
the guardian, destroying a large quantity of important papers, and by an
extraordinary fatality the guardian died. William chose, at this time, to
go to the house of a relative in the upper part of New Hampshire, where he
supposed he might have leisure to study, which was already a decided passion with him.

But he was presently shocked by the tone of this family, which seemed
to him to be singularly irreflective, and wholly given to enjoying the goods
of this world in the form of good eating. He, therefore, determined to
leave them; and, as he afterwards said, wishing to break in upon the dul-
ness of their life by at least a little inconvenience, that might stir them out of
their absolute indolence with the question of "What is it?"—the last
thing he did before he left was to go on the top of the house, and stop up
the chimney. He next went to his grandfather Batchelder's, who was a
wealthy farmer, and also had a manufactory of iron ware, in which he
employed many foreign workmen. While William was there, one of these
was killed by an accident; and, during the last few hours of his life, William sat by his bedside, talking to him of death and the world to come.
He talked as a Protestant, and perhaps the workmen were Catholics; but
at any rate this talk offended them; and, after the Funeral, when the old
man had sent them all to their rooms to meditate on death and judgment,
while he himself was devoutly reading the Scriptures at home, the workmen,

gathering in one of the rooms, called William to them, and told him that they were going to punish him for what he had said to their dying friend. They proceeded to undress him and wrap him in a winding sheet, and stretch him out on the boards upon which the corpse had been laid, and there they bound him down like a corpse, and left him, as it were, for the night. Nevertheless, every now and then, they would come in with a light, and look at him, as if watching the dead.

He amused himself with drumming with his fingers,—the only motion he could make; and had strength enough of mind to resist the ghastly impression, which might have been permanently injurious to his nervous system, had not his courage been as great as his imagination was excitable. In the morning he was released, but the whole thing was so painful to him that he did not care to expose himself to any repetition of the same kind of tricks, while he was too generous to tell his grandfather, who would, he felt certain, have discharged all the workmen, as sacrilegious, for thus trifling with the semblance of death. He concluded, therefore, to leave in silence, and he walked off the next day, and, after a time, arriving in Andover, he offered himself to a blacksmith as apprentice, whose good wife took him into the house, on his representing himself as an orphan and destitute.

Here it was his fancy to play a singular prank. The old woman offered to teach him to read, and the Catechism; and he assented with alacrity. The Catechism was easily taught by rote; but the stupidity about learning his letters seemed intense. Nevertheless he was a very great favourite with the old woman; for his disposition was very sweet, his bodily activity great, and his individuality altogether singularly attractive. One day the old woman observed on the clean white pannel over the fire-place, a verse of poetry, in an elegant handwriting, and asked who wrote it; to which one of the men replied that he saw William writing it. She said,—"Pshaw, William cannot read his letters;" but to her utter bewilderment, and even vexation, William, who was appealed to, did not deny it. No explanation was possible, and he did not attempt any; but, suddenly struck with a sense of having insulted her kindness, he felt that he could not stay to brook her reproaches; and, resorting to his usual mode of cutting short difficulties, left immediately.

He wandered off till he came to the Merrimack River, where he saw a man on a raft going down the river: he called to him and asked for a passage, and the man took him on. As he passed Haverhill, over against the Baptist meeting-house, where he afterwards ministered, he saw upon the banks the congregation assembled to witness an act of Baptism by immersion. Is it not quite possible that this expressive symbol, entering in among the images of his mind, at this eventful period of his life, may have lain there silently working, as a word of the great Truth, which subsequently called him from death unto life?

Having arrived at Newburyport, he sought employment as cabin boy in a Lettre de Marque of twenty-two guns, which was going to Cape François, Porto Rico, for salt. It was now 1783; and when three days out, they fell in with a Bermuda Privateer and had a battle. On this occasion William displayed undaunted courage and zeal in the management of a swivel on the main top; and gained great esteem of the ship's company.

The Captain and mate were excellent persons, and became very much attached to the beautiful, talented, active and self-relying boy; and set him to keep the reckoning of the ship, as he was a good mathematician, and had even studied the application of mathematics to navigation, while a school boy in Boston. A storm now drove them into the Gulf of Mexico, and several of the crew were washed overboard by terrific seas, and among others, the Captain himself. After great pains, he at last reached Cape François, the ship's destination.

While there, William and four sailors were sent in a long flat boat, twenty miles along the coast for the salt. This boat was upset on the Westerly end of the Island, and lost, and they all had to swim ashore, which was nearly a mile off, and in a place generally infested with sharks; but none molested them. When they got upon shore, the question arose, which way they should go to reach the ship; and William was quite sure of one route, while the sailors took an opposite direction. He was without hat, jacket and shoes, having lost in the sea every thing but shirt and pantaloons. After walking many hours, he went up a rising ground, and reached the top just as the sun was setting. Here he was startled by seeing a multitude of human beings gazing upon the sun; and, after some observation, he found they were performing rites of worship to that luminary. These were savage in their character. His daughter has heard him describe this scene to brother ministers at his own fireside, and the strong impression it made on his imagination. He was somewhat alarmed with respect to his own reception among these Pagans, but he needed refreshment, and concluded to go down the hill to a small hut which he saw at its foot, and see what he could do by the sign language to conciliate some hospitality, and learn the way to Cape François. In going into the hut, he saw lying on the floor a gigantic looking man, all rags and shaggy, who was not a negro, but seemed a savage of a peculiar species. William, however, addressed him with gestures, on which the creature rose, gazed at him a moment, and then rushed forward, and clasped him in his arms. Mr. Batchelder, in telling this story, used to say that he really believed, for the moment, it was the devil, who had caught him at last, in punishment for all his wickedness (which, however, consisted in nothing more than such freaks as have been related above; for he was singularly free from vicious propensity.) But presently the words,—" William Batchelder, don't you know Pedro?"—undid the mystery in part. It was a Portuguese sailor, once shipwrecked in the harbour of Boston, to whom, in his extremity, William had administered Christian charity, some years before, as almoner of his grandfather Crosley. The revulsion of feeling was so great that he nearly fainted; but he was tenderly cared for by the grateful sailor, and, with the assistance of a guinea, which Pedro gave him, got back to the place where the ship lay. The sense of a Divine Providence was brought home to his heart with great power by this singular incident.

The sailors whom he had left to take their different route, did not get back till some days afterwards. They then loaded their ship, and returned towards Newburyport. It happened, however, that the mate, who was serving as Captain, died on his way home, and, although William was not sixteen years old, he selected him as the only one of the crew capable of navigating the ship, and his last words besought the sailors to obey him implicitly. Thus installed as Captain, William steered the vessel home safely, for which he was handsomely paid by the grateful owners.

He now determined to return to study, and actually made some advance in medical science. But his mind had been very deeply impressed with the remarkable Providence which had seemed to watch over his life, and he finally resolved to study Theology, though rather, perhaps, with the idea of knowing what was true, than with the purpose of preaching. Among his papers is found a memorandum of the extraordinary course of reading he took up, comprising not only all the leading writers of the several sects of Christianity, but even the principal Infidel writers.

But, before entering on this portion of his life, I cannot but pause to call your attention to the remarkable character the above account exhibits, especially the self-dependance and independence, the fulness of life, the adventurous spirit, the calm sense of inward power. He had never yet doubted that he had wealth, upon which he should finally fall back—he now saw that it was gone irretrievably, but he felt that there was that within himself out of which he could live. His conversion to the Baptist persuasion, even to the Christian life, was not brought about by any ministration of others, but his studies at last led him to the Bible as the original fountain, or at least the sure stream from the fountain of God. Drinking there with the fulness of youthful life, and with the fresh sensibility of an exquisitely organized heart, not without some wide observation of men in actual life and in the world of books, he came to that absolute humility, which is man's only legitimate attitude before the majesty of God's law, and the ineffable beauty of Christ's love; and seeing that human nature of itself is nothing but "life in death," he threw himself at the foot of the cross, and was buried in that Baptism, out of which the children of Adam may rise one with Christ to the Father, to go forth the fervent single-hearted apostle of the Crucified to those his Master had died to save. Mr. Batchelder, in the midst of the cares of a family of his own, of a parish with whose every progressive interest he identified himself, indeed of humanity itself, so far as it could be compassed by his immense Christian energy, was truly an example of living above the world, while he lived in it. He showed his full reception of the benefits of his Saviour's love by the bounty with which he spread the glad tidings, deeming it an honour and glory to work as well as suffer for the cause of causes.

For the several first years of his ministry, he preached without settlement, in the manner of the old-fashioned Baptists. On the 29th of November,* 1796, he was ordained Pastor of a Church at Berwick, his principle of decision as to locality being, as he himself said, to find "the least attractive place, where the greatest good could be done." At Berwick, his salary consisted of a small farm and house, and the services of a man servant abroad and a woman servant at home. Here he worked on his farm, kept school for children in the day, and adults in the evening, preached at various localities within several miles three times on Sunday, and sometimes in the week days. The story of his wonderful ministrations of the Gospel is the cherished tradition of the whole country around Berwick.

* Another account says, the 14th of August.

His daughter tells many anecdotes, showing how he educated his children to economy and generosity at once; how infinitely he was removed above complaining of poverty; and how his versatile talent, applied to every species of labour, supplied the house with comforts. On one occasion he made a sleigh, going to the workshops of mechanics to make the different parts, and taking this occasion of intercourse to establish a gracious influence over their minds. There was no office of usefulness so humble that he could not perform it, and ennoble it with a gracious dignity. For in this intercourse, so various, he always preserved the dignity of genuine superiority. Ardent and independent as he was in youth, he never seemed to descend to the arena of personal altercation in his maturity, under any provocation whatever. From the time he felt constrained to preach the Gospel of Christ, he seemed lifted forever above all temptations of earthly strife. Those who understand the composition of New England society in the country towns, well know how to appreciate this. On one occasion, a Deacon of his church, having wronged and maligned him, afterwards expressed some doubts as to the facts. Mr. Batchelder immediately went to his house and met him near the door. The Deacon said something about going half way to meet him. "I will go the whole way," said Mr. Batchelder.

At the suggestion of Dr. Baldwin, Mr. Batchelder was invited to Haverhill to fill an important place, where many persons distinguished for mind, position and wealth, composed the orthodox Congregational Church. He accepted the invitation and was installed on the 4th of December, 1805. Here his salary was somewhat larger, and his activity could be more exclusively confined to his profession. And I must tell one thing more to show how truly he was above the temptations of the world.

His aunt, Jane Crosley, had married an English officer of the East India Company, and carried her own fortune to join with his at Madras. She became there a rich widow; and when she died, an advertisement called for her next of kin to go to England and receive her estate. Mr. Batchelder never, for one moment, entertained the idea that he could leave the spiritual work to which he believed he had a special call, and which was crowned with such successes, to go and get earthly wealth. But he empowered lawyers, and sent out papers, and his presence was necessary, as George the Fourth put in a claim on the ground that the heir did not appear in person. But this did not disturb him or his purpose. The property was, therefore, confiscated to the Crown.

Now observe a contrast. He had taken great interest in Mrs. Judson, and her husband's missionary enterprise to the East, though he had nothing to do with it officially, as they were of the Orthodox Congregationalists, and he was a Baptist. But, after a period, the news came from India that they had become Baptists, and they called on the denomination in this country to send them comfort and aid. This news caused in Mr. Batchelder all the excitement which the news of personal chances for fortune could not do. His family describe the peace and rapture that illumined his countenance, the energy with which he brought all things to bear, that he might go to Boston, and meet his brethren, and commune upon ways and means to answer this Divine call, as he believed it. Greatly by means of his personal energy the Baptist Mission to the East had its organization.

He also lost his life by the zeal with which, in the winter of 1817–18, he went about among the Baptists of Maine to raise funds to establish Waterville Theological Seminary and College. Strongly impressed with the importance of this institution, he was the most successful of agents to raise enthusiasm for it and money. His success carried him beyond his personal power, and he took a violent cold, resulting in a lung fever, which carried him off on the 8th of April, 1818, at the age of fifty-one.

On the day of his Funeral, all business was suspended at Haverhill. The shops were shut, and all the people of all sects came forth to mourn for what was felt to be a general public calamity.

Mr. Batchelder seldom wrote out a sermon. There are among his papers numerous skeletons of sermons which show that he premeditated what he delivered ; but his fluent eloquence required no previous writing out in detail.

His hearers would testify that, however comfortable they were in mind, as they sat down to hear him, he inevitably tore to pieces all their robes of self-righteousness, and left them naked, and imploring for the garment of salvation at the hands of Christ, the Redeemer.

The exaltation he produced in his hearers, he also often produced in himself. One evening, after baptizing a crew of sailors in a rocky nook of the shores of the ocean, near Berwick, he said to his friends that it seemed to him that the rocks were covered with supernatural lights, and these continued on the roadsides and trees all his way home.

A flood of exaltation also descended upon his dying hour, and his last words were,—" I see this glory," and then a shout—" Glory." This is the more noteworthy, as he was habitually the opposite of talkative or demonstrative. A sweet, quiet dignity characterized his usual demeanour.

Mr. Batchelder's only publications, as far as I can learn, are a Sermon preached at Buxton, Me., at the Ordination of Abner Flanders, 1802, and a Masonic Discourse at Danvers, 1810. They evince very considerable ability.

Mr. Batchelder was married, in 1790, to Huldah, daughter of Benjamin Sanborn, a Deacon of the Congregational Church in Deerfield, N. H. They had several children. Mrs. Batchelder died in 1846, at the age of seventy-nine.

Yours truly,
ELIZABETH P. PEABODY.

FROM THE REV. IRAH CHASE, D. D.
PROFESSOR IN THE NEWTON THEOLOGICAL SEMINARY.

Boston, May 25, 1855.

Rev. and dear Sir: I cherish a very endearing recollection of the Rev. William Batchelder. If I mistake not, I met with him first in this city at Dr. Baldwin's. During my residence at Andover, as a student in the Theological Seminary, my acquaintance with him was increased. I can never forget the paternal kindness with which, when I was exceedingly ill, he invited and conveyed me to his house in Haverhill. Nor can I forget the cheerful and timely attentions which I there received. Under God, they contributed much to the restoration of my health, and they made a deep impression on my heart.

When my studies at Andover were completed, he was about to make a journey to the State of Maine, for the purpose of attending the first meeting of the Trustees of the Baptist Literary and Theological Seminary in that State. He invited me to accompany him, and gave me a seat in his chaise. We passed, without haste, through the wide field where, in earlier days, he had laboured as a minister of the Gospel. Everywhere he was received with the warmest Christian love. He was welcomed as a father, and the people came in crowds to hear him preach.

The meeting of the Trustees was at the house of Governor King, in Bath, and the principal business was to locate the Seminary. It was delightful to see Mr. Batchelder amidst the loved and venerated men there assembled; with many of whom he had toiled and prayed long before they had thought of ever being permitted to meet on such an occasion as now called them together. Waterville was selected as the place for the incipient Seminary, which has since become Waterville College.

During the journey, he availed himself most happily of the ample opportunities afforded for conversation. He related many instructive incidents connected with the early history of the churches within the sphere of his labours. His whole deportment, as it came under my observation, was kind, courteous and cheerful. It gave "lucid proof that he was honest in the sacred cause," and that he felt the importance of doing good in his daily intercourse with men, as well as in his ministrations from the pulpit.

Since the time referred to, nearly forty-one years have passed away. I saw him no more. For, upon our return to Haverhill, I hastened from Massachusetts to enter on my duties as a Missionary in the Western part of Virginia; and not long afterwards he finished his career. But his tall, slender frame and his expressive countenance still seem to be before me. I love to think of him, and of such as he was. It is adapted to awaken gratitude for the Gospel, to purify and elevate the soul, and to endear the hope of Heaven.

Most respectfully yours,
IRAH CHASE.

ASA MESSER, D. D. LL. D.*
1792—1836.

ASA MESSER, son of Asa and Abiah Messer, was born in Methuen, Mass., in the year 1769. His father was a farmer on the banks of the Merrimack. At the age of thirteen, he left the town school in his native place, and went to live at Haverhill, where he was clerk in a store for nearly a year. Having given up his clerkship, he studied for a short time under the instruction of the Rev. Dr. Hezekiah Smith, of Haverhill, and then went to Windham, N. H., where he completed his preparation for College under the Rev. Mr. Williams, a Scotch clergyman, who was in high repute for both talents and education. At the age of seventeen, he entered Brown University, a year and nine months in advance. He graduated in 1790; and his reputation for scholarship may be inferred from the

* Prof. Elton's Memoir of Dr. Maxcy.—MS. from Hon. T. Metcalf.

fact that the next year he was chosen a Tutor in his Alma Mater. In this office he continued till 1796, when he was elected Professor of the Learned Languages in the same institution. He was licensed to preach by the First Baptist Church in Providence in 1792, and was ordained in 1801. In 1799, he was elected to the Professorship of Mathematics and Natural Philosophy, and continued in it till the resignation of President Maxcy in 1802, when he was appointed President of the College. After having been connected with the institution, as a pupil and an officer, for nearly forty years, he resigned the office of President in the year 1826. He preached occasionally, both while Professor and President, for congregations of different denominations. His sermons were always written, and delivered with the manuscript before him. After retiring from the Presidential chair, he was elected by the citizens of Providence, for several years, to important civil trusts, which he discharged with ability and fidelity. His last years were occupied chiefly in superintending a small farm, in social intercourse, and reading. He died at Providence, October 11, 1836, aged sixty-seven years.

President Messer received the honorary degree of Doctor of Divinity from Brown University in 1806, and from Harvard University in 1820; and that of Doctor of Laws from the University of Vermont, in 1812.

He was married to Deborah Angell, and had four children,—three daughters and one son. The son died in infancy. The second daughter was married to the Hon. Sidney Williams, of Taunton, Mass; the youngest married the Hon. Horace Mann, of Boston; and the eldest remains (1850) unmarried. His widow still survives.

The following is a list of President Messer's publications:—A Discourse delivered on Thanksgiving Day, at the Congregational meeting-house in the First Precinct in Rehoboth, 1798. A Discourse delivered in the Chapel of Rhode Island College to the Senior Class, on the Sunday preceding the Commencement, 1799. An Oration delivered at Providence in the Baptist meeting-house on the Fourth of July, 1803. An Address delivered to the Graduates of Rhode Island College, at the Public Commencement, 1803. An Oration delivered before the Providence Association of Mechanics and Manufacturers, at their Annual Election, 1803. An Address delivered to the Graduates of Brown University, at the Commencement, 1810. A Discourse delivered before the Warren (R. I.) Association, 1812.

Professor Elton, in his Memoir of President Maxcy, has inserted an Address of President Messer to the Graduates of Brown University at the Commencement in 1811; stating, however, that it was then (1844) *first* published from the original manuscript.

FROM THE REV. E. A. PARK, D. D.

ANDOVER THEOLOGICAL SEMINARY, }
June 17, 1857. }

Dear Sir: I cannot remember the time when I was not familiar with the countenance of President Messer. Before I entered College I saw him every week, and while I was a member of College I saw him every day, and no one who has ever seen him can ever forget him.

His individuality was made unmistakable by his physical frame. This, while it was above the average height, was also in breadth an emblem of the expansiveness of his mental capacity. A "*long* head" was vulgarly ascribed to him, but it was breadth that marked his forehead; there was an expressive breadth in his maxillary bones; his broad shoulders were a sign of the weight which he was able to bear; his manner of walking was a noticeable symbol of the reach of his mind; he swung his cane far and wide as he walked, and no observer would doubt that he was an independent man; he gesticulated broadly as he preached; his enunciation was forcible, now and then overwhelming, sometimes shrill, but was characterized by a breadth of tone and a prolonged emphasis which added to its momentum, and made an indelible impress on the memory. His pupils, when they had been unfaithful, trembled before his expansive frown, as it portended a rebuke which would well-nigh devour them; and they felt a dilating of the whole soul when they were greeted with his good and honest and broad smile.

That his mental capabilities outstretched those of ordinary men might be inferred from the mere record of his life. Before he fitted for College he was a faithful clerk in a wholesale grocery store at Haverhill, Mass., and at the age of twenty-one, he left the College with high honours. For delicate philological analysis he had no peculiar aptitude; yet, one year after his graduation, he was chosen to the Classical Tutorship in the University over which the accomplished Maxcy presided, and only three of the Alumni of the College had ever been elected to that office before him. So acceptable were his classical instructions that, after the five years of his Tutorship, he was honoured by his Alma Mater in being elected her first Professor of the Learned Languages. After a creditable service of three years in this office, he was chosen Professor of Mathematics and Natural Philosophy, and after a still more honourable career of three years in this, to him, more congenial department, he was elected President of the Institution. In the Presidential chair he proved himself to be a sound political economist, and a logical and often powerful reasoner in various branches of ethics. He was born in the year when the first class was graduated at the College; seventeen years afterwards he entered the Institution, as a pupil; and after the lapse of only twelve years from the day when he ceased to be a pupil, he became the President of the University. He was then but thirty-three years old. His predecessor had taken the Presidential chair at the still earlier age of twenty-four. For a man of thirty-three, to administer an office so recently honoured by Maxcy and Manning, demanded a wide expansion of mind and heart; yet when he entered on this high station, no class in the College had contained more than twenty-eight members, and when he left it, he had instructed classes of forty, forty-one, forty-seven and forty-eight pupils, and among them many scholars eminent in church and state: he had raised the finances of the College to a prosperous condition, and had added depth and breadth to the groundwork of one of our noblest Universities. He was only fifty-seven years of age when he retired from Academic life, but he had then been connected with the College as a pupil or instructer thirty-nine years. During all this time he was noted for a round-about, strong sense, for a vein of humour, if not of broad wit, for a terse idiomatic Saxon style. In grave counsel few men have been so far-sighted and self-collected, who were likewise in the social circle so quick at repartee, and so irresistibly amusing. I have seldom known a veteran in the government of a College, who was so strict a disciplinarian, so clear-headed a diplomatist, and at the same time so apt in uttering kindly words to the boys whom he met in the street, so ready with a cheering proverb or a sprightly turn with the care-worn and down-hearted. As a financier he was sagacious and circumspect. In all the details of business he was far more exact than clergymen are wont to be. Punctuality in fulfilling engagements was one of his most noted excellencies. He was an earnest and sometimes a conspicuous politician. His fellow-citizens were glad to honour him with civil offices, after he had left the University. A seat on the bench of the Supreme Judicial Court of Rhode Island was once tendered to him, but he declined accepting it. He laboured in the service of free schools, at a time when his efforts were imperatively needed, and of all charities which were not sectarian he was a discreet friend. He knew men. He understood the world. His original, shrewd maxims are not yet forgotten. In his Baccalaureate Address of 1811 he said to the Senior Class, "Should you choose no profession at all, you would, having no stimulus, be likely to live with no industry or enterprise; and of course with no usefulness, respectability or satisfaction. Should you, while nature would give you *one* profession, give yourselves *another*, this might even be worse than none at all: it might keep you ever struggling both against wind and tide." "If money is your object, you may gain it better by ploughing than preaching." *Appendix to President Maxcy's Remains, pp.* 415, 418. In his Baccalaureate Address of 1803 he said, "You will find most men alive to their own interest, and in general it will be the most safe to commit yourselves to them only so far as that interest may induce them to befriend you." *Ibid. p.,* 440.

It is as a Theologian, that President Messer is in the truest sense a study. He felt an affectionate regard for Nathaniel Emmons and for John Thornton Kirkland, and thus illustrated the broadness of his catholicism. Tough as he was and often stern, he recoiled from religious debate. "You should allow nothing but a sense of duty," he advised the class of 1811, "to carry you into the field of theological controversy; for then you will be liable to sacrifice the truth of God, not less than the love and peace of men." *Appendix to Pres. Maxcy's Remains, p.* 419. Many sharp observers have regarded him as a decided and thorough-going Unitarian. Some have looked upon him as substantially orthodox, and others have consigned him to various intermediate positions.

In the seven pamphlets which I have read from his pen there is no *decisive* indication, that he differed in any essential doctrine from the evangelical divines of New England. Perhaps he did not regard himself, at that period, as *confidently* holding any opinion which was at variance with the accepted faith of his denomination. His early education had been acquired on the banks of the Merrimack; he was early familiar with the vague terms of the "Merrimack theology," and that was proverbially far from the *high* Orthodox standard. In favour of the inspiration of the Scriptures, Dr. Messer uses, in these pamphlets, the most unequivocal language, and he takes a strong and bold position against the popular infidelity of the times. The first of these pamphlets was published when he was thirty years old, and is entitled "A Discourse delivered in the Chapel of Rhode Island College to the Senior Class on the Sunday preceding their Commencement, 1799." Here he speaks of the Bible as proving its own Divinity by "the way of salvation which it discloses by Jesus Christ," and says: "No where can we find a way in which such imperfect, sinful creatures, as men are, can be just with God, and made happy forever, but in Him, who *is the way, the truth, and the life.*" Pp. 8, 9. "You have no way to obtain his smiles but through the merciful interposition of his glorious Son." P. 14.

The latest of Dr. Messer's pamphlets was published when he was forty-three years of age, and bears the title, "A Discourse delivered before the Warren Association, met at Warren on Tuesday, September 8th, 1812." This Discourse, from the text, I. Peter v. 1, 4,—"The *Elders* which are among you," &c., is an historical curiosity. It abounds with utterances as decisive as the following: " The difference, therefore, between friends and foes, right and wrong, black and white, is not more striking than is the difference between the characteristics of other men and of the disciples of Christ. What a difference between a crown of glory and a lake of fire! between eternal life and eternal death! between the mansions of joy and the dungeons of woe! between the songs of the ransomed of the Lord, and weeping, wailing, and gnashing of teeth! And yet this is the difference between the prospect of the disciples of Christ and of other men; of him who serveth God, and of him who serveth Him not." P. 18.

Of these " other men," it is added: " Their condition is not safe. The most awful calamities hang over them. They are not the friends of God. They are the enemies of God, and He has threatened to pour out on them the vials of his wrath. Remaining as they are, they should tremble for the prospect before them. It is a horrible tempest. It is tribulation and anguish. It is weeping, wailing and gnashing of teeth. It is everlasting destruction from the presence of the Lord and from the glory of his power." P. 8.

How can these men be made sons of God? " In one view," says President Messer, " this effect lies beyond the power of man. It is not of him that willeth, nor of him that runneth, but of God that showeth mercy. Not any thing but the power of God can bring sinners to repentance. To them all the preaching, however learned or eloquent, which the Spirit of God will not apply, is nothing better than a ' sounding brass, or a tinkling cymbal.' The preacher must ever be careful to exhibit men as the truth exhibits them, fallen, helpless, perishing sinners, and he also must ever be careful to let them know, what the truth will let them know, that not any thing but the mercy of God can save them: but that, at the same time, this mercy is rich and free, and equal to the salvation of the very chief of sinners. Hence the truth which the *Elder* is bound to explain and enforce, will at once suggest reformations, revivals of religion;—such blessed effects as, since this Association last assembled in this place, have been seen in Warren; such as, for the last several months, have been seen in Harwich, in Barnstable and in Providence, and such as, at this very time, and in a wonderful manner, may be seen in Bristol." Pp. 16, 17.

The conflicting rumours with regard to President Messer as a theologian, may be explained by supposing that he modified his views as he studied the Unitarian controversy. I have no evidence that he ever abandoned the doctrines, that man is by nature entirely devoid of love to God, and that he needs a radical change of heart in order to be saved. It is said by some of his intimate friends, that, in his earlier ministry, he believed in the doctrine of a strictly vicarious atonement; but it is said by others yet more intimate, that, if he ever believed this doctrine, he decidedly abandoned it in his later years. During a large, perhaps the larger part of his public life, he probably adopted the Arian view of the person of Christ, and, in the main, coincided with the General Baptists of England, more nearly than with any other denomination of Christians. While he remained President of Brown University, he continued to attend the First Baptist Church in Providence, but after he retired from Academic life he attended a Freewill Baptist Church. He considered himself a student of theology until the day of his death, and on some points did not pretend to have fully established his opinion. It was therefore a question often discussed, and never fully decided, how far and for how long a time he doubted or disbelieved various doctrines of the evangelical faith.

There was a resemblance, as well as a contrast, between the theological career of President Maxcy and that of President Messer. Dr. Maxcy became more and more orthodox, while he remained at Brown University; Dr. Messer less and less. A few months before Dr. Maxcy's elevation to the Presidency, he wrote: "For my own part, I can safely say that I have never been disposed to confine myself to the peculiar tenets of any sect of religionists whatever. Great and good men have appeared among all denominations of Christians, and I see not why all do not deserve an equal share of attention and regard." "An entire coincidence in sentiment, even in important doctrines, is by no means essential to Christian society, or the attainment of eternal felicity. How many are there, who appear to have been subjects of regeneration, who have scarcely an entire comprehensive view of one doctrine in the Bible!" *Maxcy's Remains, pp.* 149, 151. Dr. Messer often made similar remarks. He was a Rhode Islander in freedom of thought, and freedom of speech. He has given his own autobiography, to some extent, in his letter to Rev. William Richards, D. D., of Lynn, England. It was doubtless an honest letter, but none the less adroit or profitable. It exhibits Dr. Messer as he was, an uncompromising Independent in Ecclesiastical Polity, and an earnest friend of the College whose finances he enriched, and in whose favour he enlisted the sympathies of the General Baptists of England. Dr. Richards was a prominent divine among the General Baptists, and to him the far-seeing President writes thus, on the 18th of September, 1818:

"This Literary Institution (Brown University) was founded by men who breathed the very spirit of religious freedom, which you, as expressed in your letter, breathe yourself. Though the charter of it requires that the President shall forever be a Baptist, it allows neither him, in his official character, nor any other officer of instruction, to inculcate any sectarian doctrine: it forbids all religious *tests*, and it requires that all denominations of Christians behaving alike, shall be treated alike. This charter is congenial with the whole of the civil government established here by the venerable Roger Williams, who allowed no religious tests, and no pre-eminence of one denomination over another; and none has here been allowed unto this day. This charter is also congenial with the present spirit of this State, and of this town. Nothing here would be more unpopular than an attempt to place one religious sect above another. The ancient Baptist Church in this town never had in it, and probably never will have in it, any creed but the word of *God*, and it is very large and very flourishing. Of the value of this spirit of religious freedom, no man perhaps has a higher estimation than I myself. I abhor a bigot, and I should be unwilling to live among men unwilling that I should think for myself. My sentiments on this subject (if, indeed, it may be lawful for a man to quote himself,) were lately, in a discourse which I delivered before the Bible Society of this State, expressed in the following words: 'Denominational attachments, I know, are very natural, and when kept within the bounds of moderation, they are very commendable; but when carried beyond them, they become bigotry, and bigotry in its worst form is a fury as haggard as the worst of those which flew from the box of Pandora.' 'Religious bigotry indeed, and religious tyranny, both belong to the same kennel, and God grant that, by driving them back to their native dungeon, Bible Societies may be made the means of accelerating the progress of that 'charity which beareth all things, believeth all things, hopeth all things, endureth all things.'—These thoughts were addressed to a large assembly in this town, and they were well received. Hence you may learn a little of the town, and also of me, and then of the College, and this little I hope will not discourage your design of becoming one of its generous benefactors."

These words of Dr. Messer struck the right chord in the soul of Dr. Richards. Mr. Evans, the biographer of Richards, appends to them the following remark: "Gratified with this letter of the President of Rhode Island College, which breathes the spirit of unadulterated Christianity, Mr. Richards now resolved to become one of its generous benefactors. In his will he bequeathed his Library, consisting of nearly thirteen hundred volumes of Theology, History and Biography to Brown University."

As strength of style comes from strength of character, it is natural to infer that the robust mind and energetic impulses of President Messer would be developed in vehement language, and this, when uttered with his massive and sometimes tumultuous voice, would rouse up the drowsiest auditors. "Yes, young gentlemen," he said in his Baccalaureate of 1799, "on the same principle that you deny the existence of God, you must deny the most plain mathematical axioms; you must deny your own existence; you must deny the existence of any thing and every thing in the lump. None but a fool, none but a madman, can say in his heart,—'There is no God.'"—"Yes, if you will not believe there is a God, you must adopt the ghastly, murderous doctrine that you have no Creator, no Preserver, no Benefactor; that you sprang you know not from what, that you are bound you know not where; that there is no virtue, no vice, no heaven, no hell, no immortal state, no day of righteous retribution, no nothing which can elevate a man above an ox. O cruel, foolish, desperate doctrine! Let me rather be swallowed up alive in the yawning earth, than embrace a doctrine so full of blasphemy, desperation, madness and misery." Pp. 12, 13. "The enemies of our government are the enemies of our religion, our country, and of mankind. It is not difficult to divine what would be the consequence, if these murmuring spirits could obtain their object—the most licentious and infernal manners, politics, irreligion and plunder would soon be the torment of America; and all the peace, safety, religion, liberty and republicanism on earth would soon be buried in chaos. I exhort you, therefore, my friends, to consider the enemies of our government the enemies of yourselves. Banish them from your company; and associate with none but men of sound, patriotic, American principles." P. 14. In his Baccalaureate of 1803, he said: "If a man's belief has no influence on his practice, that practice will be as destitute of moral quality as is the running of a horse, or the flouncing of a whale." P. 13.

After these quotations it may be superfluous to add that when President Messer was bent on giving a racy expression to a sterling thought, he did not allow himself to be disheartened by trifles. In his sound and wholesome oration before the Providence Association of Mechanics and Manufacturers, he asks: "Can we be independent of other nations, while we cannot print a book without their types, nor make a pen without their penknife, nor a shirt without their needle, nor even a shoe without their awl?" P. 14. And again he says: "It is a trite but true adage that 'a Jack at all trades is good at none.'" P. 8.

In his conversation and familiar lectures, Dr. Messer would often excite a smile by his homely, if not uncouth phrases. Hence it has been inferred that he was, both in principle and in habit, careless of his diction. This is not true. In general he studied a rhythmical cadence, and we often see a marked antithetic structure in his sentences. Thus, in his Baccalaureate of 1810, we read: "At noon encircled with all the lures of life, you may at night be encircled with all the pangs of death." P. 7. To the Class of 1803, he said: "Be guarded, then, against these two extremes: against distracting your minds by roaming at random among all subjects indifferently, and against contracting them by attending to only a few subjects exclusively." P. 4.

Little as it might have been expected of him, he certainly does, here and there, betray a desire to search out unusual expressions, and he speaks of "every thing which sublimes our natures," and of "rulers who distinguish us with all our peace," and of "the most salubrious antidote ever administered to the sorrows of men." By this occasional effort to avoid commonplace remarks, he now and then throws a haziness over his phraseology, which, in the general, was precise and clear. Thus he meant to express a thought more profound than appears at first sight, in these words: "It is obvious that inveterate and confirmed habits become very rigid and inflexible." *Fourth July Oration at Providence*, 1803, *p.* 9. It is obvious that with this occasional obscurity of style, and with his facetious tendencies, he would let fall many a remark which would be stored up in the archives of Academic anecdote.

Still, he is remembered by his friends, not chiefly as a man of wit, or of far-reaching understanding, or of rare practical skill, or of punctuality and exactness in discharging his varied and complicated duties, Academic, Civil and Ecclesiastical,—although we gladly recall these distinguishing traits of his character,—but he is remembered by his friends with the kindliest emotion on account of the rich virtues of his domestic life; the tenderness with which his capacious mind watched over the children of his love, the confiding affection which he delighted to repose in his most excellent and exemplary wife, the habitual cheerfulness which he diffused through the entire circle of his family. As a son, brother, husband, father, he was the central object of attraction, and the beams of joy and love uniformly radiated from him over all the inmates of his happy home. On these, his most signal excellencies, however, it is not fitting that I dilate now and here.

Very respectfully, your friend and servant,

EDWARDS A. PARK.

FROM THE HON. WILLIAM L. MARCY.

ALBANY, November 27, 1849.

My dear Sir: During my college life,—from 1805 to 1808,—I had that sort of acquaintance with Dr. Messer which generally exists between students of College and their President. I formed a definite opinion of his character at that time, and though I occasionally saw him afterwards, my early impressions concerning him were not modified by those few interviews. You must, therefore, take what I am to say as the testimony of a College student, whose observations were of course made from a stand-point, not the most favourable to a familiar and thorough view of the inner man.

Dr. Messer sustained his position as President of the College in a highly creditable manner, and was generally esteemed and beloved by the students. He was regarded as a man of even temper, honest in his purposes, free from prejudice, and well adapted to exercise that kind of authority which pertained to his office. He always met his class (for he was one of our instructers during the Senior year) with a kindly spirit and manner, and never assumed any offensive official airs, or did any thing that seemed designed to impress us with a sense of his superiority. He was often very familiar in our recitations, and sometimes introduced anecdotes, by way of illustration, that we thought more remarkable for good-humour and appropriateness than for the highest literary refinement.

Dr. Messer was far from being a graceful man,—indeed some might have thought him even inclining to be awkward,—but there was that in his movements and general manner, that betokened great simplicity and honesty of purpose, and made up for the lack of artificial accomplishments. His pronunciation of certain words was quite peculiar, and yet he was evidently unconscious of it; for I well remember that some of the roguish students used, sometimes, in the exercise of declamation, to adopt these peculiarities in his presence, and, so far from their escaping his attention, or receiving his approbation, he would instantly detect them, and criticise them, much to the amusement of the students, with the utmost freedom and good-nature. I am inclined to think that he did not bestow any great attention upon what may be called the *minutiæ* of literature; and yet he was a substantial, competent instructer, and was certainly distinguished for the kindly and paternal supervision which he exercised over all who were placed under his care.

Of his character as a preacher, I am perhaps hardly a competent witness, as I heard him only occasionally, when he supplied the pulpit, in the absence of the regular Pastor, and do not remember ever to have read any of his sermons. I think he was practical rather than doctrinal; logical rather than imaginative and ornate; and, though his style of preaching was too plain to suit the taste of the mass of College students, I believe it was always well received by the more mature and sober part of his audience. It used to be whispered, even at that period, that he had some tendencies to Arianism; and I have learned, from a source entitled to full credit, that his views, afterwards, became more decided in favour of that system. But I never heard of his introducing in the pulpit any speculations not in accordance with the commonly accredited orthodoxy.

On the whole, my recollections of President Messer are very pleasant, and, though I trust you will receive better aid than I have been able to render, in your effort to transmit to posterity some just idea of his virtues and usefulness, I confess that this very slight offering to his memory has been with me only a labour of love.

I am, very respectfully,
Your obedient servant,
W. L. MARCY.

WILLIAM STAUGHTON, D. D.*
1793—1829.

WILLIAM STAUGHTON was descended from a respectable and pious ancestry, and was born at Coventry, in Warwickshire, England, January 4, 1770. His parents were Sutton and Keziah Staughton, both persons of decidedly religious character. They had seven children, of whom William was the eldest. The church with which his parents were connected, and in which he passed his earliest years, was the Baptist Church in Coventry, then under the pastoral care of the Rev. John Butterworth, author of the Concordance that bears his name. The family subsequently removed from Coventry to London, where they were under the pastoral charge of the late Dr. Rippon.

The subject of this sketch gave indications, in early youth, of superior talents, and especially an exuberant fancy, which occasionally discovered itself in poetical efforts of considerable merit. His parents designed him for a mechanical trade; and, at the age of fourteen, he was sent to Birmingham to learn the business of a silversmith. He had previously had the advantage of a good English education; but so ardent were his aspirations for knowledge that he studiously availed himself of every opportunity for acquiring it. Up to the period of his going to Birmingham, he had given little evidence of religious sensibility or reflection; but, shortly after, he became deeply awakened, under an earnest and pungent dis-

* Lynd's Memoir.—MS. from H. G. Jones, Esq.

course, to a sense of his sinfulness, and for eight or nine months was a subject of overwhelming convictions. So seriously was his bodily health affected by the state of his mind that he was for some time under medical treatment; and one of his physicians, regarding it as a case of religious phrenzy, prescribed the reading of novels and romances; but so much was he shocked by the prescription that he would never afterwards suffer that physician to visit him. At length, as he lay writhing in agony upon his bed, the peace that passeth understanding was brought to his spirit, through that most cheering passage,—"Come now and let us reason together, saith the Lord: though your sins be as scarlet, they shall be white as snow; though they be red like crimson, they shall be as wool." Not long after this, he was admitted to the Baptist Church in Birmingham, under the pastoral care of the Rev. Samuel Pearce.

About this time, when he was only seventeen years of age, he published, as it would seem rather to gratify the wishes of some of his friends than from the dictates of his own judgment, a small volume, entitled "Juvenile Poems." But the great purpose of his life was now changed. Instead of continuing at his trade, he went to Bristol, and became a member of the Baptist Theological Institution there, with a view to prepare himself for the work of the ministry. He soon commenced preaching in the neighbouring churches, and such was his popularity that, even before his theological course was completed, he came to be regarded as quite a star in the denomination. He received several calls to settle, and among others one from the very respectable church in Northampton, which had been rendered vacant by the removal of Dr. Ryland to the Presidency of the Bristol Institution. He, however, declined them all, having his eye upon this country as the ultimate field of his ministerial labours.

About this time, the Rev. Mr. (afterwards Dr.) Furman, of Charleston, wrote to some of his brethren in England, requesting that they would send out some young man of good promise to take a pastoral charge in Georgetown, S. C. The letter being read at a meeting of ministers, they unanimously agreed that Staughton was the man best qualified for the mission; and, as the suggestion was in accordance with all his predilections and intentions, he gladly availed himself of it, and made his arrangements without delay for crossing the ocean. He arrived in Charleston, S. C., in the autumn of 1793, bringing with him strong recommendatory letters from several of the most eminent clergymen of his denomination in England. He was received with great cordiality by his brethren in South Carolina, and, without much delay, commenced his ministerial labours in Georgetown. He was married almost immediately after his arrival, by Dr. Furman, to Maria Hanson.

In this new field he quickly acquired a very extensive popularity; and when it was found that he was inclined to withdraw from it, the most flattering offers and vigorous efforts were made to detain him. But, after having resided there about seventeen months, during which time a church had been constituted and he had accepted the pastoral charge, he became satisfied that the climate was unfriendly to his health; and this, together with his strong repugnance to the system of slavery, determined him to seek a Northern residence. Accordingly, he removed with his family to

New York, at the close of 1795, where also he was met with tokens of marked respect and kindness.

Scarcely had he reached New York before the Yellow Fever—that awful scourge of humanity—made its appearance. He suffered a severe attack of it, insomuch that not only was his case considered hopeless, but a report went abroad and reached his friends in England that he was actually dead; and, while they were preparing to go into mourning for him, they were relieved by a letter written by himself announcing his recovery. He did not, however, *entirely* regain his health for a considerable time, being subject, after the fever left him, to a violent rheumatic and spasmodic affection.

Having, in the course of the winter, received an invitation from the Rev. Dr. Allison to succeed him in the charge of his Academy in Bordentown, N. J., he accepted the proposals, and removed thither the ensuing spring. In June of this year, (1797,) he was ordained at Bordentown, according to the custom of the Baptist Churches in this country; and, during the period of his connection with the Academy, he preached frequently to one or two churches of his own communion in the immediate vicinity. His expectations seem not to have been met by the establishment at Bordentown, in consequence of which he removed, towards the close of 1798, to the neighbouring town of Burlington. Here he had a large and flourishing school, to which he devoted regularly eight hours of each day, and at the same time supplied two churches on the Sabbath, besides occasional services in the week. The Baptist Church in Burlington originated in his efforts; and the number of its members increased, during the brief period of his ministry there, from fourteen to ninety-three.

In 1801, when he was only twenty-eight years old, the degree of Doctor of Divinity was conferred upon him by the College of New Jersey. It was understood to have been done at the instance of the late Governor Bloomfield.

Dr. Staughton having, during his residence at Burlington, become well known at Philadelphia, the first Baptist Church in that city resolved to make an effort to obtain his constant services as a minister. Accordingly, about the commencement of the year 1805, they extended to him an invitation to supply their pulpit for one year; giving as a reason for the limitation, that they were embarrassed in their financial affairs, and that, at the end of a year, they hoped to be able to meet the expenses incident to the regular support of a minister. He accepted their invitation, and the effect of his labours upon the prosperity of the congregation fully justified the most sanguine expectations concerning it; so that he was not only called at the close of the year to the pastoral care of the church, but such was the growth of the congregation that they found it necessary, after a short time, to enlarge their place of worship. During his ministry among them, more than a hundred persons were added from other churches, and nearly three hundred on a profession of their faith. Two new churches also were formed out of this body,—the third Baptist, and the First African, of Philadelphia; and a new impulse was given by his instrumentality to the interests of the denomination throughout the city.

Dr. Staughton continued the Pastor of the First Church until the year 1811, when he was induced to identify himself with a new enterprise,—namely, the formation of a church, and the erection of an edifice for public worship, in Sansom Street. For a while after their organization, the new church worshipped in the Court House on Chestnut Street, and afterwards in the Academy on Fourth Street; but, after a reasonable period, they erected a large circular building, ninety feet in diameter, at an expense of forty thousand dollars. Here was the theatre of his greatest popularity, and perhaps also of his greatest usefulness. The house, capacious as it is, was ordinarily well filled, and on Sabbath evening was generally thronged; and the frequent additions to the communion of the church indicated that, while he was admired for his eloquence, a Divine power attended his ministrations.

The labours of Dr. Staughton, during his residence in Philadelphia, it would have seemed scarcely possible for any human constitution to endure. He preached regularly thrice, and often four times, on the Sabbath, and once or twice during the week. He was engaged also, during a part of every day, in the instruction of youth, besides directing the studies of a number of young men in their preparation for the ministry, and having, a great part of the time, the editorial responsibility of a religious periodical. He was also the active friend and patron of many of the benevolent enterprises of the day, and was always ready to lend his influence where he thought it might advance in any degree the interests of humanity. He was among those who had a leading influence in originating the Philadelphia Bible Society, and from its commencement was its Recording Secretary, and afterwards one of its Vice Presidents. He assisted also in the formation of the Female Bible Society of Philadelphia,—the first Female Bible Society, so far as is known, that was ever organized. In the Sunday School cause he was most deeply interested; and not only his eloquent tongue but his eloquent pen was put in requisition to illustrate its importance and urge its claims. And, in addition to all this, there were a thousand nameless inroads upon his time, from an extensive circle of acquaintance, and from being a sort of centre of influence for his denomination in a large city.

When the Columbian College,—an institution designed to educate for the ministry young men of the Baptist denomination, was established in the vicinity of Washington, Dr. Staughton was appointed its President; and, though he was inducted to office in January, 1822, he did not remove from Philadelphia till the autumn of 1823, but supplied his place by an occasional visit of a few weeks. In the interval between his acceptance of the appointment and his removal to Washington, he suffered a most severe domestic affliction in the death of his wife. But her death was peaceful, even triumphant; and his behaviour in view of it, showed that he was no stranger to the joy in tribulation. He received from many quarters, and especially from his brethren in the ministry of various denominations, the most marked expressions of sympathy and respect; and when the news of his bereavement reached the students of the College at Washington, they testified their affectionate condolence in a highly appropriate and touching communication.

It was no easy thing for him to break the cord that bound him to his congregation in Sansom Street. A vigorous effort was made to retain him; and it was only a strong sense of duty that led him to accept the appointment. His introduction to his new sphere of labour seemed to augur well for both his comfort and usefulness. His Address at the opening of the College was highly popular; his condescending and affable deportment towards the young men conciliated their regards; and the friends of the institution congratulated themselves that their prospects were every thing they could desire. It turned out, however, that these high hopes were fallacious. It was quickly discovered that the very existence of the institution was in jeopardy, by reason of pecuniary embarrassment; and, though Dr. Staughton himself was one of the last to be convinced of this, yet he was ultimately constrained to admit it, and to act in view of it. In 1826, after he had been for some time desponding in regard to the ultimate success of the enterprise, some change occurred which he deemed auspicious; and, in the commencement of the year 1827, he made a journey through the Southern States, with a view, if possible, to secure the means of delivering the College from its embarrassments. While he was in Charleston, he received intelligence from Washington, that led him at once to tender the resignation of his office as President. And when this came to be known, the other officers quickly followed his example, and the College was virtually disbanded. Dr. Staughton remained a few weeks at the South, after resigning his place, and then took passage by water directly to Philadelphia.

For a short time after his return to Philadelphia, he preached to the congregation in New Market Street; but just as they were about giving him a call to become their Pastor, an application for his services was made from a distant part of the Union, to which he ultimately determined to yield. The Baptists in the State of Kentucky were now establishing a Literary and Theological Institution at Georgetown, and Dr. Staughton was chosen its first President. Though he felt reluctant to remove so far from the field of his former labours, and from the circle of his most endeared associations, yet, after having duly considered the case in all its bearings, he made up his mind to accept, and in due time signified his acceptance of the invitation. Provision had been made for a liberal endowment of the institution; some of the leading men of the State were enlisted vigorously for its support; and, with a man of so much ability and influence as Dr. Staughton at the head of it, nothing seemed wanting to ensure its prosperity.

On the 27th of August, 1829, a few days before he announced his acceptance of the Presidency at Georgetown, he was married to Anna C., daughter of James Peale, Esq., of Philadelphia.

On the 20th of October, he left Philadelphia for his new field of labour, which, however, he was never destined to reach. On parting with his old friends, he received many testimonies of their affectionate regard; and the New Market Street Church particularly, which he had supplied for some time previous, addressed him in a communication expressive of their gratitude for his ministrations and their interest in his welfare. When he reached Baltimore, it was apparent to his friends that he was the subject of a serious, and they feared an alarming, malady. He, however, after remaining a few days with them, proceeded to Washington, where, after a little time, his strength seemed to be somewhat recruited, insomuch that he actually performed one public service on the Sabbath. This, however, was the last which he was destined to perform; for before the next Sabbath, his disease had assumed a more aggravated form, and on the 12th of December, 1829, he sunk calmly to rest, aged fifty-nine years, eleven months, and eight days. He evinced, during his whole illness, the most unqualified resignation to the Divine will, and sometimes uttered himself in the language of joyful confidence and triumph. His Funeral was attended by a large concourse, and the services on the occasion were performed by several clergymen of different denominations. His remains were interred in the Episcopal burying-ground in Washington City; and, having rested there for nearly three years, were removed to the Sansom Street cemetery in Philadelphia, where they now repose, beside those of his first wife.

The following is a list of Dr Staughton's publications:—A Discourse occasioned by the sudden Death of three young persons, by Drowning; delivered at the Baptist Meeting House in Bordentown, N. J., 1797. Missionary Encouragement: A Discourse delivered before the Philadelphia Missionary Society, and the Congregation of the Baptist Meeting House, Philadelphia, 1798. An Eulogium on Dr. Benjamin Rush, 1813. A Sermon commemorative of the Rev. Samuel Jones, D. D., 1814. An Address delivered at the Opening of the Columbian College, 1822.

Dr. Staughton had four children,—two sons, and two daughters,—all by the first marriage. The eldest son died in infancy. The other son, *James*, studied medicine, was for some time Professor of Surgery in the Medical department of the Columbian College, D. C., and afterwards, till the time of his death, occupied the same chair in the Medical College of Ohio. His eldest daughter, *Maria Leonora*, was married to the Rev. Dr. Samuel Lynd, for several years Pastor of the Baptist Church in Cincinnati, and afterwards President of the Theological Institution at Georgetown, Ky.; and his youngest, *Elizabeth Ann*, to Dr. John Temple of Virginia. The second Mrs. Staughton survived her husband, and has since become the wife of General William Duncan, of Philadelphia.

FROM THE REV. DANIEL SHARP, D. D.

Boston, November 8, 1848.

My dear Sir: The name of Dr. Staughton awakens in my bosom the most delightful recollections. He was one of the most amiable, talented, noble-hearted and useful men with whom I have ever been acquainted. I was first introduced to him in the spring of 1807. The circumstances which gave rise to that event, and his invariable kindness towards me subsequently, were, I believe, in perfect accordance with the feelings which governed his whole life.

Hearing by a mutual friend that I had been licensed to preach, but was desirous of increasing my little stock of literary and theological knowledge, before I devoted myself exclusively to the work of the ministry, he addressed to me a most affectionate letter, in which he confirmed my views and purposes, invited me to his house, and assured me of his readiness to aid me in a course of study, to the best of his ability.

I accepted his invitation, and on the evening of the twenty-first of March, in the year already mentioned, I found myself in his hospitable dwelling. Although his engagements were numerous,—for besides preaching three times on the Sabbath, and twice during the week, he gave instruction in two of the most respectable Female Seminaries then in Philadelphia,—yet I recited to him once or twice every day, except on the Sabbath. In addition to the course of study which was prescribed, the almost unreserved intercourse which he permitted me to enjoy with him, was of no small advantage. His instructive remarks,—the result of his own experience and observation, concerning ministerial and pastoral duties; his amiable manners in private life, and his able and eloquent discourses in public,—for he was then at the zenith of his ministerial career,—were not, I trust, wholly lost upon me. I am sure, while I possess the power of memory, these seasons of delightful and profitable intercourse can never be forgotten. They are treasured recollections, which, even at this distance of time, cheer many a solitary hour.

The interest which Dr. Staughton felt for his pupils did not subside when they were removed from his immediate care. His letters followed them to their scenes of labour, fraught with expressions of friendship, and the counsels of experience and wisdom. He felt for them a paternal regard. If they were faithful, successful and respected, they were his glory and his joy. He loved to speak of them as his sons in the ministry of reconciliation.

In return, his pupils felt for him a filial veneration and love. The mention of his name has often operated as a spell in charming away the sadness which the coldness and selfishness of others had produced, by calling up vividly to remembrance those sunlight seasons in which they held intercourse with one, whose dignity as a teacher was so blended with the affability and kindness of the man as to inspire the most timid with confidence, and the most bold with respectful regard.

Dr. Staughton possessed an uncommonly active and vigorous mind. I now feel admiration and surprise, while I think of the amount of his intellectual labours. Although his sermons were not wholly written, yet they were by no means extemporaneous effusions—they were the product of much and varied reading, and of deep and patient thought. In the earlier years of his ministry, so laborious was his preparation for the pulpit that it frequently occasioned serious inroads upon his health. During the period I was with him, I never heard him on the Sabbath, more than once or twice, when he had not notes of his discourse, more or less copious. These, however, he used so expertly that persons who did not see them, had no suspicions of any paper being before him.

But his intellectual efforts were not confined to his preparations for the pulpit. He composed and delivered lectures on Botany, Chemistry, and Sacred and Profane History, to the young ladies at the two Seminaries already named. And for two years at least, he was virtually, although not nominally, the editor of a monthly religious periodical,—a large, if not the largest, portion of the original and selected matter in the work, during that period, having been contributed by him. From that publication, and the "Latter Day Luminary,"—a very interesting volume containing the productions of his pen, might be compiled. It would be a treasury of able essays, ingenious criticisms, striking anecdotes, and beautiful poetry.

Dr. Staughton was a truly benevolent man—he was so, both from sympathy, and from principle. I have accompanied him many a time to the habitations of the poor, and to the couches of the sick and the dying; and he never seemed more happy than when he was ministering to their wants, and when, by the utterance of the tenderest feelings, in the tenderest language, he evidently soothed their sorrows. I need say nothing of his untiring, powerful, and disinterested support of the religious and humane charities of the age. Every one, acquainted with their rise and progress, knows that he most readily gave his time, his talents, and his whole influence in advancing their prosperity. In his most favourite plans, I believe, he had never his own aggrandizement in view. Some of them might have been impracticable, but they were not selfish. His errors were those of a generous and too confiding soul. I have known him suffer wrong in patient silence; but, although I knew him intimately and long, I never knew him do a mean, unkind or unjust action.

As a Preacher, he was at times surpassingly eloquent. It is difficult to describe the manner in which he illustrated and enforced the great truths of Christianity. No one can convey to those who never heard him a correct idea of his action, so suited to his words; or of his countenance, so expressive of what was passing within; or of the intonations of his voice, which penetrated the chambers of the soul, and awakened emotions of joy or grief, of terror or transport, at his bidding.

There were occasions, however, when it seemed to me that he had more action and voice than his subject required. But when he appeared in the pulpit, prepared by suitable reflection to discuss some great truth, as his imagination kindled, and his soul expanded with his theme, he would pour forth such strains of lofty and yet melting eloquence, as I never heard from any other man. Many a time I have seen a crowded assembly, now held in breathless silence,—now all in tears,—and now scarcely able to remain on their seats, while listening to "the glorious Gospel of the blessed God," delivered with such sublime and thrilling pathos, that if angels had been spectators, they must have been enraptured with the scene.

He was not more happy in his manner than in his selection of subjects. He was an attentive observer of passing events. Whether these affected nations, families, or individuals, if they were of a character to excite public attention, he felt that

"To give to them a tongue was wise in man."

His texts on these occasions were like "apples of gold in pictures of silver." Every one perceived their appropriateness. Attention was awakened, and the instruction thus imparted could not easily be erased from the mind.

It may, perhaps, be interesting to record some instances of his peculiarly happy talent in this respect. When intelligence was received from Spain of the downfall of the infamous Goday, who was styled the "Prince of Peace," he delivered on the following Sabbath a most interesting discourse from the passage in Isaiah,—"He shall be called the Prince of Peace." I distinctly remember that, after alluding to the event, he described, in brilliant contrast, the infinite superiority of the Lord Jesus over all earthly princes, as to his personal dignity, the extent and duration of his authority, and the beneficence of his reign. At another time, when a great encampment in Europe had been surprised and routed by an opposing army, he preached a sermon from the words,—"The angel of the Lord encampeth round about them that fear Him, and delivereth them," which almost electrified his hearers. Placing them in imagination in sight of the camp, listening to the clash of arms, and the roar of cannon, and witnessing the carnage that ensued, he then directed their contemplations to the peaceful tents of the righteous, and to their certain and complete protection, afforded by the unlimited and encircling power of the Almighty. In the summer, Dr. Staughton preached in the open air, in Southwark, on Sabbath mornings, at five o'clock. I heard him there, just as the orb of day was ascending above the horizon, announce for his text,— "Unto you that fear my name, shall the Sun of Righteousness arise with healing in his wings." In that discourse he drew a beautiful parallel between the glorious effects of the sun on all animated nature, and those which are produced by Him, who is "the Light of the world, and the Life of men." I might easily adduce other instances of his felicitous manner in seizing on the incidents of the times, and improving them so luminously and impressively that the truths which he taught could scarcely ever be forgotten.

Dr. Staughton was a man of great catholicity of spirit. He was true to his own convictions, but he cherished and manifested a large and habitual charity for Christians of other sects, and he taught his pupils to do the same. On a Dedication occasion, he once said,—"I know I am but adding a voice to the thoughts of my brother through whose ministrations this house has been raised, and of the members of the Church in general, when I give a cordial welcome to every preacher of Jesus to assist in its holy services. The points in which we differ from our Christian brethren of other denominations, compared with those in which we all agree, bear no greater proportion to each other, than does the trembling lustre of a star to the meridian blaze of the summer sun. While Christian ingenuousness proceeds to state religious sentiment with plainness and simplicity, Christian love looks anxiously for the moment when bigotry shall expire with the flames it has kindled."

What he thus praised he practised. On baptismal occasions he was admirable. While he gave free utterance to his own convictions, there was not the semblance of invective in his remarks. He spake what he deemed to be the truth, but always in love. He beautifully exemplified the advice which he gave to one of his students—"At the water side," said he, "ever be calm, affectionate and firm—show the people that you respect them, and they will manifest respect for you." There was a calm dignity in his appeals, which commanded respect; and in my most confiding intercourse with him, for a long succession of years, he was always affectionate in his expressions concerning Christians of other denominations.

But although he commanded general respect and admiration, and was indeed a public man, yet no one could feel a greater sympathy in the pains and pleasures of private life. The following letter to my daughter, who was pursuing her studies at the Asylum for the Deaf and Dumb at Hartford, is a striking illustration of his affectionate interest for those who were the subjects of affliction:—

"NEW YORK, April 28, 1826.

"MY DEAR CHILD:

"I have seen, with great satisfaction, some specimens of your handwriting. I am surprised at the degree of improvement. Only go on to improve, and, with your neat hand, you will write a letter equal to any of us.

"I presume you remember me. If you do not, look at my picture in the parlour of your dear parents, and then take up your pen and write the words,—'That is a friend that loves me.'

"By the return of your father, if the Lord spare my life, I will write you a full sheet. I am rather much engaged this morning; but I cannot help expressing my joy that you seem desirous of knowing and loving the Lord Jesus. Pray to Him—though you do not speak to Him, He can hear the language of your heart, and make you his own dear child forever and ever. He will take you, when you die, to his bosom, and you will sing his holy praises to all eternity.

"Give my affectionate regards to your beloved mother, and to your brothers and sisters. The Lord bless you.

"I am, my dear Ann,
Yours very truly,
"WILLIAM STAUGHTON."

I feel that I have given but a faint sketch of the virtues and talents of Dr. Staughton. I might have used more freely the language of eulogy, and yet not have exceeded the truth. Any who knew him as intimately as I did, will recognise the likeness. But a feeling of disappointment will come over them, and they will say "it is not so beautiful and splendid as was the original."

Wishing you all success in your undertaking,

I am, dear Sir, affectionately yours,

DANIEL SHARP.

FROM THOMAS D. MITCHELL, M. D.

PHILADELPHIA, February 14, 1859.

Dear Sir: Having been very well acquainted with the late William Staughton, D. D., when he was Pastor of the First Baptist Church in this city, and subsequently, when he served the church on Sansom Street, I venture to communicate to you a few things concerning him, which may perhaps aid in the just presentation of his character, in your forthcoming volume on the Baptist Clergy.

Although born and educated in the Third Presbyterian Church, of which the late Doctors Milledoler and Alexander were Pastors, I well remember the frequent attendance of my father and others of the family on the ministrations of Dr. Staughton,—especially his Sabbath-night services. The crowded state of the ancient edifice, known as the Old Second Street Meeting House, soon called for enlargement, not once merely, but several times, till at length the audience-room was equal in capacity to almost any other in the city.

Dr. Staughton's preaching seems to me to have been eminently adapted to win souls. He did not aim at mere rhetorical glare on the one hand, or at metaphysical abstractions on the other; but his grand object seemed to be to exhibit the Cross in all its attractive power. His manner was always solemn and impressive, and sometimes deeply affecting. No one else ever read the lines,—

"All hail the power of Jesus' name," &c.,

as they flowed from his lips. At least so I thought, and such, I know, was the opinion of thousands. And in like manner,

" Jesus, lover of my soul,"

carried with it more of the Heavenly inspiration, as well as the inspiration of poetry, as read by him, than as I ever heard it read by any other person.

To the young his manner was especially pleasing; and *there* was, in fact, the secret of a large portion of his ministerial success. I was then a youth; and I am quite sure that the high regard which I have ever since cherished for him, had its rise in the hold he got of my sympathies, at that early period. Well do I remember a prayer-meeting, started and carried on by him for several years, near the residence of my father, in a school-house, owned by a member of the First Presbyterian Church. Indeed, the Presbyterians had much to do in originating this meeting, and the place was frequently filled to overflowing.

But the most signal efforts of Dr. Staughton were those which he put forth at what was then the extreme Southern border of Philadelphia, near the Navy Yard. Two or more of the family of Captain Beasley were converts under the Doctor's ministry, and at their instance a sunrise meeting was commenced on the lawn in front of the Captain's house. That service, being on the Sabbath, added one to the ordinary pulpit services, so that he delivered four discourses on each Sabbath, during nearly the entire summer. I was myself far from being pious at that time, but there was a charm about those sunrise services, that drew me to them, though I was obliged to walk three-quarters of a mile. Large congregations were gathered under the venerable willows of the premises, and if the true God was ever worshipped in spirit any where in Philadelphia, it was just at the place to which I now refer. Scores of individuals were there converted, and became, as subsequent years proved, devoted servants of Christ. If I do not greatly mistake, those labours mark the most magnificent epoch in the history of the Baptists of Pennsylvania. From two church edifices and a handful of members, they began to spread out, and at length acquired the position in this region that has made them, as a Society, what they now are. To this result the efforts of Dr. Staughton, out of the pulpit as well as in it, were powerfully auxiliary. And when to all this we add the fact that in his own dwelling in this city was commenced the first Baptist Theological School in this country,—the same in which some of the brightest lights of the denomination, living and dead, have been educated, you have a clue to the rapid progress of the Society of Baptists, not in this city merely, but, to a great extent, in the entire country. I may safely say that it is a rare thing that a minister of any denomination enjoys so extensive a popularity, and for so long a period, as did the venerable man of whom I am writing.

Allow me to close this brief communication with an announcement made to-day at the prayer-meeting held in Sansom Street Baptist meeting-house, by a venerable man from Indiana, who turned in to see for himself what the noonday prayer-meeting really was. Said the old man,—"I bless God that I am permitted to be once more in this sacred place. Here it was that I was born again, forty years ago, under the faithful preaching of Dr. Staughton. I never can forget his tender and affectionate appeals."

Very truly yours,
THOMAS D. MITCHELL.

MORGAN JOHN RHEES.
1794—1804.

FROM THE REV. NICHOLAS MURRAY, D. D.

ELIZABETH, N. J., September 10, 1855.

My dear Dr. Sprague: I regret to say that the material for a memoir of the life of the Rev. Morgan John Rhees is much less ample than could be desired. As he was the father of my wife, I suppose that I am in possession of all the leading facts, illustrative of his history or character, that are now accessible. In what follows, I believe you have the substance of all that can now be gathered concerning him.

Europe was profoundly agitated by great and stirring events during the last half of the eighteenth, and the beginning of the present, century. These events gave rise to many noble characters in Church and State; and such was the commingling of the moral, religious and political elements as not unfrequently to convert politicians into preachers, and the ministers of the Gospel into soldiers and politicians. And of this, the subject of this sketch, who has recorded his name, both in Britain and America, as an eloquent minister of the Gospel, and as an ardent and devoted advocate of democratic principles, was at once proof and illustration.

MORGAN JOHN RHEES was born in Glamorganshire, Wales, on the 8th of December, 1760,—the son of highly respectable and pious parents. As he early evinced superior talents, and a great love for study, they gave him a finished education. He first devoted himself to teaching, and soon acquired a high reputation for brilliant writing and eloquence. He became hopefully pious, and connected himself with the Baptist Church, which was the Church of his fathers. After a full consideration of his duty, he consecrated himself to the work of the ministry; and, to prepare for his high calling, he entered the Baptist College at Bristol. On leaving the College, he was ordained over the Church of Peny-garn, in Monmouth, where he laboured with great ability and success; and where traditions, illustrating his power and eloquence, are yet abroad among the people. Whilst here, he wrote many sacred lyrics, and other poetical pieces, which are yet in high repute among his countrymen.

With a soul all alive to the wrongs of the oppressed, and to the universal extension of liberty, he became an enthusiastic advocate, at its commencement, of the French Revolution. Indeed, he resigned his charge, and went over to France, in order to witness the glorious triumphs of liberty. He was, however, soon convinced of the unprincipled selfishness of the chief actors in that memorable drama, and returned to Wales, determined to defend his own principles the more zealously, and, for this purpose, he established a quarterly magazine, called "The Welsh Treasury." In this, with high eloquence and terrible sarcasm, he exposed the policy of the English ministry. But he was compelled to relinquish it, and, knowing that he was suspected of being friendly to the French interests, and that the Tory ministry only needed a fair pretext to subject him to prosecution, he called many of his friends around him, and, as the protector of a Welsh colony, came to America, where he landed in February, 1794.

He was most kindly received by the Rev. Dr. Rodgers, then Pastor of the First Baptist Church in Philadelphia, and Provost of the University of Pennsylvania. Between these two there existed, ever after, a cordial friendship. Finding the civil institutions of the country in harmony with all his political views, and nothing, in the way of religious intolerance, to fan his excitable feelings, the religious sentiment soon rose to the supremacy in his heart; and, as if he had never turned aside from the ministry, he again preached the Gospel with great power and success. He was followed by admiring crowds wherever he spoke; and preached Christ with an earnestness and an unction, but rarely witnessed since the days of Whitefield. He travelled extensively through the Southern and Western States, preaching the Gospel of the Kingdom, and in search of a suitable location for his colony. On his return to Philadelphia, he married the daughter of Col. Benjamin Loxley, of that city, who was an officer of the army of the Revolution, and a man of high character and standing. After two years residence in Philadelphia, he, in connection with Dr. Benjamin Rush, purchased a large tract of land in Pennsylvania, which, in honour of his native country, he called Cambria. He also located and planned the capital of the county, to which he gave the name of Beulah. To this place he removed his own family, with a company of Welsh emigrants, in 1798, which was increased, from year to year, by others from the Principality.

Here he was intensely occupied, for several years, with the duties which devolved upon him, as a large landed proprietor, and as Pastor of the Church of Beulah. For the benefit of his increasing family, he was induced to remove to Somerset, in Somerset County, where he died of a sudden attack of pleurisy, and in the triumphs of faith, on the 17th of September, 1804, in the forty-fourth year of his age. Indeed, his departure seemed rather a translation than a death. He left a widow and five children to mourn his loss.

The following letter was addressed by Dr. Rush to Mrs. Rhees, in reference to the death of her husband; and it shows the writer's exquisite sensibility and sympathy, as well as his high appreciation of Mr. Rhees' character :—

" MY DEAR MADAM:

" Accept of my sympathy in your affliction. While you deplore the loss of an excellent husband, I lament the loss of a sincere and worthy friend. His memory will always be dear to me. Be assured of my regard for you and your little family. May a kind and gracious Providence support you! And may you yet have reason to praise the orphan's Father, and the widow's God, in the land of the living !"

" From, my dear Madam,

Your sincere friend,

" PHILADELPHIA, January 26, 1805." BENJAMIN RUSH."

A glowing but chastened enthusiasm was a leading characteristic of Mr. Rhees, and gave form and hue to his entire life. He had a highly poetic temperament. This was apparent from his earliest life,—not merely from the lyrics of which he was the author, but from the ardour with which he devoted himself to every subject which interested him. He was, whilst orthodox himself, a liberal in religion, and a democrat in politics. Hence he was a lover of all good men, and threw the mantle of charity even over persons whose opinions he considered honest, though unsound. Hence he was the intimate friend of Dr. Priestly and of Jefferson, whilst utterly eschewing their religious opinions,—because they agreed with him on the agitating political topics of the day. He was a most fervent preacher and orator, and gave to his sentiments a point and intensity which made them deeply felt. And down to the present day, his name is as ointment poured forth among the old settlers of Cambria and Beulah. And if any excuse is necessary for the degree to which he united the religious and the political in his life, it may be found in the circumstances of his times, which induced many of the ablest divines of his native and adopted country to pursue the same course.

Mrs. Rhees was a woman of high character. On her great bereavement, she returned to her native home, where, upon her patrimonial inheritance, she educated her children, and lived to see them all not only members of the Church of Christ, but filling posts of high honour and usefulness. Endowed with a mind of the strongest original texture, polished by education, stored by reading and reflection, and by grace subdued to the most humble obedience to the truth, she was efficient in action, wise in counsel, strong in faith, and untiring in doing good. A spirit of self-sacrifice, connected with the deepest humility, was her leading characteristic. But few have lived a life more consistent and lovely, or died a death more cheerful, calm and confiding. She rested from her labours on the 11th of April 1849, in the seventy-fourth year of her age.

The earlier productions of Mr. Rhees were published in the Welsh language, but few of them have been translated. The few Orations and Discourses, written and published by him in this country, exhibit great vivacity and eloquence.

With great regard,

Truly your friend,

NICHOLAS MURRAY.

— ◆◆ —

ZENAS LOCKWOOD LEONARD.*

1794—1841.

ZENAS LOCKWOOD LEONARD was a descendant, in the fifth generation, of Solomon Leonard, who emigrated from Holland about 1630, and is believed to have been a member of John Robinson's congregation at Leyden. He first settled in Duxbury, and afterwards became an original proprietor, and one of the first settlers, of Bridgewater.

The subject of this sketch was the second of thirteen children of Capt. David and Mary (Hall) Leonard, and was born at Bridgewater, Mass., January 16, 1773. His father, though not a professor of religion, was a worthy and exemplary man. He was twin brother of Jonathan Leonard, father of the late lamented Dr. Jonathan Leonard of Sandwich, a graduate of Harvard College, of the class of 1786. His mother was a daughter of Deacon Joseph Hall, of Taunton, and was distinguished for her fervent piety, great energy and industry, and uncommon intelligence.

His early years were passed on his father's farm, where he acquired habits of industry and a knowledge of agriculture, that he turned to good account in after life. In March, 1790, when he was about seventeen years of age, his mind first became deeply impressed with eternal realities, and about the middle of June following, he obtained evidence, as he believed, of a renovated heart. For a short time he was somewhat perplexed and agitated on the subject of Baptism, but he finally became satisfied that immersion is the scriptural mode of administering that ordinance, and he was, accordingly, baptized in that way on the 1st of July following, and immediately after connected himself with the First Baptist Church in Middleborough, then under the pastoral care of the Rev. Isaac Backus; of which his excellent mother had been a member for several years.

Shortly after this, he commenced a course of study preparatory to entering College. He was assisted partly by his elder brother, *David A.—* then a member of Brown University, and partly by the Rev. Dr. Fobes, a Professor in the same University, but having his residence and a pastoral

* MS. from his son, M. Leonard. Esq.—Communication from Hon. W. L. Marcy.

charge in the adjoining town of Raynham; and, during part of the time, he studied without an instructer, and in connection with his labours upon the farm. In May, 1792, he was admitted to the Sophomore class of Brown University, and, during his whole College course, was distinguished for diligence in study, exemplary deportment, and earnest piety. He graduated with honour in September, 1794.

On leaving College, he commenced a course of theological study under the direction of the Rev. William Williams of Wrentham, Mass.; but, at the urgent request of his friends, he began almost immediately to preach, being regularly licensed, according to the order of his denomination, by the Church in Bridgewater. He spent the next winter in Sandwich, and some of the adjoining places, and early in the spring, was permitted to take part in a powerful revival of religion in Provincetown,—a place situated on the extreme Northwestern point of Cape Cod. After this, he went, by invitation, to Templeton, and remained there about two months, when he determined to prosecute, what he had previously meditated, a tour through the New England States, and the State of New York. He, accordingly, set out; but, on arriving at Sturbridge, Mass., at the close of his second day's journey, he was led to abandon the project, and accept an invitation to preach to the Baptist church in that town. On the 30th of January, 1796, he received a unanimous call from the Church and Society to become their Pastor; and, having accepted it, he was ordained on the 15th of September following,—the Rev. Dr. Baldwin of Boston preaching the Ordination Sermon.

With such zeal and energy did Mr. Leonard now apply himself to the work of the ministry, that his health soon began to fail, and in the summer of 1797 he was obliged to suspend his labours for several months, which he spent upon the sea-shore. In the autumn he was so much improved that he commenced a grammar school in the immediate vicinity of his own dwelling, which he continued, with one or two exceptions, for thirteen successive seasons; and for several years he had in his family a number of young men fitting for College, or more immediately for some of the higher walks of active usefulness. In the spring of 1798, his health again became very feeble, and serious fears were entertained of an incipient disease of the lungs, which might oblige him to desist from public speaking altogether. He again availed himself, for a while, of the sea air, but with little or no apparent advantage. Afterwards, he journeyed into the Northern part of Vermont, and in the autumn made a visit to Cape Cod; but his health still continued feeble. About this time, he resumed his early habit of regular labour in the open air; and this was the means of restoring him to a comfortable state of health, which continued till near the close of life.

On the 1st of September, 1799, he was married to Sally, daughter of Deacon Henry Fiske, of Sturbridge,—a lady distinguished for excellent judgment, discreet management of her household affairs, and all those qualities which are most desirable in the female head of a family. She survives (1857) in a green old age.

Mr. Leonard was active in procuring a division of the Warren (Rhode Island) Baptist Association. A Convention of ministers and private members of the church was held at Sturbridge, November 3, 1801, which resulted in the formation of the Sturbridge Association. Their first meeting was held at Charlton, September 30, 1802, and, for more than a quarter of a century, he was one of the leading spirits of the body. He enlisted with great zeal for the promotion of several of the prominent benevolent objects of the day,—particularly the Sabbath School, the Temperance cause, and the cause of African Colonization, and was President of the Society for Worcester County and Vicinity, auxiliary to the Baptist Board of Missions. He also repeatedly accepted and conscientiously discharged civil trusts conferred upon him by his fellow-citizens. His uncommon industry and perseverance, and scrupulous regard to system, enabled him to accomplish a great amount of labour.

It was his often expressed desire that he might not outlive the period of his usefulness; and it was a mysterious dispensation of Providence that, while in the midst of vigorous manhood, he was visited with a malady (softening of the brain) which gradually brought a cloud over his intellect.

On the 13th of October, 1832, he was, by his own request, dismissed from the immediate charge of the congregation, which he had ably and faithfully served, during a period of thirty-six years. The next year, the citizens of the town signified their continued confidence in his fidelity and ability, by electing him, for the sixth time, to represent them in the Councils of the State. For some years he continued a constant attendant in the sanctuary, and occasionally took part in conference and prayer meetings. It had been his custom to visit annually his pious mother, and the friends and home of his youth, in the Eastern part of the State, and generally, in going or returning, to attend Commencement at Brown University. His last journey thither was made in 1833. In the autumn of 1835, accompanied by his son, he made a tour through a part of New Hampshire and Vermont, which he seemed greatly to enjoy, but was glad to return home " to rest." He died on the 24th of June, 1841, in the sixty-ninth year of his age, and his Funeral Sermon was preached by the Rev. Joel Kinney, then Pastor of the Baptist Church in Sturbridge, from II. Timothy iv. 7, 8.

Mr. Leonard was the father of seven children,—three sons and four daughters. The eldest,—*Henry Fiske*, was graduated at Brown University in 1826, and studied Law with the late Nathaniel Searl, LL.D., of Providence, a classmate and friend of his father. He died soon after he was admitted to the Bar. All the remaining children survived their father.

The only productions of Mr. Leonard's pen, that are known to have been printed, with the exception of contributions to various periodicals, are the Circular Letters to the Sturbridge Association, for the years 1802, 1810, 1822, and 1825, and an Oration delivered on the Fourth of July, 1816.

DAVID A. LEONARD, an elder brother of the Rev. Zenas L. Leonard, was born at Bridgewater, September 15, 1771; was baptized and admitted a member of the First Church in Providence, March 7, 1790; was graduated at Brown University in 1792; was ordained as an Evangelist at Bridgewater, December 17, 1794; afterwards preached two years at Nantucket, and for about the same period at Asonet (now Freetown); and was stated supply, for some time, at the Gold Street Baptist Church in New York. He removed to Bristol, R. I., in June, 1805, and shortly after became a Unitarian. He now withdrew from the active duties of the ministry, and engaged in mercantile pursuits, and about the same time was appointed Postmaster, which office he held twelve years. He was also Secretary of the Bristol Insurance Company, and was editor and proprietor of the Bristol Republican, a paper warmly devoted to the interest of the then Democratic party. In the hope of improving both his health and his worldly circumstances, he removed to the West in the autumn of 1817, and died in Harrison township, Boone County, Ia., on the 22d of July following.

He was married to Mary Pierce of Middleborough, February 9, 1797, by whom he had eleven children,—three sons and eight daughters. One of the daughters was married to the Hon. David Merriwether, late U. S. Senator from Kentucky, and Governor of New Mexico, and another to the Hon. William P. Thompson of Louisville, late Member of Congress from that District.

Mr. Leonard was distinguished as a scholar, and especially as a philologist, and he occasionally indulged in writing poetry. He published a Sermon delivered at Holmes' Harbour, Martha's Vineyard, on the Death of Mr. John Holmes, 1795; an Oration delivered at Nantucket, at the Celebration of the Festival of St. John, 1796; a Funeral Sermon delivered in Gold Street Church, New York, 1800; an Oration delivered at Raynham, Mass., on the 5th of July, 1802; an Oration delivered at Dighton, on the Fourth of July, 1803; and an Oration delivered at Raynham, on the Acquisition of Louisiana, 1804.

FROM THE REV. ALVAN BOND, D. D.

Norwich, Conn., April 6, 1857.

My dear Sir: It gives me pleasure to learn that the name of the Rev. Zenas L. Leonard is to find a place in your "Annals of the American Pulpit," as it does to contribute any reminiscences of that excellent man, which I may be able now to command. My acquaintance with him commenced in the year 1820, when I became his neighbour by assuming the Pastorate of the Congregational Church in Sturbridge. Though many years have passed since my intercourse with him ceased, in consequence of my removal to another field of labour, yet I have many distinct recollections of him which it is pleasant to revive.

Mr. Leonard was of about the medium height, with a robust, fully developed form, erect and firm, but rather moderate, in his movement. His complexion was light, with a clear blue eye; and his face, as a whole, though not conformed to a classic model, was expressive of intelligence, firmness, benignity, and cheerfulness. His deportment was manly; and his manners, though not highly polished, were affable and gentlemanly. He understood and practised the courtesies and hospitalities of life, and in his social intercourse he was an agreeable companion,—fluent and instructive in conversation. He was free from eccentricity, and not given to such license in the use of his tongue as detracts from the dignity and propriety which should characterize the Christian minister.

In regard to his talents, and especially executive force of character, he ranked much above the ordinary type. By his literary attainments and general intellectual culture, he acquired a position and influence that commanded deference among the ministers of his own order, as well as the respect of his Congregational brethren, with whom he maintained kind and fraternal relations. It is not claimed that he excelled in those attractive qualities which secure the highest degree of popularity; but he undoubtedly possessed those sound, discriminating, earnest and energetic elements of mind, which are favourable to the highest usefulness, and which secured to him a solid and lasting reputation.

As a writer, he had a good command of language, and expressed himself with ease, force, and perspicuity. His elocution was good, and his style of reading the Scriptures excellent. The deep, mellow tones of his voice, modulated to the gravity of manner, with which he was accustomed to enunciate the Holy Word, gave uncommon significance and impressiveness to the portions which he read.

His Christian character, though not marked by any extraordinary developments, was of that calm, sincere and steadfast stamp, the moral efficiency of which did not depend on the exciting influence of objective agencies, so much as on the power of an interior, healthful vitality, supplied by grace. In his habitual deportment and conversation, he manifested supreme deference to the authority, truth, and spirit of the Gospel; stability and persistency of purpose; uncompromising advocacy of the cause of freedom, righteousness, and public virtue; and unwearied activity in performing the various duties of his profession. His was a piety of steady progress, which mellowed richly and ripened fruitfully, as his sun gradually went down behind the cloud of death.

When Mr. Leonard was invested with the responsibilities of a settled Pastor, he was quite young, and his theological training had been less thorough than he had intended it should be. At that period, too, disheartening forms of antagonism challenged the ministry to polemic encounter. The extravagances of Separatism, the leaven of Antinomianism, and the blighting spirit of French Infidelity, had so unsettled the foundations of religious belief, that spiritual religion burned with a dim light, and but little sympathy was felt for a direct, earnest, evangelical tone of preaching. To a young man, just putting on his armour, as a Christian minister, such a state of things must have seemed not a little discouraging. But, having enjoyed educational advantages above most of the Baptist ministers of that period, and having, from a literary stand-point, surveyed the condition and studied the resources of the enemy, he was enabled to sustain himself, amidst his labours and conflicts, with decided advantage. His progress was gradual but constant, till he secured a commanding position among his brethren, and was regarded as one of their ablest leaders. The fact that, for a period of thirty-six years, he officiated to the satisfaction of a highly intelligent Society, as a Preacher and Pastor, is an historic attestation to both his capability and fidelity.

In his public services he was earnest, though not vehement,—grave and instructive, and not unfrequently highly pathetic and impressive. His salary being inadequate to the support of his family, he was under the necessity of devoting a portion of his time to agricultural pursuits. He did not, however, neglect his professional studies, though he never aimed at the refinements of esthetic culture, or the reputation of brilliant scholarship. The position he occupied did not offer much stimulus to literary ambition. His views and habits partook very much of a practical character. His sermons, though unwritten, were not unstudied; and if they did not show the graces of classic composition, or the attractions of rhetorical ornament, they abounded in manly thought and apt illustration, and were listened to with pleasure and profit. His church flourished under his care, and, though never very numerous, the stability and Christian intelligence which marked the religious character of the mass of those who composed it, showed the practical value and evangelical spirit of his teachings.

Though honest and decided in his adherence to the distinctive views of his denomination, he was far from excluding from the circle of his charity those who differed from him in respect to mere ecclesiastical forms, or minor points of doctrine. In building up his own church and denomination, to whose prosperity he was ardently devoted, he adopted a method that was open and manly, conscious of his ability to maintain his ground, without recourse to the selfish policy of an exclusive sectarism. Consequently he lived at peace with his brethren of other denominations, and enjoyed their respect and confidence. During the period of my ministry, of more than ten years, 1 maintained with him relations of an official and social character, which were never disturbed by the slightest misunderstanding As Pastors of different flocks, which were intermingled by domestic alliances, we dwelt together in unity; and between the people of the respective congregations there was a reciprocity of neighbourly kindnesses, and Christian sympathy, uninterrupted and unmarred by sectarian jealousy and bitterness.

When Mr. Leonard was settled, the laws of the State secured privileges to the Congregationalists, or as they were sometimes called,—"the Standing Order," not enjoyed by Societies of other denominations. He early took ground against this monopoly of privileges, and contended that all denominations of Christians were entitled to an equality of religious rights, and that the precedence of one over another was an infringement of such rights, which ought to be remedied by appropriate legislation. He maintained that all ecclesiastical monopoly is a violation of the fundamental principles of the Democracy, that gives form and vitality to our civil institutions. If his zeal on this subject sometimes brought him into an antagonistic position with the Congregational Society, in public meetings, it was with him a contest for principle,—not the spirit of animosity towards those from whom he differed. It has long since been conceded by all denominations that the principle for which he contended,—namely, the equality of legal protection and privilege to every Christian sect, is right; but the warmth which he manifested, while the question was yet unsettled, never interfered in the least with the agreeable relations that existed between himself and his Congregational brethren. As an illustration of the conciliatory spirit which they both cherished, it is worthy of remark that, at a time when the Congregational church was destitute of a Pastor, he was invited to supply their pulpit for a season, and his people to unite with them in the services of the Sabbath; and this arrangement actually took effect, to the mutual satisfaction of both congregations.

In seasons of special religious interest, there was such a mutual understanding and harmony of action between the two ministers, that the good work was in no instance disturbed, as it has too often been in other places, by an exciting denominational controversy. Union meetings for religious purposes were occasionally held, with satisfactory results. Those persons who can recollect these "times of refreshing," when both churches were revived and enlarged by the visitation of the gracious Spirit, and the ingathering of converts; when fraternal sympathies and mutual labours furnished an example of the sweet charities of vital religion, will bear their testimony to the power and preciousness of those spiritual harvest seasons. The shepherds were not afraid to call their respective flocks together, on certain occasions, that they might feed in the same green pasture, and by the side of the same still waters. While they returned to their respective folds, neither shepherd missed any of his own flock. The spirit of Christian brotherhood, cherished at these union gatherings, gave fervour and efficiency to prayer, and produced a cordial outflow of a Heavenly fellowship, responsive to the sentiment,—

"O, sweet it is, through life's dark way,
"In Christian fellowship to move,
"Illumed by one unclouded ray,
"And one in faith, in hope, in love."

The time was when the cause of education found but slender support from a portion of the people attached to the Baptist denomination. This prejudice was somewhat prevalent in the earlier period of Mr. Leonard's ministry. Knowing the advantages of a liberal mental culture, he entered heartily into such measures as promised improvement and elevation to the public schools. He was a strong advocate for the free and thorough education of the masses, and favoured liberal appropriations for this important object. By personal, persevering efforts, he contributed not a little in aid of the cause of education in the town. He shared cheerfully the arduous services which this work devolved upon a few, and never was disposed to shirk responsibility, when an appeal was made for his co-operation. He served on School Committees and Boards of Visiters, with a cheerful and constant devotion of time and attention to the work. He urged a liberal and enlightened policy in the maintenance of Free Schools; and he lived to have cheering proof that the efforts which he put forth in this cause were not in vain.

As a Citizen, he identified himself with the municipal interests of the town. The circle of his ecclesiastical relations and labours did not limit his activities or his influence. He consulted for public improvements, and aided in accomplishing them. By his devotion to the public welfare, by his stern integrity, his sound common sense, and his enlightened views on great political questions, he won public consideration and confidence. Though his own Society constituted but a minority of the population of the town, such was the estimation in which he was held that he was repeatedly elected to represent the intelligent constituency of the place; and when the Constitution of the State was revised, he was chosen a delegate to the Convention to which that important business was entrusted.

Though he never would descend from the high ground he occupied as a Christian minister, to wield the carnal weapons of political strife, he claimed the right to canvass political measures and principles, fearlessly to avow and maintain his own opinions, and, as a citizen, to avail himself of the elective franchise. Though he was not in the habit of preaching political sermons, except occasionally on Fast or Thanksgiving days, yet he maintained that the pulpit must be free to speak, where the great interests of national morality and safety are concerned, or it must cease to be

"The most important and effectual guard,
"Support and ornament of Virtue's cause."

Mr. Leonard's theological views were strictly evangelical. Jesus Christ and Him crucified was the central theme of his ministrations. In his views of Conversion, and Christian experience generally, he was clear and discriminating; and was therefore a judicious counsellor to persons inquiring after the way of salvation. As an early and decided friend of religious revivals, he preached, and prayed, and laboured, with a view to their promotion among his people. During his ministry, he was repeatedly blessed with ' times of refreshing from the presence of the Lord."

As it respects measures of religious progress, and the cure of great moral and social evils, he was earnest and aggressive. He regarded it as the Christian's duty, not only to keep his own vineyard, but to labour also in a wider field, which is the world. He, accordingly, both by example and appeal, urged on his church the duty of going forward, in obedience to the calls of Providence, in the prosecution of every good work.

Thus, as a Citizen, a Christian, and a Minister of the Gospel, did this venerable servant of God, by a faithful and uncompromising devotion to the cause of human improvement, and the advancement of the Redeemer's Kingdom, serve his generation. The evening of his life was saddened by infirmities, which reached beyond the body to the mind; but the horizon of his faith and hope was luminous and cheerful. Though his public career was not signalized by any extraordinary intellectual demonstration, it was not because he was not capable of making efforts that would have greatly distinguished him; but because he instinctively shrunk from notoriety—as an instance of which I may mention that, when the proffer of literary honours was made to him by his *Alma Mater*, he unhesitatingly discouraged it. Pursuing the even tenor of his way, he made and left his mark on the Religious Society to which he ministered, and on the town with whose varied interests he identified himself. Among that people who honoured and revered him while living, his memory is still fragrant, and his good influence gratefully acknowledged.

Truly your friend and brother,

ALVAN BOND.

JOHN HEALEY.

1794—1848.

FROM THE REV. GEORGE F. ADAMS.

BALTIMORE, Md., March 29, 1859.

My dear Sir: With my excellent brother and predecessor, the Rev. John Healey, I enjoyed an intimate acquaintance, for about ten years, and had therefore a good opportunity of forming a correct judgment of his character. In complying with your request, I have not only availed myself of my own personal recollections, but have examined the Records of the Church with which he was so long connected, and the very few memoranda which he left in the possession of his family. None of the friends of this venerable man would claim for him any remarkable intellectual endowments, or any high professional distinction, and yet the position which he held in the Church, in connection with his great moral and Christian excellence, justly entitles him to a grateful commemoration.

JOHN HEALEY was born in Leicester, England, October 31, 1764. His parents were members of the Established Church of England, and the rite of Confirmation was administered to him at the age of fourteen. About the same time, he was apprenticed to a silk dyer; and at this trade he continued to work for many years after he was settled in this country. When he was about seventeen, he began to attend the preaching of the Rev. John Deacon, a minister of what is now called in England "the General Baptist Church." Under his ministry he became, as he believed, a new creature in Christ Jesus, and received Baptism at his hands. As it was customary, in the social meetings of the Church, for any who were thus disposed, to speak of their experience in Divine things, Mr. Healey used occasionally to avail himself of the opportunity to address his fellow disciples. He commenced preaching in or about the year 1792,—several years after he made a profession of his faith. In 1794, he, with several of his neighbours, mostly members of the same church, came to this country, having, before leaving England, covenanted together as a Christian community, and Mr. Healey was chosen as their spiritual guide. They landed in New York in October, and remained in that city till February of the following year, when they came to Baltimore,—the place to which their minds were directed before leaving England. They worshipped, for some time, in a warehouse, which had been fitted up for that purpose by some members of the Episcopal Church over which the Rev. Dr. Bend presided as minister. It is due to the Christian kindness of Dr. Bend to state that Mr. Healey was allowed to occupy this room three Sabbaths each month, free of rent. He continued to minister to this little band for about two years, without any formal organization. The church was regularly constituted, with only five members, on the 11th of June, 1797, and Mr. Healey was publicly ordained by the Rev. Messrs. Joshua Jones and John Austin, on the 20th of July, 1798. He continued in the Pastorship until December, 1747, when, on account of infirmity incident to his advanced age, he resigned his charge. He died on the 17th of June, 1848, at the age of nearly eighty-four years.

Mr. Healey was married, May 15, 1789,—five years before coming to America, to Mrs. Mary Martha Leech, whose maiden name was Brodair. She was a widow, with one daughter,—now the highly respected widow of the late William Young, Esq., of Baltimore. He had several children, but only two of them lived to maturity. His eldest son, *Joseph Ward*, born in England, died at sea, at the age of thirty. His only surviving daughter, *Elizabeth*, is the wife of Timothy Stevens, Esq., of Baltimore County, a lady of great respectability and moral worth. Mrs. Healey died December 22, 1803. In June, 1805, Mr. Healey married Mrs. Elizabeth Hunt, a widow, who was one of the little band who came with him to this country, and one of the original constituents of his church. They lived in happy union until her death, which took place May, 11, 1843. She was a woman of kindred spirit with her husband, and in all respects "a help-meet for him." She had no child.

Mr. Healey, though, as I have already intimated, not distinguished for either talents or learning, possessed good common sense and a sound judgment, had read quite extensively, and had acquired considerable knowledge of the Greek and Hebrew languages. His piety was at once ardent and consistent. Through his long career, as a Christian and a minister, he maintained a spotless reputation.

He was a steady friend and supporter of the various efforts of Christians to spread the Gospel throughout the world. He was one of the constituent members of the Baptist General Convention for Missionary purposes, formed in Philadelphia in April, 1814, and, with other worthy brethren, was appointed one of its Board of Managers. One of its earliest auxiliary Societies was formed under his auspices.

As a preacher, I cannot say that Mr. Healey was eminently successful, if his success be judged of by the numerical growth of his church. During his ministry, he admitted to the communion four hundred and forty-six, besides the original members. The number of communicants, however, seldom exceeded one hundred and fifty at any one time. It should be stated that, during a large portion of his ministry, he was obliged to devote much of his time to secular business, the church never having been able to give him a support for his family. Indeed, he himself was accustomed,

for many years, to give not only his time but also his substance to defray
the incidental expenses of maintaining public worship.   During his ministry, the church erected two houses of worship, to both of which enterprises the Pastor lent both his time and his means.   Yet, with these drafts
upon him, beside the support of his family, and the constant hospitality to
which a minister of the Gospel must be given, he saved enough, by industry
and economy, to possess a comfortable house.   During the last twelve or
fifteen years of his life, he was enabled, by means of what he had accumulated in business, and what the church could pay for his services, to devote
himself exclusively to the duties of his sacred office.

Between Mr. Healey and the people of his charge, there existed a strong
mutual attachment.   He moved about among them with an earnest desire
to do them good, and he was especially particular to "visit the widows
and fatherless in their affliction."   He was an eminently good man in all
his various relations, and his record is on high.

Very faithfully yours,
GEORGE F. ADAMS.

FROM THE REV. B. T. WELCH, D. D.

Newton Corners, June 16, 1859.

My dear Sir: Your request for my recollections of Father Healey touches a
tender chord in my heart.   I knew him from 1817 till his death.   I resided in
Baltimore for some years, and sat under his ministry, and it was especially
through his instrumentality, in connection with that of his church, that I was
myself introduced to the privileges and responsibilities of the sacred office.
He was accustomed to call upon me to pray and exhort in our social religious
meetings; and, after he had read a chapter, he expected me to follow it with
such comments as I was able to make.   When I expressed to him my conviction that I was incompetent to speak to edification, he said "No,—go on, and
if you get it crooked, I'll make it straight;" and when I had finished my
remarks, he would follow with some remarks of his own, and would sometimes say,—" The young man has spoken to you the truth, and it will be well
for you if you receive the truth at his lips."   Thus began my training for the
ministry; and, at no distant period, the Church, acting of course, under his
counsel and guidance, gave me a license to preach the Gospel wherever, in the
Providence of God, there might be an opening.

It was not long after I was licensed before the good old man accompanied
me on a preaching tour of forty days, on both sides of the Juniata River, on
the borders of Maryland and Pennsylvania; and, during this mission, I had
opportunity to make full proof of his wisdom, benevolence, devotion, and, I
may add, good-humour.   One or two circumstances that occurred on this journey, which are still perfectly fresh in my remembrance, I will mention as
giving you a better idea of some of his characteristics than I can convey in
any other way.

It had fallen to my lot to preach on one occasion, and the object of my discourse was to explain and defend the doctrine of Election.   Among my
hearers was a certain lady, who was a very zealous Arminian, and of course
had no sympathy with the views which I had undertaken to put forth.   It so
happened that, after the service, we were invited to her house to dine; and
she availed herself of the opportunity to let me know that the system of
doctrine which I preached found no favour in her eyes.   The castigation she
gave me, I received with exemplary deference, and neither Father Healey nor

myself thought proper to enter into any discussion with her on the subject. When we came out to mount our horses, the old gentleman, whose faith in the doctrine of my sermon was as firm as a mountain, simply said, with a most expressive look—" As it was in the beginning, is now, and ever shall be, world without end."

Another incident illustrative of a different characteristic. One night where we lodged, it became a matter of convenience for us to occupy the same bed. I happened to be awake some time in the night, but, supposing my companion was asleep, I did not venture to speak to him. At length, however, I heard from him a low whisper, in which I instantly recognized the breathings of devotion. For some time, he prayed most fervently for himself, supplicating blessings with reference to his own peculiar needs. He then commenced a most earnest and affectionate intercession for me,—regarding my circumstances especially as a young preacher,—the temptations and dangers to which I should be exposed, and, with an almost matchless fervour, imploring for me large measures of Divine grace, that I might be preserved and carried forward in a career of eminent ministerial usefulness. Those moments, during which I was listening to the supplications of that man of God in my behalf, I have always thought had more of blessing crowded into them than perhaps any period of my life since I entered upon the Christian course. The idea that the venerable saint was thus wrestling with God for me, in the stillness of midnight, when he supposed that no ear this side of Heaven was awake to his tender and imploring utterances, so wrought upon my inmost soul, that I found it difficult to prevent my emotions from taking on an audible form. I felt then that the prayer that was going up for me was the effectual fervent prayer of the righteous man; and, while I have never lost the savour of that nightly exercise, it has always been with me a cherished impression that not a few of the great blessings with which my life has been crowned, may have had a connection, in the Providence of God, with those devout whispers to which I then listened.

While Father Healey was eminent for a devotional spirit, and was one of the finest models of Christian character that I remember to have met with, he had naturally one of the most lovely and loving of dispositions. One incident illustrative of this trait, that came within my immediate knowledge, I can never forget. On my return to Baltimore, some time after I came to the North, I was prompted alike by filial duty and filial love, to call upon him soon after my arrival. The moment I entered the room in which he was, he sprang from his chair, rushed up to me, threw his arms around my neck, laid his head upon my shoulder, and burst into tears. It was the overflowing of one of the kindest, warmest hearts that God ever placed in a human bosom. It was not easy to say how much of the benevolence that came out in his life was to be set to the account of nature, and how much to that of grace; but it was impossible to mark the generous and kindly workings of his spirit from day to day, and resist the impression that he was a debtor to both in a higher degree than often falls to the lot of humanity.

Father Healey was far from being a popular preacher. His sermons were not distinguished for either the logical or the imaginative—they were little more than familiar talks—and yet they were always sensible, and always embodied material for useful reflection. His manner as well as his matter was characterized by the utmost simplicity, and uniformly impressed you with the idea that he was striving to do you good. His salary was so small that he might almost be said to have rendered his services gratuitously; and the necessity of connecting with his professional engagements a secular occupation as a means of supporting his family, no doubt greatly lessened the force and attractiveness of his public ministrations.

In his personal appearance, Father Healey was a fine specimen of an Englishman. He was rather inclined to a plethoric habit. He had an intelligent face, a keen eye, and while his countenance readily took on an arch expression, it was always blazing forth in the warm glow of hearty good-will. Though nobody regarded him as, in the common acceptation of the word, a great preacher or a great man, every body esteemed, honoured and loved him; and I venture to say that if I were to revisit the scene of his labours, I should find that his name there is still a household word, and that, with all the surviving members of his flock at least, his memory is as fragrant as ever.

Very fraternally yours,
B. T. WELCH.

JOHN WILLIAMS.*
1795—1825.

JOHN WILLIAMS was born at Carnarvonshire, Wales, March 8, (O. S.) 1767. His father's name was *William* Roberts, from which, according to an ancient Welsh custom, of deriving the Surname of the children from the Christian name of the father, he took the name of *Williams*. His father was a farmer, as his more remote ancestors had also been for several generations. He went at an early age to live with his maternal grandfather, whose residence was a few miles distant from his father's: here he passed the years of his boyhood; and, as both his father's and grandfather's families were strongly attached to the Established Church, his earliest religious associations were altogether with that Body. Being, by a constitutional lameness, unfitted for agricultural pursuits, it was his father's wish that he might receive such an education as should qualify him to enter the ministry in the Established Church; but his unwillingness to be dependant on his family led him to prefer a trade. With a view to carry out this purpose he went to reside in the County town of Carnarvon. But before he had been long there an event occurred, which gave a new complexion to his character, and a new direction to his pursuits. Under the preaching of David Morris, a devoted Calvinistic Methodist minister, he was brought to receive Christianity in its life and power; and, shortly after, when he had about completed his nineteenth year, he united with the Independent Church in the neighbourhood, then under the care of the Rev. Dr. Lewis, a man distinguished alike for talents and acquirements.

Not long after he had made a public profession of his faith, encouraged by his judicious and excellent Pastor, he resolved to devote himself to the ministry; and very soon commenced his public labours. Before long, he began to entertain doubts as to the validity of Infant Baptism; and those doubts were not a little confirmed by a remark that fell from Dr. Lewis, who did not suspect the tendencies of his mind, in reply to an inquiry he made of him in regard to the meaning of the passage,—" Buried with him in Baptism." The Doctor's answer was,—" I really think the Baptists have, in that text, the advantage over us." He soon revealed his doubts to Dr. Lewis, who did his utmost to remove them; but all his efforts proved unavailing. In due time, he felt constrained, in obedience to his honest and mature convictions, to receive Baptism by immersion; and, in doing so, he became a member of the Horeb Baptist Church at Garn. But this change in his views and church relations did not at all affect the warm friendship which had existed between him and Dr. Lewis: Mr. Williams, to the close of his life, continued to speak of his former Pastor, in terms of the strongest affection.

Shortly after Mr. Williams connected himself with the Horeb Church, he became their Pastor. Before entering upon this charge, some of his friends advised him to study for a while at the Bristol Baptist Academy; and, in subsequent life, he regretted that he had not followed their advice; but he seems to have been determined to a different course by an apprehension, growing out of what he thought were signs of consumption, that his period for labour was short, and that he needed it all to devote directly to his Master's service. The circumstances in which he was placed by this early settlement, put in requisition all his energies of both mind and body; for the Horeb Church was composed of several branches, and met at different places of worship; and, in addition to this, he travelled extensively through North and South Wales, collecting funds for building two meeting-houses for the accommodation of his people. By this means he became generally known and greatly respected throughout the Principality; and, at the same time, the tone of his physical constitution was much improved, and the unfavourable symptoms, which had awakened his apprehensions, were in a great degree removed. He often travelled in company with the celebrated Christmas Evans, who was his intimate friend, and with whom he kept up a correspondence to the close of life.

Mr. Williams at length formed the purpose of seeking a home on this side of the ocean. In the multitudes who were emigrating from Great Britain to this country, there were many of the mountaineers of Wales, not a small portion of whom had no knowledge of the English language; and it was with special reference to the wants of this class that he resolved to come hither, and cast in his lot among them. He landed at New York on the 25th of July, 1795, bringing warm recommendations from his church, who had parted with him with extreme reluctance, and from various others, among whom was his former Pastor, Dr. Lewis.

Within a fortnight after he arrived in the country, a younger brother, who had come with him, died very suddenly in the neighbourhood of Newark, N. J. Mr. Williams was in New York when the tidings reached him; and he immediately set out and travelled on foot to the place where his brother had died. This exertion, in connection with the severity and suddenness of the blow, threw him into a violent fever. In the distress and agitation of mind which ensued, he began to doubt whether, in coming to this country, he had not run before he was sent; he prayed that one, though it were but one, soul might be given him as the fruit of his labours in America; and, when he recovered from his illness, he addressed himself to his work with greater zeal than ever. He had intended to plant himself in the neighbourhood of some Welsh settlement, and to continue his labours in his native language; and, with this view, his attention had been directed to Beulah in Pennsylvania, and Steuben in New York. His first sermon in America was in Welsh, and was preached in the meeting-house then occupied by the Rev. John Stanford, in Fair (now Fulton) Street.

The Baptist Church in Oliver (then Fayette) Street, consisting of about thirty members, worshipped in an unfinished building, only thirty feet square, with scarcely decent accommodations; and here Mr. Williams was allowed, occasionally, to preach for the benefit of his countrymen. Up to this time his knowledge of the English language was too imperfect to justify his attempting to preach in it; but, by request of the church, he gave himself to the study of it, and very soon had made such progress that he ventured one service in English on the Sabbath, while the other was still performed in Welsh. The English part of his congregation became constantly more and more interested in his pulpit efforts, as well as in his private character; and, having already made several unsuccessful attempts to procure a supply, they began to fix their attention upon *him* as a suitable person to fill the place. After a trial of nine months, they gave him a unanimous call; and, on the 28th of August, 1798, he was formally constituted Pastor of the church. The Yellow Fever, just about this time, appeared in New York in uncommon virulence, and Mr. Williams was very early attacked by it. By the use of prompt and decisive means, however, the disease was arrested, and his life, which had been despaired of, mercifully preserved.

Mr. Williams, from the time of his settlement over this church, was constantly growing in both favour and usefulness. The place soon became too strait, and in 1800 the meeting-house was enlarged, and in other respects rendered more commodious. In the course of years, this place also became insufficient; and was succeeded by a noble stone edifice which compared well with the largest and most attractive places of worship then in the city. His congregation, as these changes would indicate, was constantly upon the increase; his church was greatly enlarged and strengthened; and, during his connection with them, about four hundred and forty persons were baptized, exclusive of others baptized on Long Island and in other parts of the State. In the early part of the year 1823, the Rev. Spencer H. Cone, of Alexandria, D. C., became his colleague in the pastoral office.

About this time, his bodily strength began perceptibly to decline, and his mind seemed to be losing its wonted energy. In the course of the winter, he was attacked by a violent influenza, from which he suffered great prostration; but he still cherished the hope that it would occasion nothing more than a temporary suspension of his labours. For two or three weeks previous to his death, he seemed to be gaining strength, and his friends were becoming somewhat encouraged in respect to his recovery. Saturday night, however, he passed without rest, and on Sabbath morning his whole appearance indicated an unfavourable change. In the course of the morning, he was occupied in reading from a favourite work,—President Edwards' work on the Religious Affections; and he also held a brief conversation with a brother minister who had called to see him. Having requested his friend to employ himself with a book, he walked into an adjoining room and threw himself upon the bed. He almost immediately expressed a wish to rise, and, being helped by his wife into a chair, he passed away in a moment and without a struggle. This event occurred on the 25th of May, 1825. His Funeral was attended at the meeting-house in Oliver Street, and a Sermon on the occasion was preached by his intimate and long-tried friend, the venerable John Stanford.

Mr. Williams' publications are a Sermon preached before the New York Missionary Society, and several Association Letters.

A son of Mr. Williams,—the Rev. Dr. William R. Williams, of New York, is well known as one of the ablest preachers, and most accomplished writers, of the day.

FROM THE REV. CHARLES G. SOMMERS, D. D.

New York, May 12, 1853.

Dear Sir: I knew the Rev. John Williams well, and it gives me pleasure to bear my testimony to his remarkably elevated character and useful life. My acquaintance with him commenced about the time that I came to this city, in the year 1810, and I may say that I was on terms of intimacy with him almost from that time till his death. Before I was myself in the ministry, I was often a visiter at his house, and often heard him preach, though he was not the Pastor of the church with which I was more immediately connected. After I commenced preaching, my relations with him became still more intimate, and I have never ceased to regard him as eminently deserving the appellation of a model Christian and a model Minister.

Looking first at his outer man, I may say that there was nothing about him externally that was particularly striking or attractive. In stature, he was of about the middle height; his face was very much of the Welsh character,— round and full, and beaming with kind and generous feeling. His voice was strong, and had somewhat of the Welsh accent; but was marked by another peculiarity, not easily described, which never struck a stranger pleasantly. If you had met him casually in the street, and heard him speak only enough to catch the sound of his voice, and then had been called upon to offer a conjectural opinion of his character as a preacher, your judgment would almost certainly have been very wide of the mark. For though, when he entered the pulpit, you saw the same man, and heard the same voice, yet the man, under the influence of the great truths he was delivering, seemed to have brightened into a superior being, and, in your admiration of what was said, you quite forgot the imperfection of the voice which uttered it. Though he had but little gesture, yet such was the earnestness of his spirit that his whole frame would sometimes seem tremulous under the power of his emotions. He was accustomed to elaborate his discourses thoroughly in his own mind, and to commit the outline to paper, and then to trust for the language to the impulse of the moment at the time of delivery. He was a most diligent student of the Bible, and his great object in preaching seemed to be, not only to bring out the mind of the Spirit, but to bring it in contact with the thoughts and feelings of his hearers in all its Divine power; and in this I must say that he succeeded beyond most persons whom I have known. Though the basis of all his discourses was evangelical truth, he was accustomed to view truth in its most practical bearings; and no one could ever listen attentively to his preaching, without feeling that he had prescribed something to be done as well as to be believed. He had excellent powers of reasoning, though his preaching was not generally of an argumentative cast. As the Welsh was his native language, he was of course familiar with that version of the Scriptures; and I used to think that, owing to this, he sometimes arrived at shades of difference in the construction of a text, which gave him an advantage over most other preachers. His prayers were remarkable specimens of the simplicity as well as fervour of devotion. I think it must have been difficult for any man—no matter how wicked he may have been—to have heard him pray without being impressed with the thought that he was in actual communion with God.

For nothing, perhaps, was Mr. Williams more distinguished than for the natural gentleness and amiableness of his spirit. He loved peace, some might perhaps say, even to excess: for rather than see it interrupted, he would sometimes yield his own opinion, where his friends thought he had better have adhered to it. His congregation were devotedly attached to him,—the youth and little children equally with the adults. In his social intercourse he was always pleasant and cheerful, but never even seemed to lay aside the dignity of the Christian minister. He had in his natural constitution a rich vein of wit; but so careful was he to avoid the appearance of evil, that he always kept it under rigid control, though it would now and then give a bright hue to some of his remarks. He was one of the most modest and retiring of men. Not only was it impossible that he should ever obtrude himself where his presence or his influence was not demanded, but it often required some effort to draw out an expression of his opinions where circumstances rendered it especially desirable. In our Associations and public meetings of different kinds, his voice was rarely heard, unless he was directly called upon to speak; but then he always spoke with composure, and dignity, and point; and no man's opinion was perhaps more generally respected. He was an earnest Baptist, but he had a strong fellow-feeling with true Christians of every name.

I would say of him, in one word, that he was distinguished for a clear, sound and strong mind, for an amiable and a retiring spirit, for an effective eloquence, and for an intense and glowing devotion to the best interests of his fellow-men and the honour of his Master.

Very truly yours,
CHARLES G. SOMMERS.

WILLIAM PARKINSON.*
1796—1848.

WILLIAM PARKINSON, second son of Thomas and Dinah Parkinson, was born in Frederick County, Md., November 8, 1774. His mind was first awakened to a sense of his condition as a sinner, under the preaching of Elder Lewis Richards, of Baltimore, in 1794; and he was baptized, near Woodsberry, Frederick County, by Elder Absalom Bainbridge, on the 17th of June, 1796. His parents, at the time of his birth, were both Episcopalians, and his mother especially he regarded as a devout and earnest Christian. To her, chiefly, he was indebted for his early training; and it is not known that he ever had any other teacher, except in the study of the Hebrew language.

While he was yet a mere boy, his parents, through the instrumentality of Elder John Davis, a somewhat distinguished Baptist preacher of that day, were led to embrace the distinctive views of the Baptists, and travelled on horseback thirty miles to have the ordinance administered to them by immersion. This circumstance made a strong impression on the mind of the son; but, being soon after entered as a clerk in a mercantile establishment in Baltimore, he seems to have banished all serious thoughts, and to have become passionately fond of worldly gaiety. At the age of about twenty, however, his mind took a different direction, and the salvation of his soul became with him the object of supreme concern. He derived great advantage, at this period, from his intercourse with a pious old slave in Baltimore, who was unremitting in his efforts to lead him to embrace the Saviour. At length his mind reposed in the gracious promises of the Gospel, and he made a public profession of his faith shortly after he had completed his twenty-first year.

Having now an increasing desire for reading and study, he abandoned his clerkship, and, in the latter part of 1794 or early in 1795, returned to Frederick County, and opened a school at Carroll's Manor. Here he devoted all the leisure that he could command to the culture of his mind, and all the money he could spare to the purchase of books. Having occasion, soon after he was baptized, to travel a considerable distance from home, he was attracted to a particular place to hear a celebrated preacher, who had made an appointment there for that day. A large audience assembled, but the preacher did not come. It was proposed to have a prayer-meeting, and Mr. Parkinson, being known to be a professor of religion and a schoolmaster, was invited to share in the exercises. He read a portion of Scripture and commenced speaking; and, as he proceeded, the passage revealed to him new treasures, and he spoke with increased earnestness and power, until, to his great astonishment and mortification, he found that his address had occupied upwards of three hours. On his return home, he made an acknowledgment to the church of this irregular procedure, (as he deemed it,) but their own estimate of the case may be inferred from the fact that they proceeded almost immediately to give him a regular license to preach the Gospel. He was ordained to the work of the ministry, by Elders Jeremiah Moore and Lewis Richards, on the 1st of April, 1798.

Mr. Parkinson's predilections were in favour of becoming a missionary, and on this ground he objected for some time to taking a regular pastoral charge. In 1801, he was chosen Chaplain to Congress, and was re-elected for two successive years; but he had the privilege, during this time, of travelling through the week, and preaching every day where he had previously made appointments. He was also particularly interested in the cause of education, and was instrumental in the establishment of one or two Academies.

In 1802, Mr. Parkinson made a visit to the city of New York, and his services in the First Baptist Church were so acceptable that he was invited to return and spend a few months with them; but he preferred to labour as an itinerant. In November, 1804, they renewed their invitation, and he accepted it, though not with any intention of remaining longer than through the winter. In February following, they gave him a call to become their Pastor, which, in view of all the circumstances of the case, he accepted early in April. In the spring of 1805, a revival of religion commenced under his ministry, which continued six years, adding a greater or less number to the church, each successive month.

But in the midst of this high degree of prosperity, Mr. Parkinson's prospects of usefulness were, temporarily at least, clouded by reports unfavourable to his moral character. It is sufficient, however, to say that they became the subject of legal investigation, and he was acquitted of the several charges, and left in regular standing in the church.

During the last ten years of his ministry in the First Church, various circumstances conspired to reduce its numbers. His constitution had become impaired by excessive labour, insomuch that he felt himself no longer adequate to perform all the duties of his office; and in 1840 a proposal was made to have an assistant minister. This measure, however, did not seem likely to succeed according to his mind, in consequence of which he tendered the resignation of his charge. The church reluctantly accepted it, and gave him a dismission to the Church in Frederick, Md., with which he had originally been connected.

The Bethesda Baptist Church in New York, constituted principally of members dismissed from the First Church, very soon presented him a call, and, as he felt himself adequate to the moderate amount of labour that would here be required of him, he accepted it, and became their Pastor in 1841. This connection, however, was of brief continuance. In December of that year, he had a fall which injured him so severely as, in the judgment of many of his friends, to render him unfit for any further public service. He, however, persevered in his labours, amidst all his debility and suffering, resolved not to leave the pulpit as long as he could make himself heard in the delivery of his message. From August, 1847 till March following, he was confined to his bed. The last few days of his life were days of great suffering, but he endured it with the utmost submission, and in the full confidence that it was the harbinger of eternal rest. He died on the 10th of March, 1848, in the seventy-fourth year of his age. His Funeral was attended in the First Baptist Church, and an appropriate Discourse delivered by the Rev. Daniel Dodge, of Philadelphia.

Mr. Parkinson published A Treatise on the Public Ministry of the Word, especially as under the Gospel Dispensation, 1818; and A Series of Sermons on the xxxiii Chapter of Deuteronomy, in two volumes, octavo, 1831. On the cover of the above mentioned Treatise appears the following advertisement—"Preparing for press a work entitled An Attempt to shed light upon several disputed points in Divinity, among which are I. The True Standard by which Fallen Man is tried and condemned; II. The Aggravations of his Condemnation; III. The Nature and Extent of the Atonement made by Christ; IV. The Covenant of Redemption; V. The Natural and Moral Ability and Inability of Man; VI. The Gospel Call to Repentance." Whether this work was ever published, I have not been able to ascertain.

FROM THE REV. B. T WELCH, D. D.

NEWTON CORNERS, June 6, 1859.

My dear Sir: I had but just entered the ministry in 1826, when I made the acquaintance of the late Rev. William Parkinson, of whom you ask me to give you some account. He took me by the hand, with great kindness, and asked me to preach for him; and I well remember that his congregation was, at that time, one of the largest, and most imposing in its appearance, that I had ever seen. Such was the interest that he manifested in me and for me, that I ventured, soon after, to address a letter to him, requesting that he would favour me with his suggestions and counsels with a view to aid me in the great work on which I was entering. His answer was characterized by great kindness and wisdom, and was designed especially to impress me with the importance of looking immediately to the Holy Scriptures, and the Holy Spirit that dictated them, for the light which I needed in the prosecution of my ministry.

In person, Mr. Parkinson was of about the middle stature, rather inclined to be stout, and at that time had a full face, and a sedate and kindly expression. I always found him exceedingly amiable, and disposed to oblige me by every means in his power. He was rather deliberate in his movements, and his whole appearance gave you the impression of a thoughtful and earnest mind.

It was, I believe, conceded by all who knew him, that his intellectual powers were quite extraordinary. As a scholar, too, particularly in the department of Biblical learning, he was probably unsurpassed by any in his denomination at that day. He studied the Scriptures, in their original languages, most closely and critically, and the results of his learning were manifest, both in his conversation and his public discourses. He was profoundly versed in the Levitical Law, and delighted to trace the foreshadowings of another and a sublimer dispensation in the institutions and rites of the ancient economy. Indeed, this became well-nigh a passion with him, insomuch that it constituted a striking, if not a predominating, feature of his public ministrations.

He was, during a part of his ministry at least, one of the most popular preachers which New York, or perhaps I may say any other of our cities, has ever had in it. No church would contain the number which, at some periods, would throng to hear him; and hence he sometimes preached to a congregation of some thousands assembled in the Park. He preached without notes, but always spoke with ease and fluency, and seemed to have the best language fully at command. Without any remarkable power of voice, his enunciation was so distinct that he could be easily heard and understood at a very considerable distance. His gesture was appropriate and graceful, though not very abundant; and his attitudes and whole bearing in the pulpit were in a high degree manly and dignified. The tone of his preaching was strikingly evangelical, and whatever might be the exterior of his subject, he was sure to find Christ in it before he had finished. His discourses were marked by great concentration and consecutiveness of thought, which interested and delighted the intelligent, while yet they were so luminous, impressive, I might almost say majestic, that the multitude were attracted by them. I think he rarely preached less than an hour, but I believe his hearers never wearied under him, and indeed, at that period, an hour was not considered, by any means, an extraordinary length.

Mr. Parkinson had the reputation of being a man of sound judgment and great practical wisdom, and for many years he exerted a commanding influence in his denomination.

Yours fraternally,

B. T. WELCH.

STEPHEN SMITH NELSON.
1796—1853.

FROM THE REV. ROBERT TURNBULL, D. D.

HARTFORD, Conn., July 22, 1856.

Rev. and dear Sir: In complying with your request for some account of the Rev. Mr. Nelson, first Pastor of the First Baptist Church in this city, I have the advantage of drawing, to some extent, upon my own personal recollections, of living among the people whom he served in the pastoral relation, for several years,—though chiefly of another generation; and, in addition to this, I have explored every source of information concerning him within my reach. The result of my observations and inquiries will, I hope, prove to be substantially what you have requested of me.

STEPHEN SMITH NELSON, a son of Thomas and Ann Nelson, was born in Middleborough, Mass., October 5, 1772. The training of pious parents was blessed to his conversion at the early age of fourteen. In his sixteenth year, he was baptized by the Rev. William Nelson, and united with the Baptist Church in Middleborough, then under the pastoral care of Isaac Backus, the venerable Annalist of the Baptist denomination, and the earnest advocate, in early times, of the rights of conscience, and the true freedom of the soul. He was graduated at Brown University in 1794, and was, from 1819 to 1831, a member of the Board of Trustees of that institution. On leaving College, he studied Theology with the Rev. Dr. Stillman, the devout and eloquent Pastor of the First Baptist Church in Boston, and frequently assisted him in his labours by visiting and otherwise. By this means he acquired a thorough practical training for the work of the ministry. In his twenty-fourth year he was licensed to preach the Gospel. After labouring two years with the church in Hartford, as a stated supply, he was ordained in 1798, as their Pastor, preaching to them at first in "an upper room," or in the old Court House. The church, however, soon secured a convenient place of worship, which, though humble in its appearance, and rough in its furniture, was found to be a true Bethel,— "the House of God and the very Gate of Heaven."

At this time, Mr. Nelson was the only liberally educated Baptist minister in Connecticut; and there is no doubt that his accurate scholarship, courteous manners, and consistent piety, served greatly to aid in the establishment and increase of the Baptist Church, especially in this city. He was actively engaged in the remarkable revival of religion that occurred about the close of the last century, and which added so many converts to the churches of all Christian denominations in Hartford and elsewhere.

Decided in his peculiar views and usages as a Baptist, he was the cordial friend and brother of all good men. On that account, he was in the most friendly and intimate relations with Doctors Strong and Flint, at that time the only Congregational ministers in Hartford, and cheerfully co-operated with them in the cause of Christ.

Though Mr. Nelson's pastoral charge was in Hartford, his occasional labours extended to several of the neighbouring towns, particularly Middletown; and the First Baptist Church in Upper Middletown (now Cromwell) was established by his efforts.

Mr. Nelson, as well as several other prominent Baptist clergymen of that day, was not only the firm friend but open advocate of civil and religious liberty, as the inalienable birthright of the human soul; and, during his residence in Hartford, took an active part in preparing and urging upon the public attention "The Baptist Petition,"—a Remonstrance addressed to the Connecticut Legislature, complaining of the civil disabilities which "Dissenters" from the "Standing Order" were compelled to suffer, and urging upon them the great doctrine of absolute "soul liberty,"—in other words, the entire freedom of conscience, worship, and action, in the domain of religion,—which petition, constantly pressed by the Baptists, and other lovers of liberty, who united with them, at last severed, in Connecticut, the union of Church and State, by securing that Constitution of civil government, which, in 1818, gave to all equal civil and religious rights.

At the first election of Mr. Jefferson to the Presidency of the United States, Mr. Nelson was appointed, with others, by the Danbury (now the Hartford) Baptist Association, in behalf of that Body, to prepare and forward to him a Congratulatory Address, recognizing his acknowledged attachment to civil and religious liberty.

In 1801, Mr. Nelson resigned his charge in Hartford, and became, for a number of years, Principal of a large and flourishing Academy at Mount Pleasant, now Sing Sing, N. Y., at the same time taking charge of an infant church in that village. Both the Church and Academy flourished under his care until the War with Great Britain came on, in consequence of which he removed in 1815 to Attleborough, Mass., where an extensive revival took place under his labours, which brought into the church upwards of a hundred and fifty persons. After this, he had the charge, for a short time, successively, of the churches in Plymouth, Mass., and Canton, Conn.

In 1825, he removed to Amherst, Mass., for the purpose of availing himself of the facilities there furnished in the education of his family. During the first year of his residence there, he took charge of the church in Belchertown; but being unable, on account of the distance, to perform the duties to his own satisfaction, he resigned it. He was accustomed, however, almost till his dying day, to preach to feeble and destitute churches in the neighbourhood and elsewhere, as he had opportunity. In these gratuitous labours he enjoyed the abundant blessing of God.

For the last few years of his life, his rapid progress in spirituality was obvious to all his friends. He was filled with peace. He longed for the salvation of God, both here and hereafter. Hundreds at least were brought to Christ by his agency, through his long career, and his last days were crowned by the reviving influences of God's Spirit upon the churches around him, in which he also was permitted to share. A delightful visit to his son in Greenfield, a short time before his decease, was a season of refreshing to both himself and many others. He lived to see all his children and some of his grandchildren gathered into the fold of the Good Shepherd,—some of whom are on this side, and some on the other side, of the flood. For the accomplishment of this object he laboured and prayed much during the last years of his life. He established a monthly Sabbath evening Concert of Prayer throughout the different families of his children for the conversion of all their relatives, which is kept up to this day; and, as another means to the same end, he addressed, on his seventy-eighth birth-day, to each of his grandchildren the memorial of a selected text of Scripture, accompanied by a word of patriarchal counsel. His ruling passion was to do some good while life lasted, so that he might be a burden neither to himself nor to others. His desire was fulfilled. The illness of which he died, which was erysipelas in the head, lasted but six days. His mind was calm and composed. He comforted his comforters. Tranquilly he stepped into the dark waters of Death's river; speedily and pleasantly he gained the farther shore; and while his friends and family were gazing with mingled grief and joy, he was lost to their sight amid the glories of the Heavenly Canaan. He died at Amherst on the 8th of December, 1853, in the eighty-second year of his age. His Funeral drew together a great concourse of his friends and neighbours, ministers and private members of the Church, from his own and other denominations; and a Sermon was preached on the occasion by the Pastor of the Baptist church, which was followed by an impressive Address from one of the Professors in Amherst College. "As we have known him," was the utterance of one of these, "he appeared as the pilgrim who had passed the hill of difficulty, the valley of the shadow of death, the giants and the lions. His strifes were over. He was walking in the land of Beulah, fanned by refreshing breezes, and calmed by the gentle strains that floated on the ear of his listening spirit. Such was his place among us. We looked for him, and he had gone over to the celestial city."

Mr. Nelson was about five feet, six inches in height, erect in his gait, neat in his appearance, prompt in his movements, and remarkably urbane in his manners. When I knew him, his hair was silver gray, his eye bright and penetrating, and his movements as vivacious nearly as those of a young man. Brief, pointed, earnest, evangelical, his preaching was eminently fitted to do good. His voice was clear and ringing; his manner impressive and dignified, as became an ambassador for Christ. His life was simple, serene, and, especially in his later years, heavenly. "He seemed," said a dear friend and relative, "to move among men in the quietness of his own reflections, above and aside from the cares and conflicts of outward life, at peace with God, at peace with men."

Mr. Nelson was married, on the 15th of October, 1798, to Emelia, third daughter of Deacon Ephraim Robins, of Hartford,—who still survives.* They had nine children,—four sons and five daughters. Two of the sons were graduates of Amherst College. One of these, *Ephraim Robins*, had the ministry in view, and was contemplating the work of a Foreign Missionary, but died, greatly lamented, in 1831, while filling the office of Tutor in the Columbian College, D. C. His elder brother, *William Francis*, after pursuing a course of Theology at the Newton Theological

* Mrs. N. has deceased since the commencement of the year 1859.

Institute, became a Professor in Richmond College, Va.; but has since become Pastor of the Church in Wickford, R. I.

I am yours truly and fraternally,

ROBERT TURNBULL.

ISAAC SAWYER.*

1797—1847.

ISAAC SAWYER, a son of Isaac Sawyer, was born in the town of Hoosick, N. Y., on the 22d of November, 1770. His parents were Pedobaptists,— his father being a Presbyterian, and his mother an Episcopalian. His father's ancestors came from England; his mother's from Ireland. When he was a small boy, his father was taken captive by the Indians, a large number of whom surprised him in the night; and he, with another white man, was started off (the family having been stripped of every thing the Indians could carry away) for the Falls of Niagara, where the famous Captain Brant then was, with a large company of his men. Mr. Sawyer, as he was leaving his house, caught up a leaf of some book, and pretending to the Indians that it was part of the Bible, obtained permission from them to read it, in company with his friend; and, while they professed to be reading it, they were actually devising means for their escape. On the eleventh night of their captivity, when they were on one of the branches of the Susquehannah River, in Pennsylvania, the party of their captors having separated, and only four of them having the charge of the two whites, Mr. Sawyer, taking advantage of this circumstance, carefully drew himself out from between the two Indians who were sleeping on either side of him, and with an axe instantly killed them both. This aroused the others; and, in order to despatch them both at once, he dropped his axe, and caught up a gun and snapped it; but, finding that it was not loaded, he seized a hatchet with which he killed one, and wounded the other. The latter made his escape; and Mr. Sawyer and his friend, after traversing the wilderness fifteen days, and subsisting on roots and berries of winter greens, at length reached a settlement of whites at a place then called Minisink, on the Susquehannah, nearly famished, and exhausted by fatigue. Mr. Sawyer's family were removed to Albany after his return, and remained there during the greater part of the War; but, towards its close, they settled in Pittstown, N. Y., where Mrs. Sawyer died, when her son Isaac was about eleven years of age. Three years after, his father died of a disease contracted during his captivity. Thus young Sawyer was left an orphan at the early age of fourteen.

Two years after this, he bound himself out to a man by the name of Herrick, who, soon after, removed to the town of Monkton, Addison County, Vt. That country was then a wilderness, without schools, churches, or any other institutions for the promotion of intellectual, moral or religious culture; and it was in such circumstances that this young man lived

* MS. from his son, Rev. Conant Sawyer.

till he attained the age of twenty-one. His associates were, like himself, utterly regardless of the claims of religion; and he and they mingled together in scenes that were fitted to exclude God from their thoughts, and paralyze their moral sensibilities.

On the 20th of September, 1792, he was married to Mary, daughter of Joseph Willoughby, of Monkton, with whom he shared the highest domestic enjoyment during the long period of fifty-five years. They had ten children,—nine sons, and one daughter; all of whom survived both their parents; all of whom became professors of religion and were baptized by their father; and five of whom are now (1858) ministers of the Gospel. Mrs. Sawyer died in Jay, Essex County, N. Y., on the 26th of August, 1849.

In the year 1793, Monkton was visited with a revival of religion,—the first that Mr. Sawyer ever witnessed; and it was then that he became hopefully a subject of renewing grace. For a long time he was overwhelmed with a sense of his own sinfulness, and sometimes trembling on the borders of despair. He sought to make himself better, that he might have something to offer in the way of personal righteousness, as a ground of his justification; but, after a long course of fruitless effort, was brought, as he believed, to welcome Christ as his Saviour, and accept of salvation as a free gift. In referring to the commencement of his Christian course, after he was far advanced in life, he said,—"The hope I was then permitted to cherish, I have enjoyed from that day to the present, though not without some attacks of unbelief. At an early period of my experience, however, I had so full a confirmation of the truth and Divinity of Christianity, that the enemy has not been permitted since to shake my confidence in it; nor have I indulged the least doubt but that those who die impenitent will be forever banished from the pure and peaceful presence of God." Very few of the young people with whom he had been more immediately associated became subjects of the revival, and he found the utmost circumspection and firmness necessary in order to resist the influences they brought to bear upon him.

At that period, there was no church of any denomination in the town in which he lived; nor was there any ordained minister within forty miles of him. His relatives, so far as he knew, were all Pedobaptists; and he himself had been baptized in infancy; but still he felt disposed to examine the subject of Baptism for himself. As the result of an earnest and somewhat protracted investigation, he reached the conclusion that there was no warrant in Scripture for Infant Baptism, and that it was his duty to be baptized by immersion, upon a profession of his own faith. As soon, therefore, as an administrator could be obtained, he, and ten others, were baptized and organized into a Baptist church. It was the first church of that denomination formed in the county. And, although he was the youngest of the company, he was soon chosen Deacon, and served in that capacity until he began to preach.

He was called by the church to "exercise his gift" in preaching in 1797; but so deeply was he impressed with a sense of his own unfitness that he hesitated long before he could make up his mind to go forward. One day, when at work in the field, these words were constantly passing through his mind,—"Let the dead bury their dead." On his return home at evening, he took up his Bible to ascertain the connection of the words; but he did not know where to look for them. Much to his surprise, on opening the sacred volume, they were the first words on which his eye rested. And greater still was his astonishment when he read the connection,—"But go thou and preach the Gospel." He exclaimed,—"This certainly cannot be for me"—he could not for a moment admit the idea that he was called to the sacred office,—such was his sense of incompetency; and had it not been for the urgent solicitations of the church, he would probably have never had any other than a secular vocation.

On the 29th of June, 1799, a Council was called, consisting of five ministers and several lay delegates, who, after due examination, ordained him to the work of the ministry. He remained at Monkton some thirteen years after his ordination, during which time the church increased to about one hundred members, and enjoyed in other respects a good degree of prosperity. But, as some became dissatisfied in consequence of his taking legal measures to secure a glebe lot which was offered by law to the first ordained minister in every town, in which, after a seven years' law suit, he succeeded,—this, in connection with the influence of party politics, led him to leave Monkton, and remove to Fairfield, in the same State, in March, 1812. While he was Pastor of the Church at Monkton, he performed several missionary tours in the Northern Counties of New York, in some of which his labours were eminently blessed; and many of the large and flourishing churches, now existing in that part of the country, were gathered through his instrumentality. He was generally sent out by the Association to which he belonged, and was absent from home six or eight weeks at a time. He was accustomed, as long as he lived, to revert with great satisfaction to these missionary labours, as having been among the most pleasant and successful of his whole ministry.

In consequence of the breaking out of the War with Great Britain, he remained in Fairfield but a single year. In 1813, he removed to Orwell, Rutland County, where he spent four years, and witnessed a powerful revival of religion in connection with his labours.

About this time, he seriously meditated the purpose of finding a home in the West. He had an uncle in Harpersfield, O., who was very desirous that he should settle in that part of the country, and, as an inducement to him to do so, offered him a valuable farm. He consented to settle with the Church at West Haven, with the understanding, however, that he should visit the State of Ohio in the course of the year, and, if he thought best, should ultimately remove his family thither. He made the contemplated journey to Ohio, and was much pleased with the country; but, at the earnest solicitation of the Church in Brandon, he relinquished the idea of settling in the West, and removed to Brandon in the spring of 1818. Here he remained as Pastor of the church seven years, and, during that time, witnessed one of the most powerful revivals that ever occurred under his ministry. In 1825, he removed to Bethel, on the East side of the Mountain, in Windsor County, where he remained till 1828, performing the duties of a Pastor during a large portion of the time, and occasionally labouring as a Missionary and an agent of the Hamilton Literary and Theological Institution. After spending three years here, he removed to Westport, Essex County, N. Y., where he remained six years, and witnessed three extensive revivals. During his residence in this place, he baptized a hundred and fifty persons on a profession of their faith, more than two thirds of whom were added to the Church in Westport. In 1834, he left Essex County, and removed to Knowlesville, Orleans County; and after this lived successively in Stockton, Chautauque County, and Lewiston, in the County of Niagara. In the two last named places he lived and laboured but a short time.

The last six or seven years of his life, he spent chiefly with his son and daughter in Essex County. His death occurred suddenly. He attended church on the Sabbath, was taken ill on Monday, died on Thursday, and was buried the next Sabbath. His disease, which was of the nature of cholera, resisted all medical treatment, and reached a fatal termination on the 30th of September, 1847. A few hours before his death, his son said to him,—"Father, you feel that you have got almost home, do you not?" He said,—"I do." "And does not the near prospect of Heaven fill you with joy?" He answered,—"I cannot say that I feel any particular ecstacy, but I have a hope that is like an anchor to the soul." His end was eminently peaceful and happy; and none who knew him doubted that it marked the beginning of an eternal rest.

Mr. Sawyer baptized, during his ministry, upwards of eleven hundred persons, and among them a greater number who became ministers than have been baptized by any other minister in Vermont. He lived to be seventy years of age, and was for half a century a preacher of the Gospel. He was the first President of the Vermont Baptist State Convention, and held this office several years. He was the friend of Education, and laboured much at home and abroad to promote the interests of the Baptist Education Society. He was also the friend of Missions, of Temperance, of Emancipation, of every cause which involved the present or future well being of his fellow-men.

FROM THE REV. S. S. CUTTING, D. D.
PROFESSOR IN THE ROCHESTER UNIVERSITY.

ROCHESTER, January 15, 1859.

Rev. and dear Sir: My earliest recollection of the Rev. Isaac Sawyer is associated with an incident illustrative of his character. It was, I think, in the summer of 1827, before the tender of the cup had ceased to be an acknowledged part of the hospitalities of a Christian family. The minister of our church,—the Baptist church in Westport, N. Y.,—had resigned, and Mr. Sawyer had been invited to visit the place with a view to the pastoral office. He, with the retiring minister, was a guest at my father's house, between the services of the Sabbath day. I, as the boy on whom that duty naturally devolved, was directed to bear to our Reverend visiters the refreshment of brandy and water, with sugar attached; and this I did without a thought to that moment of any connection between conscience and drinking, except that conscience forbade intemperate drinking. With the air of the true gentleman, quietly but firmly, Mr. Sawyer declined the cup. "It is a point of conscience with me," said the already venerable man; "I have united with some of my brethren in an obligation to abstain entirely." "A point of conscience!"

thought the astonished boy,—and he never forgot the lesson, or ceased to honour the minister of religion from whose lips those few words had fallen. Thank Heaven, the cup ceased to be among the hospitalities of that home.

All my subsequent impressions of Mr. Sawyer's character were outgrowths of this original incident. He was of medium stature, rather slightly formed, erect, and possessing that kind of dignity which, while it never repelled a proper approach, prohibited rude familiarity. There was nothing sanctimonious in his manner or bearing, but there was sanctity, and nobody presumed to trifle in his presence. There had been a powerful revival of religion in the town, and the church had had large accessions. His ministry was of the kind to establish Christian character, to promote Christian growth, and to prepare the church for wider usefulness and greater extension. Other revivals succeeded, and it is my impression that I have not been accustomed to see, generally, in later years, so much of thoroughness in the foundations of Christian life, as distinguished his ministry at such seasons. I well remember a revival which occurred in 1831. I was a student at the time, at home in search of health. On my arrival, I found preparations in progress for a "Four Days Meeting." The frame of the house of worship had been for some time raised, but the work had proceeded slowly. Roof and rough boarding were now hurried on; a loose flooring was laid; rude benches were to furnish sittings for the congregation, and a carpenter's bench a platform for the preachers. The moral preparations seemed to be less adequate. A meeting largely attended was held in a school-house on the evening previous to the great gathering in the unfinished church. The Providence of God had brought to the village, on that evening, the venerable Father Comstock, a Congregational minister, long known and honoured in Northern New York. On these aged men devolved the duty of the religious instructions of that evening. Father Comstock preached, making the union of Christians in love, and prayers, and labours, the burden of his message, and reaching a strain of Christian eloquence which it has never been my lot to witness on any other occasion. Father Sawyer followed, reiterating and applying these instructions, and, before the evening closed, the members of the church, to that hour so languid and so wanting in faith as well-nigh to quench the hope of a blessing, were brought upon their knees in confessions and prayers which were the sure precursors of a great ingathering of souls. This great revival was, I believe, the last under the ministry of Father Sawyer at Westport, and illustrated, as it seems to me, the excellence and height of his power as a Christian Pastor.

I was best acquainted with Father Sawyer's ministry when I was too young for a critical estimate of his intellectual power. He always, I believe, preached extemporaneously, and I well remember that his quiet but earnest and impressive facility of speech seemed to me remarkable, and I think his clearness, method, and correctness were not less noticeable. I do not know the extent of his acquisitions. I know that he valued highly intellectual cultivation as a preparation for the ministry, for he encouraged and stimulated my own purposes in regard to an education. His attention to the education of his own family, several of whom became ministers, equally attested the same fact. I met him but seldom after this period. Once I saw him in his extreme old age, sustaining still the dignity of former years, and looking serenely for the rest which remaineth for the people of God.

Very respectfully yours,

S. S. CUTTING.

DANIEL DODGE.

1797—1851.

FROM THE REV. HENRY C. FISH.

NEWARK, N. J., July 12, 1855.

My dear Sir: I cheerfully comply with your request for such an account as I am able to give of the late Rev. Daniel Dodge, who was known, for many years, as one of the prominent ministers of the Baptist denomination in this country. What I shall write, is partly from personal knowledge, and partly from diligent inquiry among his surviving friends. I have also the advantage of living in the midst of the congregation which he served for several years.

DANIEL DODGE was born in Annapolis, Nova Scotia, December 1, 1777; his father having migrated to that Province from Ipswich, Mass. His father's sympathy with the American cause, during the Revolutionary struggle, led him to return to his native country, while the War was yet in progress, and to settle again in Massachusetts. His mother, who was a Miss Conant, of Massachusetts, was a devout member of the Episcopal Church; but, while Daniel was yet very young, she embraced the Baptist faith,—a circumstance by which he seems to have been very strongly impressed. He was exceedingly fond of his mother, and is said never to have been guilty of but a single act of disobedience towards her, and that of a very trivial character; but it occasioned him, ever after, the deepest regret, and contributed not a little to that conviction of his guilt which preceded his acceptance of the Saviour.

Of the circumstances of his conversion little is now known; but it is known that, at the age of eighteen, he indulged the hope that he had passed from death unto life, and united with the Baptist Church in Woodstock, Vt., then under the pastoral care of Elder Elisha Ransom. He began almost immediately to feel a strong desire to become a preacher of the Gospel. To remove an impediment in the way of realizing the object of his desires, he purchased his time of a ship builder, to whom his father had apprenticed him. He agreed to pay to his employer the sum of one hundred dollars, to acquire which he went to sea; and, while upon his voyage, was taken, with others, by a French Privateer vessel, and caused to pass through many trials, and much suffering. In the good Providence of God, he at last escaped, placed in the hands of his former employer the stipulated sum, and, not long after, in 1797, realized his wishes in becoming a minister of the Gospel. He received license to preach from the Baptist Church in Baltimore, under the pastoral care of the Rev. Mr. Richards. He preached some time in different churches in Maryland and Virginia. About 1802, he became Pastor of a Church in Wilmington, De., where he laboured with great success, baptizing sixty persons in one year. He preached in Wilmington nearly twenty years, and then went to Piscataway, in New Jersey, where he had the charge of a church about fourteen years. From Piscataway he was called to the pastoral care of the church in Newark, in June, 1832. He accepted the call, and in the month of August, entered fully upon his labours. This proved in all respects a happy choice, as was soon apparent in the increase of harmony among the brethren, in a better attendance upon the means of grace, in the awakening of the careless and the increase of the faithful. In November, 1837, he resigned his charge at Newark, on account of the inadequacy of his support; but the Church were unwilling to be deprived of his valuable services, and induced him to withdraw his resignation. He continued with them until December, 1839, when he became the Pastor of a church in Philadelphia, where he resided at the time of his death. For a year and a half previous to that time, he had been unable to perform his pastoral labours ; but such was the affectionate esteem of his people towards him, that they would not consent to accept his resignation, until two or three months previous to his decease. At intervals, especially during the early period of his last illness, his mind was somewhat clouded with doubts. God gave him grace, however, for the most part, to triumph in hope and joy. Particularly was this true in the few last months of his earthly sojourn.

A brother in the ministry,—the Rev. Dr. Kennard of Philadelphia, in calling upon him, when he was suffering much, directed his mind towards Christ and Heaven, and repeated the passage,—" We shall see Him as He is." At this, the old man threw up both his hands, and with gushing tears exclaimed,—" Too much, too much !" On another occasion, this brother spoke to him of the many happy souls now in Heaven, and ready to welcome him there—to which he replied with much emotion,—" Do you think so ?"—and the suggestion filled him with joyful surprise. He bore his protracted sufferings without complaint, but waited for his change to come. When informed of the death of an aged brother in the ministry, whom he had long and intimately known, he cried out,—" Is he gone before me ? Why does my Heavenly Father keep me here ?" He died on the 13th of May, 1851, aged seventy-five years. After his death, and before his burial, persons of all ages, even down to little children, flocked with most intense interest, to look upon his face once more, before his remains should be carried to their final resting place. It was estimated that his Funeral was attended by fully two thousand persons, among whom were about thirty clergymen. The Funeral Sermon was preached by the Rev. Dr. Kennard.

Mr. Dodge was married, soon after he entered the ministry, to a Miss Ragan of Virginia, a lady of eminent piety. After her death, he was married a second time to Miss Letitia Mankin, of Baltimore, who, with one daughter, survived him.

My first acquaintance with Mr. Dodge was in the spring of 1844, at the meeting of the American Baptist Triennial Convention in Philadelphia. He was at that time one of the more active members of the Body, and entered into the various discussions and business transactions with much interest and enthusiasm. His head was crowned with thick, short, white hair, and his brow was wrinkled with age ; but the fire and force of other days were not abated. His form was quite commanding—tall, erect, massive, with a countenance indicative of a genial heart, and an earnestness of purpose. His pulpit ministrations were not especially marked, but always highly acceptable ; especially while dwelling upon his favourite topic,—the doctrine of Divine Grace. The entire bearings of the man, both in his social and public intercourse, were adapted to impress one with his plain, round-about common sense, his keen insight into human nature, and his marked sincerity and devotion.

During his extended ministry, he always bore an irreproachable character, and was greatly esteemed in every community in which his lot was cast. He was a man of enlarged Christian sympathies, and hailed every one as a brother in whom he recognized the Master's image; while yet he was a consistent Baptist, always showing himself faithful to his own convictions. Though he had never had the advantages of a liberal education, he had by no means neglected the culture of his own mind, and never appeared on any occasion otherwise than with propriety and dignity. His sound judgment and excellent common sense, as well as his peaceable and conciliatory spirit, were often put in requisition in cases of controversy; and few were more successful than he in healing divisions. He was sure to be cordially welcomed at all public meetings of general interest, as well as in Associations of his own denomination; for he had always something to say to enlighten, or encourage, or help. Many are they who hold his memory in hallowed recollection; and many are the fruits of his ministry, attesting to his protracted and successful labours.

I am most truly yours,
HENRY C. FISH.

WILLIAM COLLIER.*
1798—1843.

WILLIAM COLLIER was born in Scituate, Mass., October 11, 1771. He was the eldest son of Isaac and Tamsen Collier, whose family consisted of twelve children. The father pursued the occupation of a farmer, and was much respected for intelligence and integrity. Under the influence of a pious mother, he developed, in his youth, a simplicity of character, and conscientious regard to moral obligation, which distinguished him through life.

He early evinced a distaste for sea-faring pursuits, in which most of his youthful associates became engaged, and was soon led to Boston for the purpose of learning the trade of a carpenter. Here he attended upon the ministry of Doctors Stillman and Baldwin, and, a few years later, at the age of twenty-one, he united with the Second Baptist Church, under the pastoral care of Dr. Baldwin. Having completed his apprenticeship, and feeling a strong desire to spend his life in preaching the Gospel, he entered upon a course of study with reference to that object. In the year 1793, he entered Rhode Island College, (now Brown University,) and graduated in 1797. He afterwards studied Theology under the President of the College, the Rev. Dr. Maxcy, and was licensed to preach the Gospel by what is now the Baldwin Place Church, on the 3d of June, 1798.

* MSS. from his son,—Mr. W. R. Collier, and Rev. Gurdon Robins.

Mr. Collier was ordained at Boston, July 11, 1799, the Sermon being preached by Dr. Baldwin, the Charge delivered by Dr. Stillman, and the Right Hand of Fellowship given by Dr. Gano. He was ordained as a Minister at Large, but was almost immediately settled as Pastor of the Baptist Church in Newport, R. I., where he remained, however, but one year, being then called to the Pastorate of the First Baptist Church in New York City. This station he occupied for a term of four years. From this place he was transferred, without any intermediate loss of time, to Charlestown, Mass. Here he became Pastor of the Baptist Church in the year 1804, and held the position for sixteen years. This, as it was his largest term of service, also presents the field to which we are chiefly to look, as a test of the value of his labours. Here he became intimately associated with those fathers in the ministry, Doctors Stillman and Baldwin, and other clergy of his denomination, maintaining among them a good standing, as Pastor of a prominent church, and enjoying the uniform confidence and affection of his people, and the respect of the community in which he lived. Though he exercised his ministry during a period in which the country was greatly agitated by political conflicts, and the churches suffered a corresponding depression, he sustained himself with great dignity as an active and successful minister of the Gospel. During part of his ministry at Charlestown, he shared with Dr. Morse the Chaplaincy of the State Prison. He resigned his charge, on account of the failure of his health, in the year 1820.

Immediately after this, he removed to Boston, where he spent the remainder of his life. Here he commenced a long and varied service as Minister at Large, thus closing his ministerial life as he began it; and, during the whole of the period last named, he was widely and favourably known for his labours in connection with the City Mission, and other kindred enterprises. He was one of the pioneers in the Temperance Reform, and, in addition to a great amount of previous labour in aid of it, he undertook, in the year 1826, the publication of a weekly Temperance newspaper, called *The National Philanthropist*,—the first paper of the kind, as far as is known, that was ever printed. It was sustained by him for two years, and proved a very efficient auxiliary to the cause.

About the 12th of February, 1843, Mr. Collier was suddenly prostrated, while actively engaged in City Missionary labours,—his exertions in that work having been for some months obviously far beyond his strength. He soon became aware that his sickness was unto death,—the effect of which was greatly to quicken his religious feelings. His chief anxiety seemed to be to bear a dying testimony to the truth as it is in Jesus. He then turned his attention to the settlement of his worldly affairs, and, with the utmost tranquillity of spirit, gave the most minute directions in respect to all that concerned him. It then seemed as though his work was done, and nothing remained for him but to await calmly the summons which he knew was at hand. He resumed his natural manner, and, as far as his weakness and suffering permitted, his sick chamber became the scene of the same genial and social influences which had ever attended his personal presence through life. Thus he lingered till the 19th of March, 1843, when, without a struggle, his spirit passed from its earthly tenement, to mingle in higher scenes. A Funeral Discourse was delivered in the Second Baptist Church, of which he was a member, by the Rev. Dr. Rollin H. Neale, and the numerous attendance from all classes evinced a high and general appreciation of his character, and a deep sense of the loss that had been sustained, especially in the circles in which he had moved.

Mr. Collier published a Sermon preached before the Massachusetts Baptist Missionary Society in 1816, and a Sermon preached at Lyme, Conn., at the Ordination of G. W. Appleton, in 1819. He compiled a Hymn Book; edited the Baptist Preacher,—a monthly publication consisting of Sermons from living ministers, commenced in 1827; and superintended an edition of Saurin's Sermons, of a work in four volumes, entitled " The Gospel Treasury," of Andrew Fuller's Works, &c., &c.

Mr. Collier was married on the 10th of August, 1799, to Abigail, daughter of Deacon Ephraim Robins, of Hartford. Conn. By this, his only marriage, he had seven children, two of whom died in early life. *Ephraim*, his youngest son, survived to the age of twenty-seven. He graduated at Harvard College in 1826, and was a young man of great purity of character, rare classical tastes, and excellent scholarship. He was, however, of feeble constitution, and just as he entered on the work of the ministry to which he was consecrated, he was called to mingle in higher scenes. He died in 1840. The eldest son and three daughters still (1858) survive.

FROM THE REV. BARON STOW, D. D.

BOSTON, September 6, 1858.

Rev. and dear Sir: My acquaintance with the Rev. William Collier commenced about the year 1825. He was then actively engaged as a Minister at Large, in Boston, and was regarded by a large circle, of various denominations, as a man of warm Christian philanthropy, and an industrious, useful labourer. He had then passed his prime, and was on the descending side of life. In person, he was rather above medium size, moderate in his movements, and a little stooping in his gait. His head was well formed, with no part especially protuberant, or indicative of marked intellectual character. His hair was light and thin, his complexion fair, his eye soft, and his whole expression of face bland and amiable. My first impression was, that he must be a man of great humility and meekness, shrinking from notoriety, oblivious of self, and regardful of the good of others. That impression I never had occasion to correct. From 1832 till the time of his death, I sustained to him the relation of Pastor, and therefore had ample opportunity to observe the traits of his character. Uniformly he honoured my position, and I never had occasion to suspect him of a disposition to counterwork my plans, or control church action. He was ever ready for service as a private member, demanding no preference or pre-eminence on account of either his age or his ministerial office. He was invariably my helper and friend, and I could have gone through the longest Pastorate, with a hundred such as Mr. Collier in the membership, and found the relation only agreeable. In the church he was respected and beloved as eminently a man of God, and his death was most sincerely lamented. And here I may add that my esteemed predecessors, the Rev. Dr. Baldwin, and the Rev. James D. Knowles, were accustomed to speak of him as a quiet, unobtrusive member, and a useful coadjutor.

The character of Mr. C. was peculiarly harmonious. His faculties and affections were admirably balanced, and consequently he was not adapted to be a leader where great boldness or daring was requisite, nor was he a man to produce a sensation in the masses. He had a low estimate of himself, and never ventured into prominence, even where the general respect for his character would have tolerated much assumption. If he erred in judgment, it was always in matters affecting his personal interest, and never bringing damage to others. Though eminently conservative, yet he was sufficiently progressive, and to the last was interested in every movement that promised good to humanity. He struck out no large plans of action, and yet, in some things, he was the originator and the pioneer of good enterprises. Hating every thing wrong, he was charitable towards wrong-doers, and sought, through kindness, to benefit them. I never heard him speak ill of any person; I have often known him to seek for the best possible construction of the designs and motives of such as others were earnest to condemn. I think no man has lived in this community who better deserved the name of peacemaker.

Mr. Collier had strong faith in the Bible as the word of God, and he loved the book, and studied it with docility and success. His views of Christian doctrine were clear, strong and symmetrical. The plan of salvation, as a plan of Grace, he admired and habitually commended. I never met with his superior in the exposition of Paul's strongest passages relating to Justification by Faith. And yet, when near his end, he said to me:—"Many years ago I was much impressed by those words of the Apostle,—'Wherefore we labour, that, whether present or absent, we may be accepted of Him.' I have long been labouring at that point, anxious so to demean myself in all respects as to secure final acceptance. But I now perceive that I have unconsciously been manufacturing as pretty a piece of self-righteousness as ever was put together. I renounce the whole, and turn to the finished work of Christ as my all. If I am not accepted in the Beloved, I am lost forever. Warn Christians, my brother, not to put any measure of sanctification in the place of Christ's justifying righteousness."

The memory of Mr. Collier is fragrant in this community. The sphere that he filled was not large, but he filled it well. He walked with God.

Your brother in heart,
BARON STOW.

CLARK KENDRICK.*
1799—1824.

CLARK KENDRICK was a descendant, in the fifth generation, of John Kendrick, who was born in England in 1605; came to Boston in 1639; settled in Newton, Mass., and died on the 29th of August, 1686, aged eighty-one years. He was a son of Ebenezer and Anna (Davenport) Kendrick, and was born in Hanover, N. H., on the 6th of October, 1775,—his parents having removed thither, a short time before, from Connecticut. His father became hopefully pious near the close of his life, and joined the Congregational Church; but his mother, though distinguished for her good sense and brilliant wit, was not a professor of religion, and evinced no special interest in it. It is said that his father, who was killed by the fall of a tree, was engaged, in his last moments, in prayer for the salvation of his family; and all his children have become exemplary members of the Church.

* Amer. Bapt. Mag., 1831.—MS. from his son,—Rev. Dr. Kendrick.

Some time before the death of his father, Clark was placed in the family of an uncle, in the vicinity, who afterwards removed to Bethel, Vt. Having lived with him, labouring on a farm, till he was seventeen, he removed to Plainfield, in the same State, where he continued in the same occupation for two years,—until he lost his health. He then left Vermont, made a short visit to Connecticut, for the sake of enjoying the sea air, and again took up his residence in Hanover. Here he qualified himself for teaching, and spent about three years in that employment before he left the place. During this period, in the summer of 1797, he became hopefully the subject of a spiritual renovation.

The circumstances attending his conversion were deeply interesting. On a certain evening, he and the friend in whose family he was boarding fell into a conversation on the subject of religion, which gradually assumed an unwonted solemnity, and left upon Mr. Kendrick's mind a deep impression of the importance of eternal realities. By Mr. K.'s request, his friend detailed to him some of the particulars of his Christian experience; and this heightened not a little his own sense both of obligation and of need. For six weeks, he suffered, without interruption, the most intense anguish of spirit, insomuch that his friends greatly feared either that his bodily health would sink, or that his mind would become unstrung. Meanwhile others, from witnessing his agony, became similarly impressed; a general awakening ensued; and numbers were rejoicing in the hope of the Gospel, while he was yet oppressed with the wild horrors of despair. At length, however, the dark cloud which had enveloped him passed off, and while he reposed a joyful confidence in his Redeemer, he became an earnest and efficient auxiliary in sustaining and advancing the work which had so singularly originated with himself.

Mr. Kendrick, who had now reached the age of twenty-two, soon became impressed with the conviction that it was his duty to preach the Gospel; but so reluctant was he, from a distrust of his abilities and a consciousness of his limited attainments, to yield to it, that he actually left New Hampshire, crossed the Green Mountains on foot, and came to Salem, N. Y., where he engaged in teaching a school, in the hope of being able to banish these unwelcome thoughts from his mind. He did not succeed, however, in accomplishing his object; for the sense of obligation to this duty still remained with him, and, on the appearance of something like an awakening in the place, he lost all his diffidence and entered into it with the utmost zeal and efficiency. The Rev. Obed Warren,* who was, at that time, Pastor of the Baptist Church in Salem, became at once deeply interested in Mr.

---

* OBED WARREN was born in Plainfield, Conn., March 18, 1760, and supposed himself to have been converted at the early age of seven years; but it was not till he was fifteen years old, and after his parents had removed to Dudley, Mass., that he made a profession of religion by uniting with the Baptist Church. In that town he commenced preaching, and on the day that he was twenty-one years old, delivered his first sermon. Shortly after this, he accepted a call to the Church in Halifax, Vt., where he laboured several years, and about the year 1790, removed to Salem, N. Y., and took charge of the Baptist Church in that place. But in the spring of 1812, he was dismissed by his own request, and accepted a call to the Cambridge Baptist Church, in which connection he remained till the spring of 1816, when he became for a short time the Pastor of the Hoosick Church. He subsequently removed to Delphi, Onondaga County, N. Y., where he laboured two years; thence to Scipio, Cayuga County, where he spent one year; and thence to Eaton, Madison County, where he had the charge of the First Baptist Church for three years; and finally to Covert, Seneca County, where he died on the 29th of August, 1823, in the sixty-fourth year of his age, and the forty-third of his ministry. He was a man of sound judgment, sterling integrity, and great efficiency and public spirit.

Kendrick, seconded his views in regard to the ministry, and rendered him all the assistance in his power.

After having lived at Salem about two years, Mr. Kendrick commenced preaching, and the year following was invited to visit Poultney, Vt., and the consequence of his visit was an immediate effort on the part of the people there to engage him as their Pastor. The circumstances attending his call were peculiar; as it came not from the Baptist Society, but from the town, which had hitherto been controlled by Congregational influence. The Baptists, whose numbers scarcely exceeded thirty, had, in consequence of their distance from a church of their own communion, uniformly worshipped with the Congregationalists, and assisted in the support of their minister. When the Congregational church became vacant by the removal of their Pastor, it was understood that they would unite in the support of any minister whom the town might call; though they doubtless expected that it would be one of their own order. Mr. Kendrick visited them in the spring of 1801; and, in the early part of 1802, received an invitation from the town to settle among them. Owing to divisions, partly religious and partly political, then existing in that community, his prospects for a quiet ministry were by no means promising; but he still thought it his duty to accept, and did accept, the call. A Baptist church was duly organized on the 8th of April, and his ordination took place on the 20th of the next month. In October following, he was married to Esther, daughter of David Thompson, who had removed to Poultney from Goshen, Conn. They had twelve children, four of whom died in infancy, the rest all survived their father.

His church which, at its organization, consisted of thirty-four members, was nearly doubled during the first year of his ministry. The next year the Congregationalists withdrew, and both they and the Baptists built for themselves each a separate and commodious place of worship. In 1805, Mr. Kendrick, owing, as it would seem, to circumstances connected with his settlement, was subjected to severe trials, and both the press and the Court of Justice were put in requisition to establish charges against him. The case was deemed so serious that an Ecclesiastical Council convened at Poultney for the purpose of inquiring and judging in respect to its merits. He seems to have been fully vindicated from the offensive charges, and even those who had manifested towards him the greatest hostility, afterwards became some of his most cordial friends.

From this period Mr. Kendrick's ministry was comparatively smooth and unembarrassed. Revivals of religion, of greater or less extent, occasionally attended his labours; but, in 1816, one, more powerful than any which had preceded, occurred, which added upwards of a hundred to his church, and numbered many more as its hopeful subjects.

One object which very early awakened Mr. Kendrick's special interest was the Vermont Association, to which, in 1800, while a member of Mr. Warren's Church at Salem, he had been appointed a delegate. At the time he became a member of it, he found it in a distracted and broken condition. He immediately set himself to heal the divisions which existed in it, and his efforts were not without success. The meetings of the Body soon became entirely harmonious, and Mr. Kendrick remained an active and useful member of it till the close of life.

In this Association, the missionary spirit was early cherished, and measures were adopted for carrying the Gospel into the destitute regions round about. In the Northern parts of Vermont and New York, as well as in Canada, there were vast districts where scarcely a church or a minister was to be found. The Association, as a Body, and some of the churches individually, had, for some time, been in the habit of making an annual contribution with reference to these destitute regions; but there was no Missionary Society formed in Vermont until 1812. Mr. Kendrick, however, had previously made several missionary tours into various parts of the above named districts,—the first of which was in the summer of 1808, under the patronage of the Baptist Missionary Society of Massachusetts, when he spent three months in visiting the churches in Upper Canada. In 1810 and 1812, he made short excursions into the Northern parts of Vermont and New York, and on the borders of the Canadas. In 1813, he visited the Western part of New York, and, while engaged in this mission, his health, owing to excessive labour, in connection with the severity of the season, sustained a shock from which it never recovered. In 1814, he made another, but less extended, tour, which closed his missionary labours. His zeal in the cause of missions, however, continued unabated, and a plan of wider extent was now going into operation, in whose origin and promotion he was actively enlisted.

On the return of the Rev. Luther Rice from India, in 1813, an unusual interest was awakened in the Baptist churches in Vermont, as well as in other parts of the country, in behalf of Foreign Missions; and, immediately after the formation of the Baptist General Convention for the promotion of Missions, an Auxiliary Society was formed in Vermont, with some of the leading ministers in the State at its head. Mr. Kendrick was originally its Vice-President, but in 1817, became its Corresponding Secretary, and held the office until his death. The same year he was appointed Chaplain to the Vermont Legislature, and his services in the pulpit were there received with marked approbation.

In 1819, the honorary degree of Master of Arts was conferred upon him by Middlebury College.

While he was thus engaged in public labours, his constitution was gradually giving way, under the power of a disease which affected his head and preyed upon his spirits, sometimes occasioning a distressing mental depression. Yet nothing even damped his interest in the prosperity of the Church. The subject which now especially occupied his thoughts, was the importance of a higher standard of education for the ministry; and, having associated with him a few others whose views and feelings on the subject were similar to his own, he was chiefly instrumental in forming the Baptist Education Society of the State of Vermont, the immediate object of which was to support indigent young men in their preparation for the sacred office. Of this Society Mr. Kendrick was chosen President, and, subsequently, was appointed an Agent, to visit the Churches and procure funds in its behalf. The Society had been constituted previous to the year 1817; and in 1820 they were contemplating the establishment of a school, when a change of measures was deemed expedient.

In September, 1817, the Baptists of the Central and Western Districts of the State of New York formed a Society for a purpose similar to that of the one in Vermont, and immediately proceeded to take under their patronage indigent young men who were preparing for the ministry. These they maintained at different institutions until the year 1820, when, the number of their beneficiaries having increased to about twelve, they opened a school in Hamilton, Madison County, trusting to the liberality of the denomination for its support and enlargement. While on an agency in New York, soliciting aid for his own institution, it was proposed to him to relinquish the idea of opening a School in his own State, and to use his influence to induce the Vermont Society to co-operate with the Society in New York for the support of the School already established at Hamilton. Mr. Kendrick was favourably impressed by the proposal, and, on his return to Vermont, having laid the matter before his own Society, and secured their concurrence, the proposed combination was immediately effected. Mr. Kendrick was now appointed General Agent of the Society for the State of Vermont, and he continued in the faithful discharge of the duties thus devolved upon him, until his death.

His interest in the progress of this Institution never faltered during the rest of his life. He never lost an opportunity to secure to it private beneficence, or to commend it to public regard. In June, 1823, nearly a year before his death, he visited Hamilton, and attended the examination of the School, the exhibition of the graduating class, and the meeting of the Board. In an Address to the Board, he manifested the utmost confidence in the success of the Institution, and, on his return, assembled the people of his charge, and gave them an animated account of its condition and prospects.

During the winter preceding his death, his health had been manifestly declining. The affection of his head had increased, and was attended by a dizziness, that sometimes almost incapacitated him for his public duties; though he continued to discharge them till about three weeks before his death. Even then, no immediate danger was apprehended, and his friends allowed themselves to hope that the return of spring might relieve and invigorate him. No material change in his symptoms occurred until the Wednesday evening preceding his death, when he was struck with paralysis. Being now aware that the time of his departure was at hand, he called his family around him, and prayed for them, for himself, for the Church, and the world; and closed by saying,—" The prayers of David, the son of Jesse, are ended." He lingered through the Sabbath following, and at twelve o'clock at night requested to be placed in a chair,— which having been done, his head fell back, and without a struggle or a groan he expired. He died on the 29th of February, 1824, in the forty-ninth year of his age. A Discourse was delivered at his Funeral by the Rev. Mr. Dillaway of Granville, from the words which closed his last audible earthly supplication,—" The prayers of David, the son of Jesse, are ended."

Mr. Kendrick's publications were a pamphlet on Close Communion, entitled "Plain dealing with the Pedobaptists, &c.;" A Sermon before the Legislature of Vermont; and one or two Funeral Sermons.

FROM THE REV. NATHANIEL COLVER.

CINCINNATI, July 16, 1857.

Dear Sir: Will you accept a brief reminiscence of the late Rev. Clark Kendrick of Vermont, from one who cherishes his memory with veneration and love. Clark Kendrick was, alike as a Man, a Christian, and a Minister of Jesus Christ, aside from and above the common order. There were features of character which strongly distinguished him from all other men with whom I have been acquainted. His light hair and light complexion gave him a youthful appearance; there was a timid, delicate play of mirthfulness about his countenance; but through it all, and over all, there was ever a gentle, uncompromising and commanding dignity. He seemed to possess a fund of wit that would ever and anon be breaking out, yet was so controlled as never to detract from that gravity which adorned his ministerial character. I can scarcely better express it than by saying that in his conversation there was a gentle flow of wit, chastened by an unaffected gravity and unassuming wisdom, which made him at once among the most companionable and dignified of all the men of whom it has been my privilege to have personal knowledge.

Among his ministerial brethren he was a delightful model of fraternal kindness. Especially did his young brethren feel that they had in him a father and a friend. He could and did at times criticise their performances with great fidelity, but at the same time with such a frank, redeeming tenderness, that none ever thought of taking offence. To a young brother in the ministry, not over skilled in rhetoric, he once said,—"My brother, God has given you a wonderful voice. I almost envy you a voice so sweet and full; but you sometimes let it break,—and it seems harsh enough to rive an oak that has stood for years hardening in the sun." The young brother took care not to let his voice break again.

He was not less peculiar in his family. He sat like a king, but a benignant one. He seemed to take for granted that his word was law, and so it was. I do not know that he ever used corporeal punishment, but if he looked disturbed, and said, as none but he could say it, "J——, can't you be clever?"— it was enough. Occasionally he would resort to some eccentric mode of administering reproof, in order to render it effectual. On one occasion, in a high pew in the gallery of one of the old fashioned churches, some boys, during the time of worship, got to cracking and eating nuts. His keen eye perceived it, and that one of his own sons was with them. He stopped and, with a countenance both grieved and vexed, said: "D——, come and sit on the pulpit stairs and eat your nuts." D—— came and sat on one of the pulpit steps; and though more than one of his sons had a habit of cracking nuts, as Bunyan would say, I believe none of them ever afterwards ventured to eat nuts in meeting time.

He had a happy way of quoting old sayings, especially the Proverbs. They seemed in fact almost to have been made for his especial use. On one occasion, he was desired to interfere in a matter of personal difficulty. He begged to be excused, saying,—"Solomon says, 'He that passeth by, and meddleth with strife belonging not to him, is like one that taketh a dog by the ears—if you hold him you must have a tussle with him; and if you let him go, he is sure to bite."

As a speaker, he was a little heavy in manner, but this was atoned for by the richness of his matter, and the never failing "point." His manner was quite peculiar. A disease in his head (which, before his death, became very troublesome, caused ossification, and probably shortened his life) led him to contract a certain habit of hemming and snuffing, as if to remove some obstruction from his throat. This habit, although a little unpleasant to a stranger, became, to his constant hearers, inoffensive and almost agreeable. A moment or two of hesitation while removing the apparent obstruction, and then there would burst forth some thought so rich, so striking, as more than to compensate for the waiting, and to cause all physical peculiarities to be wholly lost sight of. As a sermonizer, too, he was peculiar. He did not carry you with a storm of eloquence, or with an outburst of passion; but he never failed to entertain, enchain, and instruct. His discourses had a natural order and easy development, illustrating the rhetorical requisition of a beginning, a middle, and an end. They abounded in common sense and solid truth, and none who had heard him once failed to desire to hear him again.

As a Counsellor, he was unsurpassed. I love to remember him in scenes of church difficulty, with his intuitive grasping and fatherly disposal of the matter. His plain and faithful language, couched often in homely, but forcible, imagery, was almost sure to reach its aim. " Brother B——," he would say, " is a little apt to be putting his flukes into somebody; he needs to be checked a little." " Brother R——, you confess enough, but you keep taking it all back; do let it stay." And as he said this with a look half playful and half serious, and a manner at once kind and severe, Brother B. and Brother R. would own the justice of the rebuke, and the one allow that he needed to be " checked " and the other permit his confession to " stay." In short, his counsels of severity, but of righteousness, rarely failed of success. The denomination throughout the State felt his power as a counsellor, and mourned his loss, when he fell, as that of a leader in Israel.

The character of his piety was modified by the peculiar structure of his mind. Surpassed by many in passionate zeal and in flights of holy fervour, he may have been; but by none in the childlike simplicity and fidelity of his faith. I know of none of whom I could say more heartily that he was without guile. It seems to me that he never thought of flinching from the truth, never doubted its power, never relied for a moment on anything but God and truth for success. In his church, and with his people, his words of consolation, counsel or reproof, ever fell with weight. In illustration I could relate many anecdotes which still linger in the memories of those who knew him: I will mention but one. His church had occasion to exclude for covetousness a member who refused to pay his church dues. A few days after, the excluded member met his Pastor, and, as in former times, said.—" How do you do Brother Kendrick?" But Brother Kendrick declined the recognition, saying, as he alone could say it,—" You need not call me brother. I belong to a brotherhood that hold all for God as his steward. You do not belong to that brotherhood; you must not call me brother." The countenance of the man fell: he went away in grief: but at the next covenant meeting he came to the church, and said,—" Brethren, I wish you would take me back and try me; when I first joined the church I made a mistake. I kept my farm out. This time I wish to put in all I have." He was readmitted into the church, and his Pastor again called him brother.

I love to remember Clark Kendrick as one belonging to, but in advance of, the past generation of ministers. At the time of our acquaintance, I was just entering with much fear and trembling upon the work of the ministry; he was in his meridian strength. I found in him a tender father and a true friend, and gathered inspiration from his noble spirit and the strength and vigour of his thoughts. He preached my Ordination Sermon, and laid his hands on me at my consecration. Our acquaintance was as intimate as it

well could be, considering the disparity of our years. I loved him with veneration, and his maxims yet remain with me. When I remember his sunny
face, his mind well-balanced and of large proportions, his sound discretion,
his loving heart, his dropping wisdom, I long to meet him in Heaven. I love
to think of him among the great and good that have gone before him, and
above all with that Saviour whom on earth he served with such distinguished
ability and devotion.

I am, dear Sir, truly yours,

NATHANIEL COLVER.

ASAHEL MORSE.*

1799—1838.

ASAHEL MORSE was a son of the Rev. Joshua Morse, who was born in
South Kingston, R. I., on the 10th of April 1726. He (the father) was
hopefully converted under the preaching of Whitefield, at the age of sixteen. The next year he commenced preaching as an itinerant. At length,
after preaching in several different places in Connecticut, in which he was
subjected to severe trials from the intolerance of the times, he gathered a
Church in the North parish of New London, (now Montville,) and was
ordained as its Pastor on the 17th of May, 1751. He married Susannah,
daughter of Joseph Babcock, of Westerly, R. I., with whom he lived happily forty-five years. They had eleven children, all of whom lived to
maturity. The distress occasioned by the Revolutionary War led him to
remove from New London to Sandisfield, Mass., where he settled in 1779;
gathered a church soon after, and lived to see it number a hundred members. He died in 1795, in his seventieth year: his wife survived him fifteen years, and died in her eightieth year.

Asahel Morse was born at New London, (Montville,) on the 10th of
November, 1771, and was a little less than eight years old when his father
removed to Sandisfield. He evinced an early fondness for books, and at
the age of nine had made himself quite familiar with the writings of
Josephus, and was also a diligent and constant reader of the Bible. During
several subsequent years, he devoted much time to the study of History
and Geography, and to reading books of Travels; and at nineteen he
taught a winter's school, and in the spring following went to a school of a
higher order, in which he studied Algebra, and some kindred branches.
He had, at this period, an irrepressible desire to obtain a liberal education.

He began to be the subject of serious impressions when he was in his
tenth year; and, after alternations of anxiety and indifference, which were
protracted through nearly two years, he supposed that he had cordially
acquiesced in the terms of the Gospel, and was the subject of true evangelical exercises. It was not long, however, before the world began to
regain its ascendancy over him, and he gradually sunk back into a state of

* Autobiog. in Bapt. Mem., 1844.—MS. from his son.

habitual carelessness. When he was nineteen, he taught a school during the winter in Stockbridge, Mass.; and, after he had closed his school, availed himself for some time of the instructions of Mr. Samuel Whelpley, who had then a number of young men under his care, and who had been, for two or three years, a Baptist preacher. Though he was then a vain and trifling young man, Mr. Whelpley often conversed with him on the subject of religion, and was so much impressed by his knowledge of Scripture, and his ability in sustaining his own positions, that he used to tell him that "he wished he would throw by his nonsense and go to preaching." He subsequently taught a school in Canaan, where his mind was again roused to serious reflection, though his views and feelings were yet far from being established; and, after this, he became still more unsettled, by reading Paine's Age of Reason, and some other works of infidel tendency. It was not till the latter part of the year 1798 that he was enabled finally to rest, as he believed, on the Rock of Ages. There being an unusual attention to religion in the neighbourhood in which he lived, he was induced to attend some of the meetings, and, after a season of great anxiety and terrible conflict, aggravated not a little by the recollection of his having trifled with his own previous convictions, he was enabled to cherish an enduring hope in God's forgiving mercy. He was baptized, on the 9th of November, 1798, by the Rev. Rufus Babcock,* of Colebrook, Conn., when he was within one day of being twenty-seven years old.

* RUFUS BABCOCK was born in North Stonington, Conn., April 22, 1758, (the eighth generation from the progenitor of most, if not all, of this name in the United States,—James Babcock, of Essex, England, who, as one of the Puritans, migrated to Leyden, in Holland, and thence to Plymouth, where he arrived in June, 1623.) His father, Elias Babcock, who belonged to that division of the Baptists known as Separates, removed, during the minority of his youngest son, Rufus, to North Canaan, Conn., about the year 1775. The latter was two or three times called out as a soldier in the Revolution, serving in Captain Timothy Morse's company, whose daughter he subsequently married. In 1783, he was baptized by the Rev. Joshua Morse, and joined the Baptist Church in the adjacent town of Sandisfield, Mass., by which church, some years later, he was licensed to preach. He gathered a church in Colebrook, Conn., where he was ordained in 1794,—the first minister of any denomination settled in the township. When he first went there to visit, by request, a few Baptist families, the Congregationalists, who had a meeting-house in an unfinished state, but had no Pastor, met, for a while, with their Baptist brethren, and Mr. Babcock preached acceptably to the united congregations. Early in 1794, a small Baptist Church was regularly constituted, and he was ordained, the same day, their Pastor. For want of adequate accommodations elsewhere, the services were conducted in a large barn, though it was in mid-winter. He continued to serve this Church as its Pastor, until he was seventy-three years old, with good success; above five hundred members having been added during his connection with it. The church gathered members from several neighbouring towns, where no Baptist organization then existed. In some of these he commenced regular preaching stations, and churches of the same faith have since been gathered. His labours were thus widely extended and very arduous. He mainly supported his family by his and their hard earnings and careful savings on his small farm; and was, moreover, enabled to educate his two younger sons for the ministry at Brown University. Against the earnest protestations of many of the church, he insisted on their accepting his resignation, when he had passed his threescore and ten years, more than half of which he had spent in their service. He also gave them a parsonage, and continued to nurse the church with fatherly care during the rest of his life. Without any great advantages for early culture, without fluency of speech or any of the graces of an orator, he had such native soundness and vigour of mind, coupled with good sense and indefatigable industry, that he was highly and deservedly esteemed, not only in his own communion, but by intelligent and learned ministers of other denominations. One of his sons (*Cyrus Giles*) was graduated at Brown University in 1816, and licensed to preach, and called to the Pastorship of the Baptist Church in Bedford, Mass.; but he declined the call on account of ill health, and came home, to his father's, to die. Dr. Chauncey Lee, of the Congregational Church in the same town, preached his Funeral Sermon in the pulpit of his bereaved brother, to their united congregations, in March, 1817. Another son, bearing his own name, was graduated in 1821, and is now the Rev. Dr. Babcock, well known as one of the most prominent ministers in the Church. Mr. Babcock, the father, died in November, 1842.

After making a public profession of religion, he began almost immediately to exhort, not only in private circles but in public meetings; and he was really exercising his gifts in preaching almost before he was aware of it. He was formally licensed to preach by the Baptist Church in Sandisfield, of which he was a member, in the spring of 1799; and, during that year, divided his labours in preaching between Sandisfield and some other places. He made repeated visits to Enfield, Conn., where a rich blessing seemed to attend his labours.

In the spring of 1800, Mr. Morse commenced preaching in Winsted, Conn., one half of the time; and he removed his family thither in the autumn following. He was ordained there in May, 1801; after which, he travelled in various parts of Connecticut, preaching in almost every town through which he passed. He remained at Winsted, supplying a small Society there, the greater part of the time, for two years and seven months; but, as the Society was unable to contribute much to his support, he gave part of his time, during the last year, to Winchester and Torrington.

In the autumn of 1802, the Baptist Church in Stratfield, Conn. invited him to visit them; and this led to a negotiation which resulted in his removal thither in June, 1803. Here he continued nine years and three months, during which time he was in the habit of preaching six times a week, except in the months of July and August. His salary here consisted of two hundred dollars a year, besides many valuable presents.

In 1807, he accepted an appointment from the Shaftsbury Baptist Association to take a missionary tour into Upper Canada. He left home on the 15th of August, and passed through the Genesee country to Niagara. He remained in the Province a little more than a month, during which time he attended fifty-four meetings, preached fifty-one sermons, baptized four persons, and gave fellowship to a church in Clinton, at the Thirty Mile Creek. The tour seems to have been one of great interest to him, though attended by considerable exposure and hardship.

In 1810, Mr. Morse was invited to take charge of the First Baptist Church in Suffield, Conn., their Pastor,—the Rev. John Hastings, being so much enfeebled by age and disease as to be inadequate to discharge any longer the duties of the place. This overture occasioned him great embarrassment and hesitation; but the result was that, after two years, he dissolved his relation with the Church at Stratfield, and took charge of that at Suffield.

In 1818, he was a member of the Convention which was held at Hartford for framing a Constitution for the State of Connecticut. In the object of this meeting, he, with the Baptist denomination generally, felt the deepest interest. In April, 1820, he went to Philadelphia, as a delegate from the Connecticut Baptist Missionary Board to the Baptist General Convention;—an occasion which brought him in contact with many excellent ministers, and supplied the material for many grateful recollections.

During his residence at Suffield, he was invited to take charge of several churches, particularly at Cheshire and Pittsfield, in Massachusetts, and Springfield, in New York; and he had sometimes entertained the idea of making a change; but, in 1828, he came to the resolution, in view of his advancing years, and his pleasant relations with his people, to remain at Suffield during the rest of his life. Scarcely, however, had this resolution been taken, before his congregation became the scene of a violent commotion, in the issue of which he resigned his pastoral charge; and the next spring he united with the Baptist Church in Hartford.

After this, he preached in various places, and was disposed to remove to Ohio, but was prevented by not being able to dispose of his real estate in Suffield. He at length engaged to supply a very feeble church in Colebrook, Conn., for one year, and removed thither in October, 1831. At the close of that engagement, being still unable to dispose of his property at Suffield, he consented to remain at Colebrook for an indefinite period; and, in the autumn of 1832, became the Pastor of the Second Baptist Church in that town. Here he remained four years; but, during this period, he became conscious that he was the subject of a physical affection, against which his energies could not long hold out. A paralytic stroke came upon him, while he was addressing his congregation, and so shattered his mind that, though he afterwards partially regained his health, he was never able to comprehend the subject on which he was speaking, notwithstanding it had previously been entirely familiar to him. He removed back to Suffield in the year 1836, his faculties having by this time so far declined that he was incapable of performing any ministerial duties. Here he remained until his death, which occurred on the 10th of June, 1838, in the sixty-seventh year of his age. About seven weeks previous, he had been struck with apoplexy; but he so far recovered from this as to be able to converse with his family and friends, and to testify to the all-sustaining power of the Gospel which he had preached.

Mr. Morse was married on the 24th of August, 1795, to Rachel, eldest daughter of Amos and Lucy (Fargo) Chapel, of New Marlborough, Mass. They had eight children,—all sons.

FROM THE REV. RUFUS BABCOCK, D. D.

PATERSON, N. J., 25th March, 1858.

My dear Sir: My acquaintance with the late Rev. Asahel Morse began in my early childhood. My father's house, in North Colebrook, Conn., was the welcome home of his brother ministers of different denominations, several of whom you have embalmed in your volumes already published. Dr. Jonathan Edwards and Dr. Chauncey Lee were successively Pastors of the Congregational Church in the same town; and they, learned and noble men as they were, fully appreciated the strong and manly good sense and ardent devotedness to the cause of Christ of their less erudite Baptist brother, and visited him as frequently, and co-operated with him as cordially, as with those of their own communion. Beneath his humble roof were often gathered the wise and good of that early day; and my recollection, reaching back almost to the beginning of this century, brings up a long array of departed worthies, who, in their journeyings to preach the Gospel and perform other ecclesiastical services, found it convenient to turn in for a night and share the hospitalities of the Pastor of North Colebrook. The personal appearance of such men as Daniel Wildman, John Hastings, and many others of Connecticut, and an equal number from Rhode Island, Massachusetts, and New York, is indelibly impressed on my memory. Among them came the good Mr. Morse. I cannot remember when I first saw him: his form, his smile, his voice were familiar to me from my earliest years. Some of these visiters seemed to belong only to my father, and talked with him almost exclusively. Others gave their attention to the adults of the family generally; but Mr. Morse belonged to us children just as much as to any of the rest. We felt that we could claim our share of him, and that claim was never repudiated. He talked with us about our school studies, and thus enhanced our interest in them; about our general reading, and was always leading us on to something higher and better; and he could enter into the spirit of our work and our sports, and seemed to be hearty in it all. In all this condescension there was nothing to impair in the least his dignity as a Christian minister. He was just about the last of my father's guests that rude and roguish boys would have thought of treating with indecorum or undue familiarity.

The music of his powerful voice is the first thing I remember concerning him in the pulpit. His robust frame, his erect position, the perfect self-possession with which, without a scrap of manuscript, he would pour forth his well matured and weighty thoughts by the hour, and the somewhat wider range of thought and illustration which he indulged in than we were accustomed to hear from others, next impressed themselves upon my memory. Near the close of a precious revival, in the end of the autumn of 1815, he exchanged with my father, and spent a week or more, visiting from one neighbourhood to another, and preaching day and night. On the Sabbath, he administered Baptism and the Lord's Supper. I was myself one of the candidates, and it is no marvel that I can never forget the circumstances. The day proved stormy—the cold sleet was falling fast as we gathered on the banks of the stream, raised our voices in a brief song of praise, and he bared that broad brow of his, and looked up to God in prayer. It seemed as if we almost saw the Heavens again opened, and witnessed another dove-like descent of the Holy Spirit. Taking the first candidate by the hand, with a generous assuring smile, he repeated the familiar lines of a hymn written by his much loved friend, John Leland:

> " Brethren, if your hearts be warm,
> " Ice and snow can do no harm;
> " If the Saviour you have prized,
> " Believe, arise, and be baptized."

His manner of administering the ordinance was at once inimitably simple, solemn and tender. It gave the impression of one utterly forgetful of self, and absorbed in the purpose of honouring his beloved and gracious Saviour. The outlines of his sermons on that day I could readily reproduce from memory, after an interval of nearly forty-three years. But I will only say that they were characteristic of the man and the times, developing much of Gospel truth and practical duty from some parts of the Levitical dispensation,—its furniture, even the carvings and ornaments of the tabernacle,—which, to common readers, would convey no such meaning. In this respect he followed Dr. John Gill, who, in Rabbinical lore, has had few, if any, superiors. The doctrinal system of this profound and learned, but somewhat ultra, Calvinist, was, I believe, substantially adopted by Mr. Morse; but Owen, Booth, Fuller, and McEwen were also among his favourite authors, and probably each of them may have had something to do in modifying his views.

After I was licensed to preach, he once or twice heard me, and I well remember a correction he suggested on some point of Theology, where he thought I might improve. Some young ministers regarded him as unduly severe, but nothing could be more genial and considerate than his manner towards me.

One who knew him better than I did, and in whose judgment and recollection I have entire confidence, writes thus concerning him:—"His characteristics were varied. Blunt and outspoken, never calculating with a conservative foresight, which a prudent regard for the feelings of others might demand, he ever fearlessly upheld what he believed to be truth, whether men would hear or forbear. Scarcely could he be regarded dogmatic, and still less disposed to maintain a point for the sake of argument. Truth with him admitted of no compromises—hence he might always have been regarded as a radical man. Warm in his attachments, he loved both to exercise hospitality and to receive it. Religion with him was a matter of deep-seated principle, and he had no sympathy with spasmodic piety. His temperament must have been of a sanguine character in early life, though in later years it assumed a lymphatic type. His physical courage was remarkable. If requisite, he would have suffered amputation or the rack without exhibiting a sign of pain; yet his eyes would moisten in his pulpit ministrations, especially in prayer.

"Always happy in the bosom of his family, he lived his boyhood over again in the favourite sports of his children. Every where he was a favourite with the young. Until his sixtieth year his vigour was unimpaired, and he would mount his horse, heavy as he was, with the ease of a boy. He was in a small way a practical farmer, and rather prided himself on being a superior mower."

Mr. Morse was a self made, but a well made, man. His acquisitions in some departments were both extensive and accurate. The study of History, ancient and modern, sacred and civil, was ever his delight; and his iron memory preserved and reproduced his acquisitions at pleasure. The same reliance on memory enabled him to dispense with notes in preaching. His sermons, as to the subject matter, and even the illustrations he intended to employ, were faithfully studied beforehand; but he could safely trust to the inspiration of the moment for the fitting language. His, therefore, was not, so far as the words were concerned, memoriter preaching. It was eminently instructive and suggestive also. He rarely exhausted any topic, but said just enough to excite the minds of his hearers to further and independent reflection.

Like his eccentric and highly gifted friend, John Leland, he took a deep interest in the politics of the day, though he never degraded the ministry by mingling in partisan conflicts. No wonder that he and most of the Baptist ministers of that period were opposed to the party called Federalists, from the apprehension they entertained that their influence would perpetuate the union of Church and State, so oppressive to all who were not of the "Standing" or established "Order." This will account for his action in the Convention for forming a Constitution in Connecticut, abolishing these odious religious distinctions. He also regretted the agitations on Antimasonry, considering them uncalled for and profitless.

His home life was quiet and agreeable. He was habitually an early riser, and loved invigorating exercise before breakfast. The press was not then as prolific as it is now; but whatever new and good books, suited to his tastes and his object, came in his way, he read immediately, without regard to system. But his recollections of what he had thus made his own were so systematized, mentally, as to be always at his command. Certain devotional volumes, as Buck's Treatise on Religious Experience, Booth's Reign of Grace, Bunyan's Allegorical Works, Cowper's, Hart's and Newton's Hymns, he greatly delighted in. He was quite fond of music, vocal and instrumental. Old Hundred and China were among his favourite Church tunes.

The malady which carried him to the grave, impaired all his faculties, mental and physical, several years before his decease; but those whose recollections of him reach back to his prime, very uniformly speak of him as not

only impressive but often truly eloquent in the pulpit. Feeling the power of
his subject, he would make those who listened to him feel it too. Of the
purity of his life and the unaffected goodness of his heart, no one who knew
him could entertain a doubt. His name is fairly entitled to a place among
the most excellent and influential ministers of that portion of the Church to
which he belonged.   Yours fraternally,

                                                    RUFUS BABCOCK.

ELISHA SCOTT WILLIAMS.*
1799—1845.

ELISHA SCOTT WILLIAMS, a son of the Rev. Eliphalet Williams, D. D.,
was born in East Hartford, Conn., October 7, 1757. His father was, for
many years, Pastor of the Congregational Church in that place; and his
grandfather, the Rev. Solomon Williams, of Lebanon, was among the most
eminent Congregational ministers of New England. He was graduated at
Yale College in 1775, at the early age of eighteen. Possessing naturally
a somewhat adventurous spirit, and being deeply imbued with the love of
his country, he entered the army in 1776, as Adjutant of a regiment of
young men from his native State, many of whom were from within the
range of his own acquaintance. He crossed the Delaware with Washington, and was in the battles of Trenton and Princeton. Having acquitted
himself with much honour on the land, he went on board the privateer
Hancock, of twenty-eight guns, in which, after some weeks' cruise, they
encountered, somewhere on the coast of Bermuda, the British frigate
Levant, of thirty guns, and, after a most desperate engagement, the latter
blew up. In this action, Captain Hardy, the brave commander of the
Hancock, was shot down by Mr. Williams' side. After this, he returned
to his father's house in East Hartford; but in 1780 he went to live in
Stockbridge, Mass., where he was engaged in some kind of business for
about ten years. The same year he was married to Abigail Livermore of
Waltham, Mass.

In the year 1790, he removed to the District of Maine, and took up his
residence in the then newly settled town of Livermore, where his father-
in-law, from whom the town was named, then lived. Here he was employed
as a schoolmaster, and also held the office of Justice of the Peace. It was
here too that his mind underwent a great, and as he believed, radical,
change on the subject of religion. Hitherto he had felt no sympathy with
the system of Christian doctrine to which he had been educated, which
recognizes the merits of Christ as the only foundation of the sinner's hope.
On a certain evening, he was led, from curiosity, to attend the preaching
of a Baptist minister by the name of Smith,† in an adjacent town; and

* Bapt. Mem. 1845.—MS. from his family.
† ELIPHALET SMITH laboured as an Evangelist in Fayette and its vicinity as early as 1790,
and was Pastor of that Church from 1792 to 1798; and united with the Rev. Oliver Billings in
supplying it several years afterwards.
Mr. BILLINGS, above referred to, was ordained as an Evangelist in 1800, and was the acting
Pastor of the Church in Fayette for more than twenty years, and Senior Pastor till his death,
which occurred on the 31st of July, 1842.

the discourse, being of a very searching and pungent character, only supplied Mr. Williams with fresh grounds for cavil and opposition. He was, however, drawn irresistibly to hear the same preacher the next evening, when he was thrown into a state of extreme agitation and anguish of spirit, under a conviction of his own sinfulness, from which he quickly passed, as he believed, to a state of reconciliation with God through the death of his Son. His views of the glory of Christ in the work of redemption were such as to fill him with surprise and rapture.

As he received his first religious impressions in connection with the preaching of a Baptist minister, he seems at once to have embraced the peculiar views of that denomination, and to have been identified with them from that period to the close of his life. His friends began almost immediately to urge him to enter the ministry; but, for some time, he resisted their importunity. He, however, consented to aid them in their more private religious meetings; and in this way his gifts were gradually developed, so that, after a few months, he consented to preach in public. His very first effort proved instrumental of the conversion of an individual, who became an eminently devoted and useful Christian. This greatly encouraged him to persevere. He was ordained as an Evangelist at the meeting of the Bowdoinham Association, in August, 1799, and shortly after commenced preaching, half of the time in Brunswick, and the other half in Topsham. In 1800, he became the Pastor of the Church in Brunswick, and continued in this relation about three years. During the whole period of his residence in Maine after he commenced preaching, he was actively engaged in planting and cherishing churches of his own denomination.

In the summer of 1803, he received a call from the First Baptist Church in Beverly to become their Pastor. This call he accepted; and the first sermon he preached there was from Acts x. 29—"Therefore came I unto you without gainsaying, as soon as I was sent for. I ask, therefore, for what intent ye have sent for me." He remained Pastor of this church until the autumn of 1812. During his ministry here, there were two revivals of religion, which resulted in an addition to the church of a hundred and fifty-seven members.

In 1812, having been, by his own request, dismissed from his charge, he took up his residence in Boston, and acted in the capacity of a Minister at Large during the rest of his life. Here he became intimately associated with Dr. Baldwin, and other prominent clergymen, and rendered important aid in forming new churches, and assisting feeble ones, in Boston and its vicinity. Not only his active services, but his pecuniary means, were liberally expended in thus doing good.

After having been thus engaged in Boston for some twenty-five years, he returned, about the year 1837, to Beverly, to pass the evening of his days in the scene of his former labours. During the last year of his life, he suffered much from a disease incident to old age, and which, at last, wore out his life. He died on the 3d of February, 1845, in the eighty-eighth year of his age.

Mr. Williams' first wife died in Boston in July, 1817. By this marriage he had eleven children,—three sons and eight daughters. He married, about the year 1821, for a second wife, Rebecca Bridge, of Boston, who died in Beverly, in March, 1842, aged seventy-six. There were no children by the second marriage.

Mr. Williams' publications are a Serious and Familiar Dialogue concerning the Divine Ordinance of Baptism, by a Friend of Truth; and a Sermon in the Baptist Preacher.

FROM THE REV. IRAH CHASE, D. D.

BOSTON, April 10, 1858.

Dear Sir: My opportunities of knowing the Rev. Elisha Scott Williams were limited almost exclusively to meeting with him a few times on public occasions, and to incidental remarks from those to whom he was well known.

In personal appearance he was above the ordinary size,—tall, erect and well proportioned. His eyes were blue, and his countenance was somewhat florid. His whole aspect and demeanour made the impression that he firmly believed what he professed, and that he was habitually mindful of his high and holy calling. Not only in the pulpit, but out of it also, he was " simple, grave, sincere." His manners were those of a gentleman of the old school. If, in trying circumstances, he sometimes uttered a harsh or unkind word, he, with frankness, expressed his regret, and promptly made all needed reparation. His theological reading and the structure and habits of his mind led him rather to the cool and didactic manner, than to the glowing and impressive, in the ministrations of the pulpit. And yet there was ample evidence that his heart sympathized with deep religious feeling. He loved to trace and exhibit the experience of Christians. And he set a high value on a Pastor's free and familiar intercourse, especially with the more devout and lowly members of his flock, as contributing to his own spirituality, and to his ministerial usefulness.

Yours, dear Sir, with much esteem,

and with best wishes,

IRAH CHASE.

BENJAMIN TITCOMB.

1799—1848.

FROM THE REV. THOMAS B. RIPLEY.

PORTLAND, October 2, 1857.

My dear Sir: In compliance with your request, I have gathered all the more important facts in connection with the life of the Rev. Benjamin Titcomb, within my reach, and herewith embody them in a narrative which I hope may suit your purpose. The material has been drawn from the most authentic sources.

BENJAMIN TITCOMB was born in Falmouth, now Portland, Me., in July, 1761. Of the particulars of his early life, and especially of the time and circumstances of his conversion, I am not informed. But it is ascertained that both himself and his wife were, for some time, members of the First Congregational Church in Portland, and that they left that Church in consequence of a change in their views of religious truth, and associated themselves with others, who, about the same time, (early in

1796,) had hopefully embraced Christianity in its life and power. These individuals, from an examination of the Scriptures and other religious books, had been brought to conclusions respecting Christian truth and duty, which resulted in their separating themselves from the Ecclesiastical Societies then existing in Portland.

To this little company Benjamin Titcomb opened his doors, and their meetings were held for some time under his roof. For the first three months, not more than five or six constantly attended. The meetings, which were conducted by prayer and praise to God, and the reading of sermons, began, after a while, to grow formal—the result, it was thought, on inquiry, of thus reading printed discourses. The practice was, therefore, laid aside, and, instead of it, the reading of the Scriptures was introduced; and this was followed almost immediately by a revival of religious feeling. The number of attendants began now to increase, and soon the place of meeting was crowded. During this time, Mr. Titcomb was accustomed to address the people thus convened at his house, offering generally expository remarks upon the Scriptures. This was the commencement of his ministerial course.

In 1797, a school-house was hired for the place of meeting. Previously, however, to that, Mr. Titcomb had been baptized in North Yarmouth, by Dr. Thomas Green,* Pastor of the Baptist Church in that place. Several others began now to think very seriously, and with deep interest, on the subject of Christian Baptism. " What does the Bible teach on this subject ?" was, I suppose, their inquiry. Ministers, residing at some distance, commenced visiting them ; and, within the space of about a year and a half, eight or nine persons were baptized on a profession of their faith in Christ, and stood ready to be constituted a distinct church.

Mr. Titcomb received the approbation of the Church in North Yarmouth, of which he was a member, to enter upon the work of the ministry. He was ordained in that town, in 1801, at the Anniversary of the Bowdoinham Association. Some may read with interest the names of the ministers who took part in the services—The Rev. Dr. Baldwin, of Boston, led in the Introductory Prayer. The Sermon was preached by the Pastor of the Church. In the Prayer, accompanied by the laying on of the hands of the Presbytery, the Rev. Mr. Stinson,† of West Bowdoin, officiated. The Rev. Elisha Williams, of Brunswick, gave the Charge ; the Rev. John Tripp, of Hebron, presented the Right Hand of Fellowship ; and the Rev. Robert Low,‡ of New Gloucester, led in the Concluding Prayer.

In January, 1801, the brethren in Portland hired a large upper room in a brick store for their place of worship. In March following, those who

---

* DR. THOMAS GREEN was first a physician, but subsequently became a minister, and was ordained Pastor of the Church in North Yarmouth in January, 1797, where he continued, useful and beloved, until his death, which occurred on the 29th of May, 1814.

† WILLIAM STINSON was ordained at Bowdoin, (Litchfield) in June, 1792, as Pastor of the church in that place, having previously been one of its members. His connection with that church continued till 1822.

‡ ROBERT LOW was ordained Pastor of the Church in New Gloucester in 1800, and officiated in that church from 1800 to 1807, and from 1815 to 1820. He also discharged the duties of Pastor in Readfield from 1807 to 1815, and from 1832 to 1834. After supplying the Wayne Church, and others destitute of a stated ministry, from 1820, he became Pastor of Livermore (third) in 1824, and remained there till 1832. From 1834, he was nearly laid by on account of the infirmities of age.

had been baptized, adopted certain Articles of Faith, expressive of their views, and agreed to unite in Church relation. At their request, a Council from the neighbouring churches convened; who, having obtained satisfactory evidence of the mutual fellowship of these individuals, and having examined their Covenant and Articles of Belief, proceeded to constitute them a regular Church of Christ. Of this little flock Mr. Titcomb became the Pastor in September, 1801. Such was the origin of the Baptist Church in Portland.

Mr. Titcomb continued his labours with this church until 1804. In September of that year, he was dismissed to join the Baptist Church in Brunswick, Me., of which he then became Pastor, and continued such till 1827.

In regard to this long period, I am not able to present any very definite statements, except in relation to an interesting revival which occurred in Brunswick, in 1816. That was a gloomy year to the farmers of New England. In Maine, I well remember, frosts came every month, and the fruits of the earth were cut off. How dreary and strange an aspect did the fields present! The standing corn was black with frost, even in August. But the garden of the Lord flourished—the dews and the sunshine of Heaven were upon it. Revivals extensively prevailed. Multitudes were gathered into the fold of the Good Shepherd. Brunswick shared largely in the Heavenly visitation. And here occurred a memorable scene, on Monday morning, July 22d. Dr. Baldwin, of Boston, had spent the preceding day in Bath, and on his way to Yarmouth and Portland, where he was expected to take part in the services of two ordinations, he preached by appointment in Brunswick, in a hall frequently opened for religious meetings. Many individuals were deeply impressed by the truth, and awakened to anxious inquiry. Mr. Titcomb estimated that the number was more than fifty. No impassioned oratory wrought this wonderful result. It was not " the wind, great and strong," nor " the earthquake," nor " the fire ;" but " the still small voice " was there. The preacher's manner was ordinarily, and I suppose also on that occasion, rather calm than vehement. He spoke the truth in love, seriously and earnestly, and the power of the Holy Spirit attended it. The revival went on. Among the number of those who obeyed the Gospel, was Mr. Titcomb's son Benjamin, who afterwards entered the ministry, but finished his course long before his father.*

---

* BENJAMIN TITCOMB, JR., was born in Standish, Me., December 4, 1787. He was fitted for College at Phillips' Academy, Exeter, and was graduated at Bowdoin College in 1806. He commenced the study of the Law with Judge Mellen of Portland, but abandoned it after two years, and for several succeeding years lived in Brunswick, and was occupied chiefly in the indulgence of his literary tastes. In 1816, during a revival in Brunswick, he became, hopefully, a subject of renewing grace. In April, 1817, he commenced preaching, and soon after accepted an invitation to labour with the Baptist Church at Freeport, Me. In September, 1821, he accepted a similar invitation from the Baptist Church in Charlestown, Mass. In January, 1822, he returned to Brunswick to receive ordination as an Evangelist; but scarcely had he resumed his labours at Charlestown before his prospects of usefulness were clouded by the failure of his health. In the summer following, he took leave of his people, and went again to Brunswick to live with his father. But his apprehensions in regard to a speedy death were not realized. He continued, for several years, preaching occasionally in various places, and especially in Freeport, the scene of his early labours. In 1824 and 1825, he edited the Maine Baptist Herald, a weekly religious newspaper published in Brunswick. In November, 1828, he was attacked with a lung fever, which run into a pulmonary consumption, that, in about four months, terminated his life. He died, in the tranquillity of a joyful hope, on the 29th of March, 1829.

Respecting this revival—Mr. Titcomb, in a letter dated April 17, 1817,—addressed, I suppose, to Dr. Baldwin,—states that the whole number added to the church by Baptism, since October, 1815, was a hundred and fifty-two. He adds that the revival was preceded by an uncommon attention to meetings, which, for more than twelve months before, had been held in all parts of the town. The church likewise was much stirred up to prayer and supplication. Days were especially set apart for fasting and prayer, and were attended with an unusual blessing. The ordinance of Baptism was of remarkable religious benefit to those who witnessed it, as were also the exhortations of converts. Persons of all ages, from eighty years down to nine, shared in the blessing.

To this church Mr. Titcomb sustained the pastoral relation about twenty-two years. In 1829, a new church was formed in Brunswick, called the Village Church, of which the same year he became Pastor, and so continued, until 1836, at which time his pastorate ceased; and thenceforward till his death, which occurred, September 30, 1848, his pulpit labours were occasional only, and, I believe, ceased entirely, some years before his decease.

Of his wife, who long shared with him the anxieties and cares of ministerial life, it is fitting that some mention should be made. She was born in Saco, Me., May 22, 1768, and was a daughter of the Rev. John Fairfield,* of that town. She was married to Mr. Titcomb in 1786; and, from that time till her death, July 24, 1838, a period of fifty-two years, they were fellow-helpers on the journey of life. She was of the number of those who were organized as the First Baptist Church in Portland, just thirty-seven years before her death.

In his latter years, Mr. Titcomb was wont to speak of death with a smile. A Christian friend, who had called at his house,—looking at the portrait of Mrs. Titcomb, inquired,—"Is she living?" "Oh, no," replied the aged man, "she has gone home long ago;" and, with a smile, added,— "My Master will send for me soon, and I am all ready." His death seemed no less pleasant than his anticipations of it had been. He appeared perfectly sensible in the last conflict, and said,—"This is death— I shall soon be discharged." He survived almost all his early contemporaries, and reached the great age of eighty-seven.

Mr. Titcomb was the father of thirteen children,—six sons and seven daughters, nine of whom survived him.

For the substance of what I am about to state in respect to Mr. Titcomb's personal appearance and habits, I am indebted chiefly to two of his surviving daughters.

His person was rather above the ordinary height of men. In his countenance there were peculiar and striking lineaments which, once seen, would not soon be forgotten. His hair, which inclined to curl, was of a chestnut colour. From early life, the crown of his head was bald, giving a marked conspicuousness to his forehead. His eyes were bright, and of a clear blue colour. His complexion was florid, his frame muscular, his

---

* JOHN FAIRFIELD was a native of Boston; was graduated at Harvard College in 1757; was ordained Pastor of the Congregational Church in Saco, October 27, 1762, was dismissed in July, 1799, and died in 1819.

temperament sanguine and nervous. In walking, his step was firm and elastic, his head tending somewhat forward, and his pace rapid. His dress was plain and scrupulously neat: his manners were dignified and somewhat reserved.

As may be said of almost every man who reaches fourscore, he was an early riser. He loved retired life, yet did he heartily enjoy the social circle; enlivening the conversation by occasionally relating such anecdotes as he had stored in his retentive memory.

He loved music; and to him praise was a delightful part of worship; whether public, in which he always joined, or private, when he led in the service with a clear musical voice. "One of my earliest recollections of him," writes his daughter, Sarah, "is, as he walked about the room,—his hands clasped behind him,—singing hymns."

A kind and faithful husband, he was deeply afflicted by the death of his wife, with whom he took sweet counsel for more than half a century. His love to his children also was very strong. When his eldest son, Benjamin, died, the father felt the stroke severely. His strong frame shook, and he was removed from the bedside, entirely overcome. When he recovered, he said,—"I went down into the dark valley with him."

As a Preacher, his style was plain, simple and concise. The Bible was his daily study. He was never known to decline any religious service on the plea of not being prepared. He invited a young minister, who was at his house, to preach on the Sabbath; but the reply was,—"I am not prepared." "Not prepared," said the Elder; "a soldier should always have his armour on."

Hoping that these notices of one of our most useful and venerated ministers may suit your purpose, I am respectfully,

Your brother,
THOMAS B. RIPLEY.

FROM THE REV. R. W. CUSHMAN.

BOSTON, March 18, 1858.

My dear Sir: The request contained in your note received yesterday, is one with which it gives me pleasure to comply,—not only because it furnishes me with an occasion to express my gratification with the laudable work in which you are engaged, but because the contribution you have asked from me recalls the memory of one whom, though I am not a "Churchman," I love to think of as my godfather. It was as one of the lambs of his flock that I learned to love and revere him; and, for a series of years, had the benefit of his shepherd care.

Father Titcomb was then—at least to the eye of my youth—an old man. I remember him as of a somewhat tall and well-developed frame, though not portly. His face was rather sharp, and of oval contour, with prominent aquiline nose. His brow was high; his head quite bald; what hair he had was worn quite short. His voice was not loud, but it was musical, and of manly tone.

I believe he was considered, by people who did not know him intimately, as distant and unsocial; and perhaps this notion was not wholly without foundation. His early life had been passed amid the trials of a pioneer Baptist ministry—himself a convert from the Pedobaptist faith, who had sundered dear ties, and sacrificed worldly interests, to preach a faith at that time everywhere spoken against. But those who knew him best were strongly attached to him, and could testify to the warmth of his heart. This must certainly have been true of his own people.

In all my intercourse with them,—and it was very extensive,—I do not remember ever to have heard among them a word adapted to chill my own youthful love and reverence for him.

As a Preacher, he was not what people would now call interesting: no gesticulation, unimpassioned, monotonous. He spoke without seeming to be sensible of the presence of the people, and wholly absorbed with the thought of what he was saying. But it was evident from his whole manner that he had a deep sense of the presence of God, and of his own responsibility. He seemed, however, to regard the simple utterance of the truth as all that became him. He seemed to look on himself as the mere vehicle—the *statue* for the emission of the Divine oracle.

He was a doctrinal and expository, rather than a hortatory, preacher. His belief was that Christ had a people, to be saved by the word *spoken* through human lips, but made *efficacious* solely by the Spirit; and he seemed to regard anything beyond its simplest enunciation as a human admixture. This idea, as we know, was very much a characteristic of the Baptist ministry of by-gone days. But, as the people of those days were imbued with deep convictions, strong prejudices, and peculiar notions, in reference to Divine truth and the preaching of it, there was the less need of the adjuncts of eloquence, which are now deemed so necessary in a preacher. Father Titcomb's ministry, notwithstanding these deficiencies, was a successful one. I remember to have heard him say, in a devotional meeting in the awakening of 1816, that it was the *nineteenth* " reformation " in which he had laboured.

Of the later years of his life I have little knowledge. The last time I saw him was in the summer of 1842. He was then very aged; yet remarkably active. The powers of his mind had yielded somewhat to the weight of years; but his heart had certainly grown young. He was much more social and affable; and all his thoughts were of the home to which he was approaching. It was at his own hospitable board, on an Associational occasion, that I last remember him. He was surrounded by the patriarchs, Case, Kendall,* and others with whom he had been a fellow-labourer in their early years, in Church planting and culture in the wilds of Maine. The conversation turned from the past—so natural for old warriors—to the future. Father Titcomb became so filled with joy at the thought of what was before him, that his face became radiant with his emotion. He dropped his knife and fork on his plate, and clapped his hands, and exclaimed: " I shall behold the land that is very far off ; and mine eyes shall see the King in his beauty!"

Very respectfully and fraternally yours,

R. W. CUSHMAN.

* HENRY KENDALL was born in Sanford, Me., July 3, 1774; became hopefully pious at nineteen; was licensed to preach in 1801; was ordained at Mount Vernon, Me., in 1805; and the same year became Pastor of the Church in Litchfield. Here he remained labouring acceptably and usefully until 1818, when he removed to Topsham, and took charge of the church in that place. In 1828, he resigned this charge, after which he devoted himself to missionary labour, and was, for some time, employed as an agent of the Maine Domestic Missionary Society.

JOSHUA BRADLEY.*
1799—1855.

JOSHUA BRADLEY, the youngest son of his parents, was born in Randolph, Mass., July 5, 1773. The ancestors of his family are traceable to an emigration from England of five brothers, in the year 1636. One of these brothers settled in Boston, another in New Haven, and the other three are believed to have settled farther South. The father of Joshua was Hopestill Bradley, a descendant of the Boston branch. He was a soldier in the Revolutionary War, and was wounded in the battle of Bunker Hill. He died at the house of his son, Hope Bradley, in Randolph, Vt., in 1813, aged one hundred years.

The parents of Joshua Bradley were poor, but were professedly religious, and members of a Congregational church; and he was taught by them to repeat a form of prayer every night, and required to recite a portion of the Catechism every Sabbath. He was accustomed also, at the close of every day, to go through a certain form of self-examination; and if he found that he had done anything that appeared to him sinful, he would satisfy his conscience by repeating his prayer a second time. At the age of fourteen, he was apprenticed to a Mr. Thayer, a shoemaker in his native town, till he was twenty-one. In the summer of 1790, he was awakened to an awful conviction of his sinfulness by a dream in which the scenes of the final judgment were made to pass most vividly before him. After struggling for some time under the burden of guilt and fearful apprehension, he became, on the 8th of October following, suddenly enraptured by a view of the glory of the Saviour, and overwhelmed by a sense of forgiving mercy. Shortly after this, he joined the Baptist Church in Randolph, then under the care of the Rev. Mr. Briggs. It began now to be impressed upon his mind that it was his duty to preach the Gospel; but, as his circumstances seemed altogether adverse to it, he endeavoured to dismiss the idea as a temptation of the adversary; but it would still return upon him with irresistible power; and the more, as he saw that his efforts to awaken the attention of his youthful companions and others around him to the concerns of their souls were manifestly attended with the Divine blessing. At length he made an arrangement with Mr. T., to whom he was apprenticed, to go to school four weeks, that he might learn to read the Bible— for until then he was unable to read a verse in it, without spelling each word. This only quickened his ambition to proceed in a literary course; and, being much encouraged by his teacher, Mr. Benjamin Turner,—who had then (1791) just graduated at Harvard College, he resolved to enter upon a course of study with a view to a liberal education. Obtaining a Latin Grammar, he hung it up before his shoe-bench, studying as he worked, and reciting to Mr. Turner as he had opportunity. As soon as the period of his apprenticeship had expired, he devoted himself vigorously to his preparation for College, studying about twelve hours daily, besides making a pair of shoes each day to pay for his board. He entered the

*MS. Autobiog.—MS. from Rev. Dr. Babcock.

Academy of the Rev. William Williams, at Wrentham, in 1795, and two years after became a member of the Junior class in Brown University. Too poor to pay the full price for his board, he sat at the second table for the first year, at a very reduced rate, and taught a school during his vacations, to enable him to pay his College bills. Jeremiah Chaplin (afterwards the Rev. Dr. Chaplin, first President of Waterville College) was the only other Baptist student in the College at that time. They held a prayer meeting in their room every Saturday evening, and on the Sabbath between meetings. They read together Edwards on Redemption, Hopkins' Body of Divinity, and other similar works. They also established and conducted a Young People's prayer meeting in Providence, on Wednesday evenings, at which they exhorted, expounded the Scriptures, &c. They both graduated on the 4th of September, 1799. The theme of Bradley's Oration was " The impossibility of exterminating Christianity from the earth." He says " The clergy seemed pleased, and I was invited to visit some of them."

Immediately after his graduation, he was licensed to preach by the church in his native town. For six months, he divided his time, as a supply, between the Baptist Church in Attleborough, Mass., and a new Society in Pawtucket, R. I.—the latter, encouraged by the attendance on his ministrations, erected their first meeting-house, which was soon filled. Having completed this engagement, he travelled some weeks in New Hampshire and Maine. He was invited to become a colleague with Dr. Stillman of Boston, and with the Rev. Isaac Backus of Middleboro'; but he finally accepted an invitation to share with the venerable Gardiner Thurston the pastoral care of the Second Baptist Church in Newport, R. I. He was ordained on the 13th of May, 1801,—Dr. Gano, and the Rev. Messrs. Luther Baker, John Pitman, and Joel Briggs taking part in the service. A cheering revival immediately commenced, and continued for six years, during which two hundred and forty-seven were added to the church. It extended also to neighbouring churches, both in Rhode Island and Massachusetts. Beside his abundant labours at home and in the vicinity, he was accustomed to travel and preach about six weeks in each year, wherever the Providence of God seemed to open the way; and much good often resulted. In this way, during his six years' settlement in Newport, he visited nine States, attended many Associations, and became extensively acquainted with ministers and churches. In 1807, finding himself wearied out by his manifold labours, he resigned his charge, and removed to Mansfield, Conn., dividing his ministrations between that place, and the neighbouring town of Tolland. In both places his labours were highly acceptable—in Tolland a Baptist church was soon formed, and in Mansfield a Baptist meeting-house was built and filled. The Baptist Church in Middletown now earnestly requested his services; and he accordingly went thither, first occupying the Court House as a place for preaching, but, as that was soon filled, they erected a convenient house for public worship. In 1809, by the solicitation of various persons, especially of some young men who were candidates for the ministry, he opened an Academy in Wallingford, Conn., and the next year a fine, commodious edifice was built, where he generally had about one hundred pupils from several different

States. While conducting this Academy, he preached in North Haven, where he formed a Baptist church, and also officiated Saturday evenings at New Haven, in Masonic Hall, which he himself hired for the purpose. Here he was subjected to a severe trial in being prosecuted for the alleged crime of forgery. He was charged by certain parties with having forged the name of Dr. Welch of Mansfield, and falsely pretending to be a regularly ordained minister—the case came to trial before the Court, in August, 1812, and he was triumphantly acquitted. A narrative of the whole affair was subsequently published and widely circulated.

Several families, who had sat under Mr. Bradley's ministry at Newport, having removed to Windsor, Vt., sent an earnest request to him to come and preach to them. He, accordingly, removed thither, in October, 1813, and commenced preaching in the Court House. As this was soon over-flowing, larger accommodations were called for, and a commodious brick church edifice was erected. Here he continued about four years, and was occupied at the same time in teaching a school in his own house, chiefly for those who were looking forward to the ministry. In 1817, he started for Ohio, with a view to establish a literary institution in that State; but circumstances prevented him from carrying out his purpose. The Baptist Church in Albany, which had been for some time in a divided state, invited him to become their Pastor; and his acceptance of their invitation was the means of restoring them to harmony. As their small meeting-house soon became inadequate to their accommodation, he suggested that the theatre should be purchased, and transformed into a place of worship; and this was accordingly done, at an expense of ten thousand dollars. It was dedi-cated on the 18th of January, 1819, the Sermon on the occasion being preached by President Nott, which secured a large collection in aid of the enterprise.

In November following, Mr. Bradley was induced to accept an invi-tation from Middlebury, N. Y., to take charge of a new Seminary, and also of a Baptist church, in that village. A revival soon commenced, in connection with his labours, the influence of which was widely and benignly felt. He remained here until 1824, when, on account of Mrs. Bradley's infirm health, he resigned the place, both as teacher and preacher, and travelled, preaching as he had opportunity, in the Northwestern part of New York. In Ellisburgh, Jefferson County, he established a Seminary,—obtaining an incorporation, and six thousand dollars for its endowment. Here also he was successful as a Pastor. While in the State of New York, he and his pupils were instrumental in establishing six new churches in as many years.

In 1826, he was invited to visit Pittsburg, Pa.; and, finding the Baptist church there much distracted, he commenced a school for his support. He divided his labours on the Sabbath between Pittsburg and Alleghany City, and his influence in resuscitating the Baptist interest in that neighbourhood soon became perceptible. His school was large, consisting of a hundred and sixty pupils; and a considerable revival of religion attended his min-istry. In 1827, he was earnestly solicited by the Rev. John M. Peck* to

---

* JOHN MASON PECK, the only child of Asa and Hannah Peck, was born in Litchfield, (South Farms,) Conn., October 31, 1789. His father was a lineal descendant, in the fourth

go to Illinois, to take charge of a new Seminary at Rock Spring,—which subsequently grew into Shurtleff College at Upper Alton. The fact that it was to be a Manual Labour Institution was the circumstance which especially attracted Mr. Bradley to it, and led him, without much hesitation, to consent to become its Principal. He reached St. Louis in June, 1827; and, as the Seminary buildings were not completed, he preached there and at Edwardsville, Ill., during the summer; and a large number were gathered into the church through his instrumentality. In the autumn, Rock Spring Seminary was opened; and within one year it numbered a hundred and thirty pupils. To secure the better medical aid for his wife, he left the Institution, after having been connected with it about a year, and fixed himself for a season in Louisville, Ky., where he preached, and taught a Young Ladies' School. In 1829, he removed to Middletown, O., where he

generation, of Deacon Paul Peck, who came from England in the Defiance, in 1634, and accompanied the Rev. Thomas Hooker to Hartford, and was an officer in his church till his (Mr. Peck's) death, which occurred on the 23d of December, 1695, at the age of eighty-seven. John M. enjoyed no other advantages of early education than those which were furnished by the Common School; but he made the best of them, and, when he reached manhood, he spent his winters in teaching a school, and his summers in labouring on a farm. On the 8th of May, 1809, he was married to Sarah Paine; and about this time they both joined the Congregational church in his native place. Two years later, he removed to Greene County, N. Y., and there, after much consideration, joined a Baptist church, by which, the next year, he was licensed to preach. He was ordained in Catskill, N. Y., on the 9th of June, 1813. The year following he became Pastor of the Baptist Church in Amenia, Dutchess County, N. Y.; and, while there, studied the Greek Testament, under Daniel H. Barnes, in Poughkeepsie, twenty-five miles distant. The next year, (1815,) he became acquainted with Luther Rice, who was instrumental in giving a fresh impulse to his missionary zeal. By his advice, Mr. Peck repaired, early in 1816, to Philadelphia, and entered the Theological School of Dr. Staughton, where he pursued his studies with great vigour and success for one year. In May, 1817, he was set apart as a Missionary of the Baptist General Convention, for the West; and he reached his destination (St. Louis) about the close of that year. For the next nine years he was engaged as an itinerant missionary, and a teacher of a select school, ranging through Missouri and Illinois, and residing in St. Louis, then in St. Charles, Mo., and ultimately fixing his home at Rock Spring, St. Clair County, Ill. In 1826, he visited New England and New York, soliciting aid for the West, both to sustain missionaries and to assist in founding a Literary and Theological Institution for educating Common School teachers and Ministers of the Gospel. This object was secured, and the Rock Spring Seminary was built on ground given by Mr. Peck. In April, 1829, he commenced, as both editor and publisher, "The Pioneer,"—the first Baptist newspaper established in the Western States. This paper he continued for about a dozen years, at an annual expense to himself of some two hundred dollars. In March, 1830, he was obliged to accept the Principalship of the Seminary, which had failed, in some respects, to meet public expectation; but, after an experiment of some fifteen months, his health failed, and he found it necessary to return to more active life. In the summer of 1831, he spent three months with the Rev. Dr. Going, in planning the American Baptist Home Missionary Society. Early in 1832, he published a small but very useful volume, entitled "The Emigrant's Guide;" and, shortly after, commenced a monthly periodical, entitled "The Illinois Sunday School Banner." In 1834, he published the Gazetteer of Illinois. In 1835, Shurtleff College was founded at Upper Alton, Ill., to take the place, and carry out the designs, of the Rock Spring Seminary; and in this enterprise he was the principal agent. He travelled nearly six thousand miles, and collected twenty thousand dollars, to endow the institution. In watching over and helping forward these varied interests, and aiding in the establishment of a Theological Institution at Covington, Ky., he was occupied till 1843, which year, with the two following, he spent at Philadelphia, as Corresponding Secretary and Financial Agent of the American Baptist Publication Society. Returning then to his Western home, he resumed his labours in that field with renewed ardour. He was Pastor of several important churches in Missouri, Illinois, and Kentucky; was a large contributor to Reviews and Newspapers; wrote the Life of Daniel Boone for Sparks' American Biography; edited a second edition of "Annals of the West,"—a large octavo volume; compiled the Memoir of Father Clark, a Western preacher; and made important contributions to nearly all the Historical Societies of the Northwestern States and Territories. He died in great peace, at his home at Rock Spring, March 15, 1858. After about a month, his remains were, by the special desire of many of his friends, removed and interred in the Bellefontaine Cemetery, St. Louis. The degree of Doctor of Divinity was conferred upon him by Harvard College in 1852. His large and valuable collection of newspapers and pamphlets was destroyed by fire a few years before his death; but his immense manuscript collections were, by his will, placed in the hands of the Rev. Rufus Babcock, D. D., from whom the public are expecting, ere long, one or more volumes consisting of his Life and Remains. He was the father of ten children, six of whom survived him. He was undoubtedly one of the most remarkable self-made men of his day.

soon had several hundred pupils under his care. The next year, he attended the Baptist Convention in Lebanon, and awakened an interest in behalf of education, which resulted in the establishment of Granville College,—for the endowment of which he subsequently obtained about two thousand dollars. In visiting Indiana, where there were about three hundred Baptist churches, and no Seminary, he was invited to become Principal of a Seminary in Connersville, the capital town of Fayette County. He opened the Institution on the 4th of October, 1830, and soon had about a hundred and seventy pupils. He was invited to deliver an Oration, on the next Fourth of July, at Indianapolis, and was there instrumental in forming an Education Society. He there opened a School in the Baptist meeting-house, and had a hundred and twelve pupils from November till the following May. The next year, (1833,) Mrs. Bradley died; and her husband, while travelling and preaching in Kentucky, took the fever and ague, and suffered severely from it for some time. He then returned to Pittsburg, and again engaged there both in teaching and preaching. In 1835, he delivered an Address on Education before the Monongahela Association, which resulted in a partially successful effort to establish and endow a literary institution for Western Pennsylvania, and Western Virginia. Such a College was finally established by him in Harrison County, Va., since called Rector College, of which, at the instance of Mr. B., the Rev. Charles Wheeler * became President. During his agency for this College, he secured the purchase of a valuable site, and buildings for a Female College at Bottetourt Springs, Va., in May, 1843, and obtained a charter for it the following winter. In March, 1847, he visited Brownsville, Pa., and, by desire of the inhabitants, opened a Seminary in the Masonic Hall. The next year he visited the scene of his former labours in New York and Rhode Island, and preached several month's for the Fourth Baptist Church in Newport. In 1849, he visited Lansingburg, N. Y., and was instrumental in forming an Education Society, of which he became General Agent. In September, 1850, by the desire of his son, Joshua T. Bradley,

---

* CHARLES WHEELER, a son of Samuel and Catharine (Adams) Wheeler, was born at Rowley, Mass., on the 8th of April, 1784. His father was graduated at Harvard College in 1771, and was licensed to preach in the Congregational Church. He (the son) became hopefully pious, about the year 1801, and joined the Congregational church in his native place, under the pastoral care of the Rev. Mr. Bramin; and he began to prepare for College under his instruction. While he was prosecuting his studies, he embraced the views of the Baptists, and transferred his relation to a neighbouring church of that communion. In due time he became a member of Brown University, and graduated in 1807. After leaving College, he was employed for some time in teaching a school, first in Wiscasset, Me.; afterwards in Salem, Mass.; and subsequently in Middleborough, where he was licensed to preach. In 1812, he supplied, for several months, the First Baptist Church in Boston. His mother having, about this time, removed to Pennsylvania, induced him to follow her; though he seems to have consented very reluctantly. He left Boston for Pittsburg, in June, 1813; having been married, in March preceding, to a daughter of the Rev. Samuel Nelson, of Middleborough; and shortly after opened a school in Washington, twenty-five miles West of Pittsburg, and at the same time commenced preaching to a large congregation in the Court House. In October, 1814, he was ordained, and a church constituted in Washington, of which he became the Pastor. Here he continued for twenty-six years, preaching not only to his own church, but frequently to several other churches in the neighbourhood. Meanwhile he also continued his connection with the school. In 1839, he was chosen President of Rector College, and about the same time visited New England to solicit aid in its behalf. He removed his family to Pruntytown, the seat of the College, in 1840, and exerted himself to the utmost to bring forward the infant institution. In his devotion to this object he overtasked both his physical and intellectual energies, and brought on a hemorrhage of the lungs, and subsequently an enlargement of the heart, which terminated in death, on the 11th of January, 1851. He was an accomplished scholar, an excellent teacher, and an able, earnest and successful minister.

Esq., of St. Louis, he accompanied him to St. Paul, Min., where he made his home till his death. From this point he made occasional excursions to Illinois, Iowa, and even to St. Louis, visiting old friends, and preaching and performing such services as his strength allowed.

Mr. Bradley died at St. Paul, on the 22d of November, 1855, in the eighty-fourth year of his age. He had for several weeks been confined to his bed, but, during his whole illness, exhibited the most unqualified resignation. Just before he expired, he gave utterance to his feelings in strains of the most intense and sublime rapture, declaring his full assurance that he was standing on the verge of Heaven. His life was one of incessant but diversified labour, and eminent usefulness. His remains were, by his own request, removed to Pittsburg, Pa., and deposited in the vault of his son-in-law, Asa P. Childs, near those of his beloved daughter, Mrs. Frances Childs.

Mr. Bradley was married, in the year 1799, or 1800, to Leah Thayer, of Massachusetts. She died at Indianapolis, Ind., on the 5th of July, 1833, aged fifty-one years. The next year, he married Mrs. Harriet M. Brown, who still (1859) survives. He had nine children by the first marriage, and two by the second. All his children are now deceased, except two—a son, *Joshua T.*, and a daughter, who is married to William B. Collard, of Wyoming, N. Y.

Besides several minor productions in pamphlet form, Mr. Bradley published two small volumes,—one on " Revivals," and another on " Free-Masonry."

FROM THE REV. RUFUS BABCOCK, D. D.

PATERSON, N. J., February 10, 1859.

My dear Sir: My earliest recollections of the Rev. Joshua Bradley are connected with the attendance of my brother, next older than myself, at the Academy taught by him at Wallingford, Conn., in the year 1810. More than once, in that and the following year, I accompanied this brother on his return to the Academy, after a visit at home, and this gave me an opportunity of seeing something of the Principal in his relations to both the instruction and the management of his school. The impression he then made upon me was too deep not to be enduring. He was between thirty-five and forty years of age. He was of medium height; of dark complexion; with a piercing black eye, and a rotund face, bearing the general aspect of fine health and spirits and great activity. In all his intercourse with his pupils, his manner seemed free and genial, but somewhat decided and exacting. He was just about the last man you would think of taking liberties with, and yet you might be assured of his kindness if you deserved it. You felt, both in and out of the school, that the religious man and the minister predominated over the mere officialities of the Preceptor. On one occasion I was present at the semi-annual exhibition of the Academy, and I was much impressed by his unusual capability and tact in getting up and managing to the best advantage such showy demonstrations of the capacities of all classes of his pupils. He was, in short, a very popular teacher, and within his own range a very good one.

In the autumn of 1811, my mother died suddenly; and, as my brother was sent for to attend her Funeral, his worthy Preceptor, Mr. Bradley, came with him. He preached the Funeral Sermon; and the text he selected,—" Blessed are the dead that die in the Lord," in connection with the occasion, gave fine scope to his sympathetic nature, while it made him, to the bereaved circle, emphatically a minister of consolation. I well remember that, in the evening, after the Funeral, he interested me not a little by a somewhat detailed account of his own life; and I can recall much of his very language even to this day. "My earliest recollections," said he, "are of the battle of Bunker Hill. My mother held me up in her arms, and while she was thrown into a paroxysm, by the flashes and the roar of artillery, as she pressed me to her bosom, and then lifted me above her head, she cried,—'There, there, child, is your father, fighting for his country.'" Then he gave us an account of his apprenticeship, and the hardships he endured in connection with it. He related the impressive dream he had of the final judgment, which was the first step in that process of mind that issued in his conversion. He told us of his struggles to obtain an education, contrasting his early condition with the more favoured lot of my father's sons, who had all the requisite paternal aid. The years in which he so overtasked his energies at Newport, and the various persecutions he had endured in my native State, also passed under review. The story was told without the semblance of ostentation, and it was hardly possible that any one should have listened to some portions of it without being moved.

During my College course,—probably in 1819,—he visited Providence, and spent a week or two in that city and vicinity. I think he was still soliciting funds for defraying the expense that had been incurred by the purchasing and fitting up of the Albany theatre as a house of worship. He had still many old friends in that city; and so deeply were many of the College students interested in him, that they were sure to be present wherever they knew he was to preach. He was, probably, at that time, at the height of his popularity as a preacher.

Again in 1824, while I was Pastor of the Baptist Church in Poughkeepsie, he passed a Sabbath with me, preaching once, and insisting on once listening to "the son of his dear friend and brother," as he called my father. The next day I accompanied him some little distance out of town on his way, and I well remember with what a cordial and fatherly spirit he made various useful suggestions to me,—the result of his own ample experience. He had been a very active Freemason; and I had a little before declined an overture to be advanced in that fraternity; but he fully approved my course. In speaking of the delivery of his sermons, I remember his saying, with some degree of earnestness,—"If your heart prompts to tears, do not suppress them;" and this advice was quite in harmony with his own practice. After this, I met him casually several times, North, South, and West, but generally only in public convocations, where there was little opportunity of familiar intercourse. But I was kept tolerably well informed of his various efforts and sacrifices, especially in promoting the nascent educational enterprises of our Baptist communities. Occasionally, too, we corresponded. Once again, in the winter of 1847–48, I met him in Newport, R. I., where he was regularly officiating in a small destitute church. We passed considerable time together at the house of an intimate mutual friend. His heart seemed just as warm and genial as when I had first known him, nearly forty years before. We talked on various topics connected with the great progress of the Baptist cause during the nearly half century, in which he had been publicly identified with it. There was in his manner a delightful absence of all sourness or captiousness,—nothing to indicate that he had ever been ill-treated or slighted, or had not always been walking in sunshine. He seemed to dwell with great interest upon the past, as furnishing matter of gratitude to God, for having enabled him to do and to sacrifice so much for the promotion of a cause dearer to him than life. His sermons there were said to be (for I did not hear him preach, being engaged in another church at the hour of his service) highly charactoristic. They were not profound, or logically very coherent; but they were full of the marrow of the Gospel, abounded in touching incidents, and were delivered with all the fervour and unction of his youth. Such had been the whole course of his life as to utterly preclude large theological or biblical attainments. Himself, and his estimable classmate, Dr. Chaplin, were fitting complements of one perfect circle,—one having very fully what the other lacked, while both were eminently good and useful in their respective spheres. Probably, as an instructer, he might now be deemed lacking in the exactness, thoroughness, and broad compass of modern scholarship, both literary and scientific. But he could kindle many a fire which demanded more solid fuel for its continuance, but which would never have begun to burn, but for such appliances as he could furnish. I cannot but regard him, therefore, as one of the most self-denying, enterprising and useful men I have ever known.

Yours most fraternally,

RUFUS BABCOCK.

JOHN STERRY.

1800—1823.

FROM THE REV. FREDERIC DENISON.

NORWICH, Conn., February 22, 1859.

Dear Sir: The following sketch of John Sterry has been drawn from the books and papers that emanated from his pen, from letters and oral statements communicated to me by his children, from the records of the church over which he presided, and from recollections furnished by persons who knew him in his business relations, and were privileged to sit under his ministry. I am unable to furnish *personal* recollections of him, but, as I have often heard him described, and have been assured by many who were his cotemporaries to whom I have read the outline of my sketch, that I have fairly, though roughly, pictured his life, I trust you will accept with confidence what I have been able to gather.

JOHN STERRY was born in Providence, R. I., in 1766. His father, Roger Sterry, was an Englishman. His mother, Abby Holmes, was from Stonington, Conn. The family was every way worthy, though not favoured with wealth. On account of a connection, by marriage, with the family of Gov. Fenner, the children were favoured with unusual educational advantages. John improved his opportunities faithfully, and even studied in Brown University, though he did not take the full collegiate course. His gifts and scholarship, as evinced in his youth, and confirmed by the labours of his life, were far above mediocrity. He was a superior mathematician; as was also his brother, Consider Sterry: and both brothers distinguished themselves not only as mathematicians, but as mechanics and writers. When but a little past their majority, they jointly produced and published a large mathematical work. While this work was passing through the press, under the supervision of John, one of the compositors was taken sick. John immediately stepped into the compositor's place, and successfully handled the "stick." This was the beginning of his career as a printer.

About the year 1790, Mr. Sterry removed to Norwich, Conn., and soon established himself as a printer, book-binder, book-seller, paper-maker, author, and publisher. After a few years, he entered into business relations with Epaphras Porter: and the firm of Sterry and Porter became very widely and honourably known.

Mr. Sterry was married in 1792 to Rebecca Bromley of Preston, Conn. Though Rebecca was but sixteen at her marriage, she proved an excellent wife, fully adequate to all her important duties. Mr. Sterry had ten children,—six sons and four daughters, all respectable and useful. His eldest son is a worthy Deacon of a Baptist Church in Utica, N. Y.

Previous to Mr. Sterry's conversion, he, with his brother, Consider, wrote quite a large book in favour of the doctrine of Universal Salvation. Before completing the volume, John thought that some proof of the doctrine should be drawn from the Bible. But, in searching for it, he became convinced that his favourite position could not be sustained. He wished to drop the enterprise of publishing; but his brother urged it forward, especially in consideration of their having obtained a large number of subscribers for the work. John yielded very reluctantly, and went forward till the sheets were ready for binding. He then insisted that half the volumes should be set out to him, that he might do with them as he should choose. Immediately, upon the division, he took his portion of the sheets, and carrying them into the back yard, and piling them up, set fire to the whole, declaring that he could never be responsible for giving to the world what he did not believe to be true.

Mr. Sterry was converted after his removal to Norwich, through the instrumentality of a little band of Baptists, made up in part of Separatists, then maintaining themselves as a branch of the Rev. William Northup's Church in Kingston, R. I. Immediately upon his conversion, he united with this little company, among whom his gifts and graces were soon recognized and honoured. They selected him as their leader, and gave him liberty to "improve his gift" in preaching. Early in the year 1800, this little band took measures to become a regular and independent church; and on the 12th of July they were publicly recognized, by suitable advice and assistance from a council, as the First Baptist Church in the city of Norwich. As Mr. Sterry had already won the entire confidence of the church, and a large measure of popularity as a preacher, the church, in October following, called him to ordination. And, on the 25th of December, 1800, he was appropriately set apart to the work of the ministry. His Ordination Sermon was preached by the Rev. Silas Burrows, from Acts xx. 28.

As the church was at first very small and very poor, worshipping in private houses, a school-house, or a rope-walk, and sometimes, in warm weather, on account of the numbers that desired to attend, in a grove,—the meeting-house raised in 1801 not being finished till 1807; and as the religious usages of the more wealthy portion of the community, together with the ecclesiastical laws of Connecticut, were as yet quite unfavourable to the Baptists, Mr. Sterry's trials and toils were neither few nor light. A less independent, self-reliant, truth-loving, and persevering man would have been quite disheartened. And such was the poverty of the church, during the whole period of his ministry, though greatly prospered under his labours, that in no year did they pay him a salary exceeding one hundred and fifty dollars. His circumstances, therefore, as well as his natural tastes, prompted him to continue his mechanical and literary pursuits through life. Nevertheless, he was the devoted Pastor of this church; and he also preached much in adjoining towns, and even in Rhode Island and Massachusetts. For a time he preached regularly, once a month, at Preston, during the early history of the Baptist Church in that place.

Several memorable revivals were enjoyed by the church under Mr. Sterry's ministry. The years 1816 and 1817 brought large numbers into it. Another happy season of refreshing was experienced in 1819. The whole number received to the church by Baptism, during the twenty-three years of his ministry, was one hundred and seventy-seven.

Mr. Sterry's originality of mind was evinced by at least two valuable inventions. He invented the art of marbling paper,—an art which has since been carried to great perfection, and spread over the civilized world. His patent was sold for a consideration to Epaphras Porter. He also discovered an improved method of bleaching cottons, and this he disposed of to Rhode Island manufacturers.

Mr. Sterry also distinguished himself as an author. As I have already intimated, while he was yet a very young man, he, with his brother Consider, had prepared a large mathematical work—it consisted of two parts, an Arithmetic and an Algebra, and was entitled "The American Youth." This octavo volume of three hundred and seventy-seven pages was put to press in 1790, and was not only highly commended by teachers and Professors in Colleges in this country, but was favourably noticed in Europe. In 1795, the brothers prepared and published an "Arithmetic for the use of Schools in the United States." Mr. Sterry was accustomed, yearly, for a while at least, to assist Mr. Nathan Daboll in the preparation of his celebrated Almanacs.

Soon after he entered the ministry, he rendered important aid to the Rev. William Northup in preparing and publishing a Hymn Book, entitled "Divine Songs,"—a Collection that, for a season, was widely used in our Baptist Churches. In June, 1804, Sterry and Porter (though Mr. Sterry was the prominent writer) edited and published a newspaper called "The True Republican,"—a very spirited, popular and useful sheet. Mr. Sterry was an able writer and editor. He was a democrat, of course, and was honest to the core. Though his paper provoked strong opposition from the Federalists of the day, he never treated his opponents otherwise than with respectful consideration. The favourite motto of his political papers was indicative of the man,—"Nothing extenuate, nor aught set down in malice." He contended for a protective tariff; a reform in the mode of conducting elections, so as to secure fairness; and especially for Religious Liberty and a new State Constitution. The last two great objects, for which he wrote vigorously and sacrificed freely, he lived to see happily secured in 1818. All his writings are clear, well-tempered, racy, and abounding in great and sound principles.

The last few years of Mr. Sterry's life were somewhat clouded,—first, on account of certain unhappy misunderstandings in his church, and secondly, on account of reverses in his pecuniary affairs. He experienced a great loss of property from purchasing in Boston a large quantity of Italian silk, which he attempted to reel, but found it had been damaged by salt water. This loss was augmented and aggravated by the unskilfulness and deceit of an English silk manufacturer, whom he employed to construct machinery, and aid him in the process of reeling.

Mr. Sterry's naturally studious turn of mind and capability of mental abstraction may be illustrated by an amusing anecdote. One of his business tours to Boston he made on horseback. On his return, when he rode up to his house, he was met by his son, who informed him that he had somewhere exchanged horses. The fact of the exchange was as new to Mr. Sterry as it was to Robert, while the horse in hand was but half as valuable as his own.

Mr. Sterry was six feet in height, well formed, erect, with a pleasant and commanding countenance. His mental powers were suited to his physical,—strong, solid, well proportioned. As a speaker, he was plain, usually energetic, sometimes fervid. His preaching was logical and forcible, with less of the hortative than marked that of some of his brethren, and occasionally nobly eloquent. He was executive rather than diplomatic. In sound judgment and prudence he had few superiors. Hence he was often selected by his brethren in the ministry for duties and stations that were alike honourable and responsible.

In short, Mr. Sterry was an able and good man. He was laborious, faithful, true to great principles, unambitious of place and preferments, glorying only in the Cross of Christ. He was the true and beloved yoke-fellow of John G. Wightman, Roswell Burrows, Asa Wilcox, William Palmer, the worthy Miners, and all the veteran labourers in Eastern Connecticut. For the age in which he lived, he was a workman that needed not to be ashamed, as is sufficiently attested by his writings, found in his books and papers, and in the Circular and Corresponding Letters he prepared for the Groton Union Conference and the New London Baptist Association.

His wife survived him ten years. She died of consumption in October 1833, aged fifty-seven.

The disease that terminated Mr. Sterry's life, was an affection of the liver. He suffered severely but a few weeks. On the 5th of November, 1823, in his own house in Norwich town, and in the fifty-seventh year of his age, he departed triumphantly to his rest. His Funeral Sermon was preached to a mourning community, by the Rev. Wm. Palmer, from Matt. xxv. 21. His remains were tearfully buried in the Town Plot Cemetery, where

" The rude forefathers of the hamlet sleep."

Yours fraternally,
FREDERIC DENISON.

EZRA BUTLER.*

1800—1838.

EZRA BUTLER, the third son of Asaph and Jane (McAllister) Butler, was born in Lancaster, Mass., in September, 1763. His mother, who was of Scotch parentage, died when he was a mere boy; but, from what he had heard, as well as from what he remembered, of her, he supposed that she was a truly pious person, though not a professor of religion. His father lived to a somewhat advanced age, and in his later years not only made a public profession of his faith, but was apparently a devout Christian. The first six years of the son's life were spent in his native place, and in Warwick, Mass. After the death of his mother, his father's family was partially separated, and he lived for a few years with his eldest brother. This brother and his wife were both exemplary members of the Congregational Church; and their fidelity to his spiritual interests seems to have left an enduring impression upon his mind. His sister-in-law especially was careful to teach him forms of prayer, which he found of use many years after, when his own diffidence suggested their adoption, to some extent, in first commencing family devotions. *Joel Butler*, the brother referred to, joined the Baptists in 1780, and commenced preaching and was ordained at Woodstock in 1785. He moved from field to field, through the State of New York, Westwardly, and died at Geneva, Ind., September 13, 1822, in his seventy-first year. His eldest son (*Ora*) was also a Baptist minister in good repute.

At the age of about fourteen, Ezra Butler went to live with Dr. Stearns, of Claremont, N. H.; and, with the exception of a few months, remained there during the rest of his minority. The Doctor soon entrusted to him the management of his large farm, while he himself attended to the duties of his profession. At the age of sixteen he enlisted as a soldier in the Revolution, but, after having served about six months, returned to his place as manager of Dr. Stearns' farm. A few months after he had reached his majority, he, with his brother Asaph, about two years older than himself, left Weathersfield, Vt,—to which place his father had in the mean time removed,—to try their fortunes in the Valley of Onion River. The last twenty-five miles of their route they travelled on snow shoes, (the snow being about four feet deep,) transporting the few articles they took with them, on a hand-sled. They reached what is now Waterbury, their place of destination, on the 20th of March, 1785. The place was then entirely new, there being but one family in it, and not more than half a dozen dwellings for a distance of twenty-five miles, both above and below the town, on Onion River. All that portion of the State, for nearly sixty miles, extending from Lake Champlain almost to White River, was one dense forest, without roads. and, with the above exceptions, without inhabitants. Here Mr. Butler, being then in his twenty-second year, commenced a farm for himself, depending for success entirely on his own honest industry, and here he remained till he was summoned to his long home.

* Memoir by a Lady.—MS. from his son, Russell Butler, Esq.

Mr. Butler was married on the 13th of June, 1785, at Weathersfield, Vt., to Tryphena Diggins, formerly of Windsor, Conn.; though he did not move his family to Waterbury until September of the next year.

At the age of twenty-seven he became hopefully a subject of renewing grace. In his early years he had been more or less thoughtful in regard to his immortal interests, but, after his removal to Waterbury,—exiled as he was from the public means of grace,—his mind settled into a habit of utter indifference in regard to spiritual things. Being obliged to labour hard during the week, he was accustomed to spend part of the Sabbath in sleep; and, on a certain Sabbath, as he woke from sleep, he observed his wife reading a pamphlet, and asked her to read it aloud. As its title-page was gone, he never knew either its title, or the name of its author; but the subject was one which, in former years, had occasioned him great perplexity,—namely, how a man can be blameable for possessing an evil disposition which he did not create for himself; and hence he listened with earnest attention. After she had read aloud for some time, he stopped her with the simple exclamation,—"If this is true, we are *undone.*" Though he said nothing more, he was thrown into the most intense agony of spirit, which continued until the Friday following, when he carried his wife to pass the night with a friend whose residence was four or five miles distant from his own. Being alone that night, he resolved that he would read the Bible, and endeavoured to settle the question intelligently whether his condition as a sinner was really such as the pamphlet to which he had listened had led him to apprehend. The following is his own account of the exercises of his mind at this period, given by a friend to whom he communicated it :—

"I performed my necessary labour as soon as possible, and then sat down with my Bible. I read the Epistle to the Romans—it all condemned me. It was plain that I was a sinner, utterly condemned before God, and must be lost. I felt as sure of this as if my sentence had actually been pronounced in my hearing Sometimes the thought would enter my mind that God had mercy on sinners—He had mercy on Saul of Tarsus—He may have mercy on me. But no, I am more vile than any other sinner. Saul had not the light that I have—he did what he thought was right—I have done what I knew was wrong.

"I finally thought that I would fall down and once more bemoan my condition before God. I could not think of *praying*, but I resolved to utter my lamentations for the last time, and then never attempt to address God again. I had many times tried to pray, and had always done so standing,—except that I had sometimes prostrated myself on my face; but now I fell upon my knees and bemoaned my lost state. My mind was occupied upon myself. My own case was the engrossing consideration. After a time I lost sight of myself, and was wholly absorbed in contemplating the glory of God. Such glory and excellency as I beheld I had never conceived of. The room seemed filled with the manifestation of God's glory. The law of God then appeared to me exceedingly beautiful and excellent After rising from my knees, and being, for some time, rapt in these contemplations, my mind reverted to my own state. And can I ever be permitted to behold this glory; or must I be banished from the presence of God, and be left to continue his enemy?—was my inward inquiry. Again I took up my Bible, and read over the same portions I had been reading in the early part of the evening; but I did not find the same things that I had then discovered; and I read on with all haste in order to find what had before made such an impression upon me. I came to the expression,—'Love is the fulfilling of the law.' Here I paused—I had read this portion of Scripture many times before, but I never before saw this expression—What does this mean? I pondered. Can this mean that love to the law is the fulfilling of the law? I see not but it does. And why should not the law be loved? What more worthy of love? And do I not love this law? Here some faint idea entered my mind that I must have passed the change called regeneration; but it was not distinct enough for me to fasten upon.

"I retired to my bed, but soon such discoveries were made to me of the glory of God that I could not rest. I felt as if surrounded with his visible presence and glory. I arose, rekindled the fire, and lighted a candle; and, filled with these overwhelming views, I spent most of the night. Towards morning I slept a short time; but at the dawn of day I arose full of the same thoughts and feelings.

"Before night I brought my wife home, and, hastening to finish my usual labours, I sat down in the evening, and began to talk to her of the glory of God, as being every where visible, and exceeding every thing else. I talked on till, after some time, she said she could see nothing of this. In my astonishment I exclaimed,—' Why you are as blind as the chimney-back!' But it occurred to me instantly that, a few days ago, I was equally blind.

"That evening a Baptist minister, by the name of Call,* who resided at Woodstock, and whom I had formerly seen, being on a journey, called to spend the night with me. I never was so glad to see any man, before nor since. My first salutation expressed the state of my mind. He preached in the house of one of the inhabitants the next day, which was Sunday; and, after he had closed, I got up, and, with tears and sobs, tried to tell my neighbours how things appeared to me. They were struck with wonder. Every mouth was open, and all hands upraised in astonishment. After the Sabbath was passed, I was again left without any human being near, who could counsel me, or even enter into my feelings.

"'As yet' I observed, 'you seem, Sir, not to have had a manifestation of Jesus Christ as a Saviour—how and when did this take place?'

"True," he replied, "I had not; but during Monday morning I was greatly distressed to know what God would do with me. And now I think I exercised submission as I scarcely have at any other time. My anxiety was extreme to be permitted to enjoy the presence of God, and behold his glory—still I felt that He would do right, and I could acquiesce in his disposal of me. In an agony of feeling, I was walking to a neighbour's, and, while on my way, Jesus Christ was set before me as *the Saviour of sinners.* This was my first apprehension of the way of salvation. The Gospel plan was unfolded to my view, and I went on my way rejoicing in the application of the atonement to my soul, my views of the glory of God more enrapturing than ever. The views I then had of Christ as my Saviour I did not lose for many years, nor should I do right to say I have ever lost them. On arriving at my neighbour's, in a flood of tears I tried to tell him my feelings, but they were entirely beyond his comprehension."

As there was no church within forty miles of Mr. Butler's residence, he had no opportunity, for some time, of making a public profession of religion. Besides, his views were not at once settled in respect to Baptism; though the result of his reading and reflection on the subject was that he was brought into full sympathy with the Baptists. The next winter, about one year from the time of his former visit, Mr. Call again passed through Waterbury, and stopped long enough to preach a sermon and baptize Mr. Butler. During the service preparatory to the Baptism, his mind became greatly clouded, and he was led to fear that all his previous experiences had been delusion; but before the ordinance was actually administered, the cloud passed away, and he went down into the water full of peace and joy.

After this, Mr. Butler was ready to avail himself of every opportunity, whether in public or private, to help forward the cause of his Master. About the beginning of the year 1800, he was called to the ministry by the church in Bolton, of which he had been a member several years. As the population in the surrounding country increased, new churches were established; and when a Baptist church was organized in Waterbury, towards the close of the year 1800, he was chosen and ordained as its Pastor,—an office which he continued to hold thirty-two or three years.

Mr. Butler united, at different periods, various civil offices with that of a minister of the Gospel—indeed he had held some of these several years previous to his ordination. After the organization of the town in 1790, he was the first Town Clerk; and was not long after appointed Justice of

* ELDER CALL was an itinerant preacher or evangelist, who, though his family resided at Woodstock, travelled extensively in Vermont, and it is believed in other New England States also, in the exercise of his ministry.

the Peace; and, about 1797 or '98, was chosen Representative to the General Assembly, and was subsequently several times re-elected. In 1806, he was elected one of the Council of Censors, and about the same time,—perhaps a year or two earlier,—was appointed a Judge of the County Court,—his residence then being in Chittenden County, and the sessions held at Burlington. After the organization of Washington County,—his residence being within its limits,—he was appointed Chief Justice for Washington, as he had previously been for Chittenden, and was reappointed every year, with one or two exceptions, until 1825. He was, for many years previous to this date, elected by the State a member of the Legislative Council. He was a member of Congress two years,—from 1813 to 1815; and was Governor of the State of Vermont for an equal period,—from 1826 to 1828. His administration as Governor was distinguished chiefly by a vigorous and successful effort for the suppression of Lotteries, and by some essential improvements in the system of Common School education. The last public act he performed, was to officiate as Elector of President of the United States, in 1836; having been appointed by the other Electors to supply the place of an absent member of the Electoral College.

An extensive revival of religion occurred in Waterbury, during the time that he held the office of Governor, which resulted in considerable additions to the several churches, and in which his own family had a liberal share. Notwithstanding the cares and burdens incident to the high civil station which he held, he sympathized deeply in the religious movement, always cherishing an intense interest in the progress of Christ's Kingdom, and never losing sight of the fact that his highest office was that of a minister of Christ.

Governor Butler, during a considerable part of his life, was the subject of much bodily infirmity and suffering. For several years previous to his death, his decline was very perceptible, and he was able to go little from home. For four days immediately preceding that event, he had been confined to his room; and for the last day or two was evidently aware that he was approaching his end; but his extreme weakness, accompanied with a degree of drowsiness, rendered him incapable of much conversation. Every thing, however, indicated perfect composure of spirit; and these signs were confirmed into certainty by the higher testimony of a long course of Christian activity and devotion. He died on the morning of July 12, 1838, in the seventy-fifth year of his age.

Mrs. Butler, who had long lived an exemplary Christian life, died on the 9th of March, 1843, in her seventy-sixth year. They had eleven children, three of whom died very young; the eldest daughter died in 1821, aged thirty-three; and the remaining seven,—three sons and four daughters still (1859) survive, scattered in four different States, and occupying different positions of respectability and usefulness.

When the Rev. Dr. Cox and the Rev. Mr. Hoby, two distinguished Baptist ministers in England, came to this country, a few years since, as a deputation to the American Baptist Churches, the latter called on Governor Butler; and in the joint Report of their Travels, which they subsequently published, Mr. Hoby thus refers to the interview:—

"At Waterbury, I paid a visit to Governor Butler, who, you remember, though a Pastor in our denomination, had once the honour of being Governor of the State of Vermont. His eye is not so dimmed with age, but that you may clearly discern it was once expressive of the intelligence and energy equal to the responsibilities of such an office, however undesirable it may be to blend it with pastoral engagements. Forever let his name be honoured among those who steadfastly determined, and laboured with untiring zeal, to disencumber the State of the burden of a religious establishment, and religion of the manifold evils of State patronage. As he walked towards the town, he told me that, fifty years ago, he cleared the first spot in this cultivated district, which was then all wilderness—now his children's children are growing up around him, to inherit the land and the liberties they owe so literally to their fathers."

FROM THE REV. ALVAH SABIN.

GEORGIA PLAIN, Vt., October 24, 1857.

Dear Sir: The first time that I ever saw the Rev. Ezra Butler was at an Ecclesiastical Council convened at Morristown, Vt., about the year 1818. He was then, and, as he informed me, had been for some time, in very infirm health, his disease being an inveterate asthma. I well recollect my surprise at seeing him so far from home, when he was manifestly in so feeble a state. Some one asked him if he attempted to labour at all; and his answer was,— "Yes—not that my labours amount to any thing; but if I did not tire myself, I could not rest." He was of about the ordinary stature, but his shoulders were bowed, and his gait slow, and almost tottering. His complexion was dark; his hair black; his forehead prominent; his eyes deeply sunken, but black and piercing; and when engaged in debate, he would raise them and fix them on an opponent in a way that could not fail to convince him that he had a clear headed man to deal with. I noticed that he was evidently fond of debate, though he always treated his opponent with profound respect.

My next opportunity for gaining a personal knowledge of him was in October, 1826,—the year he was appointed Governor of the State of Vermont, and the Rev. Aaron Leland, another Baptist minister, was Lieutenant Governor. I was myself that year a Representative in the Legislature from my native town; and it so happened that, during my stay in Montpelier, I boarded in the same house with these two venerable men, and became quite intimate with Governor Butler. When he had got his annual speech printed, as was customary, before it was delivered, he asked me to go with him to his room; and, putting his speech into my hands,—"Now," said he, "do you sit down, and read that speech to me, and let me see how it appears." I did so; and when I had finished reading it, he simply remarked,—"Well, I am sure that little thing cost me more than it is worth." During the session, the members had a general caucus for the purpose of nominating a candidate for Governor the succeeding year; and some of his opponents advised his particular friends to suggest to him that he had better take himself out of the way, as he would thereby save himself the mortification of a defeat. After the meeting, he inquired what was done: and I stated, among other things, what some of the would be leaders in the political affairs of the State had graciously volunteered to advise in respect to himself. His reply was illustrative of his prodigious energy of will, and fearlessness of all opposing influences—"If every man in that house were opposed to my next election," said he, "I would have it, though it should cost me every cent I am worth on earth." Butler and Leland were often engaged in animated conversation: the former was lean and cool blooded; the latter was portly and corpulent. As they would walk the room together, talking earnestly, Leland would raise the latch, and jerk the door wide open; and, after a turn or two, Butler would walk softly and close the door: after a turn or two more, Leland would again go through the same process of raising the latch and flirting the door open; and Butler would soon proceed to close it; and thus they would alternately open and close the door half a dozen times in one conversation,—neither observing what the other had done, but each indicating the temperature of his own blood.

The next year I was sent for to spend a week with the church in Waterbury. It was a time of some revival, and the Governor took a deep interest in the work. I shall not soon forget the tears of affection and joy that he shed on witnessing the Baptism of, I think, five of his children, and two or three of his grand-children, at the close of the week I was there.

At the early period when Governor Butler commenced his ministry, there were but few churches, and those were very poor and small; and no inconsiderable portion of the Baptists had scruples as to paying their preachers any thing for their services. Governor Butler told me that he would give me his whole history in connection with the matter of salary, in two anecdotes. They were the following:—

At one time, a certain brother N——, voluntarily, and from his own conviction of duty, brought him two bushels of wheat, which, of course, he did not hesitate to receive. The next year, the crops of the farmers being somewhat stinted, and Brother N——'s among the rest, he concluded, in order to help out the deficiency, to go and demand of his minister the wheat which he had *generously* given him the year before. He, accordingly, did go, and made the demand in person; alleging that, as the season was, Mr. Butler could better afford to return it than he could to do without it. Mr. B. remonstrated against the injustice, to say nothing of the indelicacy, of the demand; but his parishioner could neither be convinced nor shamed, and even shadowed forth a threat that if the wheat was not returned, he would bring the matter to the notice and adjudication of the church. Mr. B., for the sake of peace, finally yielded to the strange and unrighteous exaction, and the man went off with the same quantity of wheat which he had brought the year before.

The other case was this—A parishioner called on him to attend a Funeral at his house; and, after the service was over, and the Governor was about leaving for home, the man put into his hands one silver dollar; " and that," said he, " is the sum of all I ever received for preaching, though, for a great many years, I preached regularly to this church, and answered the calls that were made upon me far and near."

I regret that my acquaintance with Governor Butler does not enable me to go into the minute details of his character; but perhaps what I have written may give you some idea of its more prominent features.

With great respect,
I am your obedient servant,
ALVAH SABIN.

Other Solid Ground Titles

In addition to the book in your hand, Solid Ground is honored to offer other uncovered treasure, many for the first time in more than a century:

www.ingramcontent.com/pod-product-compliance
Lightning Source LLC
Chambersburg PA
CBHW070858140426
R18135300001B/R181353PG42812CBX00001B/1